ALFRED HITCHCOCK

ALL THE FILMS

THE STORY BEHIND EVERY
MOVIE, EPISODE, AND SHORT

ALFRED HITCHCOCK
ALL THE FILMS

THE STORY BEHIND EVERY MOVIE, EPISODE, AND SHORT

BERNARD BENOLIEL, GILLES ESPOSITO,
MURIELLE JOUDET, JEAN-FRANÇOIS RAUGER

BLACK DOG
& LEVENTHAL
PUBLISHERS
NEW YORK

Contents

For each Alfred Hitchcock film, the year given is the year in which filming was completed.

Alfred Hitchcock, a Life in the Making

"I've become a body of films, not a man; I am all those films."

Alfred Hitchcock

February 1927 saw the release in London of a young man's third film, shot the previous year and almost left on the shelf because one of his investors found it so different from current productions: *The Lodger* was inspired by an atmospheric novel, which was itself inspired by the memory, still very present at the time, of the terrible acts of Jack the Ripper. Fifty feature films later, Alfred Hitchcock, no longer a young man in 1971, returned to London to direct his penultimate opus: *Frenzy*, the story of a psychopath who strangles his victims with a necktie.

Taking Control of the World

It is no exaggeration to say that Hitchcock is a constant presence in the popular culture, both because of his undying love of the macabre (peppered with black humor), which reveals the true passions of humankind, and because of his obligation to make his presence known. More than any other filmmaker, Hitchcock was the willing victim of a worldwide success story, a prisoner of his immense reputation and the renewed expectations of an audience that he himself created. Jean-Luc Godard's voice-over in his *Histoire(s) du cinéma* best describes the extent to which this artist was able to capture the imagination of twentieth-century audiences: "Alfred Hitchcock succeeded where Alexander, Julius Caesar, and Napoleon failed: in taking control of the world." Hitchcock's breathless films, with their heady figures and motifs, fulfilled a totalitarian dream of cinema: to appeal to the whole world (which required the impactful power of the Hollywood film industry). He succeeded better than the great Soviet filmmakers, who dreamed of speaking to the masses rather than

to the sum total of individuals suggested by "the general public."

"Life is not just about breathing, it's about being breathless." (Hitchcock)

A twentieth-century art form that remained figurative and narrative out of loyalty to the great narratives and representations of the previous century (theater, painting, serial novels), relegating plastic abstraction to its margins, cinema invented both its audience and its language: Hitchcock is the man who brought the science of filmmaking to a degree of near absolute perfection. Surely suspense, the feeling experienced by the spectator to which the filmmaker's reputation remains most attached, is the consequence of the use of classical film editing as invented by the American filmmaker David Wark Griffith in the mid-1910s: not only a way of making images follow each other logically, but also the parallel presentation of two competing or rival actions whose coincidence ends up resolving an expectation, a fear, an anguish. Undoubtedly more than Soviet filmmakers in general, and Eisenstein in particular, Hitchcock used film editing as a means of stirring the emotions of the spectator, whose unconscious the author of *Battleship Potemkin* dreamed of "plowing through."

Fear and Trembling

If the director of *The Birds* (1962) invented a machine to frighten the viewer, it is because he was first and foremost an artist who lived through, described, criticized, and analyzed the twentieth century, perceived as a period of war and terror. Totalitarianism, whether Nazi or Stalinist, forms the backdrop to some of

his films (*Foreign Correspondent*, 1940; *Saboteur*, 1942; *Lifeboat*, 1943; *Notorious*, 1946; *Torn Curtain*, 1966; *Topaz*, 1969), which convey the image of a world structured solely by fear: The twentieth century is therefore "Hitchcockian." Hitchcock unmasked another threat, that of the wretchedness of the democratic subject, whether British or American citizen, the ordinary man confronted with his own miserable impulses. Behind his feverish, illusory romanticism (*Vertigo*, 1957), Hitchcock's work is a relentless exposure of the individual reduced to his needs and appetites (*Psycho*, 1960; *Frenzy*). This impulsive individual was Hitchcock himself. For the filmmaker, fiction was also a means of calming the fire of his desire by providing it with the outlet of a work of art. Many films celebrate the "Hitchcock blonde," the mirage he observed with pain and passion, sadism and adoration. He knew how to create beauty from his unavowable desires, sublimating his sexual frustration to reveal and shape actresses: Joan Fontaine, Ingrid Bergman, Grace Kelly, Tippi Hedren...

The Art of Fear

When Hitchcock talked about his beloved art of fear, it is hardly surprising that this child of the century had recourse to a metaphor taken from war: "Fear in cinema is my special field, and I have, perhaps dogmatically, but I think with good cause, split cinematic fear into two broad categories—terror and suspense. The difference is comparable to the difference between a buzz bomb and a V-2. To anyone who has experienced attacks by both bombs, the distinction will be clear. The buzz bomb made a noise like an outboard motor, and its chugging in the air above served as notice of its impending arrival. When the motor stopped, the bomb was beginning its descent and would shortly explode. The moments between the time the motor was first heard and the final explosion were moments of suspense. The V-2, on the other hand, was noiseless until the moment of its explosion. Anyone who heard a V-2 explode, and lived, had experienced terror."[1]

"It is in form that we need to look for depth"[2]

Hitchcock, more than any other, worked to ensure that cinema achieved a status reserved for the so called noble arts. And it was necessary, in a grandiose paradox, for this metamorphosis to involve a director long considered a master of entertainment, a champion of the "fairground attraction," all qualities that should have condemned cinema to remain specifically a trivial form of amusement. From then on, it was the French critics of the 1950s, mainly those of the *Cahiers du cinéma*, who were the first to recognize and bring to light the metaphysical concerns underlying this work. But if Alfred Hitchcock, an English Catholic, is now perceived as a filmmaker of the realms of sin and the Fall, of the damnation of man, who is immediately and irremediably guilty, it is as much through the exposition of religious motifs and themes (*I Confess*, 1952) as through his formal or dramatic choices (the shadow that draws a cross on Ivor Novello's face in *The Lodger*, or James Stewart on the edge of the void in *Vertigo*).

"Self-plagiarism is style" (Hitchcock)

Hitchcock's entire oeuvre describes an evolution that seems to encompass the entire history of cinema. The division of the latter into "classical," "modern," and "postmodern" periods applies as if in miniature to his films, which he progressively adopted, self-criticized, redeployed, and subjected to a mannerist deformation, taking them from the classical age to modern times. He was a director who shot remakes of his own films, becoming his own first successor: *North by Northwest* (1958), a film about a chase across a continent, takes *The 39 Steps* (1935) and *Saboteur* (1942) as its starting point, extending and diverging from them. He even permitted himself to make the "same" film twice, *The Man Who Knew Too Much* (1934 and 1955), the first version lasting just over an hour and the second almost twice as long.

Experimentations

However, the filmmaker was never content to simply plow the same furrow. The filmography of the man who has often been referred to as a "shrewd shopkeeper" is, in truth, full of insane risk-taking and experimentation of all kinds: Salvador Dalí's "signature" dream in *Spellbound* (1944) and James Stewart's nightmare in *Vertigo* (1957); an hour-and-twenty-minute film shot in eleven sequence shots (*Rope*, 1948) and a shower scene in forty-five seconds and seventy-eight shots (*Psycho*); a historical work

(*Under Capricorn*, 1948) and a science fiction one (*The Birds*); insanely complex set designs (*Lifeboat, Rope, Rear Window*, 1954); films in VistaVision and Technicolor (*To Catch a Thief*, 1954), and, from 1955 onward, square-picture black-and-white TV movies (*Alfred Hitchcock Presents*); "visions" (*The Island That Wants to Be Visited* [*Mary Rose*], 1964) and visual experiments (*Kaleidoscope*, 1964–1967) so astonishing that Hitchcock was prevented from making them by his producers. He sought to break his own image, to thwart the expectations of the system, to challenge the common perception of his art, at the risk of commercial failure (the dry realism of *The Wrong Man*, 1956; the clinical case of *Marnie*, 1964) or unexpected success (the brutality of *Psycho*).

The Man Who Knew Everything

Such films convey the impression of a coherent, terrible world, along with a sense of unrivaled formal and technical mastery, to the point where the director gives the impression of an omniscience that intimidates every analyst and commentator: Hitchcock or the man who knew everything…If the viewer does not understand something in an Alfred Hitchcock film, the spectator can be sure that the filmmaker has the answer. This art of total control over both the detail and the overall picture is rare in the history of cinema, and probably only Stanley Kubrick could have achieved such demiurge-like status. Hence the certainty that nothing in a film directed by Hitchcock is devoid of meaning. This infallibility does not, of course, imply a license to make his cinema say anything, but rather implies the impossibility of exhausting its secrets. In fact, from the 1950s onward, such a work contributed to the seemingly infinite number of aesthetic and poetic reflections on the human sciences (sociology, psychoanalysis, philosophy…).

"'Pure cinema' is what I believe in" (Hitchcock)

And why Hitchcock now? Precisely because he is inexhaustible, and therefore always rewards revisiting. Because his name has become synonymous with his art, a man who, trained in the silent era, sought to express himself only in visual terms ("pure cinema," as he put it). Because the influence of his work is gigantic, and far exceeds the remakes and conscious rereadings of his films. Hitchcock forever laid the foundations for transforming the rules of contemporary entertainment. There is not one Hollywood thriller, from the exploits of James Bond to the works of Steven Spielberg, not one adventure or horror film, in the US, Italy, or Korea, that does not pay tribute to the author of *Psycho*. It was an oeuvre of enduring relevance that has yet to have its last word.

Fifty-Three Feature Films

From 1925 (*The Pleasure Garden*) to 1975 (*Family Plot*), from London to Hollywood, Alfred Hitchcock created a total of fifty-three feature films, some of which are the most famous in the history of film: *Blackmail* (1929), *The 39 Steps*, *The Lady Vanishes* (1938), *Rebecca* (1939), *Notorious*, *Rear Window*, *Vertigo*, *North by Northwest*, *Psycho*, *The Birds*...And other lesser-known or more controversial works, well worth (re)discovering: *The Ring* (1927), *Rich and Strange* (1931), the first version of *The Man Who Knew Too Much*, *Secret Agent* (1935), *Stage Fright* (1949), *The Trouble with Harry* (1954), *Marnie*...

Twenty TV Movies

But this total of fifty-three does not by any means account for everything. He also made twenty films for television, between 1955 and 1962, as part of his celebrated series *Alfred Hitchcock Presents* and *The Alfred Hitchcock Hour* (ten seasons between them, 1955–1965). These TV films, placed here in the context of the filmography, have long been considered secondary, an appendix to the main body of work. But can we imagine Hitchcock, a born experimenter, indulging in bread-and-butter work rather than seizing this new form and using it as a laboratory? We need to see "One More Mile to Go" (1957) or "Lamb to the Slaughter" (1958) again and again to gauge the extent to which these "short forms" prepared the way for *Psycho*, itself intentionally filmed under the economic conditions of television. We need to see "Mr. Blanchard's Secret" (1956) and, above all, "The Crystal Trench" (1959) again and again to realize that both, like variations on a theme, continue *Rear Window* and *Vertigo*. We need to see "Revenge" (1955), "The Case of Mr. Pelham" (1955), "Four O'Clock" (1957), and "Bang! You're Dead" (1961) over and over again to feel that the filmmaker is using the new medium, which had entered American homes

on a massive scale, to hold up a merciless mirror to all his (TV) audience. By means of television, which is nonetheless also subject to the censors' gaze, he could freely explore one of the dimensions of his cinema: the humdrum of everyday life, sexual frustration to the point of madness, the horror of married life, the savagery beneath the thin veneer of civilization. Beyond "Uncle Alfred's" debonair, ever-joking demeanor, the Hitchcock universe is one of total pessimism, where everything—from access to material comfort to the advent of true love—is a deadly illusion.

War Films

Fifty-three plus twenty...still not the complete list. To this we need to add the "war films"—his two propaganda shorts (*Bon voyage, Aventure malgache*, 1944) and his photo dramatization published in *Life* in 1942 ("Have You Heard?")—and also list the films on which he "helped out" on behalf of the war effort, without being credited. Of these, the most important and crucial has long been known as *Memory of the Camps*. In the summer of 1945, Hitchcock, who had been living in Los Angeles for six years, returned to London at the request of his friend and producer Sidney Bernstein to help him make a film from unprecedented images: those of the liberation of the Nazi concentration camps and death camps. The filmmaker had a month in the English capital, but the shock waves of what he saw were to spread, either beneath the surface or clearly visible, through the American work that followed.

All the Films...

To be truly comprehensive, we must also mention all the unrealized projects (and they are numerous) and identify the documentaries and other small films to which Hitchcock contributed, often for his own reasons. Cinema came to this somewhat strange and solitary child, who, though frightened of police officers from an early age, found pleasure in the meticulous and insatiable observation of the world around him.

Hitchcock Before Hitchcock (1899–1925)

"Fear [...] is a feeling that people like to feel when they are certain of being in safety."

Alfred Hitchcock

Prologue

• On February 20, 1896, at London's Finsbury Technical College, Robert William Paul presented his invention, the Theatrograph, the first English projector, to be marketed. On the same day, at the Polytechnic Institution in Regent Street (West End), the Lumière brothers' correspondent showed films made with their brand-new Cinématographe, both camera and projector.

August 13, 1899

• Born in Leytonstone, a suburb northeast of London, Alfred Joseph Hitchcock was the third and last child of William Hitchcock, the third generation of a family of fruit and vegetable merchants, and Emma Jane Whelan, of Irish descent and the daughter of a police constable. He came from a Catholic family, "which in England is almost an eccentricity."[1]

1899 and Early Years

• His father's shop was located in a working-class district of London, at 517 High Road (the house was on the second floor), amid butcher shops, workshops, theaters, newsagents… Alfred's earliest memories include the smell of ripening bananas and walnuts being shelled for sale. Alfred often accompanied his father, William, on deliveries to London's Covent Garden Market. His father was stern, hardworking, nervous, emotionally awkward, and a stickler for order.

Covent Garden: *Sabotage*, 1936; *Frenzy*, 1971.

January 22, 1901

• Queen Victoria died. One of her sons, Edward VII, became King of the United Kingdom and the member countries of the Empire (Canada, Australia, New Zealand, Newfoundland), as well as Emperor of India. He reigned until his death in 1910. In the June 1, 1960, issue of the French magazine *Arts*, Hitchcock took the Proust questionnaire: "Who is your favorite historical figure?" Answer: "Edward VII. He led a pleasant life and he made the Entente Cordiale" [an allusion to the diplomatic agreements signed in 1904 between the United Kingdom and France].

1904 or 1905?

• This is one of Hitchcock's most famous stories, and one he has told many times. When Alfred was five or six years old, his father sent him to the police station with a note. The officer read it, locked the boy in a cell without comment (for no more than five minutes, of course), and, as he was let out, delivered the sentence "This is what we do to naughty boys." This very young "wrong man" was also a born storyteller: He did not hesitate to dramatize this episode of unverifiable veracity, declaring that "the metallic clang of the imposing door closing and the brutal slamming of the bolt" were engraved forever in his memory.

Imprisonment: *The Mountain Eagle*, 1926; *Blackmail*, 1929; *Murder!*, 1930; *The Paradine Case*, 1947; *Dial M for Murder*, 1953; *The Wrong Man*, 1956; *Frenzy*, 1971.

A "prison" memory for the young Alfred Hitchcock? Henry Fonda (*The Wrong Man*, 1956).

Confession: Montgomery Clift, O. E. Hasse (*I Confess*, 1952).

Around 1905

• At the theater, one scene definitively caught his imagination: The heroine appeared lit in pink, while the traitor appeared in a halo of green light.

• "I was what they call a well-behaved child." At family gatherings: "I would sit quietly in a corner, saying nothing. I looked and observed a great deal." […] "can't even remember having had a playmate. I played by myself, inventing my own games."

A halo of green light: Kim Novak in *Vertigo*, 1957; *Mary Rose* (unrealized project), 1964.

1906

• By the age of seven, Alfred was the only child in his parents' home: "Fear? It influenced my life and my career […] It was a Sunday. My parents put me to bed and went for a walk. […] Then, by misfortune, I woke up. I called out, but no one answered. It's dark all around me. Groping, I get up, wander around the empty, dark house, arrive in the kitchen and find a piece of cold meat, which I eat, sprinkling it with my tears."

• The young boy was educated at Howrah House, a private school located in a convent run by the Faithful Companions of Jesus in Poplar, a neighboring district of Leytonstone.

1907 or 1908

• The Hitchcocks moved to Salmon Lane, in the lively East London district of Limehouse, where Alfred's father opened two fishmonger shops.

• For years, Alfred had to confess his entire day at the foot of his mother's bed every evening, without leaving out a single detail. It was something he would always remember.

Confession, Catholicism, the Last Judgment:
The Manxman, 1928; *Spellbound*, 1944; *I Confess*, 1952; *The Wrong Man*, 1956; "The Horseplayer" (TV), 1961; *The Birds*, 1962…

1908

• A reader of railroad signs and travelogues, able to memorize the grid map of New York and recite the names of the stations on the Orient Express route, himself a traveler on the Thames and to the terminus of every London tramway line, young Alfred dreamed about transportation. On his bedroom wall, he pinned a planisphere and sharpened his sense of precision by plotting the comings and goings of British merchant ships, represented by so many little flags. At the cinema or a fair, he saw *Aboard a Crazy Train*, a film shot from the front of a locomotive and ending with a simulated accident. Forty years later, and with a number of suspense films to his credit, Hitchcock published a text in *Good Housekeeping* magazine entitled "The Enjoyment of Fear" (February 1949).

Train: *Number Seventeen*, 1932; *The 39 Steps*, 1935; *Secret Agent*, 1935; *The Lady Vanishes*, 1938; *Shadow of a Doubt*, 1942; *Spellbound*, 1944; *Strangers on a Train*, 1950; *North by Northwest*, 1958…
Boat: *Downhill*, 1927; *Champagne*, 1928; *The Manxman*, 1928; *Rich and Strange*, 1931; *Jamaica Inn*, 1938; *Lifeboat*, 1943; "Dip in the Pool" (TV), 1958; *Marnie*, 1964; *Torn Curtain*, 1966… In 1939, for his first American film, Hitchcock planned to tell the story of the *Titanic*…
Bus: *Downhill*, 1927; *Number Seventeen*, 1932; *Sabotage*, 1936; *To Catch a Thief*, 1954; *The Man Who Knew Too Much*, 1955; *Torn Curtain*, 1966…

1910

• Like the rest of London, the young Hitchcock followed the case of Dr. Crippen, hanged for killing his wife and burying her dismembered body in the coal cellar of the marital home. Fleeing with his mistress to Canada, he was recognized by the captain of the transatlantic liner, who used a new means of communication—wireless telegraphy—to alert the English authorities, thereby facilitating his arrest.

In response to Proust's question "What are your favorite heroines in real life?," the filmmaker replied, "Grace Kelly, or Adelaide Bartlett," the alleged murderer of her husband in a case (ménage à trois, chloroform poisoning) that led to a resounding trial in 1886—two years before the abominable murders of Jack the Ripper terrorized and captivated Londoners for a long time to come. "Crime has always fascinated me. To my mind, it's a uniquely English problem."
• From October 5, for three years Hitchcock attended St. Ignatius College in Stamford Hill, run by the Jesuits, a Catholic congregation vowed to poverty, chastity ("the angelic virtue"), and obedience. Mass preceded each school day. The priests' teaching ranged from religious instruction ("the power of Jesuitical reasoning") to the study of languages, from history to mathematics, from science to literature (Shakespeare, Dante, Dickens), from singing to drawing. Young Alfred, a studious day pupil, every year finished "second or third in the class. This is far better than being top of the class. Otherwise people expect too much of you, and the pressure is too great."

Good education was also based on order and discipline, not to say correction. An extract from the rule: "A well-informed pedagogue cannot underestimate the importance of corporal punishment.

Corporal punishment is healthy. And it is English." Hitchcock would say on many occasions that the threat of punishment with the ferule, a flat instrument like a ruler, made of wood or hard rubber, fortified his sense of fear (physical fear, fear of sin) and taught him suspense, with the punished pupil deciding for himself when the punishment would come, and living from then on in expectation of receiving his punishment. Hitchcock would also say that these corrections, from which his good behavior seems to have exempted him, impressed him with "a certain sense of drama."
• The rather plump and subsequently chubby young man never practiced any sport, refraining from doing so for most of his life (with the exception of a bit of tennis). "I expend all my energy above the neck. I observe." Hitchcock was already the master observer.

Dr. Crippen: *Rear Window*, 1954; "Back for Christmas" (TV), 1956; *Vertigo*, 1957.
Jack the Ripper: *The Lodger*, 1926; *Frenzy*, 1971.
Tennis: *Easy Virtue*, 1927; *Strangers on a Train*, 1950.
Voyeur: *The Pleasure Garden*, 1925; *Rear Window*, 1954; "Mr. Blanchard's Secret" (TV), 1956; *Vertigo*, 1957; *Psycho*, 1960…

1913

• In the autumn, Hitchcock enrolled at the London County School of Engineering and Navigation in Poplar, where he studied electricity, mechanics, and industrial design. He also attended evening classes at the University of London.

From August 1914

• On August 4, 1914, the British Empire declared war on Germany and, through the interplay of alliances, entered into a global conflict. From May 1915 until the end of the war, German aircraft bombed England's capital. On at least two occasions, explosions occurred very close to the Salmon Lane house. "Through the window we could see—an extraordinary sight!—flak shells exploding around a zeppelin illuminated by searchlights."

1914–1921

• Hitchcock was employed by Henley's Telegraph Works, an electric cable company. He was quickly promoted: Starting out as a grader, he was transferred to the sales department, then to advertising (1918), where he put to good use his taste for drawing and promotion and his ability to anticipate public reactions. Esteemed for his talent and humor, he began to socialize to some extent.

Mary Rose, J. M. Barrie's play about a ghost, was first performed in April 1920 at London's Haymarket Theatre. In the title role, Fay Compton. The young Alfred Hitchcock, who attended one of the performances that year, would remember it for the rest of his life.

The profile of Madeleine: Kim Novak (*Vertigo*, 1957).

The ghost: Kim Novak (*Vertigo*, 1957).

December 12, 1914

• At the age of fifty-two, William Hitchcock died suddenly. Alfred's sister Nellie told him: "*Your* father is dead." The eldest brother, William Jr., took over the two fishmongers on Salmon Lane.

1915

• Gaumont, a French film production company, opened the huge Lime Grove Studios in Shepherd's Bush, West London, where Hitchcock would later make four films.

• Hitchcock attended Goldsmiths College (University of London), where he studied drawing, painting, and art history.

Lime Grove Studios: *The Man Who Knew Too Much*, 1934; *The 39 Steps*, 1935; *Secret Agent*, 1935; *Sabotage*, 1936.

1915–1918

• Solitary and shy, especially with women, the teenager began to assert his interests by frequenting music halls and theaters. He went to the movies a lot and bought specialized magazines, *The Bioscope* and *The Kinematograph and Lantern Weekly*, in a store in Leicester Square. He visited Madame Tussauds' wax figure museum and its Chamber of Horrors. He attended court hearings at the Old Bailey.

Alfred Hitchcock read John Buchan's *The Thirty-Nine Steps*, published in 1915, discovered Flaubert's *Madame Bovary* and the work of Edgar Allan Poe: "Without wishing to sound immodest, I can't help comparing what I try to put into my films to what Poe put into his stories: a perfectly incredible story told to readers following a logic so hallucinatory that it gives everyone the impression that the same story could happen to him tomorrow."

He indulged his passion for food and, with his first wages, went in particular to Simpson's in the Strand, a restaurant on one of London's main streets. This also contributed to his stoutness.

• At eighteen, old enough to be called up but exempted from active duty, Hitchcock joined the Royal Engineers volunteer corps. He moved from his home on Salmon Lane to the heart of London.

Music hall, theater: *The Pleasure Garden*, 1925; *Downhill*, 1927; *Rich and Strange*, 1931; *The 39 Steps*, 1935; *Stage Fright*, 1949…
Cinema: *Sabotage*, 1936; *Saboteur*, 1942.
The Old Bailey: *Flames of Passion* (Graham Cutts; assistant: Alfred Hitchcock), 1922; *The Paradine Case*, 1947; *Frenzy*, 1971.
John Buchan: *The 39 Steps*, 1935.
Simpson's in the Strand: *Sabotage*, 1936.

1919–1921

• In June 1919, Hitchcock published his first text in the *Henley Telegraph*, a company magazine of which he was founder and editor, a short story entitled "Gas" and signed "Hitch" ("It's 'Hitch'…without the 'cock,'" he often joked), a frightening tale with a comic punch line. Up to March 1921, he published six other short stories, all in the same tone, designed to surprise and entertain. The second, *The Woman's Part* (September 1919), is told from the "blocked" point of view of a voyeuristic spectator who suffers and enjoys his impotence.

• An avid moviegoer ("I didn't miss a thing"), he preferred American films, by D. W. Griffith ("the Christopher Columbus of the screen"), Chaplin, Cecil B. DeMille, and those starring Mary Pickford. He admired their sense of editing and dynamism: "Whereas English films presented a flat image, mixing foreground and background, American films were lit from behind so that the figures and characters in the foreground stood out better from the background."

1920

• *Mary Rose*, a play by J. M. Barrie (author of *Peter Pan*), was performed at the Haymarket Theatre (West End), with Fay Compton in the title role. Hitchcock never forgot this ghost story, and in the 1960s he even tried in vain to adapt it for the screen.

Fay Compton: *Waltzes from Vienna*, 1933.

1921

• In April, Hitchcock resigned from his position at Henley's Telegraph Works to officially join the Islington-based film studios in North London, with which he had already been working since the end of the previous year. Indeed, he had read in the trade press that the Hollywood studio Famous Players–Lasky, which had opened well-equipped and organized studios in the British capital in 1919, was hiring writers and illustrators of intertitles (captions; the texts and drawings that, onscreen, add "dialogue" to the plot in silent films). To secure a job, he presented a portfolio of sketches, brochures, and intertitle designs, all examples of his skill and calm determination.

Islington Studios: *The Lodger*, 1926; *Downhill*, 1927; *Easy Virtue*, 1927.

1921–1924

• In December 1921, Alfred Hitchcock became one of the four hundred members of the Kinema Club,

Italy, summer 1925: Alfred Hitchcock during the filming of *The Pleasure Garden*.

a Central London–based association of English film production professionals. He remained a member until 1924.

1921–1925

• Over a period of five years, Hitchcock took part in nineteen films as an "intertitler," set designer (starting with George Fitzmaurice's *Three Live Ghosts*, 1922, with Clare Greet), and, from 1923, co-writer and assistant director. He also attempted to direct *Number Thirteen* and co-directed *Always Tell Your Wife*. His drawings as a set designer and art director helped him

visualize the best angle for a director, and where to place the camera.

In an interview in the 1960s, Hitchcock recalled his early days at Islington Studios for British Famous Players–Lasky: "You must remember that I was trained in the American way. When you pushed open the studio doors, it was like being in Hollywood. Everyone was American. The screenwriters were American, the directors were American."

Early 1922

• Famous Players–Lasky stopped producing films in Islington, unsatisfied with the box-office results in

September–December 1924: shooting of *The Blackguard* (Graham Cutts). Twenty-five-year-old Hitchcock was screenwriter, set designer, and assistant director.

the UK and the US. Hitchcock's first film, *Number Thirteen* (or *Mrs. Peabody*), unfinished and now lost, was thus a semi-independent venture. The scenario is Chaplinesque: A woman wins the lottery and dreams that she is entertaining her friends in her mansion, while her enemies have become her servants. In the lead roles: Ernest Thesiger, who acted in J. M. Barrie's *Mary Rose* at its premiere, and Clare Greet, playing Mrs. Peabody. Due to a lack of funds, filming was interrupted, despite financial help from the actress's father and an uncle of the hapless director. On this occasion, Hitchcock learned the importance of meticulous preproduction, from financial editing to preparatory drawings (later storyboards). All that remains of the film are a few photos.

Clare Greet: *The Ring*, 1927; *The Manxman*, 1928; *Murder!*, 1930; *The Man Who Knew Too Much*, 1934; *Sabotage*, 1936; *Jamaica Inn*, 1938.

July–August 1922

• Graham Cutts shot *The Flames of Passion*. Hitchcock took part, in various capacities, in seven films by this English director, one of the most renowned of the period. The same year, Cutts directed *Paddy the Next Best Thing*, with Hitchcock as assistant, Eliot Stannard as scriptwriter, and actresses Marie Ault and Marie Wright.

Eliot Stannard: *The Pleasure Garden*, 1925; *The Mountain Eagle*, 1926; *The Lodger*, 1926; *Downhill*, 1927; *Easy Virtue*, 1927; *The Ring*, 1927; *The Farmer's Wife*, 1927; *Champagne*, 1928; *The Manxman*, 1928.
Marie Ault: *The Lodger*, 1926; *Jamaica Inn*, 1938.
Marie Wright: *Murder!*, 1930.

September 1922

• *Spanish Jade* by John S. Robertson was released, Hitchcock's eleventh contribution as title designer. This work on intertitles introduced him to their effects and, consequently, to the effects of editing on the film's meaning. In other words, editing provides the viewer with the emotions intended by the director. Later, Hitchcock would become fascinated with the "Kuleshov effect," which would become his breviary of editing and directing.

Editing and directing: *Sabotage*, 1936; *I Confess*, 1952; *Torn Curtain*, 1966...

1923

• On January 9, 1923, Edith Thompson, suspected of involvement in the murder of her husband with the complicity of her lover, was hanged. It was a case, trial, and execution that made headlines. The deceased was the daughter of William Graydon, who taught the young Hitchcock to waltz in the late 1910s, when he was working at Henley's. He knew the story in great detail and remembered it for the rest of his life, respectfully sending Edith Thompson's sister a Christmas card every year.
• In February, Hitchcock was production manager on *Always Tell Your Wife*, a short film produced by comic actor Seymour Hicks. Halfway through the film, he replaced the director, who had been fired by the producer, and co-wrote this "two-reeler" with the actor. In his autobiography (1949), Hicks described him as "a fat young man [...] terribly enthusiastic and eager to try his hand at directing." The cinematographer was Claude L. McDonnell. The story is about a husband, his wife, and his mistress, with shots of a caged bird. The film seems never to have been distributed. Only one of two reels remains.
• Wyndham's Theatre (West End) presented *The Dancers*, a play that was a great public success. The main attraction was a young actress with a husky voice and singular charm named Tallulah Bankhead.

Allusion to the Edith Thompson affair: *Stage Fright*, 1949.
A woman caught between two men: *The Mountain Eagle*, 1926; *The Lodger*, 1926; *The Ring*, 1927; *The Manxman*,

1928; *Rich and Strange*, 1931; *Secret Agent*, 1935; *Notorious*, 1946; *Under Capricorn*, 1948; *Dial M for Murder*, 1953; *North by Northwest*, 1958; "Mrs. Bixby and the Colonel's Coat" (TV), 1960...
Claude L. McDonnell: *Downhill*, 1927; *Easy Virtue*, 1927.
Bird in a cage: *Sabotage*, 1936; *Psycho*, 1960; *The Birds*, 1962.
Tallulah Bankhead: *Lifeboat*, 1943.

April–May 1923

• *Woman to Woman*, shot in Islington, was the first film co-produced by Michael Balcon; it was directed by Graham Cutts, with actress Betty Compson. Hitchcock adapted the play, designed the sets, and assisted with the direction: "It was the first film I really took in hand." He recruited the continuity girl and film joiner Alma Reville, whom he had noticed earlier and who had just lost her job in Islington. Together, they made five Cutts films between 1923 and 1925.
• To prepare for *Woman to Woman*, Hitchcock traveled to Paris for the first time: He attended mass at the Madeleine church, then went to the Moulin Rouge to study the architecture of the famous cabaret and create a replica of it in the film.

Betty Compson: *Mr. & Mrs. Smith*, 1940.

Spring 1924

• Michael Balcon founded Gainsborough Pictures and took over Islington Studios. He produced *The Passionate Adventure*, directed by Graham Cutts and starring Lillian Hall-Davis, for which Hitchcock, among others, wrote the screenplay. In the course of the plot, the heroine plunges a knife into the villain's back—a visual surprise and a stabbing shock that the future director was to make a specialty.

Lillian Hall-Davis: *The Ring*, 1927; *The Farmer's Wife*, 1927.
The stabbing: *Blackmail*, 1929; *Sabotage*, 1936; *Dial M for Murder*, 1953; *Psycho*, 1960...

September–December 1924

• Following a co-production agreement between Gainsborough Pictures and UFA (Erich Pommer), a highly reputed German film production company, Alfred Hitchcock and Alma Reville traveled to Babelsberg, on the outskirts of Berlin, to prepare for Graham Cutts's new film, *The Blackguard*, with Bernhard Goetzke in one of the lead roles. The young screenwriter and assistant director was also responsible for the sets, in particular that of an imposing dream sequence set in paradise, with numerous "angelic" extras and, (already), a gigantic staircase. Another set, for a concert hall, was inspired

Alfred Hitchcock, early 1920s.

by London's Royal Albert Hall. Through signs and sketches, Hitchcock communicated with German set designers and with Theodor Sparkuhl, the cinematographer on several Ernst Lubitsch films.

• While Hitchcock, a cinephile and film apprentice, already admired the science of lighting in Hollywood films, he was equally inspired by the monumentality of the sets in German expressionist films, in contrast to their attention to detail (Fritz Lang: "There are no details"), the audacity of their framing, and their often aerial or "unchained" camerawork. On one of the huge sets at Babelsberg Studios, he witnessed a day's shooting of F. W. Murnau's *The Last Man* (*Der letzte Mann*), a film so obsessed with visual expression that it is almost entirely narrated without the aid of intertitles. Hitchcock was impressed by a scene with a reconstructed station platform, a real train car in the foreground, and another real train car at the far end of the same shot, from which passengers were alighting. Between the two, perspective was forced by spectacular trickery to create an impressive illusion. And Murnau declared, formulating the future credo of the author of *Rear Window*: "It doesn't matter what you see on the set. What matters is what you see on the screen." It does not matter what the bottle is (the reality of the shoot), as long as you have the intoxication (the viewer's emotion). It does not even matter if this illusion is visible in the image, only the effect and impression obtained.

Erich Pommer: *The Pleasure Garden*, 1925; *Jamaica Inn*, 1938.
Bernhard Goetzke: *The Mountain Eagle*, 1926.
Staircases: *Easy Virtue*, 1927; *Number Seventeen*, 1932; *Rebecca*, 1939; *Suspicion*, 1941; *Shadow of a Doubt*, 1942; *Notorious*, 1946; *Strangers on a Train*, 1950; *The Man Who Knew Too Much*, 1955; *Vertigo*, 1957; *Psycho*, 1960; *Frenzy*, 1971…
Royal Albert Hall: *The Ring*, 1927; *The Man Who Knew Too Much*, 1934 and 1955.
German expressionism: *The Lodger*, 1926; *The Man Who Knew Too Much*, 1934; *Strangers on a Train*, 1950…

February 1925

• Hitchcock films *The Prude's Fall* with actor Miles Mander. This would be the last Cutts-Hitchcock collaboration.

Miles Mander: *The Pleasure Garden*, 1925; *Murder!*, 1930.

Spring 1925

• Michael Balcon negotiated a co-production agreement for five films involving Gainsborough Pictures and Emelka (MLK), a German company based in Munich. Alfred Hitchcock returned to Germany, but for the first time as director of a project entitled *The Pleasure Garden*. He was twenty-six years old.

October 1925

• October 25 saw the first screening by the Film Society, a Regent Street cine-club dedicated to films by French directors (Marcel L'Herbier, Jean Epstein), Germans (Robert Wiene, Fritz Lang, Walter Ruttmann, G. W. Pabst), and Soviets (Vsevolod Pudovkin, S. M. Eisenstein). None of these films—an art form in their own right—were distributed, or they were heavily censored in Great Britain. Alfred Hitchcock was an assiduous spectator at these monthly screenings, and four of the Film Society's founders and animators were to become his collaborators: Adrian Brunel, Ivor Montagu, Walter Charles Mycroft, and Sidney Bernstein.

Adrian Brunel: *Elstree Calling*, 1930 (co-scriptwriter and supervision).
Ivor Montagu: *The Lodger*, 1926; *Downhill*, 1927; *Easy Virtue*, 1927 (montage); *The Man Who Knew Too Much*, 1934; *The 39 Steps*, 1935; *Secret Agent*, 1935; *Sabotage*, 1936 (associate producer).
Walter C. Mycroft: *The Ring*, 1927; *Champagne*, 1928; *Elstree Calling*, 1930; *Murder!*, 1930 (co-scriptwriter and adaptor).
Sidney Bernstein: *Memory of the Camps*, 1945; *Rope*, 1948; *Under Capricorn*, 1948; *I Confess*, 1952 (co-producer).

Epilogue…

• On December 2, 1926, Alfred Hitchcock and Alma Reville were married at the London Oratory, a Catholic church on Brompton Road (in Westminster).

Marriage: *Easy Virtue*, 1927; *The Ring*, 1927; *Rich and Strange*, 1931; *Rebecca*, 1939; *Mr. & Mrs. Smith*, 1940; *Notorious*, 1946; *Marnie*, 1964…

English Hitchcock

The Pleasure Garden

1925

Great Britain/Germany • 1 hr 15 (20 images/second) • Black and White • Silent • 1.33:1

Production Dates: Summer 1925
Release Date in Germany: November 3, 1925 (Munich)
Release Date in Great Britain: April 12, 1926 (London), January 14, 1927 (outside London)

Production: Gainsborough Pictures, Münchner Lichtspielkunst AG (Emelka)
Producer: Michael Balcon

Based on the novel of the same name by Oliver Sandys (1923)
Screenplay: Eliot Stannard
Director of Photography: Gaetano di Ventimiglia
Assistant Director, Continuity: Alma Reville
Art Direction: Ludwig Reiber

Starring: Virginia Valli (Patsy Brand), Carmelita Geraghty (Jill Cheyne), Miles Mander (Levet), John Stuart (Hugh Fielding), Ferdinand Martini (Mr. Sidey), Florence Helminger (Mrs. Sidey), Georg H. Schnell (Oscar Hamilton), Karl Falkenberg (Prince Ivan), Louis Brody (Carruthers), Elizabeth Pappritz (young native woman)…

"Awake! for Morning
in the Bowl of Night /
Has flung the
Stone that puts the
Stars to Flight."

—

Omar Khayyam, "The Rubaiyat of
Omar Khayyam"

SYNOPSIS

—

Patsy, a dancer at the Pleasure Garden Theatre, a London music hall, is courted by rich, flesh-loving patrons. She befriends Jill, who manages to get into the troupe by seducing the owner. The two young women stay with an elderly couple, the Sideys. Jill is engaged to Hugh, an engineer who is preparing to spend several months in the tropics on business. Her comrade and colleague, Levet, falls in love with Patsy. While Hugh is away, the pushy Jill is romantically involved with Prince Ivan. Disappointed with Jill, Patsy distances herself from her friend and marries Levet. The two spend their honeymoon at Lake Como. From there, Levet leaves to find Hugh, who learns of his fiancée's infidelity from the tabloids, sinks into despair, and falls ill. Patsy decides to join Levet, believing him to be unwell, although he has used this condition as an excuse to dissuade her from coming. Jill, though well taken care of and lavishly accommodated, refuses to finance her trip. In the end, the Sideys lend her the money she needs. Patsy leaves without announcing her arrival and discovers that her husband is living with a native woman. Caught in the act, Levet chases off his mistress, then drowns her in the sea. While taking care of Hugh, Patsy realizes that she is in love with him. Driven mad by jealousy and guilt, Levet tries to kill his wife with a scimitar, only to be shot dead with a revolver by one of Hugh's friends. Patsy returns to England with the young man, now cured.

GENESIS

Alfred Hitchcock joined the English film industry in 1920. For five years, he trained with enthusiasm and talent in various trades—intertitle designer, set designer, scriptwriter, location manager, assistant director...at the Islington Studios, acquired by producer Michael Balcon in 1924. In 1925, at the age of twenty-six, Hitchcock was ready.

His Foot in the Stirrup

Hitchcock's first film was also the first co-production between Michael Balcon's company, Gainsborough Pictures, and Münchner Lichtspielkunst, aka Emelka (the pronunciation of the acronym MLK). Based in Munich, the German production company was counting on this alliance to rival UFA, the country's largest studio, based in Berlin. *The Pleasure Garden* was the first of five titles in the contract between Gainsborough Pictures and Emelka.

The screenplay, adapted from a novel by Oliver Sandys, one of the many pseudonyms of the prolific British bestselling author Marguerite Florence Laura Jarvis, was entrusted to Eliot Stannard. Author of almost ninety films between 1914 and 1933, the screenwriter would go on to write for Alfred Hitchcock eight more times.

CASTING

Among the leading male roles, that of Levet, the bigamist husband, was played by Miles Mander, who joined Hitchcock again in 1930 for *Murder!*. The actor had been touring since 1920, playing numerous supporting roles in England and Hollywood until his death in 1946. He was most notably seen in Albert Lewin's *The Picture of Dorian Gray* in 1945. Mander also worked as a screenwriter, writer, director (six feature films between 1928 and 1936), and producer.

The Idealistic Lover

Hugh Fielding, the idealistic lover, was played by John Stuart, born in Edinburgh in 1898, who enjoyed a long and prolific film career until his death in London in 1979. He played supporting roles in numerous British films, including Henry Cass's *Blood of the Vampire* and Terence Fisher's *The Revenge of Frankenstein* in 1958, and Wolf Rilla's *Village of the Damned* in 1960. He also frequently appeared in episodes of TV series. In 1931, Hitchcock rehired him for *Number Seventeen*.

An American Star

Convinced that the film needed an international star to break into the American market, Balcon brought Virginia Valli over from Hollywood to play Patsy, the big-hearted girl. She had made her debut at Essanay Studios in 1915 and was now a star at the peak of her career, filming for Fox and Universal. In 1924, the actress starred in King Vidor's *Wild Oranges*.

The other main female character, the cynical Jill, was played by Carmelita Geraghty, an American actress and close friend of Virginia Valli's, who made her debut in Maurice Tourneur's *Les deux gosses* (Jealous Husbands) in 1923. She left the film business in 1935 to become a painter.

Actresses' Caprices

Hitchcock's fiancée, Alma Reville, who was also his editor and assistant director, welcomed the two American actresses in Cherbourg and moved with them to Paris. To meet their requirements, they stayed at the Claridge Hotel, which immediately put a strain on the film's low budget. Alma Reville also took them to various boutiques to choose the dresses they would wear in the film.

FILMING AND PRODUCTION

Given that this was a co-production, interiors were shot at the Geiselgasteig Studios near Munich, and exteriors in Italy. Italy also provided the setting for the final sequences, which were supposed to take place in the tropics, in a place called "The East," presumably a British colony in the Middle East.

A Nightmarish Shoot

While Alma was in Paris with the two actresses, trying to rein in their expenses, Hitchcock left Munich for Genoa, accompanied by his cinematographer, Gaetano di Ventimiglia (known as "Baron Ventimiglia"), a cameraman, Miles Mander, and Elizabeth Pappritz, a young actress who played the unfaithful Levet's native mistress and for whom this would be her only film role. Di Ventimiglia, a Sicilian-born nobleman who had worked for the Associated Press and the *Newark Times* newspaper before entering the film industry, was reunited with Hitchcock on his next two films, *The Mountain Eagle* and *The Lodger*.

This first shoot was a nightmare for the young director. Mander nearly missed the train when he went to retrieve his makeup box, which he had left in a cab. The blank film, which di Ventimiglia had suggested Hitchcock should not declare at customs,

Karl Falkenberg, Carmelita Geraghty.

was confiscated at the Austrian-Italian border. The cameraman was sent to Milan to buy more, but on his return, the expense proved unnecessary: The seized film had been cleared through customs, in exchange for a fine…

A Revelation

The crew began shooting in the port of Genoa, then moved to San Remo for the beach scenes. Hitchcock was fond of recounting how, during filming, when Elizabeth Pappritz was indisposed and refusing to get into the water for the drowning scene, and being still very ignorant of the secrets of female physiology, he had to have the technical crew explain to him the existence of menstruation.

The waitress at a local hotel is said to have replaced the actress. Hitchcock referred to one shot in particular as a laborious, burlesque moment, his actor struggling to carry the drowned actress out of the water. However, this sequence does not exist in the longest version of the film known to date. Could Hitchcock have decided against it? Furthermore, it was the actress Elizabeth Pappritz who appeared in this dramatic scene. Could Hitchcock have shot it again, after the young actress's "indisposition," to replace the shots filmed with the improvised understudy? Either way, this was the first murder scene in a Hitchcock film, with an underwater shot of rare violence, showing the young woman struggling in vain against her assailant.

A Holiday Location

Summer 1925. The honeymoon sequence was shot on Lake Como, Italy, and the film couple stayed at the sumptuous Villa d'Este. Alfred Hitchcock and Alma Reville liked the place so much that they spent their own honeymoon there at the end of the following year. They would return frequently on vacation until the 1970s.

Elizabeth Pappritz, soon to be the victim of the first murder scene in a Hitchcock film.

Running Out of Resources

The film's budget was stretched by the purchase of film stock and Parisian expenses (luxury hotels and other high-cost items), forcing Hitchcock, who also had his wallet stolen, to write a letter to Balcon asking for an advance on his salary. He had to borrow money from the actors. Alma Reville and the actresses finally joined the team in Italy, at the Villa d'Este on Lake Como, where a few shots were canned. Always short of resources, Hitchcock sent his fiancée to ask the star of his film to lend him some money...

The filmmaker also took advantage of this moment and the setting to modify certain aspects of the script. The return journey was eventful. Hitchcock paid for excess luggage because of the large number of trunks brought by Virginia Valli. The team missed their connection in Zurich and had to find a hotel. While unloading the many suitcases from the train, a window was broken and had to be paid for.

The interior sequences were finally shot at the end of July 1925 in Munich, at the co-producer's studios.

A Tragedy of Desire

Despite a complicated and disorganized shoot, this film by a young director already gives an impression of mastery. One of the major themes in Hitchcock's work is immediately apparent: guilt. The guilt felt by Levet after the murder of his mistress manifests itself in the superimposed appearance of her ghostly body and face, which come to haunt him.

The Pleasure Garden is particularly striking for the strong erotic dimension of its narrative and direction. There are many fetishistic shots, such as the one showing Patsy's legs, one of them bare after her stocking falls on her shoe. For this melodrama is also a tragedy of destructive sexual desire, announced right from the opening credits. A dancer shimmies in a beam of light, foreshadowing the milieu described—that of the music hall and its chorus girls—and arousing the viewer's excitement. The predatory intensity of the male gaze is staged in the opening sequence: a shot of young women tumbling down a spiral staircase, followed by one of a line of dancers onstage, waving their arms and raising their legs. This is followed by a long tracking shot

of a row of male spectators thrilled by the show. One of them observes the girls' legs through theatrical binoculars. From the very first images by Alfred Hitchcock, the motif of voyeurism and the close-up technique express the filmmaker's intention to divide the body into objects of desire.

RECEPTION

On discovering the film in the small screening room at the Munich studio, Michael Balcon exclaimed that, given its technical qualities, *The Pleasure Garden* looked more like an American production than a European one.

A Frustrated Theater Release

The film displeased C. M. Woolf, head of the Gainsborough film distribution company, who was certain that audiences would be disconcerted by the formal staging effects (camera movements, super-impositions, contrasting lighting). Judging *The Pleasure Garden* insufficiently commercial and too "European" (i.e., too intellectual), he decided not to release it in the regions at first, to the great displeasure of the filmmaker. *The Pleasure Garden* was not shown throughout England until a year and a half later, in January 1927, before the distribution of *The Lodger*. The film was released in the US in September 1926, where its promotion relied exclusively on the presence of its female star, Virginia Valli.

Beginnings Considered to Be Promising

More than thirty years later, Alfred Hitchcock would recall that the *Daily Express (London)* had already described him in 1926 as "a young man with a master's brain." *The Observer* added that the filmmaker "has made some of the source material so interesting as to make one eager and optimistic for his future."

Until recently, however, *The Pleasure Garden* was not widely regarded by film historians. For a long time, it was seen as the first attempt by a filmmaker whose genius, according to them, would only manifest itself somewhat later.

Incomplete Copies

Hitchcock himself paid little heed to the film, conceding "a few interesting scenes" but preferring to tell his interlocutors about the chaotic shooting of the film. It is also true that, for a long time, *The Pleasure Garden* circulated in the form of truncated, poor-quality copies, with missing intertitles and mutilated sequences. It was not until it was restored by the British Film Institute in 2012 that the original version of an already highly personal work was discovered, in which is found, in embryonic form, a number of obsessions characteristic of Hitchcock cinema.

A Seemingly Moralistic Melodrama

The film's narrative structure consists of two parallel plots, those of the sentimental and moral journeys of two couples intersecting. With this apparently conventional scenario, the producer had doubtless no other intention than to offer audiences a commercial melodrama based on mediocre literature—a melodrama that condemns immorality and debauchery and rewards virtue.

The pairing of the two heroines, on the other hand, takes on an ambiguous sexual dimension, noted by François Truffaut in his interviews with the filmmaker. The two young women live together and sleep in the same bed. One of them wears pajamas, while the other wears a nightdress, a stereotypical translation of the masculine-feminine duo formed by Patsy and Jill.

Freeze Frame

Between two spaces and two widely separated times, Hitchcock imagined a particularly cruel and cynical form of connection. When Levet leaves Italy and sets sail for the tropics, Patsy, his wife, who has stayed behind, waves her handkerchief at him as he departs. A superimposed shot replaces the close-up of Patsy's hand with that of Levet's native mistress, who gives her lover the same welcoming wave. By the sheer force of the montage of these two hands, one woman has replaced another, almost naturally.

An Impulsive Violence

It is in the final section that the passions long held in check are unleashed with a violence that was almost scandalous for the time.

Desperate over Patsy's arrival, which provokes her immediate repudiation, Levet's native mistress sinks into the sea to drown herself. She is joined by her lover, who one imagines is trying to save her from suicide. When he reaches her, he grasps her in an embrace that is both erotic and deadly…as he buries her head underwater. Sex and death are thus irrevocably intertwined, and the sudden violence of the murder foreshadows the sordid assassinations in *Frenzy*, for example, filmed almost fifty years later. A similar confusion is suggested earlier in the film by the menacing shadow of Levet approaching Patsy when he wants to seduce her.

The impulsive explosion that asserts itself in the final minutes of *The Pleasure Garden* brings the film closer to the brutal naturalism of the cinema of Erich von Stroheim (*Foolish Wives* in 1922, *Greed* in 1924), who would describe the steamy, decadent atmosphere of the tropics at the end of his film *Queen Kelly* (1928). Before romantic harmony resumed with the formation of the Hugh-Patsy couple, this Hitchcockian pleasure garden was the less-than-Eden-like scene of a fatal confusion between Eros and Thanatos.

On the Pleasure Garden stage, time for the chorus line.

Alfred Hitchcock in the foreground; behind him, Alma Reville; behind the camera,
Gaetano di Ventimiglia. A fake production photo, a real promotional photo…

The Mountain Eagle

1926

Great Britain/ Germany • 1 hr 23 • Black and White • Silent • 1.33:1

Production Dates: October 1925–January 1926
Release Date in Germany: May 1926
Release Date in Great Britain: June 1927

Production: Gainsborough Pictures, Münchner Lichtspielkunst AG (Emelka)
Producer: Michael Balcon

Based on an original story by Charles Lapworth, "Fear o' God" (undated)
Screenplay: Eliot Stannard, Max Ferner
Director of Photography: Gaetano di Ventimiglia
Assistant Director, Continuity: Alma Reville
Artistic Directors: Ludwig Reiber, Willy Reiber

Starring: Nita Naldi (Beatrice), Malcolm Keen (John "Fear o' God" Fulton),
Bernhard Goetzke (Pettigrew), John Hamilton (Edward Pettigrew),
Ferdinand Martini (the dog Major)

> "It was a very bad movie and I'm not sorry there are no known prints."
>
> ——
>
> Alfred Hitchcock

> "Among the most 'wanted' of all missing films [...], something of a Holy Grail for film historians."
>
> ——
>
> Mark Duguid, British Film Institute

SYNOPSIS

——

Beatrice, the schoolteacher in a Kentucky mountain village, gives evening lessons to Edward Pettigrew, a crippled young man. She shows him a great deal of attention, arousing the jealousy of his father, Pettigrew, a justice of the peace and businessman, who tries to seduce her. She rebuffs him. Furious, he makes Beatrice look like a loose woman in the eyes of the villagers, prompting her to flee to the mountains. The young schoolteacher is taken in by a hermit, John Fulton, known as "Fear o' God," who, to suppress the scandal, forces Pettigrew to marry them, promising to divorce her as soon as she wishes. But Beatrice discovers that this new, unexpected life suits her perfectly. When Edward disappears, her father takes advantage of the situation to have Fulton arrested, accused without evidence of his son's murder and thrown into prison. After a year in solitary confinement, the false culprit escapes, returns to the mountains, and is reunited with his wife, who has had a child by their union. When the infant falls ill, Fulton braves the cold and snow to return to the village in search of a doctor. He comes across Pettigrew, and the confrontation is inevitable. But the worst is averted when Edward reappears. The father, who had been driven by an ancient anger against Fulton that goes back to the time of his son's birth, finally makes peace with his rival.[1]

Alfred Hitchcock, Alma Reville, Malcolm Keen: location scouting.

GENESIS

The financial setup for Hitchcock's second directorial effort resembled that of *The Pleasure Garden*: an Anglo-German co-production that should enable costs to be shared between the two countries and double the box-office receipts. An American star was also announced in the credits so that the film could be exported across the Atlantic.

The Hitchcock Cliché

Charles Lapworth, editorial director of Gainsborough Pictures, was the man behind the story. While Eliot Stannard tried to turn this heavy melodrama into a possible screenplay, Hitchcock, in October 1925, set out in search of photogenic exteriors. He described what he was looking for in an article published twelve years later: a pretty thatched-roof village, with snow-capped mountains in the background and beautiful trees in the foreground, and nothing modern in the shot. In short, it was an idealized, rustic image. Hitchcock had a fascinating conception of the cliché. He could reproduce well-known locations and use them dramatically (the Swiss chocolate factory and the rugged mountains in *Secret Agent*, 1935; the flower market and the Grande Corniche in Nice in *To Catch a Thief*, 1954) or, on the contrary, "avoid the cliché," as he put it, countering it to create surprise (in *North by Northwest*, 1958, the daylight "film noir scene" with a man in a business suit in a cornfield…).

CASTING

In November 1925, the young director traveled to Munich to welcome his leading lady, Nita Naldi. A Hollywood star, she was famous for her roles as vamp and temptress (Cecil B. DeMille's *The Ten Commandments*, three films with Rudolph Valentino).

Hollywood on Bavaria

According to Hitchcock, Nita Naldi appeared when she got off the train as glamorous, dark, wearing four-inch heels, and a black dog to match her swathed dress. She was a vision made all the more striking by the fact that she had to embody a mountain woman "who handled a gun instead of a lipstick." Hitchcock and Alma Reville, his assistant director and fiancée, set about transforming this femme fatale into a village schoolteacher: nails, makeup, hairstyle, wardrobe—everything was reworked. Unlike his work with Grace Kelly, Kim Novak, and Tippi Hedren, the director's aim here was to erase the sex appeal of his actress, and after this essential metamorphosis, Naldi's professionalism delighted the filmmaker. The same went for the male actors, Malcolm Keen, who would be cast again in *The Lodger* (1926) and *The Manxman* (1928), and Bernhard Goetzke, a Fritz Lang actor (*Death in Destiny* [*Der müde Tod*], the chief inspector in *Doctor Mabuse the Gambler* [*Dr. Mabuse, der Spieler*]). Hitchcock, then assistant director, met Goetzke on the set of Graham Cutts's *The Blackguard* (1925).

A Lost Film

Of the fifty-three feature-length films Hitchcock made for the cinema, only one is missing: *The Mountain Eagle*, of which neither negatives nor projection prints remain, despite research by cinematheques and archives worldwide. Many films from the silent era (1895–1929) have also disappeared (around two-thirds of the Hollywood production, for example). There are two main reasons for this: For a long time, cinema was seen as an entertainment industry rather than an art form and was not carefully and systematically preserved. And in 1929, the film industry's massive transition to talkies "devalued" silent films by denying them any commercial value.

Nita Naldi, Malcolm Keen.

FILMING AND PRODUCTION

Hitchcock found the village for his film on a post-card: Obergurgl, in the Austrian Tyrol. He and his team traveled there by train and wagon and on foot, in search of a location likely to evoke Kentucky...

Too Much Snow

The location turned out to be ideal, but on the night of their arrival, it snowed so much that they had to shoot in the nearby town of Umhausen. The filming was going to take longer than expected due to the weather. In Umhausen, the snow fell so heavily that Hitchcock had to persuade the local firemen to melt it with a hose.

After one or two weeks on location, the film was completed at Munich's Emelka Studios. On set, Willy Reiber and his brother Ludwig—who had worked on the London sets of *The Pleasure Garden*—created a mountain village. The few surviving set photos testify to the attention to detail given to the interiors (the hermit's hut).

A Stormy Marriage Proposal

It was at the end of filming *The Mountain Eagle*, after leaving Munich and on board the ship taking them back to England, that Alfred Hitchcock proposed to Alma Reville. And, fittingly, the director told the story: The ship was buffeted by a heavy swell, and Alma was in bed, suffering from sea-sickness. Taking advantage of this state of weakness, he plucked up the courage to ask her the big question. With a gesture, she consented: "It was one of my best scenes, a little weak on dialogue, perhaps, but remarkably staged and soberly acted."

Nita Naldi, Malcolm Keen. With the help of Ludwig and Willy Reiber, his art directors, Hitchcock paid particular attention to the details inside the hermit's cabin.

RECEPTION

The film was distributed in Germany in May 1926, in the US from the end of 1926, and in England only in June 1927, no doubt in order to capitalize on the successful release of *The Pleasure Garden* and *The Lodger*.

Criticism of the Content, Praise for the Form

The Mountain Eagle was shown to the English press in October 1926, then shelved, partly because the few reviews obtained were mixed. For *The Bioscope*, "director Alfred Hitchcock has not been particularly well served by his author, and in spite of skilful, and at times brilliant direction, the story has an air of unreality." The same article praised "some unusually artistic lighting effects" (October 7, 1926).

On the same day, *The Kinematograph Weekly* reported that the director had "slowed the pace too much" and told "a story with too many unconvincing twists and turns." Still, the journalist praises Bernhard Goetzke's performance: "You can almost feel his train of thought through his expressions." Later, the *Gloucestershire Echo*, sensitive to the story's emotional crescendo, also praised Goetzke's performance: "a particularly vigorous facial study" (August 9, 1927). And in the *Gloucester Citizen* (August 23, 1927): "There are some striking snow scenes and fine mountain scenery and many exciting moments—instances in which the suspense is very ably contrived."

An Unknown Filmmaker, but Not for Long

At the beginning of 1926, Alfred Hitchcock was twenty-six years old and had received a sound training. He had already made two feature films, and his rise was rapid. But at the time, with films still on the shelf, he was still a director unknown to the public, only noticed by the specialized press for his earlier work as a screenwriter. However, he had the full confidence of his producer, Michael Balcon, who, at the beginning of 1926, had already announced a program of nine films, one of which was immediately assigned to Hitchcock: *The Lodger*.

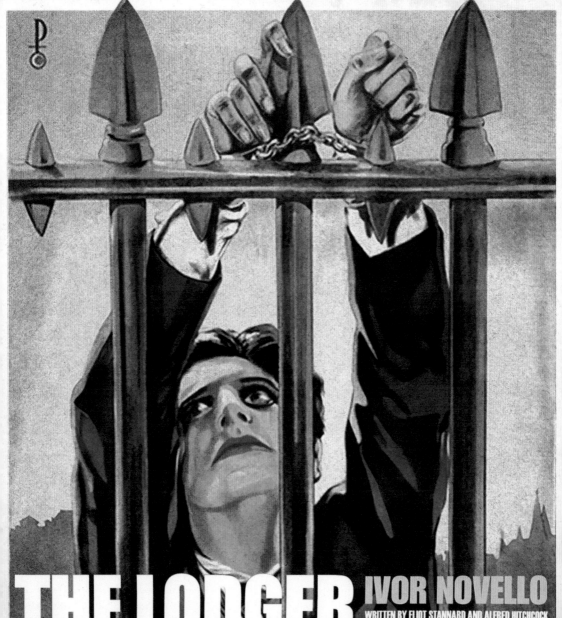

The Lodger

Great Britain

1 h 32
(20 images/second)

Black and White

Silent

1.33:1

Production Dates: Early March–mid-April 1926
Release Date in Great Britain: February 14, 1927
Release Date in the United States: June 10, 1928

Production: Gainsborough Pictures, Carlyle Blackwell
Productions / Piccadilly Pictures
Producers: Michael Balcon, Carlyle Blackwell

Based on a novel of the same name by Marie Belloc Lowndes (1913)
Screenplay: Eliot Stannard
Director of Photography: Gaetano di Ventimiglia
Assistant Director: Alma Reville
Scripts: Renie Morrison, Alma Reville
Artistic Directors: C. Wilfred Arnold, Bertram Evans
Costumes: Gilbert Adrian
Second Editing, Intertitles: Ivor Montagu
Intertitles Design: Edward McKnight Kauffer

Starring: Ivor Novello (the lodger), Marie Ault (the landlady), Arthur Chesney
(husband of the landlady), June Tripp (Daisy), Malcolm Keen (Joe, policeman),
Reginald Gardiner (a dancer at the ball), Alfred Hitchcock (a man seen from behind,
in the newspaper offices, and perhaps also during the attack by the crowd)…

> "Those who have dreamed of him [...] assure us that Jack the Ripper presented himself to them as an extremely elegant man, with a dark, handsome face, extremely slender hands and wrists whose slenderness did not preclude robustness."

— Robert Desnos, Jack l'Eventreur (*Jack the Ripper*), 1928

SYNOPSIS

—

An "avenger" is roaming London, particularly in the Bloomsbury district. Every Tuesday evening, in the fog, this elusive man murders a young woman, always a blonde, and signs his crime with a triangle drawn on a piece of paper. This is the seventh time he has done this. The newspapers increase their circulation, the police stall, and the public panics. One evening, a stranger knocks on the door of a local boardinghouse and moves in upstairs. Strange and seductive, he soon develops strong feelings for Daisy, the landlady's daughter and a model, herself troubled but engaged to Joe, a policeman working to arrest the "Avenger." One Tuesday evening, the tenant takes advantage of the darkness to slip out. Shortly afterward, a new crime is reported. The landlady, who has seen him come and go, has no doubts. She tries to keep Daisy away, but Daisy finds herself increasingly attracted to this handsome stranger with his disturbing manner. Blinded by jealousy, Joe convinces himself of the tenant's guilt and handcuffs him. The man flees, pursued by a lynch mob. Fortunately, at the same time, the arrest of the Avenger is announced. The false culprit explains himself: His sister having been killed by the Avenger, he has decided to imitate him in every way in order to find and eliminate him. Innocent, the tenant—in reality the owner of a large mansion—can now marry the woman he loves and who loves him.

Ivor Novello, the man in the scarf.

GENESIS

In December 1925, the English trade press announced a new Gainsborough production, *The Lodger: A Story of the London Fog.*

This would be the third feature for the twenty-six-year-old Hitchcock, who had just directed several scenes from *The Mountain Eagle* in Munich. His producer, Michael Balcon, had acquired the rights to the bestselling novel by the prolific Marie Belloc Lowndes and was inspired to entrust its adaptation to his young protégé.

A Haunting Story

Hitchcock was very fond of *The Lodger*, a novel published in 1913, about a mysterious lodger whose entire household anxiously wonders whether he is the killer of young London women. This imaginary tale was inspired by the still vivid memory of the demented and very real crimes of Jack the Ripper, who brought an atmosphere of terror to the capital in 1888. And the man known as the Whitechapel Killer lived in a neighborhood not so far from Leytonstone, where little Alfred was born in 1899…

By the age of seventeen, Hitchcock had already seen a theatrical adaptation of *Who Is He?*. The novel would haunt him for the rest of his life. In July 1940, he made a broadcast of it for CBS Radio, and that same year tried to bring about an American remake in color and talkies. He also used the story in other films (notably *Shadow of a Doubt*, 1942). In 1971, *Frenzy*, his penultimate film shot in London, opened like *The Lodger*: a murdered woman, a bank of the Thames, a crowd bending over to view an inanimate body, with the killer's distinctive sign—a scarf in *The Lodger*, and a necktie in *Frenzy*.

Some Minor Changes

As with his two previous films, Hitchcock wrote the screenplay with Eliot Stannard. Son of a novelist, an insatiable worker, an avid reader, and a smooth talker, Stannard held an unrivaled record (except for Hitchcock's wife, Alma Reville, who was in a different category): Between 1925 and 1929, he wrote the screenplays for nine of the director's first ten films. Between January and February 1926, the two men embarked on an essentially faithful adaptation of *The Lodger.*

Admittedly, Stannard and Hitchcock made some changes: The character of the landlady, the protagonist of the novel, is less important in the film. On the contrary, they expanded Daisy's role, giving rise to the first Hitchcock blonde. Another difference: Whereas in the novel, the penultimate chapter takes place in the Chamber of Horrors at Madame Tussauds' waxworks museum, Hitchcock did not use this location. His forthcoming cinematic work suggests that the young filmmaker must have been reluctant to give up such a memorable set piece. The film does, however, introduce an accessory with a promising future in the Hitchcock world: handcuffs. Another promising motif is a beautiful and disturbing bathroom scene: Daisy enters her bathtub, her nudity conveniently protected by a cloud of steam. When, suddenly, more than thirty years before the shower scene in *Psycho*, the disturbing tenant's hand grips the doorknob and the man almost enters…

For Hitchcock Addicts

In the novel, not all the Avenger's victims are blond. The choice of blondness was a matter of the imagination of the two screenwriters, or of Hitchcock's fantasies. For example, he forced June Tripp, the lead actress, to wear a blond wig.

Frances Bavier, Jack Palance, in *Man in the Attic*, one of the remakes of *The Lodger*.

A Series of Adaptations

Following Hitchcock's 1926 adaptation of Marie Belloc Lowndes's novel, there were several others: a British film by Maurice Elvey, with Ivor Novello once again in the title role (*The Lodger*, 1932). Then there was John Brahm's film for 20th Century-Fox, with the disturbing Laird Cregar as the lodger (*The Lodger*, 1944). Argentine director Hugo Fregonese offered another version with Jack Palance (*Man in the Attic*, 1953). Hitchcock told Truffaut that he found these remakes "too laborious." In 2009, there was another Jack the Ripper (*The Lodger*) by David Ondaatje, starring Simon Baker.

CASTING

It is the tenant, Mr. Sleuth in the novel and an unnamed man onscreen, who brings about the most significant change from book to film.

"The most handsome man in England"

Although forgotten today, Ivor Novello was a star in 1926. Born in Wales, composer of popular songs, author of one-act plays, and successful film actor (*The Rat*, Graham Cutts, 1925), Novello was known above all as an *homme fatal*. Adored by female audiences, he embodied a local version of Rudolph Valentino. In the first half of the 1920s, the American press dubbed him "the most handsome man in England." Onscreen, this tall figure exuded androgynous beauty and masochistic acting, culminating in a scene in *The Lodger* where he hung from a railing by his handcuffs, unable to free himself. Such fragility and celebrity certainly demands some consideration…The directive not to portray Novello as a real-life serial killer, in order to preserve his popularity, came from C. M. Woolf, the all-powerful distributor and president of Gainsborough Pictures. In the novel, however, there is no doubt as to the guilt of this enlightened tenant. Hitchcock dreamed of an

outcome similar to the one in the novel, and more ambiguous than the one into which he was abruptly forced. The presumed murderer disappears into the fog, just as the real Jack the Ripper's crimes abruptly cease without ever being solved.

A Short Lesson in Suspense

The main character must be a wrongly identified suspect. Screenwriters are free to allow suspicion to hang over the hero for a while, so long as they exonerate him at the end…without a shadow of a doubt. An obligation, justified by the actor's untouchable image, to which Hitchcock would return when concluding *Suspicion* (1941): Cary Grant could never be a murdering husband. But this constraint in *The Lodger* proves to be productive in three ways.

First, it forcibly introduces the recurring motif of the falsely accused individual and the fine line between good and evil. Secondly, it inaugurates the Catholic vein of Hitchcockian inspiration, turning the executioner of the novel into a martyr in the film, a Christ reliving his Passion (evident in the close-up where a shadowy crucifix is emblazoned on Novello's white face). The tenant, although he has the manner of a guilty man, now bears the stigma of the innocent.

Freeze Frame

A brief sequence in *The Lodger* is particularly striking: The disturbing tenant paces back and forth in his room, his comings and goings suddenly visualized by the landlady on the floor below through a transparent ceiling, while the chandelier sways with the vibrations. The glass ceiling, the sequence of overhead and low-angle shots, the vibrating chandelier, all contribute to making the footsteps of a restless man "heard" in this silent film.

Lastly, this obligatory twist (guilty? not guilty?) heightens the film's suspense and involves the audience: "You achieve more suspense if the audience is worried about a known person than if it concerns an unknown person. The audience may go into convulsions at the thought of Clark Gable being murdered, but if it is an unknown actor, they will wonder, 'Who is that?'"[1]

Writing a Score

While solving his main casting problem, which affected the current script, Hitchcock established the subdivision into scenes, which in turn were divided into shots. Shot by shot, he made a drawing or had one made, specifying the position of the actors and the location of the camera, as well as the scenery and furniture required, and even listing the props on the back of the sketch. From the outset, the filmmaker knew how to visualize a script, which itself already contained highly visual ideas. From the very

start, and to use a comparison to which he would often resort, Hitchcock behaved like a composer creating a symphony alone on the screen of his mind, then on paper, long before assembling his full orchestra. In other words, a score cannot be improvised on the day of its performance. The same goes for a shoot.

FILMING AND PRODUCTION

The six weeks of filming, from early March to mid-April 1926, also included editing, no doubt carried out by Alma Reville. During that time, the filmmaker, though still a novice, never ceased to expand his horizons.

Like a Fish in Water

Despite the hurtful gossip spread by Graham Cutts—the "in-house" director who, fearful of being supplanted by his former assistant, told anyone who would listen that the film would be "incomprehensible"—Hitchcock felt "like a fish in water" in Islington Studios. And the finished film is astonishingly inventive. This aspect is in evidence from the very first scene: The close-up face of a young blond woman screaming is placed on a glass background and lit from below to enhance the expressiveness and bring out the victim's golden hair. Then the blurred outdoor backgrounds to represent the London fog are obtained with a piece of gauze placed in front of the camera lens. In the film's opening minutes too, faces seen in close-up are superimposed on one another, one expressing concern, the other dismay or fear—a visual idea that would be reused, forty years later, in the opening credits of *Torn Curtain* (1966).

Film Direction Under the Influence

From his third feature, Hitchcock established both a clean, almost clinical framing of people and objects, and a penetrating filming style, as though he wanted to get closer and closer, to see what is forbidden (a naked body, an injured body). His staging plays with doors that open and close in the same shot; with a staircase shot from above or below; with the mezzanine and upstairs of the boardinghouse, a foreshadowing of the house in *Psycho*. And of course, he played with the most disquieting and suggestive ways of lighting a shot. In the last months of 1924, Hitchcock spent time at the UFA studios in Berlin. *The Lodger* was influenced by German expressionism (*Nosferatu*, F. W. Murnau, 1922; *The Street* [*Die Straße*], Karl Grune, 1923), an art form that

revolutionized set design and unleashed the power of light and shadow.

RECEPTION

By May 1926, the production company was able to arrange the first private screenings, in particular for the dreaded C. M. Woolf, who, it was said, tended to listen to the advice of Graham Cutts…a screening so dreaded that Hitchcock, rather than attend, preferred to take his wife on an aimless walk through London. On their return, the verdict was clear: *The Lodger* was an arty film for intellectuals, condemned to remain on the shelf.

Ivor Montagu to the Rescue
Initially distraught, Michael Balcon, the producer, came up with the idea of showing the film to Ivor Montagu. The son of a banker and a young intellectual of the Far Left, Montagu was—like Hitchcock—a regular viewer of Soviet films shown from October 1925 onward at the Film Society in London, the avant-garde film club he had co-founded. Montagu loved *The Lodger* and, encouraged by Balcon, suggested improvements. In particular, he suggested reducing the number of intertitles, which too often interrupted tension or action that was perfectly legible without onscreen text. He also commissioned Edward McKnight Kauffer, an American graphic artist based in London, to design the credits and play with the killer's trademark triangle in some of the intertitles. Hitchcock approved of this

external intervention, which he later passed over in silence, no doubt to leave the impression of having controlled everything. Finally, Montagu, as a translator of texts by Eisenstein and Pudovkin, suggested giving the final chase—that intense moment when the tenant is almost killed by the pursuing mob—a "Soviet-style montage" feel, with more short, dynamic shots. In August 1926, new shots were filmed and inserted into the film. All in all, *The Lodger*'s budget would have been around £12,000, which seems about average for English productions of the time.

Hitherto Unknown
In mid-September, Balcon organized a press screening—double or nothing. Iris Barry in the English *Daily Mail* called the film "brilliant." For *The Bioscope*, it was nothing short of "the best British production to date" (September 16, 1926). Many of the film's first audiences shared this impression of experiencing the hitherto unknown, at least in their own country. At the very beginning of 1927, the success of *The Lodger*'s public release confirmed in the eyes of the profession the advent of a new talent named Hitchcock. This was a source of pride for English cinema, which, at the time, was very uncomfortable with the glare of Hollywood production.

The Birth of "Pure Cinema"
The director would often say that he considered his third film to be the first true "Hitchcock picture." He was particularly proud of the first fifteen minutes of *The Lodger*. In this fine example of "pure cinema,"

he showed, through the sheer power of shots and editing, the journey of a news item, the way a crime becomes a news item that pervades an entire town at high speed: telephone, ticker tape, newspaper headlines, radio, illuminated banners, and so on, with Hitchcock each time adding a detail about the murderer for the audience's attention.

Certainly, at the start of 1927, *The Lodger*'s audience was both surprised and sensitive to this disturbing and erotic vision of the modern world: a world that had suddenly moved from the horse-drawn carriage to the car and from gas to electricity. It was a new world in which the devastating power of something suppressed could suddenly manifest itself.

Much later, Ivor Montagu would remember that time, the group of English film buffs, intellectuals, and apprentice filmmakers of the 1920s, and Hitchcock among them. He remembers the feeling that this young director was surely "the only one of [them] who could achieve his goal." Montagu added: "He lived to make films."[2]

Where Is Hitchcock?

It was in *The Lodger* that Hitch-cock first appeared in one of his own films: at the beginning, on the telephone and from behind, in the offices of the *Evening Standard*, and, it seems, at the end, among the crowd who want to tear the fugitive apart. The film-maker often said that his first cameos were to make up for the lack of extras. What became a signature, and almost a trade-mark, may well have started out as a private joke and a nod to a few journalists.

It seems that in 1926, when shooting *The Lodger*, the young Hitchcock wanted above all to imitate one of his idols, Charlie Chaplin, who, in *Public Opinion* (1923)—a film not including Charlie Chaplin—appeared, un-recognizable, for the duration of one shot.

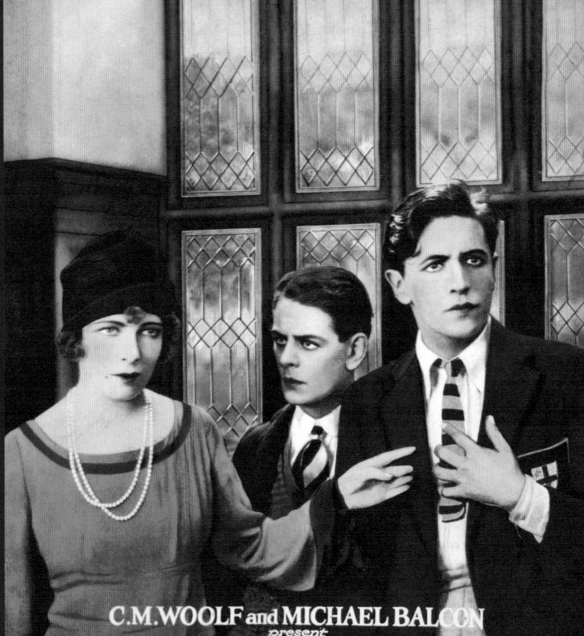

C.M. WOOLF and MICHAEL BALCON
present
IVOR NOVELLO
in
"DOWNHILL"
with
ISABEL JEANS

Downhill

Great Britain · **1 hr 14** (20 images/second) · **Black and White** · **Silent** · **1.33:1**

SYNOPSIS

Production Dates: January 17–early April 1927
Release Date in Great Britain: October 24, 1927 (London)
Release Date in the United States: 1928

Production: Gainsborough Pictures
Producers: Michael Balcon, C. M. Woolf

Based on a play of the same name by David L'Estrange (pseudonym of Ivor Novello and Constance Collier)
Screenplay: Eliot Stannard
Director of Photography: Claude L. McDonnell
Assistant Director: Frank Mills
Art Direction: Bertram Evans
Film Editing: Lionel Rich, Ivor Montagu

Starring: Ivor Novello (Roddy Berwick), Isabel Jeans (Julia), Ben Webster (Dr. Dowson), Norman McKinnel (Sir Thomas Berwick), Robin Irvine (Tim Wakeley), Jerrold Robertshaw (the Reverend Henry Wakeley), Sybil Rhoda (Sybil Wakeley), Lilian Braithwaite (Lady Berwick), Ian Hunter (Archie), Violet Farebrother (the poetess)…

The star of his rugby team, Roddy Berwick is the most popular student at school. His friend is Tim, who is dating a young cake-shop girl. One day, the latter tells the principal that she has been dishonored by one of the two young men…and accuses Roddy. Knowing that Tim, of modest means, will not be able to obtain a scholarship if he is expelled, Roddy refrains from denouncing him. He is expelled from the school, then leaves the family home, with his father not believing in his innocence. He ends up in Paris as an extra in a variety theater, where he befriends the star of the show, Julia. Roddy is surprised to receive a substantial inheritance from his godmother. The actress leaves her lover to marry the rich young man. The money is soon swallowed up by Julia, who spends lavishly and maintains a relationship with her lover without her husband's knowledge. Roddy is once again in decline, until he ends up, sick and half-mad, in a slum in the port of Marseille. There, some sailors have the idea of taking him back to England, in the hope of receiving money from his relatives. Once on the English coast, Roddy slips away to return to his family home. But while he had feared his father's wrath, the latter announces that he had discovered the truth and asks his son to forgive him. The family is reunited.

"Here is a tale of two school-boys who made a pact of loyalty. One of them kept it—at a price."

Opening credits card sequence of *Downhill*

GENESIS AND CASTING

In September 1926, *The Lodger* was presented to the press and film professionals. Its screening made such an impression that Alfred Hitchcock was offered a good contract by a new company, British International Pictures. However, the filmmaker still owed Gainsborough Pictures, the successful producer of *The Lodger*, six months' work. Studio boss Michael Balcon decided to make use of his protégé for as long as possible.

A Thirty-Four-Year-Old Teenager

For the screenplay, the choice fell on *Down Hill*, a play that Ivor Novello, the unsettling tenant of the previous film, had already performed onstage, and which he had co-written with Constance Collier, under the joint pseudonym of David L'Estrange.

In the silent film, star Ivor Novello took on the role of Roddy Berwick onscreen, despite a detail that is far more embarrassing on the silver screen than on the stage. At the time, he was thirty-four years old, whereas at the start of the film, his character was still a teenager. Hitchcock told François Truffaut that the play was rather mediocre. Nevertheless, he endeavored to make the most of a commission that he renamed *Downhill*, in a single word, and for which he himself wrote the opening credits card: "Here is a tale of two school-boys who made a pact of loyalty. One of them kept it—at a price." This is the first of the director's many films in which one character is made to take the rap for another, after his or her trust has been abused.

FILMING AND PRODUCTION

Hitchcock tried to enhance a very melodramatic story with ingenious inventions, sometimes flirting with comedy. Some of these survived the final cut, but the filmmaker claims to have shot some comic digressions that were cut by the producers, including a fight treated in burlesque mode.

The Fall

Hitchcock's main concern was to symbolically represent the moral and social decline of the hero—in the sense of a downward slope. When he is expelled from school, a very wide shot shows him as a tiny speck, lost in the monumental architecture

Freeze Frame

One scene shows Roddy flirting with Julia, while her lover stands aside to mix himself a cocktail. This is followed by a framing shot in which the glass takes up a large part of the image, with the two suitors in the background. And just as the seltzer gushes into the drink, Roddy leaves the room, as if driven out by a huge water cannon!

of the college. And after the break with his parents, an underground station escalator takes him down toward a dark destiny. Hitchcock himself found the symbolism of the fall rather conventional. However, he recounted an amusing anecdote about this shot: As it was to be filmed during the nighttime closure of the underground network, the filmmaker directed the scene dressed in a tuxedo, having spent the evening at the theater!

Russian Dolls

Hitchcock used a play of Russian dolls to show what became of Roddy in Paris. A close-up shows him as a playboy in formal wear, before the frame widens to show him as a waiter in a restaurant. But a sideways camera movement turns the tables again, revealing the characters performing a musical on the stage of a theater.

For Hitchcock Addicts

When Roddy enters Julia's dressing room, she sits with her back to the door, tilting her head back to see who the newcomer is. A subjective shot, following the young woman's gaze, then shows Roddy upside down. Hitchcock used this visual gag in a famous scene from *Notorious* (1946), starring Ingrid Bergman and Cary Grant.

Green Hell

Hitchcock declared himself quite proud of the sequence in which the feverish hero is overcome by hallucinations on the cargo ship taking him back to England. The character's nausea and remorse are expressed by the greenish tinting of the image. This postproduction process replaced the blurring and fading effects that accompanied dream and nightmare scenes in most films of the period.

RECEPTION

When the film was released exclusively in London, it was accompanied by a surprising attraction: the projection suddenly stopped, and actors Ivor Novello and Robin Irvine took to the stage to perform an additional scene absent from the feature. Nevertheless, *Downhill* received a lukewarm reception, with critics praising its brilliant direction but criticizing its insipid storyline.

Melodramatic Clichés and Visual Creativity

The final version of the film is marked by melodramatic excesses, some of which today seem close to misogyny. For example, the hero, now a social ("taxi") driver, meets a benevolent lady, but the eruption of sunlight soon reveals the aged, ungracious features of his date, making him realize the horror of his condition as a gigolo.

Nevertheless, a number of passages show that Alfred Hitchcock already possessed the purely visual expression that is the hallmark of the great silent film artists. For example, the cake-shop girl's accusations are represented not by dialogue cards, but by a whole series of images superimposed on the young woman's face. These mental images are taken from earlier scenes, and we can guess that the denouncer is perverting their meaning to overwhelm the poor schoolboy.

C.M. WOOLF & MICHAEL BALCON
present

ISABEL JEANS

with

ROBIN IRVINE

Adapted from
play by NOEL
COWARD

EASY VIRTUE

A *Gainsborough Picture*
directed by ALFRED HITCHCOCK

TRADE PRESENTATION
LONDON HIPPODROME
TUESDAY AUGUST 30ᵗʰ AT 3 P.M.

All seats reserved --

Easy Virtue

Great Britain •

1 hr 20
(21 images/second) •

Black and White •

Silent •

⬓
1.33:1

Production Dates: March–May 1927
Release Date in Great Britain:
September 1927 (London), March 1928
(outside London)
Release Date in the United States:
June 1928

Production: Gainsborough Pictures
Producers: Michael Balcon, C. M. Woolf

**Based on a play of the same name by
Noël Coward (1924)**
Adaptation: Eliot Stannard
Director of Photography: Claude L.
McDonnell
Assistant Director: Frank Mills
Art Direction: Clifford Pember
Film Editing: Ivor Montagu

Starring: Isabel Jeans (Larita Filton),
Franklin Dyall (Aubrey Filton), Eric Bransby
Williams (Claude Robson), Ian Hunter (Mr.
Greene), Robin Irvine (John Whittaker),
Violet Farebrother (Mrs. Whittaker), Frank
Elliott (Colonel Whittaker), Dacia Deane
(Marion Whittaker), Benita Hume
(switchboard operator), Alfred Hitchcock
(the man near the tennis court?)…

SYNOPSIS

L arita Filton is involved in a trial in a dramatic divorce case. A flashback shows her torn between a young painter who courts her and an alcoholic, jealous husband who mistreats her. One day, the two men have an altercation, at the end of which the artist, mistakenly believing he has killed the husband, commits suicide. Acknowledged as being responsible for the painter's fate, Larita loses the case. To escape the scandal, she goes to the Côte d'Azur, where she meets a young man, John Whittaker. Whittaker, who refuses to hear about her past, insists on marrying her. But as soon as the couple arrive at the Whittakers' English home, Larita encounters hostility from John's mother and sisters, who do their utmost to convince him of the error of this hasty marriage. The conflict comes to a head when the family identifies the young woman as the protagonist in the high-profile divorce and suicide affair. Her mother-in-law forbids Larita to attend a Whittaker party. The young woman pulls off a coup by attending the festivities anyway. There she meets up with her first husband's lawyer, who assures her that she can get a quiet divorce if she does not stand up for her rights. The second separation is finalized, but with journalists recognizing her as the defendant in the famous "Filton scandal," Larita is once again the prey of photographers as she leaves the courtroom.

"'Virtue is its own reward' they say—but 'easy virtue' is society's reward for a slandered reputation."

—

Opening credits card of *Easy Virtue*

GENESIS AND CASTING

March 1927: With his contract with Alfred Hitchcock due to expire in June, producer Michael Balcon put his protégé to work nonstop.

Two Birds with One Stone

At the end of March, the filmmaker headed for the Côte d'Azur to kill two birds with one stone. On the one hand, he shot the final images of *Downhill*, filming actor Ivor Novello on the rooftop of a hotel in Nice. On the other, he shot the exteriors for *Easy Virtue*. It is hardly surprising, then, that these two silent features have many actors in common. For example, Isabel Jeans, seen as a fickle wife in *Downhill*, played the lead role in *Easy Virtue*. She moved to Hollywood in 1937, where she was reunited with Hitchcock for *Suspicion* (1941).

The Plot Before the Plot

Easy Virtue is adapted from the play of the same name by prominent young playwright Noël Coward. However, the stage play, which begins with the arrival of the newlyweds at the Whittaker home, only provides material for the second half of the film. In its first forty minutes, the Hitchcock version shows events that are merely referred to in the play's dialogue: the news item leading to the heroine's divorce, then her remarriage during a stay on the Côte d'Azur. Coward, who had met Hitchcock at the start of the project but had not collaborated on the screenplay, took no issue with these changes. The two men remained friends for a long time, and twenty years later, the playwright was one of the personalities invited to the set of *Rope* (1948) to help promote the technical challenge of this unusual shoot.

FILMING AND PRODUCTION

While Noël Coward's play is a corrosive comedy of manners, Hitchcock delivered a darker work, emphasizing the hypocrisy of upright English society, reluctant to accommodate a free-spirited woman.

Scandal!

The story begins with the painter's suicide, a kind of mini crime film inserted in flashback within a trial sequence.

This latter sequence enables Hitchcock to add a theme absent from the play: the denunciation of the excesses of the tabloid press. On leaving court, the heroine has to run the gauntlet of the flashbulbs of predatory reporters. Later, her fear of having her past revealed is symbolized by superimposed or close-up shots of a camera. Finally, the film's conclusion is entirely different from that of the play, where the curtain falls as the heroine leaves the Whittakers' social gathering. In Hitchcock's film, we return to the first scene: Larita attends the trial of her second divorce and, despite her precautions, is once again harassed by journalists.

Deadly Purpose

During their discussions in the early 1960s, Hitchcock told Truffaut that the worst intertitle he had ever written was the one that closes *Easy Virtue*, when the heroine calls out to the photographers:

◉ *Where Is Hitchcock?*

Some may think that they recognize the filmmaker in the tennis game scene. Sitting on the edge of the court, Larita makes John's acquaintance when he comes to her to apologize after she has been struck by a ball. Just before the incident, a man walks past actress Isabel Jeans to leave the courts. Is it Hitchcock?

Freeze Frame

When Larita telephones John to give him the answer to his marriage proposal, Hitchcock dispenses with dialogue cards…and even images of the two involved! The scene consists of a fixed shot of a switchboard operator listening to the conversation; her facial expressions let the viewer know that the proposal has been accepted.

Freeze Frame

At the very beginning of the film, the courtroom is shown from the judge's point of view, then the magistrate's monocle enters the frame, so that the lawyer's face appears magnified as if by a magnifying glass. The shot is seamless, courtesy of a trick invented by Hitchcock. To create a sharp image with full depth, he had a giant replica of the monocle built, then replaced the glass with a mirror. The actor playing the lawyer is placed behind the camera, while an understudy in the distance represents him in the long shot.

"Shoot, there's nothing left to kill!" However, despite its emphatic nature, this card inaugurates a recurrent theme throughout the filmmaker's work: the equating of the photographic lens to an instrument of death. In *Foreign Correspondent* (1940), for example, a diplomat is assassinated in a crowd by a bogus journalist holding a pistol against his camera.

RECEPTION

Easy Virtue was a huge commercial failure, which critics attributed to its artificial depiction of the characters' social milieu. But while the film is indeed a rather bombastic melodrama, it nonetheless contains the seeds of two of the director's major works.

A Stranger in Her Own Home

The initial situation—a young wife isolated in a foreign home—was developed further in *Rebecca* (1939), which also begins with a hurried marriage on the Côte d'Azur, and in *Notorious* (1946). In the latter, Ingrid Bergman's character also falls victim to the tabloid press and is confronted by a mother-in-law who, as in *Easy Virtue*, draws up her austere silhouette at the top of a monumental staircase.

So even Hitchcock's most minor films contain elements essential to an understanding of his work.

Gordon Harker, Carl Brisson (aka "One Round Jack"), Harry Terry.

The Ring

Great Britain · **1 h 29** (20 images/second) · **Black and White** · **Silent** · **1.33:1**

Production Dates: July–August 1927
Release Date in Great Britain: October 1, 1927

Production: British International Pictures
Producer: John Maxwell

Based on an original story by Alfred Hitchcock
Screenplay: Alfred Hitchcock, Eliot Stannard, Walter C. Mycroft
Director of Photography: Jack E. Cox
Visual Effects: W. Percy Day, Fortunino Matania
Assistant Director: Frank Mills
Art Direction: C. Wilfred Arnold
Continuity: Alma Reville

Starring: Carl Brisson (Jack Sander, known as "One Round Jack"), Lillian Hall-Davis (Mabel), Ian Hunter (Bob Corby), Forrester Harvey (James Ware, the promoter), Harry Terry (the showman), Gordon Harker (Jack's trainer), Eugene Corri (referee), Charles Farrell (the second), Clare Greet (the fortune-teller), Tom Helmore (a spectator), Minnie Rayner (boxing contestant's wife), Billy Wells (the boxer), Brandy Walker (a spectator)…

> "[In *The Ring*,] marriage is depicted as one long fight divided into a series of rounds that comprise a long struggle."
>
> ———
>
> Donald Spoto, Hitchcock biographer

SYNOPSIS

———

Jack is a fairground boxer, a well-built man who challenges anyone to last more than one round against him. An elegant stranger, susceptible to the charm of Jack's fiancée, Mabel, takes up the gauntlet and, to everyone's surprise, wins with a knockout. He is in fact Bob Corby, Australian heavyweight champion. To keep Mabel close to him, Bob offers Jack the chance to become his sparring partner and protégé. Bob secretly gives the young woman a snake-shaped bracelet and kisses her. Jack, surrounded by his fairground friends, marries Mabel and wins victory after victory but suffers more and more from the irresistible attraction his wife feels for his rival. His trainer, however benevolent, proves powerless to reassure him. So much so that on the very night Jack wins his title match, the couple quarrel violently and separate. On the day of the big fight at the Royal Albert Hall between Jack and Bob, the hall is packed and overheated. The outcome is uncertain for a long time, but Jack, spotting Mabel sitting in the opponent's camp, lets his guard down and almost gets beaten. Moved to see him in distress, and rediscovering her feelings for her husband, she sides with him and gives him the strength to put Bob down. Loving and appeased, the young woman finally discards the bracelet given to her by her lover and leaves the jewel at ringside. Bob, more seducer than lover, seems to have come to his senses, ready for a new conquest.

Elstree Studios (in the county of Hertfordshire), owned by British International Pictures, founded in 1927.

GENESIS

In June 1927, having just finished shooting *Easy Virtue*, Alfred Hitchcock left Gainsborough Pictures and Michael Balcon, with whom he had made his first five films, to join British International Pictures (BIP).

The Early Days of British International Pictures

BIP was founded by John Maxwell, a Scottish-born barrister and a businessman at heart: Operator of a circuit of cinemas, then distributor (Wardour Films), in 1927 he took over the Elstree Studios (in Hertfordshire, north of London) and modernized them. Above all, he founded BIP with the intention of taking advantage of the impending Cinematograph Films Act, a protectionist law passed in December 1927, which introduced quotas to favor national productions to the detriment of American competition. The perverse effect of this policy was to encourage the rapid release of many cheap, mediocre films ("quota quickies"), an effect from which Hitchcock's own productions were not entirely immune (*Champagne*, 1928; *Juno and the Paycock*, 1929). John Maxwell, who recruited the fashionable director in the hope that his talent would help him penetrate the overseas market, produced a total of eleven Hitchcock films between 1927 and 1932, from *The Ring* to *Number Seventeen*.

The newly formed BIP offered Hitchcock a better salary: The press of the time exaggeratedly quoted £17,000 for four films a year, but it was more like £13,000. Either way, at the age of twenty-eight, Hitchcock became England's highest-paid director. This change was also supposed to give him greater creative freedom, a promise that would prove true at least with *The Ring*, his first film made in this context.

Boxing and Behind the Scenes

Even before joining BIP, Hitchcock had an idea for a story: a sentimental intrigue set in the world of boxing. The young man knew the world of boxing fairly well, since he was a fan of fights, notably at London's Royal Albert Hall. But he was less interested in the sport itself than in what went on behind the scenes, using his gift for observation, as always, to capture "glimpses" in his film. For example, the spectators in the front rows were dressed as if at the opera to enjoy a brutal and popular spectacle, or the superstitious custom of pouring the contents of a bottle of champagne over the boxer's head before the thirteenth round.

Right from the start of the writing, Hitchcock also played subtly with his title. *The Ring* refers both to the place where the boxers fight and to the circular structure of a plot that begins and ends with a fight between the same two opponents, but also to the wedding ring, symbolizing the vow of fidelity at the heart of the film.

A Little Helping Hand

The screenplay was written almost exclusively by the director. However, his regular scriptwriter, Eliot Stannard, unofficially lent him a hand, as did

Lillian Hall-Davis, Carl Brisson: a couple on the ropes.

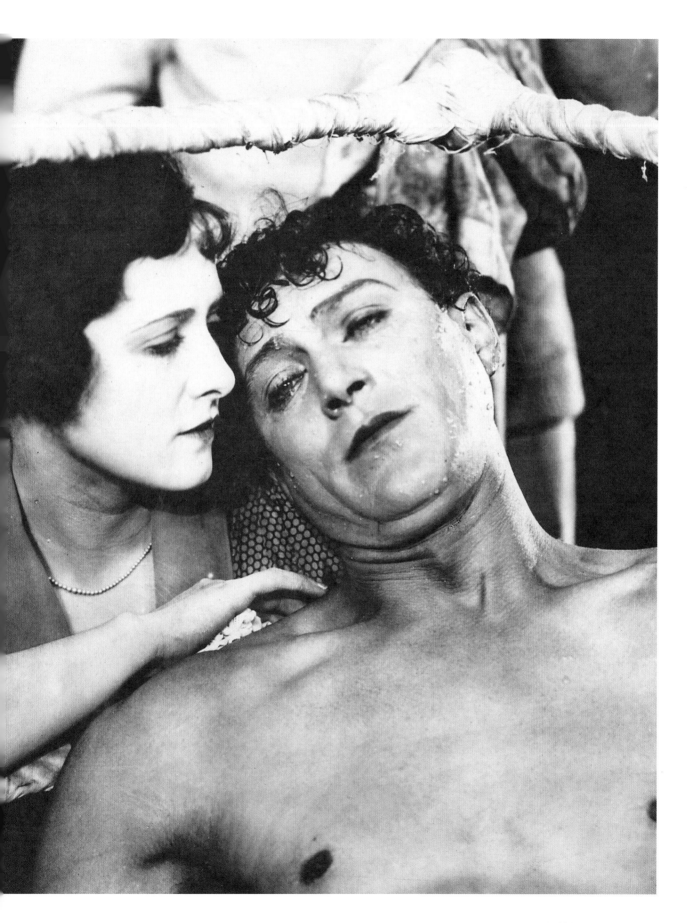

In training, Gordon Harker and Carl Brisson.

Walter C. Mycroft, whom Hitchcock had known since his days at the Film Society film club; this former *Evening Standard* critic had recently become head of the script department at British International Pictures. By early summer 1927, the whole story was ready, including the cutting. It was the first film produced by BIP and Hitchcock's first original screenplay—one without a murder or anyone falsely accused.

CASTING

The Ring was a first in an additional way. Claude L. McDonnell, the cinematographer on Hitchcock's two previous films, withdrew after the production refused him a pay raise. The director recruited John Jaffray Cox, known as Jack Cox, a young but already experienced cameraman, and made him his cinematographer. Described by future director Michael Powell as quick to set up his lights, "kind and genial," Cox would be involved in over a hundred films during his career. But years after his last collaboration with Hitchcock, it's still the Master he'll always remember for his quick wit, his astonishing and stimulating visual ideas, his taste for a job well done. Together, they were responsible for the ten films the director made for BIP as well as *The Lady Vanishes* in 1938.

Popular Actors

At liberty this time to hire the actors of his choice, Hitchcock recruited Carl Brisson for the role of Jack "One Round," an authentic Danish boxer who made his real acting debut in *The Ring*. Ian Hunter, who played the rival, Bob, was originally from South Africa. After *Downhill* and *Easy Virtue* in the same year, 1927, this was his third and most important role in a Hitchcock film. Lillian Hall-Davis, an English silent film star appreciated by Hitchcock even more for her vivacity in life than on a film set (although she committed suicide in 1933), played a character that was to recur in the filmmaker's work: that of the woman caught between two men. Above all, Hitchcock offered his film debut to a colorful stage actor, Gordon Harker. Hitchcock was so pleased with Harker's phlegmatic demeanor that he cast him in his next two films, as well as giving him an appearance in *Elstree Calling* (1929). Harker was the epitome of the cockney, the working-class Londoner (like the director) whose slang, accent, and humor made him stand out. Furthermore, Harker had a memorable face. He looked as though he was straight out of the suburbs, precisely the people Hitchcock hoped would come to see his films.

One night, when Mabel comes home particularly late, Jack, her husband, makes a scene. The tension between them escalates to the point where he rips off the strap of her evening gown, revealing her slip and part of her body. Shocked and furious, the wife has an unexpected and revealing reflex: facing her husband, she covers herself with the portrait of her lover and, thus "dressed," walks to the door, through which she disappears. In this way, Mabel violently displays her preference. But on the scale of the film, more than the choice of one or the other, the young woman is above all excited by the repeated spectacle of two men fighting over her.

FILMING AND PRODUCTION

Right from the opening, *The Ring* sets the scene and asserts its style as a series of short shots of a fun-fair—reconstructed on the grounds of the Elstree Studios. Its attractions included images of a crowd of surprised onlookers (so many extras) and a close-up of a barker's mouth…

From Life

Hitchcock had a keen eye for the picturesque, expressive, even grotesque details, with many portraits and caricatures taken from life. The beginning of the film, and throughout, is full of visual discoveries that give *The Ring*, a fictional film for the general public, a taste of the avant-garde: distorted or stretched images, short cuts, reflections and mirrors, and plays with the off-screen, as in the gag of a fight so fast that the camera, instead of following the amateur boxer into the ring, waits for him in his corner, knowing in advance that he will soon reappear in a sorry state.

In Church

Jack and Mabel's wedding scene is just one example of the young director's mastery of cinematographic language in the final years of the silent era. He begins by parading Jack's friends and witnesses into the church nave, all of them from the fairground world: his noisy boss, his hair slicked back, obviously entering the place for the first time in his life; Siamese twins, one of whom wants to sit on the left and the other on the right; a dwarf followed by a giant…This is a strange parade ("Hitchcock saw himself as a monster" ["Hitchcock se voyait comme un monstre"], said Truffaut), including a number of kindly freaks who foreshadow others in a crucial scene in *Saboteur*, made fifteen years later.

The Wedding Ring and the Bracelet

At the same time as sketching this droll, very human background, Hitchcock chisels out the moment of the exchange of vows between the bride and groom, the "wedding ring" sequence, under the amused gaze of the bride's potential lover. As the smitten Jack places the ring on Mabel's finger, the snake-shaped jewel, a gift from Bob, which she wears on her upper left arm, suddenly leaves its place and falls onto her wrist. The director brings the ring and bracelet together in the same close-up, two circles that contradict each other, a mismatch that expresses the young woman's conflicting desires in a single image. Hitchcock played with this bracelet and its significance throughout the film, making it appear and disappear according to the situation and the repression or otherwise of Mabel's sexual attraction to the other boxer. As a young married man writing and shooting *The Ring*, Hitchcock's commentary on the sacred bonds of marriage is ambivalent, to say the least.

Technical Challenges

For the final showdown at the Royal Albert Hall, the director had to marshal all his know-how. For the first time in his career, he used a German special effect known as the "Schüfftan process," which Fritz Lang had just used for *Metropolis*. This trompe-l'oeil technique uses a tilted, semi-reflective mirror to

Behind the camera, Jack E. Cox (a cinematographer who made eleven films with Hitchcock, from *The Ring* to *The Lady Vanishes*). In the center, a reflector to redirect the light. On the right, the filmmaker.

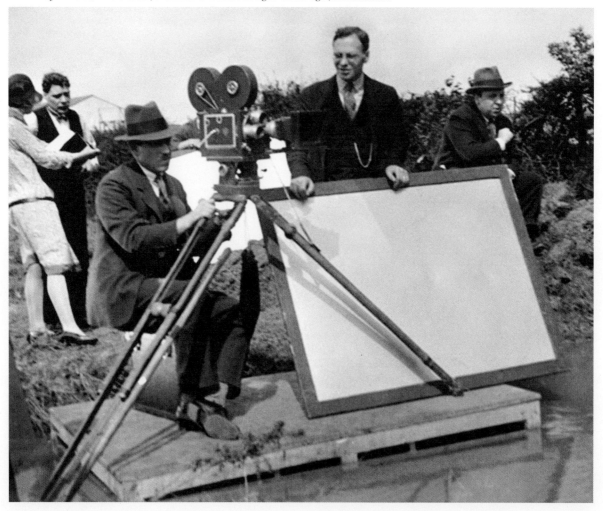

combine life-size bodies and scenery (the ring, the boxers, the front rows with real spectators) with a model ("dummy" spectators painted on the mirror) in the same shot, to create the impression of a single reality through a forced perspective. In this way, Hitchcock creates the illusion of a packed house at minimum cost.

At the climax of the fight between the two rivals, Hitchcock finds a way to represent the moment of the knockout from the point of view of the boxer about to hit the mat: blurred shots, a play with the dancing lines of the ropes, a downward camera movement to represent the fighter's collapse, large halos of light in place of the overhanging ring lights. The combination of the director and the new cinematographer worked wonders, and Jack Cox became renowned precisely for his ability to create "in-camera" blurs, cross-fades, and superimpositions. Decades later, Hitchcock would still remember

For Hitchcock Addicts

The couple's handsome London apartment bears witness to their upward social mobility, due to Jack's success in the ring and his wife's new acquaintances. The main room is a vast living room, with a large bay window at the back overlooking the city lights. This bay window and night view of houses and neon signs foreshadowed, twenty years ahead of time, the unique set of *Rope* (1948) and its spectacular panorama of New York City, also entirely re-created in the studio.

that, at the dress rehearsal for *The Ring*, a montage sequence—undoubtedly the knockout sequence—was applauded. Another first for the director.

RECEPTION

Hitchcock, who liked *The Ring*, later commented that the film did not make any money but that it was a success in its own right. It was an understatement, to say the least, given the English press's national pride and joy in the director and the film.

Unanimous

The Bioscope declared, "This is the most magnificent British film ever made." It published a double-page spread of all the praise in the press and addressed Hitchcock directly, urging him, on behalf of an industry that owed him a debt of gratitude, to maintain such quality and to continue working in his native country (October 6, 1927). The *Western Morning News* (October 3) considered *The Ring* the best riposte to those who might claim that good films are not made in England. In the *Guardian* (November 9), the journalist praised the humor of certain situations and the inventiveness of the staging. The *Times* (November 22) in particular praised the opening scene at the fair and, on the whole, a film that stood head and shoulders above current productions. For the *Sunday Express*, "the film is significant mainly because Hitchcock himself is significant."

Obsessions

The Ring retains intact its formal qualities and the sense of detail that constantly enhances the conventions of the plot—a poignant interrogation of the "joys of matrimony" and the temptation of adultery. Furthermore, the film displays a very Hitchcockian obsession with original sin (the snake bracelet) and the quest for redemption. For example, as Jack sits in the corner of the ring, groggy, his face streaming with water, sweat, and blood, his hair forming a kind of crown of thorns, Mabel is at his side, as if at the foot of the Cross. It is only at the price of such suffering that his long ordeal will come to an end. Even as a young man, Hitchcock was already observing the eternal turmoil of the human condition with both humor and concern.

The Third Man

It was the real Eugene Corri (c. 1857–1933) who in 1907 broke the tie in the final bout and was reputed to have refereed from inside the ring rather than sitting outside it. He would have been the "third man" in some one thousand matches over the course of his career, including the famous Dempsey versus Carpentier match (1921). A boxer himself in his youth, author of several books on the art of pugilism, he was also known for his elegance—in *The Ring*, he officiates in a tuxedo—and his passion for cigars.

"VANITY FAIR" SUPPLEMENT   MEN OF THE DAY No. 1318.

"a typical Englishman"

BRITISH INTERNATIONAL PICTURES, LTD.
Present
EDEN PHILLPOTT'S Record Breaking Stage Success

THE FARMER'S WIFE

featuring

JAMESON THOMAS
LILIAN HALL-DAVIS
GORDON HARKER
GIBB McLAUGHLIN
MAUD GILL.

Directed by

ALFRED HITCHCOCK

WARDOUR
FILMS LIMITED
Head Office - 173 Wardour Street. London W1

The Farmer's Wife

Great Britain

2 hr 9
(21 images/second)

Black and White

Silent

☐
1.33:1

SYNOPSIS

Production Dates: October–December 1927
Release Date in Great Britain: March 2, 1928
Release Date in the United States: January 4, 1930

Production: British International Pictures
Producer: John Maxwell

Based on a novel and a play by Eden Phillpotts, *Widecombe Fair* **(1913) and** *The Farmer's Wife* **(performed for the first time in London in 1924)**
Adaptation: Eliot Stannard
Director of Photography: Jack E. Cox
Assistant Director: Frank Mills
Art Direction: C. Wilfred Arnold
Film Editing: Alfred Booth

Starring: Jameson Thomas (Samuel Sweetland), Lillian Hall-Davis (Araminta Dench), Gordon Harker (Churdles Ash), Gibb McLaughlin (Henry Coaker), Maud Gill (Thirza Tapper), Louie Pounds (Louisa Windeatt), Olga Slade (Mary Hearn), Ruth Maitland (Mercy Bassett), Antonia Brough (Susan), Haward Watts (Dick Coaker), Mollie Ellis (Sibley Sweetland)…

After marrying off his daughter, wealthy farmer Samuel Sweetland decides to end his five-year widowhood. With his devoted servant, Araminta Dench, nicknamed Minta, he draws up a list of single women to court. Sweetland first visits Louisa Windeatt, a widow who refuses his advances to maintain her independence. The farmer then courts the shy and nervous Thirza Tapper, on the verge of fainting upon hearing his proposal, who lets him know that she has no need of a man in her life. Then it is the turn of Mary Hearn, surprised and laughing at the man she finds too old for her. Exasperated, the widower hurls scathing criticism at her, provoking the young woman into a fit of hysteria. Sweetland makes one last attempt with Mercy Bassett, a waitress, but is again rejected. Alone and desperate, the farmer has an epiphany and finally turns his attention to Minta: His loyal and devoted servant appears to him to be the ideal wife. Although Thirza Tapper and Mary Hearn change their minds, the farmer stands by his choice. Minta accepts the proposal. Sweetland proposes a toast to his future union to the few friends gathered at his home, while Miss Hearn has another attack of nerves.

"Beer drinking don't do 'alf the 'arm of love-making."

Churdles Ash (Gordon Harker), in *The Farmer's Wife*

GENESIS AND CASTING

The Ring had only just been released on the cinema circuits when Alfred Hitchcock and his crew headed out into the English countryside to shoot the exteriors of his fourth film of 1927, his second for British International Pictures (BIP).

A Repeated Success

This was a bucolic comedy adapted from *The Farmer's Wife*, a successful play by British playwright and writer Eden Phillpotts, itself a stage adaptation of one of his novels, *Widecombe Fair*, published in 1913. The triumph of *The Farmer's Wife* in 1924, which was revived in 1928, led BIP to entrust the film adaptation to its star director. Eliot Stannard, Hitchcock's loyal screenwriter, took charge of the adaptation. *The Farmer's Wife*, in its theatrical version, contains a lot of dialogue, and the main challenge was to keep the intertitles to a minimum so as not to overload the film with text.

The film crew at teatime: in the chaise longue, Gordon Harker; behind the camera, Jack E. Cox; at the table, Alfred Hitchcock, Jameson Thomas, Maud Gill.

Old Hands and New

Jameson Thomas played Samuel Sweetland, the farmer determined to remarry after five years of widowhood. Thomas had a prolific film and stage career behind him but had not appeared in any of the stage versions of *The Farmer's Wife*. Actress Lillian Hall-Davis, already seen in *The Ring*, was cast as the devoted maid who proves to be the ideal wife. Only Maud Gill, the spinster, had appeared in the original play. Gordon Harker (*The Ring, Champagne*) played Churdles Ash, Sweetland's picturesque handyman.

FILMING AND PRODUCTION

Just before shooting, Hitchcock confided to a journalist from the *Western Daily* his desire to film nature and rural landscapes as the backdrop for a film representative of the old English country way of life. Once the exteriors had been filmed, the technical and artistic team returned to the Elstree Studios to shoot the interiors in two weeks.

A Manifesto

Hitchcock may have been delighted to be filming in the countryside, but he nevertheless made a film that had little to do with him. Although he carried out the commission without batting an eyelid, the filmmaker published a text in the *London Evening News* on November 16, 1927 ("Films We Could Make"), that revealed his state of mind. Although he was enjoying the most prolific period of his young career, he remained dissatisfied, as he declared in this manifesto-like open letter to BIP. For him, a filmmaker must be the only master on board, not a mere

Freeze Frame

On many occasions, Hitchcock filmed an empty chair opposite the farmer's chair to represent the character's solitude. The two chairs symbolized marital union. On the empty chair, Sweetland's thoughts turn to the single women that he and his maid, Minta Dench, review. The denouement of the film is quickly revealed when, at the end of this sequence of women to be courted, Miss Dench herself comes to sit on the empty chair.

In pursuit of women, with a flower in their lapel…Gordon Harker, Jameson Thomas, Lillian Hall-Davis.

technician: "Film directors live with their pictures while they are being made. They are their babies just as much as an author's novel is the offspring of his imagination. And that seems to make it all the more certain that when moving pictures are really artistic they will be created entirely by one man."

RECEPTION

Although Hitchcock did not produce an intimate work, he did deliver a faithful adaptation of the play, ensuring its warm critical reception.

Routine Work

The *Western Mail* notes that only "the glorious 'shots' of our countryside, with a hunt in full swing, and the magnificent panorama of glorious Devon as a background, save this film from being rated second class" (April 19, 1928). This campaign seems to be the only element of *The Farmer's Wife* that finds favor with the filmmaker. In 1963, in an interview with critic Peter Bogdanovich, Hitchcock pronounced his final judgment: "It was just a routine job."

A Misogynistic Film?

Having had his various proposals of marriage rejected, Sweetland is rebuffed by the women he was courting. According to Rohmer and Chabrol,[1] it was the director himself who added this brutal twist to the script, with the farmer finally marrying his maid "because a woman is above all a housewife." The crude and sometimes misogynistic way in which

the candidates are presented, and the denouement that turns the devoted maid into the ideal spouse, strongly undermine the intent of *The Farmer's Wife*. Hitchcock sacrifices his accuracy of vision and style to a taste for the picturesque and caricature. The two French critics point out that Hitchcock would only return to atmospheric depiction when inspired by a moral conflict (*The Manxman*, 1928). This is precisely one of *The Farmer's Wife*'s major shortcomings: The film contains none of Hitchcock's own themes or obsessions.

For Hitchcock Addicts

While filming the exteriors for *The Farmer's Wife* in Devon and Surrey in October 1927, Hitchcock fell in love with the calm and beauty of the rural world. Back in London, he announced to his wife, who was pregnant at the time, his desire to buy a house in the country to get away from the hustle and bustle of London. The couple bought Winter's Grace, a house in the Surrey village of Shamley Green, just over thirty miles from the capital. The Hitchcocks installed a new kitchen, two Art Deco bathrooms, and a projection room.

Betty Balfour was a national star but "an obscene suburbanite" for Hitchcock.

Champagne

Great Britain • **1 hr 26**
(20 images/second) • **Black and White** • **Silent** • **1.33:1**

SYNOPSIS

Production Dates: February–June 1928
Release Date in Great Britain:
August 20, 1928

Production: British International Pictures
Producer: John Maxwell

Based on an original story by
Walter C. Mycroft
Adaptation: Alfred Hitchcock
Screenplay: Eliot Stannard
Director of Photography: Jack E. Cox
Camera Assistant: Alfred Wallace Roome
Assistant Director: Frank Mills
Art Direction: C. Wilfred Arnold
Set Decoration, Set Photographer:
Michael Powell

Starring: Betty Balfour (Betty), Jean
Bradin (the fiancé), Ferdinand von Alten
(the detective), Gordon Harker (the father),
Clifford Heatherley (the manager), Claude
Hulbert (club guest), Hannah Jones (club
server), Marcel Vibert (maître d'hôtel),
Balliol and Merton (dancers), Alexander
D'Arcy, Vivian Gibson, Phyllis Konstam,
Gwen Mannering, Jack Trevor, Sunday
Wilshin, Fanny Wright…

Betty, the daughter of a wealthy New York businessman, leads a frivolous life. When she decides to marry an honest young man of modest means, her father becomes worried, convinced that this suitor is only attracted by her fortune. Stubbornly, the heiress joins her lover aboard a transatlantic liner that takes them to Paris. During the crossing, a mysterious man keeps an eye on her. Betty's father joins his daughter in Paris and, to teach her a lesson, has her believe that he is ruined. The engagement seems to have been broken off, and the young woman moves in with her father in a modest hotel room. A poor but strong-willed cook, she decides to sell her jewelry to support them. On the way, the contents of her purse are stolen. Desperate, Betty meets an impresario looking for "beautiful legs" and finds herself selling flowers in a seedy cabaret. There she meets up again with the man who had spied on her on the liner to France. She also meets up with her ex-fiancé, who, shocked to see her in such a reduced situation, warns her father. To put an end to her ordeal, he reveals the deception. Relieved, Betty still holds a grudge against the two men in her life. She accepts the detective's offer to take her back to America. Waiting for her on the boat are her fiancé and her father, who confesses to having hired the man to protect her. Betty reconciles with her father and reconnects with her future husband.

"This is probably the lowest point in my filmography."

Alfred Hitchcock

GENESIS AND CASTING

Since 1927, Alfred Hitchcock had been bound by a contract with British International Pictures (BIP) stipulating that he should make twelve films in three years, for a comfortable annual salary of around £13,000. From 1928 to 1932, the filmmaker enjoyed the most productive years of his career. But Hitchcock, who wanted to make epic or more experimental works, was forced to shoot inexpensive films quickly. BIP's films were not commercially successful outside Great Britain, so John Maxwell, producer and co-founder of the studio, decided to concentrate on English audiences.

Freeze Frame

Champagne opens and closes with a shot filmed from the bottom of a champagne glass held to the lips of a stranger. This visual idea necessitated the construction of a giant champagne glass with a magnifying lens at the bottom to allow the shots to be taken. According to assistant cameraman Alfred Roome, the team didn't believe in the technique: "Most people said that of Hitch's ideas, but they almost always did work."

An Initial Screenplay

In 1927, Walter Mycroft became head of the script department at Elstree Studios. As a former film critic, Mycroft was also one of the founders of the Film Society, a cinephile association that supported the production of artistic films. It was he who inspired Hitchcock to create *Champagne*, dedicated entirely to the sparkling beverage. With his usual scriptwriter, Eliot Stannard (this was their eighth and penultimate collaboration), Hitchcock set to work to build a solid script around what was, de facto, a rather flimsy subject: the sad tale of a young woman who nails closed cases of champagne bound for Paris in Reims. As she watches the trains loaded with bottles depart, she is irresistibly drawn to the capital. There, she becomes a kind of streetwalker and experiences a series of misadventures. Disillusioned, she eventually returns home, and "every time she saw a load of champagne coming out, she thought, 'Now that's going to make someone unhappy again.'"[1]

A Sparkling Star

In October 1927, John Maxwell announced that he had hired a national star for the film, Betty Balfour. The actress, known to the general public for her ingenue roles, was sometimes dubbed "the British Mary Pickford," and sometimes crowned "Britain's Queen of Happiness." In 1927, the *Daily Mirror* named her Britain's favorite actress. From then on, the studio insisted that *Champagne* should be remade as a "sparkling" comedy…

FILMING AND PRODUCTION

Because of this change of heart, filming was postponed until the end of February 1928, which still gave Hitchcock insufficient time in which to transform his drama into a comedy. The production began with an unfinished script. Alfred Roome, the assistant cameraman, recalls that Stannard and Hitchcock wrote bits of the script on the back of envelopes on the way to the studio: "You never knew what was going to happen. This was reflected in the outcome. It made no sense."[2]

An Angry Filmmaker

Hitchcock, who had originally considered actress Anny Ondra for the role of his brazen heroine, Betty, had to deal with Betty Balfour ("a piece of suburban obscenity"). His discontent was felt on the set, and he became very short-tempered, especially with the technicians. Hitchcock discovered that BIP was using extras from *The Farmer's Wife*, his previous film. He was forced to replace them. His assistants set out to find new faces in the city's nightclubs and cabarets.

RECEPTION

The critical reception was generally frosty. *Variety* magazine described the story as "the weakest, an excuse for covering 7,000 feet of harmless celluloid with legs and close-ups [...] Technically—settings, photography and lighting—it's as good as they come. But the story, the direction and the acting are dire. Betty Balfour has a thankless role and far too many close-ups" (September 5, 1928). And the *Yorkshire Post* refers to *Champagne* as "probably the lightest thing Mr. Alfred Hitchcock has ever touched. Its story is of the worst Hollywood type, trivial, artificial and altogether worthless. But because Mr. Hitchcock is the director and because Miss Betty Balfour is the 'star' it is worth seeing" (September 3, 1928).

A Film Disowned

Unable to make the film he had hoped for, Hitchcock himself judged it harshly, and lucidly pointed out its main problem: the absence of a story. *Champagne* shows the contrast between a sparse script and a mise-en-scène brimming with mischievous observations and formal discoveries, in particular the use of the subjective shot. For example, some scenes depict a character's gaze or what he imagines: Betty's seasick fiancé sees the image of his beloved multiply and sway before his eyes. On several occasions, superimposed images reveal what one or another of the protagonists thinks is behind a door.

Virtuosity in Spite of Everything

The film's most comic idea is that of the drunk who staggers across the deck of the liner as it floats along calm seas and then, as soon as the ocean turns rough, becomes the only passenger who is able to walk upright. Never short of imagination, Hitchcock shoots a purse-snatching scene with only the legs of Betty and her assailant. The sequences in the cabaret also show an acute sense of detail: Hitchcock places behind his heroine shots of dancing or drinking that look very much like documentaries. This method of creating commotion behind his star reveals perfectly the filmmaker's relationship with *Champagne*: Everything in his film seems to interest him, with the exception of his star and his main plot.

Champagne!

Alcohol is omnipresent in the filmography of Hitchcock, himself a great lover of wines and spirits. In *The Ring* (1927), the husband serves sparkling wine to his guests while waiting all night for his wife. To signify this, Hitchcock filmed glasses that had long since stopped bubbling. In 1946, champagne and red wine played an essential role in *Notorious*.

The Manxman

Great Britain • **1 hr 50**
(20 images/second) • **Black and White** • **Silent** • **1.33:1**

SYNOPSIS

Production Dates: Early August–
end September or October 1928
Release Date in Great Britain:
January 21, 1929

Production: British International Pictures
Producer: John Maxwell

**Based on the novel of the same name
by Hall Caine (1894)**
Screenplay: Eliot Stannard
Director of Photography: Jack E. Cox
Assistant Director: Frank Mills
Art Direction: C. Wilfred Arnold
Film Editing: Emile de Ruelle
Set Photography: Michael Powell

Starring: Carl Brisson (Pete Quilliam),
Malcolm Keen (Philip Christian), Anny
Ondra (Kate Cregeen), Randle Ayrton
(Caesar Cregeen), Clare Greet (Mrs.
Cregeen), Kim Peacock (Ross Christian),
Nellie Richards (wardress), Wilfred Shine
(doctor), Harry Terry (man)…

Inseparable friends since childhood, fisherman Pete and lawyer Philip are both in love with the beautiful Kate, a waitress in a pub on the Isle of Man. The lawyer, however, keeps his feelings secret when his companion asks her to marry him. But Kate's father refuses to give his daughter to a disinherited man. So Pete sets off to South Africa to try to make a fortune there, and news of his death soon arrives. Kate and Philip, who have grown closer, can now give free rein to their love. But Pete, in reality still alive, returns home with his fortune made. The lawyer steps aside for a second time, leaving his friend to marry Kate. The young woman is not happy with the marriage, however, and no longer loves Pete. In particular, she cannot bear having to hide her former affair with Philip, the real father of the child to whom she is about to give birth. She leaves her husband, telling him that the baby is not his, without revealing the identity of the father. Pete, however, decides to keep the child. Kate then attempts to take her own life. Since suicide is a crime under the law, the young woman is brought before the court headed by Philip, who has meanwhile been appointed judge of the Isle of Man. Faced with an insoluble dilemma, the lawman publicly confesses, then resigns. Kate and Philip leave the town with their child, under the disapproving gaze of the local population.

> "Hitchcock has taken pleasure in meticulously, completely, and unflinchingly depicting the moral conflict between three people whose actions are virtually beyond reproach."

Claude Chabrol and Éric Rohmer

Carl Brisson, Malcolm Keen, Anny Ondra.

The Manxman, *First Version*

Published in 1894, Hall Caine's novel was soon treated to numerous theatrical adaptations, as well as its first transposition to film, shot as early as 1916. Although a British production, this feature film, also entitled *The Manxman*, was directed by American filmmaker George Loane Tucker and was a great success on both sides of the Atlantic. As all copies have unfortunately disappeared, it is impossible to determine whether it had any influence on Hitchcock's version.

GENESIS AND CASTING

The project was typical of British cinema during the silent era, with its many adaptations of successful literary and theatrical works. Hitchcock was commissioned to bring to the screen Hall Caine's famous novel *The Manxman* (the "man from the Isle of Man").

The Manxman was Hitchcock's ninth and last feature film scripted by the faithful Eliot Stannard. Alfred Hitchcock and his wife, Alma Reville, who had just given birth to their only daughter, would write the next half dozen films themselves.

The Love Triangle

The filmmaker once again tackled the theme of the love triangle, which he had already explored in a number of films, and in which he used some of the same actors. Dane Carl Brisson played a character not unlike the one he portrayed in *The Ring*, a good man blind to his wife's temptations, while Malcolm Keen, the jealous policeman from *The Lodger*, played his rival. At the heart of this trio, Czech actress Anny Ondra took her first steps in front of Hitchcock's camera, and rejoined him for his next feature, *Blackmail*.

FILMING AND PRODUCTION

Hitchcock initially planned to shoot on the Isle of Man, where the action took place, before settling for the Cornish coastline, which offered the same type of landscape. *The Manxman* abounds in references to life in the fishing villages, proving that the filmmaker is not afraid to leave the confined atmosphere of the studios to capture a degree of documentary reality. But the film is most striking for the extreme rigor of its direction. The exchanges of glances and the positioning of the actors perfectly express the dramatic stakes, as in two inn scenes showing Kate and Pete deep in discussion while Philip remains isolated in another shot. In the first, he notes his rival's progress with frustration, and in the second, he turns his back on the couple, expressing his resignation to the forthcoming wedding. Conversely, in moments of confrontation, the three characters are often united in the same frame.

The Complicity of the Audiences

Hitchcock's technical mastery enabled him to achieve for the first time a feat he would repeat throughout his career: that of thwarting censorship. Incredible as it may seem, Kate's pregnancy is not explained by any dialogue cards. To convey the situation and its consequences, the filmmaker relied not only upon the expressiveness of his actors, but also on the audience's complicity. In fact, after three decades of silent cinema, audiences had learned to read the lines on the actors' lips. Thus, *The Manxman* deftly dispenses with explanatory intertitles, which might have drawn the wrath of the British censorship board.

RECEPTION

According to his biographer Donald Spoto, Hitchcock was less than satisfied with *The Manxman*, an opinion shared by John Maxwell, head of British International Pictures. The latter, very disappointed by the film, put it back on the shelf and only decided

Anny Ondra, Carl Brisson.

to distribute it after having launched Hitchcock on the ambitious *Blackmail* project. Against all odds, *The Manxman* was a critical and commercial success.

No Tricks

The film's importance began to emerge in the 1950s, when commentators emphasized its singularity and its uncluttered plot, devoid of melodramatic devices. In fact, with the exception of the mistaken news of Pete's death (which, strangely enough, the illegitimate lovers do not invoke in their defense), there are no external twists to disrupt a narrative guided entirely by the evolution of the characters' feelings. In their book *Hitchcock*, future filmmakers Claude Chabrol and Éric Rohmer note, "Hitchcock has taken pleasure in meticulously, completely, and unflinchingly depicting the moral conflict between three people whose actions are virtually beyond reproach [...] Each is obliged to assume his own responsibilities, to forge his own ethics [...] The very form of the film reflects this high level of inspiration. No unnecessary artifice. The staging is deliberately focused on faces, on looks." ("Hitchcock s'est plu à décrire minutieusement, complètement et sans faux-fuyant, le conflit moral opposant trois êtres dont les actions sont pratiquement irréprochables [...] Chacun est obligé d'assumer ses propres responsabilités, de se forger une éthique [...] La forme même du film participe de cette hauteur d'inspiration. Plus d'artifice inutile. La mise en scène est délibérément axée sur les visages, sur les regards.")[1] In some respects, Hitchcock's film represents the pinnacle of his silent film expertise, which he would always define as the purest form of the seventh art, and to which he bade farewell here. Indeed, *The Manxman* was to be his last work conceived entirely as a silent film.

For Hitchcock Addicts

Some of Hitchcock's earliest works carry within them the seeds of ideas he would develop in his major films. In his book *Hitchcock's Films Revisited*, American academic Robin Wood draws a parallel between *The Manxman* and one of the director's greatest masterpieces, *Under Capricorn*, made twenty years later. What both films have in common is their focus on a woman torn between a husband from a modest background and a suitor from a good family. However, their respective conclusions could not be more different...

Alma Reville,
a Well-Guarded Secret

Alma Reville (1899–1982) was a discreet, intelligent woman, well-versed in many of cinema's crafts, who lived and worked alongside Hitchcock from his first film to his last. Convinced of her husband's cinematic genius, she was his indispensable partner and the first viewer of his films, the one whose opinion he expected, respected, and feared more than any other.

The Lure of Cinema

Alma Lucy Reville was born in Nottingham on August 14, 1899, one day after the man who would become her husband and lifelong collaborator. Her parents worked in the lace-making industry. As a child, she suffered from St. Vitus' dance (rheumatic chorea), a nervous system disease that caused her to miss two years of school. Once Alma had recovered, her family moved to Twickenham, in West London, and settled a few yards from the London Film Company studios, where her father was employed in the costume department. The young girl went there regularly to watch the filming.

In 1915, aged just sixteen, she was hired by the London Film Company as a tea girl, and then as an editor, a job then mostly given to women and requiring no experience. Alma held a number of different positions, at a time when these were still relatively undefined: She was in charge of continuity, a function that combined the jobs of script girl and editor, and sometimes helped write scripts. In 1920, she became first assistant to director Maurice Elvey, a pioneer of English silent cinema.

Mr. and Mrs. Hitchcock

Alma Reville was employed in 1921 at the British Famous Players–Lasky studios in Islington. It was there that she met Alfred Hitchcock, at the time a modest film intertitles editor. But the company soon had to downsize: Alma was made redundant, but Hitchcock kept his job. In 1923, he worked as assistant director on a Graham Cutts film, *Woman to Woman*, and offered Alma the job of editor—she would later say that he only dared to speak to her once he had become her superior. Together, they worked on five Graham Cutts productions.

In 1925, Hitchcock hired Reville as an assistant on his first film, *The Pleasure Garden*. It was the beginning of a collaboration that would end only with the director's last film, in 1975. The press took an interest in this young woman already well established in the film world. A headline in *Picturegoer* (December 1925) announced, "Alma in Wonderland: An Interesting Article, Proving that a Woman's Place Is Not Always at Home." After the Munich shooting of *The Mountain Eagle*, the filmmaker's second film, Hitchcock proposed to Alma while the ferry back to England was caught in a storm and Alma was unwell. The couple became man and wife on December 2, 1926, and two years later Alma gave birth to their only daughter, Patricia.

Twenty Films and Counting

Alma Reville (who retained the maiden name that made her a household name) is officially credited on twenty Hitchcock films, as screenwriter, assistant director, or continuity director. Whether or not her name appeared in the credits (as it did for the last time in *Stage Fright*, 1949), she was constantly exchanging ideas with Hitchcock. Her contribution at every stage of a film's development was unmistakable: She read novels and scripts likely to be adapted or filmed, was often involved in writing the screenplay and dialogues, gave her opinion on casting, sometimes visited the set, viewed the rushes, and assisted with editing.

With the passing of time, Alma Reville remained in the imposing shadow of a "publicity" filmmaker who had become an expert in the art of self-promotion. We would have to wait for the biographies devoted to the Master of Suspense to measure the importance of her contribution. One example among many: It was she who suggested that Bernard Herrmann's music be placed during the shower scene in *Psycho* (1960).

Tributes

Shortly after her death on July 6, 1982, the American critic Charles Champlin devoted a long article to her in the *Los Angeles Times*, "Alma Reville, The Unsung Partner," which he concluded as follows: "The Hitchcock touch has four hands and two of them are Alma's" (July 29, 1982). In 2003, the couple's daughter dedicated a book to her mother, *Alma Hitchcock: The Woman Behind the Man*, which looks back on her importance in the Master's creative process. On the release of *The Man Who Knew Too Much* (1955), the filmmaker himself published an article, "The Woman Who Knew Too Much," in praise of his wife and collaborator, whose modesty he lamented. But the finest tribute came on March 7, 1979, at the American Film Institute Life Achievement Award ceremony celebrating Hitchcock. He spoke of the four people who had counted most in his life: "The first of the four is a film editor, the second is a scriptwriter, the third is the mother of my daughter Pat, and the fourth is as fine a cook as ever performed miracles in a domestic kitchen—and their names are Alma Reville."

Blackmail

Great Britain

1 hr 25
(silent version
24 images/second)
1 hr 25
(sound version)

Black and White

Silent / Mono
(RCA Photophone System)

1.20:1

Production Dates: February–March 1929 (silent version), April–May 1929 (sound version)
Release Date in Great Britain: July 28, 1929 (London, sound version)

Production: British International Pictures
Producer: John Maxwell

Based on the play of the same name by Charles Bennett (1928)
Adaptation: Alfred Hitchcock
Dialogues: Benn Levy (sound version)
Director of Photography: Jack E. Cox
Camera Assistants: Michael Powell, Ronald Neame, Derick Williams
Sound: Dallas Bower, Harold V. King
Assistant Director: Frank Mills
Art Direction: C. Wilfred Arnold, Norman G. Arnold
Set Photography: Michael Powell
Film Editing: Emile de Ruelle
Music: Jimmy Campbell, Reginald Connelly
Musical Arrangements: Hubert Bath, Harry Stafford
Musical Direction: John Reynders (British International Symphony Orchestra)

Starring: Anny Ondra / Joan Barry for the dubbing (Alice White), Sara Allgood (Mrs. White), Charles Paton (Mr. White), John Longden (Police Inspector Frank Webber), Donald Calthrop (Tracy), Cyril Ritchard (artist), Hannah Jones (landlady), Sam Livesey (Chief Inspector, silent version), Harvey Braban (Chief Inspector, sound version), Detective Sergeant Bishop (detective sergeant), Johnny Ashby (boy), Johnny Butt (sergeant), Phyllis Konstam (gossiping neighbor, silent version), Phyllis Monkman (gossiping neighbor, sound version), Percy Parsons (crook), Alfred Hitchcock (man in the underground, accosted by a child)…

> "I suspected that the Producers would change their minds and need a sound film, so I planned accordingly."

—

Alfred Hitchcock

SYNOPSIS

—

In a café, Police Inspector Frank Webber argues with his fiancée, Alice White, then sees her off in the company of a stranger. The stranger, a painter, shows the young woman around his studio. Initially charming, he then tries to rape her. Alice struggles, grabs a knife, and kills her attacker. Frank, in charge of the murder investigation, finds one of his fiancée's gloves at the scene and is shocked to discover that the victim is his rival. In the tobacconist's shop run by Alice's parents, he asks Alice for an explanation. Then a burly individual, Tracy, appears at the scene: He has seen Alice enter the painter's house and demands money not to report her. However, Frank learns from the police that Tracy, an ex-convict, has been harassing the artist for some time. This makes him the prime suspect. Despite Alice's objections, Frank uses the information to turn the situation in his favor. Cornered, Tracy flees. Pursued by the police, he takes refuge in the British Museum. When he reaches the roof of the building, he falls to his death just as he is about to accuse Alice. Meanwhile, Alice has decided to go to the police station to confess her guilt but is prevented from doing so by Frank's arrival at the last minute. With Tracy now named as the killer, the case is closed.

GENESIS

Blackmail was Alfred Hitchcock's first film with sound, although a silent version also existed. The reason for this duplication is that, in England even more than in other countries, the film industry was wary of the new technology. Many producers thought sound cinema was a passing fad. Furthermore, they were unsure which recording system to opt for. Finally, they suspected that it would be some time before many British cinemas were equipped for talking pictures. As a result of all these uncertainties, *Blackmail* underwent major changes during its creation.

A Future Hitchcock Screenwriter

British International Pictures (BIP) producer John Maxwell envisaged *Blackmail* as a silent work when he acquired the rights to the play of the same name and commissioned Hitchcock to adapt it. Unbeknownst to Hitchcock, he had just found one of his most valuable collaborators in the play's author, Charles Bennett. Following the film's success, Bennett became a screenwriter. He went on to write all Hitchcock's films from *The Man Who Knew Too*

Much (1934) to *Young and Innocent* (1937). Bennett then moved to Hollywood, where he worked with Cecil B. DeMille. In sunny California, however, he reunited with his compatriot to write the screenplay for *Foreign Correspondent* (1940). He also contributed, uncredited, to the script of *Saboteur* (1942). Interviewed by Patrick McGilligan,[1] Charles Bennett denied any involvement in the film version of *Blackmail*. He added that, in any case, there was no difference between the text of his play and the film script. We do know, however, that Hitchcock worked on the script with Canadian author Garnett Weston, and then fed it into discussions with his wife Alma Reville, among others.

The Show's Highlight

In his memoirs, Michael Powell, who went on to become a famous English director, claims to have had a great deal to do with the *Blackmail* script. Only twenty-three years old at the time, he had been Hitchcock's regular set photographer for some while. According to his version, which should be treated with caution, Hitchcock had him read Charles Bennett's play on the set of *The Manxman* (1928), and used him to make the last third of the plot more

Donald Calthrop.

cinematic. Bennett suggested ending the film with a chase through the British Museum. Powell thus takes credit for one of his mentor's great trademarks: a breathless, spectacular finale set inside a well-known monument, such as the Statue of Liberty in *Saboteur* or Mount Rushmore in *North by Northwest* (1958). However, the director never confirmed his junior colleague's contributions. Moreover, *Blackmail*'s final climax follows in the footsteps of some of Hitchcock's earlier films. Indeed, he had already concluded *The Lodger* (1926) with a chase, and set the final sequence of *The Ring* (1927) in the famous Royal Albert Hall.

From Silent Films to the Talkies

Hitchcock filmed *Blackmail* between February and March 1929…then went back to the script to transform his silent film into a sound work. In fact, having long resisted talking pictures, John Maxwell decided to give them a try. In April, he set up a temporary sound stage at his Elstree Studios and asked Hitchcock to rework *Blackmail* into "the first English talking picture"—a title that would be contested by several works. At the time, many filmmakers were adding a speaking scene (usually the last sequence) at the last minute to a feature film in production. Maxwell wanted Hitchcock to adopt the same expedient. Instead, Hitchcock envisioned a film that would be almost entirely sound. With the help of successful playwright Benn Levy, he wrote the dialogue for several scenes, which he shot again, this time recording the actors' voices.

CASTING

With Tracy, the master blackmailer, Hitchcock created his first memorable scoundrel character. Suspicious-looking actor Donald Calthrop does a marvelous job in the role. The actor is even more convincing in the talking version of the film, with his smooth voice conveying the menacing insinuations the crook keeps whispering to the heroes. The filmmaker entrusted Calthrop with other equally dubious character roles in *Murder!* (1930) and *Number Seventeen* (1932).

Anny Ondra's Playback

To play the heroine, Hitchcock again called upon Anny Ondra, the star of his previous feature, *The Manxman*. In *Blackmail*, the actress once again delivers a moving performance, culminating in a

A Strange Test

The British Film Institute has preserved Anny Ondra's sound test clip. The actress, who does indeed have a pronounced Czech accent, appears alongside a jovial Hitchcock. He makes her burst out laughing by asking if she has slept with men, then concludes the fifty-second test with a barrack joke: "Come here and stay still. If you don't, it won't fit in properly, as the girl said to the soldier."

Sound test for the sound version of *Blackmail*. Alfred Hitchcock with headphones, Anny Ondra with microphone.

series of close-ups showing her distraught face as she hesitates to turn herself in to the police. However, a major difficulty arose when it came to preparing the sound version of the film. A sound test showed that her strong Czech accent was incompatible with her character as a young woman from the suburbs of London. But replacing Ondra would mean reshooting most of the film, a financially impossible solution. Hitchcock resorted to an ingenious trick: While Anny Ondra merely moved her lips, her lines were spoken by another actress outside the camera's field of vision—a kind of live playback! The result is not perfect, but it does the trick. The English actress hidden behind the scenes, Joan Barry, was rewarded two years later with the female lead in *Rich and Strange* (1931).

Two Phyllises—One Gossiping Neighbor

Almost all the actors from the silent film reprised their roles in the sound version. The exception is Phyllis Konstam, who played the chatty tobacconist's customer. Busy with other commitments, she was unable to take part in the shooting of the sound scene. Ironically, she was replaced by an actress with a name very similar to her own: Phyllis Monkman! Konstam would later appear in *Murder!* and *The Skin Game*.

FILMING AND PRODUCTION

From the very first shooting session, apart from the problem of Anny Ondra's accent, Hitchcock anticipated the eventual transformation of *Blackmail* into

a talkie. The silent version therefore includes many shots in which the actors appear from behind, leaving the filmmaker free to add dialogue and sound effects recorded after the fact in postproduction.

Scenes That Were Enhanced by Sound

The main dialogue sequences were entirely re-rendered with sound. This was a difficult operation. At the time, cameras were extremely noisy. *Blackmail*'s camera was therefore placed inside a sound-proof glass cage, equipped with wheels to allow some movement. In addition, the nascent technology of talking pictures did not yet allow for the mixing of several sound sources. So, while the actors spoke

For Hitchcock Addicts

The Duchess of York, who was to become Queen Mother when her daughter Elizabeth II acceded to the throne, visited the *Blackmail* set, keen to see the making of a talking picture. At the time, members of the royal family were not allowed to appear bareheaded in public. But Hitchcock persuaded the duchess to remove her hat so she could put on her headphones.

Freeze Frame

While inspecting the crime scene, policeman Frank whistles the melody of "Sonny Boy," a song popularized by the very first talking feature film, *The Jazz Singer*, released at London's Piccadilly Theatre at the end of September 1928. Hitchcock thus gives a nod to the American film, whose resounding success spawned the worldwide wave of sound cinema.

their lines, the sound effects were played simultaneously by specialists hidden behind the scenes. Despite these obstacles, Hitchcock used the new possibilities offered by sound to make certain scenes even more striking. For example, the painter's studio is equipped with a piano, absent from the silent version. The artist sits at the piano to sing a song to Alice, thus allaying her suspicion. Likewise, the young woman's bedroom is now home to a caged canary, whose high-pitched chirping underscores the guilt that plagues her.

"Knife! Knife!"

Not content with using sound for the first time, Hitchcock distorts it to make it expressive. This is the case in the long sequence set in the tobacconist's shop, where the filmmaker certainly drew on memories of his youth. In his father's fruit-and-vegetable store, customers would linger to discuss the latest headline news. Similarly, at the tobacconist's, everyone is talking about the murder in the neighborhood. This makes Alice, who stabbed the victim, even more nervous. The tension reaches a climax when a neighbor (played by Phyllis Monkman) starts gossiping about the method of the crime. After a while, her chatter becomes a sort of

hubbub, from which emerges only the word "Knife!," repeated ever more loudly and stridently. Hitchcock thus shifts from realistic sound to subjective listening, embracing the heroine's troubled perception. And when Frank arrives at the tobacconist's, the bell on the front door sounds like a death knell with sinister echoes.

A Silent Version Not to Be Overlooked

While the sound version of *Blackmail* was a success, its silent counterpart was by no means inferior. Nevertheless, both share the most spectacular scenes, to which the sound adaptation merely adds sound effects. After stabbing the painter, Alice wanders the streets of London all night, haunted by the memory of her crime. Looking at a neon advertising sign, she thinks she sees a knife descending vertically. And above all, haunted by the image of the artist's hand hanging lifeless, she is seized with horror at the sight of a policeman directing traffic, or the outstretched arm of a tramp sleeping on the sidewalk. As for the stalking scene in the British Museum, the idea for which Michael Powell claimed credit, Hitchcock's execution is breathtaking. It was impossible to install a film crew in the building, but Hitchcock overcame the obstacle. Using a special

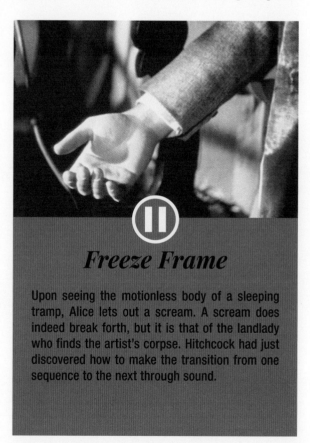

Freeze Frame

Upon seeing the motionless body of a sleeping tramp, Alice lets out a scream. A scream does indeed break forth, but it is that of the landlady who finds the artist's corpse. Hitchcock had just discovered how to make the transition from one sequence to the next through sound.

effect known as the "Schüfftan process," he embedded studio–re-created set elements, in which the actors act, within photographs of the museum's most emblematic rooms. The filmmaker had already used this process for *The Ring* (1927), but in *Blackmail*, the result is truly remarkable.

RECEPTION

The sound version of the film was released on July 28, 1929. It was preceded by a flattering assertion of patriotic pride, summed up in this phrase from the June 24 edition of the *Daily Mail*: "Best talking film yet—and British." At the end of the year, an audience poll declared *Blackmail* the best British feature film of 1929. However, this award mainly concerned the silent version, released a few months after the sound version (the date is uncertain), as this was the one most seen by audiences, since the majority of cinemas were not yet equipped for talking pictures.

An Imposed Ending

In his interviews with Truffaut, Hitchcock expressed his satisfaction with *Blackmail* but regretted not having been able to conclude with Alice's arrest. This was intended to echo the long opening sequence, which lists all the phases in the police's treatment of a criminal: arrest, interrogation, fingerprinting, imprisonment. This prologue, a kind of fast-paced mini-documentary in which the director bids farewell to the distinctive aesthetic of silent cinema, was retained in the final cut. But its repetition in the epilogue (Frank was to incarcerate his fiancée himself, concealing the fact that he had been her accomplice) was never shot, John Maxwell having insisted that the couple go free.

However, Hitchcock's intended conclusion was in line with that of the play as performed onstage. Indeed, although Bennett's original script included an unexpected twist (the rapist had in fact died of a heart attack, so the heroine was innocent!), the actress Tallulah Bankhead, who played Alice in the theater, had insisted that her character should remain guilty and eventually surrender to the police.

Guilty and Free

In *Blackmail*, guilt is dealt with in a particular way (at the denouement, Alice and Frank are left untroubled by the law) that would be found in Hitchcock's work only in the conclusion of *Sabotage* (1936). Of

Where Is Hitchcock?

At the beginning of the film, Alice and Frank are traveling on the underground. They are seated next to a rowdy boy who is annoying the passengers. In particular, the boy flicks the hat of a man played by the director. This is probably his longest film appearance: Hitchcock realizes that viewers, having already seen his picture in the press, might recognize him onscreen.

course, the young woman has killed in self-defense, and the blackmailer is a horrible character. But the blackmailer is innocent of the murder: Alice did stab the artist, and her policeman fiancé sought to conceal her crime. Moreover, the happy ending intended by the producer is not a happy ending at all. The final appearance of the painting that hung in the painter's studio (a sarcastic clown pointing an accusing finger at the heroine after she committed homicide) suggests that the heroes will have to live with the weight of their guilt. The haggard looks on Alice's and Frank's faces confirm this. Here, Hitchcock crosses a moral line that he would almost never cross again. In his later films, unjustly incriminated characters always end up being cleared of suspicion, even if they have suffered because of their mistakes. And conversely, the real culprits, no matter how motivated or attractive they may appear, are condemned by human justice.

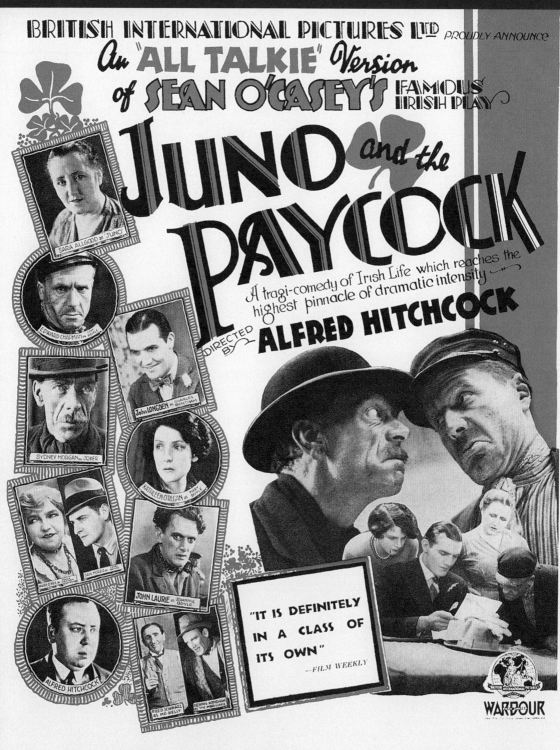

Juno and the Paycock

Great Britain • 1 hr 25 • Black and White • Mono (RCA Photophone System) • 1.20:1

Production Dates: November–December 1929
Release Date in Great Britain: September 22, 1930

Production: British International Pictures
Producer: John Maxwell

Based on the play of the same name by Sean O'Casey (1924)
Adaptation: Alfred Hitchcock
Screenplay: Alma Reville
Director of Photography: Jack E. Cox
Camera Operator: Derick Williams
Sound: Cecil Thornton
Assistant Director: Frank Mills
Artistic Directors: James Marchant, Norman G. Arnold
Film Editing: Emile de Ruelle

Starring: Barry Fitzgerald (orator), Maire O'Neill (Maisie Madigan), Edward Chapman ("Captain" Jack Boyle), Sidney Morgan ("Joxer" Daly), Sara Allgood (Juno Boyle), John Laurie (Johnny Boyle), Dave Morris (Jerry Devine), Kathleen O'Regan (Mary Boyle), John Longden (Charles Bentham), Dennis Wyndham (mobiliser), Fred Schwartz (Mr. Kelly), Donald Calthrop (Needle Nugent)…

> "The fact remains that *Juno and the Paycock* is not an Alfred Hitchcock film."

Claude Chabrol and Éric Rohmer

SYNOPSIS

In 1922, Dublin is in the midst of civil war. An orator calling for the union of republicans and other independence factions is gunned down in the street, causing panic. Lazy, alcoholic "Captain" Jack Boyle and his friend Joxer take refuge in a bar, where they learn of the murder of a republican, Robbie Tancred, betrayed by his own side. The "Captain" invites his friend to his home. The Boyle family, all together in their modest apartment (the "Captain," mother Juno, son Johnny, daughter Mary), are visited by Charles Bentham, a notary's clerk who has come to announce that they have inherited Jack's uncle's estate. Even before they receive the inheritance, the Boyles start buying on credit. Shortly afterward, they learn that the notary's clerk has been fired for improperly drafting the will. The creditors come rushing to their door to reclaim their property. One disaster follows another: Juno tells her husband that their daughter Mary is pregnant by the notary's clerk. Mary's former boyfriend offers to marry her and forget her affair with Bentham, but on hearing of her pregnancy, he flees. Only Johnny, the son, remains in the apartment. Two men come to kill him: He is the traitor who denounced Robbie Tancred. Juno learns that the police have found a body that could well be that of her son, recognizable by his amputated arm. She must identify him. Juno returns to the apartment one last time to mourn the death of her child.

GENESIS AND CASTING

After the release of *Blackmail* in 1929, British International Pictures (BIP) launched a wave of lay-offs affecting 20 percent of its workforce. Alfred Hitchcock, despite taking too long and spending too much money to make the film, was spared due to his status as a star filmmaker.

Making a Box-Office Success

Producer John Maxwell demanded that Hitchcock should pick up the pace and work on cheaper, more commercial works. The filmmaker would first supervise a few scenes from *Harmony Heaven*, a colorful musical celebrating BIP. He then accepted Maxwell's proposal to adapt a successful play by Irish playwright Sean O'Casey, *Juno and the Paycock* ("one of my favourite plays,"[1] Hitchcock later said). First performed in Dublin in 1924, the drama ran in London for over two hundred performances before embarking on a tour of the provinces. BIP believed that such a success could only lead to a successful film; more than once in his career, Alfred Hitchcock would resort to this stratagem to relaunch himself.

Remaining Faithful to the Text

Sean O'Casey, who was exiled in London, and Alfred Hitchcock met, according to the playwright's recollections, during the shooting of *Champagne* (1928).[2] O'Casey got on so well with the director that he considered writing an original screenplay for him. Like all renowned playwrights, he asked for a contract stipulating that his script, *Juno and the Paycock*, should be followed to the letter. Producer Maxwell thought that by sticking to the play, Hitchcock would have enough time to work on his next film, *Enter Sir John* (which became *Murder!*, 1930). However, O'Casey agreed to write a new opening scene set in a bar after a riot, thus diversifying the locations before the indoor scenes in the house. The script was written by Alma Reville, credited for the first time as a screenwriter on one of her husband's films.

Mixed Casting

Hitchcock established a cast that combined actors under contract to the studio with those who had already performed the play in the theater. Irish actress Sara Allgood, the heroine's mother in *Blackmail*, reprised the role of Juno, a matron as loving as she was authoritarian, which she had played in the first theatrical performances at Dublin's Abbey Theatre. Young John Longden (*Blackmail* and soon *Elstree Calling*, 1929; *The Skin Game*, 1930;

then *Young and Innocent*, 1937) portrayed Bentham, the seductive notary. And for Jack Boyle, the good-for-nothing father, the "peacock" (paycock) who is ironically nicknamed "captain," Hitchcock chose Edward Chapman, a British actor making his screen debut who appeared in three of the director's films (*Murder!* and *The Skin Game*).

A Playwright Who Disliked Movies

Sean O'Casey, a man of the theater, despised the cinema, which he saw as mere entertainment dedicated to "the glorification of insignificance." On the set of *Champagne*, the playwright was struck by the solemn atmosphere on the set and the seriousness of the film crew, who "behaved as if they were gods creating a new world." He took exception to the fact that hundreds of pounds were spent on reshooting a scene every time an actor or actress made a move too early or too late. He concluded: "I'd seen enough for one day. It was all furious and wrong."[2]

Sitting under the camera, Hitchcock prepares the scene for the reading of the will.

FILMING AND PRODUCTION

A single set (the Boyles' apartment, except for the introductory scene written for the film by Sean O'Casey) ensured that Hitchcock was able to film quickly. He filmed from November to December 1929 at Elstree Studios, north of London.

Escaping from the Confines of the Theater

To escape from the static aspect of the theater, Alfred Hitchcock favored sequence shots and sweeping camera movements.

While the camera follows the comings and goings of the characters in the Boyle family apartment, it sometimes disengages from their movements to pick out a detail in the background, as when Mrs. Boyle asks Charles Bentham if he believes in ghosts. He theorizes that some people can visualize a crime in the very place where it was committed. The camera, filming the discussion in a wide shot, slowly dollies forward, passes behind Charles Bentham, and stops in front of Johnny Boyle, tortured by guilt, as the viewer later realizes.

The Early-Stage Babbling of the Talkies

Juno and the Paycock was Hitchcock's first film made directly with sound technology. However, the technique was still in its infancy: music, noises, and dialogue all had to be recorded simultaneously at the time of shooting. This required a number of inventions and adjustments on the part of the technical team: the sound of gunshots was reproduced by a sound effects technician who whacked a sofa with a cane. For the funeral procession, a procession marched and sang live, right on the set. And because Hitchcock could not find a recording of "If You're Irish, Come into the Parlour," an Irish folk song he

Where Is Hitchcock?

The bar scene at the start of *Juno and the Paycock*, written by Sean O'Casey for the film, also served as a pretext for Hitchcock's appearance. He played a bartender. But the shot did not make the final cut. A publicity photo published in *Picturegoer* (January 1930) bears witness to this cameo.

The reading of the will: Kathleen O'Regan, John Longden, Sara Allgood, Edward Chapman.

wanted his characters to hear, a scaled-down band played the music off-screen. To reproduce the muffled sound of a recording, a soundman sang the lyrics while pinching his nose.

RECEPTION

A tale of a family's moral and economic ruin set against the backdrop of a divided Ireland, *Juno and the Paycock* received a warm critical reception when it was released on British screens in 1930. The *Times* hailed it as a "work of art; well photographed, well acted, and carrying conviction in every word and scene" but noted that Hitchcock had "been so faithful to his text as almost to forget the medium in which he was working" (January 1, 1930).

A Dissatisfied Filmmaker

Hitchcock also felt that *Juno and the Paycock* had "nothing to do with cinema"[3] and was embarrassed by its generally positive reception. Despite his best efforts, he found it hard to make people forget the theatrical setting: There was a constant struggle between O'Casey's text and the staging. Nevertheless, the growing darkness of the film and a tragic conclusion centered on Mrs. Boyle's maternal despair (the play ended with John Boyle and Joxer in a bar) remind us that *Juno and the Paycock* is indeed a work by Hitchcock.

For Hitchcock Addicts

Sean O'Casey and Hitchcock parted on bad terms: The playwright would assert throughout his career that he had never seen *Juno* and would denigrate the filmmaker. And it's said that Hitchcock's tramp who prophesies the end of the world in *The Birds* (1962) was inspired by O'Casey.

An Elastic Affair

⚑ **Great Britain** · 🕐 **10 min** · ◉ **Black and White** · 🔇 **Mono** · ▭ **1.20:1**

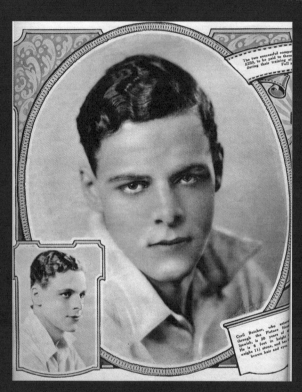

Production Dates: End 1929
Release Date in Great Britain: January 19, 1930
Production: British International Pictures
Producer: John Maxwell
Based on an idea from the magazine *Film Weekly*
Starring: Aileen Despard (girl), Cyril Butcher (boy)

Comedy short (The film is considered lost)

"I only want to thank you for tolerating this picture."

—

Cyril Butcher, addressing the audience after a screening of *An Elastic Affair*

The Life of an Employee

Between *Juno and the Paycock* and *Murder!* Hitchcock was not averse to doing odd jobs for British International Pictures (BIP), unless forced to do so by his boss, John Maxwell, who wanted to employ him between feature films. He thus directed *An Elastic Affair* and, immediately afterward, was involved in *Elstree Calling*. Only a short time later, he also created a very short subject, *Let's Go Bathing!*.

Stars of Tomorrow

An Elastic Affair is the result of a competition organized by the English magazine *Film Weekly*, in collaboration with BIP. The aim was to discover the male and female stars of tomorrow and offer them a start in their careers at the Elstree Studios. It seems that several thousand candidates took part in this competition[1] and that Hitchcock helped choose the winners. The winners each pocketed £250, signed a six-month acting contract, and were guaranteed training in their new profession, as well as a role, or rather a trial run, in a test film—*An Elastic Affair*—directed by Hitchcock, the "in-house director." Today, nothing can be said about this very short film, neither its plot, nor its form, nor even its exact duration, as the film is considered lost.

Two First-Time Actors

The lucky pair were Aileen Despard and Cyril Butcher. Irish-born Aileen Despard made her film debut with a brief but distinctive role in *Murder!* (and in *Mary*, the German version of the film), that of the victim stunned with a poker, the lifeless body discovered at the film's opening. She appeared in four more films until 1932, when she married and disappeared from the cinematic landscape.

Cyril Butcher, born in Suffolk (eastern England), landed a role in BIP's thriller *Night Birds* in 1931. A companion of the playwright and essayist Beverley Nichols, he became a director for English television in the 1950s.

Talking Picture, Silent Screening

The film was shown on January 19, 1930, at the London Palladium, in the presence of the two "talents": the budding actors received their contracts from John Maxwell. Although shot with sound, the film was projected in silent mode, as the London Palladium's projection booth lacked the necessary new equipment. This problem is symptomatic of this period of transition and uncertainty for British cinema, which had to cope with the rising production and operating costs of an industry that had suddenly switched to talking pictures. In these conditions, it cannot have been easy to fully appreciate the qualities of *An Elastic Affair*'s two first-time actors. A handful of firsthand accounts from the period describe their beginnings as sympathetic, even encouraging, but clearly still marked by amateurism.

The film had at least one other screening in London, at the Rialto cinema (with sound?), probably as the first part of the program, in the presence of Aileen Despard, announced on that day by a Hitchcock actor, Donald Calthrop (*Blackmail*).

Let's Go [Sun]*bathing!*

On February 18, 1931, Hitchcock filmed a four-minute short at Elstree Studios, in the space of just a couple of hours, which was broadcast five days later on the British Pathé News. The filming was slapdash: a few sketchy shots, barely audible, barely speaking, of a barely clothed swimsuit parade intended to help raise funds for the refurbishment of London's Middlesex Hospital. Alternately, other supposedly comic shots show a couple watching the show: While the wife, dressed in beachwear from another age, notes that it has gone out of fashion, her husband winks at the few starlets passing by, without much success. Looking at the final result, we can only assume that Hitchcock did not even bother to supervise the editing.

Elstree Calling

🏳 **Great Britain** • 🕐 **1 hr 26** • 🎞 **Black and White + Color** (Pathécolor) • 🔇 **Mono** (RCA Photophone System) • ▱ **1.20:1**

Production Dates: December 1929–January 1930

Release Date in Great Britain: February 6, 1930 (London), September 1930 (outside London)

Production: British International Pictures

Executive Producer: John Maxwell

Director of Production: James B. Sloan

Directors: Adrian Brunel, Alfred Hitchcock (additional sequences)

Staging of the Musical Sequences: Jack Hulbert, Paul Murray, André Charlot

Screenplay: Val Valentine, Adrian Brunel, Walter C. Mycroft

Director of Photography: Claude Friese-Greene

Sound: Alec Murray

Film Editing: A. C. Hammond, Emile de Ruelle (supervision)

Music: Reg Casson, Vivian Ellis, Chick Endor, Ivor Novello, Jack Strachey, Idris Lewis

Lyricists: Douglas Furber, Rowland Leigh, Donovan Parsons

Musical Direction: Sydney Baynes, Teddy Brown, John Reynders

Starring: Tommy Handley (himself, presenter), Gordon Harker (George), Hannah Jones (George's wife), Jameson Thomas (the cuckolded husband), John Longden (lover), Donald Calthrop (actor, and Petruchio in *The Taming of the Shrew*), Anna May Wong (Katherina in *The Taming of the Shrew*), and revue artistes: Will Fyffe, Cicely Courtneidge, Jack Hulbert…

"A Constellation of Stars of Stage, Screen and Broadcast Fame!"

—

Elstree Calling launch slogan

SYNOPSIS

From the studios of Elstree, near London, an announcer proudly declares that due to the marvelous invention of television, audiences will see "an all-star vaudeville and revue entertainment."

A Revue on Film

Like most of the artists under contract to British International Pictures (BIP), Alfred Hitchcock was involved in the production of *Elstree Calling*. This feature-length film was part of a genre very much in vogue in 1929–1930, when the arrival of sound cinema made it possible to transpose to the screen the collective shows called "revues" that were so popular onstage at the time. Each of the major American companies produced a luxurious sketch film, co-written by several directors and starring a host of performers. BIP followed suit with a work celebrating the glory of its Elstree Studios, where a host of stars from the English stage came together to give a variety of performances (romantic or humorous songs, ballets, music-hall numbers, comic interludes, etc.) separated by the interventions of a witty presenter (entertainer Tommy Handley, playing himself).

Hitchcock to the Rescue

Elstree Calling began as a project for director and screenwriter Adrian Brunel, who completed shooting the musical sequences at the end of 1929. However, in early 1930, he was fired by BIP's bosses, who were unhappy with the transitional scenes. Hitchcock was called in to redo or modify them. In the end, the credits attributed the direction of the film to Brunel, while Hitchcock was credited for the "sketches and other interspersed numbers." Perhaps feeling guilty about his professional betrayal of the man he had supplanted, Hitchcock always remained discreet about the extent and nature of these reworkings.

A Fatal Misunderstanding

Hitchcock is said to have shot, in whole or in part, three sequences or series of sequences. The most contentious case concerns a tragicomic sketch in which a jealous husband (Jameson Thomas, the hero of *The Farmer's Wife*, 1927) shoots an adulterous couple (the man is played by John Longden, the policeman in *Blackmail*, 1929), then realizes that he is in the wrong apartment! Brunel's script called for several variations on the same story, each treated in a different style, including that of Hitchcock. Hitchcock was even to appear onscreen, bustling around the set. This would be followed by a skit featuring the lighting effects and suspense that audiences had come to expect from him. In the end, only one version of the sketch was filmed. But who was behind the camera at the time: Brunel or Hitchcock? Nobody knows.[1]

Adrian Brunel, the Accomplice

Adrian Brunel, the principal director of *Elstree Calling*, was a close friend of Hitchcock's. In 1925, they worked together on the editing of *The Blackguard* and *The Prude's Fall*, two films by Graham Cutts for which Hitchcock was screenwriter and assistant director. By this time, both were also active in Film Society circles.

A Parody of Shakespeare

Hitchcock's involvement is more certain for *Elstree Calling*'s two narratives. One of them involves a thespian played by Donald Calthrop, *Blackmail*'s extortionist. Several times, between musical numbers, he slips onstage and tries to play Shakespeare to raise the cultural level of the show. However, he is always prevented from doing so by the technical staff. It is possible that Hitchcock directed all these recurring sequences, but in his memoirs,[2] Brunel only acknowledges that his successor turned the last one around. This time, the actor finally managed to play a scene from *The Taming of the Shrew*, but it turned out to be a parody of a recent Hollywood adaptation starring action star Douglas Fairbanks. In a delightful anachronism, Calthrop disguised as Fairbanks arrives in a sidecar in a medieval setting, where his heart's desire (played by Chinese American diva Anna May Wong) greets him with cream pies!

The First Television Satire

John Russell Taylor's authorized biography of Hitchcock asserts that the filmmaker entirely directed the second narrative,[3] made up of sequences that are the only ones not supposed to take place in the Elstree Studios. A madcap tinkerer (Gordon Harker, seen in 1927's *The Ring* and *The Farmer's Wife*, and in 1928's *Champagne*) tries to capture the broadcast of the acts on a primitive television set, but his device keeps malfunctioning. *Elstree Calling*, screened in cinemas like any other feature film, differed from American revue films in that it was presented as a "live" broadcast. However, the satirical nature of the Harker sketches is redoubled by the fact that, a quarter of a century later, Hitchcock would use television to build his personal legend.

Murder! / Mary

Great Britain/ Germany · **1 hr 32** (German version: 1 hr 18) · **Black and White** · **Mono** (RCA Photophone System) · **1.20:1**

Production Dates: March–May 1930
Release Date in Great Britain: July 31, 1930 (London)
Release Date in Germany: March 2, 1931

Production: British International Pictures, Südfilm
Producer: John Maxwell

Based on a novel by Clemence Dane and Helen Simpson,
Enter Sir John **(1928)**
Adaptation: Alfred Hitchcock, Walter C. Mycroft
(German version: Herbert Juttke, Georg C. Klaren)
Screenplay: Alma Reville
Director of Photography: Jack E. Cox
Camera Operator: Bryan Langley
Sound: Cecil Thornton
Assistant Director: Frank Mills
Art Direction: J. F. Mead
Set Decoration: Peter Proud
Film Editing: Rene Marrison, Emile de Ruelle
Music: John Reynders

Starring (English version): Herbert Marshall (Sir John Menier), Norah Baring (Diana Baring), Phyllis Konstam (Doucie Markham), Edward Chapman (Ted Markham), Miles Mander (Gordon Druce), Esme Percy (Handel Fane), Donald Calthrop (Ion Stewart), Esme V. Chaplin (prosecuting counsel), Amy Brandon-Thomas (defense counsel), Joynson Powell (judge), S. J. Warmington (Bennett), Marie Wright (Miss Mitcham), Hannah Jones (Mrs. Didsome), Una O'Connor (Mrs. Grogram), R. E. Jeffrey (jury foreman), Alan Stainer (member of the jury), Kenneth Kove (member of the jury), Guy Pelham Boulton (member of the jury), Violet Farebrother (member of the jury), Clare Greet (member of the jury), Alfred Hitchcock (man in the street)…

Starring (German version): Alfred Abel (Sir John Menier), Olga Tschechowa (Mary Baring), Paul Graetz (Bobby Brown), Lotte Stein (Bebe Brown), Miles Mander (Gordon Moore), Ekkehard Arendt (Handel Fane), John Mylong-Münz (John Stuart), Louis Ralph (Bennet), Hermine Sterler (Miss Miller), Fritz Alberti (defense counsel), Charles Landstone (member of the jury), Harry Hardt (inspector), Eugen Burg (detective), Esme V. Chaplin (attorney)…

"For years, I trained myself to apply the technique of life to the problems of my art. But today, ladies and gentlemen, that process is reversed. I find myself applying the technique of my art to a problem of real life."

———

Speech by Sir John (Herbert Marshall), in *Murder!*

SYNOPSIS

———

Edna, the wife of the director of a theater company, is found dead in the home of one of the troupe's actors, Diana. The young woman has no recollection of the events, but she is covered in blood and, above all, it is common knowledge that she was at odds with the victim. Diana is convicted of murder, despite the objections of one of the jury members, the famous actor Sir John. He believes in her innocence and starts the investigation from scratch. He soon becomes convinced that the murder was in fact committed by one of the troupe's men, who discreetly left the theater and climbed through the window into the nearby apartment. A prison interview with Diana reveals that the man is probably Fane, whose love for the young woman is made impossible by his concealed multiracial origins. To confuse him, Sir John pretends to offer him a role and has him read a scene that turns out to be an account of the murder. Fane leaves the audition in a huff. The great actor puts pressure on him again by going to the circus where he is now a trapeze artist; Fane hangs himself at the end of his act. He nevertheless leaves a written confession: Unaware that Diana already knew he was multiracial, he had killed Edna to prevent her from revealing the truth. The ex-convict, now exonerated, becomes a star of the stage alongside Sir John.

Costumed actors and backstage interrogation.

GENESIS

Noting that his two most successful feature films, *The Lodger* and *Blackmail*, were detective movies, Alfred Hitchcock set out to find a similar subject. He found one in a novel entitled *Enter Sir John*, co-authored by writers Clemence Dane and Helen Simpson.

One of Hitchcock's Rare "Whodunits"

The choice of this novel is surprising, since it falls into a category that Hitchcock often disparaged. This is a "whodunit," an Agatha Christie–style mystery in which several characters are suspected in turn, until the real culprit is unmasked at the last minute. Most of the filmmaker's films work in a completely different way: They reveal the identity of the malefactor from the outset, then build suspense by relying on the viewer's knowledge of the facts. But with *Enter Sir John*, renamed *Murder!* for the cinema, the director tackles the whodunit head-on, while making it his own in many ways. First of all, the novel provided him with a character type he would often reuse, that of the amateur sleuth, even though in this case he was trying not to exonerate himself but to clear the name of another person. In addition, Hitchcock made a number of changes to the script, allowing the echoes between theatrical fiction and reality to be fully exploited.

Art and Reality

Right at the start of the film, Hitchcock adds a sequence that initiates a constant back-and-forth between real life and the stage. Backstage at the theater, two policemen try to question the actors. The actors briefly answer the questions, then slip into character in the blink of an eye, before returning to the stage. The result is a dizzying merry-go-round, accentuated by the contrast between the seriousness of the criminal investigation and the nature of the play, which has all the hallmarks of a lighthearted comedy. However, the heart of the matter is really expressed in the famous actor Sir John's speech during the jury's deliberation, where he explains that while he usually draws inspiration from life to inform his performances, he will now have to use the resources of theater to try to influence reality. In this way, all his investigations can be read as the slow construction of a dramatic work whose final form will detail the exact circumstances of the crime.

Investigation by Means of Theater

The correspondence between investigation and theater is made explicit in the final part of the script, where Hitchcock departs from the novel to create a spectacular finale. First, the hero pretends to offer Fane a role in a play he has supposedly written, and asks him to read a passage that actually describes the premise of the murder. Already uncomfortable, the applicant is panic-stricken when he realizes that the end of the scene has been replaced by blank pages. The unmasked murderer commits suicide in the middle of a show (a circus performance). This scene is yet another addition by Hitchcock, who would include similar sequences in many of his later films. For him, the death of a guilty party is often an act of liberation, taking the form of a public confession. In *Murder!* it is followed by the reading of a confession letter from Fane, conceived as the final act of this real-life fake play.

Two Simultaneous Versions

For *Murder!* British International Pictures (BIP) teamed up with German company Südfilm to produce two versions of the film, one in English and the other in German. The advent of talking pictures had one major drawback: It became almost impossible to export films to countries where another language was spoken, whereas in the silent era, foreign distributors could simply translate the dialogue cards. A few years later, the introduction of dubbing technology solved the problem. In the meantime, however, production and distribution companies agreed to make numerous multilingual feature films, with the different versions shot simultaneously. Hitchcock applied this system: for each scene or shot, he began by directing the English actors, and then their German-speaking counterparts who re-enacted the same thing in their own language. Initially called *Mord—Sir John greift ein* (Murder—Enter Sir John), the German version was released under the title *Mary*. Although the action still takes place in England, the names of some of the characters are changed. Diana, the poor, unjustly accused heroine, is now called Mary, in what remains Hitchcock's only film in a language other than English.

CASTING

For the first time, Hitchcock had the opportunity to work with the very talented Herbert Marshall, who played Sir John. The choice was a logical one, since both actor and character were stars of the London theater. However, most of Marshall's film career would take place in Hollywood, where he

would shine in two Ernst Lubitsch films, *Trouble in Paradise* and *Angel*. In the California studios, the actor rejoined Hitchcock for *Foreign Correspondent* (1940), in which he played his usual ambiguous yet elegant role. This was a trademark image made all the more impressive by the fact that Marshall, an amputee, having been wounded in World War I, walked with an artificial leg.

The Cast of Hitchcock Actors

The whodunit genre calls for a shady-looking gallery of potential suspects, so Hitchcock called upon actors who had played villains in his earlier films. The theater manager is played by Miles Mander, the unworthy husband from *The Pleasure Garden* (1925), while the character of Ion Stewart is played by Donald Calthrop, the extortionist from *Blackmail* (1929). Two of the jurors convicting Diana are played by actresses who had already played mature, unsympathetic roles for the filmmaker: Clare Greet (the innkeeper in *The Manxman*, 1928) and Violet Farebrother (the aging seductress in *Downhill*, 1927, then the hostile mother-in-law in *Easy Virtue*, 1927). The Markham couple, who help Sir John with his investigation, are played by Edward Chapman (seen in *Juno and the Paycock*, 1929) and Phyllis Konstam, the gossiping tobacconist in the silent version of *Blackmail*. After *Murder!* the latter would appear again in *The Skin Game*, in the role of the young woman threatened by scandal.

A Soviet Spy on the Set?

The German leads were sent to London by the Berlin distributor. *Mary*'s Sir John is played by Alfred Abel, known for his roles in two of Fritz Lang's major works, *Doctor Mabuse* and *Metropolis*. As for the heroine, she is played by Olga Tschechowa, a woman with a particularly colorful life. Born in Armenia, she made her debut as an actress in Moscow, before obtaining a passport from the Soviet authorities in

For Hitchcock Addicts

Helen Simpson, co-author of the novel behind *Murder!*, also wrote the book *Under Capricorn* (1937), made into a film by Hitchcock in 1948. In the meantime, she collaborated directly with the filmmaker, helping to write the dialogue for *Sabotage* (1936). She died during World War II, in the bombing of a hospital where she was convalescing.

the midst of the civil war. She became the leading exponent of Slavic charm in German cinema, even under the Nazi regime. Arrested by the Russian occupation forces in 1945, she was transferred to Moscow and interrogated for two months, before being released and allowed to return to Germany. Persistent rumors have it that she was an undercover Soviet spy and even took part in a plot to assassinate Hitler!

The Joys of the Double Versions

Hitchcock had a much harder time casting *Mary*'s secondary roles. Actors from *Murder!* who could speak decent German were invited to reprise their characters, but of the main cast, Miles Mander was the only one suitable. For the others, the process was a laborious one, as Charles Landstone testified in his memoirs.[1] Landstone, a theater administrator and playwright, was hired to play one of the members of the jury for the sole reason that he had once performed a play in German in London. Fearing dismissal, he studied the acting of his alter ego in the English version, Kenneth Kove, and reproduced it identically when it was his turn to appear in front of the camera. Landstone was one of the few not to be fired on the spot by Hitchcock.

However, with a wry smile, the filmmaker made it clear that he had guessed his imitation technique, of which Kove seemed unaware. Landstone claims that the jury deliberation sequence, which lasts sixteen minutes onscreen, took twelve days to shoot.

FILMING AND PRODUCTION

Hitchcock, who had just completed *Juno and the Paycock*, began shooting *Murder!* with the script still unfinished. This situation, not uncommon in silent films, was much more problematic for the talkies. To save time, the director decided to let his actors improvise in front of the camera. After a week, however, he changed his mind, as the result

Fane (Esme Percy) in a drag-themed trapeze act, shortly before his suicide.

Alfred Abel, the character of Sir John in the German version.

seemed to lack momentum. Shooting began again almost from scratch.

Voice-Overs and Live Music

Murder! is surprising in its innovative use of sound. The most memorable sequence is when Sir John, while shaving in front of his mirror, decides to do everything in his power to clear the heroine's name. His state of mind is communicated to the audience by voice-over, which would pose no problem today. However, in the early days of talking pictures, it was very difficult to mix different sound sources. Hitchcock therefore came up with an ingenious solution: The voice-over, previously recorded and burned onto a disc, was broadcast by an electrophone placed outside the camera's field of vision. Similarly, musicians hidden backstage play a live aria from Wagner's *Tristan und Isolde*, which is supposed to emanate from a radio.

The Jury's Cries

The distortion of human speech, already explored in *Blackmail* (the store clerk's gossip becomes an unintelligible babble from which emerge only the words "Knife! Knife!"), is repeated in the jury deliberation scene. To convince the hero of the defendant's guilt, his counterparts crowd around him and enumerate the suspicions. Each argument is punctuated by a "What do you say to that, Sir John?," repeated ever closer and louder. Meanwhile, the framing becomes ever tighter. At the end of the sequence, the image widens again to show a bewildered Sir John standing alone at the jury table as his peers leave the room to announce the verdict. At the beginning of the scene, this large circular table is the subject of another technical innovation: the camera is positioned in the center, enabling it to multiply lateral movements as it moves from one character to another.

A Wide Range of Styles

When filming *Murder!*, Hitchcock had at his disposal a wide range of technical techniques, which he used according to the sequence to be shot. For example, the film's introduction favors a rapid montage of short shots to show the reactions of villagers

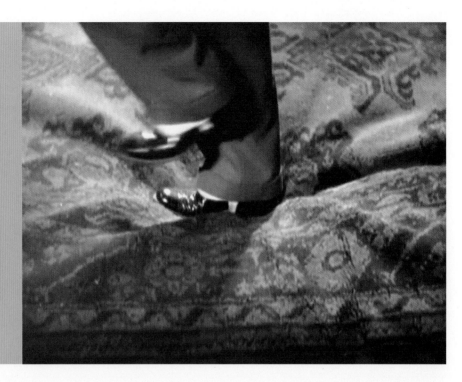

When stage manager Markham is summoned to Sir John's office, he finds himself so overawed that his legs feel like cotton wool. This image is taken literally in a brief comic shot. A trick is used to show the actor's feet sinking into a disproportionately soft, spongy carpet.

awakened by screams. But when we enter the apartment where the crime took place, the camera "calms down" for a moving close-up that slowly surveys the faces of the witnesses, before settling on Diana's haggard expression, then descending to the bloody poker lying on the floor. The same change of tone is mirrored in the final scene: Fane commits suicide in a circus plunged into dead silence, then a chorus of screams and a succession of brief shots suddenly show the crowd scattering, punctuated by inserts of a swinging segment of rope. The same variety affects the sets. Many are dark, stifling interiors, in the tradition of German cinema of the 1920s. The prison visiting room, on the other hand, is strikingly clear and uncluttered, decorated only by the reflection of a barred window.

The Caprices of the Other Alfred

Hitchcock experienced great difficulties when filming the German-language version. As he spoke fairly good German, he thought he could give the crew some technical pointers. But he soon realized that he was unable to master the rhythm and inflections of dialogue he did not fully understand. Furthermore, his collaboration with the lead actor, Alfred Abel, was not a happy one. While Herbert Marshall wore street clothes in the parlor scene,

Abel insisted on appearing in evening clothes, bizarrely arguing that a man should be dressed like that to visit a lady. Nor did the actor conceal his annoyance at the hilarious scene in which Sir John, staying overnight with the village policeman, is awakened by a hostess followed by several noisy, boisterous kids. Hitchcock thus discovered that English humor does not sit well with some Germans. In fact, in *Mary*, which is some twenty minutes shorter than *Murder!*, many sequences are stripped of details that gave flavor to the characters and the story. Despite a few variations in the direction of the shots, the interest of this German-language version is therefore rather limited.

RECEPTION

Murder! was released in London to critical and public acclaim. However, according to Hitchcock's statements to Truffaut in their interviews, the film proved too sophisticated for wide distribution in the provinces. Moreover, few copies of the alternative version, *Mary*, were released in Germany. On this point, Hitchcock confessed his mistake to Truffaut: Being satisfied with his script, he refused to accept the changes suggested by German adapters Herbert Juttke and Georg C. Klaren, even though the story

An Inspirational Trapeze Artist

To create the character of Fane, Hitchcock no doubt drew inspiration from Barbette, a Texas trapeze artist known worldwide for an act he performed dressed as a woman, before revealing his male identity to the audience at the end of the performance. Coincidentally, in 1930, the same year that *Murder!* was filmed, Barbette appeared in Jean Cocteau's *Le Sang d'un poète* (The Blood of a Poet).

should undoubtedly have been adapted to the sensibilities of German audiences.

A Metaphor for Homosexuality

The German version does, however, contain one major difference. Fane commits murder to conceal the fact that he is an escaped convict hiding under a false identity, whereas in the English version, his secret lies in his multiracial origins. According to Maurice Yacowar,[2] the novel states that Diana grew up in India and brought back the colonists' aversion to people of more than one race, which was stronger than that of the inhabitants of the metropolis. Racial barriers of this kind may seem surprising today, but Hitchcock uses them to touch on another subject, bypassing the taboos of the time. For the contemporary viewer, it is obvious that Fane is homosexual. Right from the start of the film, he is portrayed as a specialist in female theatrical roles and performs his trapeze act in a costume and makeup worthy of today's drag queens. However, Fane, unaware that Diana knows that he is multiracial (in this case construed, or manifested by appearance as gay), makes a pass at her. This is why he kills Edna, believing that she will reveal his true (sexual) orientation to the woman he covets.

No Moral Judgment

Fane is the first cross-dressing murderer in Hitchcock's oeuvre, thirty years before *Psycho*. More broadly, he paved the way for criminal characters tormented by repressed homosexuality, notably in *Rope* (1948) and *Strangers on a Train* (1950). But *Murder!* shows from the outset that Hitchcock's view of homosexuality, far from being a moral judgment, is imbued with humanity. Unusually in the filmmaker's career, the murderer is almost portrayed as a victim, or at least as someone deserving of the audience's pity. This is demonstrated in the moments leading up to his suicide: despite his haggard appearance, he finds the strength to offer the audience a final salute.

Modesty and Restraint

This deeply moving final performance is typical of a film distinguished by the modesty and restraint of its characters. The satirical touches are reserved for the picturesque Markham couple: Destitute

Where Is Hitchcock?

In the sixtieth minute, when Sir John is chatting with the Markhams outside the house where the crime took place, which they have just visited, Hitchcock passes by on the sidewalk, accompanied by a lady.

theatrical folk, they come to the rescue when called by the famous actor, and although they lend him a hand in his investigation, this is mainly in the hope of furthering their careers. Sir John, on the other hand, turns out to be a very nuanced character, who feels doubly responsible for Diana's fate. Not only does he regret not having defended her more resolutely during the trial, but he also believes he was the cause of her misfortune. In fact, he had already met her in the past: He had advised her to try her hand at touring the provinces before coming back to audition for him. He therefore believes that if he had hired her straight away, she would not have joined the troupe where the murder took place and would never have been bothered by the law. And while Sir John gradually falls in love with the young woman, this feeling is never conveyed through dialogue.

Intense Compassion

Although Diana dislikes Fane, she remains loyal to him by resolutely refusing to reveal his secret, even if it means denying herself a chance to clear her name. Indeed, she does not even exclude the possibility of her own guilt, having lost all memory of the crime. In the trial and prison scenes, the young woman expresses a touching resignation while remaining hopeful of being saved by a providential event. As Jacques Lourcelles writes, "What makes *Murder* almost unique in Hitchcock's world is that the culprit, victim and agent of human justice are all in the same boat, contemplated by the author with an intense compassion that shuns sentimentality and engenders the most poignant pathos."[3]

A woman and her blackmailer: Phyllis Konstam, Edward Chapman.

The Skin Game

🚩 **Great Britain** • 🕐 **1 hr 25** • 🎞 **Black and White** • 🔇 **Mono** (RCA Sound Recording) • ◰ **1.20:1**

SYNOPSIS

Production Dates: November–December 1930
Release Date in Great Britain: February 26, 1931

Production: British International Pictures
Producer: John Maxwell

Based on the play of the same name by John Galsworthy (1920)
Adaptation: Alfred Hitchcock
Screenplay: Alma Reville
Director of Photography: Jack E. Cox
Camera Operator: Charles Martin
Sound: Alec Murray
Assistant Director: Frank Mills
Art Direction: J. B. Maxwell
Film Editing: A. Gobbett, Rene Marrison

Starring: C. V. France (Mr. Hillcrist), Helen Haye (Mrs. Hillcrist), Jill Esmond (Jill Hillcrist), Edmund Gwenn (Mr. Hornblower), John Longden (Charles Hornblower), Phyllis Konstam (Chloe Hornblower), Frank Lawton (Rolf Hornblower), Edward Chapman (Mr. Dawker), Herbert Ross (Mr. Jackman), Dora Gregory (Mrs. Jackman), R. E. Jeffrey (first stranger), George Bancroft (second stranger), Ronald Frankau (auctioneer), Rodney Ackland (man at auction), Ivor Barnard (man at auction)…

In the English countryside, Hornblower, a nouveau riche, acquires land and evicts its modest inhabitants to create an industrial complex. The Hillcrists, from a long line of aristocrats, oppose his plans for land expansion. At an auction, Hornblower manages to buy a new plot of land, thwarting the Hillcrists' maneuvers. At the end of the auction, Mrs. Hillcrist learns that Hornblower's daughter-in-law, Chloe, had previously been paid to seduce men to ruin their marriages and incite divorce proceedings. Mrs. Hillcrist uses this information to blackmail Hornblower. He sells the property acquired at auction to the aristocrats at a loss, making them swear never to reveal what they discovered. Hornblower's son, Charles, learns of his wife's less-than-honorable past and rushes to the Hillcrists' house, where Chloe already is. Hidden behind a curtain, she hears Charles express his anger and despair. She throws herself into the Hillcrists' backyard pond and drowns. The Hillcrists are crestfallen by the misfortune that followed their getting involved with Hornblower.

"You seem to me a poor sort of creature that's bound to get left with your gout and your dignity."

The entrepreneur to the old aristocrat, in *The Skin Game*

GENESIS AND CASTING

The directors of British International Pictures (BIP) suggested that Hitchcock adapt a play for which the company owned the rights, *The Skin Game* (meaning "the swindle") by John Galsworthy. The filmmaker had discovered the play at the theater in 1920. It had already been brought to the screen in 1921 by English director B. E. Doxat-Pratt.

A Much-Admired Author

Hitchcock admired Galsworthy and knew his work inside out. It was through actor and theater producer Leon M. Lion, who appeared in *Number Seventeen* (1932), that the filmmaker met the author. Lion began writing for the stage in 1906. That same year, he published the first novel in a three-generation family story (*The Forsyte Saga*). Hitchcock particularly appreciated the erudition and refinement of the writer (who went on to win the Nobel Prize for Literature in 1932), whom he sometimes visited at his home at Bury House, Sussex. A contract binding Galsworthy to BIP stipulated that any addition of dialogue had to be approved by the author. Hitchcock was thus obliged to stay as close as possible to the original work.

From the Theater to the Cinema

The character of Mr. Hornblower, the nouveau riche, is strongly played by Edmund Gwenn. The actor had already created the role in the theater, as well as in the film version. He enjoyed a long career in English and Hollywood cinema, until his death in 1959. Hitchcock cast him as Johann Strauss the elder in *Waltzes from Vienna* (1933), followed by *Foreign Correspondent* in 1940 and *The Trouble with Harry* in 1954.

Helen Haye, who played Mrs. Hillcrist, also played the character onstage and in the 1921 film version. She appeared in Hitchcock's *The 39 Steps* in 1935.

John Longden, portraying Charles Hornblower, had a long career in British cinema. In 1929 alone, he played the detective in *Blackmail*, then appeared in *Juno and the Paycock* and *Elstree Calling*.

Sold!

Twenty-eight years later, Alfred Hitchcock would again use an auction sequence to build suspense, in *North by Northwest*. This time, a statuette containing microfilm was to be acquired.

The auction. Center, Edmund Gwenn; to his right, John Longden. On the bench, to their left, Helen Haye, C. V. France, Jill Esmond.

FILMING AND PRODUCTION

The film was shot almost entirely in the studio between November and December 1930. Contractually obliged to respect the text, Hitchcock nevertheless had fun inventing a few visual effects. During the auction sequence, for example, the camera jumps back and forth between the bidders. It darts from one face to the next, in order to portray each raise and heighten the effect of suspense.

The Mysterious Door

During a long, dramatic confrontation sequence between Chloe and Mr. Hillcrist, the filmmaker twice inserts a shot of a large closed door. These two inserts have more than just a narrative justification, in this case the possible appearance of the husband. Nobody is hiding behind the door to spy on their conversation, and the interruption of the sequence by these brief shots creates a threatening discontinuity. In this way, Hitchcock builds aesthetic suspense to heighten the tension of the scene.

RECEPTION

To the surprise of the director himself, the film was a great success with the public. Some critics took notice, including *Kinematograph Weekly* (March 5, 1931), which interpreted the dynamism of the auction sequence as "an entire avoidance of stage limitations." The *New York Times* was harsher, commenting that the film included too many interminable scenes of dialogue, although it did acknowledge a number of directorial discoveries that broke the monotony.

Nothing to Say?

The film does not have a good reputation among the most ardent Hitchcockians. For Éric Rohmer and Claude Chabrol, *The Skin Game* is the filmmaker's worst film, a slapdash work in which the author seems to have lost interest: "No trace of stylization in the acting, or precision in the direction."[1] ("Nulle trace de stylisation dans le jeu, de précision de la mise en scène.") Hitchcock himself explained to François Truffaut during their famous interviews that "there's nothing to say about it."

Although *The Skin Game* is not one of Hitchcock's major works, the script is somewhat perverse, reversing moral values at the end of the story: The noble aristocrats are ultimately more villainous than the brutal upstart. As for Mrs. Hillcrist, she is perhaps the first incarnation of the character of the monstrous, even abject mother, a character that is to be found frequently in the work of the author of *Psycho* (1960).

For Hitchcock Addicts

Hitchcock filmed a dozen takes for the sequence in which actress Phyllis Konstam, playing Hornblower's daughter-in-law, throws herself into the pond in the Hillcrists' garden. Pure sadism, perhaps. This habit of tormenting actresses was to manifest itself on other occasions throughout his career.

Henry Kendall, Joan Barry.

Rich and Strange

Great Britain · 1 h 23 · Black and White · Mono · 1.20:1

Production Dates: June–August 1931
Release Date in Great Britain: December 1931 (London),
June 13, 1932 (outside London)
Release Date in the United States: January 1, 1932

Production: British International Pictures
Producer: John Maxwell

Based on the novel of the same name by Dale Collins (1930)
Adaptation: Alfred Hitchcock, Alma Reville, Val Valentine
Photographic Direction: Jack E. Cox, Charles Martin
Camera Operator: Bryan Langley
Sound: Alec Murray
Assistant Director: Frank Mills
Art Direction: C. Wilfred Arnold
Music: Hal Dolphe

Film Editing: Winifred Cooper, Rene Marrison
Starring: Henry Kendall (Fred Hill), Joan Barry (Emily Hill), Percy Marmont
(Commander Gordon), Betty Amann (the princess), Elsie Randolph (the old maid),
Aubrey Dexter (the colonel), Hannah Jones (Mrs. Porter)…

> "A sort of intimate
> diary delivered
> to the public or a
> family album."
>
> ---
>
> Donald Spoto, Hitchcock biographer

SYNOPSIS

On his way home from work, Fred Hill confesses to his wife, Emily, his frustration at not being able to live the high life. A letter arrives from Fred's uncle, granting his nephew a fortune that will enable him to realize his dream of traveling the world. After visiting Paris, the couple embark in Marseille on a liner bound for Singapore. On board, Emily befriends Commander Gordon, a dashing bachelor in his prime. Initially discreet, their relationship becomes more serious when Fred in turn abandons his wife to court a bewitching princess. Upon their arrival in Singapore, the rupture between husband and wife seems to be complete. But Emily refuses Gordon's offer of a life together. Gordon informs her that the princess is in fact a common adventurer. Emily returns to Fred and begins to reconcile with him when he is forced to face the truth after the "princess" steals a thousand pounds and disappears. With just enough money to get home, the couple board a low-cost ship that sinks. Stuck in their cabin while the ship is evacuated, they find themselves alone on the half-submerged vessel but are rescued by a junk. As they come into contact with the barbaric yet touching customs of the Chinese sailors, Emily and Fred grow closer. They are relieved to be able to return to their small, middle-class home in the London suburbs.

GENESIS

Tired of making one film adaptation after another of plays—like *The Skin Game*, which he had just completed—Alfred Hitchcock dreamed of a more ambitious film, escaping the routine of studio shoots. The result was *Rich and Strange*, his first original screenplay since *Champagne*.

Parallel Writing

Although novelist Dale Collins's name figures prominently in the credits, this is not an adaptation as such. Collins, a specialist in maritime travel stories, developed a synopsis with Hitchcock about an ordinary English couple who set off on a cruise after receiving an inheritance. Then the two men's paths diverged. Collins wrote a novel, also entitled *Rich and Strange*, which was released simultaneously with the film. For his part, Hitchcock worked on the script to be brought to the screen, with the help of his wife, Alma Reville, and Val Valentine, a humorist and songwriter who had become a prolific scriptwriter.

Two Innocents Abroad

The inspiration for the film clearly came from the long trip the Hitchcocks took with their daughter, Patricia, in early 1931, after shooting *The Skin Game*. They traveled by sea to West Africa and the Caribbean. This experience undoubtedly contributed to the anecdotes that abound in *Rich and Strange*, in which a couple discovers life together far from the marital home and daily routine. In several interviews, the filmmaker has said that he and his wife, like the heroes of the film, were "two innocents abroad." This observation also applies to less exotic

A Shakespearean Reference

The original title *Rich and Strange* sums up the story: The sudden wealth of the two heroes leads to adventures that take a strange turn. These words come from two lines from William Shakespeare's play *The Tempest*, which form the film's title: "But doth suffer a sea-change / Into something rich and strange."

Misdirection

The film's French and American titles, *À l'est de Shanghai* and *East of Shanghai*, in no way correspond to the locations of the action. The heroes turn back to Singapore, a port some 2,300 miles southwest of the Chinese metropolis.

destinations, such as Paris, where the Hitchcock-Revilles traveled to prepare for the episode of *Rich and Strange* set in the City of Light.

Unintentional Sightings in a Brothel

As the film's characters have to visit the attractions of nocturnal Paris, Hitchcock attended the latest shows in the capital. In particular, he considered a scene in which the heroine watches a belly-dancing act. At the end, the image of the dancer's swirling navel fades into a spiral cross-fade. This sequence was never shot, but if it had been, it would have foreshadowed, twenty-six years ahead of time, the famous opening credits of *Vertigo* (1957), where the swirling image emanates from the heroine's close-up eye. However, the location scouting gave rise to a delightful anecdote. Backstage at the Folies Bergère, the filmmaker and his wife asked for a belly-dancing demonstration. They were invited to get into a cab, which took them to what turned out to be a brothel. There, the owner offered them a lesbian romp, and the two English people quickly left. This episode was not included in the *Rich and Strange* screenplay, as it would naturally have been unthinkable due to censorship. The film does, however, contain an echo of it: When the heroine, the naïve Emily Hill, discovers the very skimpy outfits of the dancers at a revue, she thinks the curtain has gone up too early and the performers have not had time to get dressed!

CASTING

For the female lead, Hitchcock auditioned several actresses. Among them, he spotted Anna Lee, a newcomer at the time, who would go on to a great career in the United States. She was to become one of John Ford's favorite actresses.

Two Strings to His Bow

In the end, however, the director agreed with the producers, who wanted to cast Joan Barry. For the

Around the table: Henry Kendall, Percy Marmont, Joan Barry, Betty Amann.

director, this actress had two assets. She had dubbed the Czech actress Anny Ondra live on the set of the talkie version of *Blackmail* (1929), for which Hitchcock was grateful. In addition, Joan Barry had just made her mark in Harry Lachman's *The Outsider*, co-written by none other than Alma Reville.

A Venerable Commander

Opposite Joan Barry, Commander Gordon was played by veteran Percy Marmont. Marmont, a former star of American silent films (Frank Borzage's *Daddy's Gone A-Hunting*, Victor Fleming's *Lord Jim*), had returned to work in his native England. After *Rich and Strange*, Hitchcock cast him in two more of his feature films, *Secret Agent* (1935) and *Young and Innocent* (1937).

Elsie's Pranks

It was a stroke of genius on the part of Hitchcock to cast Elsie Randolph, a well-known London stage entertainer, in the role of the myopic spinster whose clumsiness and indiscretion constantly disrupt the affairs of the other travelers. Initially, however, the filmmaker was concerned that Randolph's natural vivacity and charm would not suit the role. But in the middle of an audition, she picked up a pair of glasses lying on the desk, put them on, and began to declaim in a nasal, snobbish voice. The filmmaker,

immediately convinced, even gave her character, as yet unnamed in the script, the first name Elsie. During filming, the actress was the victim of one of the pranks Hitchcock liked to play on the set. Knowing that his protégée could not stand the smell of tobacco, he made her believe that she had to play a scene in a telephone booth…which suddenly filled up with a thick cloud of smoke. But this episode did not sour the friendly relationship between Elsie Randolph and her director, who would later give her a small role in *Frenzy* (1971).

FILMING AND PRODUCTION

From the outset, the British International Pictures (BIP) bosses were unhappy with the project. Moreover, they despaired of seeing their star director polish his script for months on end. They would have preferred him to spend the time adapting a successful play.

The Freezing Water of the Suez Canal

Even before the script was completed, Hitchcock sent a cameraman to the scene of the action to shoot footage with a few supporting actors. This was no doubt to give the producers something to smile about, but in the end, the shots turned out to be very useful. The sponsors cut the budget of *Rich and Strange* and demanded numerous cuts to the script. As he hoped to shoot abroad, Hitchcock had to re-create the exotic settings in the studio, with the exception of a single day's location shooting on the English coast. Actor Henry Kendall, who played Fred Hill, shot a swimming scene that was supposed to take place in the Suez Canal. However, he looked so cold onscreen that the sequence had to be cut. And although we do not know if the two events are actually linked, Kendall subsequently developed a serious illness, preventing him from working for several weeks. As a result, Hitchcock was obliged to shoot all the scenes he could without his sick actor, and then, once his lead was back on his feet, Hitchcock filmed shots of Kendall on his own and cut them into the scenes that had already been shot. As a result, Hitchcock spent a great deal of time editing, trying to integrate the shots brought back by the cameraman sent abroad.

A Cornucopia of Inventions

Despite the filming difficulties, *Rich and Strange* is a virtuosic blend of styles. The first third of the film is a veritable cornucopia of silent film innovations. The superb introduction shows a cohort of employees

In search of happiness, Mr. and Mrs. Hill (Joan Berry and Henry Kendall) are pushed to the brink.

leaving their offices at the end of the working day. This collective movement is condensed into a single sequence shot, thanks to a high-mounted camera and removable sets reminiscent of the great German films of the 1920s that Hitchcock so admired. This is followed by a burlesque scene in a crowded subway train, where the influence of Charlie Chaplin comes to the fore. As for the Paris episode, it alternates night views of streets with illuminated façades with close-ups of the bewildered faces of the two heroes. Here, Hitchcock seizes upon an avant-garde genre known at the time as the "urban symphony." This genre, whose model is Walter Ruttmann's *Berlin: Die Sinfonie der Großstadt* (Berlin: Symphony of a Metropolis, or Berlin: Symphony of a Great City) (1927), consists of a mosaic of brief, dynamic sequences covering all aspects of a city. The filmmaker creates a kind of humorous mini-pastiche, accentuating the choppy, ultra-rapid nature of the editing.

Satire and Surrealism

The ocean liner journey is the opportunity for a succession of biting sketches that pinpoint the

shortcomings of married life and the hypocrisies of adultery.

These sequences often conclude with an impromptu gag. Many of these punch lines involve Elsie's more or less willful facetiousness, while others play on the contrast with the following sequence. For example, Emily exclaims, "I like people who have fun!," while the next shot shows her husband, Fred, bedridden with seasickness. Finally, the last act plunges the film into a kind of surrealism: The sinking of the return boat takes place in a strange, cruel atmosphere. Wandering onto the sinking ship, the Hill couple see the corpse of a passenger lying on deck. Then they are stunned by the Chinese sailors who rescued them, who do not react to the accidental death of one of their own before their very eyes. Hungry, the heroes pounce on the meal they are served. But they soon spit it out overboard, having realized that it was cat meat…

Freeze Frame

When Fred secretly goes to the princess's cabin, where she has arranged to meet him, he goes to the wrong door. The soundtrack then resounds with the indignant cries of the occupants. In the same shot, the comings and goings of other passengers suggest that many of the cabins in this corridor are occupied by illicit couples. All this, however, is allusive enough to slip through the net of censorship.

Henry Kendall, suffering from seasickness: a gag that Hitchcock had already filmed in *Champagne* (1928).

For Hitchcock Addicts

In his interviews with Truffaut, Hitchcock described a particularly daring sequence he claimed to have shot but which was probably cut by the censors. As a couple swims in a pool, the woman challenges the man to swim between her legs, but when he does, she traps his head between her thighs. As he rises to the surface, he says, "You almost killed me this time," and she retorts, "Wouldn't it have been a wonderful death?"

Against All Odds

Despite its many surprising tonal shifts, *Rich and Strange* retains an impressive coherence. This is largely due to a system of echoes between elements scattered throughout the film. For example, the heroes' final bout of nausea echoes Fred's experience of seasickness at the start of the crossing. As for the black cat butchered and cooked by the Chinese sailors, this is a sort of cousin to the Hills' domestic feline. At the start of the film, Fred chases it away, the cat symbolizing for him the horror of everyday life. He does the same at the very end; the poor animal now evokes the painful memory of a disgusting meal.

RECEPTION

Rich and Strange was an unqualified commercial failure. Most reviews were scathing, such as the one in the *Yorkshire Evening Post* (January 2, 1932), which described the film as "an odd mixture of travelogue, flirtations, intrigue and maritime melodrama," whose "concoction is rather indigestible."

Freeze Frame

On their arrival in Singapore, Emily and Fred Hill are almost separated. Going their separate ways, they set off to explore the city by rickshaw. However, as fate would have it, they end up next to each other. When the time comes to set off again, the rickshaw drivers are unable to pull away, as the two rickshaws cling to each other. This gag underlines the indissoluble bond that continues to unite the couple.

A Director Already Pigeonholed

Commentators particularly highlighted the return of processes typical of silent cinema: explanatory cards, long passages devoid of dialogue. Although these elements enabled Hitchcock to focus on the visual expressiveness of his mise-en-scène, they were seen as a regression. The same *Yorkshire Evening Post* article concluded, "*Rich and Strange* is not up to the standard one expects from the producer of *Blackmail* and other notable pictures of the past." Thus, the filmmaker found himself confronted with the downside of his burgeoning popularity, as audiences refused to see him deliver anything other than a detective story.

Intimate Confessions

Hitchcock was hurt by the poor reception reserved for *Rich and Strange*. Without a doubt, this was his most personal work to date, and one of the most intimate of his entire career. This was the filmmaker's first foray into adventure cinema, and he did so with an extreme freedom of tone, which Claude Chabrol and Éric Rohmer praised in their 1957 book (*Hitchcock*). It was biographer Donald Spoto, however, who brought the film's importance to light, insisting, half a century after it was made, on its autobiographical aspects. Drawing on the very sound of the first names ("Emily" and "Fred" evoking Alma and Alfred), Spoto argues that the director and his wife/co-writer, married for five years, may

have been talking about the vicissitudes of their own married life.

The hypothesis is not without merit: Despite already having a reputation as a megalomaniac, Hitchcock would identify with the character of a fallible husband who, despite his delusions of grandeur, proved unable to manage without his wife's support.

The Mysteries of Marriage

Despite her naïveté, Emily is far more lucid than her husband, especially when she talks to her suitor about the mysterious nature of the marriage bond.

Actress Joan Barry is extraordinarily moving when she delivers this speech: "Love is a very difficult business, Mr. Gordon. You'd be surprised. It makes everything difficult and dangerous [...] You see, everything's multiplied by two. Sickness, death... the future...It all means so much more." This is the truth with which the couple are confronted during the shipwreck. Emily and Fred fall into each other's arms, and their renewed union is definitively sealed when they watch in amazement as a young Chinese woman gives birth, a miraculous event amid the horrors of the pirate junk. Alma and Alfred Hitchcock were no doubt evoking the transformation of their life together after the birth of their only daughter, Patricia, then aged three.

Professional Dissatisfaction

In a tale of learning that is both dreamlike (fortune being a providential coincidence from the very start of the film) and rooted in the most precise reality, the hero's professional dissatisfaction, which echoes that of Hitchcock himself, is another autobiographical touch.

The filmmaker was feeling increasingly cramped at BIP studios, whose bosses insisted on having him adapt dusty plays between ambitious films. The conflict was further exacerbated by the failure of *Rich and Strange*, a project that never found favor with management. Hitchcock's position at the company, where he was the star director, became precarious.

Things did not improve much with the surprising treatment he gave to his next feature, *Number Seventeen*.

Where Is Hitchcock?

Although Alfred Hitchcock does not appear in *Rich and Strange*, he did play in a scene that was cut in the editing process: At the end of their misadventures, the Hill couple meet the filmmaker in a bar and tell him their story. Ironically, the filmmaker replies that the story could not be made into a film! Had this sequence been retained, it would have been Hitchcock's only speaking role.

In the middle of his set, Alfred Hitchcock (the man in the hat) directs the first scene of *Rich and Strange*.

Ann Casson, John Stuart.

Number Seventeen

Great Britain • **1 hr 6** • **Black and White** • **Mono** • **1.20:1**

SYNOPSIS

Production Dates: End 1931–early 1932
Release Date in Great Britain:
July 18, 1932 (London), November 7, 1932
(outside London)

Production: British International Pictures
Producers: Leon M. Lion, John Maxwell

**Based on a novel and a play by
Joseph Jefferson Farjeon (1925)**
Screenplay: Alma Reville, Alfred
Hitchcock, Rodney Ackland
Photographic Direction: Jack E. Cox,
Bryan Langley
Visual Effects (miniatures):
Bill Warrington
Sound: A. D. Valentine
Assistant Director: Frank Mills
Art Direction: C. Wilfred Arnold
Music: Adolph Hallis
Film Editing: A. C. Hammond

Starring: Leon M. Lion (Ben), Anne Grey
(Nora Brant), John Stuart (Inspector
Barton), Donald Calthrop (Brant), Barry
Jones (Henry Doyle), Ann Casson (Rose
Ackroyd), Henry Caine (Mr. Ackroyd), Garry
Marsh (Sheldrake)…

It's London at night. Attracted by the light of a candle, a man enters a seemingly deserted house and meets a vagrant, Ben, who claims to be seeking shelter. They discover the body of a man they believe to be dead. While the tramp searches the "dead man's" pockets, the intruder, who claims his name is Forsythe, continues his exploration. He comes across a young woman, Miss Ackroyd, supposedly looking for her father. The corpse has disappeared. At half past midnight, Mr. Ackroyd arrives, along with a certain Sheldrake and Nora, a woman pretending to be both hearing and speech impaired, who falls instantly in love with Forsythe. Each holds a card with the number 17, which corresponds to the house number. After attempting to strangle Ben, Sheldrake retrieves a necklace hidden in the bathroom. The jewel is passed from pocket to pocket, and a climate of distrust is established. Forsythe and Miss Ackroyd are tied up by the rest of the gang, who flee. Nora frees the couple. The necklace thieves board a train bound for the coast. Forsythe hijacks a bus and tries to catch up with the train, which has gone out of control after the driver faints. He manages to jump aboard and fights with the hijackers. The train crashes into a ferry that was due to depart. Doyle, one of the suspected bandits, Ben, Nora, and Forsythe are among the survivors. Doyle pretends to be Inspector Barton, only to be unmasked by Forsythe, the real Barton. As for Ben, he has concealed the necklace on his person.

> **"Number Seventeen is an enjoyable film insofar as it shows a big kid having fun with his favorite toys."**
>
> —
>
> Claude Chabrol and Éric Rohmer

GENESIS AND CASTING

While Hitchcock was busy editing *Rich and Strange*, Walter C. Mycroft, now head of the British International Pictures (BIP) studio, asked him to adapt a successful play created in 1925 by Joseph Jefferson Farjeon, based on his detective novel *The Number Seventeen*.

The Trio Have Fun

The director worked on the script with his wife, Alma Reville, and Rodney Ackland. Ackland, who also wrote for the theater, played a small role in *The Skin Game*, filmed in 1930. He went on to write numerous screenplays for film and television until his death in 1991. The trio had fun with the unexciting source material, transforming it into a police comedy bordering on the parodic and absurd. Ackland later commented that the play was full of clichés. He also remembered working on the script at the Hitchcocks' home, the writing sessions interspersed with fits of hilarity, and an atmosphere more stimulating than that of the studio.

Disparate Casting

The director welcomed back John Stuart, whom he'd cast in *The Pleasure Garden*. The second male role, that of the tramp, a picturesque cockney, was played by Leon M. Lion, the only actor from the play and the film's co-producer. Hitchcock disliked him, regarding him as an impossible ham ("the horrible old man"). Leon M. Lion enjoyed most of his success in the theater, although he did appear in a few films up to 1939.

For Hitchcock Addicts

Alfred Hitchcock planned to turn the abandoned house where the plot begins into a shelter for the neighborhood's stray cats. One morning, a large number of felines and their owners were brought to the studio. Stagehands scattered the animals around the set. For a scene in which the frightened kitties flee, a props man fires a shot and they scamper off in all directions. The owners spent the whole day looking for their cats in every corner of the studio. The filmmaker abandoned the idea.

Freeze Frame

The pearl necklace, a manifestation of the Hitchcockian "MacGuffin," is retrieved by one of the protagonists from a toilet cistern. This taste for trivial, even scabrous detail would continue to assert itself throughout Hitchcock's career.

Born into a family of stage actors, Ann Casson had a film career that included sporadic appearances in some fifteen films up to 1990, when she made her last feature film, *I Bought a Vampire Motorcycle*.

Anne Grey, who played Nora Brant, made her film debut after a career as a journalist. In 1934, she moved to Hollywood, where she appeared in a number of films, including a Laurel and Hardy, *Bonnie Scotland*, in 1935. She quit her career for good in 1939.

FILMING AND PRODUCTION

Number Seventeen, Hitchcock's last film for BIP, also marks his penultimate collaboration with Jack E. Cox as cinematographer after nine films made together.

Maquettes and Scale Models

For the last part of the film, which features a chase between a speeding train and a speeding bus, the filmmaker used numerous models and scale models. He later admitted that only this part of the shoot really interested him. In any case, it was the first intensive use of this technique, which Hitchcock would later make frequent use of, particularly during his English period.

Pending the Masterpieces

The final chase between the train and the bus enabled the filmmaker to use all the resources of

cross-cutting to build suspense. The perfection of a film like *North by Northwest* (1958) may have its roots in some of the experiments explored in *Number Seventeen*.

RECEPTION

Number Seventeen was released in cinemas in London in July 1932 and throughout England in November of the same year.

On its release, *Variety*'s critic wrote, "Like the play, the story is vague and, despite its intended eeriness, unconvincing. It is asking a lot of an audience—even a picture one—to make them believe a woman accomplice of a band of thieves will fall in love at first sight with a detective."

A Stylistic Exercise

Alfred Hitchcock referred to *Number Seventeen* as a "disaster." A minor work in the Master's career,

the film suffers above all from the confused, almost incomprehensible nature of a story that is also rather inconsistent. It is, however, a fascinating stylistic exercise. The first part allowed the filmmaker to experiment with skillful camera movements and expressionist lighting. He deliberately contrasted the two parts of the film: one with a lot of dialogue and an enclosed space, the other in the open air and more spectacular, focusing on the purely cinematic beauty of a speeding train. A number of visual motifs also herald major moments in his work: the shot of the couple suspended above the void (*Young and Innocent*, 1937; *North by Northwest*) or the repeated use of a pair of handcuffs (*The 39 Steps*, 1935; *Saboteur*, 1942; *The Wrong Man*, 1956).

Waltzes from Vienna

Great Britain	**1 hr 20**	**Black and White**	**Mono** (British Acoustic Film Full Range Recording)	**1.37:1**

SYNOPSIS

Production Dates: End 1933
Release Date in Great Britain: February 1934

Production: Tom Arnold Production
Producer: Tom Arnold
Unit Production Manager: Henry Sherek

Based on a play by Guy Bolton, *Waltzes from Vienna*, itself adapted from the operetta *Walzer aus Wien* (Vienna, 1930)
Screenplay: Guy Bolton, Alma Reville
Director of Photography: Glen McWilliams
Sound: Alfred Birch
Assistant Director: Richard Beville
Art Direction: Oscar Friedrich Werndorff
Set Decoration: Peter Proud
Music: Johann Strauss, father and son
Screen adaptation of the music by Johann Strauss, father and son: Hubert Bath
Musical Direction: Louis Levy
Film Editing: Charles Frend

Starring: Jessie Matthews (Resi Ebezeder), Edmund Gwenn (Johann Strauss the elder), Fay Compton (Countess Helga von Stahl), Esmond Knight (Johann Strauss the younger, "Schani"), Frank Vosper (Prince Gustav von Stahl), Robert Hale (Josef Ebezeder), Charles Heslop (the valet), Hindle Edgar (Leopold), Marcus Barron (Anton Drexler)...

The scene is Vienna at the time of Emperor Franz Joseph, circa 1867. Johann Strauss, a famous composer, has a son, nicknamed "Schani." He is in love with Resi, the daughter of a confectioner. But he is also in love with musical creation, despite his father's criticism and sarcasm. Countess Helga von Stahl, out of love for the young Strauss's youth and talent, encourages him to compose a waltz to accompany a poem she has written: "The Blue Danube." Resi asks her fiancé to choose between music and pastry making, but all the young man's efforts to please the woman he loves only serve to remind him of the strength of his vocation: The rhythm of the pie makers' work sets the pace for his great work to come. With the help of music publisher Drexler, Helga arranges for Johann Strauss the elder to arrive late on the evening of an important music festival to conduct his orchestra. In his place, and to calm the impatient audience, the son conducts "The Blue Danube" for the first time and achieves a triumph. At the end of a comical love affair involving the countess's jealous and ridiculous husband, Resi and Schani are reunited and never part. As for Strauss senior, who arrives in time to hear an ovation not intended for him, he finally seems to have come to terms with the idea of having a son whose genius may well eclipse his own.

Johann Strauss the younger: "My father is a great man." The countess: "Like all great men, he has a peculiar dislike of hearing youth knocking at the door."

Fay Compton, Marcus Barron.
Vast empty spaces…

GENESIS AND CASTING

Nineteen thirty-two was a bad year for Alfred Hitchcock. He had no pleasure in supervising *Lord Camber's Ladies*, directed by Benn Levy (the dialogue writer on the talkie version of *Blackmail*). He was in open conflict with Walter C. Mycroft, now head of British International Pictures (BIP). After five years at BIP and ten feature films, England's most prominent filmmaker found himself free and without a contract.

An Unexpected Proposal

Hitchcock worked for several months with producer Alexander Korda, but no formal project came out of their working partnership. Tom Arnold, a theater impresario, offered to produce a film adaptation of *Waltzes from Vienna*, a play based on a recent Viennese operetta that had been a great success at London's Alhambra Theatre in 1931. So as not to remain idle any longer, Hitchcock agreed to shoot this romanticized episode in the life of Johann Strauss, a costume comedy far removed from his usual preoccupations. In these early years of talking pictures, he took advantage of the opportunity to experiment with the relationship between film and music, although he omitted the dance numbers.

Frictions

To play the baker in love, Arnold hired Jessie Matthews, a leading English star of stage and screen.

But she refused to take orders from Hitchcock, an "imperious young man" considered inexperienced in romantic comedies. Nor could she stand his practical jokes on the set.[1] As for the director, he was irritated by the actress's airs and graces, and in the end, the character she played was hardly sympathetic. The role of young Strauss fell to Esmond Knight, who was destined for a very long career working with the likes of Michael Powell, Laurence Olivier, Jean Renoir, and Lars von Trier. He too would not have fond memories of the shoot: "It did not give the actors confidence."[2] Hitchcock was happier to find Edmund Gwenn (*The Skin Game*, 1930) and, above all, to give a role to Fay Compton, whom he had admired onstage thirteen

For Hitchcock Addicts

After "The Blue Danube," other waltz tunes would creep into Hitchcock's films, in a more ominous or threatening way: Franz Lehár's "The Merry Widow" (*Shadow of a Doubt*, 1942), Charles B. Ward's "The Band Played On" (*Strangers on a Train*, 1950), Johann Strauss's "The Emperor Waltz" (*Torn Curtain*, 1966).

Freeze Frame

While punishing a servant, Prince von Stahl rolls him down the steps of his palace. The grand staircase is filmed in bird's-eye view so that it resembles a keyboard, and the steps are like so many keys. At the same time, in the next room, young Johann Strauss is practicing his scales. By combining sound and image, Hitchcock subtly finds a way of visualizing the music he hears.

years earlier in *Mary Rose*, a play he would dream of making into a film all his life.

FILMING AND PRODUCTION

Waltzes from Vienna was filmed at Islington Studios, then owned by Gaumont British. Hitchcock had already worked there in 1926–1927, making films for Gainsborough Pictures.

In Music

In addition to the classic script subdivision into shots, movements, and camera angles, Hitchcock sometimes established a "musical division" to ensure that the movements of the music and the film progressed optimally "in concert." At the end of 1933, while editing *Waltzes from Vienna*, he gave an interview and took the opportunity to reflect aloud on the role of music in film: "Film music and cutting have a great deal in common. The purpose of both is to create the tempo."[3]

The Return of Michael Balcon

For Hitchcock, the most important thing was to continue practicing his craft while waiting for a better opportunity. This opportunity arose on the set of *Waltzes from Vienna*. Visiting the set, producer Michael Balcon met up with the filmmaker he had discovered and asked him about his projects. The result was four films together and a successful contract with Gaumont British that lasted until the end of the 1930s.

RECEPTION

The *Times* (March 5, 1934) certainly gave Hitchcock credit for not making the mistake of just slavishly filming the play. On the contrary, his direction was described as "flexible and alive." But for the journalist, he committed a crime of lèse majesté by not making the most—far from it—of his lead actress: "He has cast her as an impudent and bad-mannered little baggage of a shop-girl and treated her as a not too important part of the film's design." Jessie Matthews could not have put it better. *Picturegoer* (April 28, 1934), on the other hand, praised the camerawork above all, which it considered to be "outstanding."

Art and Style

Although Hitchcock disparaged his film in retrospect, he was far from indifferent to it at the time. Prince Gustav von Stahl's awakening, his verbal exchange with the countess from their respective apartments, and the ensuing comedy of master and servant are all captured in a sequence lasting almost three minutes. Hitchcock's uncluttered sets create vast, surprising empty spaces on the screen, like visual echo chambers. At times, he finds visual rhymes and knows how to manage his special effects: "The Blue Danube" tune, heard in snatches throughout the film, is only played in its entirety and full majesty at the end.

Michael Balcon,
the Man Who Knew a Lot

Michael Balcon (1896–1977) produced over three hundred British films in four decades, including nine by Alfred Hitchcock. A key figure in his country's cinema, he discovered the director of *The Pleasure Garden* and put him back in the saddle at just the right moment with *The Man Who Knew Too Much*. Balcon may not have invented Hitchcock, but he certainly paved the way for him.

Relentless

"Once film production is in the blood, nothing stops the perpetuation of such follies."[1] Michael Balcon was indeed a tireless producer, a film lover with a flair for business. In the 1920s, he created Gainsborough Pictures (1924), bought Islington Studios, the best-equipped in the country (two sets),

set up co-productions with Germany, and tried to curb the hegemony of American films on English screens by encouraging high-quality nationally produced works.

In the 1930s, he became head of production at Gaumont British (1932–1936), taking the Islington and Lime Grove Studios (five sets) through the delicate technical transition to talking pictures. He put his name to a quasi-experimental documentary (Robert Flaherty's *Man of Aran*, 1934), while also creating hits for the American market (Jessie Matthews's musicals and Alfred Hitchcock's *The 39 Steps*, 1935). He then took charge of Ealing Studios (1937–1955), the birthplace of world-famous "English comedies" (*Kind Hearts and Coronets* [*Noblesse oblige*], 1949, by Robert Hamer, who had directed *Jamaica Inn* eleven years earlier). In 1963, he produced his last film, Alexander Mackendrick's ambitious *Sammy Going South*.

The Foot in the Stirrup

From their beginnings, both Balcon and Hitchcock were linked. Hitchcock, then a young jack-of-all-trades, was responsible for the script, art direction, and directing assistance on Balcon's first film, *Woman to Woman* (Graham Cutts, 1923). Its unexpected success led to four films with the same team in two years. Above all, Balcon could see what the twenty-five-year-old Hitchcock was capable of. He gave him his chance as director in 1925 with *The Pleasure Garden*, followed by four more titles, including *The Lodger*. Not only did Balcon admire Hitchcock's talent and continue to place his trust in him; he also protected him from his detractors: Graham Cutts, who slandered the newcomer for fear of losing his own star status, and C. M. Woolf, the powerful distributor of Gainsborough Productions, who hated Hitchcock's "sophisticated" films. Balcon is therefore also to be credited with preserving the integrity of a promising director's early work.

Second Chance

Not only did Balcon launch Hitchcock, but he also gave him a timely boost in the mid-1930s, at a critical time when the director found himself without a contract or a studio. He offered him a five-film contract with Gaumont British, inaugurated by *The Man Who Knew Too Much* (1934). Once again, Balcon defended the film's editing against the intractable C. M. Woolf. The time had come for Hitchcock's great English films: *The 39 Steps*, *Secret Agent*, *Sabotage* (which, its producer declared, showed "more of the real London than any other film yet made"[2]), and then, without Balcon but still with Gaumont British, *Young and Innocent* and *The Lady Vanishes*.

Ideal Conditions

Above all, Balcon enabled Hitchcock to return exclusively to his favorite genres: thrillers and spy films, whereas with British International Pictures (1927–1932), the director sometimes had to deal with imposed literary adaptations, inept comedies, or stars he had not chosen himself. At Gaumont British, Hitchcock was in tune with the American stars that Balcon managed to sign: Madeleine Carroll, Robert Young, Sylvia Sidney. He also benefited from the skilled professionals the producer knew how to surround himself with, some of whom were former friends of the filmmaker: associate producer Ivor

Montagu, story supervisor Angus MacPhail, assistant director Penrose Tennyson, editor Charles Frend, and art directors Alfred Junge and Oscar Friedrich Werndorff from Germany.

Birth of a Genre

Balcon wanted to make England a great country for cinema. Inevitably, Hitchcock's departure for Hollywood in March 1939, combined with the country's entry into the war in September and a strong upsurge in national sentiment, exasperated the producer, who attacked his former protégé in the press. Without naming him, but caricaturing him sufficiently to make him recognizable, he accused him of desertion and treason. Two days later, Hitchcock published a right of reply that did not spare the man who had discovered him. A happy professional relationship was over. Nevertheless, Michael Balcon contributed more than any other to the creation of a cinematic genre with a bright future: the Hitchcock film.

PUBLIC ENEMY NO.1
OF ALL THE WORLD··

NOVA PILBEAM
PETER LORRE
LESLIE BANKS
EDNA BEST

THE MAN WHO KNEW TOO MUCH

A PRODUCTION

Directed by ALFRED HITCHCOCK

The Man Who Knew Too Much

Great Britain • **1 hr 15** • **Black and White** • **Mono** (British Acoustic Film Full Range Recording System) • **1.37:1**

Production Dates: May 29–August 2, 1934
Release Date in Great Britain: December 9, 1934 (London),
February 1935 (outside London)
Release Date in the United States: March 21, 1935

Production: Gaumont British
Producer: Michael Balcon
Associate Producer: Ivor Montagu
Unit Production Manager: Richard Beville

Based on an original story by Charles Bennett and D. B. Wyndham Lewis
Screenplay: Edwin Greenwood, Arthur Richard Rawlinson
Additional dialogue: Emlyn Williams
Director of Photography: Curt Courant
Camera Operator: Ted Lloyd
Visual Effects: Fortunino Matania, Albert Whitlock
Sound: Frank McNally
Assistant Director: Penrose Tennyson
Art Direction: Alfred Junge
Set Decoration: Peter Proud
Music: Arthur Benjamin
Musical Direction: Louis Levy
Film Editing: H. St. C. Stewart

Starring: Leslie Banks (Bob Lawrence), Edna Best (Jill Lawrence), Peter Lorre (Abbott), Frank Vosper (Ramon Levine), Hugh Wakefield (Clive), Nova Pilbeam (Betty Lawrence), Pierre Fresnay (Louis Bernard), Cicely Oates (Agnes), D. A. Clarke-Smith (Binstead), George Curzon (Gibson), Frank Atkinson (policeman), Betty Baskcomb (Lawrence's maid), Cot D'Ordan (concierge), Tony De Lungo (hotel manager), Clare Greet (Mrs. Brockett), Pat Hagan (policeman), Joan Harrison (secretary), Frederick Piper (policeman), Alfred Hitchcock (man in the street)…

> "Politics in the midst of imaginative interests is like a pistol shot in the middle of a concert. This noise does not accord with the sound of any instrument."
>
> ─
>
> Stendhal, *Le Rouge et le Noir*

SYNOPSIS

─

Jill and Bob Lawrence spend a sporting vacation in the Swiss resort of Saint Moritz with their daughter Betty. Jill, an experienced markswoman, takes part in a rifle competition, which she loses to her rival, Ramon Levine. While there, the couple befriends a Frenchman, Louis Bernard. Bernard is shot through the heart at a party. Before dying, he tells Jill of a secret message to take to the British consul. Warned of this, Bob manages to retrieve it. The paper contains encrypted information and the name of a London district, Wapping. Terrorists plotting the murder of a senior politician in a European country kidnap Betty to force the couple into silence. With his friend Clive, Bob follows the London trail to a sect house, home to the group of criminals led by the ominous Abbott. Bob is held prisoner, but Clive manages to escape and informs Jill that the politician's assassination will take place during a concert at the Royal Albert Hall. She goes there and spots the assassin, Ramon Levine. At the fateful moment, in the middle of the concert, she lets out a scream, causing the sniper to miss. Levine, followed by the police, joins the group that has taken Bob and his daughter hostage. The police surround the building, and an intense shootout begins. Betty flees to the roof; Ramon tries to catch her. Jill grabs a rifle and shoots the pursuer. The group is eliminated to the last man, and the Lawrence family, still in shock, is finally reunited.

GENESIS

On the set of *Waltzes from Vienna*, Alfred Hitchcock received a visit from Michael Balcon, production director of Gaumont British. The producer, who had launched the filmmaker almost ten years earlier (*The Pleasure Garden*, 1925), asked about his projects. Hitchcock asked him to work with Charles Bennett on a script called *Bulldog Drummond's Baby*, inspired by the adventures of Bulldog Drummond, a famous detective novel character.

Back to Balcon

Balcon was enthusiastic about the idea and learned that John Maxwell, producer at British International Pictures (BIP), had considered the project too costly. He seized the opportunity and suggested that Hitchcock should join Gaumont British. All that remained was to acquire the rights to adapt the series of detective novels, owned by BIP. Hitchcock managed to buy them back for £250 and sold them to Balcon for twice that amount. The director and his screenwriter, who had been working for BIP since 1931, signed a five-film contract with Gaumont British. But the adaptation rights did not permit Hitchcock to use the character of Bulldog Drummond, who remained the property of BIP. So he had to change the title and, little by little, transform the story.

"The Accomplices"

Based in the Lime Grove Studios in London's Shepherd's Bush district, Bennett and Hitchcock set to work in early 1934. In the first version, private detective Bulldog Drummond unmasks an international spy ring while on vacation in Switzerland, although spies have kidnapped his baby to keep him quiet. But the script was constantly being amended with the help of seasoned screenwriter friends whom the director nicknamed "the accomplices," including Ivor Montagu, back from his trip to Hollywood with Soviet filmmaker S. M. Eisenstein, Angus MacPhail, head of Gaumont British's subjects and scripts department, and Hitchcock's wife, Alma Reville.

The film was written in a studious yet playful atmosphere. The small team met in the evening at the Hitchcocks' apartment on Cromwell Road. The "accomplices" dined, drank, and smoked; ideas were exchanged to the point where it was difficult to disentangle their origin, proof of a perfect harmony among those involved. In the end, only playwright Arthur Richard Rawlinson and writer/director Edwin Greenwood were credited with the screenplay, but no fewer than nine collaborators (including Welsh actor Emlyn Williams) worked on the expanded story right up to the start of filming.

Overflowing Topicality

Although Hitchcock was reluctant to divulge his political opinions in his films, he found himself surrounded by an anti-fascist, socialist team, and even a communist (Montagu). This atmosphere influenced the screenplay, while the filmmaker drew on current events and recent political events for fascinating fictional material. The year 1933 saw the burning of the Reichstag, Germany's parliament building, as well as the attempted assassination of US president Franklin Roosevelt by an Italian anarchist. The scriptwriters also recall the Sidney Street siege, or the Battle of Stepney, which took place in 1911 in London's East End: Winston Churchill, then home secretary, led the attack on two revolutionaries barricaded in a building. The kidnapping of aviator Charles Lindbergh's baby in March 1932 is another likely source of inspiration. Fueled by these events and the collective ebullience of the screenwriting team, *Bulldog Drummond's Baby* became *The Man Who Knew Too Much*, a title Hitchcock borrowed from a collection of detective stories by British writer and journalist G. K. Chesterton.

The One-Note Man

The climax of *The Man Who Knew Too Much* is inspired by a comic strip by H. M. Bateman, *The One-Note Man*, published in 1921 in *Punch* magazine, of which Hitchcock was a loyal reader. This

A preparatory drawing by Alfred Junge, art director of *The Man Who Knew Too Much*.

humorous comic strip recounts the daily life of a musician who wakes up in the morning and prepares to play a single note at his orchestra's evening concert before going home to bed. Hitchcock's idea was to build a sequence in which the stakes rested entirely on waiting for a single cymbal stroke, corresponding to the moment when the assassin was to shoot the politician. Hitchcock asked composer Arthur Benjamin to create a cantata especially for this concert scene.

CASTING

Attending the premiere of a play in London, Hitchcock discovered actor Pierre Fresnay, then a member of the Comédie-Française, and offered him the role of Louis Bernard, the secret agent. After giving actor and playwright Frank Vosper a comic role in *Waltzes from Vienna*, Hitchcock cast him as Ramon Levine, the sinister sniper. Leslie Banks and Edna Best, two English actors, played Bob and Jill Lawrence, the close-knit, humorous couple who have to cope with the kidnapping of their child, played with great emotion by Nova Pilbeam, a fourteen-year-old actress to whom Hitchcock would give the lead role in *Young and Innocent* three years later.

Public Enemy Number 1

The real audacity of the casting lies in the choice of Peter Lorre to play Abbott, the terrorist leader. The Hungarian actor became famous for lending his eerie, boyish good looks to the character of the child murderer in Fritz Lang's *M*. Lorre fled Hitler's Germany in 1933, taking refuge in Paris. Ivor Montagu brought him to London. The actor barely understood English, but Hitchcock fell under the spell of this man with his atypical physique and big, sad eyes. Inspired by this newcomer, Hitchcock went on to develop the character of Abbott, the spy chief, into a captivating villain, both bloodthirsty and Shakespearean. It was also this sardonic face, with its scar and blond streak, that illustrated the film's poster with the tagline "Public Enemy No. 1 of All the World."

Recomposing the Technical Team

With his usual technicians still under contract to BIP, Hitchcock had to reassemble a team. Balcon recommended a twenty-year-old named Penrose Tennyson, as assistant director.

The producer also endeavored to attract German refugees from the film world to London, including artistic director Alfred Junge and cinematographer Curt Courant. However, Hitchcock insisted on hiring an English editor with whom he could communicate well and chose the twenty-three-year-old

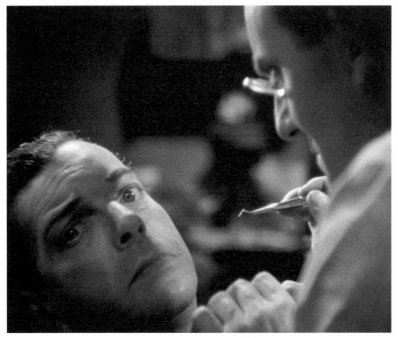

A real fake dentist: the familiar and the frightening (left, Leslie Banks).

Where Is Hitchcock?

Hitchcock's silhouette appears furtively. As Bob and Clive cross the street on their way to the Tabernacle of the Sun sect, he passes behind their backs, wearing a hat and a long, eccentric black oilskin. The collar almost completely conceals his face, and it is his silhouette that gives away his identity.

H. St. C. Stewart. Albert Whitlock, in charge of models and miniatures, also made his appearance in the filmmaker's world. Throughout his career, Hitch took great pleasure in training young people, "Hitch's boys."

FILMING AND PRODUCTION

Filming at the Lime Grove Studios lasted two months, from late May to early August 1934. The atmosphere on the set was just as stimulating as that during script development. In the evenings and on weekends, Hitchcock hosted parties at Cromwell Road for members of the crew, both stars and technicians, helping to strengthen the spirit of camaraderie on the set.

A Postcard

The Man Who Knew Too Much begins with the image of a table covered with guidebooks and tourist brochures on Switzerland, browsed by an anonymous hand. A cross-fade reveals the mountainous landscape of the winter sports resort of Saint Moritz (a mixture of painted canvases and shots filmed by a second crew). This postcard-style opening, a technique favored by the filmmaker, gives the viewer a sense of security that in no way foreshadows the horror to come. This introduction also presages the end of the film, where the tone will have changed completely: at the beginning, Jill Lawrence, an excellent markswoman, takes on Ramon Levine, a man who is as skilled as she is, for fun, and who wins the shooting contest. Amused and unaware of the threat he represents, she exclaims that they are "sworn enemies!," then both promise a rematch. In the end, it is the same gunman she intercepts in the middle of a concert at the Royal Albert Hall, then shoots from afar, just as she did in the competition. Between the beginning and the end, he becomes the target.

The Illusionist

With a tight budget (£49,000), Hitchcock had to use his talents as an illusionist to create spectacular scenes. With its ostensibly costly sequence in the Royal Albert Hall, Hitchcock used the Schüfftan process, named after its inventor, a German cinematographer. A tilted mirror is used to combine life-size and model sets in the same shot, giving the illusion of a continuous, larger-than-life set. Hitchcock had already employed this trick—used as early as *Metropolis* (Fritz Lang, 1927) and often in expressionist and fantasy films—in *The Ring* (1927) and *Blackmail* (1929). Above all, it spared him the need to hire hundreds of extras and, by enabling the addition of hand-drawn silhouettes to represent an audience, helped him create the illusion of a packed concert hall. "Then in the box we had a woman opening a program, and so forth, and the eye immediately went to the movement. All the rest was static."[1]

American Influence

The best-known sequences in *The Man Who Knew Too Much* are distinguished by their virtuosic, taut editing. The audience at the Royal Albert Hall attending a concert is matched by the mass of onlookers witnessing the shootout between police and terrorists hiding in a building. These two audiences—the cultured elite and the "man in the street"—indicate that Hitchcock saw action (and even violence) as a spectacle that appeals to the broadest possible audience. With its brutality (the policemen killed) and feverish realism, its portrayal of lawless yet charismatic villains (the character played by Peter Lorre), the shooting sequence evokes an American gangster film, a genre that was very popular in the 1930s, and evokes Howard Hawks's *Scarface* (1932) in particular.

RECEPTION

The producers of *The Man Who Knew Too Much* were targeting the English market as a priority, while hoping for US distribution. But the film fell foul of censors on both sides of the Atlantic.

Freeze Frame

During the concert at the Royal Albert Hall, the editing combines several actions, spaces, and characters: Jill Lawrence on the lookout for the gunman (the camera extends her gaze and sweeps the hall's balconies) while keeping an eye on the politician; the group of terrorists listening to the concert on the radio, waiting for the fateful note; the musician, an unwilling accomplice in the crime in the making; the choir singing ("nameless fear" [...] "All save the child"); the gunman behind a curtain, with only the barrel of the weapon visible. So the real cinematic spectacle is not only onstage, but also in the auditorium and dressing rooms.

When the Censors Become Involved

The British Board of Film Censors (BBFC), the British government's censorship board, demanded the removal of shots of the final shootout in which London police officers appear with weapons—in England, policemen did not normally carry firearms. It was felt that such depictions would be detrimental to the reputation of the national police force. The sequence was amended, but Hitchcock retained a scene in which the police commandeer the stock of a local gunsmith. In the US, *The Man Who Knew Too Much* came up against a censorship system designed to curb, among other things, the violence of gangster films. The head of the Production

More Than an Assistant

In 1933, in search of a new assistant, Hitchcock placed an advertisement in several British newspapers: He was looking for a "young lady, highest educational qualifications, must be able to speak, read and write French and German fluently," for film producer. Joan Harrison, a twenty-one-year-old student, applied. Although she did not speak German, she was hired as an assistant on *The Man Who Knew Too Much*. Her job included reading stories and screenplays for the filmmaker. Her role soon extended beyond her initial function: She helped to write some of the screenplays and became one of the producers of the *Alfred Hitchcock Presents* series.

Code Administration (PCA) declared that the film contained "too much slaughter; too much gunplay; too much murdering of policemen [...] The final two reels of the film presents a slaughter the like of which we have not seen since the days of *Scarface*."[2] Gaumont British had no choice but to re-edit these scenes, but did not entirely satisfy the PCA.

The Critics Were Impressed

The Scottish magazine *Cinema Quarterly* found the filmmaker more at ease and inspired with this political drama than he had been with the romantic musical *Waltzes from Vienna* (1933). British critic C. A. Lejeune wrote in the *Observer* of a filmmaker who had "thrown critics and intellectuals overboard with one of his incomparable rude gestures, and gone in for making pictures for the people" (December 9, 1934). Lejeune concluded that the film was probably his best. In the US, the *New York Times* critic called the film "directed with a fascinating staccato violence [...] it is the swiftest screen melodrama this column can recall" (March 23, 1935).

In Praise of the Film's Scenic Style

Still influenced by German expressionism (shadows projected onto a staircase wall, disturbing close-ups of faces), *The Man Who Knew Too Much* also inaugurated a new genre: spy thrillers. In their essay[3] on *The Man Who Knew Too Much*, Rohmer and Chabrol consider that the film definitively established Hitchcock's status as a showman with audiences and critics alike, but criticize it for "implications timidly expressed, significant details sparingly distributed" ("des implications timidement exprimées, des détails significatifs chichement distribués"). It does, however, contain a reference to the Sarajevo assassination in 1914, an explicit allusion to the risk of a new world war. But the film's lack of emphasis on political issues, which appear to be mere pretexts for all kinds of adventures, bears witness to the filmmaker's philosophy at work in *The Man Who Knew Too Much*. Because the political implications are barely sketched out, in favor of a dazzlingly long plot and frenetic twists and turns, Hitchcock designates his mise-en-scène as the true focus of the film, a momentum that sweeps everything along in its path, a blast that fires on all cylinders.

From White to Black

With its short running time (seventy-five minutes), this compact feature film successfully performs the feat of taking the viewer through an uninterrupted series of perilous adventures. Starting with the kidnapping of Betty Lawrence, the film plunges the viewer into an underworld of suspense: the scene at the fake dentist's, the ceremony and brawl at the Tabernacle of the Sun sect, the concert at the Royal Albert Hall, the final shootout... *The Man Who Knew Too Much* opens on the immaculate whiteness of the Swiss mountains and then transports its audience to the sticky blackness of the London night.

H. M. Bateman *The One-Note Man*, *Punch*, December 14, 1921.

THE ONE-NOTE MAN—I

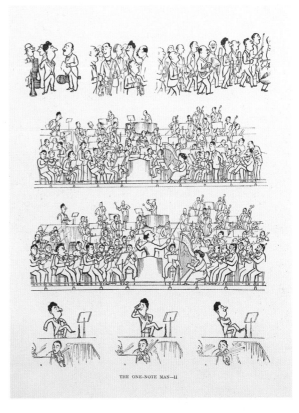

THE ONE-NOTE MAN—II

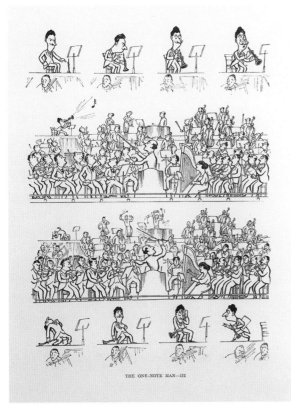

THE ONE-NOTE MAN—III

THE ONE-NOTE MAN—IV

Paul Newman, Ludwig Donath in *Torn Curtain* (1966).
Right: Roscoe Lee Browne, Donald Randolph in *Topaz* (1969).

The MacGuffin,
a Very Ridiculous Secret

In his interviews with François Truffaut,[1] following an allusion to the secret clause of a diplomatic treaty, the object of the quest of the Nazi spies in *Foreign Correspondent* (1940), Alfred Hitchcock describes one of his most famous theories: that of the MacGuffin. "It's a bias, a trick, a ploy, we call it a gimmick." Truffaut, in search of a definition, then asks, "The MacGuffin is the pretext, is that right?"

A Funny Story

Hitchcock continues his discussion with the young filmmaker, referring to the British Army's espionage missions on the border of India and Afghanistan, the aim of which was to steal the plans of a fortress or some other secret: "MacGuffin is the name we give to this kind of action: stealing papers, stealing documents." For the filmmaker, these papers, documents,

or secrets must be extremely important to the characters, but not to the narrator. He adds that the origin and meaning of the MacGuffin can be found in a funny story. Two men are on a train. One of them asks the other about the parcel in the net: "It is a MacGuffin, replies the interviewee.—What is a MacGuffin? asks the first.—It is a device for catching lions in the Adirondack Mountains.—But there are no lions in the Adirondacks.—In that case, it is not a MacGuffin." If Hitchcock uses this joke to define this particular concept, it is in order to emphasize its futile aspect, with no real purpose. For him, the MacGuffin is nothing but a filmmaker's tool.

Secrets of No Importance

Hitchcock's work is full of secrets and mysterious, sometimes intangible objects, to which the

characters in many of his films devote themselves and about which they fight over. Examples include the necklace in *Number Seventeen* (1932), the popular song hiding an encrypted code in *The Lady Vanishes* (1938), the uranium concealed in a bottle of wine in *Notorious* (1946), the mathematical formula memorized by Mr. Memory in *The 39 Steps* (1935) or the one stolen by the character played by Paul Newman in *Torn Curtain* (1966), and the microfilms revealing the installation of Soviet missiles in Cuba in *Topaz* (1969). Hitchcock considers his best MacGuffin, "the emptiest, the most non-existent, the most ridiculous," to be that of *North by Northwest* (1958). The CIA chief (Leo G. Carroll) refers to the spy played by James Mason as a man who trades in import-export and sells "government secrets," a hollow, imprecise phrase that vaguely describes the villain's activities.

A Means to an End

The MacGuffin as defined by Hitchcock is, of course, a concession to the commercial logic of credible or plausible scenarios. The object of the characters' quest must therefore have a concrete or virtual existence; in any case, it is a secret that generally brings the film back to its original genre, the spy thriller. Is Hitchcock cynical about

the sometimes ideological stakes of his "political" films, whether anti-Nazi or anti-Red, when he characterizes a secret apparently crucial to the plot as a "MacGuffin" in order to render it ridiculous? Some critics have accused him of this. This designation of the object of suspense as a MacGuffin is the filmmaker's way of emphasizing its unimportance. The real focus lies elsewhere. The tension and suspense in Hitchcock's films are based on psychological, sexual, and even metaphysical mechanisms that go beyond the simple detective mystery. For Hitchcock, for example, it is a mistake to attach the slightest importance to the MacGuffin (uranium hidden in wine bottles) in *Notorious*, because for him, the film is first and foremost the story of a man in love with a woman, who, as part of her mission, has to sleep with another man and even marry him—a tortuous web of desire and renunciation, frustration and resentment. The MacGuffin is merely a means to a greater end.

For François Truffaut, such a conception proved that Hitchcock was an artist with a perfect awareness of his work. It has sometimes been said that this disdain for secrecy reflects the fact that the filmmaker had nothing to say. But as the author of *Quatre Cents Coups* put it: "A filmmaker has nothing to say, his purpose is to reveal."

ROBERT
DONAT
MADELEINE
CARROLL
THE 39 STEPS
with
LUCIE MANNHEIM
GODFREY TEARLE
PEGGY ASHCROFT
DIRECTED BY
ALFRED HITCHCOCK
GB
A GB PRODUCTION

The 39 Steps

⚑ **Great Britain** • 🕐 **1 hr 26** • ◉ **Black and White** • 🔇 **Mono** (Full Range Recording System) • ▭ **1.37:1**

Production Dates: January 11–mid-March 1935
Release Date in Great Britain: June 6, 1935 (London),
November 1935 (outside London)
Release Date in the United States: July 31, 1935

Production: Gaumont British
Producer: Michael Balcon
Associate Producer: Ivor Montagu

Based on the novel of the same name by John Buchan (1915)
Adaptation: Charles Bennett
Dialogue: Ian Hay
Director of Photography: Bernard Knowles
Special Effects: Philippo Guidobaldi, Jack Whitehead
Sound: Alfred Birch
Assistant Director: Penrose Tennyson
Continuity: Alma Reville
Art Direction: Oscar Friedrich Werndorff, Albert Jullion
Set Decoration: Albert Whitlock
Costumes: Marianne, Joe Strassner
Makeup: Bob Clark
Music: Jack Beaver, Louis Levy
Film Editing: Derek N. Twist

Starring: Robert Donat (Richard Hannay), Madeleine Carroll (Pamela), Lucie Mannheim ("Annabelle Smith," the stranger), Godfrey Tearle (Professor Jordan), Helen Haye (Mrs. Jordan), John Laurie (crofter), Peggy Ashcroft (crofter's wife), Frank Cellier (sheriff), Wylie Watson ("Mr. Memory"), Hilda Trevelyan (innkeeper's wife), Gus McNaughton (commercial traveler), Jerry Verno (commercial traveler), Peggy Simpson (maid), Ivor Barnard (meeting chairman), Matthew Boulton (fake police officer), Carleton Hobbs (fake police officer), Elizabeth Inglis (daughter of Professor Jordan), Frederick Piper (milkman), Miles Malleson (Palladium manager), Charles Bennett (a passerby), Alfred Hitchcock (a passerby)…

SYNOPSIS

—

A brawl breaks out in the London music hall where Mr. Memory, a juggler with a phenomenal memory, is performing. In the chaos, Richard Hannay meets a mysterious stranger who urges him to take her home. She tells him she is an international spy being pursued by two killers because she is working to prevent the hijacking of a British military secret by an organization called "the 39 Steps." Hannay does not believe it, but during the night, the young woman is murdered. In her hand is a map with the name of a small Scottish town circled on it. Knowing that he will be accused of the murder, Hannay sets off for Scotland, hunted by both the police and the killers. During his journey, the fugitive is almost shot by the head of the enemy network, Professor Jordan, and is twice denounced by a stubborn young woman, Pamela. However, Pamela recognizes his innocence when she overhears a conversation revealing that Jordan needs to contact someone at a show at the London Palladium. Seeing Mr. Memory arrive onstage, Hannay understands everything: the plans for a new British warplane are about to leave the country thanks to the artist, who has memorized them. Surrounded by the police, he shouts to the entertainer: "What are the 39 Steps?" Caught in his act, Memory replies that it is a foreign spy ring, before being shot by Jordan. Jordan is arrested, and Hannay is finally cleared.

GENESIS

In devising *The Man Who Knew Too Much* (1934), Hitchcock drew heavily on a writer he had read assiduously in his youth, John Buchan. At the beginning of the twentieth century, Buchan revolutionized the spy novel, replacing the traditional schema of intrigue between various governments and secret services with the tribulations of a character plunged by chance into the subterranean struggle between states. This approach is in line with that of Hitchcock, who from the start of his career had enjoyed showing ordinary people grappling with extraordinary events. With the aim of making a new spy thriller to confirm the success of *The Man Who Knew Too Much*, the director decided to adapt one of Buchan's many novels centered on the hero Richard Hannay.

A Dual Pursuit

Initially, Hitchcock wanted to bring Buchan's *Greenmantle* to the screen. However, as the plot was set in different countries, the project proved financially unfeasible. The director therefore fell back on Hannay's first adventure, *The Thirty-Nine Steps* (1915), set entirely in Great Britain. In the end, the choice was a fortunate one, as this novel is famous for having invented from scratch a narrative structure that has remained effective ever since: a character unjustly accused of a murder committed by spies finds himself pursued by both the spies and the police, and must single-handedly unmask the conspirators to prove his innocence. Hitchcock would reuse this framework in many later works, right up to *North by Northwest* (1958).

Same Structure, Different Scenes

When he reread the novel, Hitchcock liked the pace and hectic action but found the story lacking in humor and psychological depth. With his screenwriter Charles Bennett, he applied some major changes to the story. Only the overall architecture of the book remains: In possession of clues to an international conspiracy, Hannay sets off to investigate in Scotland, where he inadvertently stumbles across the head of the enemy network and escapes him at the last moment, then returns to London to prevent the disclosure of a military secret. On the other hand, many episodes have been modified or replaced by completely new scenes. The character of Mr. Memory, absent from the novel, was invented for the film *The 39 Steps*—Hitchcock converted the word "thirty-nine" into numbers.

For Hitchcock Addicts

In John Buchan's novel, the hero is pursued by a plane as he crosses the Scottish moors. This situation inverts the usual parameters of danger, which no longer arise from a confined space, but from an immense expanse devoid of potential shelter. Due to a lack of resources, Hitchcock did not exploit this idea in *The 39 Steps*, with the exception of a brief shot of a model helicopter. But a quarter century later, he would remember it for the famous scene in *North by Northwest* where Cary Grant is attacked by a plane in open country.

Character Development in the Extreme

Mr. Memory's act consists of soliciting questions from the audience, to which he always gives accurate answers using his prodigious memory. This talent has inspired an original technique for the spies: on their behalf, the artist learns secret plans by heart, so that no theft of documents is ever recorded. But Hannay turns this trait on its head by asking Mr. Memory about the 39 Steps. In a kind of professional reflex, the entertainer cannot help but reveal the truth in public. Mortally wounded, he finds the strength to recite the series of equations he has learned, in a liberating confession reminiscent of the sacrificial suicide of the murderous trapeze artist in *Murder!* (1930). In his interviews with François Truffaut, Hitchcock admitted that Mr. Memory is typical of his method of establishing the essential traits of a character, then pushing them to their ultimate consequences as the screenplay is written.[1]

CASTING

Whereas Buchan's novel has very few female protagonists, they are more numerous in *The 39 Steps*. In the book, the character murdered in Hannay's apartment is a man. Onscreen, it is a woman, who presents herself as an international spy selling her services to the UK. The role is played by Lucie Mannheim, a German actress who became involved in English cinema after fleeing Nazism. Her accent implies that the members of the enemy network are agents of the Third Reich, without the latter being specifically named.

A set by Albert Whitlock, based on a preparatory drawing by Oscar Friedrich Werndorff (right).

Salty Banter

The major difference between the book and the film lies in the creation of the character of Pamela, a strong-willed young woman who crosses Hannay's path twice. They are constantly engaged in salty verbal skirmishes, although the viewer senses that they are gradually falling in love with each other, and this banter is one of the main charms of *The 39 Steps*. To play this quarrelsome couple, Hitchcock and his producers cast Madeleine Carroll and Robert Donat, two English actors who had already starred in Hollywood films, in the hope of promoting the film's export to the US. Following the same logic, Hannay is transformed from a South African in the novel to a Canadian onscreen, no doubt so that North American viewers can better identify with him.

The Model for the Hitchcock Blonde

The filmmaker would often remark that Madeleine Carroll was the model for the "Hitchcock blonde." While this was no small compliment, the director was no less intent on unsettling his actress at every opportunity. From their very first meeting, he surprised her by asking her to abandon her genteel mannerisms and allow the lively, spontaneous personality

he sensed in her to express itself. Furthermore, the script places Pamela in some very risqué situations for the time. She meets Hannay when, hounded by the police, he forcibly kisses her to mislead them, posing as an enamored fiancé. Outraged, she denounces him, as she would do again subsequently. This time, however, the so-called police turn out to be killers of the 39 Steps. Hannay manages to escape…taking with him Pamela, to whom he has meanwhile been handcuffed. The pair take refuge

"The 39 Steps"?

The novel's title refers to a concrete detail: the number of steps on a staircase leading to a secluded cove where a spy ship must drop anchor. In the film, "the 39 Steps" is simply the name of the spy network. Another difference: The book's plot takes place on the threshold of World War I, while the feature film transposes the action twenty years later, to the time of its shooting.

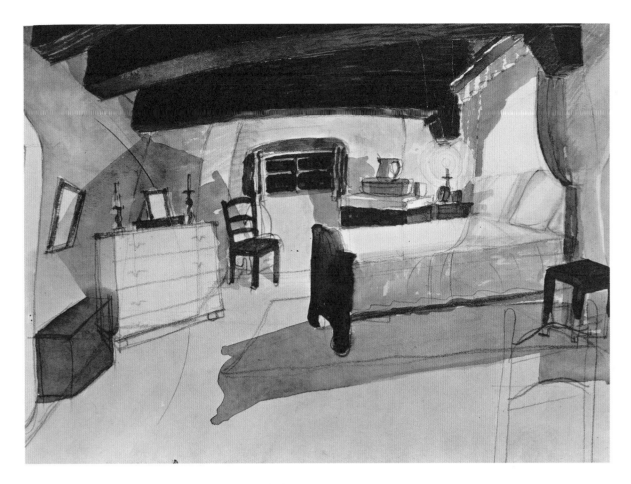

in a pub guest room, where they have to cohabit as best they can, the handcuffs provoking both a game of seduction and a disquieted notion of promiscuity. Hitchcock delves deeper into the sexual symbolism of handcuffs, which he inaugurated in a famous scene in *The Lodger* (1926).

A Devious Trick

To create chemistry between his two lead actors, Hitchcock used an unusual stratagem. After arranging for Madeleine Carroll and Robert Donat *not to meet* beforehand, he began the first day's shooting by having them rehearse a shot in which, bound by handcuffs, they run across a Scottish moor setting. The director then left the set for a long time, taking the key with him. Bound together against their will, the two stars became annoyed, then began to laugh at the situation. By the time Hitchcock returned, they had gotten to know each other. Even though members of the team might have found the tactic questionable, it paid off: Onscreen, Carroll and Donat demonstrate exactly the blend of antagonism and complicity that Hitchcock was looking for.

FILMING AND PRODUCTION

Hitchcock conceived *The 39 Steps* as a fast-moving film. The usual explanatory passages are reduced to a minimum, in favor of a juxtaposition of episodes that act as "movies within a movie," each with its own atmosphere. The result is a succession

The Real Mr. Memory

In several interviews, screenwriter Charles Bennett took the credit for the creation of Mr. Memory. However, he was inspired by a real-life character, Datas, who took his name from his ability to remember dates. Hitchcock saw him onstage as a child and remembers the gag that concluded his act. An audience member asked when Good Friday "fell" on a Tuesday, and Datas replied that a horse named Good Friday had fallen at a horse race on Tuesday, June 2, 1874!

In the studio and in front of the camera: Madeleine Carroll, Robert Donat.

of striking contrasts. One example among many: In a dramatic moment, Hannay is shot by Jordan, the spy chief; a scene later, he is alive and well and explains to a superintendent that the bullet was miraculously stopped by the Bible in his coat pocket. Hitchcock does not show how Hannay, feigning death, managed to leave Jordan's house and return to the police station. He leaves it to the viewer to imagine what, onscreen, would have resulted in laborious scenes that detracted from the overall pace.

General Disbelief

Despite the tonal diversity of its episodes, the film retains great unity, due to the aspect of disbelief. In this respect, it adopts the opposite tack from the novel, where Hannay meets a series of generous characters who readily accept his incredible story of espionage and lend him a helping hand. In Hitchcock's work, it is the precise opposite: The hero constantly insists that he is telling the truth, but almost everyone thinks that he is lying and that he is indeed a murderer. This situation produces intense moments of suspense, but also some hilarious scenes. For example, the Scottish commissioner

assures Hannay at length that he is now convinced by his version of events…and then orders his arrest, saying that the locals are not as stupid and naïve as Londoners think!

Love: Stronger than Doubt

The only character who immediately believes in Hannay's innocence is the unfortunate young wife of a stingy, puritanical old farmer. Troubled by the hero, she lets him escape when his pursuers arrive, even though it means incurring her husband's wrath. This episode, undoubtedly the darkest in a film with a generally lighthearted tone, is also one of the most beautiful. This is due in no small part to the moving performance by Peggy Ashcroft, a stage actress with very few film credits, and one whom Hitchcock greatly admired. The innkeeper, played by Hilda Trevelyan, is another female character who is very sensitive to the impulses of the heart. She believes Hannay when he claims that he and Pamela are a couple on the run, and she diverts the killers when they arrive. But this is much more than naïveté: The brave innkeeper has sensed the attraction between the two young people from the outset, of which they themselves are not yet aware.

Some Virtuosic Initial Long Shots

Although she is clearly increasingly attracted to Hannay, Pamela still believes him to be guilty for a long time. She only changes her mind when she succeeds in removing her hand from the handcuffs while the hero is asleep. Just as she is about to flee, she overhears a phone call from the bogus policemen in the pub, proving that the fugitive is telling the truth. In fact, the romance between Pamela and Hannay does not materialize until the very last moment of the film, when Mr. Memory makes his poignant confession. This scene is handled in a single take, concluding with the two lovers joining hands in the foreground. In several sequences of *The 39 Steps*, Hitchcock began experimenting with the virtuosic long shots that were to become his trademark during his American period.

RECEPTION

The 39 Steps received a triumphant reception at its London premiere. Invited to the festivities, John Buchan himself even proclaimed that the film was superior to his own novel. Reviews were equally enthusiastic, not only in England but also in the US. In fact, the film was a commercial success in a number of English-speaking countries, including Australia and Canada. The Gaumont British company thus made a real breakthrough on the international market, achieving what British International Pictures had tried in vain to accomplish with Hitchcock's first talking pictures. For almost forty years, the director toyed with the idea of a sequel to *The 39 Steps*, adapting another Richard Hannay adventure written by Buchan, *Greenmantle*. Although revived on numerous occasions, the project never saw the light of day.

Remakes Galore

The English cinema produced a remake of *The 39 Steps* every twenty or thirty years or so, without the involvement of Hitchcock. The first, directed by Ralph Thomas, dates from 1959. This was followed by another feature film, by Don Sharp (1978), and a BBC TV movie (2008). With amateur counterespionage stories now seeming outdated and ill-suited to contemporary geopolitics, these two latest versions return in part to the novel's roots, setting the action on the eve of the First World War. However, the shadow of Hitchcock still looms large. The 1978 film concludes with a typically Hitchcockian dramatic climax: Hannay, trying to prevent a bomb from exploding, finds himself hanging from one of the hands of the clock of Big Ben. Finally, a play entitled *The 39 Steps* was performed

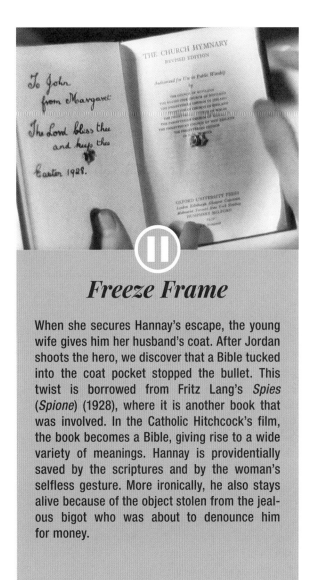

Freeze Frame

When she secures Hannay's escape, the young wife gives him her husband's coat. After Jordan shoots the hero, we discover that a Bible tucked into the coat pocket stopped the bullet. This twist is borrowed from Fritz Lang's *Spies* (*Spione*) (1928), where it is another book that was involved. In the Catholic Hitchcock's film, the book becomes a Bible, giving rise to a wide variety of meanings. Hannay is providentially saved by the scriptures and by the woman's selfless gesture. More ironically, he also stays alive because of the object stolen from the jealous bigot who was about to denounce him for money.

in a London theater from 2006 to 2015, then revived in New York. This is a parodic comedy evoking the humor of Monty Python. It was the latest proof that, in the public mind, the title is indissolubly linked to the filmmaker's name.

In the Collective Memory

In 1999, the British Film Institute organized a survey of a thousand national film professionals to draw up a list of the hundred best English films of the twentieth century. *The 39 Steps* came in fourth, beaten only by Carol Reed's *The Third Man* and two David Lean films, *Brief Encounter* and *Lawrence of Arabia*. Although Hitchcock's previous masterpieces include *The Lodger*, *Rich and Strange*, and *Murder!*, this is chronologically the first of his feature-length films to register in the collective memory.

![eye icon]

Where Is Hitchcock?

When Hannay and the mysterious stranger board a bus as they leave the music hall, the filmmaker walks along the sidewalk in the foreground, throwing an empty box or package to the ground.

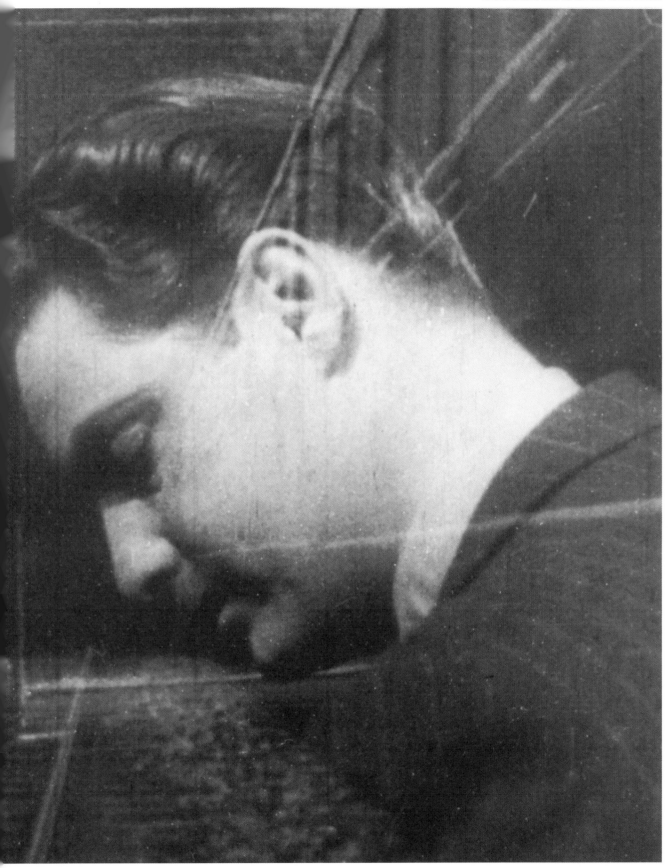

Madeleine Carroll and Robert Donat.

SECRET AGENT

STARRING

Madeleine **CARROLL**

Peter **LORRE**

John **GIELGUD**

Robert **YOUNG**

From the play by Campbell Dixon
Based on the novel "ASHENDEN" by
W. SOMERSET MAUGHAM

DIRECTED BY
ALFRED HITCHCOCK

A  PRODUCTION

Secret Agent

Great Britain · **1 hr 26** · **Black and White** · **Mono** (Full Range Recording System) · **1.37:1**

Production Dates: October–November 1935
Release Date in Great Britain: May 1936
Release Date in the United States: June 15, 1936

Production: Gaumont British
Producer: Michael Balcon
Associate Producer: Ivor Montagu

**Based on a collection of short stories by W. Somerset Maugham,
Ashenden: Or the British Agent (1927); and a play by Campbell Dixon
itself inspired by the same collection of short stories**
Screenplay: Charles Bennett
Dialogue: Ian Hay
Additional Dialogue: Jesse Lasky Jr.
Director of Photography: Bernard Knowles
Camera Operator: Stephen Dade
Sound: Philip Dorté
Assistant Director: Penrose Tennyson
Continuity: Alma Reville
Art Direction: Oscar Friedrich Werndorff
Costumes (dresses): Joe Strassner
Music: John Greenwood, Louis Levy
Film Editing: Charles Frend

Starring: Madeleine Carroll (Elsa Carrington), John Gielgud (Edgar Brodie /
Richard Ashenden), Peter Lorre (the General), Robert Young (Robert Marvin), Percy
Marmont (Mr. Caypor), Florence Kahn (Mrs. Caypor), Charles Carson ("R"), Lilli
Palmer (Lilli), Tom Helmore (Colonel Anderson), Howard Marion-Crawford (Karl,
Lilli's fiancé), Rene Ray (maid), Michael Rennie (the captain), Michel Saint-Denis
(coachman), Andreas Malandrinos (casino manager)…

"Does a film have to make sense when life does not?"

—

Alfred Hitchcock

SYNOPSIS

—

It is London, 1916. In the midst of World War I, the British secret service passes novelist Edgar Brodie off as dead. Under the identity of Richard Ashenden, he is sent to Switzerland by his superior, "R," to unmask and eliminate a German agent. Once he is in situ, two other spies help him: the "Mexican," a professional killer, and Elsa, officially Ashenden's wife and relentlessly courted by an American on vacation, Robert Marvin. A suit button found in the hand of an informant (a murdered church organist) puts Ashenden and the Mexican on the trail of their enemy, an Englishman named Caypor, married to a German woman, whom they identify among their hotel guests. The spies sympathize with the traitor and persuade him to accompany them on a high-mountain trek. While Ashenden, horrified, follows the scene with a telescopic sight, the Mexican precipitates the man into the void...only to discover shortly afterward that there has been a mistaken identity. Crushed, Elsa and Ashenden declare their love for each other and want to give it all up, when the Mexican returns with a new lead. The two men dismantle a nest of spies using a chocolate factory as a cover...and finally learn the name of the real traitor: Robert Marvin. The four spies find themselves in the same train compartment, the Mexican pulls out his knife, but the train, bombed by the British, derails. In the wreckage, Marvin, mortally wounded, asks for a weapon to put him out of his misery. But, traitor to the end, before succumbing, he shoots the Mexican with the same revolver. Only Elsa and Ashenden can return home, their mission accomplished.

GENESIS

Since 1934, Alfred Hitchcock had been under contract to Gaumont British, a studio in West London run by Michael Balcon. Although he decided on budgets and intervened in casting, the enterprising producer placed his trust in the filmmaker, giving him a period of great creative freedom. This freedom was justified and reinforced by the recent success of two spy films—"comedy thrillers,"[1] as the director described them—*The Man Who Knew Too Much* and, even more so, *The 39 Steps*.

Old Acquaintances

At Lime Grove, home to several film sets and the production company's offices, Hitchcock was reunited with old acquaintances and friends: Angus MacPhail, head of the script department; Ivor Montagu, whom he had met at the time of *Blackmail* (1929) and who was associate producer on four of his films from the mid-1930s; and Charles Bennett, a playwright and screenwriter whom he had met at the time of *Blackmail* (1929). In 1980, Montagu recalled the happy atmosphere that presided over their work sessions, at Lime Grove or Cromwell Road, where the Hitchcocks lived at the time: "The script meetings were a feast of fantasy and dialectic, a mixture of crosswords to be composed and solved, all bound together with humour."[2]

Codename: Ashenden

The filmmaker and his friends chose to adapt a play by *Daily Telegraph* film critic Campbell Dixon, based on Somerset Maugham's 1928 collection of short stories, *Ashenden: Or the British Agent*. The famous English novelist was active in the ranks of the Secret Intelligence Service (SIS) during World War I. Drawing on his notes, memories, and imagination, he created the postwar character of Ashenden, a distinguished writer and secret agent in the service of His Majesty. He was an autobiographical figure, but only in part according to Maugham, who considered reality a poor storyteller and deliberately created surprise effects in his fiction: "Cymbal blows or reversals of situation are faults only in clumsy hands." Hitchcock held the same sentiments and said he conceived of a film not as a slice of life, but as a slice of cake. He declared: "What is fiction, after all, if not life from which the dull parts have been removed?"

From "R" to "M"

In creating James Bond, aka 007, novelist Ian Fleming, himself a British secret service agent during World War II, was inspired by the character of Ashenden, created by Somerset Maugham (1874–1965). Fleming is said to have paid homage to Maugham in "Quantum of Solace" (1960), a short story inspired by His Excellency, which appeared in 1928 in the collection *Ashenden: Or the British Agent*. Similarly, "R," the director of the Secret Intelligence Service, who gives Ashenden his orders, becomes "M" in Fleming's celebrated novels. Finally, in *Secret Agent*, Ashenden obtains authorization to eliminate his enemy—a license to kill.

A Free Adaptation

Of the eight short stories that make up *Ashenden: Or the British Agent* (fourteen others, deemed too politically sensitive, were reportedly censored before publication by Winston Churchill), the Lime Grove scriptwriters retained only two: "The Traitor" and "The Hairless Mexican." From the former, they retained only the characters of Caypor, his German wife, and their dog, as well as the Swiss setting. The second provided them with the extravagant character of the Mexican, described by Maugham as repulsive, ridiculous, and fascinating, bald including his eyelashes and eyebrows, his fingernails painted red and trimmed to a point…Above all, the screenwriters had fun interweaving the two plots: the fatal error of the Mexican, who in the story executes an innocent man instead of the real spy, shifts to Caypor, a proven traitor from the start of the story, who becomes, in the film, the innocent victim of a tragic misunderstanding. As for the character of Elsa Carrington and the romance between the two spies, Bennett and Hitchcock import them from Dixon's play.

Firing on All Cylinders

The adaptation is very free, all the more so as the scriptwriters also imagine certain sequences and oddities from scratch. Among the most Hitchcockian are the organist's death, the chocolate factory as a spy hideout, a musical instrument made from a coin that keeps rolling around in a container, the train accident…At this time, Hitchcock and his crew—Bennett, Montagu, Alma Hitchcock, and Joan Harrison, his personal assistant since 1934—were firing on all cylinders: a novel, a play, a newspaper article, a show, something seen in the street…If a face, a situation, or a place impressed him, Hitchcock worked it into the script with his screenwriter. For him, the "scene to be created" was more important than maintaining the logic of the plot. Hitchcock would always favor spectacle over plausibility. "A story may be implausible, but it should never be banal." Somerset Maugham echoed that sentiment: "If the work is successful, the reader believes it to be true."

Final Preparations

As always, Charles Bennett provided the first version, without dialogue. In October 1935, Bennett, Hitchcock, and Montagu met in Switzerland to find inspiration and locations. Hitchcock then traveled alone to the Balkans in preparation for the last scene, the train crash. Finally, he returned to London to finish the script and casting, before moving on to shoot *Secret Agent*. For the writing of the dialogue, he rehired Ian Hay, an English novelist and humorist, to whom we can attribute, among other things, this exceedingly British exchange at the beginning of the film, when Ashenden, supposedly deceased, reappears in uniform: "R: Do you love your country?—Ashenden: I've just died for it."

In keeping with his habit of accumulating screenwriters, or helping hands, Hitchcock also recruited Jesse Lasky Jr., the son of Paramount studio's co-founder, specifically to write the dialogue for the American character, Robert Marvin.

CASTING

For *Secret Agent*, Hitchcock wanted to reunite the *39 Steps* duo of Robert Donat and Madeleine Carroll.

A Glossy Beauty

With Madeleine Carroll, the motif of the sophisticated and witty Hitchcock blonde reaches its early culmination thanks to her appearance in two of his films: *The 39 Steps* and *Secret Agent*. In this new feature, from the very first shot in which she appears, she is shown with her face covered in makeup remover. In the next scene, she finds herself in a bathroom, between a bathtub and a roll of toilet paper, clearly visible in the shot. Here, Hitchcock revealed his ambivalent desire, recurrent throughout his filmography, to both sublimate an actress and degrade her magnified image.

A Shakespearean Actor

With Robert Donat unavailable, Michael Balcon, still keen to reach the American market, contacted producer Jack Warner in the hope of recruiting the actor Leslie Howard. But in the end, the presence of Madeleine Carroll, who was very popular in the US (*The World Moves On*, John Ford, 1934), and Robert Young, a charming young Hollywood leading man, made it possible to hire an English star to play the role of Ashenden. Hence Hitchcock's idea of casting John Gielgud. A well-known Shakespearean actor, Gielgud had only made a few films and was wary of the cinema: He did not believe he could really act in the sense that he understood it in the theater, since filming does not respect the chronology of a plot or the duration of a situation. To convince him, Hitchcock suggested that Ashenden was a modern Hamlet, a hero torn between his humanist values and his duty to kill in wartime.

Madeleine Carroll, Peter Lorre, and John Gielgud, three spies.

The Mexican and Other Roles

For the colorful character of the Mexican, the director brought back Peter Lorre, his actor from *The Man Who Knew Too Much* and a regular in hallucinatory roles in Germany, the US, and England, following his stunning performance in Fritz Lang's *M* (1931). Also of note, in a small soubrette role, is Lilli Palmer: Like Peter Lorre and Oscar Werndorff, the artistic director for *Secret Agent*, this young actress fled Nazi Germany in the early 1930s. Still a novice, she was destined for a long career on Broadway and in Hollywood, then in Europe. Conversely, Florence Kahn, playing the German wife, a former actress at the Old Vic theater in London, made her only screen appearance in *Secret Agent*—according to Hitchcock, she had never set foot in a studio or even "seen a film in her life"![1]

Saint-Denis, a Small Role, and a Major Figure

Unusually for such a farsighted filmmaker, Hitchcock improvised a scene on the set of *Secret Agent*: Elsa Carrington (Madeleine Carroll) and Robert Marvin (Robert Young) were exchanging witty banter in a moonlit carriage, and the presence of the coachman provided material for further bon mots. The coachman was played by Michel Saint-Denis, who was visiting John Gielgud that day. He was a disciple of Jacques Copeau, founder of the London Theatre Studio in August 1935, director of Radio Londres during World War II and host of a column under the pseudonym Jacques Duchesne until 1944.

FILMING AND PRODUCTION

Filming was not an enjoyable experience for John Gielgud, who felt that he was out of place and dull. After *Secret Agent*, he made only one film in almost twenty years… And in fact, Hitchcock seemed to be interested only in Madeleine Carroll, perhaps thinking that his lead actor was not up to the job after all.

A Strange Profession

John Gielgud had his work cut out for him, competing with a blonde whose cinematographer, Bernard Knowles (*The 39 Steps*), gently illuminated her.

And Robert Young played a villain more attractive than the official hero. Then there was Peter Lorre: a morphine addict, sometimes nowhere to be found when filming, but when he finally did perform, his bulging eyes, his complexion, his earring, his curly wig, and his crazy mimicry stole the viewer's attention.

Above all, John Gielgud, a stage actor, posed the same problem for the filmmaker as Montgomery Clift (*I Confess*, 1952) and Paul Newman (*Torn Curtain*, 1966): They all came with an already acquired acting technique that hampered the direction more than it helped, whereas Hitchcock wanted to impart feelings to an actor almost solely through the suggestive force of his editing.

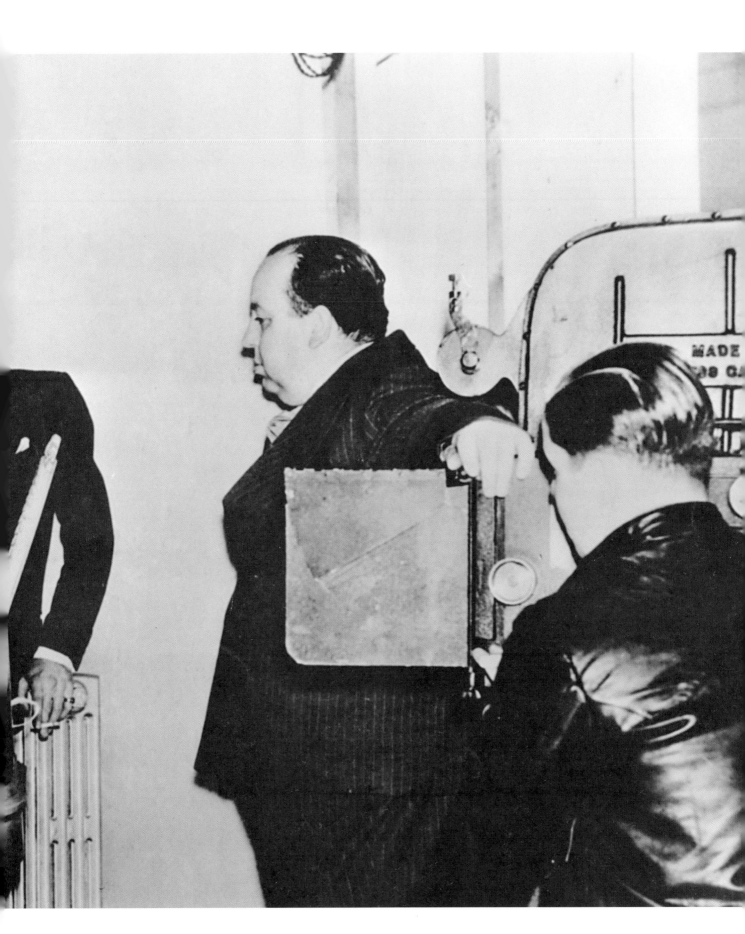

Two Endings for One Film

The British Board of Film Censors (BBFC) and the Production Code Administration (PCA) having read the script beforehand,[3] Hitchcock was faced with another shooting difficulty. The reading produced a list of "recommendations," fortunately not always acted upon: The Mexican must be of indefinite nationality, so as not to offend Mexicans; the bogus spouses are strongly urged to sleep in separate bedrooms; all bathroom scenes must be eliminated (toilet paper, a provocation by Hitchcock?); salacious gags must be avoided; the Swiss must not be offended, and so on...Above all, the American censors demanded that the Mexican should die to atone for his sins. On this point, the protestations of Ivor Montagu, the associate producer, were in vain. For this reason, the director would have filmed two endings. First, that of his screenplay: after the train crash, Robert Marvin, the mortally wounded felon, asks for a drink. The good-natured Mexican passes him his flask of whiskey before aiming for his heart. Liquid pours from the traitor's mouth. The Mexican drinks in turn, a smile on his face. Then, at the studio's behest, Hitchcock shot the film's other ending: The traitor shoots the Mexican before succumbing to his wounds.

A Part for the Whole

Under contract to Gaumont British between 1934 and 1938, Hitchcock acquired a real mastery of cinematographic technique and a great art of "previsualization": he designed and built, not a complete set, but only the part he knew would appear in the shot and in the film format on the screen. In doing so, he saved production costs and earned the respect of his production crews.

A Crime Under the Magnifying Glass

Secret Agent is one of the most exciting films of Hitchcock's English period, and not only because it weaves together the threads of macabre thriller, psychological realism, and unbridled comedy. An audiovisual climax, the scene of Caypor's death, when the innocent man is mistaken for the guilty one, produces genuine aesthetic suspense. From the large, squared-off window of a mountain observatory, Hitchcock films a wide shot of a snowy landscape and, in the distance, two small silhouettes approaching a precipice. ("In fact, they were two figures on cotton wool. In a film studio, the people who have the most fun are the model makers."[4]) This panorama corresponds to what Ashenden sees with the naked eye, before looking through a telescope. The camera abruptly moves to a view through the telescope. This movement suddenly creates a magnifying-glass effect, an unbearable proximity to the murder to the point of making the hero, an accomplice at a distance, scream. To these shots, Hitchcock adds, in an alternating montage, those of Caypor's little dog, left at the hotel dozens of kilometers away, who starts howling desperately, a veritable "telepath" of his master's disappearance. The dog's howling even fills the soundtrack of some of

the mountain views. And watching the animal's distress, Elsa, a spy "just for fun" until that point, a scatterbrain in search of thrills, also begins to appreciate what is at stake. Finally, she buries her beautiful face in her guilty hands.

Stridencies

Hitchcock dares to experiment with sound: witness the editing of the Caypor assassination sequence, like many other moments in the film. It was not until *The Birds* (1962) that such aural innovation was seen again. It would be impossible here to list every sonic tour de force, which, more than once covering the dialogue, recalls in its own way the expressiveness of the silent film era. Among the most significant moments are, right from the opening, the impact of bombs falling on London; later, the continuous ringing of a telephone; the deafening alarm in the chocolate factory; in the folk song scene, the shrillness of a device in which a coin keeps spinning in an earthenware container, testing Elsa's already frayed nerves.

Death of an Organist

In the church scene, the entire action unfolds under the influence of a single, throbbing, mysterious note.

Freeze Frame

Hitchcock always delighted in dark humor. *Secret Agent*'s first sequence was a coffin surrounded by grieving dignitaries. Once the room is empty, the one-armed mortician takes out a pack of cigarettes, extracts one with his only able-bodied hand, and lights it at one of the large candles surrounding the catafalque. Then, with great difficulty, he sets about straightening and opening up the coffin: empty! *Secret Agent* was to be "a film for laughs," so the moment of real death would be all the more striking.

The spectator/listener understands it at the same time as Ashenden and the Mexican: This "music" comes from the clenched hands on the keyboard of the murdered organist, his body held in rigor mortis. The villagers come running, and the heroes take refuge in the church belfry as the sound of bells deafens them: Hitchcock focuses on the mouth of one protagonist and the ear of the other, both striving to speak and hear each other.

"In *Secret Agent*, music is potential noise"[5] and sound is synonymous with disruption and chaos. It is the chaos of the world and of morality three years after Hitler's rise to power, so that the side of good also indulges in reprehensible acts such as Caypor's assassination. Can there be good reasons for killing a man? That is a serious question for a "spy comedy." In the end, Hitchcock was right to evoke *Hamlet*: to kill or not to kill, that is the question.

RECEPTION

In 1937, *Film Weekly* ran a readers' poll to elect the best British film of the previous year: *Secret Agent* came in fifth.

"Gentlemen of Verisimilitude"

The reception from the Anglo-Saxon press, however, was more mixed than for the release of the director's two previous films. For the *Times* journalist (May 11, 1936), the film failed to reconcile humor and suspense like two instruments each playing its own score. The *Monthly Film Bulletin* (May 1936) criticized the director for favoring bravura moments, such as the chocolate factory sequence or the train crash, at the expense of plot coherence. Hitchcock would later refer to this category of journalists as "gentlemen of verisimilitude." The same criticism came from a thriller specialist who was also concerned about the moral ambiguity of the world in the 1930s: Novelist Graham Greene, who was writing the *Spectator*'s film column at the time, acknowledged the filmmaker's talent but accused him of "lacking a sense of reality […] and as an author [of having] no sense of what life is all about" (May 15, 1936).[6]

On the other side of the Atlantic, the *New York Times* (June 13, 1936) even criticized the staging and editing, singling out only Madeleine Carroll's beauty (misused in the reviewer's opinion) and Peter Lorre's acting.

A Modern Hero

Hitchcock himself, always on the lookout for the "magic formula" for producing a film that worked both onscreen and at the box office, would not spare *Secret Agent* in the name of this dual ambition. He took a particularly critical look at what he and his screenwriter had done with Ashenden, the man who pursues "a negative goal" (killing an innocent). And why should viewers identify with a hero who would rather not be one? On the contrary, *Time*'s American critic appreciated *Secret Agent*'s lack of self-confidence, as opposed to the superhuman gifts of Sherlock Holmes: "Ashenden belongs to that modern school of sleuths whose fallibility makes them credible" (June 15, 1936). And it is this weakness and the doubts of the "hero" that make him an already modern character in the eyes of today's audiences.

A Film on Fire

Once he had finished shooting *Secret Agent*, never short of ideas, Hitchcock called upon Len Lye. The New Zealand–born artist, who had lived in London since the 1920s, was one of the pioneers of frame-by-frame film painting. To make the railway accident at the end of the film even more spectacular, he created color effects to give the impression that not only the train, but the film itself was on fire. Was this too realistic? In any case, it was removed after the first test screening, for fear of creating panic both in the booths and in the cinemas… And yet, surely this cinematic "panic" represents the ultimate Hitchcock dream?

SYLVIA SIDNEY* OSCAR HOMOLKA

The WOMAN ALONE

JOHN LODER DESMOND TESTER
Directed by
ALFRED HITCHCOCK
FROM THE NOVEL BY JOSEPH CONRAD
A ⬦ PRODUCTION
* COURTESY OF WALTER WANGER PRODUCTIONS, INC.

Sabotage

Great Britain	1 hr 16	Black and White	Mono (Full Range Recording System)	1.37:1

Production Dates: July 1936
Release Date in Great Britain: December 2, 1936 (London)
Release Date in the United States: January 11, 1937

Production: Gaumont British
Producer: Michael Balcon
Associate Producer: Ivor Montagu

Based on a novel by Joseph Conrad, *The Secret Agent: A Simple Tale* **(1907)**
Screenplay: Charles Bennett
Dialogue: Ian Hay, Helen Simpson
Additional Dialogue: E. V. H. Emmett
Director of Photography: Bernard Knowles
Camera Operator: Stephen Dade
Sound: A. Cameron
Assistant Director: Penrose Tennyson
Continuity: Alma Reville
Artistic Directors: Oscar Friedrich Werndorff, Albert Jullion
Set Decoration: Albert Whitlock
Costumes: Joe Strassner, Marianne
Music: Hubert Bath, Jack Beaver, Louis Levy
Film Editing: Charles Frend
By agreement with, and acknowledgments to, Walt Disney for the scene from the cartoon *Who Killed Cock Robin?* **(1935)**

Starring: Sylvia Sidney (Mrs. Verloc), Oskar Homolka (Karl Anton Verloc), Desmond Tester (Stevie), John Loder (Ted Spencer), Joyce Barbour (Renee), Matthew Boulton (Superintendent Talbot), S. J. Warmington (Hollingshead), William Dewhurst ("professor" Chatman), Martita Hunt (daughter of the "professor"), Pamela Bevan (granddaughter of the "professor"), Peter Bull (Michaelis, a conspirator), Clare Greet (Mrs. Jones), Charles Hawtrey (studious youth at the aquarium), J. Hubert Leslie (a conspirator), Aubrey Mather (greengrocer), Frederick Piper (bus driver), Fred Schwartz (tailor), Torin Thatcher (Yunct, a conspirator), Austin Trevor (Vladimir), Alfred Hitchcock (a passerby in front of the cinema?)…

"London must not laugh on Saturday."

Message from the organization, in *Sabotage*

SYNOPSIS

—

A cinema called the Bijou is set in a working-class district of London. The owner, Verloc, lives in a house behind the screen, with his wife and her beloved younger brother, Stevie. Next door, a greengrocer employs Ted Spencer, a Scotland Yard inspector assigned to keep an eye on Verloc. The latter is a saboteur working for a secret organization, using the cinema as a front. His wife is unaware of his shadowy activities. His superior orders him to strike a blow: to explode a bomb in Piccadilly Circus on the day of the Lord Mayor's celebration. A bomb maker who runs a bird shop prepares the time bomb and delivers it to him in a birdcage on the day. But without any contact with his acolytes and spied on by the police, Verloc entrusts Stevie with the dangerous package and asks him to deliver it, along with two rolls of film, without fail, before 1:45 p.m. Stevie dawdles on the way, eventually boarding a bus that explodes at the appointed time. The remains of one of the film reels Stevie was carrying help Mrs. Verloc understand that her brother is dead and her husband the culprit. That evening, at the dinner table, in a daze, she grabs the carving knife and stabs the criminal. When Ted arrives at the scene, he finds her prostrate. He confesses his love for her and offers to run away with her. The bird man also comes to the Bijou, to retrieve the birdcage. But, trailed by the police and about to be arrested, he blows up everything, including the dead man's body. Distraught and yet beyond suspicion, Mrs. Verloc blends into the crowd on Ted's arm.

A studio reconstruction of a movie theater; next door, a greengrocer.

GENESIS

Hitchcock's new project was based on *The Secret Agent*, a novel by the Polish-born English writer Joseph Conrad. This was the filmmaker's ninth and final collaboration with producer Michael Balcon since 1925's *The Pleasure Garden*.

A Question of Titles

Hitchcock had just released a film called *Secret Agent* (*Quatre de l'espionnage* in French), and to avoid confusion, Gaumont British did not want to use the title of Conrad's book. So the original version of *Secret Agent* is called *Sabotage*. The new title also reflects the liberties taken by the director and his screenwriter, Charles Bennett, in adapting the novel, even though it is one of the great works of this respected writer. In general, Hitchcock did not like adapting masterpieces of world literature; in fact, he was wary of them. Above all, he was looking for the best stories for the cinema and, even more so, for *his* cinema.

From Gas to Electricity

There are many differences between the novel and the film. The plot moves from the Victorian era (1886) to contemporary London, from gas to electricity (a light bulb is switched on in the very first shot). Conrad's Russian anarchists and double agent in the pay of an imperial embassy become saboteurs of uncertain nationality, ideology, hierarchy, and motivation, other than a desire to disrupt public order.

Some characters, such as Mrs. Verloc's mother and the deputy prefect, disappear or remain only for the duration of a scene. Others are transformed from top to bottom. Inspector Heat, austere and determined in the novel, renamed Spencer in the film, is now boastful and amorous. Stevie, the simple-minded young boy, becomes playful and prankster-like but continues to embody the figure of the innocent. In the book's conclusion, Mrs. Verloc, in despair, commits suicide by going overboard after leaving her wedding ring on the deck of a ship; at the end of the film, overwhelmed by her misfortunes but in love, she is safe and sound.

The Bijou

The most spectacular change is in the setting: Joseph Conrad's Verloc runs a store in Soho, a sort of grimy stall selling comic papers, an anarchist publication, a few obscene books, and other kinds of shady merchandise. It is a small business that serves as a cover for the secret agent. The same character seen by Hitchcock and Bennett owns a cinema in a populous neighborhood, the Bijou, which literally serves as a screen for his activities. At the back of the cinema, just behind the screen, is his house. The protagonists (the saboteur, his wife, Stevie, the inspector, and the small band of patient conspirators) must cross the projection room to reach the noisy street on one side, and the home on the other, which is home to both a family and a network of seditionists.

His Name Was Adolf

In *Sabotage*, the criminal conspiracy never reveals its purpose or the identities of its sponsors, for two reasons. First, explanations and justifications are of little importance to Hitchcock; the only things that matter to him are the situations and their visual potential. Second, to avoid censorship, producer Michael Balcon made sure that no country or political system was explicitly named. Thus, the character of Verloc, named Adolf in the 1907 novel, is renamed Karl Anton in 1936, three years after the rise of Hitler.

Paradise Lost

Despite all these changes, the screenwriters remained faithful to the atmosphere of the novel, which is Dostoyevskian, dense, dark, twisted, and pessimistic. Unlike *The 39 Steps* or *Secret Agent*, *Sabotage* is not a film "for laughs"; it is never ironic, but constantly disturbing, suffocating in its concentration of febrile, feverish beings. It is certainly with a view to portraying this end-of-the-world atmosphere that the filmmaker imagined some surprising counterpoints: the large turtles swimming in the London Zoo Aquarium (a setting absent from the novel), the birdhouse where the bomb is made (also absent from the novel), the puppies awaiting adoption playing in a shop window, the conversation about the sex life of oysters…Caged, locked up, separated, the animals are a reminder of a natural, innocent way of life, a lost paradise with which the worst of the species—humans caught up in the deadly game of mad passions—rubs shoulders, and which it ignores. Bennett and Hitchcock created two worlds that are mutually inaccessible.

Structural Work and the Finishing Touches

As usual, Charles Bennett was responsible for the structure of the story. He completed a first version of the script in the spring of 1936, including the denouement. Bennett described himself as "a first-class constructionist […] The great essence of construction is to know your end before you know your beginning […]

To just start off and wander on the way isn't any good whatever…because you're wallowing."[1]

Hitchcock then called upon dialogue writers to tie the whole thing together: Ian Hay (*The 39 Steps*, *Secret Agent*), Helen Simpson (co-author of a novel adapted by Hitchcock in 1930 under the title *Murder!*) and E. V. H. Emmett (the voice of Gaumont British newsreels).

CASTING

The director wanted to cast the facetious Robert Donat (*The 39 Steps*) in the role of Inspector Spencer. But his chronic asthma would have made him unavailable, or perhaps the English producer Alexander Korda, with whom he was under contract, would actually have refused to release him. Hitchcock therefore turned to the more conventional John Loder. Charles Bennett, a close friend of the actor, confirmed that Loder was not Donat: "I think that made a 100 percent difference to the movie."[1]

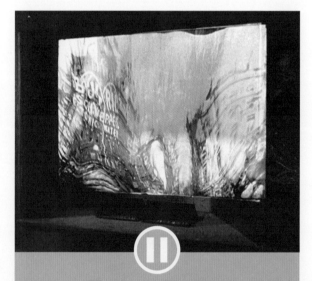

Freeze Frame

Verloc, the saboteur, meets his superior at London Zoo. His mission is to detonate a bomb. Hitchcock visualizes Verloc's thoughts by filming the glass of an aquarium, which fades into a silent view of Piccadilly Circus at rush hour. The sound of a detonation is then added, and a trick is used to "melt" the image: the buildings collapse as if under the effect of the explosion. There is a return to the face of Verloc, who cannot believe his eyes.

Thirty-five years later, when shooting *Frenzy* in England, the director encountered the same difficulty with Jon Finch, who, in his opinion, was not very charismatic.

Supporting Roles

Other roles were better allocated: Desmond Tester (Stevie), only seventeen at the time of *Sabotage*, was England's best-known child actor (that same year, 1936, he played Asticot in *The Beloved Vagabond*, with Maurice Chevalier). William Dewhurst, a stage actor, took on his first film role (he died suddenly the following year): that of the ominous "professor" who makes bombs in his dining room, surrounded by his granddaughter's dolls. Oskar Homolka, born in Vienna, Austria-Hungary, a theater and film actor in Germany, left the country in 1933, when the Nazis came to power. He made three films in Great Britain in 1936, before spending part of his career in the United States, often playing spies or villains.

The Girl with the Big Sad Eyes

Producer Michael Balcon took advantage of one of his trips across the Atlantic to convince Sylvia Sidney to come and film in England, especially as the actress had recently expressed her wish to give it a try. Trained as a theater actress, she became a star in 1931 (that same year, she made films with Rouben Mamoulian, Josef von Sternberg, and King Vidor), and by then Sidney had become a very famous American actress. Hitchcock and Bennett insisted that she should take on the role of Mrs. Verloc: they liked the way her round face, her prominent cheekbones, her large sad eyes, and the sudden illumination of her smile expressed concern, sometimes a fleeting relief, and more often the intimate suffering of her characters. She had also just starred in *Fury*, the first American film by German director Fritz Lang, released in London in June 1936, and an important director for Hitchcock (he saw his silent films and cast the actor from *M*, Peter Lorre, in *The Man Who Knew Too Much* and *Secret Agent*).

FILMING AND PRODUCTION

Although some of the streets and squares in the novel were invented and many built for the film, at the Lime Grove Studio in Shepherd's Bush, Hitchcock insisted on precise locations: Scotland Yard; Liverpool Road, in Islington, where the bird man had his store; Piccadilly Circus; the East End, where the Bijou is located. The cinema, the setting for much of the drama, adjoins a greengrocer's store

The City World

Like *Frenzy* much later on, *Sabotage* focuses on the bustle of London streets: crowds in all directions, traffic, markets, attractions, and hucksters. Hitchcock's re-creation of this anonymous hustle and bustle, both good-natured and possibly threatening, corresponds to his idea of an ever-latent danger. It is also in keeping with the novel's descriptions and its vision of an enormous, monstrous city, "more populous than some continents [...] a cruel devourer of the world's light" (Joseph Conrad, "Author's Note," *The Secret Agent*).

with a stall overlooking the street. The latter evokes the profession of Hitchcock's father at the turn of the century. Fruit and vegetables on one side, a movie theater on the other: These two places, side by side, form a precipitate of the filmmaker's childhood and adolescence, "a juxtaposition of Hitchcock's own formative milieu."[2]

"She wanted to go home."

Filming was not without its misunderstandings and complications. Sylvia Sidney said she was baffled by the director's piecemeal approach, shooting the shots he needed in no particular order, without even filming the entire scene to which those shots belonged. He might decide, several days later, to add more takes to complete a montage that was only visible in his head…The actress wanted to rely on dramatic continuity to experience and convey her character's emotion. But instead, she had to give the camera an isolated look or deliver an expression taken out of context. Ivor Montagu, *Sabotage*'s associate producer, recounted how, on more than one occasion, he had to go onto the set to reassure the actress, who had returned to her dressing room: "she was not to be consoled. She wanted to go home."[3]

A woman, her husband, and a carving knife: Sylvia Sidney, Oskar Homolka.

At the Table

The climax of Sylvia Sidney's "crisis" was reached during the dinner scene after the death of Stevie, the innocent, at the husband's hands: At the table, Mr. and Mrs. Verloc face each other. Gradually, the wife's irrepressible desire to commit murder and the husband's intuition of his wife's secret thoughts come to the fore. The action unfolds over a long period of time, almost wordlessly. The actress was disheartened about shooting this sequence, but Montagu convinced her to wait until she saw the first cut. On the day in question, Sidney, Montagu, Hitchcock, and his editor, Charles Frend (who made four films with Hitchcock in the 1930s) met in a small projection room. Dazzled by the result, the actress turned to the filmmaker and said, "Hollywood must hear of this."

Where Is Hitchcock?

In *Sabotage*, Hitchcock does not appear, as he would almost invariably do from his next film onward (*Young and Innocent*, 1937). If it is indeed Hitchcock, he merely appears as an extra, from behind, wearing a hat and raincoat, five minutes from the end. With other pedestrians, he walks along the sidewalk in front of the Bijou, while the "professor" gets out of a cab to retrieve the birdcage used to hide the bomb.

The murder scene (twenty-four images for thirty-two shots) as first reproduced by François
Truffaut in his book of interviews with the filmmaker (*Le Cinéma selon Hitchcock*, 1966).   →

Thirty-Two Shots

The breathtaking dinner scene was reproduced by
François Truffaut, in his book of interviews with
the Master, in a series of double-page photograms.
Montagu, for his part, describes it using words such
as *close-ups and inserts*, *eyes*, *expressions*, *forks*,
potatoes, and *cabbages*.

The whole thing lasts just under three and a half
minutes for thirty-two shots in which the director
varies the length of the segments and alternates the
scales of the frame. The whole is a perfect example
of the "pure cinema" toward which Hitchcock's art
tends. From the actors' faces to the objects and camera movements, every element contributes equally to the final impression. The carving knife keeps

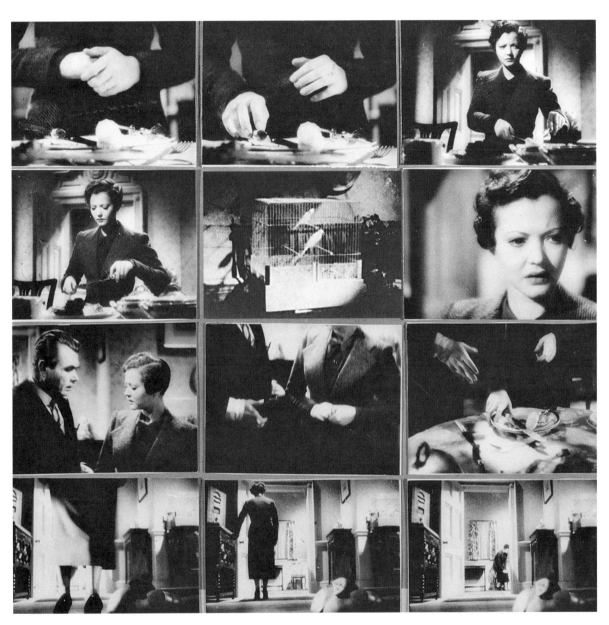

returning to Mrs. Verloc's hand, "like a magnet," as Hitchcock put it. The husband approaches his wife slowly, the silence in the room disturbed only by the crunch of his soles; he advances toward the camera to such an extent, Hitchcock would say, that the spectator would almost recoil in their seat to let this enormous face pass. In the end, we cannot tell whether Karl Anton Verloc is murdered by his wife or whether he "goes to the knife," as if consenting to his punishment. The Hitchcockian direction of the emotions, however, keeps the audience on the side of the character played by Sylvia Sidney.

Hitchcock Wants a Tramway

For the film's other great moment, the scene where Stevie, unknowingly carrying a bomb around

London, uses public transport, Hitchcock wanted a tramway line built. Ivor Montagu, in charge of the budget on behalf of the production, considered that a bus would be cheaper and would do just as well, especially as Gaumont British was going through a serious financial crisis. At the end of 1936, the company was decimated by a wave of redundancies, including Balcon and Montagu.

The filmmaker did not get his tram. Nevertheless, this ten-minute sequence does not suffer. This too will go down in the "Hitchcock annals" as a model for the development of suspense: clockwork shots counting down the minutes, music sounding like a countdown, a shot of the inside of the package revealing the workings of a relentless mechanism, superimposed images recalling the fateful hour of the explosion, a bus carrying the bomb stopping at a red light, and an emphasis on the film reel canisters that Stevie is carrying along with the bomb, as if the very essence of cinema were at stake at this moment in the film.

RECEPTION

The scene of the bus explosion and the boy's death determined some of the film's critical reception. Even before writing her article for the *Observer*, British journalist C. A. Lejeune lashed out at the director after the film's premiere. She did not take kindly to the fact that he had made the child die, even going so far as to show the disintegration of the bus. According to Lejeune, a very acerbic conversation ensued. She also attacked Charles Bennett, omitting to point out that the novel does not "show" Stevie's death, only its effects.

Mea Culpa

Upset by this altercation, especially as he liked C. A. Lejeune and her critical judgment, Hitchcock, aware of the spectacular power of the cinematic image, would later indulge in self-criticism, confessing what he came to regard as a fault. With François Truffaut, in the early 1960s, or on *The Dick Cavett Show* (ABC, June 8, 1972), he would return to "The Boy with the Bomb" to say that he should never have let the bus and the "kid" blow up. And if everything was going to explode, since the plot depended on it, it should have been done off-screen, out of sight of the viewer. Throughout this sequence, the audience has too much time to become attached to the child, and therefore to resent the film for such a denouement. And Hitchcock takes the opportunity to differentiate between suspense and surprise. In the one case, the

Who Killed Cock Robin?

Mrs. Verloc has just learned of the terrible death of her little brother. In a state of shock, before joining her husband for a fatal dinner, she passes by the cinema, where a Walt Disney cartoon, *Who Killed Cock Robin?* (1935, Silly Symphonies series), is being shown. When the bird on-screen receives an arrow through the heart and falls from the tree, the nursery rhyme "Who Killed Cock Robin?" resounds. With this nagging question in mind, she gets up and goes to join her husband. Walt Disney is thanked in the credits for *Sabotage*.

viewer is aware of the danger, fears it or desires it. In the other, they expect nothing and are startled.

An (Almost) Perfect Accord

The rest of the British critics were in favor of the film. Even the writer and journalist Graham Greene, who had little appreciation for the director's adaptations and wrote as much in his review of *Secret Agent*, considered *Sabotage* a success, partly because the film captured some of the ruthless brutality of the novel (*The Spectator*, December 11, 1936).

In the United States, which the filmmaker visited for the first time in the spring of 1937 to promote *Sabotage*, the American version of which was titled *The Woman Alone*, articles in the *New York Times* and the *New Yorker* were positive, even laudatory. The same is true of the December 16, 1936, issue of *Variety*, although the magazine's critic regretted that the terrorists' motivation remained unknown, "as a result, the audience watches the piece and its suspensive moments with interest, and when it is over, is still hazy as to the why and wherefore."

On the Art of Conspiracy

The American critic of the *Nation* (March 13, 1937) sensed the profound truth of *Sabotage*: "Mr. Hitchcock knows exactly what a movie should be and do [...] a live wire seems to run backward from any of his films to all the best films one can remember, connecting them with it in a conspiracy to shock us into a special state of consciousness with respect to the art." Cinema, a conspiracy? This is how *Sabotage* begins, since even before the credits roll, a dictionary page appears, with a focus on the definition of the word "sabotage": a violent action "with the object of alarming a group of persons or inspiring public uneasiness." Surely this is the very definition of Hitchcock's desired effect in general, and in this film in particular, which serves as a manifesto. *Sabotage* is a film in which cinema is constantly represented in concrete terms: the theater, the reels, the projection, the spectators. Hitchcock was a troublemaker and a crowd manipulator.

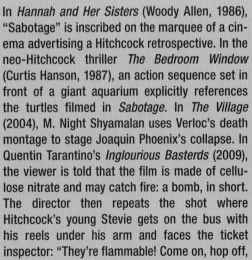

For Hitchcock Addicts

In *Hannah and Her Sisters* (Woody Allen, 1986), "Sabotage" is inscribed on the marquee of a cinema advertising a Hitchcock retrospective. In the neo-Hitchcock thriller *The Bedroom Window* (Curtis Hanson, 1987), an action sequence set in front of a giant aquarium explicitly references the turtles filmed in *Sabotage*. In *The Village* (2004), M. Night Shyamalan uses Verloc's death montage to stage Joaquin Phoenix's collapse. In Quentin Tarantino's *Inglourious Basterds* (2009), the viewer is told that the film is made of cellulose nitrate and may catch fire: a bomb, in short. The director then repeats the shot where Hitchcock's young Stevie gets on the bus with his reels under his arm and faces the ticket inspector: "They're flammable! Come on, hop off, big boy!"

The Successor to "39 Steps"

NOVA PILBEAM

IN "THE Girl Was Young"

WITH DERRICK DE MARNEY

Directed by ALFRED HITCHCOCK

A GB PICTURE

Young and Innocent was originally released in the United States under the title *The Girl Was Young.*

Young and Innocent

Great Britain • **1 hr 23** • **Black and White** • **Mono** (Western Electric Mirrophonic Recording) • **1.37:1**

Production Dates: March 1937
Release Date in Great Britain: November 1937
Release Date in the United States: February 17, 1938

Production: Gainsborough Pictures (Gaumont British)
Producer: Edward Black

Based on a novel by Josephine Tey, *A Shilling for Candles* **(1936)**
Screenplay: Charles Bennett, Edwin Greenwood, Anthony Armstrong
Dialogue: Gerald Savory
Director of Photography: Bernard Knowles
Camera Operator: Stephen Dade
Sound: A. O'Donoghue
Assistant Director: Penrose Tennyson
Continuity, Script: Alma Reville
Art Direction: Alfred Junge
Set Decoration: Albert Whitlock
Costumes: Marianne
Music: Jack Beaver, Louis Levy
Songs: Samuel Lerner, Al Goodhart, Al Hoffman
Film Editing: Charles Frend

Starring: Nova Pilbeam (Erica Burgoyne), Derrick De Marney (Robert Tisdall), Percy Marmont (Colonel Burgoyne), Edward Rigby (Old Will), Mary Clare (Erica's aunt), Basil Radford (Erica's uncle), John Longden (Inspector Kent), George Curzon (Guy), Pamela Carme (Christine), George Merritt (Detective Sergeant Miller), J. H. Roberts (Mr. Briggs), Jerry Verno (lorry driver), H. F. Maltby (police sergeant), Clive Baxter (Burgoyne boy), John Miller (policeman), Alfred Hitchcock (photographer outside the courthouse)...

"This is cinema at large, but which imposes upon itself the iron discipline of seducing, of captivating the audience, notably due to a dizzying rhythm where every second is bursting with invention and expectation."

Jacques Lourcelles, film critic

SYNOPSIS

One night, a couple are quarreling. The man, at the height of his anger, is afflicted by a tic that makes him blink. The next day, the woman is found lifeless on a beach, strangled with a raincoat belt. Robert Tisdall, a relative of the victim, spotted by two female walkers at the scene of the crime, is accused. The evidence is overwhelming: The belt is from his raincoat, stolen the day before. Placed in custody, Robert flees just as his trial is about to begin, taking with him Erica Burgoyne, the daughter of the investigating superintendent. At first coerced, then less reluctant, Erica follows him in his quest for the raincoat that will exonerate him. The two young people's closeness gradually develops into a loving complicity. They find the raincoat on a vagrant, Will, but the coveted belt has disappeared. Will says he got it from a man with a twitch in his eye. While Robert continues to flee, Erica is arrested by the police and returned to her family. A matchbox found in his raincoat pocket enables her to trace the real culprit to the city's Grand Hotel. Erica searches the hotel for the man with the tic, who is none other than the orchestra's drummer, disguised as a black man. At the sight of the police looking for Erica, he faints. Erica quickly revives him. When he wakes up, the man is immediately seized by a nervous tic. Unmasked, he confesses to the crime. Robert is cleared on the spot and Erica, radiant, is finally able to introduce the man she loves to her father.

GENESIS

Alfred Hitchcock began writing *Young and Innocent* in a climate of economic crisis. The brothers Isidore and Maurice Ostrer, bankers at the head of the Gaumont British board of directors, decided to close the Lime Grove Studio, where the director had shot all his films since *Waltzes from Vienna* (1933). Several hundred employees were laid off, including Michael Balcon, producer of Hitchcock films at Gaumont British since *The Man Who Knew Too Much* (1934). If the filmmaker escaped this "clean sweep," it was because he still owed the company two films. *Young and Innocent*, however, was produced by Gainsborough Pictures, a secondary production unit belonging to Gaumont British, which now confined itself to distribution.

A Producer at the Service of His Director

Balcon was replaced by Edward "Ted" Black, former owner and manager of a cinema circuit who had moved into production in the 1930s, taking over the Islington and Lime Grove Studios. The new producer's personality was the exact opposite of his predecessor's: Balcon loved publicity and gala dinners; Black shunned receptions and all forms of worldliness. Ted Black was a discreet perfectionist who enjoyed long meetings spent polishing a screenplay. Black was "solid and hard-working,"[1] and unlike Michael Balcon, he solved the problems presented to him on his own. Balcon's cosmopolitanism was matched by Ted Black's typically British spirit, as he preferred to cast English celebrities rather than big Hollywood stars. In his eyes, the success of a film depended above all on the soundness of the script. A dedicated producer and great admirer of Hitchcock, for whom he acted as intermediary with the Ostrer brothers of Gaumont British, Black did everything in his power to facilitate the filmmaker's work, even inflating the budget when the situation allowed. Their collaboration, which lasted for two films (*Young and Innocent*, *The Lady Vanishes*), went off without a hitch.

Nine Screenwriters for One Film

Hitchcock set about adapting *A Shilling for Candles* by Josephine Tey, one of the pseudonyms of British novelist Elizabeth Mackintosh. The filmmaker; his wife, Alma; his assistant, Joan Harrison, to whom he entrusted more and more responsibilities; and screenwriter Charles Bennett spent the Christmas vacation of 1936 in Saint Moritz, where they alternated between work sessions and skiing—except for Hitchcock, who was content to don a skier's outfit and read on the veranda. It was at this time that Charles Bennett received a contract offer from Myron Selznick for Universal. Unable to refuse such an offer, he interrupted his work and flew to Hollywood, where a long career as a screenwriter specializing in action films awaited him. Although Hitchcock had lost a loyal collaborator, he nevertheless wished him a safe journey with a small party.

The script was far from finished, however, and Hitchcock compensated for Bennett's departure by bringing together, as he often did, the energies of several screenwriters: among them Anthony Armstrong, writer for the satirical weekly *Punch*, playwright Gerald Savory, and Edwin Greenwood, who had worked on the screenplay for *The Man Who Knew Too Much*. Angus MacPhail, Hitchcock's friend and story editor, unofficially orchestrated the meeting. Up to nine people would have worked on the script.

A Girl at the Heart of the Story

The detective storyline of Tey's novel was gradually diluted in the film's various registers (adventure, chase, romantic comedy), so that the original crime and its resolution became entirely secondary. The novel's central character, Inspector Grant, was reduced to a mere silhouette, with the two young people on the run becoming the film's real heroes. The story was reworked to such an extent that the studio agreed to give the film a new title: *Young and Innocent*. As for the American title, now forgotten, it draws attention to the film's real heroine: *The Girl Was Young*. The director sums up what bringing a literary work to the screen could mean for him: "In the book, the girl disappears from the story. In the film, the girl is the story."[2]

CASTING

In keeping with Ted Black's policy, the two stars chosen to play the fugitive and the girl who falls in love with him are English. For the role of Robert Tisdall, "the wrong man," Hitchcock chose the young stage and screen actor Derrick De Marney. Nova Pilbeam, an eighteen-year-old actress who had played the English couple's daughter in *The Man Who Knew Too Much*, was chosen to play Erica Burgoyne, the superintendent's daughter.

Feminine Intuition

Hitchcock's preference for his actress fueled the plot and direction of *Young and Innocent*. Indeed, the character played by Nova Pilbeam belongs to an unprecedented category of Hitchcock blondes. Erica Burgoyne is an intelligent, resourceful young woman, the only one capable of administering first aid to Robert Tisdall when he collapses during interrogation. Of all the characters, often professional investigators, she alone has the almost immediate intuition that the presumed culprit is innocent. In Hitchcock's work, this presentiment is intimately linked to the birth of feelings of love: It is because she senses that Tisdall is innocent that she begins to love him, and vice versa. Her acuity sets her above the other characters. She is the heroine: adventurous, clear-sighted, autonomous.

This is one of the few times when Hitchcock did not film a female character as something intrinsically alien, different, that he can sublimate to the point of delusion. Erica is real. She is grounded to the point of nearly being swallowed up by the ground collapsing beneath her car in the film's most spectacular scene, set in a disused mine serving as a precarious refuge for the fugitives. Perhaps Hitchcock saw his heroine as both a woman and a man (he desires her and identifies with her), and this unprecedented blend is the character's greatest charm.

FILMING AND PRODUCTION

Hitchcock once again enlisted the help of cinematographer Bernard Knowles and editor Charles Frend. Alfred Junge, who had worked on *The Man Who Knew Too Much*, supervised the film's spectacular sets.

Tense Filming

Shooting began in March 1937 at Lime Grove, but after a few days the studio was forced to close due to an internal dispute at Gaumont British. The crew moved to the much more modern and comfortable Pinewood Studios, which offered the director and art director vast spaces in which to build their sets. But even so, shooting *Young and Innocent* was not without its difficulties. Hitchcock was irritable, certainly anxious about risking public failure. His unhappiness was evident in his physique: He put on an enormous amount of weight. His lead actor, Derrick De Marney, was the victim of sarcasm and vexation throughout the shoot and spread the rumor that the

filmmaker dozed off while shooting a scene, only to wake up as soon as it was over. The press picked up the story. Only Nova Pilbeam, spared the moodiness of Hitchcock, who behaved as a true gentleman with her, received preferential treatment. Years later, the actress would refer to the film as "the sunniest" she had ever been involved in.

Anthology Scenes

Young and Innocent is a mixture of adventure film, police investigation, love story, and story of initiation. Although it lasts less than an hour and a half, it is a succession of adventures in extremely varied tones. Two scenes in particular are regarded as bravura masterpieces.

The first is the scene in which the couple and the vagrant accompanying them, who have taken refuge in an abandoned mine, see the ground give way beneath their feet. To shoot this sequence, Hitchcock used Pinewood's largest studio and built the set five meters high, so that he could film a car sinking into the ground. Robert and the vagrant manage to escape; Erica is almost swallowed up but is caught at the last moment by Robert's outstretched hand. The cutting of the action, the setting that verges on abstraction, and the cavernous rumble of the soundtrack create an expressionist parenthesis within the film.

The final sequence in the Grand Hotel is one of the most unforgettable scenes in Hitchcock's filmography. In a very long tracking shot, the camera starts from the ceiling, crosses the ballroom, passes between the dancers, crosses the stage where the musicians are playing, and stops just ten centimeters from the guilty party's tense face. Two days of setup, numerous extras, and the largest crane in England were needed to shoot this sequence, in which the camera moves over forty-five meters. The camera seems to free itself from the narrative, revealing the key of the enigma to the viewer, who is then one step ahead of the characters.

A Complicity with the Audience

While Hitchcock created an optical complicity with the audience in the final scene through the use of tracking shots, this is because suspense depended on it. The question is no longer "Who is the culprit?" but "How will the heroes identify the culprit before

The murderer unmasked after a tracking shot of over 145 feet. This film includes an extended scene featuring a character in black face, an abhorrent but distressingly common trope of the age.

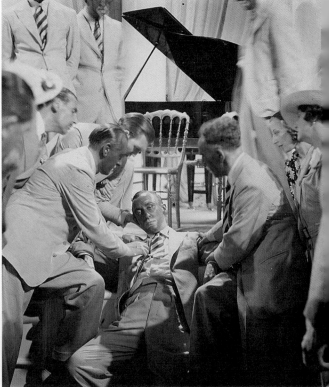

it is too late?" In Hitchcock's cinema, this reversal of what is at stake in a scene is a key way of engaging the viewer in the plot and keeping him or her captive. At the tea dance, the band plays a song whose refrain names the real culprit: "No One Can Like the Drummer Man." Hitchcock commissioned the lyrics and music from three Americans: Sammy Lerner, Al Goodhart, and Al Hoffman. After the drummer's arrest and confession, *Young and Innocent* begins a brief, happy denouement that enables the police and sentimental intrigue to conclude. Erica has cleared Robert's name, and her father accepts the idea of another man in his daughter's life.

RECEPTION

The film was released in British cinemas in November 1937 to a warm reception. The *Monthly Film Bulletin* praised the subtlety of the filmmaker's vision: "One of the great charms of the film is that it evokes the everyday lives of ordinary people living in a typically English environment [...] Countless small details testify to Hitchcock's keen and penetrating observation and knowledge of human nature. Comedy, romance, and thrills are skilfully combined. The love story between the two young characters develops simply and naturally, without an ounce of sentimentality." Journalist C. A. Lejeune, in *The Observer*, also

emphasized the humanity and warmth of the filmmaker's work.

Enthusiastic Americans

Young and Innocent was released in the US in early February 1938, under the title *The Girl Was Young*. Producer David O. Selznick considered the film to be splendid. Frank S. Nugent of the *New York Times* wrote of Hitchcock's ability to turn the familiar into the disturbing: "A serene English countryside under his glance suddenly grows ugly and threatening; a rail road yard can be made as ominous and mysterious as Herr Frankenstein's castle; a crowded dance floor in a hotel dining room becomes sinister and dread." (February 11, 1938).

A Typically Hitchcockian Scenario

As critic Alain Bergala[3] notes, *Young and Innocent* features a typical scenario that the filmmaker would repeat on several occasions, notably in *Psycho*, *The Birds*, and *North by Northwest*: in these films, a man who is mature enough to begin his sexual life is unable to do so under the influence of his mother. At the end of a journey punctuated by incredible trials, he finally achieves independence, finds love, and renounces "superior" authority. Only the hero of *Psycho* fails, in the symbolic sense, to "kill his mother."

Free

Young and Innocent laid the foundations, albeit in inverted terms, for an intimately Hitchcockian scenario: a young woman must escape her father's authority in order to take a step forward. Erica is the eldest of an otherwise all-male sibling group raised by her widowed father, the town's police superintendent. As the only female in the household, she plays the role of older sister and surrogate mother. Her elopement with a man presumed to be guilty, with whom she falls in love, represents her entry into adulthood and the transgression involved in assuming independence, especially from a father who, as a policeman, is doubly symbolic of the context of the law.

For Hitchcock Addicts

The scene stopping off at Erica's aunt's house, where a childish party delays the young couple's escape, would be considered incidental and was cut when the film was released in the US. "It was stupid," Hitchcock would say, "because it was the very essence of the film." Indeed, despite its apparent gratuitousness, it proves to be a pure moment of Hitchcockian virtuosity, where oppressive suspense emerges against a backdrop of lightness and humor.

Nova Pilbeam, the Little Dog, and the Fiancé

On the set Hitchcock redoubled his attention toward Nova Pilbeam. The actress confided that she and the director shared a love for the little dog that, in the film, belongs to the character she played. When the animal had to leave after completing all her scenes, Pilbeam and Hitchcock were so distressed that Hitchcock, she says, "decided to write another sequence for the dog, so [they] could keep the animal with [them] for another five or six days." Also, when filming the scene of the ground collapsing in the mine, the filmmaker, aware of Pilbeam's feelings for his assistant director, Penrose Tennyson, chose to film the close-ups of the hand stretched out to save her using his assistant's hand. Pilbeam and Tennyson married after the shoot.

Passport to Hollywood

In many ways, *Young and Innocent* foreshadowed the second half of Hitchcock's career. This opus would inspire numerous sequences in his American films: The woman's corpse on the beach and the unexpected shot of seagulls, seen as carrion birds, foreshadow *The Birds*; the scene in the mine of the hand extended at the last moment evokes the finale on the edge of the void in *North by Northwest*; the long tracking shot that starts from the ceiling, crosses an entire expanse, and finally captures a detail is repeated in the scene of the reception of *Notorious* (the key hidden in the palm of Ingrid Bergman's hand).

To date, Hitchcock had not responded to any offers from American studios. The director had enjoyed real prestige and a comfortable situation in his homeland since the mid-1930s. But with the British film industry in crisis, as evidenced by Gaumont British's difficulties, the temptation of an American career became ever stronger. Shortly after the filming of *Young and Innocent* was completed, the director rushed to find a ready-made script

An Initial Approach

In August 1937, Hitchcock, accompanied by Joan Harrison; his daughter, Patricia; and his wife, Alma (shown above from left to right), set off for New York on a trip that was presented as leisurely but was far from being disinterested. When he arrived, Hitchcock was surprised by the number of his admirers. Several British actors and directors had already established themselves in Hollywood, as had his screenwriter Charles Bennett most recently. On hearing of Hitchcock's arrival in the United States, New York representatives of the major studios tried to approach him, in particular Katherine Brown, on behalf of Hollywood producer David O. Selznick (*Anna Karenina*, *A Star Is Born*). Hitchcock and his wife spent a few days at Brown's country house, discussing the possibility of a contract with Selznick. Negotiations came to nothing. This was to be only a postponement.

he could film quickly, in order to free himself from his contract with the British studio, to whom he still owed a title.

Although not his last English film, *Young and Innocent* seems in retrospect to be the director's true intimate passport to Hollywood: a typically British work, as intended by his producer Ted Black, but already, in many ways, with its head in America.

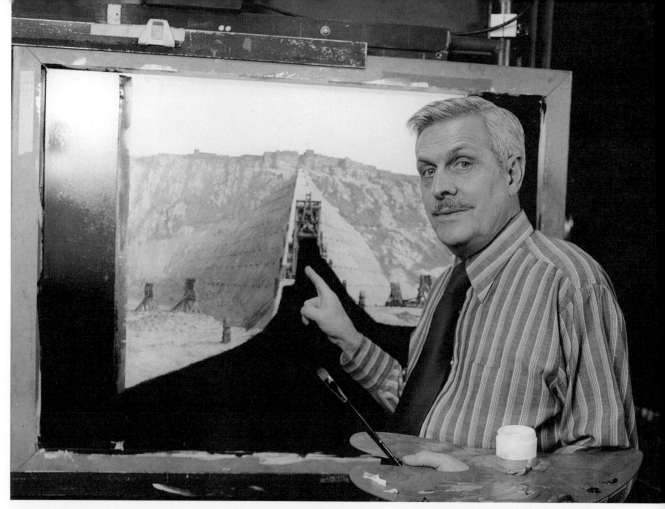

Albert Whitlock; profession: matte artist.
Right: Albert Whitlock's preparatory study for a famous shot (*The Birds*, 1962).

Albert Whitlock,
the Illusionist

Trained as a painter, Albert Whitlock (1915–1999) came to prominence in the second half of the twentieth century for his ingenious matte painting technique. He worked with Hitchcock during both his English and American periods. Together, they made six films in the 1930s, the period of their London youth, and another six during the last fifteen years of the Master's creative career, a period in which Whitlock acquired his reputation. But what is a matte painter?

A Deceptive Art

Born in London, Whitlock joined Gaumont British in 1929, at the age of fourteen, as a young jack-of-all-trades: stagehand, set builder…It was at the same studio that he first worked on a Hitchcock film, *The Man Who Knew Too Much* (1934). He was employed to fake the concert scene at the Royal Albert Hall, painting miniature spectators in the background to create the illusion of a full house in projection. From the outset, this was Albert Whitlock's art: making the impossible possible, making a false reality become real, all at the lowest possible cost. On the set of *The 39 Steps* (1935), he painted all the set signs. Never acknowledged in the credits, but recognized as a scenic artist, he was involved in four other English films by Hitchcock in the second half of the 1930s: *Sabotage, Young and Innocent, The Lady Vanishes*, and *Jamaica Inn*.

From Disney to Universal

During and after World War II, Whitlock perfected his technique of painting on glass (and later,

original negative matte painting). Impressed, in 1954 Walt Disney himself convinced him to come to the United States to work on his live-action productions (*Twenty Thousand Leagues Under the Sea*). In 1961, Whitlock was hired by Universal, which Alfred Hitchcock had also just joined. This time, he was listed in the credits (as a pictorial designer) and became a leading technical and artistic collaborator, deploying his matte painting skills on all the Master's films, from *The Birds* (1962) to *Family Plot* (1975), via *Marnie* (1964), *Torn Curtain* (1966), *Topaz* (1969), and *Frenzy* (1971). Proof that he had become indispensable to the filmmaker, in 1964 he also created a large number of preparatory drawings for *Mary Rose*, a project that never came to fruition but that Hitchcock dreamed of for the rest of his life.

A Cinema Painter

Matte painting is the art of combining, in the same shot, a real view (the action shot beforehand) and a painting that completes, hollows out, or extends the space represented. This "additional reality" is achieved by placing one or more black matte covers in front of the lens, thus masking part of the filmed shot and creating a free space for painting a rural or urban setting, adding a church, a street, or clouds: a sky and a village seen from a lake (*The Birds*), a docked Soviet cargo ship (*Torn Curtain*), an office building (Rutland & Co. in *Marnie*)—all these are additions that are more real than life. The matte painter is a film painter.

Skies

In *The Birds*, two matte paintings remain famous for their Hitchcockian effect: the town of Bodega Bay, entirely redrawn and colored by Whitlock, suddenly seen from the sky ("God's point of view," as the filmmaker put it[1]). And then, the film's final shot: an end-of-the-world sky (or the dawn of another), a barn on its side. And everywhere birds, some alive, some fake: an unforgettable finale, saturated with hostile presences, which leaves the survivors' car a narrow path to an uncertain outcome.

Trompe L'Oeil

Among so many other feats, the scene in *Torn Curtain* at the museum in East Berlin (reinvented at Universal City: two minutes of film, six matte paintings) remains a masterpiece. All the sets through which Paul Newman passes are partly or wholly painted by Whitlock: not only the walls, the marble floor and its gigantic motif, the galleries, a staircase, but also the paintings in the museum! In short, painted pictures on painted walls: a double trompe l'oeil. At the time of shooting, Newman performed in an empty space. Always concerned with his character's thoughts to justify his actions, the actor asked Hitchcock: "What is my motivation for walking straight?" Answer: "If you don't, you'll disappear behind the matte painting."[2]

Craft(manship)

Albert Whitlock's astonishing skills long predate digital special effects, green screens, computer tricks, and other computer-generated images. Nonetheless, his art (and craft) of matte painting was capable of passing off an illusion as reality. It is a detectable or invisible illusion that both reassures and disconcerts the viewer's eye: nothing less than the ambition of Hitchcock's cinema.

The Lady Vanishes

🏳 Great Britain • 🕐 1 hr 36 • 🎞 Black and White • 🔇 Mono (British Acoustic Film Full Range Recording) • ▱ 1.37:1

Production Dates: March–April 1938
Release Date in Great Britain: October 7, 1938 (London),
January 2, 1939 (outside London)
Release Date in the United States: November 1, 1938

Production: Gainsborough Pictures (Gaumont British)
Producer: Edward Black

Based on the novel by Ethel Lina White, *The Wheel Spins* (1936)
Screenplay: Sidney Gilliat, Frank Launder
Director of Photography: Jack E. Cox
Camera Operator: Leslie Gilliat
Sound: Sydney Wiles
Assistant Directors: Tom D. Connochie, Roy Ward Baker
Continuity: Alma Reville
Artistic Directors: Alex Vetchinsky, Albert Whitlock
Music: Louis Levy, Charles Williams
Film Editing: R. E. Dearing, Alfred Wallace Roome

Starring: Margaret Lockwood (Iris Henderson), Michael Redgrave (Gilbert), Paul Lukas (Dr. Hartz), Dame May Whitty (Miss Froy), Cecil Parker (Mr. Todhunter), Linden Travers ("Mrs." Todhunter), Naunton Wayne (Caldicott), Basil Radford (Charters), Mary Clare (Baroness Athona), Emile Boreo (hotel manager), Googie Withers (Blanche), Sally Stewart (Julie), Philip Leaver (Signor Doppo), Selma Vaz Dias (Signora Doppo), Catherine Lacey (nun), Josephine Wilson (Mrs. Kummer), Charles Oliver (officer), Kathleen Tremaine (Anna), Alfred Hitchcock (man at Victoria Station in London)…

> "National self-criticism has never been taken further than in Hitchcock's *The Lady Vanishes.*"

André Bazin

SYNOPSIS

———

Bandrika, a country in Central Europe. Following an avalanche, the passengers of a train are stranded for the night at an inn. Among them is young Iris Henderson, returning to England to get married. The next morning, the train can set off again. Iris is hit on the head by an object and nearly faints. Miss Froy, a governess, helps her to regain her composure, and the two travelers become acquainted over tea. The young woman dozes off, and when she wakes up, Miss Froy has disappeared. The other passengers claim never to have seen the governess. No one believes Iris's story except Gilbert, a folk music specialist intrigued by her tale. A so-called Miss Froy appears in the same clothes as the governess. Iris suspects a plot. With Gilbert, she embarks on a quest fraught with danger. They discover that the train is full of spies and finally find the real Miss Froy, held by Dr. Hartz, who has covered her with bandages. Once freed, she confides in them that she is a British secret service agent whose mission is to transmit a coded message hidden in a musical tune. The train stops in the middle of the track, and a shootout breaks out between the soldiers led by Dr. Hartz and the train's passengers, who have finally rallied behind Iris. The crew sets off again, finally arriving in England. The enemies are unmasked. Iris and Gilbert, now a couple, with the code, meet the governess at the offices of Scotland Yard.

GENESIS

After a stay in the US, where he honed his British humor with the press and began talks with Hollywood producers, Hitchcock returned to Islington Studios, where he finalized the editing of *Young and Innocent*. In October 1937, short of ideas for his next film, he asked his producer, Edward "Ted" Black, head of Gainsborough Pictures, if he had a project for him. This was an unprecedented request from the filmmaker, who was reluctant to receive a finished script. He was no doubt in a hurry to terminate his contract.

Ready to Use

The producer had a ready-made script. In 1936, on the recommendation of screenwriter Frank Launder, he acquired the rights to *The Wheel Spins* by Ethel Lina White, a British novelist whose plots, several times adapted for Hollywood, often feature young women in danger. Frank Launder and Sidney Gilliat delivered a screenplay based on White's novel, and American director Roy William Neill began work on the film. But after a series of setbacks, filming was interrupted.

A Dynamic Duo

Launder and Gilliat were experienced screenwriters, used to mixing thriller and comedy. They were also no strangers to plots set on board a train, a popular literary and cinematic theme at the time, not least because of the growing popularity of this means of transport and the democratization of foreign travel.[1] The pair made significant changes to Ethel Lina White's novel: They added two English gentlemen who were cricket fanatics, as well as the romance between the heroine and a folk music specialist (who encapsulates two of the novel's characters), the only passenger to believe her version of an inexplicable disappearance. In the end, the novel's initial atmosphere is transformed into a picturesque tale with many witty repartees. Hitchcock was enthusiastic when he read this script, which had already been approved by the studio. He undoubtedly detected in it a number of ingredients typical of his cinema: suspense, the theme of suspicion, English humor, a train, a young man and a young woman bound by the same belief who come together through a series of adventures. The director declared himself ready to make the film in less than a month.

A Paternity Dispute

Hitchcock claims to have been behind the adaptation of *The Wheel Spins*. In reality, although he made a few changes to Launder and Gilliat's work, these mainly concerned the film's opening and closing sequences. The filmmaker imagines the comic introduction, in which a group of people pile into a small inn, as well as the shootout between the passengers and the border police, a finale that adds Hitchcock's trademark spectacular touch to the film. As usual, Hitchcock also gave greater prominence to the secondary characters. Hitchcock's disputed authorship of the screenplay led to a stubborn disagreement between the director and his two main screenwriters, with the *New Yorker* of September 10, 1938, writing that he was "99.44%" the author of each of his films. Nevertheless, the script for *The Lady Vanishes* is undeniably his own.

CASTING

The Lady Vanishes marks the final collaboration between Hitchcock and cinematographer Jack E. Cox, with whom he had not worked since *Number Seventeen* in 1932. The filmmaker also worked with set designer Alex Vetchinsky, known for his thrifty illusionist talents, and Albert Whitlock. Their tricks, models, and transparency effects create the impression of a real train in motion.

Sally Stewart, Margaret Lockwood, Alfred Hitchcock, Googie Withers.

Theater People

For the role of Gilbert, a specialist in folk music and young Iris's main ally, Ted Black proposed Michael Redgrave. Born into a theatrical family, Redgrave was known as a director, actor, and playwright. Distrustful of cinema, he eventually accepted the generous long-term contract offered by the production company. To play the enterprising Iris, the producer recommended to Hitchcock the bubbly Margaret Lockwood, a stage actress who had made her film debut in 1934. Naunton Wayne and Basil Radford (who played Nova Pilbeam's uncle in *Young and Innocent*, 1937) played Caldicott and Charters, respectively, a typically English "pair" of friends. After *The Lady Vanishes*, Launder and Gilliat adapted this comic duo to other films, the stage, and radio. The character of Miss Froy, the affable old lady who disappears, is played by Dame May Whitty, a highly respected theatrical figure on both sides of the Atlantic, who was also pursuing a career in film.

FILMING AND PRODUCTION

The Lady Vanishes was filmed in one of Islington's smallest studios, on a set just twenty-seven meters long. The crew used just one carriage: everything else, a mixture of ingenuity and scale models, was an illusion (wasn't there a magician on board?). These modest conditions explain the excitement, but also the tension, that prevailed on the set.

A Three-Minute Rehearsal

The budget was tight, and Hitchcock was not always forthcoming. No doubt he was already dreaming of flying to Hollywood, where much more comfortable filming conditions awaited him. Michael Redgrave, the film's main star, complained that he did not have three weeks to rehearse a scene, as in the theater. Hitchcock's reply: "I'm sorry, in the cinema we have three minutes." The two leads met briefly, shortly before shooting, and Hitchcock, eager to exploit their awkwardness, filmed their characters meeting on the very first day of shooting.

"A sleepy Buddha"

Margaret Lockwood recalls a filmmaker who barely directed his actors: "He was a sleepy, waddling Buddha, with an enigmatic smile on his face."[2] In fact, Hitchcock entirely pre-planned his film before shooting it, so that the actors found themselves caught up in an extremely closely prepared framework that left them little latitude. For Hitchcock, an actor must do absolutely nothing, "which is no mean feat, by the way"; they must let themselves be used to fit in with the film as a whole. In his memoirs, published at the end of his life, Michael Redgrave was retrospectively sympathetic to a filmmaker who always knew where to place his camera and how to achieve the desired atmosphere, who had visualized everything in advance and who, once in the studio, saved everyone time.[3] A "sleepy Buddha" indeed, but with his eyes wide open…

Michael Redgrave, Margaret Lockwood, and Alfred Hitchcock (seated) during filming.

Suddenly, England goes to war...Linden Travers, Naunton Wayne, Basil Radford.

From the Familiar to the Implausible

The Lady Vanishes, like *Young and Innocent* the year before, condenses several genres: the spy/adventure film, the paranoid thriller, the comedy, and the romance. The filmmaker moves from one to the other in successive breaks of tone. The train is the perfect metaphor for these interlocking narratives: each register has its own compartment, fifteen years before *Rear Window* (1954), where a series of apartments resembles the cabins of a stationary carriage. Hitchcock mischievously takes his time before launching his spy film. The first part, in which the viewer meets the passengers stranded for the night in a hotel, enables the filmmaker to depict a gallery of characters from different social classes who make up a microcosm of British society, with all its qualities and flaws. By first constructing his film on credible ground, Hitchcock can then skillfully lead it toward the implausible.

A Political Film

Hitchcock uses entertainment to evoke the reality and moral values of his country, which he both praises and criticizes. Far from being a fallback solution, the story's fantasy makes it more effective than literal commentary.

Although the filmmaker deliberately blurs the geographical lines (is Bandrika an imaginary country in Central Europe, Switzerland? Austria? Czechoslovakia?), *The Lady Vanishes* is nonetheless a political metaphor in the form of a warning and a film that takes sides. In the spring of 1938, the world was on the eve of World War II, and Nazism had already engulfed parts of Europe. During the exchange of fire between the passengers and the military, one of the passengers is killed after surrendering while waving a white handkerchief. Hitchcock clearly points out the impasse of pacifism and defends England's entry into the war against Germany. Through fiction, he castigates the politics

The enemy's response: Paul Lukas (in profile) and Mary Clare against the tree.

of appeasement and the resignation of the democracies in the face of Hitler—in this respect, the film prophesies the Munich Agreement of September 29, 1938, a Franco-English capitulation to the demands of the Reich chancellor ("We have sustained a defeat without a war," as Churchill would say). For a long time, the passengers refuse to believe in the disappearance of the old lady, but their sudden awareness of the danger enables their exaggerated individualities (a metaphor for the isolationism that prevailed in England at the time) to form a collective that did not hesitate to take action.

Individual interests finally take a back seat to the general peril.

RECEPTION

The Lady Vanishes was released in London in October 1938 and in the US a month later. Hitchcock had created such a very British drama, but the film was a critical and public triumph on both sides of the Atlantic, becoming the biggest success of the period for a British film.

Where Is Hitchcock?

A few minutes before the end of the film, Hitchcock appears, mingling with the crowd of Londoners, on a platform at Victoria Station. He makes a furtive, comic appearance: cigarette in mouth, hat and tiny briefcase in each hand, the filmmaker passes by with a strange shrug of the shoulders.

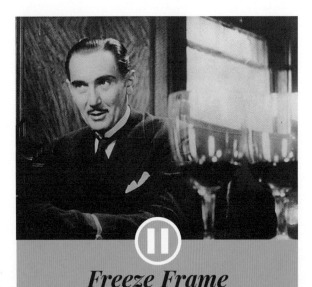

Freeze Frame

A fan of poisoned drinks (*Suspicion*, 1941), Hitchcock employed a clever trick in *The Lady Vanishes*. Rather than using dialogue to heighten tension, he translates danger visually by filming part of a scene through glasses, so that the viewer's gaze never wavers from them, attracted by the magnifying effect, while the characters' conversation continues. He had oversized glasses made for this purpose, a process he had already used in *Champagne* (1928) and would return to in *Notorious* (1946).

An English and American Success

C. A. Lejeune, in the *Observer* (October 19, 1938), believed that Hitchcock "has reached the point when every new film of his can be regarded as a blind date for connoisseurs of mystery fiction." Campbell Dixon of *World Film News* (November 1938) called it "the best Hitchcock and the best thriller ever made in England." Journalist Alistair Cooke testified on the radio to the enthusiasm of New York audiences: "I have never known an audience in a movie theatre anywhere applaud so whole-heartedly together as the Broadway audiences are applauding *The Lady Vanishes*" (BBC, January 19, 1939). The *New York Times* named *The Lady Vanishes* best film of 1938, and Alfred Hitchcock received the 1939 Best Director Award from the New York Film Critics Circle, the only award of his career as a director.

The Unbelievable Truth

The Lady Vanishes, a political and prophetic film, is also a dreamlike, philosophical work. This veritable manifesto against what the filmmaker calls "our friends the verisimilitude" praises the implausible, the enjoyment it provokes often being aroused by the unreality of situations (the brawl in the luggage car with magic props, the tune that acts as a coded message, the nun in heels). For the first time, the filmmaker suggests that the train journey may just be a dream for Iris, a young woman in search of sensations. The whole film becomes her initiatory tale, half-real, half-fantasy. *The Lady Vanishes* is also a vertiginous reflection on the concept of reality: In the end, reality is no more than a convention accepted by the majority, and anyone who does not adhere to it is considered insane. Hitchcock would return, notably in *Vertigo* (1957) and *North by Northwest* (1958), to this idea of a reality apparently accepted by all but also seen as a generalized conspiracy.

Are Actors Cattle?

Hitchcock is renowned for "roughing up" his actors to achieve the effects he wanted onscreen. According to Michael Redgrave, the director believed that "they will sometimes play better if they are insulted with humour,"[3] British actors being prime targets. At the time, British actors were wary of cinema and despised the still young art form as inferior in every way to the "noble art" of theater. "I don't know if his famous remark, 'Actors are cattle,' was uttered in my honor," said Michael Redgrave, "but I distinctly remember hearing it." Often questioned about the meaning of this provocation, Hitchcock always corrected...in his own way: "I never said that actors were cattle. What I said was that they should be treated as such."

CHARLES LAUGHTON

JAMAICA INN

MAUREEN O'HARA · LESLIE BANKS
EMLYN WILLIAMS · ROBERT NEWTON
Directed by ALFRED HITCHCOCK
PRODUCED BY ERICH POMMER

A POMMER-LAUGHTON MAYFLOWER Production
VERITY FILMS, INC.

LITHO IN U.S.A

Jamaica Inn

Great Britain · **1 hr 38** · **Black and White** · **Mono** (RCA Photophone System) · **1.37:1**

Production Dates: October–November 1938
Release Date in Great Britain: May 12, 1939 (London),
October 1939 (outside London)
Release Date in the United States: October 11, 1939

Production: Mayflower Pictures
Producer: Erich Pommer, Charles Laughton
Unit Production Manager: Hugh Perceval

Based on the novel of the same name by Daphne Du Maurier (1936)
Screenplay: Clemence Dane, Sidney Gilliat, Joan Harrison
Dialogue: Sidney Gilliat
Additional Dialogue: J. B. Priestley, Emlyn Williams
Photographic Direction: Harry Stradling, Bernard Knowles
Camera Operator: Gus Drisse
Special Effects: Harry Watt
Visual Effects: W. Percy Day
Sound: Jack Rogerson
Assistant Directors: Roy Goddard, Edward Joseph
Continuity: Alma Reville
Set Decoration: Thomas Morahan, Albert Whitlock
Costumes: Molly McArthur
Makeup: Ern Westmore
Music: Eric Fenby
Musical Direction: Frederic Lewis
Film Editing: Robert Hamer

Starring: Charles Laughton (Sir Humphrey Pengallan), Horace Hodges (Chadwick, Sir Humphrey's butler), Hay Petrie (Sir Humphrey's groom), Frederick Piper (Sir Humphrey's agent), Herbert Lomas, Clare Greet, William Devlin (Sir Humphrey's tenants), Jeanne de Casalis, Mabel Terry-Lewis, Bromley Davenport, George Curzon, Basil Radford (Sir Humphrey's friends), Leslie Banks (Joss Merlyn), Maureen O'Hara (Mary, Joss's niece), Marie Ney (Patience Merlyn), Emlyn Williams (Harry, the peddler), Robert Newton (Jem Trehearne), John Longden (Captain Johnson), Wylie Watson (Salvation Watkins, Sir Humphrey's gang), Morland Graham (Sydney), Edwin Greenwood (Dandy), Mervyn Johns (Thomas), Stephen Haggard (Willie Penhale)…

"The hardest things to photograph are dogs, babies, and Charles Laughton."

Alfred Hitchcock

SYNOPSIS

A band of shipwreckers in nineteenth-century Cornwall cause a ship to run aground by masking the light of a beacon. The brigands kill the crew and steal the cargo. Leaving Ireland after her mother's death, young Mary travels to Cornwall to stay with her uncle Joss and aunt Patience, proprietors of the Jamaica Inn. The inn has such a bad reputation that the coach driver first drops her off at the home of Sir Humphrey Pengallan, the local justice of the peace, who falls under the young woman's spell and resigns himself to taking her to the inn, a den of shipwreckers. During the night, Mary saves Trehearne, one of the gang, from hanging, on suspicion of embezzling merchandise. She escapes with him and takes refuge in Pengallan's house. As Trehearne confesses to the judge that he is in fact an undercover policeman, Mary leaves to warn her aunt and uncle of the imminent arrival of the police, followed by Pengallan and Trehearne. Pengallan reveals that he is the leader of the shipwrecking gang and ties up Trehearne. Leaving Trehearne in Patience's care, Joss takes his men to organize another shipwreck. Meanwhile, Mary convinces her aunt to release the young man, then goes to the coast to prevent the shipwreck by lighting a fire on the cliff. The constables arrest the thugs. Pengallan, who has gone mad, kidnaps Mary to take her to America. When his ship is surrounded, he climbs a mast and throws himself into the void.

Standing, center, Charles Laughton.

GENESIS

In 1938, Alfred Hitchcock was in negotiations with American producer David O. Selznick when he was offered the chance to shoot *Jamaica Inn*, his last film in Great Britain. Charles Laughton was to star in the film, as well as producing it, since he had acquired the rights to Daphne Du Maurier's novel. At the same time, the filmmaker was considering the adaptation of another of the novelist's books, *Rebecca*.

A New Showcase for Charles Laughton

Laughton teamed up with German producer Erich Pommer, former head of Universum Film AG (UFA), responsible for a number of 1920s masterpieces by Lang, Murnau, and Pabst, as well as Hitchcock's first film, *The Pleasure Garden* (1925). Pommer had been in exile since the Nazis came to power in 1933. Their company, Mayflower Pictures, had already produced two successful feature films in 1938, *Vessel of Wrath* and *Sidewalks of London*, both starring Laughton. The *Jamaica Inn* project also gave Laughton a starring role.

Familiar Surroundings

Absorbed by his imminent departure for Hollywood, Hitchcock tackled the commission with little enthusiasm. He did not get on well with Pommer. Daphne Du Maurier's novel was first adapted by playwright Clemence Dane (the author of the novel behind

Murder!, 1930), before Sidney Gilliat (*The Lady Vanishes*, 1938) and Joan Harrison took over. It was Hitchcock who imposed Joan Harrison as co-writer. His loyal assistant since 1933 was credited for the first time as a screenwriter on one of his films. She followed him to Hollywood, where he called upon her talent on several occasions (*Rebecca*, *Foreign Correspondent*, *Suspicion*, *Saboteur*) and where she produced the television series *Alfred Hitchcock Presents*.

Three Times Daphne Du Maurier

Jamaica Inn (1938), *Rebecca* (1939), *The Birds* (1962): Alfred Hitchcock adapted two novels and a short story by best-selling British novelist Daphne Du Maurier (1907–1989). Unhappy with *Jamaica Inn*'s treatment, the writer considered blocking the rights to adapt *Rebecca*.

From Minister to Justice of the Peace

Taking advantage of the Hitchcocks' trip to the United States, Pommer reworked the script. The character of the shipwreckers' leader, a clergyman in the novel, was transformed into a justice of the peace to avoid offending censors, particularly the American censors, who prohibited a "villain" from being a member of the clergy.

CASTING

Jamaica Inn is a film made by and for Charles Laughton, who played one of the most spectacular roles in a career that was not short of such roles.

An Extraordinary Actor

Born in 1899, Laughton studied at London's Royal Academy of Dramatic Art and made his stage debut in 1926. His astonishing physical presence combined with impeccable diction caused a sensation.

By the time he was filming *Jamaica Inn*, his whimsical genius had already left its mark on films by Erle C. Kenton (*Island of Lost Souls*), Alexander Korda (*The Private Life of Henry VIII*, in a role that won him an Oscar), Leo McCarey (*Ruggles of Red Gap*), and Frank Lloyd (*Mutiny on the Bounty*). Hitchcock admired him. However, filming was made extremely difficult by the actor's whims and apprehensions: He demanded numerous takes, left the set to find inspiration, and sometimes broke down in tears. He required the director to frame him to the waist only until he had established the right manner of walking for his character. He found this to the tune of Carl Maria von Weber's "Invitation to the Dance" ("Aufforderung zum Tanz," 1819). Hitchcock told the press: "Directors can't direct a Laughton picture. The best they can hope for is a chance to 'referee.'" The two men would meet again in 1947, in the United States, on the set of *The Paradine Case*.

Costume Films

In cinema, Hitchcock preferred contemporary plots to historical narratives, as he considered it impossible for characters in period costume to behave credibly. *Jamaica Inn* is nevertheless the second of his three "costume" films, after *Waltzes from Vienna* (1933) and before *Under Capricorn* (1948).

A Revelation

It was Charles Laughton who cast Maureen O'Hara in the female lead role. Enlisted at the age of fourteen at Dublin's prestigious Abbey Theatre, Maureen FitzSimons (her real name) was spotted a few years later by Laughton, who discovered her in a screen test and was fascinated. She traveled with him to the United States in the months following the filming of *Jamaica Inn* and played Esmeralda in William Dieterle's adaptation of *The Hunchback of Notre Dame*. This flamboyant redhead enjoyed a great career in Hollywood, and it was with John Ford that she made her finest films (*How Green Was My Valley*, *Rio Grande*, *The Quiet Man*, *The Long Gray Line*, *Wings of Eagles*).

In Familiar Territory

For the rest of the cast, Hitchcock was reunited with a number of actors who had worked with him before: Wylie Watson (*The 39 Steps*), Frederick Piper (*The Man Who Knew Too Much*, *The 39 Steps*, *Sabotage*, and *Young and Innocent*), Clare Greet (*Murder!*, *The Man Who Knew Too Much*, and *Sabotage*). Actor Emlyn Williams, the whistling shipwrecker, collaborated on the dialogue, as he did for *The Man Who Knew Too Much*. Leslie Banks, who played the father of the kidnapped child in 1934's *The Man Who Knew Too Much*, played Joss, the innkeeper leading the shipwreckers. His greatest role came seven years before *Jamaica Inn*, as the cruel aristocrat Count Zaroff in *The Most Dangerous Game*.

FILMING AND PRODUCTION

The film was shot at Elstree Studios, north of London, where Hitchcock had gigantic sets built. The spectacular shipwreck at the beginning was re-created on large sets, with giant wind tunnels and artificial waterspouts simulating the storm.

Memories of Expressionism

Harry Stradling, who began his career in 1920 as a cinematographer, worked with the faithful Bernard Knowles on the film's photography. This was his first collaboration with Hitchcock, who would work with him again in Hollywood on *Mr. & Mrs. Smith* (1940) and *Suspicion* (1941). The use of contrasting lighting, and the Gothic atmosphere created by the elaborate lighting, recalled at times the shadow play of German expressionism. Thomas Morahan's impressive labyrinthine set and the robbers' tavern, a veritable maze of staircases and multilevel openings, are further reminiscences of this aesthetic from across the Rhine.

Music, but Only Sparingly

The musical accompaniment is by Eric Fenby, his only film composition. Hitchcock used it sparingly, essentially confining it to the opening and closing credits, forgoing this dramatic device during the narrative. He repeated this approach in 1962 in *The Birds*.

RECEPTION

Hitchcock and his family had been living in the United States for two months when the film was released in London on May 12, 1939. It was a huge public success in Great Britain.

A Critical Disappointment

The Anglo-Saxon press was disappointed, however, not recognizing the work of the man who had become the world's most famous English director. "A Penny dreadful," wrote *Film Weekly*. For *New York Times* critic Frank S. Nugent, future screenwriter for John Ford, it "will not be remembered as a Hitchcock picture but as a Charles Laughton picture." The *New York Herald Tribune* lamented that the film was "surprisingly dull and uninspired." It deplored the way Charles Laughton "has given a show" and speaks of a "a mannered and highly lackadaisical melodrama."

A Game of Villains

Hitchcock considered *Jamaica Inn* an "absurd enterprise." For him, the unveiling of the true identity of Laughton's character, a seemingly respectable man who in reality pulls all the strings, should have come at the end of the film. Nevertheless, he admitted that the "Jekyll and Hyde" dimension of this double-identity character had interested him. *Jamaica Inn* is also markedly different from the costume melodramas of the time in its cruelty: Sailors' throats are slit, the spy is hanged, the main character commits suicide after going mad…

American
Hitchcock

David O. Selznick,
or, the Perfect Disharmony

"I consider myself responsible for everything."[1] So says David Oliver Selznick (1902–1965). Or rather, as "DOS" writes in the memos ("my famous or infamous memorandums")[1] with which he inundates those close to him, collaborators and rivals. Discoverer of stars (Vivien Leigh, Ingrid Bergman, Joan Fontaine), screenwriter (*A Star Is Born, Duel in the Sun*), this all-powerful producer (*Gone with the Wind*) brought Hitchcock to Hollywood in 1939. As was his wont, Selznick was to establish a relationship with the English filmmaker "under his command" until 1947, in which power and creativity were inextricably intertwined.

Working His Way up from the Bottom (to the Top)

Born of Lithuanian-Jewish parents, Selznick learned the film business from his father, a bankrupt distributor in 1923. Immediately enterprising and arrogant, indefatigable and exhausting, honest and rigid, indispensable and omnipresent, within ten years the young man had worked his way through the studio system: reader at MGM (1926), director of the script department and assistant to the boss at Paramount (1928), production manager at RKO (1931), vice president of MGM (1933). At the end of 1935, at the age of thirty-three, he set up his own company, Selznick International. At the end of the 1930s, while overseeing the *Gone with the Wind* adventure, he launched *Rebecca*, his first film with Hitchcock.

The Boss and the Employee

In July 1938, Hitchcock signed a seven-year contract with the producer for a starting salary of $2,500 a week, which in fact lasted until 1947. Together and against each other, they made three films: *Rebecca* (1939), *Spellbound* (1944), and *The Paradine Case* (1947). Hitchcock, who had started out in England with an American company (Famous Players–Lasky, later Paramount) and had dreamed of Hollywood, came to the United States to move from a poor production economy to the glitz and glamour of the California studios, that unique place that Orson Welles, in the same year, 1939, referred to as "the biggest electric train set any boy ever had."[1] In return, Hitchcock learned and experienced, particularly with Selznick, the principle of authority governing such an organization: The director was a salaried employee serving the will of the producer, who, from script to edit, controlled the film.

A Successful Launch

When Hitchcock was not filming for Selznick, the latter "rented" him out to other companies. This was the case for *Notorious* (1946), a film sold to RKO after the producer had contributed to the script and decided on the casting (some consider it their best "collaboration"). Hitchcock, annoyed by this practice of "lending," which paid off more for DOS than for himself, made seven films in seven years. In fact, he familiarized himself with other studios (RKO, Universal, 20th Century-Fox), proved his "employability," and accelerated his professional integration in his adopted country. Also benefiting from the promotional power of Selznick International, the popularity of the Master of Suspense grew. Selznick, who had an economic interest in this reputation, nevertheless promoted the director's fame and visibility like no other—except for Hitchcock himself.

Incompatibilities

Hitchcock and Selznick had opposing conceptions and practices, particularly when it came to adapting a novel. Hitchcock favored the greatest freedom, sacrificing plot and characters where necessary. The latter advocated maximum fidelity to the book. From this point of view, the long memo DOS addressed to the filmmaker on June 12, 1939, on receipt of his first work based on Daphne Du Maurier's *Rebecca*, is a model of its kind, a "lesson"—Selznick uses the word—and a point-by-point dismantling: "I must say bluntly that I find the adaptation very bad, and that it is easier to make another one than to fix this one."[1] Selznick would never stop meddling with

David O. Selznick and Alfred Hitchcock on the set of *Rebecca* (1939).

everything, from trimming Joan Fontaine's eyelashes in one of her close-ups (*Rebecca*) to re-editing entire sequences (*Spellbound*), not to mention writing an entire screenplay: "It is obvious that, even if I keep working eighteen to twenty hours a day, *The Paradine Case* won't be what it should be."[1]

Captain of His Own Ship

There is no doubt that Hitchcock brought Selznick a darker romanticism, and the producer for his part contributed a greater attention to his characters.[2] Their antagonism, whether fruitful (*Rebecca*) or counterproductive (*The Paradine Case*), was also a sign in the first half of the 1940s of the slow evolution in Hollywood of the perception of the importance of filmmakers, increasingly eager for independence (Hitchcock, Welles, Preston Sturges). So, in 1946, rather than renew his contract with Selznick, Hitchcock chose to set up his own company, Transatlantic Pictures, to become his own producer for a few films, and sole captain of his own ship.

Selznick International
PRESENTS
Rebecca
with
Laurence OLIVIER
·
Joan FONTAINE
DIRECTED BY
ALFRED HITCHCOCK
From
DAVID O. SELZNICK
Producer of
GONE WITH THE WIND
Based On the Novel by
DAPHNE DU MAURIER
Released thru UNITED ARTISTS

Rebecca

United States • 2 hrs 10 • Black and White • Mono (Western Electric Noiseless Recording) • 1.37:1

Production Dates: September 8–November 20, 1939
Release Date in the United States: March 28, 1940 (New York),
April 12, 1940 (United States)

Production: Selznick International Pictures
Producer: David O. Selznick
Based on the novel of the same name by
Daphne Du Maurier (1938)

Adaptation: Philip MacDonald, Michael Hogan
Screenplay: Robert E. Sherwood, Joan Harrison
Screenplay Assistant: Barbara Keon
Director of Photography: George Barnes
Special Effects: Jack Cosgrove
Visual Effects: Albert Simpson
Sound: Jack Noyes, Arthur Johns
Assistant Directors: Edmond F. Bernoudy, Eric Stacey
Artistic Directors: Lyle Wheeler, William Cameron Menzies
Set Decoration: Joseph B. Platt, Howard Bristol, Dorothea Holt
Makeup: Monte Westmore
Costumes: Eugene Joseff
Music: Franz Waxman, Lou Forbes
Film Editing: Hal C. Kern, W. Donn Hayes, James E. Newcom

Starring: Laurence Olivier ("Maxim" de Winter), Joan Fontaine (the second Mrs. de Winter), George Sanders (Jack Favell), Judith Anderson (Mrs. Danvers), Nigel Bruce (Major Giles Lacy), Reginald Denny (Frank Crawley), C. Aubrey Smith (Colonel Julyan), Gladys Cooper (Beatrice Lacy), Florence Bates (Mrs. Van Hopper), Melville Cooper (coroner), Leo G. Carroll (Dr. Baker), Leonard Carey (Ben), Lumsden Hare (Tabbs), Edward Fielding (Frith), Philip Winter (Robert), Forrester Harvey (Chalcroft), Alfred Hitchcock (the man passing in front of the telephone booth)…

"Last night, I dreamt I went to Manderley again. It seemed to me I stood by the iron gate leading to the drive [...] Then, like all dreamers, I was possessed of a sudden with supernatural powers and passed like a spirit through the barrier before me."

Voice-over at the opening of *Rebecca*

SYNOPSIS

Mrs. Van Hopper, a wealthy widow, is on vacation in Monte Carlo with her lady-in-waiting. The two women cross paths with Maxim de Winter, an aristocrat devastated by the death of his wife, Rebecca. In her spare time, the lady-in-waiting grows closer and closer to Maxim de Winter, who falls in love with her and asks for her hand in marriage. The newly-weds return to England and travel to Manderley, the impressive family manor in which the new Mrs. de Winter struggles to find her place. Rebecca's former housekeeper, Mrs. Danvers, has an undiminished passion for her deceased mistress and tries to intimidate the "intruder." She treacherously suggests that the second Mrs. de Winter wear the dress Rebecca wore to a costume ball the day before her death. At the height of her dismay at her husband's anger, the young wife is about to commit the ultimate act when she learns of the recovery of a sunken boat containing Rebecca's body. An investigation is launched. The dead woman's former lover accuses Maxim de Winter of killing his wife, who was pregnant by another man. Maxim confesses to his new wife that Rebecca, whom he hated, died accidentally during one of their arguments, and that he made it look like suicide. But a doctor reveals that, far from being pregnant, Rebecca was suffering from incurable cancer. The possibility of suicide seems credible and Maxim de Winter is cleared. The couple return to Manderley to find the manor in flames: As guardian of the temple, Mrs. Danvers has set fire to the house and perishes surrounded by Rebecca's memories.

GENESIS

In the midst of preparing *Jamaica Inn*, Alfred Hitchcock was approached by several Hollywood studios. Tempted by various offers, the filmmaker nevertheless declared to a London journalist in the spring of 1938: "If I go to Hollywood, it will only be to work with [David O.] Selznick."[1]

The Call of Hollywood

An independent studio ruled with an iron fist by a perfectionist and megalomaniac producer, Selznick International Pictures had always shown a keen interest in Hitchcock. But at the time, David O. Selznick, known to all as "DOS," was preoccupied with his own big project: the adaptation of Margaret Mitchell's novel *Gone with the Wind*. However, his agency was urging him to sort out the filmmaker's file, which was in danger of slipping through his fingers. Irritated by Selznick's procrastination and courted from all sides, the filmmaker raised the stakes. He also wanted to know what project awaited him before going to America. On July 2, 1938, urged on by his brother Myron Selznick, DOS proposed that the director work on a screenplay about the sinking of the *Titanic*. The producer offered him an exclusive contract for two films a year, that is, two times twenty weeks' work, and $50,000 for his first "Selznick film."

From *Titanic* to *Rebecca*

Hitchcock gathered all existing documentation on the sinking of the transatlantic liner and set to work. His second film for Selznick International Pictures was already set: It was to be an adaptation of *Rebecca*, Daphne Du Maurier's Gothic novel, which was a huge success at the time, enthralling both DOS and Hitchcock. Selznick, known for launching the careers of female actresses, considered that the character of Mrs. de Winter "probably exemplifies the feeling that most young women have about themselves."[2] He acquired the rights to adapt the novel for $50,000. In mid-November 1938, the producer decided that *Rebecca* would be Hitchcock's first film for Selznick International Pictures.

The Start of the Trouble

During the winter of 1938–1939, Hitchcock wrote a first draft with his wife, Alma, as well as Joan Harrison and Michael Hogan, a popular radio personality. However, Hitchcock and Selznick had different ideas about adapting a novel for the screen: The producer advocated absolute fidelity to the original material and wanted to retain as many elements as possible. For the filmmaker, on the other hand, every literary work offered a narrative skeleton that he could rework as he saw fit, with the help of his collaborators.

A Big Journey…and More Problems

On March 4, 1939, with an unfinished draft under their arm, the Hitchcock family left England, accompanied by Joan Harrison. The little tribe arrived in California on April 5, settling into an apartment not far from the Selznick International Pictures offices. In early June 1939, Hitchcock's first draft for his producer shocked the latter "beyond words."[2] He did not appreciate the comic observations that the filmmaker invariably added to his adaptations, since he wanted to produce serious, solemn entertainment.

Even though he was busy shooting *Gone with the Wind*, DOS kept a close eye on the work of his new recruit. His untimely interventions consisted of long memorandums in which he set out his views, corrected, and ordered modifications. To the director, he summed up his wishes in a laconic formula: "We bought 'REBECCA' and we intend to make 'REBECCA.'"[2] Selznick reinstated as much dialogue as possible from the novel and fine-tuned the characters' psychology, while Hitchcock was more interested in translating the book visually. After a total of seven screenwriters, *Rebecca*'s script was completed, and a shooting date set.

A Novel That Makes Its Mark

Rebecca draws on the world of the Victorian Gothic novel, blending romance, fantasy, and the macabre in plots where the present is haunted by the ghosts of the past. Daphne Du Maurier's work was a great success when it was released in 1938. It was adapted into a radio drama and a play and also appeared as a serial in the *New York Daily Mirror*. Selznick sold the American radio rights to Orson Welles.

The second Mrs. de Winter (Joan Fontaine) caught between the first (painting) and the accusing gaze of the housekeeper (Judith Anderson).

Joan Fontaine, Laurence Olivier.

CASTING

Katherine Brown, the studio's New York representative, recommended British stage actress Judith Anderson for the role of the disquieting housekeeper haunted by the memory of Rebecca. This choice proved so memorable that it inspired Walt Disney to create the character of the stepmother in *Cinderella* (1950).

The Struggle Continues

Producer and director struggled over the roles of Maxim de Winter and his second wife. They finally settled on British actor Laurence Olivier, famous for his great Shakespearean interpretations in the theater. The actor insisted that his wife, Vivien Leigh (*Gone with the Wind*'s Scarlett O'Hara), should play Mrs. de Winter, but Hitchcock insisted on hiring an American actress to emphasize his heroine's cultural and almost linguistic isolation in Manderley manor. To add a touch of humor, the director entrusted the role of Jack Favell, Rebecca's

cousin and ex-lover, to the lively George Sanders. The producer insisted on using cinematographer George Barnes, whom he borrowed from Warner Bros. A specialist in vaporous lighting, Barnes was known for his ability to bring out the best in female stars. The artistic direction of the sets, essential to the baroque madness of the plot, was entrusted to Selznick International Pictures' resident set designer, Lyle Wheeler.

A Young Leading Lady

Two weeks before shooting was due to begin, *Rebecca* still had not found her leading lady. Hitchcock auditioned more than thirty actresses and finally chose Joan Fontaine, a twenty-one-year-old performer who had never played any significant role. Unconvinced by her attempts, the filmmaker was nevertheless cornered by a producer enchanted by the young actress's photogenic qualities. Privately, Alma Reville did not share this infatuation, appreciating neither her "coy and simpering" manner nor her "extremely irritating" voice.[2]

Work session: Alfred Hitchcock, Joan Harrison.

FILMING AND PRODUCTION

Filming on *Rebecca* began on September 8, 1939. A few days before, England had declared war on Germany, a fact that deeply affected the predominantly British cast. Years later, Laurence Olivier summed up the general atmosphere: "We felt blighted right through," Olivier recalled, "careers, lives, hopes."[2]

Filming That Did Not Look Promising

The international cataclysm overshadowed a shoot strewn with pitfalls: Technicians went on strike, Joan Fontaine fell ill, and Hitchcock did not film fast enough in the eyes of Selznick, who controlled everything from a distance. Accustomed to being unencumbered by the British producers, Hitchcock discovered the experience of the interventionism of the American moguls, who were the real masters of Hollywood at the time—and Selznick more so than any other.

A Burlesque Heroine

Joan Fontaine, a late arrival on the project, did not fit in well with the rest of the team, and the director took advantage of this to exploit the discomfort that characterizes Mrs. de Winter. He decided to shoot the heroine's arrival at Manderley first: Of modest

extraction, the young woman was petrified by so much pomp. Sequences in which the character gets lost in the rooms, breaks a statuette, and behaves like a guest or a blameworthy child when she is the mistress of the house are filmed as veritable burlesque moments wrested from the cultural gravitas imposed by Selznick.

The Story of a House

Although absent throughout the film, Rebecca haunts characters, objects, and places: Manderley ends up personifying her. The new Mrs. de Winter has to battle against an inhospitable home that turns the dead into the living. Hitchcock confided that *Rebecca* is "the story of a house; it could also be said that the house is one of the three main characters in the film" (original text in French).[3] Twenty years before *Psycho*, Hitchcock used the motif of the mysterious house in the middle of nowhere for the first time. For the exterior shots of Manderley, Hitchcock exaggerated the visual impression, using a large model for close-ups and a smaller one for distant shots. The opening, in which Mrs. de Winter's dreamy voice recalls her stay at Manderley as the camera glides along the path leading to the manor house, immediately plunges the viewer into a fairy-tale world—Rebecca's cousin nicknames the new Mrs. de Winter "Cinderella."

The Hold

Displaced and somewhat abused by his producer, Hitchcock nevertheless proved that his genius could adapt to any situation, and he excelled in scenes depicting the psychological complexities of the film.

Mrs. Danvers tests her prey by forcing her to take a guided tour of Rebecca's world, which has become both a museum and a mausoleum. The more the housekeeper reveals of her former mistress's private life (her furs, her underwear, her nightdress), the more present and alive she makes her, and the more her replacement becomes a shadow of the former Mrs. de Winter. Hitchcock returns again and again to Joan Fontaine's face, increasingly impressed and soon collapsing. Filmed like a scene from a cruel fairy tale, the visit to the bedroom also reveals Mrs. Danvers's fetishistic, deadly devotion to Rebecca.

An Artistic Battle at Every Moment

Rebecca took nine weeks to film, three weeks longer than planned. The Hitchcock/Selznick war continued right up to the very last shot. The producer wanted a cloud of smoke to rise into the sky to form a gigantic "R," but the Hitchcockian option was chosen: The camera moved into the burning bedroom and stopped in front of the "R" embroidered

An Illicit Passion

Joseph I. Breen, chairman of the Production Code Administration (the American censorship board), was adamant: "There must be no suggestion whatever of a perverted relationship between Mrs. Danvers and Rebecca."[2] Yet there is no doubt that the housekeeper nurtured a passionate love affair with her former mistress. Rather than emphasizing this through dialogue, Hitchcock entrusted Judith Anderson with the task of suggesting, through her acting alone, the sexual bond that united the two women (and which is also suggested in the novel).

on Rebecca's pillow. Selznick had won the screenplay battle, Hitchcock the filming battle. The editing war remained to be fought, but Hitchcock had ensured that only the required footage was shot, leaving Selznick with few options. A few days before Christmas, the producer organized a public preview of the film: The reactions prompted him to reshoot some scenes and rerecord some inaudible dialogue. While Hitchcock was already at work on *Foreign Correspondent*, DOS took care of the entire postproduction phase, as well as incorporating Franz Waxman's eerie, enchanting, and "enveloping" score.

RECEPTION

After a New York preview covered by *Variety* magazine—it was headlined "David O. Selznick's *Rebecca* Gives Radio Music City Hall the Biggest Opening Business in Its History!"—the film was released across the US on April 12, 1940, to triumphant acclaim.

A Hollywood Filmmaker Is Born

The *New Yorker*'s John Mosher considered that Hitchcock had "labored hard to capture every tragic or ominous nuance, and presents a romance which is, I think, even more stirring than the novel" (March 29, 1940). *Film Daily* pointed out that *Rebecca* "should have special appeal to [female] fans" (March 26, 1940). Through the magic of Hollywood, Hitchcock turned a young, inexperienced actress into a star. *Rebecca* brought in a profit of $700,000 for Selznick International Pictures, a decent result but one that left the producer dissatisfied. He was paying the price for his independence: His distribution network was too weak compared to that of a major studio. Yet this was a record for a Hitchcock film. Nominated in eleven categories, *Rebecca* won the Oscar for Best Picture and Best Cinematography.

A Joint Effort

Years later, the filmmaker would confide that he did not consider *Rebecca* "a Hitchcock film," but rather a kind of nineteenth-century tale. In other words, the film belonged more to its producer than to the director, who was drawn to the subjects of his own time. In fact, *Rebecca* expresses two equally antagonistic artistic wills, but the incessant power struggles resulted in an exciting collaboration that was more harmonious than director and producer were willing to admit. Selznick believed in the effectiveness of his muscular method: "Many people do their best when

Where Is Hitchcock?

Hitchcock's appearance is easily missed by all but the most die-hard fans of the Master's cameos. Almost at the end of the film, with a hat and a raised coat collar, he passes behind the back of the character played by George Sanders (Jack Favell) as the latter emerges from a telephone booth and converses with a policeman.

they work for me. I bully them, harangue them, coach them into doing better."[2]

A Question of Feelings

Selznick forced the filmmaker to break with his habits and explore uncharted territory. Hitchcock created a work whose dramatic tension is based less on a frenetic sequence of actions than on psychological triggers. *Rebecca* is not without its inconsistencies and implausibilities (the discovery of Rebecca's incurable illness, the belated revelation of Maxim de Winter's hatred of his wife), but these do not hinder the viewer. If Hitchcock never had any regard for verisimilitude, he proved here that this requirement became entirely secondary when one was more concerned with rendering the slightest inflection of the protagonists' feelings. Hitchcock, a filmmaker with a penchant for clashing plots and mixed genres, learned from the American producer to be more romantic and to put stars and characters at the heart of the film.

The Birth of Hitchcockian Romanticism

Hitchcock always had a penchant for female characters. His British heroines were adventurous and humorous women of action. Mrs. de Winter is the opposite: Her moods prevent her from acting and taking control of Manderley. She is overcome by a permanent sense of unworthiness: toward her husband and his social standing, toward Mrs. Danvers, and, above all, toward her rival from beyond the grave. *Rebecca* lays the groundwork for a new type of Hitchcock character, one who stands on the sidelines of the action but fails to be part of it. It's also about how to win the love of a man who is apparently in love with a dead woman. In this way, the film inaugurates an entire dreamlike aspect of Hitchcock's work and foreshadows his melancholy films tinged with morbid romanticism, from *Under Capricorn* (1948) to *Vertigo* (1957).

Walter Wanger
presents
ALFRED HITCHCOCK'S
PRODUCTION OF

FOREIGN CORRESPONDENT

The Thrill Spectacle of the Year!

starring

JOEL McCREA

with

Laraine Day · Herbert Marshall
George Sanders · Albert Basserman
Robert Benchley

Directed by ALFRED HITCHCOCK
Released thru United Artists

Foreign Correspondent

Great Britain • **2 hrs** • **Black and White** • **Mono** (Western Electric Mirrophonic Recording) • **1.37:1**

Production Dates: March 18–June 5, 1940
Release Date in the United States: August 1940

Production: Walter Wanger Productions
Producer: Walter Wanger
Unit Production Manager: James Dent

Screenplay: Charles Bennett, Joan Harrison
Dialogues: James Hilton, Robert Benchley
Director of Photography: Rudolph Maté
Visual Effects: Paul Eagler
Special Effects: William Cameron Menzies
Sound: Frank Maher
Assistant Director: Edmond F. Bernoudy
Art Direction: Alexander Golitzen
Set Decoration: Julia Heron, Richard Irvine
Hair stylist: Carmen Dirigo
Makeup: Norman Pringle
Costumes (supplied by): I. Magnin & Co.
Music: Alfred Newman
Film Editing: Dorothy Spencer, Otho Lovering

Starring: Joel McCrea (John Jones / Huntley Haverstock), Laraine Day (Carol Fisher), Herbert Marshall (Stephen Fisher), George Sanders (Scott ffolliott), Albert Bassermann (Van Meer), Robert Benchley (Stebbins), Edmund Gwenn (Rowley), Eduardo Ciannelli (Mr. Krug), Harry Davenport (Mr. Powers), Martin Kosleck (tramp), Frances Carson (Mrs. Sprague), Ian Wolfe (Stiles), Charles Wagenheim (assassin), Edward Conrad (Latvian), Charles Halton (Bradley), Barbara Pepper (Dorine), Emory Parnell (Captain "Mohican"), Roy Gordon (Mr. Brood), Gertrude Hoffman (Mrs. Benson), Alfred Hitchcock (man in the street with newspaper)…

"A.H. is the filmmaker
for an age of terror."

Jean-Patrick Manchette, French
novelist

SYNOPSIS

An American journalist, John Jones, is dispatched to Europe in August 1939 to report on an impending conflict. He meets Stephen Fisher, leader of a peace association and organizer of a banquet in honor of Mr. Van Meer, the Dutch diplomat responsible for negotiating a treaty between European countries. During the reception at the Hotel Europe, Jones tries to seduce Fisher's daughter Carol, while Van Meer disappears. But he is announced as being in Amsterdam. On the spot, Jones witnesses the diplomat's assassination. Aided by Carol and English journalist Scott ffolliott, he pursues the killer and locates him and his accomplices in a windmill. There, he also spots Van Meer, who has been kidnapped and drugged; a look-alike has been shot in his place. The thugs flee before the police arrive. Jones, back at the Hotel Europe, avoids being kidnapped. Fisher, in reality the head of the spy ring that masterminded the diplomat's kidnapping, provides Jones with a bodyguard who tries twice, unsuccessfully, to kill him. Jones and ffolliott, convinced that Fisher is a traitor, want him to believe that his daughter has been kidnapped. Fisher goes to a house where Van Meer is being tortured in order to deliver the terms of a secret clause in a diplomatic treaty. Jones and ffolliott intervene. The spies flee. The two journalists take an airliner to the United States. On board are Fisher and his daughter. Hit by antiaircraft fire, the plane plunges into the sea. Her father sacrifices himself to save Carol. Back in London, Jones makes a speech on the radio urging America to prepare its defense as the bombs begin to fall.

GENESIS

The contract binding Alfred Hitchcock to David O. Selznick beginning in April 1939 provided for the possibility of "renting" the filmmaker to other producers. Busy with the completion of *Rebecca* and the costly promotion of *Gone with the Wind*, Selznick agreed, for $5,000 a week, to "loan" Hitchcock to Walter Wanger, an independent and progressive producer obsessed with the idea of using cinema to bear witness to history in the making. He was already responsible for Fritz Lang's *You Only Live Once*, John Ford's *Stagecoach*, and William Dieterle's *Blockade*, about the Spanish Civil War. He quickly hit it off with Hitchcock, who found himself relieved to escape Selznick's dictatorial demands for his second American film.

Writing and Rewriting

Since 1936, Walter Wanger had owned the rights to *Personal History*, the memoirs of Vincent Sheean, an American journalist who worked as a foreign correspondent. Before Hitchcock arrived on the scene, he had already had several screenwriters work on adapting the book: John Howard Lawson, then Budd Schulberg and Harold Clurman. The latter two transposed the action of the story to Nazi Germany. William Dieterle was approached to direct. But the project ran into opposition from the Bank of America, which was afraid of financing a film that would break with America's policy of neutrality. When he finally found the funds, Wanger hired John Lay and John Meehan to rework the script and considered Charles Boyer and Claudette Colbert for the lead roles.

A Screenplay in Constant Evolution

When the project finally came back to Hitchcock, he suggested that Wanger should hire his compatriot and former collaborator Charles Bennett (*The Man Who Knew Too Much, The 39 Steps, Secret Agent, Sabotage, Young and Innocent*), who would be joined by the faithful Joan Harrison. The idea was to turn the project into a spy comedy and recapture the picaresque spirit of *The 39 Steps*. To achieve this, the screenwriters used John Buchan's novel of the same name, as well as *Greenmantle*, another of his writings, as inspiration for several sequences. Annoying the filmmaker, Wanger often intervened during the

writing process, and even during the shooting, to have the script altered to reflect the current upheaval (the invasion of Poland, which led to France's and England's declarations of war in September 1939; the advance of German troops; the successive defeats and capitulations in Europe at the beginning of 1940). Richard Maibaum ("I was writer about number thirty on *Foreign Correspondant*"),[1] future screenwriter of the James Bond series, was asked to flesh out the character of the kidnapped old Dutch diplomat. When he expressed reservations about the logic of the script, Hitchcock replied that he was only interested in effects: "If the audience ever thinks about logic, it's on their way home after the show, and by that time, you see, they've paid for their tickets."[1]

Peace in Danger

Certain that an air attack on England was imminent, Wanger wanted to add an ending to the film that would warn America. Hitchcock suggested asking prolific playwright and screenwriter Ben Hecht to write it. He did so in one day. The actors

Freeze Frame

To escape his abduction, the hero climbs out of his bedroom window and onto the ledge of the Hotel Europe. As he tries to lean on the neon sign, he suddenly turns off the "el" in the word *hotel*.

In bombed-out London, an appeal to the forces of the free world. Last scene of the film (Laraine Day, Joel McCrea).

Anti-Nazi Hollywood

Prior to the United States' entry into the war in December 1941, Hollywood tried to respect the principle of neutrality in American international policy by avoiding the production of overtly anti-Nazi films. There were exceptions, however, such as Anatole Litvak's *Confessions of a Nazi Spy* (1939), Frank Borzage's *The Mortal Storm* (1940), and, of course, Charlie Chaplin's *The Great Dictator* (1940).

were called back to the set for the scene in which Jones delivers a fiery speech imploring his country to arm itself against the threats to peace that now hang over it. Despite this, the final speech attempts to avoid a direct call for the United States to enter the war, in keeping with its official policy of neutrality and nonintervention. This ending replaces the one intended by Hitchcock: a sardonic, disillusioned observation by the English journalist explaining how the Germans were going to deny the attack on the passenger plane by an antiaircraft battery and blame it on the British.

CASTING

Hitchcock dreamed of casting Gary Cooper and Barbara Stanwyck, who had just shot *Meet John Doe* under the direction of Frank Capra. As Stanwyck was unavailable, the female lead was eventually played

by Laraine Day, an actress known for her role as a nurse in a series of successful films (the *Dr. Kildare* films).

Naïve American and Witty Englishman

Gary Cooper turned down the offer. According to Hitchcock, it was probably the actor's entourage, doubting the quality of the director's films, who advised him against accepting. Cooper later admitted that he had made a mistake in refusing the role. Cary Grant was considered for the role but turned out to be working with Howard Hawks on *Only Angels Have Wings*. Joel McCrea played the lead role, that of an American journalist caught up in an espionage plot in a Europe on the brink of war. Although he lacked the reputation of Cooper, McCrea, who began his career in 1927, had already appeared in several notable films (*The Most Dangerous Game* in 1932; Cecil B. DeMille's *Union Pacific* in 1940). Hitchcock was disappointed with this "second choice" and criticized the actor's nonchalance, a quality perfectly suited to his character of a glib, intuitive, and candid American reporter.

Hitchcock welcomed back George Sanders. In contrast to his role in *Rebecca*, he played a sympathetic character, the journalist "ffolliott" (no capital letter), a model of English wit, intelligence, and phlegm, who joins forces with the American reporter and contrasts with the latter's somewhat gauche rudeness.

A Seductive Villain

Herbert Marshall, a British actor with whom Hitchcock reunited ten years after his starring role in *Murder!*, played Fisher, the chief spy disguised as a politician working for peace. In the interim, he had embarked on a Hollywood career and had already worked with such greats as Josef von Sternberg (*Blonde Venus*) and Ernst Lubitsch (*Trouble in Paradise*, *Angel*). He is one of Hitchcock's most successful villains. Concealing his activities as an unscrupulous Nazi spy behind an affable exterior

and seductive irony, his character becomes more human as he is torn between his love for his daughter and his patriotic duty. His final sacrifice brutally lends him a kind of dignity.

Secondary Roles

The character of the disillusioned Dutch diplomat is played by Albert Bassermann, a great German classical actor who was a member of Max Reinhardt's troupe. He fled Nazi Germany on Lubitsch's advice because his wife was Jewish. As he spoke no English, he learned his dialogue phonetically. He was nominated for an Oscar for Best Supporting Actor.

Actor, screenwriter, and humorist Robert Benchley played Stebbins, the American correspondent in London who greets Jones on his arrival. To the director's satisfaction, he wrote his own witty dialogue.

Edmund Gwenn, who previously acted for Hitchcock in *The Skin Game* (1930) and *Waltzes from Vienna* (1933), played the creepy bodyguard who tries to kill Jones on two occasions.

FILMING AND PRODUCTION

The film was shot at producer Samuel Goldwyn's Hollywood studios. Large sets were built to reproduce various locations in London and Amsterdam, as well as a windmill with gigantic gears and the interior of an aircraft. Some shots without actors were filmed by a second crew in the two European capitals. The cameraman's boat was torpedoed at sea; having lost all his equipment, he had to make the trip a second time.

Complex Staging

Rudolph Maté was responsible for the film's sophisticated photography, full of contrasts, backlighting, and chiaroscuro. Born in Poland, he started out in the film industry in Hungary as assistant cameraman to producer and director Alexander Korda before moving to Germany, where he had the opportunity to work with Karl Freund, a genius of expressionist

For Hitchcock Addicts

One of the film's greatest admirers was Joseph Goebbels, then Reich minister of propaganda. He called the film "[a] masterpiece of propaganda, a first-class production which no doubt will make a certain impression upon the broad masses of the people in enemy countries."[2]

A murdered ambassador (Albert Bassermann) and a killer on the run (Charles Wagenheim).

images. After working as cinematographer on Carl Theodor Dreyer's *The Passion of Joan of Arc* (1928), he moved to Hollywood in 1935, where he photographed a number of major films (William Wyler's *Dodsworth*, King Vidor's *Stella Dallas*, Orson Welles's *The Lady from Shanghai*). As a director from 1947 onward, he distinguished himself in almost every genre (Western, science fiction, and, above all, film noir). His work on *Foreign Correspondent* earned him an Oscar nomination.

The man in charge of special effects, William Cameron Menzies, had just been working on the set of *Gone with the Wind*. He began his long career as an art director and designer in 1917, working until his death in 1957. He also directed a number of films, some of them science fiction: *Things to Come* in 1936, *Invaders from Mars* in 1953...

The Price of Realism

The scene of the plane crashing into the ocean gave Hitchcock the opportunity to devise a trick to create the illusion of spectacular realism. He installed

Where Is Hitchcock?

Hitchcock is a passerby in a London street, absorbed in reading a newspaper (preoccupied by the alarming news of the day?). He passes American John Jones (Joel McCrea) coming out of his hotel.

Another Aircraft Story

Around the time of *Foreign Correspondent*, Hitchcock did Walter Wanger a favor on another of his productions. He shot a brief, amusing scene in an airplane between an amateur pilot and an airsick passenger (Walter Pidgeon and Joan Bennett in *The House Across the Bay*, 1940).

a cameraman in a plane that swooped down and approached the water at full speed. These shots were then projected transparently in front of a set that reproduced the cockpit. A tank had been placed behind the paper screen onto which images of the inexorably approaching sea were projected. At just the right moment, the screen ripped open, allowing gallons of water to spill out, invading the set and submerging pilots and passengers alike.

Although the producer had planned a budget of $750,000, the film ended up costing a million and a half.

RECEPTION

Foreign Correspondent was released in the US in August 1940 to great critical acclaim. Critics were enthusiastic but overlooked the film's political dimension and saw it mainly as quality entertainment.

Approval and Reticence

For the American press, the film was essentially a particularly successful thriller. The artifices, naïvetés, and implausibilities it revealed were largely offset by a masterful art of action and suspense and an inimitable sense of playing with the audience's nerves. They also did not dwell on its political dimension.

The film was released in Great Britain in October 1940, when the Battle of Britain had already begun, a week before the air raids on London. Although reviews were favorable, Jones's final tirade, in which he sees America as the world's last light, provoked some irritated reactions, notably from documentary filmmaker Paul Rotha, who, along with others, wrote an op-ed in the *Documentary News Letter*. Rejecting the idea that the light no longer shone in Great

Britain, he criticized the film for its defeatism and lack of understanding of the British state of mind.

The film was not released in France until after the war, in October 1948, in a version shortened by seventeen minutes. It found no favor in the eyes of the fierce Jean-Jacques Gautier of *Le Figaro* (October 29, 1948), who spoke of "a gigantic turnip skilfully cultivated by a high-class horticulturist" ("un navet gigantesque cultivé avec talent par un horticulteur de classe").

From Humor to Terror

The film features a recurring narrative structure in Hitchcock's postwar films: a female character caught between two men, one of whom explicitly embodies a father figure from whom she must emancipate herself.

But *Foreign Correspondent* is above all shot through with two seemingly incompatible qualities. The film seems to continue the tradition that the director brought to a high degree of perfection in the latter part of his English period with films like *The 39 Steps* and *The Lady Vanishes*: that of the spy comedy, the humorous film chase at the end of which a couple is formed. But Hitchcock's second Hollywood title is also a rainy, windswept film, darker and more terrifying than its predecessors. Hitchcock's denunciation of Nazism and his depiction of a Europe on the brink of war enabled him to envision disturbing shots, sometimes bordering on the abstract (the killer's run making the umbrellas wave, the windmill's sails turning upside down), even frightening (Edmund Gwenn's hands advancing toward the camera as he attempts to push the hero into the void). *Foreign Correspondent* depicts an anguished world caught up in a fatal spiral.

CAROLE LOMBARD
ROBERT MONTGOMERY
IN
Mr. & Mrs. Smith
with
GENE RAYMOND
JACK CARSON
PHILIP MERIVALE
LUCILE WATSON
Story and Screen Play
by NORMAN KRASNA
DIRECTED BY
ALFRED HITCHCOCK
RKO RADIO PICTURES
1A
Country of Origin U.S.A.
411/16

Mr. & Mrs. Smith

United States · **1 hr 35** · **Black and White** · **Mono** (RCA Sound System) · **1.37:1**

SYNOPSIS

Production Dates: September 5–November 2, 1940
Release Date in the United States: January 31, 1941

Production: RKO Radio Pictures
Executive Producer: Harry E. Edington

Based on an original story by Norman Krasna
Screenplay: Norman Krasna
Director of Photography: Harry Stradling
Special Effects: Vernon L. Walker
Sound: John E. Tribby
Assistant Director: Dewey Starkey
Artistic Directors: Van Nest Polglase, Lawrence P. Williams
Set Decoration: Darrell Silvera
Makeup: Mel Berns
Costumes: Irene
Music: Edward Ward
Film Editing: William Hamilton

Starring: Carole Lombard (Ann Krausheimer Smith), Robert Montgomery (David Smith), Gene Raymond (Jeff Custer), Jack Carson (Chuck Benson), Philip Merivale (Mr. Ashley Custer), Lucile Watson (Mrs. Custer), William Tracy (Sammy), Charles Halton (Harry Deever), Alfred Hitchcock (a passerby)…

Park Avenue, New York, 1940. For three years, the Smiths, Ann and David, have loved each other as much as they love to quarrel, only to reconcile. However, they each learn that an irregularity in their marriage contract makes their union illegal. Ann takes exception to David's delay in asking her to marry him again and kicks him out of their home. He is forced to take a room at his club. He tries to win his wife back, following her everywhere, day and night, while she continues to vaunt her newfound independence. While trying to bring them together, Jeff Custer, David's lawyer and business partner, falls in love with Ann. To arouse her ex-husband's jealousy, she declares herself receptive to his advances despite a disastrous evening when they end up stuck on top of a fairground attraction in the pouring rain. Undeterred by this misadventure, Ann and Jeff head off on a winter vacation to Lake Placid in the Adirondack Mountains. They are preceded by David, whom they discover unconscious in the cottage next door, apparently freezing. This ruse to awaken Ann's tender feelings for him only works for a while before sparking another argument. But in the face of so much mutual love despite the apparent hostility, Jeff decides to step aside and the Smiths fall back into each other's arms.

Ann: "If you had it all to do over again, would you still have married me?" / David: "Honestly, no."

Mr. & Mrs. Smith

The irresistible Carole Lombard.

GENESIS AND CASTING

After his first two American successes (*Rebecca* and *Foreign Correspondent*), Hitchcock developed several personal projects and received offers from all the major studios. Producer David O. Selznick, who had him under contract, had no trouble "renting out" his director at a good price. He "loaned" him to RKO for two films: *Mr. & Mrs. Smith*, then *Before the Fact*, which became *Suspicion* in 1941, and which excited the director even more.

Anything for Carole Lombard

Mr. & Mrs. Smith was the work of screenwriter Norman Krasna, a specialist in screwball comedy and other "remarriage comedies."[1] The film exists above all to showcase Carole Lombard. A delightful star of successful entertainments (*Twentieth Century, My Man Godfrey, Nothing Sacred…*) and one of Hollywood's most influential actresses, Lombard insisted that her friend Alfred Hitchcock, with whom she shared a similar sense of humor, should direct the film. The filmmaker, who received the script in early May 1940 and took a month to read it, was persuaded out of admiration for the star ("a moment of weakness," as he later put it).

Typically American?

No doubt Hitchcock also accepted this unusual commission to demonstrate that he could work quickly and well in different genres. He also wanted to move away from the "English" (*Rebecca*) or "continental" (*Foreign Correspondent*) atmosphere for a while and become more rooted in his adopted country: "I want to direct a typical American comedy about typical Americans." Assuming that the Smiths, who live on Park Avenue, are indeed typical Americans…

Where Is Hitchcock?

Hitchcock passes the Smiths' apartment building as the husband and lover emerge, heading in opposite directions. This appearance is filmed by Carole Lombard, herself under the gaze of a *Life* photographer…To "get even" for the actors' profession, she reportedly had the filmmaker redo the take several times.

Republican Versus Democrat

For the male lead, Hitchcock hoped for Cary Grant but got Robert Montgomery, a likable young leading man whose career until then had been devoted almost exclusively to light roles. Montgomery got on well with Lombard, even though one was a Republican and the other a fervent Democrat, against the backdrop of an election campaign in which Franklin D. Roosevelt was seeking a third term. As soon as Montgomery's back was turned, Lombard covered the windshield of his car with leaflets praising the president of the United States.

FILMING AND PRODUCTION

Filming took place in an almost lighthearted atmosphere. On the first day, Lombard prepared a much-publicized surprise for Hitchcock: On the set, in a cattle pen, three heifers wore the names of the three main actors around their necks. It was a way of mocking the director's now-famous phrase about treating actors like cattle.

Small Finds

The pace of this Hollywood comedy, which is considered typical or conventional, is uneven. Some of the repartee and situations hit the mark, other aspects less so. A few scenes escape stereotypical comedy, such as Montgomery's attempt to make his nose bleed, or the incongruous plumbing noises that interrupt a meeting of virtuous people in the bathroom. The film also thumbs its nose at the censors, who force an unmarried man and woman onscreen to sleep in separate beds. The Smiths share the same bed, but soon learn, and the viewer with them, that they were never legally married…In this little war of the sexes, in which the leading role goes to the woman, Carole Lombard, with the help of Harry Stradling's lighting, regales the camera with seductive facial expressions.

RECEPTION

Thanks mainly to its star, Carole Lombard, the film did well for the studio ($750,000 in receipts). Critical reception was more mixed. *Variety* (December 31, 1940) noted that "Alfred Hitchcock pilots the story in a straight farcical groove," while the *New York Times* (February 21, 1941) pointed to the "moments of dullness" in this supposedly hectic comedy. As for Otis Ferguson in the *New Republic*, he doubted that the viewers' laughter would last as long as the film…

Freeze Frame

Hitchcock said he was happy to film the script. Film historian Bill Krohn does, however, note one of the Master's great ideas.[2] During the breakfast scene, he first films a close-up of Carole Lombard gazing lovingly at her husband above the table. The next day, to express the same feeling, he replaces this shot with a less conventional framing: under the table this time, she slips her elegant little bare feet into her husband's trouser legs, then the camera moves up to eye level.

A Sense of Humor

Hitchcock's strong sense of humor, including its dark side, is evident in all his films, and is one of the essential dimensions of his "couple" comedies. We find it in the tone of certain scenes in *Rich and Strange* (1931), the first half hour of *The Lady Vanishes* (1938), the dinner table exchanges between Inspector Oxford and his wife in *Frenzy* (1971)…But the strength of this humor is that it serves as a counterpoint, contrasting with other moments of radically different tone. Hitchcock's humor serves his art of mixing genres. But *Mr. & Mrs. Smith*, a comedy in the strict sense of the word, lacks this blend, and the fact that it was created by the Master of Suspense doesn't seem to upset its comedic sensibilities.

CARY GRANT
JOAN FONTAINE

IN

Suspicion

with

SIR CEDRIC HARDWICKE
NIGEL BRUCE
DAME MAY WHITTY

Directed by
ALFRED HITCHCOCK

RKO RADIO PICTURES

Screen play by Samson Raphaelson, Joan Harrison, Alma Reville

Suspicion

United States • **1 hr 39** • **Black and White** • **Mono** (RCA Sound System) • **1.37:1**

Production Dates: February 10–May 16, 1941
Release Date in the United States: November 1941

Production: RKO Radio Pictures
Executive Producer: Harry E. Edington

Based on a novel by Francis Iles (Anthony Berkeley Cox),
Before the Fact **(1932)**
Adaptation: Joan Harrison, Alma Reville, Samson Raphaelson
Director of Photography: Harry Stradling
Special Effects: Vernon L. Walker
Sound: John E. Tribby
Assistant Director: Dewey Starkey
Artistic Directors: Van Nest Polglase, Carroll Clark
Set Decoration: Darrell Silvera
Makeup: Mel Berns
Costumes: Edward Stevenson
Music: Franz Waxman
Film Editing: William Hamilton

Starring: Cary Grant (Johnnie Aysgarth), Joan Fontaine (Lina McLaidlaw Aysgarth), Cedric Hardwicke (General McLaidlaw), Nigel Bruce (Gordon Cochran Thwaite, alias "Beaky"), Dame May Whitty (Mrs. McLaidlaw), Isabel Jeans (Mrs. Newsham), Heather Angel (Ethel), Auriol Lee (Isobel Sedbusk), Reginald Sheffield (Reggie Wetherby), Leo G. Carroll (Captain Melbeck), Billy Bevan (ticket collector), Carol Curtis-Brown (Jessie Barham), Faith Brook (Alice Barham), Violet Campbell (Mrs. Barham), Leonard Carey (Burton), Alfred Hitchcock (the man posting a letter)…

"Suspicion is a tenuous thing, so impalpable that the exact moment of its birth is not easy to determine."

Francis Iles, *Before the Fact*

On a train, Lina McLaidlaw is confronted by a man traveling first-class with a third-class ticket. The young Englishwoman recognizes Johnnie Aysgarth, playboy and tabloid star. They cross paths at a hunt, then meet again at a ball. Johnnie engages in a heartfelt courtship of the young woman, who becomes increasingly smitten and succumbs to his desire. They marry on the spot, despite the opposition of Lina's family. After a European honeymoon, the couple return to England and settle into a sumptuous home. But the young bride becomes aware that her husband is living beyond his means and squandering his money at the racecourse. He does not hesitate to sell the McLaidlaw parents' wedding present to satisfy his passion. Johnnie embarks with Beaky, a wealthy friend, on the development of a cliffside property to build a hotel. Lina fears that her husband wants to kill his partner in order to dispossess him. The young woman later learns of Beaky's death as a result of a stupid bet. Her doubts increase further after a discussion with a friend, a mystery writer. Lina is now convinced that her husband wants to kill her with a glass of poisoned milk. She decides to go to her mother's house, but he insists on accompanying her. On the way, a fearful Lina almost falls out of the car, but Johnnie catches her. She confesses her suspicions to him, while he confesses that he had intended to commit suicide to put an end to his money problems. Appeased, the couple return home.

GENESIS

While filming *Mr. & Mrs. Smith*, Alfred Hitchcock was already focusing on the next film to be delivered to the RKO studio: an adaptation of the crime novel *Before the Fact*, by Francis Iles, one of the pseudonyms of British writer Anthony Berkeley Cox. Hitchcock considered *Before the Fact* a masterpiece of the genre. Since its publication in 1932, RKO had owned the rights to the story but was unable to produce a screenplay to satisfy the Hays office, Hollywood's censorship body.

Murder, Suicide, and Adultery

Before the Fact tells the story of a woman madly in love with her husband even though she knows him to be a con man, a womanizer, and ultimately a murderer. Murder, suicide, and adultery are at the heart of the novel, the adaptation of which posed a real challenge in terms of censorship. This obstacle, far from discouraging Hitchcock, excited his creativity: He had taken up a similar challenge when filming *Rebecca* (1939), suggesting in particular a lesbian relationship and a near suicide. To allay producer Harry E. Edington's fears, Hitchcock assured him that he would tell the story from the wife's point of view, the husband being infamous only in her vivid imagination.

An Illustrious Assistant

In November 1940, Alma Reville, Hitchcock's wife, and Joan Harrison, his closest collaborator, drafted the first version. To develop it into a screenplay and write the dialogue, the filmmaker called on the services of a prestigious playwright and screenwriter, Samson Raphaelson, author of the play that gave rise to the first talking picture in cinema history, *The Jazz Singer* (1927), and co-writer of Ernst Lubitsch's brilliant comedies (*Trouble in Paradise, The Merry Widow, Angel…*). The writer arrived in Hollywood at the beginning of December and worked daily with the filmmaker. He cleaned up his treatment of secondary plots and characters in order to focus on the main couple. Hitchcock accepted Raphaelson's ideas but warned him about the risk of censorship. The two men thus removed a number of elements from the source material: the couple's adulterous relationships, the heroine's devotion to love, even the masking of her own death as suicide when she realized that her husband wished to murder her. After five weeks of respectful and cordial collaboration, the writer returned to New York.

CASTING

To play the seductive Johnnie Aysgarth, RKO considered Laurence Olivier or Orson Welles. But when Hitchcock took over the project, his first choice was the recently naturalized English actor Cary Grant.

A Romantic Comedy Star

During the 1930s, Cary Grant starred in sparkling romantic comedies directed by Hollywood masters George Cukor, Leo McCarey, and Howard Hawks. He refused to star in *Mr. & Mrs. Smith*, deeming his character too predictable. But this time, the filmmaker wanted to cast him in the opposite role, of a husband suspected of murder. By casting such a charismatic and popular actor, Hitchcock anticipated the inevitable public sympathy for the villain's character. *Suspicion*, still entitled *Before the Fact* at this point, inaugurated a collaboration of four films over almost twenty years between filmmaker and actor.

In Memory of *Rebecca*

Actress Michèle Morgan, who had just arrived in Hollywood after fleeing occupied France, was considered for the role of Lina McLaidlaw, but Hitchcock rejected her because of her French accent. In any case, RKO preferred Joan Fontaine, who had become a star since her first Hitchcock film. The actress read *Before the Fact* and saw in it the possibility of a new *Rebecca*. At the height of her enthusiasm, she was even willing to work without pay… David O. Selznick, who had produced *Rebecca*, was not so generous and agreed to "lend" his actress to RKO for $7,500 a week.

England in Hollywood

With *Before the Fact*, as with *Rebecca*, Hitchcock, who needed to re-create a typically British atmosphere in Hollywood, wanted to hire as many English actors as possible who had been exiled to the US because of the war. Dame May Whitty, already seen in *The Lady Vanishes*, played Lina McLaidlaw's mother; Nigel Bruce, seen in *Rebecca*, played Johnnie's sidekick, Beaky; actress Isabel Jeans, who appeared in 1927 in *Downhill* and *Easy Virtue*, was cast as Mrs. Newsham. To play the character of the picturesque mystery writer, Hitchcock chose Auriol Lee, a former English theater star turned Broadway director and producer. It would be her only appearance in an American film.

FILMING AND PRODUCTION

Hitchcock reunited with cinematographer Harry Stradling and editor William Hamilton, who had worked on *Mr. & Mrs. Smith*. After his contribution to *Rebecca*, composer Franz Waxman wrote the spirited, romantic score for *Suspicion*. But in February 1941, filming began with an unfinished script; Hitchcock was making a film whose conclusion had not yet been determined, which confused the actors, who still did not know the purpose of their behavior and actions.

A Series of Hitches

Difficulties followed thick and fast: Hitchcock fell ill, and filming was delayed for several weeks. When he returned to the set, Joan Fontaine felt neglected by a director who seemed to have no interest in her or the film. Production became alarmed, Fontaine fell ill, and there was even talk of stopping the filming for good. Edington and Dan Winkler, the two men who had hired Hitchcock at RKO, were dismissed as responsible for the studio's poor results following the financial failure of Orson Welles's *Citizen Kane* (1941). President George Schaefer took the strange step of hiring Joseph Breen, then in charge of enforcing the Hollywood censorship code, known as the Hays Code, as temporary director of RKO—he would remain in the post for eight

For Hitchcock Addicts

In the previews, audiences failed to grasp the meaning of the original title, *Before the Fact*, which refers to a legal expression: "accessory before the fact." In the novel, Lina is an accomplice in her own murder. A list of titles was drawn up according to the endings envisaged. Hitchcock suggested *Johnnie*, to focus attention on his male star. RKO chose *Suspicion*, a word that appears in the second paragraph of the novel. The filmmaker found the title "banal and cheap."

months before returning to the Production Code Administration.

In Search of an Ending

RKO found itself in the midst of a crisis during shooting and took the film's censorship problems increasingly seriously. The script underwent further reworking, but the main question was the ending, since suicide and unpunished murder were forbidden by the Hays Code. Hitchcock would later make contradictory statements on the subject: He would sometimes claim that he had always wanted the film to take place inside the head of a paranoid wife, and sometimes that he had dreamed of an ending faithful to the novel, with Johnnie as the murderer. Throughout the shooting, no fewer than twenty possible endings were envisaged! There was even talk of a patriotic ending: Johnnie, out of contrition, enlists in the Royal Air Force and dies a hero's death.

Preview and Happy Ending

In one of the film's endings, Lina drinks the milk she imagines to be poisoned. When she realizes her mistake, she goes into the next room and prevents the anguished Johnnie from ingesting the poison himself. Lina saves him at the last minute, Johnnie confesses his wrongdoing, and the couple reconcile. This ending was shown at a preview screening, an opportunity to gather audience reactions. The audience booed the film. According to Hitchcock, the audience did not understand why Lina deliberately poisoned herself, and they rejected Johnnie's long confession scene. In an interview published in the *New York Herald Tribune* a month after the film's release (December 7, 1941), Hitchcock confided that he had known from reading the book that he would have to change the ending. For him, a film is not comparable to a novel or a play, but rather to a short story: "The short story and the screenplay have in common unity and pace, and what is more, they each require, in my opinion, a final twist." *Suspicion*'s sudden, precipitous happy ending not only satisfies the public and the censors, but is also, in his eyes, "aesthetically just."[1]

A Film Disappears...

On June 25, 1941, on a trip to New York to take part in a radio program, Hitchcock hurried back to Los

Freeze Frame

In her huge bedroom, Lina, dressed in white, lies on her bed like a fairy-tale heroine. One shot, tilting horizontally, films a beam of light in which Johnnie's shadow is cast on the entrance hall floor. He emerges from the kitchen and climbs the stairs to his bedroom in the half-light. The whiteness of the glass of supposedly poisoned milk he brings Lina glows in the darkness. Hitchcock, never at a loss for tricks to imbue a familiar object with ominous significance, has placed a lamp at the bottom of the glass to increase its luminescence. Johnnie walks slowly over to his bedridden wife, places the glass on her bedside table, and his "Good night, Lina" sounds like a farewell. The next morning, the glass is still in its place, untouched.

Angeles after learning that a producer, Sol Lesser, was reworking *Before the Fact* and deleting all the scenes that made Johnnie look like a murderer. The film thus redacted ran for fifty-five minutes...The story of this "butchering" reverberated throughout Hollywood, and after numerous protests, including those from the Selznick brothers, the film's integrity was restored—and Sol Lesser was "thanked."

An English Madame Bovary

The story of *Suspicion*'s production can be told from either a negative or positive perspective. Negatively, Hitchcock was prevented from developing the plot as he wished by Hollywood censors. Positively, the filmmaker, as usual, transformed the source material to create a personal work, shot through on all sides with his obsessions. Right down to the title, which he did not like, *Suspicion* is a purely Hitchcockian work that seems to correspond perfectly to the director's initial vision. In particular, the film revives the sense of feminine melodrama introduced by *Rebecca*. Joan Fontaine plays an English Madame Bovary. A bespectacled old maid immersed in her reading, she allows herself to be seduced by a playboy who turns her head. As in *Rebecca*, Hitchcock films the emotional reactions of a heroine who is constantly shifting from one state of mind to another. Joan Fontaine's acting, unique in the way it brings shy, fragile heroines to life, succeeds in expressing this internal struggle between certainty of love and doubt about her husband's true identity.

The Interplay of Genres

With *Suspicion*, Hitchcock rediscovered the mix of genres he loved so much, moving from light to shade, from comedy to thriller, in the same film. The filmmaker also proved that he could appropriate any genre (even romantic comedy), any actor (even Cary Grant), and instill the poison of doubt. This meeting of romance and thriller is personified by the film's star couple: Joan Fontaine plays on a melodramatic chord, just as she did in *Rebecca*, while Cary Grant brings a lightness and ironic distance to the film.

RECEPTION

Despite a long and chaotic shoot, an ending that was frequently altered on paper and even on the set, and a sudden, hasty happy ending, *Suspicion* was an instant hit with audiences and critics alike when it was released in the US in November 1941. The *New York Herald Tribune* found it "far better than *Rebecca*"; many critics hailed it as a psychological thriller with breathtaking suspense. The *Times*, however, was disappointed by the incomprehensible ending: "Up to the last few minutes Mr. Hitchcock follows the book faithfully, and his methods—sudden, uneasy silences, an effective, if a little crude, use of shadow, some cleverly taken close-ups—enhance the drama, but he then suddenly and unforgivably reverses all the points he has been at such pains to make, and kills the psychological significance of the story by clearing Johnnie of all suspicion [and offering a happy ending]" (December 4, 1941).

Interpretations

Hitchcock often commented on the ending of *Suspicion*. To Peter Bogdanovich, he confided his desire for a different conclusion: "I think it would have been more successful if I'd shown them both in the car and if he'd just glanced regretfully over his shoulder—because he didn't push her."[2] For Truffaut,[3] the psychological depth of *Suspicion* lies precisely in its distance from the original work: Whereas in the novel, a wife *discovers* that her husband is a murderer, in the film she *believes* that her husband is a murderer. And the ending, sufficiently implausible, allows the viewer to make the most worrying assumptions about Lina's future.

Shadows and Light

This shift from *discovery* to *belief*, as Truffaut points out, places *Suspicion* in a mental world where Lina's psyche casts light and shadow on every scene. Witness the sequence in which she believes Johnnie has killed his best friend: The living room is plunged into gloom, and when her husband appears accompanied by Beaky, unharmed, Lina drops her dark coat as the first notes of a waltz escape from the phonograph. Almost imperceptibly, Hitchcock gradually brings the scene back into the light as the shadow slowly fades from Lina's consciousness.

Compulsion

French critic Pascal Kané went so far as to propose an analytical reading of the heroine's discovery of

Where Is Hitchcock?

Halfway through the film, the filmmaker appears from a distance, in profile, recognizable only by his silhouette. Dressed in a dark suit and hat, he posts a letter next to the bookshop where Lina is.

sexual pleasure and the ensuing slavery to love when Lina is finally married to Johnnie.[4] For Hitchcock, even the feeling of love is permeated by a metaphysical questioning of good and evil. The filmmaker has little sympathy for this sentiment, which he films as a kind of psychic compulsion. Through love, Hitchcock's heroes find themselves dispossessed of themselves and enter a world governed by irrational affects such as paranoia.

An Initiating Nightmare

With its simple, tightly focused plot, sober expressionism, and twisted fairy-tale art, *Suspicion* has all the makings of a mythological canvas that Hitchcock would reuse on several occasions. The film is a story of initiation: From a spinster who refuses the company of men, Lina becomes a woman who experiences the world as well as love and doubt, at the risk of her life. From *Shadow of a Doubt* (1942) to *Marnie* (1964), not forgetting *Notorious* (1946) and *Under Capricorn* (1948), Hitchcock, a director of tried-and-tested heroines, would follow the vein of female initiation and growth throughout his career.

The visions of Lina (Joan Fontaine):
fantasy or premonition?

Hitchcock at War

From March 1939, Alfred Hitchcock was an Englishman in America. Settled with his wife and daughter in Los Angeles to conceive fantasies for the Hollywood dream factory, he was nonetheless aware of the war that broke out in Europe in September. His enviable situation as an expatriate tormented him all the more, as his mother, brother, sister, friends, and former colleagues were living in London, under bombardment from 1940 onward. Until 1945, in parallel with his work as a thriller director, he seized every opportunity, without ever mentioning or advertising it, to place his know-how at the service of the anti-Nazi propaganda of the British and American governments.

Commitments

Although he was admittedly not a very political filmmaker, Hitchcock nonetheless produced clear-sighted, *engaged* fictions before the war (*The Man Who Knew Too Much*, 1934; *The Lady Vanishes*, 1938)

and during the war (*Foreign Correspondent*, 1940; *Saboteur*, 1942; *Lifeboat*, 1943). But faced with the reality of the global conflict, and with a desire to make himself useful, he also directed two propaganda documentaries in London in early 1944 (*Bon voyage, Aventure malgache*). In the summer of 1945, still in London, he worked on a compilation of images from the Nazi extermination camps, entitled *Memory of the Camps*. In addition to these, other wartime works, one fiction and four documentaries, unsigned by the filmmaker and unpaid, deserve mention.[1]

Forever and a Day (1940–1942)

An RKO production, an episodic drama, and a patriotic effort on the part of Hollywood's British community (with proceeds going to organizations helping refugees), *Forever and a Day* had seven directors, all English except for Frenchman René Clair, who was to replace Hitchcock. As early as 1940, Hitchcock was working on the script for his sketch (*1897*) with his accomplice Charles Bennett, one of his most important screenwriters of the 1930s. But in 1942, caught up in the production of *Saboteur*, he was unable to find the time to direct it. Although the love story takes place in Victorian England, it is all about what, in 1940, embodied the hope of the free world. Indeed, when a character asks the young Englishwoman played by Ida Lupino where she is running so fast, she replies, "America!" End of episode.

Men of Lightship "61" (1940–1941), Target for Tonight (1941)

In early 1941, Sidney Bernstein, a friend of Hitchcock's who had become head of the Ministry of Information (MOI) film department in London, asked the filmmaker to supervise the American version of two British propaganda documentaries. The aim was to reach audiences on the other side of the Atlantic, both by securing theatrical distribution and by stirring an opinion that would remain largely neutral until the attack on Pearl Harbor on December 7, 1941.

During the summer, Hitchcock was slightly involved in *Target for Tonight*, a film recounting the preparations and execution of a British air raid on Germany—Churchill would have seen the English version at least three times, such was his appreciation for the story. Essentially, the filmmaker tightened the editing at the beginning of the film to bring the American viewer into the action more quickly.

Hitchcock's intervention is more significant on *Men of the Lightship*, renamed *Men of Lightship "61"* for the occasion, and bears witness to his meticulous work. Here again, to help the film's reception by an American audience he knew better than his compatriots, he made a number of changes: He deleted entire scenes, compressed others, simplified the narrative, and cut out typically English undertones (humor, references) while retaining some of the boldness of the initial cut. From one version to the next, the film running time changes from twenty-four to sixteen minutes. He also asked Robert E. Sherwood (*Rebecca*) to rewrite the commentary on the images, to be voiced by Robert Montgomery (*Mr. & Mrs. Smith*). He also had some of the voices dubbed to replace one accent with another, hoping to give this English film, which praises the spirit of resistance, its best chance in the United States.

The Fighting Generation (1944)

Made by Hitchcock in one day, on October 9, 1944, at Selznick's studios, *The Fighting Generation*, which lasts just under two minutes, is set in a hospital room. A nurse initially seen from behind turns around, and, facing the camera, actress Jennifer Jones, superbly photographed by cinematographer Gregg Toland (*The Grapes of Wrath*, *Citizen Kane*), speaks in close-up to the American nation, urging it to continue financing the war effort by buying war bonds. Twelve thousand copies of this little film were printed and seen throughout the United States.

Watchtower over Tomorrow (1945)

In December 1944, Hitchcock was commissioned by the US State Department to make a film to help create a United Nations organization—the future UN—so that the immediate postwar period would be one of long peace. On December 26, accompanied by screenwriter Ben Hecht (*Spellbound*, *Notorious*), Hitchcock traveled to Washington, and during the night the two men drafted the first version of *Watchtower over Tomorrow*, a mixture of archival footage and transitional sketches. Although this treatment seems to have met with official approval, and although Hitchcock was scheduled to direct it, it seems that the filmmaker's contribution to the project ended there, although this is not certain. Some have seen the Master's signature in one scene, or at least an idea he may have initiated on the night of December 26: A sequence shot starts with a child playing on the floor with an electric train, a dog at his side. The camera pans up to a table on which rests a framed photo of a soldier, surely the boy's father. It continues to the right, to weeping parents reading a letter, no doubt informing them of their son's death in battle.

The headquarters of the United Nations would make a memorable return to Hitchcock's cinema: It is in this gigantic New York building that Roger O. Thornhill (Cary Grant) goes to meet a man who, for all the world to see, dies in his arms, stabbed to death. And so begins a mad chase across the American continent, this time during the Cold War (*North by Northwest*, 1958).

You'd like to say —
IT CAN'T HAPPEN HERE!
...but every jolting scene is TRUE!!

FRANK LLOYD Productions, Inc., Presents

Priscilla   Robert
LANE CUMMINGS
in
ALFRED HITCHCOCK'S
Saboteur

with

Norman LLOYD   Otto KRUGER   Alan BAXTER
Alma KRUGER   Dorothy PETERSON   Clem BEVANS

Directed by ALFRED HITCHCOCK   A UNIVERSAL PICTURE   Associate Producer, JACK H. SKIRBALL
ORIGINAL SCREEN PLAY, PETER VIERTEL   JOAN HARRISON   DOROTHY PARKER

Saboteur

United States • 1 hr 49 • Black and White • Mono (Western Electric Mirrophonic Recording) • 1.37:1

Production Dates: December 17, 1941–February 1942
Release Date in the United States: April 24, 1942

Production: Frank Lloyd Productions, Universal Pictures
Producer: Frank Lloyd
Associate Producer: Jack H. Skirball

Based on a story by Alfred Hitchcock
Screenplay: Joan Harrison, John Houseman, Peter Viertel, Dorothy Parker
Director of Photography: Joseph Valentine
Camera Operator: James V. King
Trick Photography: John P. Fulton
Sound: Bernard B. Brown
Assistant Director: Fred Frank
Art Direction: Jack Otterson, Robert Boyle
Set Decoration: Russell A. Gausman
Music: Frank Skinner
Film Editing: Otto Ludwig

Starring: Priscilla Lane (Patricia "Pat" Martin), Robert Cummings (Barry Kane), Otto Kruger (Charles Tobin), Alan Baxter (Mr. Freeman), Clem Bevans (Neilson), Norman Lloyd (Frank Fry), Alma Kruger (Mrs. Henrietta Sutton), Vaughan Glaser (Philip Martin), Dorothy Peterson (Mrs. Mason), Ian Wolfe (Robert), Frances Carson (society woman), Murray Alper (truck driver), Kathryn Adams (Mrs. Brown), Pedro de Cordoba ("Bones"), Billy Curtis (little person), Marie Le Deaux (circus performer), Anita Bolster (Lorelei, bearded lady), Jeanne Romer (Siamese twin), Lynn Romer (Siamese twin), Alfred Hitchcock (man in front of a New York drugstore)...

> "*Saboteur* is
> Hitchcock's first
> American film about
> the United States
> that uses America
> as a setting."
>
> ▬
>
> Peter Viertel, co-screenwriter,
> *Saboteur*

SYNOPSIS

▬

A fire breaks out in an American aeronautical factory. A worker, Barry Kane, gives a fire extinguisher to his best friend, who is immediately burned to death. The cylinder turns out to have been full of gasoline, and Barry is suspected by the police. He sets out to find Fry, the suspicious worker who gave him the booby-trapped extinguisher. He arrives at a ranch and discovers that the wealthy owner is part of a sabotage ring. Unable to prove it, Barry is arrested. He escapes from the police car and takes refuge in the cottage of a blind man who believes in his innocence. The disabled man's niece, Pat, thinks he is guilty and tries to hand over the fugitive. However, as their journey progresses, she becomes convinced that he is telling the truth. After following the trail, the two young people find themselves trapped in the New York lair of the saboteurs, who are preparing to carry out an attack on the city. Barry manages to escape, and realizing that a ship is to be sunk in the Brooklyn shipyard, at the last moment he thwarts the attack, whose perpetrator is none other than Fry. Under threat from Fry, he is taken back to the terrorists' headquarters. But Pat has managed to lure the police there. Fry flees and hides in the Statue of Liberty. At the top of the statue, a fight ensues between Barry and the odious Fry, who falls to his death.

The couple on the run, saved by the circus troupe: Jeanne and Lynn Romer, Marie Le Deaux, Pedro de Cordoba, Billy Curtis, and Anita Bolster surround Priscilla Lane and Robert Cummings.

GENESIS

Still under contract to David O. Selznick, Hitchcock developed various projects that his boss could either produce himself or sell as turnkey projects to a Hollywood company, making a substantial profit on the monthly salary paid to the filmmaker. Even before he had completed *Suspicion* (1941), Hitchcock was considering a color talking remake of *The Lodger* (1926). But on the advice of Jack H. Skirball, a producer working for Universal Studios, he settled on a story about a young man unjustly accused of sabotage. In fact, Selznick lost interest in the project, and Skirball obtained the right to make the film, entitled *Saboteur*.

War Breaks Out During Scriptwriting

The plot of *Saboteur* compiles numerous elements from Hitchcock's previous spy films, notably *The 39 Steps* (1935): the hero hunted by both the police and foreign agents, the young woman who gradually takes up the fugitive's cause, the spy chief with the suave, aristocratic manner. Hitchcock developed the story with the faithful Joan Harrison, but she left her mentor to become a screenwriter in Hollywood. She was replaced by one of Selznick's right-hand men, John Houseman, a former theater collaborator

of Orson Welles's, and by a very young novelist, Peter Viertel. With them, Hitchcock gave the script a more didactic turn, including fascist tirades delivered by wealthy traitors, to which the hero responds with speeches extolling American values. While the script was being written, the situation was changed by the Japanese attack on the American base at Pearl Harbor on December 7, 1941. Previously, the authorities had ensured that films remained strictly neutral with regard to the ongoing conflict in Europe. Now, on the contrary, the political powers that be were asking Hollywood to stimulate the spirit of patriotism.

The First Purely American Hitchcock

At the end of the writing phase, satirical columnist Dorothy Parker was called in to polish up the local color of typically Yankee characters: a boastful truck driver who picks up the hero hitchhiking and then helps him escape, members of a circus troupe who—in a very American gesture—vote democratically to decide to protect the fleeing couple. With Hitchcock's previous Hollywood films set outside the US—with the exception of *Mr. & Mrs. Smith* (1940), a commissioned work—*Saboteur* is in fact the first feature where the filmmaker adapts his own type of storytelling to the reality of his adopted country. Thus, for once, the spies' purpose is hardly a MacGuffin, a pretext soon forgotten by the audience. On the contrary, their targets are very specific: an aeronautics factory dedicated to supporting the war effort, the Boulder Dam recently inaugurated by President Roosevelt, a ship about to set sail from the Brooklyn shipyard. Following the same logic as he once did with London's landmarks, Hitchcock sets his spectacular scenes in famous New York locations: Fry opens fire in the grand auditorium of Radio City Music Hall, then meets his death at the top of the Statue of Liberty.

CASTING

While Selznick was still considering producing *Saboteur* himself, he was thinking of casting Broadway musical star Gene Kelly in the lead role, thus giving him his screen debut. Things became more complicated when the project went to Universal, one of the least wealthy of the major Hollywood companies. Furthermore, the film's budget was already burdened by the royalties paid to Selznick. Hitchcock therefore failed to hire top-notch actors.

Lesser-Known Actors

Initially, Hitchcock wanted Henry Fonda or Gary Cooper to play the hero. But the other major studios refused to rearrange their schedules to make these stars available. Joel McCrea, who had played a similar role in *Foreign Correspondent* (1940), was not available either. The director turned to Robert Cummings. Hitchcock would later say that Cummings was a solid actor of light comedy but not very capable of expressing gravity in the face of danger.[1]

Nonetheless, Cummings played his role as a worker well, one of the few in the filmmaker's oeuvre. In fact, the Master would use the actor again in *Dial M for Murder* (1953). But the choice of a little-known actor like Cummings dashed any hopes of hiring Barbara Stanwyck or Margaret Sullavan, two big stars Hitchcock had managed to interest in the script. To play Pat, he allowed Universal to impose Priscilla Lane, declaring later that she did not fit the character.[1] In fact, this former singer was far from having the same "swagger" as Madeleine Carroll in her turbulent relationship with the hero of *The 39 Steps*.

Villains of Varying Degrees of Success

Hitchcock had a hard time getting Otto Kruger, who plays Tobin, the leader of the saboteurs, to deliver a performance full of innuendo. Initially, Hitchcock wanted Harry Carey to play him. At the time, this very popular actor symbolized the American patriarch, and audiences would have been extremely surprised to see him play a terrorist. But Carey—and his wife, even more so—were outraged at the idea of him playing a traitor to the nation. On the other hand, the episodic role of bomber Fry left a lasting impression on viewers, courtesy of actor Norman Lloyd's sly demeanor. Lloyd was recommended by John Houseman, who knew him when they were both members of Orson Welles's theater troupe. Lloyd also played in *Spellbound* (1944) and Charlie Chaplin's *Limelight*. Later a producer for the small screen, he was above all an essential cog in the television series instigated by Hitchcock in the 1950s, directing many episodes himself. Another important new member of the director's entourage was cinematographer Joseph Valentine, who would soon illuminate *Shadow of a Doubt* (1942) and then *Rope* (1948).

FILMING AND PRODUCTION

Jack H. Skirball, a great admirer of Hitchcock's, supported the latter's requests to the other producer, Frank Lloyd, a former director who had notably created the first version of *Mutiny on the Bounty* with Clark Gable. Spacious sets at Universal Studios were

Hitchcock's Western?

Although he worked in Hollywood for four decades, Hitchcock never directed a Western. He did, however, dabble in the genre in *Saboteur*, when Barry escapes on horseback from Tobin's ranch, pursued by horsemen who capture him with a lasso. A touch of the Western also permeates the mining town that has become a ghost town, where the saboteurs hide out to keep an eye on the dam that is to be destroyed.

thus allocated to re-create an enclosed river whose rapids enabled the hero to escape from the police, or the desert expanses of the American West. But on a tight budget, Hitchcock had to counterbalance these expenses using clever and economical means.

The Art of Accommodating Remnants

In the early 1940s, Universal's most lucrative productions were the films featuring teenage star Deanna Durbin, for which set elements were built and housed in the studio's storerooms. The ballroom in *Saboteur*, for example, is built around a monumental staircase created for a Durbin picture and features a scene that conveys Hitchcock's theme of incredulity: Pat and Barry tell the wealthy guests that their respectable hostess is actually part of a spy ring, but their listeners inevitably mistake them for intruders or jokers. Tobin's ranch is a house already seen in a film starring Deanna Durbin, built in the studio's backyard. Returning to Universal two decades later, Hitchcock reused it as the home of the Brenner family in *The Birds* (1962). The factory bombing that opens the film is stylized to the extreme. The factory's façade is represented by a simple shed, and incisive, rapid editing reduces the explosion to significant details: thick black smoke passing in front of a corrugated iron partition, followed by a detonation.

Simulated Depths

The greatest technical challenge lay in the night scene where the police inspect the fairground trailers. As the convoy is shown in a deep, wide shot, Hitchcock had to rig the perspective to keep costs down. Real trailers were placed in the foreground, but those following were models or simple cardboard cutouts. Policemen were supposed to inspect the vehicles along their entire length. The filmmaker's idea was to position large extras as close as possible to the camera, with smaller men and even little people behind them. In the background, they are nothing more than puppets with miniature electric flashlights in their hands.[2] Fry's fatal fall created the opportunity for a spectacular trick. Set against a black background, actor Norman Lloyd was attached to a wire that made him spin around while the camera performed a rapid tracking shot. The image was then embedded in a still shot featuring reconstructed details of the Statue of Liberty. The whole shot gives the impression of the spy falling into a void.

RECEPTION

Saboteur was a commercial success to almost everyone's surprise. The studio had little faith in the project, and the mixed press presented the film as a series of effective scenes linked by sloppy, implausible transitions. In various interviews, Hitchcock expressed similar reservations, adding that he had a particular regret about the final sequence. Thrown over the railing, Fry is held by the sleeve by Barry, who tries in vain to save him. Hitchcock felt that, to keep the audience's attention, it was the hero who should have been dangling dangerously over the

The Nazi spy (Norman Lloyd) held back by his adversary (Robert Cummings) and "eliminated" by the Statue of Liberty.

A stylized attack with corrugated iron, black smoke, then a detonation.

Freeze Frame

The great verbal confrontation between Barry and the traitorous Tobin is the subject of a very significant shot–reverse shot cut. The young hero stands, framed at the waist, while a very wide shot shows the traitor comfortably seated on a sofa. This difference in scale underscores the contrast between Barry's rebelliousness and Tobin's arrogant fascist rhetoric.

void. However, Hitchcock included a similar scene at the end of *To Catch a Thief* (1954).

Hot News

Saboteur undoubtedly owes its success to the fact that it coincided with the height of tumultuous current events. The attack on Pearl Harbor occurred just as the screenplay was being written, making it one of the very first American feature films to deal with World War II since the country entered the war. At the time, the general public was very concerned about the possible presence of Nazi sympathizers in the country. On several occasions, Hitchcock claimed to have been inspired by the pro-German associations that had developed in the preceding years, advocating a kind of American fascism, and which were disbanded shortly before Pearl Harbor. In the course of editing, the filmmaker also included images of the liner *Normandie* grounded in New York Harbor, connected with a shot of Fry smirking. Rumor had it that the ship had been sabotaged, prompting the US Navy to protest against the film. Eventually, the investigation determined that the sinking of the *Normandie* was accidental, but this detail further accentuates the resonance between *Saboteur* and the concerns of the public at the time.

A Return to Serious Matters

The success of *Saboteur* led to a wave of films about spies and saboteurs in Hollywood. Most of these productions, however, did not go so far: They showed German agents infiltrating the United States, whereas Hitchcock showed American citizens collaborating with the Nazi enemy. Nevertheless, after a few months, the authorities and studio bosses agreed that these stories exaggerated the domestic threat and risked undermining public morale. From 1943 onward, the majority of films dealing with the war were therefore set on foreign fronts. Hitchcock no doubt realized that with *Foreign Correspondent* and *Saboteur* he had reached the end of the cycle of semi-parodic variations on *The 39 Steps*. His next spy film, *Notorious* (1946), was more serious. He returned to the wild chase motif in *North by Northwest* (1958), but with infinitely more complex themes. In the short term, however, the success of *Saboteur* put the filmmaker on good terms with Universal, which immediately allowed him to film one of his most personal masterpieces, *Shadow of a Doubt* (1942).

Where Is Hitchcock?

At the start of the New York episode, the film-maker is seen standing next to a woman in front of a drugstore. Initially, Hitchcock planned for his character to be a deaf person making obscene gestures. But the was idea abandoned to avoid disrespecting those who cannot hear.

"Have You Heard?"
A Photo-Story by
Alfred Hitchcock

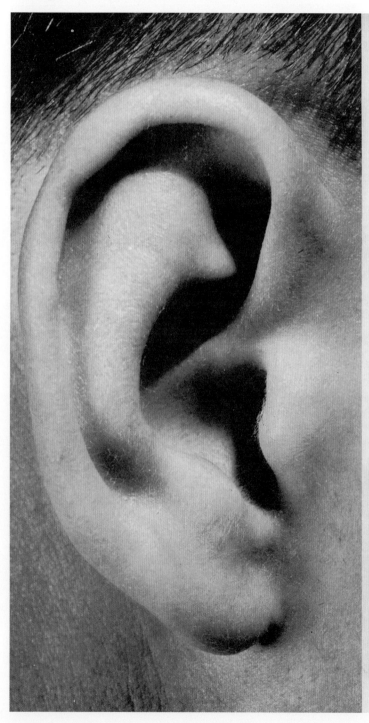

LIFE PRESENTS

"HAVE YOU HEARD?"

THE STORY OF WARTIME RUMORS

Suggested by . . . . STEPHEN EARLY

Directed by . . . . ALFRED HITCHCOCK

Photographed by . . . . ELIOT ELISOFON

From Stephen Early, secretary to President Roosevelt, recently came the suggestion that LIFE tell a picture story of wartime rumors and the damage they are liable to do. In accordance with this request, the Editors asked Alfred Hitchcock, famed Hollywood movie director, to produce such a story, with LIFE Photographer Eliot Elisofon as his cameraman. When Mr. Hitchcock graciously agreed, a script was prepared, the director picked his characters from the ranks of movie professionals and LIFE's Los Angeles staff, and shooting commenced in Hollywood.

Have You Heard?, which LIFE presents on the following six pages, is the result of their cooperation in photo-dramatization. A simple sexless story, it shows how patriotic but talkative Americans pass along information, true or false, until finally deadly damage is done to their country's war effort. One false rumor is silenced by a man of goodwill who later is unwittingly responsible for starting a true rumor which ends in a great catastrophe. Moral: Keep your mouth shut.

A church congregation in the city of Zenith hears its minister offer a special prayer for "our boys in the armed services who even now may be sailing for such far places as Alaska."

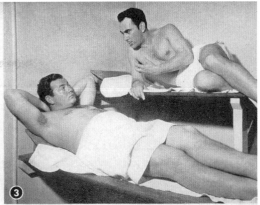

Bussing home from Sunday services, the blonde girl in the funny hat tells her friend: "I'm sure now. Those Zenith soldiers are sailing for Alaska. He didn't ask us to pray last Sunday, so they must be leaving this week." In bus seat behind them, a musician leans forward to overhear their conversation.

At Zenith's Steam Palace, the bus-riding violinist confides to a local hardware salesman: "Have you heard? Troopships are sailing to Alaska this week. They say thousands of boys are going up there. Preachers are already praying for them around the city."

At a Zenith restaurant that Sunday evening the hardware salesman entertains some friends. "Have you heard?" he asks. "No? Well, we are sending thousands of boys up to Alaska. Their troopship sails on Wednesday or Thursday, I understand, and they'll be convoyed by six destroyers on their trip up there."

One of the dinner guests, a gas-station proprietor with a liking for bow ties, chats with his customers next morning: "Have you heard about the large convoy of troopships going to Alaska? Friend of mine who really knows says they're leaving Wednesday night."

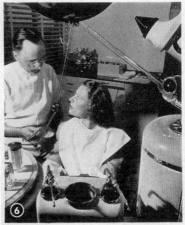

At the dentist's, pretty dinner companion of the hardware salesman passes on the secret news. "They're sailing Thursday afternoon. It means a new front. The man who told me knows one of the officers."

"There's going to be a blackout so that no one will know when the troopships go out Friday midnight for Alaska," confides another young woman, who was at the salesman's dinner, to her roommate.

"I never listen to rumors," replies a Zenith haberdasher to customer who repeats troopship story. "You shouldn't spread such talk. Nothing but rumors!"

BUT_____

Based on an idea by Stephen Early, President Roosevelt's personal mouthpiece, *Life* published a photo-drama on July 13, 1942, directed by Hitchcock. Six pages and eighteen numbered shots (by Eliot Elisofon, one of the magazine's star photographers) set the scene to remind the American public of the dangers of spreading rumors and the sometimes dramatic consequences of innocent word of mouth. In wartime, there was only one watchword: "Keep your mouth shut!"

In frame 14 (and 15) of his "film," the filmmaker makes his traditional appearance.

A dozen tropical shirts are ordered by a young Army lieutenant in the store of the Zenith haberdasher the next evening just before closing time. But the sleeves are too long and will have to be altered. The lieutenant says: "If you can't get them done and delivered to my hotel by 9 o'clock Friday night, never mind the order. I won't be able to pay for them if I've gone when they're delivered. Understand?" The haberdasher says he understands. But he muses to himself: "Tropical shirts. This young fellow must be headed for Australia."

An hour late for dinner, the haberdasher arrives home to find his wife and children already finishing their meal. He explains his tardiness: "Last customer held me up at the store. A lieutenant. Couldn't be helped. He took a dozen tropical shirts. He had to have the sleeves altered. I guess he's been ordered to Australia. I've got to get his order done by 9 o'clock Friday night. I suppose he's sailing on a troopship Friday midnight and that's why he's in such a rush." The haberdasher's son Christopher, a little pitcher with big ears, takes in every word.

70

Playing with "the gang" down the block the next afternoon, Christopher seeks to impress his older friends: "Gee, my dad's making shirts for almost the whole Army. He sold lots to soldiers going to Australia to fight. He's working now so the troopships can sail Friday midnight."

Bursting with excitement, Christopher's older pal arrives home to find his mother's afternoon bridge club in session. "You know what, Mom? Christopher's father's making shirts for a whole boatload of soldiers. He says they're all sailing for Australia at midnight next Friday."

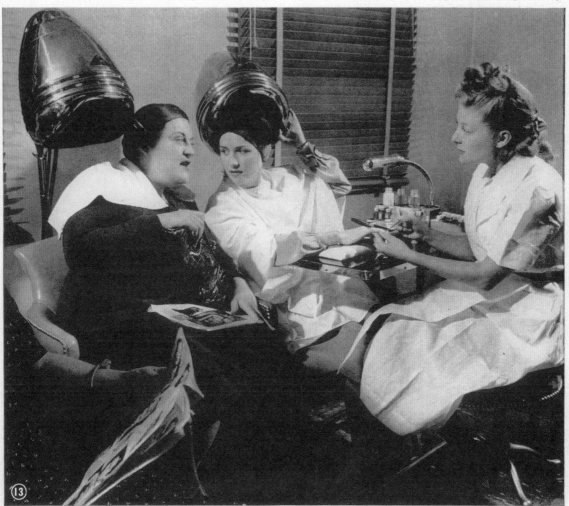

Next morning, the plumpish member of the bridge club makes her regular weekly visit to one of Zenith's beauty parlors. An ardent gossip, she can hardly wait to get out of the drier and tell her friend and the manicurist the "news" she heard the day before. "My dear, have you heard about the troopships sailing for Australia? Yes, my dear, they're going out at midnight Friday—lots of them. I'll bet General MacArthur'll be glad to hear about this. Don't you think it would be thrilling to go down to the docks Friday night and watch them leave!"

CONTINUED ON NEXT PAGE

14 At the Friendship Cafe the manicurist tells her boy friend: "A customer told me today that lots of our troopships are sailing to Australia on Friday at midnight." The shady-looking man standing next to them listens attentively. (Note bartender played by Alfred Hitchcock, *center*).

15 The mysterious man, whose ears were even more attentive than the manicurist's boy friend, leaves the cafe, remembering these important words: "Troopships . . . Australia . . . Friday at midnight." His business is to check all rumors, not pass them along for social conversation.

16 A midnight rendezvous is held by the mysterious man, an Axis agent, with a U-boat officer and seaman who have paddled ashore in a small rubber boat. In a dark cove, the secret military information the haberdasher so innocently revealed to his family at last reaches the enemy.

17 "How does the enemy find out about these ships?" exclaims the irate Zenith haberdasher, who habitually rejects all rumors, as his morning paper tells him what happened to the troopship aboard which was the young lieutenant who bought the dozen tropical shirts (*see opposite page*).

72

Shadow of a Doubt

1942

United States · 1 hr 48 · Black and White · Mono (Western Electric Recording) · 1.37:1

Production: Universal Pictures
Producer: Jack H. Skirball

Production Dates: July 31–October 28, 1942
Release Date in the United States: January 15, 1943

Based on an original story by Gordon McDonell
Screenplay: Thornton Wilder, Sally Benson, Alma Reville
Director of Photography: Joseph Valentine
Visual Effects: John P. Fulton
Sound: Bernard B. Brown
Assistant Director: William Tummel
Script: Adele Cannon
Artistic Directors: John B. Goodman, Robert Boyle
Set Decoration: Russell A. Gausman
Costumes: Vera West, Adrian (for Teresa Wright)
Music: Dimitri Tiomkin
Film Editing: Milton Carruth

Starring: Teresa Wright (Charlie Newton), Joseph Cotten (Charlie Oakley), Macdonald Carey (Jack Graham), Henry Travers (Joseph Newton), Patricia Collinge (Emma Newton), Hume Cronyn (Herbie Hawkins), Wallace Ford (Fred Saunders), Edna May Wonacott (Ann Newton), Charles Bates (Roger Newton), Irving Bacon (stationmaster), Clarence Muse (Pullman porter), Janet Shaw (Louise Finch), Estelle Jewell (Catherine), Alfred Hitchcock (bridge player, seen from behind, on the train)...

> "You look at your beloved uncle long enough, and eventually you find something."

Alfred Hitchcock

SYNOPSIS

Pursued by the police, Charles Oakley is one of two suspects wanted for the serial murders of wealthy widows. He takes refuge with his sister, Emma Newton, who is married to a bank clerk and is the mother of three children. The family lives in Santa Rosa, a peaceful California town—too peaceful, according to the eldest, Charlie. Uncle Charlie announces his arrival just as young Charlie is about to write to him, begging for a visit. This coincidence reinforces her belief that she has a special, telepathic relationship with him, inscribed in their shared first name. Uncle Newton's impromptu visit awakens the Newton family from its torpor, and the household becomes happily active. They are even selected by a journalist, accompanied by a photographer, eager to show the daily life of an average American family. But the visitors are none other than two policemen looking for the fugitive. The so-called journalist finally reveals his identity and the purpose of his visit to young Charlie, who investigates on her own, knocking the beloved figure off his pedestal. The young woman becomes suspicious and distant. Uncle Charlie knows he has been found out. He plots a series of domestic accidents aimed at eliminating his niece. The loving complicity turns into a bitter confrontation. On the train that is supposed to take Uncle Charlie away from Santa Rosa, their farewell turns into a fight to the death. The man perishes with his secret: More than anything else in the world, young Charlie wants to keep intact the idealized image her mother has always had of her beloved brother.

GENESIS

In the midst of filming *Saboteur*, Alfred Hitchcock was already thinking about the next film he would deliver to producer Jack H. Skirball for Universal Studios. Several adaptation projects were on the table, but—faced with the difficulty of obtaining the rights to a novel he was interested in—the filmmaker returned to an idea he had been working on for a long time: shooting a modern version of *The Lodger* (1926).

The Birth of Uncle Charlie

Knowing that Hitchcock wanted to shoot a crime story, the head of the literary department at David O. Selznick's production company, Margaret McDonell, invited him to lunch. She made several suggestions, and the filmmaker's choice fell on the adaptation of an unpublished text entitled *The Ventriloquist*, the story of a bigamist artist who murders his wife and, haunted by his crime, confuses his second wife with his first. Selznick considered the story too strange, but some traces of *The Ventriloquist* (notably the second wife's fall from a cliff) were to be found in *Vertigo* (1957). The solution finally came from Margaret McDonell's husband, mystery and adventure writer Gordon McDonell, who remembered a story he had devised in 1938 when his car broke down, which he felt would appeal to the filmmaker.

On May 5, 1942, the two men had lunch together. Shortly afterward, the writer entrusted the filmmaker with a six-page draft, which the latter entitled *Uncle Charlie*. It is the story of a widow killer who, to escape the police, takes refuge in his sister's family but is soon unmasked by his favorite niece. In this first version, a dual relationship—a recurring Hitchcock motif—is already suggested between the uncle and his niece Charlotte, whom everyone calls Charlie.

A Labyrinthine Contract

Convinced that he should proceed with the project, Hitchcock set to work, but he first had to solve a major problem. This new film for Universal prevented him from fulfilling a clause stipulating that he must deliver two titles a year to Selznick International. Jack Skirball negotiated with David O. Selznick for eighteen weeks to secure Hitchcock's services. Under the terms of a labyrinthine contract, Skirball finally extended the filmmaker's availability to Universal until autumn 1942, and wrote Selznick a check for $150,000.

Any Resemblance to Real Events...

As with many Englishmen, Alfred Hitchcock's childhood was steeped in crime stories, which were to become a lifelong source of ideas and influences for his style. In the filmmaker's head, which was teeming with trivia, the criminal plot of Gordon McDonell's novel immediately echoed a famous case from the 1920s: the trial of Earle Leonard Nelson, a serial killer who murdered several married women across the United States. Hitchcock was also thinking of another lady-killer, Henri Désiré Landru, to whom Chaplin dedicated a film in 1947, *Monsieur Verdoux*. The two killers, the Hitchcockian and the Chaplinesque, share a fiercely misanthropic worldview that serves as an excuse for all their crimes.

A Quiet Little Town

Not wishing to interrupt the writing of his novel in progress, Gordon McDonell discontinued his collaboration with the filmmaker. On May 11, 1942, Alma and Alfred Hitchcock took over, writing three pages of "Notes on a possible development of the *Uncle Charlie* story for a screenplay." McDonell had specified that the plot was set in a "typical American small town" with "small people leading small, unimportant lives." Hitchcock was wary of indulging in a stereotypical treatment of the town and its inhabitants. His aim was to film a traditional town traversed by modernity, "movies, radio, jukeboxes, etc.; in other words, so to speak, small-town life lit up by neon signs."[1] As for the characters, throughout the writing process and right up to filming, he continually added to their complexity.

Modernizing the Screenplay

Hitchcock, working for the first time in ten years without his loyal collaborator, screenwriter Joan Harrison, set out to find "the best writer and connoisseur of American culture available." Miriam Howell, Samuel Goldwyn's literary agent in New York, suggested Thornton Wilder, known for his hit play *Our Town* (1938, Pulitzer Prize). Hitchcock admired Wilder's depiction of a bucolic New England town as told by its cemetery dead, and wrote to him.

Hitchcock–Wilder: Cordial Colleagues

In Los Angeles, Alfred Hitchcock and Thornton Wilder wrote a first draft of the screenplay for *Shadow of a Doubt* for a month beginning May 21, 1942. The novelist wrote to a journalist friend: "I am deeply interested in the film we are working on. Mr. Hitchcock and I get on very well. In long conversations, we concoct new plot twists, then stare at each other in a stunned silence that means, 'Do you think we can do this to them?'" In the opening credits, Hitchcock thanks Thornton Wilder for his contribution to the preparation of the film. Hitchcock would explain, "I did this because I had been moved by the qualities of this man."

Wilder was enthusiastic about the idea of working for the filmmaker but had only a month before he had to join army intelligence. Wilder met Hitchcock in Hollywood, and the two soon began working together. However, he confided to a journalist friend that he found the subject "corny." Hitchcock wanted to modernize McDonell's original script and write a striking opening. Wilder suggested preceding the uncle's arrival in the small town with a prelude showing the criminal holed up in a New Jersey boardinghouse and hunted by two detectives. The idea came from Hemingway's short story *The Killers* (1927), which opens in much the same way. The two men talked all day and exchanged stimulating ideas. This professional atmosphere of mutual respect and enjoyment of working together prevailed right up until the filming.

The Wilder Effect

With Wilder's pen, all the characters became more sympathetic, witty, and profound. We find nothing of McDonell's description of Uncle Charlie's sister as a "pushy, semi-invalid" woman. Wilder also excelled in depicting everyday scenes of family life. The small provincial town takes on a life of its own, becoming a character in its own right. At the end of May 1942, Wilder and Hitchcock had a thirty-page text and stopped work to go on location scouting with Skirball and Robert Boyle, the artistic director, in Santa Rosa, a small town of thirteen thousand inhabitants in Northern California. Hitchcock took advantage of a wartime government restriction capping the cost of building sets with new materials at $5,000 per

Hollywood film. On location, he convinced his producer to shoot the exteriors and some interiors of *Shadow of a Doubt* in Santa Rosa.

Back in Hollywood, Wilder and Hitchcock were preparing to turn their notes into a screenplay when, on June 24, the writer was forced to return to his military duties. Hitchcock confided that he was still not entirely satisfied with the script and wanted to hire a new writer. Far from being offended, Wilder understood the filmmaker's decision. His obsession remained the same: to flesh out the characters even more and make the old-fashioned aspect of the film disappear completely.

The Autobiographical Shadow

Hitchcock had returned to work alone when bad news arrived from England: His brother William informed him of their mother's condition and of her refusal to be treated in a hospital. Because he absolutely had to make progress on the script, and because it was not easy to travel to war-torn England in the summer of 1942, Hitchcock stayed in California. The constrained choice gave him a permanent feeling of guilt and anxiety. This autobiographical fact, the decline of his own mother, profoundly influenced the writing of the project and the way in which Hitchcock constantly enriched the character of the mother, who, like his own, was named Emma. It was perhaps at this precise moment that *Shadow of a Doubt* became his most personal film, intimately and secretly shaped by his own emotions.

Stroboscopic photograph by Gjon Mili (Teresa Wright and Joseph Cotten re-enacting an argument scene from *Shadow of a Doubt*), published in *Life*, 1942.

The Final Touch

Although the film tells the story of a serial killer, Hitchcock was nevertheless keen to instill a certain humor into his script. In New York, he met Sally Benson, author of the hugely successful *Junior Miss* (1941), a collection of short stories about the extravagances of a twelve-year-old girl. Her verve and talent for depicting the world of childhood added a new tone to the script. A total of five people worked on *Shadow of a Doubt*, and even six, since actress Patricia Collinge, who played Emma Newton, amended certain scenes and eliminated any trace of silliness from her character.

CASTING

To play Uncle Charlie, Hitchcock first considered William Powell, under contract to Metro-Goldwyn-Mayer, but the studio refused to loan him out, wishing to preserve his image as a likable man. The director also considered Joan Fontaine for the role of young Charlie but decided that he wanted to cast her older sister, Olivia de Havilland, who was also unavailable.

In Search of Two Charlies

Hitchcock did not have his cast when he began shooting the first outdoor scenes in New Jersey with local performers. To play his criminal hero, he finally chose Joseph Cotten, a new recruit from the Selznick stable who had made his film debut in *Too Much Johnson* (1938), then in Orson Welles's *Citizen Kane* (1941), and who had just completed *The Magnificent Ambersons* for the same director. Cotten was reluctant to take on the role of such a negative character, but Hitchcock, with his unique sense of persuasion and talent as a narrator, managed to convince him. For young Charlie, he finally settled on Teresa Wright. The actress had just been nominated for an Oscar for her portrayal of Bette Davis's daughter in William Wyler's *The Little Foxes* and had also appeared on Broadway in Thornton Wilder's play *Our Town*.

Secondary Roles

For the parents' characters, Hitchcock cast stage and screen actors Henry Travers and Patricia Collinge, who also appeared in the credits of Wyler's film. He also cast Santa Rosa residents in small roles, with Edna May Wonacott as Charlie's little sister, a grocer's daughter whose store reminded him of his father's. The casting was completed in July.

FILMING AND PRODUCTION

On July 30, 1942, the Hitchcock family visited Santa Rosa. All of them described a happy family atmosphere on the set of *Shadow of a Doubt*. This was in stark contrast to the anguish and unease that gripped the filmmaker, who was obliged to continue

A Touch of Humor?

In 1969, Hitchcock met an audience at London's National Film Theatre. Asked by an audience member, "Why have you never made a comedy?" Hitchcock replied, "But every film I make is a comedy."

filming while his mother was dying far away. The news from England was increasingly worrying: Mrs. Hitchcock's health was worsening, and war was tearing her country apart.

Dualities

At the heart of the film is the guilt that disrupts a carefree world. The uncle is the embodiment of a nightmare that forces the niece to leave behind the dreamworld of childhood. The twinship between the two Charlies is entirely suggested by the way the filmmaker presents them: from the outset, the same wide shot of their respective towns gradually narrows in on the façades of the houses, then on the windows, before penetrating inside the rooms (the filmmaker would repeat this progression at the opening of *Psycho*, 1960). Hitchcock then "captures" the "twins" in the same position: lying fully clothed on their beds, musing, eyes on the ceiling. Aptly described by François Truffaut in his book of interviews with the Master, the notion of doubles pervades the entire film: two detectives, two young children, two doctors, two cognacs, two women with glasses, two attempts on young Charlie's life, two scenes in the garage, a bar called the 'Til-Two (open until 2 a.m.)…

A Layered Film

This systematic and partly imperceptible doubling reveals itself in the image of the film, which, under the very simple guise of a painting of provincial life, conceals several levels of reading, several tonalities: thriller, even "film noir" (though the genre and expression did not yet exist), romance, a family story tinged with a comedy of manners, even a vampire film. Indeed, the first image of Uncle Charlie stretched out on the bed might evoke a Nosferatu asleep in his coffin. Other details, such as his refusal to allow himself to be photographed, point in this direction. All these strata of the story blend into one another, reflecting the collective and profoundly harmonious writing process. Similarly, *Shadow of a Doubt* has all the hallmarks of a Hitchcock film: guilt, evil, innocence, suspicion, the evil and angelic double all rolled into one.

A World Re-Created

The film reveals a quiet technical mastery, as exemplified by the ability to alternate shooting on location and, after a month spent in Santa Rosa, shooting at Universal Studios. Here, the film's artistic directors performed a feat of replicating certain parts of the

For Hitchcock Addicts

For *Shadow of a Doubt*, Alfred Hitchcock rehired Saboteur's cinematographer, Joseph Valentine, and hired a Russian composer, Dimitri Tiomkin, for the music. Both would work with the Master again (Joseph Valentine for *Rope*, Dimitri Tiomkin for *Strangers on a Train*, *I Confess*, and *Dial M for Murder*).

Newtons' home, which had become a sort of "disassemblable" house. The film is intended to be realistic, and the director had, as usual, an extremely precise vision of each shot. He achieved a number of technical and formal feats, notably a very complex and rapid camera movement that ended in a close-up during the scene in which the uncle announces his departure.

As is rarely the case in his filmography, Hitchcock focused on the everyday life of a town, its buildings, its nightlife (the scene in the seedy bar), its youth. And his view of the town was tinged with a tender melancholy, as if he sought, in what is often considered one of his very first typically American films, to reconstruct childhood memories, to create a world immersed in innocence but not so for much longer. After Wilder's departure, he wrote: "I keep remembering those things—all those old things…Everybody was good and kind, so the whole world was like that. A wonderful world. Not like today's world, not like the one we know. Being young in those days, that was something."[2]

RECEPTION

The filming and release of *Shadow of a Doubt* consolidated the filmmaker's relationship with the American press and public. For the first time, journalists were invited to follow the shooting and interview Hitchcock, who was already renowned for his witty commentaries. Unusually, promotion of a film began well before its release, a strategy sponsored by Universal's publicity department, then considered

Freeze Frame

In a crane shot at the public library, the camera rises high after the niece, suddenly "crushed," discovers in the newspaper the true identity of the man she had adored until then. On the ground, the shadow of the young girl (Teresa Wright) lengthens as she becomes more aware of the progress of evil in the world. The divorce between the two Charlies is consummated while the film's music accelerates like that of a merry-go-round running out of control.

A Personal Film

In 1964, a journalist on a Canadian TV program (*Telescope: A Talk with Hitchcock*) remarked to Hitchcock that critics had always considered *Shadow of a Doubt* to be his best film, to which the filmmaker replied, "So did I." Throughout his career, from one interview to the next, he would confirm this preference. No doubt this was a way for him to direct the gaze of critics and audiences toward his most personal film, which is both warm and tormented.

one of the best in Hollywood. Reporters from *Life*, the *New York Times*, and Los Angeles and San Francisco newspapers, as well as representatives of press agencies, visited the set to meet the real star: Hitchcock himself, who switched between directing and press interviews with a disconcerting ease. This was the beginning of the growing fame of an artist in the United States who no longer hesitated to use his own image to promote his films.

"Americana"

Released in January 1943, *Shadow of a Doubt* was a critical and popular success. The press was sensitive to the fact that Hitchcock had made a film for American audiences, an "Americana" in his own way. With this suspenseful tale set in the context of a meticulous observation of an ordinary American town and family, Hitchcock had definitely succeeded in making his mark. According to *Variety*, he "engraves in our memory the characters of this small town and this warm setting" (December 31, 1942). *Film Daily* called him "a master of suspense and a magician of mystery" whose film is "made to thrill American audiences and fill the coffers of U.S. theaters" (January 8, 1943). Bosley Crowther, in the *New York Times*, emphasized the implacable effectiveness of the filmmaker's direction, which "can raise more goose pimples to the square inch of a customer's flesh than any other director of thrillers in Hollywood" (January 13, 1943). The most laudatory words certainly came from the project's initiator.

Gordon McDonell, who previewed the film, then wrote an enthusiastic letter to Hitchcock: "I have very seldom seen a film that ceases to be one, where you forget you are sitting in a cinema, completely transported into the life projected on the screen. I have never had such an experience watching a film about a killer. I sincerely believe you have created a masterpiece."[3]

Uncle Hitchcock

The filmmaker films a lost world, laden with his own memories, and scatters a little of himself into all the characters: the little brother obsessed with problems of logic and arithmetic; the youngest daughter, who spends her time reading, in particular *Ivanhoe*, which Hitchcock himself devoured as a child; and the neighbor and father fascinated by macabre stories. But it is perhaps by blending the personalities of the two Charlies that we obtain a fairly accurate idea of the filmmaker's inner world: Hitchcock shares with Uncle Charlie, in addition to a disillusioned vision of the world, the same childhood bicycle accident that left him with an imperceptible scar on his chin. There is also something of the young Hitchcock in the young Charlie, constantly worried about her mother (her first words in the film) and trying to protect her from a shocking discovery. Emma Newton is gentle, kind, innocent—in a word, ideal—like a final tribute to Emma Hitchcock, the filmmaker's mother, who died on September 26, 1942, one month before the end of filming.

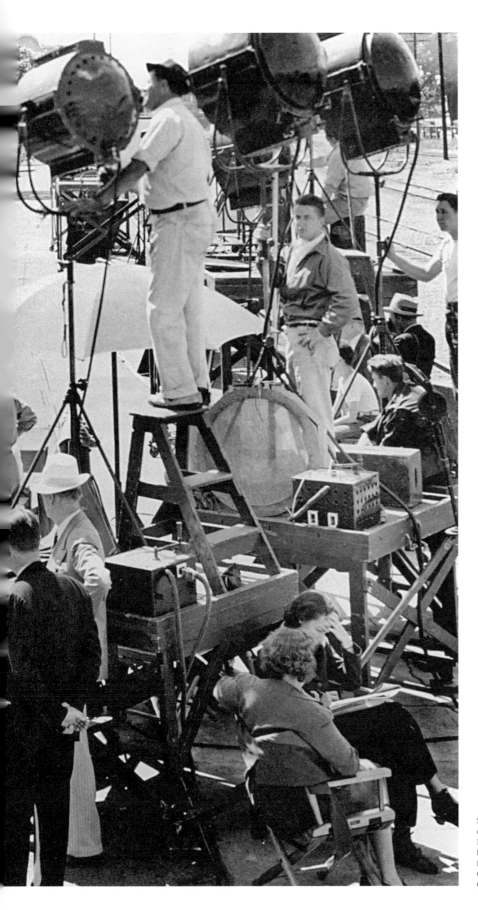

Summer 1942, on location. Hitchcock, center, directs Teresa Wright, Edna May Wonacott, Henry Travers, and Charles Bates for a scene from the beginning of the film: The Newton family comes to greet Uncle Charlie (Joseph Cotten) at the real train station in Santa Rosa, California.

ALFRED HITCHCOCK'S
production of
LIFEBOAT
by JOHN STEINBECK
starring
TALLULAH
BANKHEAD
WITH
William BENDIX ★ Walter SLEZAK ★ Mary ANDERSON
John HODIAK ★ Henry HULL ★ Heather ANGEL
Hume CRONYN ★ Canada LEE
DIRECTED BY ALFRED HITCHCOCK
PRODUCED BY KENNETH MACGOWAN
SCREEN PLAY BY JO SWERLING
20th CENTURY-FOX PICTURE
THIS POSTER IS THE PROPERTY OF THE TWENTIETH CENTURY-FOX FILM CORP. IT IS LEASED-NOT SOLD. COPYRIGHT 1943 BY TWENTIETH CENTURY-FOX FILM CORP.
TOOKER LITHO. CO. N.Y.

Lifeboat

1943

United States • 1 hr 37 • Black and White • Mono (Western Electric Recording) • 1.37:1

Production Dates: August 3–November 17, 1943
Release Date in the United States: January 28, 1944

Production: 20th Century-Fox
Producer: Kenneth Macgowan
Executive Producer: Darryl F. Zanuck, William Goetz

Based on an idea by Alfred Hitchcock and a story by John Steinbeck
Screenplay: Jo Swerling
Technical Adviser: Thomas Fitzsimmons (The National Maritime Union)
Director of Photography: Glen MacWilliams
Camera Operator: Paul Lockwood
Special Effects: Edwin Hammeras, James Curtis Havens
Visual Effects: Fred Sersen
Sound: Bernard Freericks, Roger Heman
Assistant Director: Saul Wurtzel
Artistic Directors: James Basevi, Maurice Ransford
Set Decoration: Thomas Little, Frank E. Hughes
Makeup: Guy Pearce
Costumes: René Hubert
Music: Hugo W. Friedhofer
Film Editing: Dorothy Spencer

Starring: Tallulah Bankhead (Connie Porter), William Bendix (Gus Smith), Walter Slezak (Willi), Mary Anderson (Alice MacKenzie), John Hodiak (John Kovac), Henry Hull (Charles Rittenhouse), Hume Cronyn (Stanley Garrett), Canada Lee (Joe Spencer), Heather Angel (Mrs. Higley), William Yetter Jr. (young German sailor), Alfred Hitchcock (in a photo in the newspaper)...

SYNOPSIS

———

At the height of World War II, after the torpedoing of an American liner by a German submarine, nine survivors find themselves on a lifeboat lost in the middle of the Atlantic. From very different social backgrounds and with different political sensibilities, they must learn to live together and survive, or die, like the woman who went mad after losing her child. Added to this dramatic situation is the disruptive presence of Willi, a German sailor from the submarine's crew. Suspicious, the castaways decide to keep him on board and keep a close eye on him. But they need him, as the German seems to be the only one able to steer the boat, and his medical knowledge enables him to save the life of Gus, a sailor whose gangrenous leg has to be amputated. Following a storm, the passengers lose all their provisions. Willi takes advantage of Gus's state of delirium, inducing him to throw himself overboard. Although friendships are made and couples formed, tension reigns among the exhausted crew, who gradually realize that the German is manipulating them and deliberately leading them in the wrong direction. By mutual agreement, they decide to eliminate him by throwing him out of the dinghy. Just as their cause seems hopeless, a German ship appears on the horizon, fortunately followed by an Allied vessel, which sinks the enemy ship. This is the end of the ordeal for the survivors of the shipwreck.

"I give *Lifeboat* ten days to get out of town."

———

Dorothy Thompson, in the *New York Herald Tribune*

GENESIS

Even before making *Shadow of a Doubt* (1942), Alfred Hitchcock had been thinking about a film that would "take place entirely in and around a lifeboat"—a real technical challenge, since the whole story would be filmed in the smallest possible area. He spoke to producer Jack H. Skirball, who was less than enthusiastic about the idea, anticipating the laborious writing work that lay ahead. The Master also tried to convince producer David O. Selznick, but to no avail.

A German on Board

Having just been hired by 20th Century-Fox, Hitchcock discussed his idea with William Goetz, one of the studio's founders. The filmmaker specified his desire for an allegorical film expressing his ambivalent feelings toward Germany, symbolized by the presence on board of a manipulative German. Hitchcock wanted to make him a fascinating, ambiguous character, both leader and enemy of humanity. Since his youth, he had been fascinated by German culture, particularly expressionist cinema, but also by Germany's "aggressivity." At the time of the *Lifeboat* project, Hitler's war was at its height.

John Steinbeck at the Helm

William Goetz, who was interested in the story, asked Kenneth Macgowan, a producer under contract to Fox, to approach Hitchcock. An educated man, Harvard graduate, and former theater critic, Macgowan had worked with directors such as John Ford and Fritz Lang. He helped Hitchcock sketch out an initial treatment and flesh out the characters.

Encouraged by his fruitful collaboration with author Thornton Wilder on *Shadow of a Doubt*, the filmmaker wanted to work again with a great name in American literature. His choice was Ernest Hemingway, but the writer was too busy to accept. Hitchcock then set his sights on John Steinbeck (*The Grapes of Wrath*, 1939), a novelist as celebrated as Hemingway. Furthermore, Steinbeck had just completed a novel with a theme similar to *Lifeboat*'s: *The Moon Is Down* (1942), the story of a small European town invaded by a fascist force. Interested, the writer offered to write the text in a weekend. In the end, it turned out to be a novella, which Steinbeck was able to publish under his own name. Hitchcock and Macgowan saw in this collaboration the prospect of excellent publicity for the film.

Two Visions for One Film

Steinbeck began working without a contract and without Hitchcock. By mid-January 1943, he had already written more than a hundred pages. The story is told from the point of view of a single character, a sailor. The novelist also recommended that the whole story be told in flashback. He then went to New York before heading to Europe to work as a war correspondent for the *New York Herald Tribune*. On January 14, the Hitchcock couple joined him in New York to work on the script for two weeks. Steinbeck and Hitchcock had different approaches to the character of the German: Steinbeck's version did not specify whether he was a Nazi or a submarine officer. The writer created an atmosphere of generalized paranoia without ever deciding on the status of this passenger who does not speak a word of English. As for Hitchcock, he imagined that *Lifeboat* was based on a series of betrayals by the man who gradually reveals himself to be the real enemy. Always attentive to the emotional crescendo of his films, he also wanted a finale of great dramatic violence. The two men had different films in mind, and Steinbeck had neither the time nor the inclination to edit his short story to meet the filmmaker's expectations.

In Search of the Ideal Screenwriter

Hitchcock returned to California and began looking for a screenwriter who could embrace his own

style. He met MacKinlay Kantor, author of novels and short stories about America at war, including *Glory for Me*, a novel in free verse that was later adapted into a superb film, *The Best Years of Our Lives* (William Wyler, 1946). Alma Reville and Kantor wrote an introductory scene designed to remind viewers that they were watching fiction: a sailor brings his girlfriend to the cinema before he goes to sea, while the following sequence introduces all the *Lifeboat* characters before the ship is torpedoed. After a fortnight's work, the filmmaker, dissatisfied with this introduction, which delayed the film's action, thanked Kantor.

Hitchcock finally found a rare gem in Jo Swerling, whom Macgowan presented as the best contract screenwriter available. A former journalist and playwright, Swerling arrived in Hollywood in 1929, during the transition from silent movies to talkies. He wrote for Frank Borzage, Rouben Mamoulian, William Wyler, and John Ford. He wrote the final screenplay for *It's a Wonderful Life* (Frank Capra, 1946). A seasoned screenwriter who kept a low profile but was highly respected in the profession, Swerling agreed to take over on the condition that he would not be forced to follow Steinbeck's work, which he felt was too literary to be effective on film.

CASTING

The filmmaker had to choose a cinematographer under contract to Fox, but he was keen to engage Glen MacWilliams, who did not belong to the studio and with whom he had already worked on *Waltzes from Vienna* (1933). MacWilliams created a black-and-white image that combined realism with more stylized moments, such as the scene of the dead child's funeral at sea, filmed entirely against the light to heighten the tragic solemnity of the moment. His impressive work on the film earned him an Oscar nomination for the first time in his career.

A Single Star in the Cast

From the very beginning of the project, Alfred Hitchcock had in mind the actress who would lend her features to Connie Porter, the journalist in the mink coat, the first passenger in the dinghy: It would be Tallulah Bankhead, a huge theater star. The filmmaker knew that Bankhead's presence aboard the dinghy, with her theatrical performance, distinguished bearing, impeccable fingernails, and fur coat, would seem unreal and incongruous.

The other actors in the cast were relatively unknown. Hitchcock suspected that such a strange

Jo Swerling, a Good Advocate for the Master

The only screenwriter to appear in the film's credits, Jo Swerling was a harsh critic of John Steinbeck's work. During his deposition at the novelist's plagiarism trial, he was quick to point out that internationally renowned writers can "mess up" a filmmaker's original idea, while an unknown screenwriter can turn it into a decent screenplay. He also defended Hitchcock with conviction: Every scene, every invention in *Lifeboat*, was due mainly, if not entirely, to the filmmaker.

project would not allow him to approach any major Hollywood stars. Henry Hull, a favorite of American director Raoul Walsh, was chosen to play Rittenhouse. Heather Angel played the mother who loses her baby and throws herself into the sea—Hitchcock had cast her as the maid in *Suspicion*. Mary Anderson, who appeared in *Gone with the Wind*, played Alice, the Red Cross nurse. Canada Lee, seen in plays directed by Orson Welles, was the Black sailor. William Bendix, accustomed to playing the ordinary decent American, was approached to play Gus. For the role of Kovac, who falls in love with Connie, Hitchcock, aware that he would not be able to hire a star like Gary Cooper, chose John Hodiak. Out of friendship for Hume Cronyn, revealed in *Shadow of a Doubt*, Hitchcock cast him in the role of the ship's radio operator. But the most decisive choice concerned the actor who would play Willi: Austrian Walter Slezak, who had just made a name for himself twice as a Nazi (Leo McCarey's *Once Upon a Honeymoon* in 1942 and Jean Renoir's *This Land Is Mine* in 1943), was the ideal actor.

FILMING AND PRODUCTION

When it was time to begin filming *Lifeboat*, difficulties began to mount. Fox boss Darryl Zanuck, who

had been busy on other fronts, discovered that the film had taken a record ten months to prepare and that the script had run up against censors.

OWI Becomes Involved

The Office of War Information highlighted *Lifeboat*'s problems, which were "more serious than any of your screenplays reviewed by our office in years." According to OWI, *Lifeboat* portrayed the group of Americans in an extremely negative light, "presenting an image that Nazi propagandists themselves would like to promote." All the characters were reviewed: Connie Porter was seen as "a selfish, rapacious and immoral international adventurer." Joe, the Black sailor and former pickpocket, who abstains from voting when it comes to deciding the German's fate, suggested that "he is not used to the right to vote and prefers not to exercise it." OWI went further, claiming that the Nazi was *Lifeboat*'s only hero, killed in a fit of mass fury. The scene of the German's assassination is described as an "orgasmic murder."[1] Indeed, Hitchcock later confided that the group of Americans was "like a pack of dogs"[1] at the time. Zanuck, firmly opposed to any idea of censorship, merely informed Hitchcock of the OWI report and sent no official reply to the organization.

Chaos...

Filming began in August 1943 and proved to be a trying experience, especially for the actors.

Hitchcock set himself the challenge of not taking the camera out of the dinghy. *Lifeboat* is thus a sequence of close-ups that enclose the faces and arrange them in relation to one another in striking compositions. The film was shot in a studio, with a dinghy floating in a huge tank; the sky and sea are back-projected, providing a transparent background for the shots. Hitchcock used huge fans and sprinklers to shoot the storm scene over several days. He insisted on keeping the dinghy in perpetual motion using machines to simulate the pitching motion, which meant that the protagonists had to swallow numerous anti-seasickness pills. With the alternation of hot and cold, bathing and drying, several actors fell ill, starting with Tallulah Bankhead, who caught pneumonia. Hume Cronyn testified to the difficult shooting conditions: "We were covered in a kind of sump oil and, at the end of each scene, there was at least an hour's wait to move the camera."[2]

To top it all off, the atmosphere among the cast was execrable, not least because of Tallulah Bankhead, who, true to form, continued to perform outside of the takes. This behavior annoyed the entire cast, starting with Walter Slezak, whom she called a "bloody Nazi" even when not shooting.

...and Mastery

With a plot free of digressions, as the extreme confinement of the dinghy imposes, Hitchcockian tension emerges in its raw state. The way in which Connie is gradually stripped of all her snobbish, city journalist accessories (camera, fur coat, typewriter, bracelet...) is revealing of the filmmaker's project. It is all about telling a Hitchcock-style story, creating a series of tensions with the resources at hand: faces, gestures, words, and staging.

The sequence in which Willi takes advantage of Gus's weakness to push him into the water is a typically Hitchcockian moment. The psychological climax is born of a simple shot–reverse shot cut, the suggestive power of words, and the direction of the actors. Except for the sound of the

For Hitchcock Addicts

Actress Mary Anderson, who gave Hitchcock a hard time on the set of *Lifeboat*, once asked him what he thought her best profile was. The director reportedly replied, "My dear, you're sitting on it"—a bon mot the filmmaker loved to recount...

waves, there is no music to emphasize the danger: the director's maximum efficiency is at its simplest here.

(Almost) No Music

Despite the difficulties Hitchcock encountered throughout the preparation and filming, he managed to give substance to his vision by stripping the film of anything that might have weighed it down: the political speeches of Steinbeck's characters, the opening in a cinema suggested by MacKinlay Kantor, and the traditional film score, which is conspicuous in its absence here. In fact, Hitchcock confines himself to providing music for the opening and closing credits. This radical choice is perfectly in keeping with the *Lifeboat* project: Far from civilization, the plot is also stripped bare, despite the producer's inclination to provide musical accompaniment for certain romantic scenes.

At the end of 1943, Darryl Zanuck authorized Hitchcock to travel to England to make two short propaganda films in praise of the French Resistance, *Bon voyage* and *Aventure malgache*. Alma Reville, who remained in the US, supervised the postproduction of *Lifeboat*, including Hugo W. Friedhofer's composition, directed by Emil Newman, for this almost music-free film.

RECEPTION

Zanuck viewed a first cut and found *Lifeboat* to be outstanding. He wanted to retain the director at 20th

Where Is Hitchcock?

In early 1943, Alfred Hitchcock learned of the death of his elder brother, William, six months after that of his mother. Worried about his own state of health, he embarked on a drastic diet to lose ninety pounds in record time—he weighed more than three hundred pounds at the time. The filmmaker turned this challenge into a game: Two photographs of his physique, before and after his weight loss, illustrate an advertisement for a slimming diet in a newspaper read by one of the characters in *Lifeboat*. Hitchcock thereby brilliantly solved the problem of his traditional appearance in a plot set entirely aboard a dinghy lost at sea.

Century-Fox. But he found himself somewhat out on his own in his unreserved praise of the film...

Polemic and Controversy

Lifeboat premiered in New York on January 11, 1944, while Hitchcock was still in England. The film was very well received by American audiences but provoked enormous controversy among critics. Dorothy Thompson of the *New York Herald Tribune* had harsh words for the film: "The film happens to be, from the point of direction and entertainment, brilliant," but "it is a film which, translated into German, could be presented in Berlin as a morale-builder for the Nazi's war, with only minor changes" (January 31, 1944). Although critics were receptive to the film's technical virtuosity, they were generally repelled by its exaltation of the ideal of the superman. In an initial article for the *New York Times*, Bosley Crowther conceded that "Mr. Hitchcock and Mr. Steinbeck—plus Jo Swerling, who rigged the script—have turned out a consistently exciting and technically brilliant drama of the sea" (January 13, 1944). But in another article devoted to *Lifeboat*, he saw it as a film that "sold out the democratic ideal and elevated the Nazi 'superman'" (January 23, 1944). Readers were invited to debate the film in the newspaper's columns.

This polemic was coupled with a controversy over the film's true authorship: Some attributed it to Steinbeck, others to Hitchcock. The writer, who did not recognize his work, unsuccessfully demanded that his name be removed from the credits, deeming the film "dangerous to the American war effort" and criticizing Hitchcock's treatment of the character of the Black sailor.[3]

None of this prevented *Lifeboat* from being nominated in several categories at the Oscars, or Tallulah Bankhead from receiving an award for her performance from the New York Film Critics Circle.

Ambiguity in Wartime

In the end, Hitchcock was criticized for not making an American propaganda film during wartime. *Lifeboat* assimilates the German, if not to the level of a "superman," at least to a man of strong character, reserving human weaknesses for the American side.

From One Joe to Another

On *Lifeboat*'s release, John Steinbeck received a letter from the National Association for the Advancement of Colored People (NAACP), complaining about the stereotypical treatment of Joe, the Black sailor played by Canada Lee. Steinbeck agreed. In his version, Joe is a heroic character who saves the lives of three people as he is about to be executed; he is also a nonbeliever. In the film, Joe is portrayed as a highly religious former pickpocket.

The enemy embodied by Willi possesses qualities that the ship's other passengers lack, and they find themselves, in many ways, dependent on him. Instead of drawing a clear line between good and evil, Hitchcock, as usual, prefers to reveal the ambiguity of people and situations. He chooses to film evil not as a problem that is immediately identified and easily dismissed, but as a formidable force that advances in disguise and manipulates individuals as it sees fit. While *Lifeboat*'s passengers allow themselves to be deceived one by one, it is by organizing themselves collectively that they overcome the dangerous Nazi. The moral of the story, according to Hitchcock, ignored at the time because of the passionate context, lies in the Allies' obligation to put aside their personal interests in order to work together, a sine qua non for standing up to Nazism.

Group portrait: the leg of William Bendix, John Hodiak, Walter Slezak, Hume Cronyn, Tallulah Bankhead, Heather Angel, Mary Anderson, Henry Hull.

Bon voyage

 Great Britain · **26 min**
French-language film,
subtitled in English · **Black and White** · **Mono**
(RCA Sound System) · ▱ **1.37:1**

SYNOPSIS

Production Dates: End January–
end February 1944

Production: Ministry of Information
(MOI), Phoenix Films
Producer: Sidney Bernstein

Screenplay: V. S. Pritchett,
Angus MacPhail, J. O. C. Orton
Dialogue Adviser: Claude Dauphin
Consultant: Arthur Calder-Marshall
Director of Photography:
Günther Krampf
Art Direction: J. Charles Gilbert
Music: Benjamin Frankel
Film Editing: Alan Osbiston
Starring: John Blythe (RAF Sergeant
John Dougall), Janique Joelle (Jeanne)…

**RAF Sergeant:
Au revoir,
Mademoiselle,
j'espère beaucoup
que je vous revoie.
[Farewell,
mademoiselle, I very
much hope that we
meet again.]**

**Jeanne:
Adieu, RAF. Bon
voyage!**

In London, in 1943, Sergeant John Dougall of the Royal Air Force, who has escaped from Germany, is questioned about the conditions of his journey by a French officer from the Deuxième Bureau. Dougall recalls (first flashback) his journey through occupied France, the help of the French Resistance, and his formidable escape companion, a certain Godowski. The French officer takes up the same story and reveals (second flashback) that Godowski was in fact a Gestapo agent charged with infiltrating a Resistance network and having Dougall carry a letter to a spy on English soil.

A Return to London

Having just finished shooting *Lifeboat*, Hitchcock traveled to England, staying in London from early December 1943 to late February 1944. He felt the need to contribute in his own way to the Allied war effort and to experience the atmosphere in Europe, as he saw himself as an Englishman exiled in Hollywood.

Writing a Propaganda Film

The filmmaker seized on Sidney Bernstein's offer to come and shoot first one, then two propaganda films: *Bon voyage* and *Aventure malgache*, made in French and intended for French-speaking territories that were either not occupied or progressively being liberated. A former acquaintance of the Film Society, an avant-garde film club of the 1920s, Bernstein held an important position in the film department of the Ministry of Information during the conflict. Hitchcock recalls that he made the trip in a bomber, "sitting on the floor." To recover from his rough journey between New York and London, he stayed at the Claridge. It was in his hotel room that the screenplay for *Bon voyage* was devised by several people, a script developed by writer V. S. Pritchett (who, twenty years later, would contribute to the screenplay for *The Birds*) and by Angus MacPhail, also a friend of the filmmaker's from his Film Society days. The aim of *Bon voyage* was to pay tribute to the French Resistance and to alert it to the techniques used by the enemy to infiltrate its networks.

A Cast Kept Secret

With the exception of John Blythe and Janique Joelle, two young English performers, most of the cast is made up of French actors who had taken refuge in London and whose names are not credited for security reasons. They are only mentioned in the credits as "French-speaking artists serving in Great Britain."

Far from MGM

Bon voyage and *Aventure malgache* were shot at a small studio in Welwyn, Hertfordshire. As early as October 29, 1943, in a letter, MacPhail was careful to prepare Hitchcock for the precarious shooting conditions, far from the Hollywood glitz he was now familiar with: "The pictures will not be costly; far from it. Production facilities, as you can guess, are not exactly facile. The time factor is important, so they'll have to be made pretty fast...This certainly isn't meant to scare you off the project; Sidney merely feels that it would be unfair to let you arrive under the impression that we are operating on an M.G.M. basis."[1]

A Handmade Film

To save time and money, and do the best he could with the resources available, Hitchcock drew up a storyboard as if it were one of his own feature films. He also left precise editing instructions before his departure. In fact, *Bon voyage* is a carefully crafted film including all the signature Hitchcock features: nocturnal atmospheres and shadow effects (the cinematographer had worked in Germany in the 1920s, in particular on F. W. Murnau's *Nosferatu*), eerie settings (ruins, a cellar)... The filmmaker's flashback structure enabled him to tell the same story twice, the second time proving to be a counterinvestigation that thwarts the hitherto unseen lies of the first story (Hitchcock repeated this play on points of view in "Incident at a Corner," 1960). *Bon voyage* is not lacking in humor either, as evidenced by the first sentence uttered by the English sergeant in a film intended for a French audience: "Excuse me, monsieur, French tobacco makes me cough."

Murder on the Telephone

The most striking scene comes at the end: the execution of Jeanne, the young French Resistance fighter, by the undercover Gestapo agent. As she telephones to unmask the enemy, he enters the scene: With his left hand he points a revolver at her, and with his right hand he grabs the handset. He waits—time stands still—then fires. She screams in a close-up, collapses in a wider shot, and disappears from the frame while the murderer still holds the handset and hangs up. Hitchcock adds a sordid detail: He inserts a shot of the victim's pretty wristwatch, which the killer takes off her body while making a phone call to her contact.

Circulation

Some screenings are known to have taken place in liberated Paris in October 1944; others apparently took place in September or October 1945. The film may also have circulated in Belgium. Hitchcock liked *Bon voyage* so much that he had this wartime work screened for him in 1958, when he was writing *North by Northwest* and had to resolve certain screenplay difficulties (the film alludes to a Gestapo method used in *Bon voyage*: the elimination of one of their own so as to pretend to be on the adversary's side). The filmmaker apparently briefly planned to remake this short film as a full-length feature.

Aventure malgache

🏴 **Great Britain** • 🕐 **32 min** French-language film, subtitled in English • 🎞 **Black and White** • 🔇 **Mono** (RCA Sound System) • ▭ **1.37:1**

SYNOPSIS

Production Dates: End January–end February 1944

Release Date in Great Britain: First public projection, September 3, 1993, Everyman Cinema (Hampstead, London)

Production: Ministry of Information (MOI), Phoenix Films

Producer: Sidney Bernstein

Screenplay: Jules François Clermont, Angus MacPhail

Dialogue Adviser: Claude Dauphin

Consultant: Jacques Brunius, Arthur Calder-Marshall

Director of Photography: Günther Krampf

Art Direction: J. Charles Gilbert

Film Editing: Alan Osbiston

Performance (Théâtre Molière / Molière Players): Jules François Clermont / Paul Clarus (Clarousse), Paul Bonifas (Jean Michel), Jean Dattas (man reading a telegram), André Frère (Pierrot), Paulette Preney (Yvonne), Guy Le Feuvre (general).

"The chestnuts will ripen on April 35."

Coded Resistance telegram, *Aventure malgache*

In 1944 London, a group of French actors prepare in a theater dressing room. One of them, Paul Clarus (as himself), tells his story. Flashback: In 1940, as a lawyer in Madagascar, an island in the French colonial empire, he opposed Jean Michel, head of the security forces and a collaborator. Imprisoned for acts of resistance, he was sent to prison by Michel. But the Royal Navy attacked the ship carrying him. Once freed, Clarus sent radio messages to Madagascar urging it, in all the island's languages, to choose the Allied camp. In May 1942, the British Army liberated the Madagascan colony.

War Effort

An American resident for more than four years, at the end of 1943 Hitchcock felt a compelling need to participate in the British war effort against the Axis powers. So he answered the call of Sidney Bernstein, an old acquaintance who held an important position in the film department of the British Ministry of Information. Bernstein's brief was to produce propaganda films for continental Europe as liberation approached and, in the case of two films to be directed by Hitchcock, to praise (in French) the French Resistance in France and the colonies.

A Cultural Melting Pot

In early December 1943, Hitchcock returned to London for three months. Although the subject of *Bon voyage*, another short film he was to make during the same period, had already been partly written before his arrival, the director seemed to have found the subject for *Aventure malgache* only during work sessions at the Claridge, his hotel. Surrounded by officers of the Free French forces, he noted their differences; twenty years later, he would even remember a certain Forestier, who systematically disagreed with the others. It was these divisions within the same camp that gave Hitchcock the idea for the film, as well as the true story of the adventures of a strong-willed character, Jules François Clermont, alias Paul Clarus, his stage name.

An Actor in His Own Story

As a lawyer in Madagascar, Clermont played an important role between 1940 and 1942 in the resistance to the Vichy government's administration of the Grande Île. A vociferous activist and controversial figure, openly pro-Allies in Madagascar, he turned out, once repatriated to Great Britain, to be such an individualist and Anglophile that he aroused the suspicion of the Gaullists in London. As an actor, he joined the Théâtre Molière, a troupe of French actors founded in 1943 in the English capital and directed by Paul Bonifas (Michel in *Aventure malgache*). His war experiences provide the backdrop for Hitchcock's film. By the end of December 1943, the script was ready. As with *Bon voyage*, Hitchcock added a flashback structure to the story and decided that Clermont/Clarus would play himself, with the rest of the cast going to other actors from the Théâtre Molière.

Directorial Choices

Like *Bon voyage*, and with the same technical crew, the film was shot at the modest studio in Welwyn, Hertfordshire. But unlike *Bon voyage*, *Aventure malgache* is a sparsely cut drama. It consists mainly of long still or moving shots. Frequently, two characters converse within the same frame, rather than alternating between their respective points of view (shot–reverse shot cut). Although Hitchcock would experiment more than once after the war with the value of shot length (*Rope, Under Capricorn*, 1948), this is above all a quick and inexpensive way to get the film in the can. It is also sometimes an opportunity to play with the off-screen aspect: a young man abruptly leaves his fiancée to join the Free French forces. She watches him leave, at first crestfallen, then overcome by a dark feeling, while the camera, which has not stopped rolling, pulls back to reveal a telephone at the foot of the bed. She picks it up and hands her lover over to the police.

Invisible for Fifty Years

The scene of the young woman denouncing her Resistance fiancé to the enemy may explain why the film was never distributed in France, either in 1944 or in the postwar period. No doubt it was initially banned by an authority of the Gaullist government in exile in London, or by a representative of the Resistance, on the grounds that it would be better not to show the dissension of French people, who were nonetheless on the same side. Subsequently, the British Ministry of Information probably applied a bureaucratic "precautionary principle," systematically refusing the film to anyone who requested it. This invisibility of *Aventure malgache* lasted fifty years, until its screening was authorized in 1993 in a historic London cinema (the Everyman Cinema, Hampstead, London), under the auspices of the British Film Institute.

Top Secret

In February 1957, Jules François Clermont, the hero of *Aventure malgache*, asked the British Ministry of Information for permission to borrow a copy of the film telling his story, which had never been shown since it was made. Almost fifteen years after the end of the war, the answer was negative, and would remain so...until 1993, the date of the first public screening of this propaganda drama by Alfred Hitchcock.

Dream sequence in *Spellbound*.

Psychoanalysis
According to Hitchcock

Although Sigmund Freud's first trip to the United States was in 1909, the influence of psychoanalysis in Hollywood was felt most strongly after World War II. In the aftermath of a conflict that pushed the limits of horror even further, Freudianism, which sought to explain "aberrant" human behavior, became a source of inspiration and an attempt to interpret the contemporary world. At the same time, its cinematic adaptation produced a number of simplifications and naïve representations. Hitchcock's cinema is no exception to this trend, even though his films, more than many others, have always seemed nightmarish in character, or to reflect a kind of waking dream with oedipal undertones.

Hollywood Clichés

While working on the screenplay for *Spellbound* (1944), which places at the heart of its plot a psychoanalyst madly in love with her patient and declaiming Freudian concepts with evangelical conviction, Hitchcock was fully aware that he was popularizing pseudo-psychoanalysis. Perhaps the filmmaker was mocking the Hollywood representation of psychic processes as much as, if not more than, the very seriousness of this new human science. Thus, when Hitchcock had the idea of recruiting surrealist painter Salvador Dalí to design the dream scenes in *Spellbound*, it was, among other reasons, his way of opposing the clichés of their figuration in the cinema. Here, there

The eye and the hole (*Psycho*).

is no smoke and mirrors to indicate a dreamlike moment, but spectacular visions, giant tableaux to manifest the work of the dream (i.e., the scenario written by the dreamer).

Hypnosis Versus Psychoanalysis

Is this a manifestation of the filmmaker's resistance to analysis (unlike the rest of Hollywood)? In *Spellbound*—whose title conveys this very sense of being "mesmerized"—Hitchcock plays off hypnosis against psychoanalysis: In the great scene of the first kiss, Ingrid Bergman's eyes are half-closed in close-up as Gregory Peck advances toward her; she is caught in his gaze and surrenders. Hypnosis, a technique of suggestion first experimented with and then abandoned by Freud, is the ultimate effect for a director like Hitchcock, the ideal state for the audience of his films. And there are undoubtedly three stages of development in his representation of the world: the child, the adult, and, in a higher or regressive position, the spectator.

Psychos

Although Hitchcock was fully aware of the sexual symbolism at work in his films, and enjoyed it (the train entering the tunnel in the last shot of *North by Northwest*, 1958), he was at the same time skeptical about psychoanalytic theories. Freud, for his part, had little interest in cinema and distrusted it, not believing it capable of "turning our abstractions into a plastic presentation that respects itself in the slightest."[1] Nevertheless, Hitchcock's entire oeuvre, perhaps more than any other, offers visual and dramatic equivalents to Freudian concepts such as the feeling of guilt, the development of anguish, fetishism, the drive, the discharge, the phallic woman,

the oral stage, or the missed act (Farley Granger "forgetting" his lighter in Robert Walker's compartment, thereby leaving the psychopath from *Strangers on a Train* the sign of his agreement for the latter to kill his wife in his place). Add to these the aptly named *Psycho* (1960), with its depiction of voyeurism (Anthony Perkins's eye glued to the hole in the wall) and its spectacular use of the Oedipus complex.

In a fitting counterpoint, Hitchcock's work will no doubt be among the most analyzed in the history of cinema.[2]

Red Trauma

Twenty years after *Spellbound*, Hitchcock created another overtly psychoanalytical and equally iconoclastic film. In *Marnie*, the roles are reversed: The woman (Tippi Hedren), a kleptomaniac and frigid (described as "a sex mystery" by the filmmaker), must unearth the memory of a childhood trauma, and her husband (Sean Connery) performs "savage" psychoanalysis on her. The use of the color red to represent the recollection of the trauma, along with a surge of libido, once again produces a memorable effect. Psychoanalysis is definitely of interest to Hitchcock, or at least his vision of it: that of an investigative process, a kind of imaginary pursuit or metaphysical suspense, as are his thrillers, which, in turn, convey an image of it.

The Crystal Penis

Hitchcock liked to describe his dreams. One day in 1963, he asked Jay Presson Allen, the screenwriter of *Marnie*, to interpret one: His penis was made of crystal, of great beauty and incalculable value, and Hitchcock's greatest concern was to manage to hide it from the house cook.

DAVID O. SELZNICK
presents

GREGORY PECK INGRID BERGMAN

in ALFRED HITCHCOCK'S

SPELLBOUND

A SELZNICK INTERNATIONAL PICTURE

Screenplay by Ben Hecht · *Released thru United Artists*

Spellbound

United States • **1 hr 51**
(with music for the
opening, and for the
final credits) • **Black and White + 2 red-tinted images** • **Mono**
(Western Electric
Recording) • **1.37:1**

Production Dates: June–July 1944
Release Date in the United States: October 31, 1945 (New York),
December 28, 1945 (United States, general release)

Production: Selznick International Pictures, Vanguard Films
Producer: David O. Selznick
Unit Production Manager: Richard Johnston
Production Assistant: Barbara Keon

**Based on a novel by Francis Beeding (pseudonym of John Leslie Palmer
and Hilary Aidan Saint George Saunders),
The House of Dr. Edwardes (1927)**
Adaptation: Angus MacPhail
Screenplay: Ben Hecht
Psychiatric Consultant: May E. Romm
Director of Photography: George Barnes
Camera Operator: John F. Warren
Special Effects: Jack Cosgrove, Clarence Slifer
Sound: Richard DeWeese
Assistant Director: Lowell J. Farrell
Artistic Directors: James Basevi, John Ewing
Set Decoration: Emile Kuri, William Cameron Menzies
Artistic Contributor: Salvador Dalí (dream sequence, based upon his designs)
Costumes: Howard Greer, Ann Peck
Music: Miklós Rózsa
Film Editing: Hal C. Kern, William H. Ziegler

Starring: Ingrid Bergman (Dr. Constance Petersen), Gregory Peck (John
Ballantyne), Michael Chekhov (Dr. Alexander Brulov), Leo G. Carroll (Dr. Murchison),
Rhonda Fleming (Mary Carmichael), John Emery (Dr. Fleurot), Norman Lloyd (Mr.
Garmes), Bill Goodwin (hotel house detective), Steven Geray (Dr. Graff), Donald
Curtis (Harry), Wallace Ford (stranger in the hotel lobby), Art Baker (Detective
Lieutenant Cooley), Regis Toomey (Detective Sergeant Gillespie), Paul Harvey (Dr.
Hanish), Jacqueline deWit (nurse), Alfred Hitchcock (man leaving the elevator)…

"Regarding sleep, the sinister adventure of every evening, one might say that people fall asleep with a daily boldness that would be unintelligible if we did not know that this is the result of ignorance of the danger."

Charles Baudelaire, *Fusées* (*Rockets*)

SYNOPSIS

Dr. Edwardes arrives at the Green Manors Clinic to take over from its director, Dr. Murchison. Constance Petersen, a psychoanalyst at the clinic, falls in love with him almost immediately but detects strange phobias in him, such as the color white and parallel lines. She discovers that he is an amnesiac impostor who has assumed the identity of the real Edwardes, who has disappeared. Unmasked, the man flees to New York. She joins him, determined to cure him of his amnesia by finding the source of his neuroses and "guilt complex." She takes him to Rochester to consult Dr. Brulov. At dawn, he recounts his dream of the previous night. Petersen understands his white phobia as he watches the snow fall and remembers that he last saw Edwardes when they were skiing together. Constance invites him down a slope to relive the circumstances of the trauma that caused him to lose his memory. He recalls that his guilt stems from his brother's accidental death, for which he felt responsible. His true identity, John Ballantyne, is discovered. After searching the area where the amnesiac remembers skiing with Edwardes, the police find Edwardes's body in the mountains, where he was shot dead. Ballantyne is arrested. Constance, back at Green Manors, understands from Murchison's slip of the tongue that Murchison is the real killer. He killed Edwardes so as not to have to give up his position. With his crime exposed, he commits suicide. Constance Petersen and John Ballantyne can now marry.

GENESIS

Having "loaned" Hitchcock to various production companies, David O. Selznick urged him to make the last two films in their contract. Hitchcock was in England, where he had just made two medium-length propaganda films, *Bon voyage* and *Aventure malgache*.

A Psychoanalytical Thriller

Hitchcock took advantage of his stay in London to buy the rights to a novel by Francis Beeding, the pseudonym of two British authors, John Leslie Palmer and Hilary Aidan Saint George Saunders. The action of *The House of Dr. Edwardes*, a strange thriller published in 1927, "a melodramatic and truly mad novel," said Hitchcock, is set in a psychiatric asylum. Occultism, satanism, and Freudianism are intertwined. The director sold the rights to the book to Selznick, convinced that the latter would be won over by a story featuring psychoanalysis, the science of dreams and the unconscious, which was becoming a fashionable phenomenon in Hollywood. The producer, about to leave his wife for actress Jennifer Jones, was himself undergoing analysis. While still in Great Britain, Hitchcock began work on the adaptation with Angus MacPhail, a longtime friend who had collaborated with him on *Bon voyage* and *Aventure malgache*.

Hecht and Hitch

Back in the US, Hitchcock took up the script again with playwright Ben Hecht. The two locked themselves in a room at the St. Regis hotel in New York. The filmmaker reunited with the man who had written the last scene of *Foreign Correspondent* (1940), the hero's address to the American nation at a time when Europe was already at war. The two men got on well and shared a critical and sarcastic vision of Hollywood mores. Hecht, who was also in analysis, took a keen interest in Freudian science. "Hitch," for his part, observed this discipline with interest, though he was careful not to involve himself with it personally, and though he had always regarded it

with a certain detachment. Neither he nor Hecht was fooled by the popularization, even the melodramatic vulgarity, with which Hollywood cinema used psychoanalysis to "modernize" often conventional stories. For the purposes of the script, and for the sake of authenticity, the two men visited various psychiatric hospitals.

Special Adviser

Selznick reworked the screenplay, which treated a serious subject with too much humor for his taste. He enlisted the help of his own therapist, May E. Romm, a strict Freudian who worked with a number of celebrities and who was nicknamed the "Queen of Couch Canyon" in Hollywood. She is listed in the credits as a "psychiatric consultant." Hitchcock was not particularly happy with Selznick's alterations, deletions, and revisions, which accentuated the sentimental dimension of the story.

CASTING

Ingrid Bergman had just filmed George Cukor's *Gaslight,* for which she would win the Oscar for Best Actress. Now under contract to Selznick, she was one of the biggest female American box office stars.

Hollywood and Psychoanalysis

Although psychoanalysis had already left its mark on a number of prewar Hollywood films, the success of *Spellbound* triggered a series of productions in which the science of dreams played a central role, including Fritz Lang's *Secret Beyond the Door* (1947), Anatole Litvak's *The Snake Pit* (1948), and Otto Preminger's *Whirlpool* (1949).

For Hitchcock Addicts

The film's French title, *La maison du docteur Edwardes*, is a literal translation of the title of the novel from which it is adapted (*The House of Dr. Edwardes*). The American title, *Spellbound*, was suggested by David O. Selznick's secretary.

Freeze Frame

In the first close-up kiss between Ingrid Bergman and Gregory Peck, the superimposed image of a series of open doors may have been the work of either screenwriter Ben Hecht or producer David O. Selznick.

Introducing Ingrid Bergman

Although the producer at one point considered offering the role to Greta Garbo, Hitchcock and Hecht were soon convinced that Bergman should play Dr. Constance Petersen. The star found the script mediocre and illogical but was not in a position to oppose Selznick's wishes. On the other hand, the director reassured her and convinced her to accept the fantasy dimension of the story, in particular the Hollywood treatment of psychoanalysis. Bergman recounted how Hitchcock always dispelled her doubts and reticence at the prospect of acting out an implausible scene by telling her to think about "pretending." The filmmaker was fascinated by the actress, with whom he developed a kind of romantic friendship.

A Not Very Hitchcockian Actor

Originally, the male lead was to have been Cary Grant (*Suspicion*, 1941), and the entire script was written around the actor. But Grant refused the script, which his star status allowed him to do. Hitchcock next considered Joseph Cotten (*Shadow of a Doubt*, 1942), but Selznick imposed a contract actor: Gregory Peck, who had just been nominated for an Oscar for John Stahl's *Keys of the Kingdom*. Impressed by the director's meticulousness and perfectionism, Peck, who had studied the Stanislavski method of acting in New York, often questioned Hitchcock about his character's motivations. This kind of request particularly irritated the filmmaker, who said he had no interest in what his character was thinking and advised him to eliminate all facial expressions. Having taken a liking to the young actor, however, Hitchcock amused himself by giving him advice on clothes and food, even offering him a case of vintage wine.

In his interviews with Hitchcock,[1] François Truffaut expressed his regret at the choice of Gregory Peck, finding him "empty" and completely expressionless. He was not, in his opinion, a Hitchcock actor. A year after *Spellbound*, Selznick entrusted him with the male lead in *Duel in the Sun*, the extravagant, baroque Western he produced.

Intellectuals and a Nymphomaniac

A British-born actor, Leo G. Carroll, who played Dr. Murchison, rejoined Hitchcock for *The Paradine Case* (1947), *Strangers on a Train* (1950), and *North by Northwest* (1958), where he played the head of the American Secret Service. Between 1964 and 1968, he played an equivalent role in the TV series *The Man from U.N.C.L.E.*, a sort of Hitchcock pastiche.

Russian actor Michael Chekhov plays Constance Petersen's mentor, Dr. Brulov, a benevolent and caustic father figure with no illusions about the value of human feelings. He made his stage debut in 1911; as a major figure at the Moscow Theatre, which he directed from 1922 onward, he taught acting and Stanislavski's methods, which he enriched with his own ideas on acting. After his dismissal in 1928, he moved to Hollywood, appearing in a dozen American films until his death in 1955. His most memorable role was in the Hitchcock film, for which he was nominated for an Oscar for Best Supporting Actor.

It was Rhonda Fleming, then age twenty-one, who played the troubled, nymphomaniacal, and violent young woman who appears in the opening sequence. Nicknamed the "queen of Technicolor" in the 1950s, not least because of her sumptuous red hair, she would go on to establish herself in such major films as Jacques Tourneur's *Out of the Past* (*La Griffe du passé*), Robert Siodmak's *The Spiral Staircase*, Fritz Lang's *While the City Sleeps*, and Allan Dwan's *Slightly Scarlet*.

FILMING AND PRODUCTION

Spellbound began filming in June 1944 at Selznick's studios. Photography was entrusted to George Barnes, who had already worked on *Rebecca* (1939) and created a silky image with black and white.

A Dream Conceived by Salvador Dalí

Hitchcock asked his producer to commission Salvador Dalí to design the dream sequence that holds the key to John Ballantyne's amnesia. The filmmaker felt that the Spanish artist's painting of long shadows, infinite distances, straight lines converging in perspective, featureless faces, and soft shapes would fit in perfectly with his conception of a dreamlike scene: "In all films, dream sequences are blurred. But this is not true. Dalí was the best person for dreams, because this is how dreams should be, clear."[2] But while Hitchcock "wanted" Dalí, the painter was impressed by the filmmaker, whom he found endowed with a certain mystery

rarely found in anyone else. Several of the artist's ideas seemed very complicated to realize, such as hanging real pianos above the set. He also imagined a scene in which Ingrid Bergman was transformed into a statue, and another in which she found herself covered in ants. While Hitchcock was away on a trip to London, Selznick, after a test screening, initially considered aesthete director Josef von Sternberg but eventually asked set designer William Cameron Menzies, who had already collaborated with Hitchcock on *Foreign Correspondent*, to shoot more dream scenes. The sequences he shot, based on Dalí's drawings, were included in the final version. In the end, the whole thing lasts just two minutes, and many of the original ideas (the pianos, the statue-woman) were dropped from the film. Unhappy with the result, Menzies asked not to be credited. We can only dream of what Dalí's dream would have been like in its entirety.

Where Is Hitchcock?

In the fortieth minute of the film, Hitchcock emerges with a group of people from the elevator of the Empire Hotel, where Ballantyne has taken refuge. He is holding a violin case. Three years later, it would be a cello in *The Paradine Case*. And three years later, he carries another musical instrument, a double bass, for his appearance in *Strangers on a Train*.

Violins and a Theremin

Bernard Herrmann, who had scored *Citizen Kane* and Orson Welles's *The Magnificent Ambersons*, was commissioned to write the film's score. Herrmann was unavailable, but he and Hitchcock were to meet again. Miklós Rózsa was chosen. Born in Budapest, then a composer in London, where he wrote the music for a ballet, Rózsa was introduced in 1935 to producer Alexander Korda, who suggested he score Jacques Feyder's *Knight Without Armour* (*Le Chevalier sans armure*). The musician moved to Hollywood in 1940. For *Spellbound*, he innovated by using a theremin, one of the first electronic musical instruments. For his work on this film Rózsa won the Oscar for Best Music. Hitchcock, however, did not much appreciate his work, deeming his composition sometimes too intrusive. In interviews with Truffaut,[1] he even described as "appalling" the moment when the violins start playing during the first kiss between Ingrid Bergman and Gregory Peck.

Wooden Hand and Red Images

For Murchison's suicide scene, Hitchcock built a gigantic wooden hand holding a weapon so that the clinic director's revolver could be seen in the foreground, looking back at him from a subjective camera—in other words, toward the audience. When the shot is fired, he inserted two red-tinted images to create a subliminal sensation of violence.

RECEPTION

The film was released in the US at the end of 1945 and was an immediate popular success. It grossed nearly $8 million on a budget of $2 million.

The Enthusiasm of the American Press

"David O. Selznick has fashioned a powerful drama for adults, endowing it with superb production values, and Alfred Hitchcock, in keeping with his reputation for building up thrilling situations that hold one in tense suspense, has applied his directorial skill in a masterful way" wrote *Harrison's Reports* (November 3, 1945). For Bosley Crowther of the *New York Times* (November 2, 1945), "The story… is a rather obvious and often-told tale…but the manner and quality of its telling is extraordinarily fine…the firm texture of the narration, the flow of continuity and dialogue, the shock of the unexpected, the scope of image—all are happily here." For the *New Yorker* (November 3, 1945), "When the film stops trying to be esoteric and abandons arcane mumbling for good, rousing melodrama, it moves along in the manner to which Hitchcock has accustomed us."

A Late Release in France

Invisible during the war, like all of the American productions, the film was released in France on March

Psychoanalysis at the bedside of dreams (Ingrid Bergman, Gregory Peck).

19, 1948, at the same time as *Notorious*, and suffered from this coincidence.

In *Le Parisien libéré* (March 31, 1948), critic André Bazin gave it a harsh review. He was amused that the film had gone to psychoanalysis to seek support for the implausibilities of its screenplay. "*Spellbound* sometimes manages to act on our nerves, but never, alas, on our hearts or minds."

Terror and Passion

Considered more of a minor film by Hitchcock fans, *Spellbound* is essentially a melodramatic love story, to which the highly simplified use of psychoanalysis—an aberration in clinical terms—lends its rationale. The film is the story of love at first sight that radically changes a woman. Dr. Petersen, a stern scientist with glasses and a bun, is transformed into a sensual, disheveled, and passionate lover, moving from the influence of two surrogate fathers, a "good" one (Dr. Brulov) and a "bad" one (Dr. Murchison), to the embrace of a disturbed lover, a man-child trapped in his repressed trauma.

Terror arises both from the sensation of an esoteric, almost occult-like sense of determination, of which psychoanalysis is ultimately no more than a crude disguise, and from several frightening moments offered by the film (the dream imagined by Dalí, worth more aesthetically and emotionally than a set of signs to be interpreted; the flashback restoring Ballantyne's memory of the violent death of his younger brother). The central dimension of the story (the love story) is itself conceived as a disquieting suspense. The two moments when Gregory Peck and Ingrid Bergman embrace voluptuously are fraught with a menace that the mise-en-scène accentuates. In the first, two very close-up faces approach each other in a shot–reverse shot cut; in the second, Constance Petersen's black-gloved hands, as she embraces Ballantyne, take on a slightly frightening dimension. François Truffaut was right when he said that Hitchcock filmed love scenes as murder scenes (and vice versa).

The dreamer (Gregory Peck) and his dream: a dream sequence designed by Salvador Dalí, commissioned by Hitchcock, directed by William Cameron Menzies, and edited by Selznick (sadly, the suspended orchestra scene was not included in the final cut).

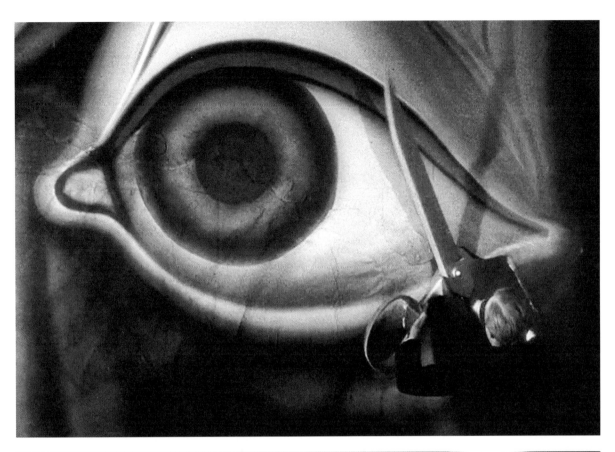

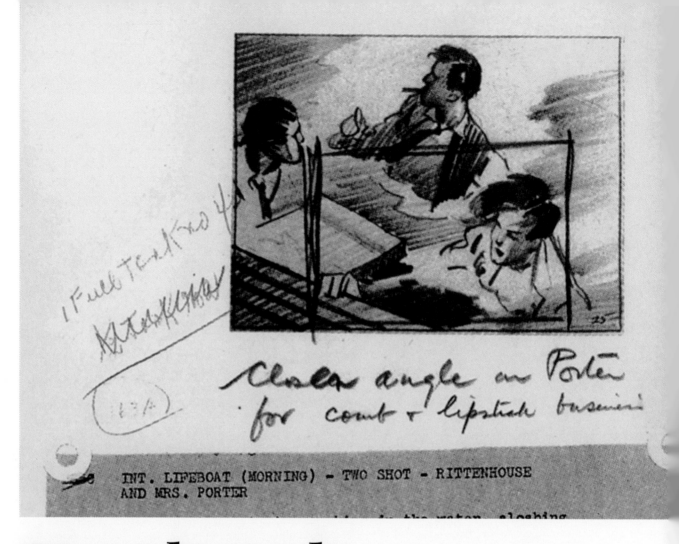

INT. LIFEBOAT (MORNING) — TWO SHOT — RITTENHOUSE
AND MRS. PORTER

Storyboards,
Films on Paper

Thomas Morahan (*Jamaica Inn*), John DeCuir (*Saboteur*), Henry Bumstead (*Vertigo*), Harold Michelson (*The Birds*), and Saul Bass (*Psycho*) were just some of Hitchcock's storyboard artists—illustrators who, in preproduction, mapped out the forthcoming film on the basis of a script and sketches by the Master, themselves documented or summary expressions of a "vision." In this way, a storyboard anticipates and suggests shot sizes, camera movements, actor paths—everything that can help control the shooting budget and give the filming process its shape.

Hitchcock's famous storyboards, these magnificent sketches, have become proof of his infallible art of anticipation and previsualization—a reality indeed, but also a legend, by virtue of their systematization. None of his scripts is entirely "storyboarded" (Hitchcock made sketches *during* shooting); script, storyboard, and technical cut were rarely definitive when shooting began; they did not have all the answers. In *Hitchcock at Work*,[1] film historian Bill Krohn documented how the filmmaker rewrote on the spot, adapting to locations, inventing scenes, changing camera positions, adding and subtracting—in short, embracing the inspiration of a shoot and its material requirements. Contrary to the myth of the all-powerful storyboard, Krohn emphasized Hitchcock's flexibility. There remained a space between the drawing and the recorded image: that of the mise-en-scène.

20th Century-Fox, *Lifeboat*, 1943: The storyboard draws a frame within a frame to indicate a close-up shot of Connie Porter (Tallulah Bankhead) fishing out her comb and lipstick in the storm.

Harold Michelson, *The Birds*, 1962.

Robert Boyle, *North by Northwest*, 1958.

Henry Bumstead, *Vertigo*, 1957.

Memory of the Camps

⚑ • 🕐 • 🎞 • 🔇 • ▱

Great Britain • **56 min** • **Black and White** • **Silent** • **1.33:1**

Production Dates: April–September 1945
Release Date in the United States: May 7, 1985 (PBS, Public Broadcasting Service)

Production: Ministry of Information (MOI)
Producer: Sidney Bernstein
Unit Production Manager: Sergei Nolbandov

Script and Commentary Adviser: Alfred Hitchcock
Script and Commentary: Colin Wills, Richard Crossman
Narrator: Trevor Howard (1985)
Research: Gordon Taylor
Scientific Adviser: Solly Zuckerman
Film Editing: Marcel Cohen, Stewart McAllister, Peter Tanner

≡

German Concentration Camps Factual Survey

⚑ • 🕐 • 🎞 • 🔊 • ▱

Great Britain • **1 h 10** • **Black and White** • **Mono** • **1.37:1**

Production Dates: April–September 1945
Release Date: February 9, 2014 (Berlin International Film Festival)

Production: Ministry of Information (MOI), Imperial War Museum (2014)
Producers: Sidney Bernstein, David Walsh (2014)

Treatment Adviser: Alfred Hitchcock
Director of Restoration: Toby Haggith (2014)
Narrator: Jasper Britton (2014)

> "We had known. The world had vaguely heard. But until now no one of us had looked on this. Even this morning we had not imagined we would look on this. It was as though we had penetrated at last to the center of the black heart, to the very crawling inside of the vicious heart."

Meyer Levin[1]

SYNOPSIS

Memory of the Camps / German Concentration Camps Factual Survey uses footage shot in the spring of 1945, during the liberation of concentration and extermination camps in Germany and Eastern Europe, to describe the horror of an unprecedented discovery: the Nazi concentration camp system, that is, the confinement, enslavement, and mass destruction of human beings. The film begins with a historical reminder, supported by archival footage: the German infatuation with Adolf Hitler, the ecstatic complicity of an entire people when he came to power in January 1933. Then, a twelve-year leap in time: April 1945, the liberation of the German Bergen-Belsen camp. Dead and dying everywhere. For more than seven days, the liberators forced the torturers to bury their countless victims in mass graves. They also forced the local authorities and the surrounding population to witness this infernal spectacle. British soldiers and doctors cared for, fed, washed, and clothed the survivors, men, women, and children of all nationalities. After Bergen-Belsen, the film moves on to other camps and mass graves in Germany, Austria, and Poland. In order of editing, they are Dachau, Buchenwald, Ebensee, Mauthausen, Ludwigslust, Ohrdruf, Thekla, Gardelegen, Auschwitz, Majdanek.

GENESIS

In the spring of 1945, on all European war fronts, the Nazis retreated and Allied forces advanced and converged on Berlin. On April 15, during its advance, the British Eleventh Armored Division discovered and liberated the German camp of Bergen-Belsen. Stunned army cameramen and newsreel operators filmed to bear witness to an appalling reality. In April and May, American and Soviet soldiers entered other concentration and extermination camps in Germany, Austria, and Poland. They also tried not to look away, in order to show the world what they were seeing. They too filmed thousands of corpses buried by torturers, emaciated and haggard survivors, facilities dedicated to mass murder.

The Film of the Allies?

From these accumulated images of atrocities—around fourteen hours of rushes—a film project was entrusted to the Englishman Sidney Bernstein, head since 1944 of the "cinema" section of the psychological action division of SHAEF (Supreme Headquarters Allied Expeditionary Force), the London-based headquarters of the Allied forces. The original plan was to produce three versions: one to be shown to Germans after the fall of the Third Reich, to make them see the crimes committed in their name but of which they claimed ignorance, to "re-educate" them and, in Bernstein's words, "shake" and "humiliate" them; another for German prisoners; and the third for the liberated populations of Europe and the United States. But at the beginning of July 1945, the American command withdrew from this project to produce its own document (*Death Mills*, Billy Wilder, 1945). Bernstein was to direct this montage film on behalf of the British Ministry of Information (MOI), incorporating footage shot by the Soviets at Auschwitz and Majdanek.

Proof Through Images

On April 20, 1945, Sidney Bernstein went to Bergen-Belsen. What he saw was so much beyond belief that he immediately sought to attest to its veracity. He tried to convey the order to film everything as far as the conditions of the war in progress and the technical means available would allow (the cameramen had no portable lights for filming interiors): the dead piled up, the children, the SS, the bloodless prisoners, the civilians in the vicinity, the mass graves, the barracks, the watchtowers, the typhus epidemic, the faces, the instruments of torture, the crematoria, the names of German industrialists inscribed on

the incinerators. British *Movietone News* operators, equipped with sound cameras, recorded in situ testimonies from executioners, victims, and British officers. In a nine-page memorandum dated April 30, the producer set out the aims of the film: to make an entire people face up to its immense responsibility and force it to accept the occupation and the justice of the Allies, and to produce irrefutable evidence of crimes against humanity for the present and for history.

Assembling a Team

Bernstein engaged Sergei Nolbandov, a director from Ealing Studios, as production assistant. To help him write an initial treatment, he recruited an Australian journalist who had reported on the liberation of Bergen-Belsen, Colin Wills, and another journalist and SHAEF member, Richard Crossman (who had seen the Dachau camp). An intelligence officer, Gordon Taylor, collected documentation on the concentration camp system. Three editors, Marcel Cohen (a French refugee), Stewart McAllister, and Peter Tanner, set to work beginning in May on assembling hours of rushes by camp and location. But how does one make a coherent, meaningful montage out such a piecemeal collection?

A Brilliant Mind

To solve his problem, Bernstein called on his friend Alfred Hitchcock, whom he had already called on in wartime to supervise the American version of two English documentaries (1940–1941), and then to direct two propaganda films, *Bon voyage* and *Aventure malgache* (1944): "I thought Hitchcock, a brilliant mind, would know how we could hold it all

together. And he did know."[2] The filmmaker, who was in Hollywood preparing *Notorious*—a drama about the persistent Nazi threat—agreed and, unable to obtain a flight, boarded an overcrowded ship. At the end of June 1945, he arrived in London. He stayed for a month.

FILMING AND PRODUCTION

In the company of Bernstein and Peter Tanner, one of the editors, Hitchcock viewed at least ten hours of footage in the MOI projection room and at Pinewood Studios. According to one account,[3] he was so shocked that it took him a week to return. In his suite at the Claridge Hotel, he discussed treatment and commentary with Colin Wills until July 16, when Wills left for Paris. Hitchcock resumed writing with Crossman until July 23, and the film evolved as the editing process took place.

Forbidden Editing

The filmmaker's obsession was the same as the producer's: Faced with such *unthinkable* horror, how can we convince public opinion of the truth of these images? How to prevent the German public in particular from challenging them? How can the film itself thwart disbelief and denial, attempts to disqualify allegedly arranged images, insinuations of manipulation of reality for propaganda purposes? Hitchcock, who usually believed in the emotional power of editing, made the opposite choice in this particular case. Knowing that every cut could be viewed with suspicion, seen as an indication of fakery, he asked his editors to leave as much of the operators' footage as possible intact in its length, since duration helps to authenticate the reality filmed. He favored the indisputable continuity of slow, painful panoramas linking corpses piled by the hundreds in mass graves, soldiers at the edge of the pit, and local authorities summoned to be present, or local inhabitants, including the SS, like slaves in their turn, obliged to carry their victims and come and go endlessly from truck to pit, pit to truck. As a filmmaker, Hitchcock responded (movement without cuts) to the suspicion, even the accusation, that these unprecedented images were staged.

Implacable Edits

Hitchcock also deliberately kept to long shots to capture as much of the reality as possible. At other times, on the contrary, he resorted to editing and its power of evocation and condemnation, showing, for example, successive still shots of piles of now-ownerless objects (suitcases, toys, wedding rings, shoes, hairbrushes, handbags, glasses).

He used another editing effect to produce a violent counterpoint. Before the British soldiers arrive at Bergen-Belsen, the film lingers for a few shots on the surrounding countryside: "Well-kept orchards and farms line the road," says the commentary. They are images of a peaceful countryside in bloom, cows grazing, children playing: a little paradise, if it were not for that smell, the commentary also says. When he presents the hell of Ebensee, in Austria, the sequence repeats the obscene juxtaposition between the healthy and happy mountain dwellers on one side and the reality of the camp on the other. Hitchcock also planned, but was unable to put his idea into practice, to draw concentric circles on maps around a focal point to emphasize

the proximity of the population. He even considered showing them the images and filming their reactions.

An Abandoned Film

Under contract to his American producer, David O. Selznick, Hitchcock left England at the beginning of August 1945. The film's commentary on the camps had been written but not recorded. Over the course of the month and into early September, the editing continued to evolve. On August 22, Peter Tanner wrote to Sidney Bernstein about the last part: "I don't think Mr. Hitchcock's ideas for this part of the film will work completely."

On September 29, the film was screened for Bernstein at the MOI: It was a five-reel cut of a planned six-reel film, as yet untitled, with a few synchronized sequences. On the thirtieth, no doubt knowing that their production was in jeopardy, he wrote to Tanner to thank him and congratulate him: "One day, you'll see that it was worth it."[3] At that point, the producer and his team's project was left almost untouched. The political aims of the postwar period had changed: It was now less a question

of punishing the Germans than of avoiding demoralizing them completely so that they would take part in the effort to rebuild their devastated country. Subsequently, Germany was to become a strategic location and a key issue in the Cold War. The film missed its moment and remained unseen for forty years.

RECEPTION

In May 1952, the five reels were transferred from the Central Office of Information (COI, successor to the MOI) to the Imperial War Museum (IWM), registered under the number F3080. A typescript of the commentary, a list of shots per reel, and editing notes were deposited with this film, which had no definitive title.

A Film Rediscovered

In December 1983, Caroline Moorehead, initially in the *Times*, then in her biography of Sidney Bernstein, recalled or revealed to many the existence in the IWM archives of a documentary on concentration camps assembled by Hitchcock at the end of the war.[4] At the same time, another biography, devoted to the editor Stewart McAllister, also mentioned it.[5]

Rediscovered, this incomplete film lasting less than an hour was shown on February 27, 1984, at the Berlin International Film Festival (the commentary was read out during the screening), then broadcast on May 7, 1985, on PBS (the American Public Broadcasting Service) program *Frontline*, under the title *Memory of the Camps*. For the occasion, the commentary, read by actor Trevor Howard, was recorded and added.[6] In September 1985, the English channel ITV (Independent Television) broadcast a seventy-minute program produced by Granada Television, Sidney Bernstein's company: *A Painful Reminder*, subtitled *Evidence for All Mankind*. The film is made up of extracts from *Memory of the Camps* (with commentary by John Graham), testimonies from three camp survivors, and interviews with Bernstein, Tanner, and a cameraman from the time. Since 2008, the Imperial War Museum has been carrying out an exemplary restoration of *Memory of the Camps*, under the title *German Concentration Camps Factual Survey* (the film is listed under this name in an MOI catalogue published in September 1945). The missing reel has been reconstituted, and the recording of the commentary redone, with the voice of theatrical actor Jasper Britton. The restoration also gave the image an unbearable and necessary sharpness. The world premiere took place at the Berlin International Film Festival on February 9, 2014.

Images of Horror

Hollywood filmmakers who had enlisted in the army saw and filmed the dead and survivors of the Nazi concentration camp system in 1945 (George Stevens, Samuel Fuller), while others edited these images or those of war operators (John Ford, Billy Wilder). Hitchcock never spoke publicly of his experience in July 1945. In the 1970s, he is said to have confided to Henri Langlois, the founder of La Cinémathèque Française: "At the end of the war, I made a film to show the reality of the concentration camps…horrible. It was more horrible than any fantasy horror. Then, nobody wanted to see it. It was too unbearable. But it stayed in my mind for all these years."[7]

This memory undeniably left a mark on his later work, whether subterranean or visible, or even affirmed by the filmmaker himself when he evoked the interminable murder of policeman Gromek in *Torn Curtain* (1966), "the scene in the gas oven," to use his own expression. His discovery, at the end of the conflict, of death on an industrial scale confirms and surpasses his vision of the world and human nature to an unimaginable extent; it clashes with and infinitely exceeds his lifelong fascination with murders, bloody news stories, the demented imagination of serial killers, and their dealings with the bodies of their victims (what to do with them?). Confronted with the images of 1945, Hitchcock faced the crime of the century.

Postwar Films

In October 1945, Sidney Bernstein came to the United States. With Hitchcock, he founded Transatlantic Pictures, an independent company that produced two films in 1948: *Rope*, a portrait of an American fascist (Brandon, played by John Dall), and *Under Capricorn*. In both, as never before in his work, the filmmaker experimented with the idea and aesthetics of a shot so long that it almost merges, at least in the viewer's mind, with the duration of the fiction itself: the ultimate dream of a film without cuts.

Two other Hitchcock films in particular emphasize the harsh handling of dead bodies: *Psycho* (1960) and *Frenzy* (1971). In 1965, the critic and essayist Robin Wood dared to explain the unprecedented darkness and horror of *Psycho*, a very somber reflection on the human race, by recalling Hitchcock's film on the camps, which was well forgotten at the time: "We can no longer be under the slightest illusion about human nature, and about the abysses around us and within us; and *Psycho* is founded on, precisely, these twin horrors."[8]

"A Murder by a Babbling Brook"

In 1954, Hitchcock made *The Trouble with Harry*, a Hollywood comedy tinged with English humor, the story of a dead man whose friendly little pastoral community spends the entire film hiding the body and trying to get rid of it. This cumbersome corpse suddenly appears right at the start, in the midst of shimmering nature, in the heart of an idyllic landscape. Hitchcock had an expression, no doubt from the start of filming and afterward, to illustrate his theory of visual counterpoint: "a murder by a babbling brook." And it was to play on this violent contrast between the splendid and the sordid that he also planned to film a murder near a waterfall in Central Park as part of an experimental project developed in the mid-1960s and then abandoned (*Kaleidoscope*). Each time, it is this image of the Bergen-Belsen countryside that returns.

CARY
GRANT
INGRID
BERGMAN
in **ALFRED HITCHCOCK'S**

Notorious!

with **CLAUDE RAINS**

LOUIS CALHERN · MADAME LEOPOLDINE KONSTANTIN
Directed by **ALFRED HITCHCOCK** *Written by* BEN HECHT

RKO
RADIO
PICTURES

Notorious

United States • **1 hr 42** • **Black and White** • **Mono** (RCA Sound System) • **1.37:1**

Production Dates: October 15, 1945–January 17, 1946
Release Date in the United States: September 6, 1946

Production: RKO Radio Pictures
Production Assistant: Barbara Keon

Based on a story by John Taintor Foote, "The Song of the Dragon" (1921)
Screenplay: Ben Hecht
Screenplay Contributor: Alfred Hitchcock
Director of Photography: Ted Tetzlaff
Director of Photography (second unit): Gregg Toland
Special Effects: Vernon L. Walker, Paul Eagler
Sound: John E. Tribby, Terry Kellum
Assistant Director: William Dorfman
Artistic Directors: Albert S. D'Agostino, Carroll Clark
Set Decoration: Darrell Silvera, Claude Carpenter
Makeup: Mel Berns
Costumes: Edith Head
Music: Roy Webb
Film Editing: Theron Warth
Stills Photographer: Robert Capa

Starring: Cary Grant (Devlin), Ingrid Bergman (Alicia Huberman), Claude Rains (Alexander Sebastian), Louis Calhern (Paul Prescott), Leopoldine Konstantin (Madame Sebastian), Reinhold Schünzel (Dr. Anderson), Moroni Olsen (Walter Beardsley), Ivan Triesault (Eric Mathis), Alexis Minotis (Joseph), Wally Brown (Mr. Hopkins), Sir Charles Mendl (the Commodore), Ricardo Costa (Dr. Barbosa), Eberhard Krumschmidt (Emil Hupka), Fay Baker (Ethel), Alfred Hitchcock (guest at the party thrown by Sebastian, drinking champagne)...

"*Notorious* is the quintessence of Hitchcock."

———

François Truffaut

SYNOPSIS

———

The action begins in Miami, on April 24, 1946. John Huberman, a Nazi spy, has been sentenced to twenty years in prison for his part in an anti-American plot. His daughter, Alicia, leads a dissolute life. At a party, she meets a man, Devlin, who seems to be courting her. As a US government agent, he actually wants to recruit her to infiltrate a group of ex-Nazis who are friends of her father's, exiled in Rio and plotting an obscure scheme. To atone for her father's guilt, the young woman accepts. In Rio, Devlin and Alicia fall in love, but she learns the purpose of her mission: to seduce Alexander Sebastian, who lives with his mother in a vast mansion where the group meets regularly. Devlin, disillusioned, becomes sarcastic and distant. Sebastian quickly falls under Alicia's spell and asks her to marry him. As she settles in, the new wife notices that the wine cellar remains locked. She grabs the key and enters the cellar with Devlin during a reception: They discover uranium ore hidden in a bottle of Pommard 1934. Sebastian notices that the key is missing from his key chain and realizes that his wife is a spy. He informs his mother and together they slowly poison her. Devlin, sensing the danger, goes to Sebastian's house. He slips into Alicia's room and helps her down the grand staircase. In front of the group of Nazis, who suspect that Sebastian's wife is a spy, Devlin gets behind the wheel of his car and forbids Sebastian to get in, abandoning him to the accusations of his fearsome accomplices.

GENESIS

In the summer of 1944, after applying the finishing touches to *Spellbound*, Alfred Hitchcock spent two months in England. With businessman Sidney Bernstein, he set about creating an independent film company, Transatlantic Pictures. The two men sought subjects, stars, and financial partners who would enable Transatlantic to compete with the big Hollywood studios. Their ambition was to bring together the best of British and American talent. Hitchcock left London having sketched out the broad outlines of the project. But back in New York, the director, eager to collaborate again with American screenwriter Ben Hecht, signed a contract extension with producer David O. Selznick for two more films, in exchange for a backdated salary increase. Transatlantic Pictures had to wait until 1948 (*Rope*) to become operational.

A Time for Female Spies

Selznick suggested that Hitchcock adapt "The Song of the Dragon," a short story by John Taintor Foote published in two parts in the *Saturday Evening Post* in 1921. He had long owned the rights to this story of a theatrical producer who finds himself forced to lend an actress to federal agents so that she can seduce an English gentleman suspected of being the head of a terrorist group. The man is in fact German and is planning an operation to sabotage American industry.

Hecht and Hitchcock began working from the short story but gradually moved away from it. They transferred the plot to Miami, then Rio, and moved from World War I to World War II. The two men also drew inspiration from the memoirs of Marthe Richard (*Ma vie d'espionne / My Life as a Spy*), a former prostitute who became an aviatrix and spy for the French secret service during World War I. The filmmaker also knew "infiltrators" who seduced potential German agents on behalf of the British Ministry of Information.

Mission: To Find a Mission!

In August 1944, Hitchcock and Hecht locked themselves away for three weeks to write a first treatment that focused the plot on the conspiracy of a group of pro-Nazi scientists who had taken refuge in South America. The film found its definitive American title, *Notorious*, in the sense of "famous" but impliedly "infamous." This alludes to Alicia Huberman's reputation as a woman of loose morals, which she belies through self-sacrifice. In December, the scriptwriters

fleshed out the main characters. One big question remained: What was Alicia's mission?

An Explosive Idea

Their work was interrupted by a trip to Washington, where they had to write and direct a short propaganda documentary (*Watchtower over Tomorrow*). Back in Hollywood in January 1945, Hecht and Hitchcock had a draft of some fifty pages. Selznick expected their work by February 1. In March, the two friends and collaborators finally had an answer to the thorny question of the MacGuffin, and in April the press was informed of the results of their research. In Washington, Hitchcock had heard references to a weapon of mass destruction being developed by a team of American scientists. Already in *Sabotage* (1936), a small newsagent exclaimed, "Big bomb sensation!" The idea came to Hitchcock that the essential element for making a bomb, uranium ore, could be hidden in the German spy's wine cellar. All that remained for the two screenwriters to do was to gather the necessary information to make this MacGuffin credible in the eyes of the public.

A Sensitive Subject

In the spring of 1945, Hitchcock and Hecht visited Dr. Robert A. Millikan at the California Institute of

Prophetic?

Alfred Hitchcock and Ben Hecht placed weapons-grade uranium at the heart of the plot of *Notorious*. To make himself seem prophetic, the filmmaker liked to say that this MacGuffin, found long before the first atomic bomb was dropped on Japan, was pure coincidence. He would even claim to have been "under government surveillance" during filming. Nothing is less certain, but it is true that Selznick, his producer, received a letter from the FBI during filming, informing him that any film featuring members of the American Secret Service must receive State Department approval before being exported abroad. Hitchcock was also advised not to develop the spy story too far.

Technology in Pasadena. Millikan, America's first Nobel Prize–winning physicist, was researching radiation, nuclear energy, and their potential military applications. The scientist responded cautiously to questions from the two scriptwriters, warning them of the dangers of their curiosity. Selznick consulted his employees, who confirmed his fears: Using uranium to make a bomb was a totally far-fetched idea. Hitchcock, for his part, persisted, justifying his point of view by the fact that, in 1945, everyone was talking about an exterminating weapon developed by the United States.

Selznick, unconvinced by the screenplay and overburdened by the budget overruns on a shoot he was much more interested in (*Duel in the Sun*, starring Jennifer Jones), threatened to sell the entire project (script, stars, and director) to producer Hal Wallis, who had long wanted to lure Hitchcock to Warner Bros. But, unconvinced by the film's argument, Wallis refused to take on *Notorious*. In June 1945, Selznick postponed the film. Hitchcock was in no hurry. He had to return to London in mid-June to make a documentary on Nazi concentration camps for the British government. Intended for German audiences, *Memory of the Camps* remained unfinished for a long time (1945–1985).

Hitchcock Liberated

The trip to Washington and the images of concentration camps he saw in London strengthened Hitchcock's resolve to see *Notorious* through. For Selznick, the project remained a burden. Negotiations began with RKO producer William Dozier. Dozier agreed to pay the astronomical sum of $800,000 for the project, and to transfer 50 percent of the profits to Selznick. At the beginning of August, the deal was almost done: Once "loaned" to RKO, Hitchcock almost became his own producer without officially being one. In fact, a clause in the contract denied Selznick, feared for his authoritarianism, any possibility of "intervening in, or supervising production."[1] At the same time, the United States dropped two atomic bombs on Hiroshima and Nagasaki, and Japan surrendered on August 15: Doubts about the relevance of the MacGuffin in *Notorious* were swept away by the terrible reality. RKO scheduled filming for the autumn.

CASTING

From the time of writing the script, Hitchcock already had in mind the two stars he would cast for the project: Ingrid Bergman as Alicia Huberman and Cary Grant as Devlin.

A Five-Star Cast

Hitchcock had already thought of bringing Ingrid Bergman and Cary Grant together onscreen in *Spellbound*. With *Notorious*, he fulfilled his wish to see them embody the ideal Hitchcockian couple. Louis Calhern was chosen to play Paul Prescott, Devlin's superior, an intelligent and insensitive man, a strategist for whom the end justifies the means. Hitchcock chose the elegant Claude Rains to play Alexander Sebastian, the ominous former Nazi, accustomed to memorable villain roles, notably in *Mr. Smith Goes to Washington* (Frank Capra, 1939) and *Casablanca* (Michael Curtiz, 1942). Leopoldine Konstantin, an Austrian film and theater actress exiled to the United States, lent her features to Sebastian's possessive, diabolical mother.

The filmmaker enjoyed the fact of having the members of the fascist group played by real German anti-fascists living in the US: Reinhold Schünzel, an actor and director from Berlin, played Dr. Anderson. Former ballet dancer Ivan Triesault played Eric Mathis, the man who executes Emil, himself played by theater director and actor Eberhard Krumschmidt. Hitchcock collaborated for the first time with cinematographer Ted Tetzlaff. Editing was entrusted to Theron Warth, who had already worked on Leo McCarey's 1942 story of Nazi spies, *Once Upon a Honeymoon*, starring Cary Grant. Carroll Clark (who collaborated with Hitchcock on *Suspicion* in 1941) and Albert S. D'Agostino, accustomed to working on horror films such as those by Jacques Tourneur, designed the sets. *Notorious* marked the beginning of a long and prolific collaboration with renowned costume designer Edith Head, whom Hitchcock "borrowed" from Paramount Studios.

FILMING AND PRODUCTION

After more than a year's preparation, shooting began on October 15, 1945. For the first time in his twenty-five-year career, Hitchcock became his own producer, although he did not have the title, and had almost complete control over his film. A relaxed, family atmosphere seemed to prevail on this shoot, during which the release of *Spellbound* was celebrated.

Writing with the Camera

The majority of camera movements were not indicated in the script and were decided at the time of filming. For Hitchcock, a film was not simply an

A very long kiss between Cary Grant and Ingrid Bergman.

illustration of a script, even though he sometimes previewed the filming down to the smallest detail. The filmmaker above all "wrote" with the camera, and this cinematic writing was never so pure, so eloquent, as in *Notorious*. The slightest object is loaded with meaning and finds its place in the plot. The cinematographer's work, which makes the film sparkle like a diamond, accentuates this impression: "The 'material,' admirably enhanced by Ted Tetzlaff's lighting (faces, metal, glass, jewels, carpets or tiles), shines with a brilliance that is alternately icy or searing."[2]

An Overlong Kiss

Notorious is packed with anthology scenes, with a total of three sequence shots. The most famous of these is the kiss between Alicia and Devlin, which thumbs its nose at the censors of the day. The censors set the maximum duration of a cinematic kiss at three seconds, so Hitchcock had the mischievous idea of filming a long, amorous conversation interspersed with fifteen brief kisses. Ingrid Bergman and Cary Grant, uncomfortable with this "interminable" scene, were invited to improvise a conversation about the dinner menu. The dialogue thus links food and sexuality, making the scene all the more sensual and unsettling. In a long sequence (over two minutes and thirty seconds), the camera follows the couple's embrace from the balcony to the front door in extreme close-up, showing Devlin's telephone conversation as the kissing continues. For Hitchcock, the camera here represents the audience,

An Obsession

While Selznick was keen to tone down references to German fascists, he shared Hitchcock's obsession with what would become of war criminals and their sympathizers after the war. Hitchcock remained marked by images of the liberation of the concentration camps. On March 29, 1945, screenwriter Hecht wrote to his wife: "Cogitated all day: had lunch with [William B.] Ziff and two million dead Jews."

At the reception given by Sebastian and Alicia, Hitchcock begins a crane movement that starts with an overhead shot of the living room where the guests are seated. The camera moves down toward Alicia, stopping just as the spy's fist opens to reveal the key to the wine cellar. Hitchcock had already used this camera movement to pick out a detail in *Young and Innocent* (1937). It enabled him to create a complicity with the viewer and tell two stories simultaneously: The couple are entertaining friends (long shot), while Alicia is on a mission (close-up).

who, because of the close-up, participate in the love scene: "It was like a temporary ménage à trois," he would say.

A Permanent State of Tension

Sexual turmoil, psychological dominance, imminent danger: *Notorious* takes viewers from one tension to another, keeping them captive. It is impossible not to fear for Alicia's life once she marries Sebastian.

Some scenes heighten this sense of insecurity: the moment when the young woman steals the key to the wine cellar, the moment when she has to reinsert it into her husband's key chain, or when she slips away from the reception with Devlin to search the wine cellar. This sequence, one of Hitchcock's most frightening, derives its effectiveness from a parallel montage. On the one hand, the filmmaker films the

party in full swing and the champagne stock dwindling, each time running the risk of forcing the husband to go downstairs and surprise the spy lovers. On the other, he shows the investigating couple and Devlin's unfortunate breakage of a bottle of 1934 Pommard containing a strange granular substance—uranium, of course, but this powder and broken bottle might also represent the hourglass that counts down the suspense to its breaking point.

RECEPTION

Filming ended in January 1946, and Ingrid Bergman would remember it as the happiest of her three collaborations with Hitchcock. The film was released progressively throughout the US between August and September 1946. In September, it was selected for

For Hitchcock Addicts

Hitchcock recounted that a distant memory inspired the idea for the long kissing scene in *Notorious*. On his way from Boulogne-sur-Mer to Paris, his train passed a factory with a large brick wall. A couple stood at the foot of the wall, the boy urinating and the girl holding his hand. "She lowered her eyes to see what he was doing, then raised them to look around, before lowering them again to check on him. And that's what gave me the idea: she wouldn't let go. A love story shouldn't be interrupted, not even by the need to urinate."[3]

Wine, Champagne, and Coffee

It was a bottle of wine that first tipped off Alicia (Ingrid Bergman) at dinner at Sebastian's; it was a bottle of champagne that made Paul Prescott realize that Devlin (Cary Grant) loved Alicia; and it was in bottles of vintage wine that the Nazis hid the uranium. Nor can the cups of poisoned coffee served to Alicia by her mother-in-law and, at the beginning of the film, the heroine's worldly alcoholism be forgotten. *Notorious* subtly deploys the theme of drinking and the motif of the bottle. Each instance, far from being merely decorative, plays a decisive role in the film's dramaturgy.

At the very beginning of the film, we may think we can see Hitchcock (a heavyset policeman with a cigar in his mouth) walking past Alicia's house. The "real" Hitchcock, however, appears furtively after an hour, at Sebastian and Alicia's big party. As the hostess worries about the number of bottles of champagne left, the filmmaker stands in front of the buffet, empties his glass, and steps out of frame.

the official competition at the Cannes Film Festival. *Notorious* was one of Hitchcock's biggest financial successes, grossing $5 million on a budget of $2 million.

Sweetness, Grace, and Elegance

The critics were unanimous: *Notorious* was a masterpiece destined for great popular success. Bosley Crowther of the *New York Times* praised the work of Ben Hecht and Alfred Hitchcock: They had written and directed "in brilliant style a romantic melodrama which is just about as thrilling as they come—velvet smooth in dramatic action...sure in its characters" (August 16, 1946). The film was released in France in March 1948; André Bazin in *L'Écran français* was far from convinced. While he admired the filmmaker's rhetoric ("the most brilliant in the world") and the complexity of his "spiral dollies," he found the scenario decidedly impossible: "The subjective camera is all very well, but there still has to be a subject!" (March 16, 1948). On the other hand, Maurice Schérer (alias Éric Rohmer), in *La Revue du cinéma* (July 1948), which devoted a series of contrasting texts to the filmmaker, praised the originality of *Notorious* and its ability "to take advantage of all the resources of Ingrid Bergman's face...*Notorious* is a film of close-ups. Its best moments are those when the actors' heads occupy the entire surface of the screen."

The Grand Style

"A cartoon could not be more precise," François Truffaut rightly confided to Hitchcock. He thus evokes the film's perfect virtuosity, in which nothing is missing and nothing is overdone. *Notorious* is brimming with ideas and visual rhymes (the last six scenes echo the first six), bringing Hitchcock's art to the highest level. Everything is eloquent, everything has meaning, and, at the same time, everything is contained in a single, wonderfully pure cinematic movement. Despite the historical backdrop and a topical MacGuffin in the form of uranium, Hitchcock would confess that "the whole film was conceived as a love story":[4] an amorous encounter thwarted by a sense of duty. As is often the case in Hitchcock's work, duty and danger are the obstacles that a man and a woman place in the way of each other's desire.

The Story of a Face

A story of love and uranium, *Notorious* also tells the story of a face: that of Ingrid Bergman. The film, a true woman's picture, can be seen as so many attempts by Hitchcock to fathom the soul of his heroine, to capture in close-up the slightest quiver, the tiniest variation on the face of his actress: sleep, illness, desire, fatigue, fear, drunkenness, suffering. The story is that of a woman in the midst of men who consider her a sinner. At the end of her mission—in other words, a series of trials and ordeals—she acquires a saint-like image, and this is one of the recurring motifs in the actress's career.

Snow White Revisited

Notorious is imbued with the Gothic novel atmosphere that Hitchcock brilliantly illustrated in *Rebecca* (1939): In one film as in the other, a vast, disquieting mansion brings together the drama and affects of the characters. This spy tale is also like a retelling of "Snow White": At the first dinner with the fascist group, there are seven men in the house (including the butler); Alicia is gradually poisoned by her stepmother, and a kiss from Devlin, her Prince Charming, awakens her from her deep slumber.

Jessica Tandy, Tippi Hedren, Rod
Taylor (*The Birds*, 1962).
Right: Joseph Cotten, Patricia
Collinge (*Shadow of a Doubt*, 1942).

"Mother!"
The Hitchcock Matriarchs

The importance of the mother figure in Hitchcock's cinema has one of its origins in the Master's biography: The filmmaker was fifteen when his father died in 1914, a death that strengthened his bond with his mother, Emma. In 1940, he insisted in vain that she leave bomb-ravaged England and join him in the United States. Emma Hitchcock died in September 1942 while her youngest son, wracked with guilt, directed *Shadow of a Doubt*, naming the mother character Emma, the most luminous and idealized protective figure in his entire filmography. Sweet, joyful Emma Newton (Patricia Collinge) sacrifices herself for her children to the point of making her daughter Charlie (Teresa Wright) feel remorse. Beyond the denouement, Charlie protects her beloved mother from the terrible truth and the experience of evil. Likewise, the filmmaker seems to have

waited, as if out of politeness, for his own mother's death before giving life to increasingly bizarre and evil mothers.

Confessions

Hitchcock recounted an astonishing anecdote about his relationship with his mother. Every evening, little Alfred was subjected to the same ritual: At the foot of Emma's bed, he would tell her about his day in minute detail, a tradition that continued into the filmmaker's adulthood. He would add that the memory of this evening confession had never left him. He transposed and demonized this memory in *Notorious* (1946): Alexander (Claude Rains) goes to the bedside of his mother (Leopoldine Konstantin) after discovering that his wife is a spy. Alex, distraught, makes no decisions until he has consulted

his mother and relies on her. It is this fairy-tale stepmother who decides to poison the intruder. *Notorious* invents the figure of the possessive, horrific mother, linked to another Hitchcock motif: the disquieting house that represents her territory and materializes the power of her hold (the "mother" house).

"A Boy's Best Friend Is His Mother" (Norman Bates)

Living in autarky with an overbearing mother, Norman Bates (*Psycho*, 1960) finds her in bed with a man one night and murders the lovers. To erase this matricide from his mind, he steals Mrs. Bates's corpse, which he insanely tries to revive by disguising himself as her. A schizophrenic, Bates oscillates between his fragile personality and that of a dead mother, "jealous" and all-powerful, who kills "in place of" his son whenever he desires a woman. The topography of the Bates territory reproduces this dual personality: on one side, the motel, site of the son's voyeuristic impulses and symbol of his sex life. On the other, the dead woman's gloomy mansion looms over him, *ad vitam aeternam*, like a castrating superego.

The Mother on Their Heels

Whether tragic or comic, Hitchcock's characters are often "aging" boys struggling to cut the umbilical cord. *North by Northwest* (1958), a spy film, is also a bizarre tale of emancipation: Roger Thornhill (Cary Grant) loses his mother's embrace and falls into the arms of the beautiful Eve Kendall (Eva Marie Saint). Grace Kelly, whose mother in *To Catch a Thief* (1954) is played by the mordant Jessie Royce Landis, follows a similar trajectory, while the film's final line heralds the beginning of trouble for Cary Grant: "So this is where you live. Oh, Mother will love it up here!"

"Poor Little Thing!"

When the beautiful Melanie (Tippi Hedren) arrives at Bodega Bay (*The Birds*, 1962), it is to seduce Mitch, a dashing lawyer (Rod Taylor). Since the death of his father, Mitch has been living with his mother, Lydia (Jessica Tandy), who bears a striking resemblance to Melanie. To protect her from jealousy, her son refrains from serious relationships. The invasion of the birds coincides with the arrival of Melanie, the first to be attacked, and may symbolize the mother's wrath, an anger that will continue to grow until it assumes the horrific form of raging clouds. In Greek mythology, a harpy is a divinity of devastation, half-woman, half-bird. At the end of the film, Melanie is left for dead by a more violent attack than the others, and Lydia finally calms down. The predatory mother even softens as she nurses the young woman back to health. Melanie is no longer a rival, but a little girl who snuggles up to her "mother" as their car pulls away from a threat that is no longer so mysterious.

"Goodbye, Sugarpop . . ."

At the very end of *Marnie* (1964), the young woman recalls the maternal murder of a lover who got too close to her little daughter. In releasing this repressed memory, Marnie makes a shocking discovery: Her mother has always loved her, because she killed for her. Freed from her trauma and pathologies, she can finally leave the territory of childhood and begin her life as a woman. For one shot, Hitchcock lingers on the grieving mother, frozen in the sadness of a final farewell to her daughter: "Goodbye, Sugarpop."

A Seven-Star HIT by the Producer and Director of SPELLBOUND

GREGORY PECK
ANN TODD
(Miss Todd appears by arrangement with J. Arthur Rank Organization)
CHARLES LAUGHTON
CHARLES COBURN
ETHEL BARRYMORE
and two new Selznick Stars
LOUIS JOURDAN
and
Valli

in DAVID O. SELZNICK'S Production of ALFRED HITCHCOCK'S

THE **PARADINE** CASE

The Paradine Case

🏳 **United States** · 🕐 **2 hrs 5** · 🎞 **Black and White** · 🔇 **Mono** (Western Electric Recording) · ▭ **1.37:1**

SYNOPSIS

Production Dates: December 19, 1946–May 7, 1947
Release Date in the United States: July 13, 1948

Production: Selznick International Pictures, Vanguard Films
Producer: David O. Selznick
Production Manager: W. Argyle Nelson

Based on the novel of the same name by Robert Hichens (1933)
Adaptation: Alma Reville, Whitfield Cook, James Bridie
Screenplay: David O. Selznick
Additional Dialogues: Ben Hecht
Director of Photography: Lee Garmes
Special Effects: Clarence Slifer
Sound: James G. Stewart, Richard Van Hessen
Assistant Director: Lowell J. Farrell
Art Direction: Joseph McMillan Johnson, Thomas Morahan
Set Decoration: Joseph B. Platt, Emile Kuri
Music: Franz Waxman
Film Editing: Hal C. Kern, John Faure

Starring: Gregory Peck (Anthony Keane), Ann Todd (Gay Keane), Charles Laughton (Judge Lord Thomas Horfield), Charles Coburn (Sir Simon Flaquer), Ethel Barrymore (Lady Sophie Horfield), Louis Jourdan (André Latour), Alida Valli (Maddalena Anna Paradine), Leo G. Carroll (Sir Joseph), Joan Tetzel (Judy Flaquer), Isabel Elsom (innkeeper), John Williams (the lawyer Collins), Alfred Hitchcock (man with a cello case)...

The setting is London. The beautiful Maddalena Paradine is accused of poisoning her blind husband, Colonel Paradine. Young lawyer Anthony Keane is assigned to defend her. From his first trips to the visiting room, he falls in love with her. The presiding judge of the court, Lord Horfield, is a cynical, lecherous character who tried to flirt with Keane's wife, Gay. She sees her husband's predicament but urges him to continue defending a woman of whose innocence he is convinced. Visiting the Paradine country house in the course of his investigations, Keane encounters André Latour, the deceased's loyal valet, who expresses the utmost contempt for Mrs. Paradine, who is described as evil. During the trial, Keane seeks to pin suspicion on Latour, whom he accuses of having tried to seduce Maddalena Paradine, of having been dismissed for this reason, and of having taken revenge. Between hearings, Latour commits suicide. In despair, Maddalena confesses to having been the valet's mistress and her husband's murderer. Keane, who has been the defendant's plaything and whose reputation has been ruined, leaves the court, devastated. At a dinner party, Horfield talks to his more sensitive wife about the need to punish criminals. Gay Keane, for her part, tries to save her marriage and, full of hope, proposes to her husband that they start afresh.

"Surprising how closely the convolutions of a walnut resemble that of the human brain."

Judge Lord Thomas Horfield (Charles Laughton), in *The Paradine Case*

Gregory Peck, Charles Laughton.

GENESIS AND CASTING

Alfred Hitchcock still owed David O. Selznick a film under the terms of their agreement. He was thinking of setting up his own production company in association with his friend Sidney Bernstein. For his part, Selznick was considering signing him to a new contract for five titles with no exclusive commitments. After the experience of *The Paradine Case*, Selznick unhesitatingly dropped the offer.

A Script in Stages

For what would prove to be their last joint production, Selznick considered adapting Robert Hichens's 1933 English novel *The Paradine Case*, a courtroom drama set in London. Hitchcock worked on the script with Alma Reville, assisted informally by Whitfield Cook, future screenwriter of *Strangers on a Train* (1950). With Selznick's agreement, Hitchcock then hired Scottish playwright James Bridie, who was based in Glasgow and discussed the script's various stages of progress with him from a distance, by means of long telegrams. The result did not please the producer. Hitchcock put Alma back to work and asked his accomplice Ben Hecht (*Spellbound*, 1944; *Notorious*, 1946), not named in the credits, to lend a hand.

Casting Disparities

The two leading male actors each found themselves in a Hitchcock film for the second time: Gregory Peck (*Spellbound*), imposed by Selznick, who had just filmed *Duel in the Sun* with him, had become a star. As for the phenomenal Charles Laughton (*Jamaica Inn*, 1938), he excelled in the role of a ruthless, libidinous judge, Lord Horfield. French actor Louis Jourdan, in his first Hollywood film, was another of the producer's choices that Hitchcock was to regret, considering him too elegant to play a character he wanted to portray more boorishly (Mrs. Paradine's valet and lover). After considering Greta Garbo for a time, Selznick wanted to make Italian actress Alida Valli a Hollywood star—but without success. The filmmaker lamented her "impassivity" and hesitant English. On the other hand, he got

Freeze Frame

While investigating the Paradine family's stately country home, Anthony Keane visits Maddalena's bedroom. The place is marked by the ghostly presence of the young woman. The camera glides over clothes left carelessly on the bed, including sophisticated undergarments. This suggestive sequence echoes a scene from *Rebecca* (1939), a fiction that also evokes a great absentee and Selznick's first production directed by Hitchcock, eight years earlier, when he had just arrived in Hollywood.

on very well with English actress Ann Todd, who played the lawyer Keane's wife.

FILMING AND PRODUCTION

During trips to England, Hitchcock identified various locations (the court, the prison) that would be reproduced in Selznick's studios. The reconstruction of the Old Bailey courtroom alone took eighty-five days, at a cost of $80,000.

The Shadow of Selznick

Filming proved particularly difficult and was one of the filmmaker's worst memories. Selznick was constantly sending Hitchcock scraps of corrected script, adding dialogue and sticking to the book. He forced Hitchcock to rework entire scenes, hating the long, sophisticated shots the filmmaker favored. Relations with cinematographer Lee Garmes (*Scarface*, *Shanghai Express*) were complicated by the conflict between director and producer. Selznick's choices, sometimes absurd and destructive, contributed to the film's academic style.

RECEPTION

The film was a commercial failure, receiving a lukewarm reception at its Los Angeles premiere on December 29, 1947.

Points of View

Bosley Crowther, for the *New York Times*: "David O. Selznick and Alfred Hitchcock have put upon the screen a slick piece of static entertainment in their garrulous *Paradine Case*" (January 8, 1948).

In France, critics were divided. Jean-Louis Tallenay, in *Radio-Cinéma-Télévision*, observed with discernment that the two most sympathetic characters on the surface, Keane and Mrs. Paradine, reveal themselves to be reprehensible and contemptible in the course of the film: "For once, we are not presented with puppets whose first gesture and first sentence definitively determine their character" (January 29, 1950).

A Film Saved by Laughton

Hitchcock disliked the film, which was made under the crushing control of the producer, saying he hated the casting choices and the confusion of the script. Admittedly, *The Paradine Case* is an unfortunately overblown work. What remains is the masterly performance of Charles Laughton, to whom Hitchcock offered a sequence of great cruelty at the end of the film: the dinner party where he reveals his ruthlessness toward his wife.

Old Bailey, the court of justice in London, reconstructed in the studio.

NOTHING
EVER
HELD
YOU
LIKE
ALFRED
HITCHCOCK'S

ROPE

STARRING

JAMES STEWART

WITH JOHN DALL · FARLEY GRANGER · SIR CEDRIC HARDWICKE

AND

CONSTANCE COLLIER · JOAN CHANDLER

Screen Play by Arthur Laurents
From the Play by Patrick Hamilton
Director of Photography,
Joseph Valentine, A.S.C.

IN COLOR BY

TECHNICOLOR

Presented by

WARNER BROS.

A TRANSATLANTIC PICTURES PRODUCTION

Rope

**United States /
Great Britain** • **1 hr 20** • **Color**
(Technicolor) • **Mono**
(RCA Sound System) • **1.37:1**

Production Dates: January 12–February 21, 1948
Release Date in the United States: September 25, 1948

Production: Transatlantic Pictures for Warner Bros.
Producers: Sidney Bernstein, Alfred Hitchcock
Production Manager: Fred Ahern

Based on the play of the same name by Patrick Hamilton (1929)
Adaptation: Hume Cronyn
Screenplay: Arthur Laurents
Directors of Photography: William V. Skall, Joseph Valentine
Camera Operator: Harry Marsh
Camera Movement Operators: Edward Fitzgerald, Paul G. Hill,
Richard Emmons, Morris Rosen
Lighting Technician: Jim Potevin
Sound: Al Riggs
Assistant Directors: Lowell J. Farrell, Claude Archer
Art Direction: Perry Ferguson
Set Decoration: Emile Kuri, Howard Bristol
Hair Stylist: Agnes Flanagan
Makeup: Perc Westmore, Ed Voight
Costumes: Adrian
Music: David Buttolph
Film Editing: William H. Ziegler

Starring: James Stewart (Rupert Cadell), John Dall (Brandon), Farley Granger
(Phillip), Cedric Hardwicke (Mr. Kentley), Constance Collier (Mrs. Atwater), Douglas
Dick (Kenneth), Edith Evanson (Mrs. Wilson), Dick Hogan (David Kentley), Joan
Chandler (Janet), Alfred Hitchcock (man walking in the street next to a woman)...

SYNOPSIS

In New York, two young men, Brandon and
Phillip, strangle David Kentley, a former university classmate. They hide his body in the living
room trunk of Brandon's spacious apartment. As the
two murderers wait for a few friends at a preholiday
party, they decide to use the trunk containing the
body as a serving tray to display food and drink for
the party. This macabre idea enables them to enjoy
their crime, which they consider perfect, and gives
them a sense of cynical superiority over the rest of
humanity, which they consider despicable. Among
the guests at the party are David Kentley's father,
his aunt, his fiancée, Janet, another university classmate, and Rupert Cadell, their former teacher and
mentor, whose Nietzschean theories on the superman encouraged their crime. The conversation turns
to Cadell's lessons. Noting David's absence, Mr.
Kentley and Janet express growing concern. Phillip's
nervousness attracts Cadell's attention and, on leaving the apartment, he discovers David's hat in the
cloakroom, a sign of his presence there only a short
time before. Claiming to have forgotten his cigarette
case, he returns and manages to extract a confession from both men, discovering the corpse in the
trunk. He expresses his contempt for their barbaric
act and alerts the police by firing shots through
the window.

Constance Collier, Joan Chandler, Douglas Dick, Cedric Hardwicke, John Dall, Farley Granger, James Stewart.

GENESIS

Rope was the first film produced by Transatlantic Pictures, the company created by Hitchcock and his partner Sidney Bernstein. The filmmaker was finally able to grant himself the artistic freedom he had long sought, after years spent under the thumb of authoritarian producer David O. Selznick. His first independent production should have been *Under Capricorn*, starring Ingrid Bergman, but the actress was unavailable. *Rope* is an audacious film on two counts: the director's technical challenge and the subject matter.

Some Guests and a Corpse

Alfred Hitchcock had long been thinking of adapting *Rope*, a play by British playwright Patrick Hamilton written in 1929. He discovered it in England in the early 1930s. The play was inspired by a 1924 incident in the United States. Nathan Leopold and Richard Loeb, two students at the University of Chicago, had executed a teenage boy, both to assert their superior nature and to enjoy a purely gratuitous gesture. Leopold and Loeb were a homosexual couple.

Hamilton's play features two cynical young men from good families hiding the body of the murdered man inside a trunk in a room where they are hosting a reception for the victim's fiancée, his parents, and a few friends.

Hidden Homosexuality

After calling on the play's author to write the adaptation, an unsatisfied Alfred Hitchcock turned to his friend, actor Hume Cronyn, who had appeared in *Shadow of a Doubt* (1942) and *Lifeboat* (1943). Cronyn had only written a few short stories and a screenplay that was never filmed, but which the filmmaker had read. Hitchcock enjoyed their long conversations and relied upon Cronyn's theatrical experience. He then asked New York playwright Arthur Laurents to take over the script. Laurents had just rewritten the screenplay for director Anatole Litvak's *The Snake Pit*. Laurents recounted that the main difficulties were the transposition of the action from England to New York and rewriting dialogue that was too typically British. It was also necessary to mask the homosexuality of the characters, which

At the blackboard, Professor Hitchcock explains to his crew (including James Stewart, seated on the right) a long camera movement in the film's only set.

was implied by various expressions such as "my dear boy," harmless in Great Britain, but too suggestive in the United States. In a Hollywood film, it was obviously out of the question to tackle such a subject head-on. Laurents's homosexuality—at that time he was the lover of Farley Granger, one of the film's actors—was also a factor in Hitchcock's decision to hire the playwright. The filmmaker wanted the characters' homosexuality to be evident without the censors noticing.

CASTING

Hitchcock considered Cary Grant for the role of Rupert Cadell, the cynical mentor, and Montgomery Clift and Farley Granger as the pair of assassins. Grant and Clift refused to take part in the film, aware that they would be exposing their own sexual orientation. John Dall was offered the role of Brandon, the dominant member of the murderous duo. He was nominated for an Academy Award for Best Supporting Actor after his performance in Irving Rapper's *The Corn Is Green*. A homosexual himself, he took on the role of Brandon in full knowledge of the situation.

A Challenge for James Stewart

Hitchcock's new agent, Lew Wasserman, who was also James Stewart's agent, convinced the actor to accept the role turned down by Cary Grant for three hundred thousand dollars and a share of the profits. Stewart's image in the eyes of the public ruled out the possibility of a homosexual relationship between the three main male characters: part of the fundamental nature of the original character thus disappeared. In addition, James Stewart did not feel comfortable in the role of a protagonist who was, after all, morally ambiguous. Yet he took up the challenge: "My professor character was the one who had unwittingly inspired the two killers…I'd never done anything like it. But Hitchcock persuaded me to do it because, in his view, James Stewart was the last person on earth you'd expect to be the instigator of such a dreadful crime. As an actor, this intrigued me. That's why I did it."[1] Moody during the shooting, he drank more than he should have, and suffered, to the point of losing sleep, from the constraints imposed by the technical conditions of the shoot and the numerous rehearsals required of him.

Secondary Roles

Hitchcock hired Cedric Hardwicke to play the vic-tim's father. The actor had already appeared in *Suspicion* (1941), and the director would direct him again in an episode of his *Alfred Hitchcock Presents*, "Wet Saturday" (1956), in a role diamet-rically opposed to that of Mr. Kentley, the honest man scandalized by Rupert Cadell's fascist, albeit ironic, remarks.

Hitchcock entrusted the role of Janet, David Kentley's fiancée, to a newcomer, Joan Chandler, who had appeared a few months earlier in Jean Negulesco's *Humoresque*. After *Rope*, she only appeared in TV series.

The whimsical Mrs. Atwater, Mr. Kentley's sister, is played by Constance Collier. Born in 1878, she made her theatrical debut in Great Britain at the end of the nineteenth century, then in the United States in 1918, two years after playing Lady Macbeth in a film by John Emerson. A great figure onstage, she also played a series of small, picturesque roles in film. She was also an old acquaintance of

Hitchcock's: Under the shared pseudonym David L'Estrange, she wrote a play with Ivor Novello (the actor in *The Lodger*), which the filmmaker adapted in 1927 as *Downhill*.

FILMING AND PRODUCTION

At the time, the average Hollywood film consisted of between four and six hundred shots. Hitchcock took the radical decision to shoot *Rope* in just elev-en shots (ten plus one for the credits), the length of which corresponded to the maximum film length allowed by the camera magazine, that is, ten minutes.

Why take such a gamble? From the outset, the filmmaker was tempted by all manner of experi-ments and technical challenges. For a long time, he had been thinking about the formal challenge that this film represented, the extreme duration of the shots being likely to make the viewer feel the irre-versible nature of time: It was a way of subjecting the audience to an experience of fatality.

Some of the technical crew on the set of *Rope*. In the center, Alfred Hitchcock.

The Illusion of Action Taking Place in Real Time

Hitchcock sought to give viewers the illusion of an uninterrupted continuity of action, as if they were attending a play, but as seen from the stage itself. The camera, mounted on a dolly developed by the filmmaker for his previous film, *The Paradine Case* (1947), follows the actors wherever they go. Depending on the camera's comings and goings, walls are lifted or slid on ("overhead tracks heavily greased with Vaseline"),[2] furniture was moved by propmen on all fours. In the film's credits, in addition to the two cinematographers and the cameraman, four technicians are credited as being "in charge of camera movements." In the words of the filmmaker, "*Rope* was a miracle of cueing" between actors, technicians, camera, and objects. Six microphones covered the entire space of the apartment, and a special floor, built above the normal floor, was completely soundproofed.

A Grueling Filming Experience

This kind of approach required numerous rehearsals, which lasted for weeks. The movements of the actors and camera were recorded on a blackboard. Filming was just as exhausting for the actors as it was for the technicians. Scenes, which could last up to ten minutes each, often had to be interrupted and then restarted from the beginning for a variety of

reasons: a stagehand in the shot, a lighting fault, an actor making a mistake when speaking his lines, a noise on the set, and so forth. Between three and six takes were required for each shot.

A False Continuity

During projection, the transition from one reel to the next should ideally be invisible onscreen. So the camera sometimes stops on an actor's back to obscure the shot and allow the next to follow imperceptibly, in the continuity of movement. In this film, however, Hitchcock changed his point of view four times when moving from one shot to the next, and a shot followed a countershot, breaking the visual continuity.

These "apparent" splices occur every twenty minutes, corresponding to the length of a film reel as configured for projection (i.e., the equivalent of two camera magazines of film). They serve as markers for the projectionist, announcing the necessary change of projector after each reel has been unwound. The existence of these "visible" splices was sometimes overlooked by commentators, who remained convinced for a long time—wrongly—of an uninterrupted visual continuity.

View of New York at Dusk

Hitchcock had a cyclorama built, a panorama of New York seen from the bay window that formed

352 *Rope*

the backdrop of the set. The model was three times larger than the set. The lights on the buildings were produced by at least six thousand small bulbs, and two hundred neon signs lit up as night fell during the course of the plot. The panorama, this "light organ for a nocturnal symphony,"[2] was meant to represent Manhattan as it might be seen from the window of an apartment between Fifty-Fourth Street and First Avenue. The smoke rising from the roofs was produced by small pipes coated with dry ice to retard condensation and reduce the speed of the vapor. The props department also used glass wool to make clouds suspended from wires.

The First Film in Color

Rope is Alfred Hitchcock's first color film. It used the Technicolor trichromatic process, which required a bulky camera, making it difficult to move the camera around, in addition to the complexity of setting up the sequence shots. According to Hitchcock, the main dramatic role of color was played by the background, New York and its sky, where all the chromatic variations take place. Consequently, violent contrasts between the costumes and the space in which the actors move should be avoided. In his interviews with François Truffaut, the Master recalled that, when he saw the film, he felt that the sunset had an exaggerated orange cast: "It was like a vulgar

postcard, totally unacceptable." For this reason, he had the last five reels returned to the film developer.

RECEPTION

After some thirty-five days of shooting in early 1948, *Rope* was released in US cinemas at the end of September. Critics were generally disappointed.

A Story of Meager Range

For the American magazine *Variety* (September 1, 1948), "Hitchcock could have chosen a more entertaining subject to use the moving camera and the

---

A Triple Session

Since everything was shot continuously, with the only limit being the end of the film in the camera magazine, the young actor who found himself locked in the wooden trunk in the first scene had to stay inside for ten minutes, long enough to shoot the three hundred meters of film. In fact, he stayed there for three times ten minutes, as this scene required at least three takes.

Where Is Hitchcock?

Hitchcock appears twice in *Rope*. The first time, during the opening credits with a bird's-eye shot of the street below the protagonists' apartment building, as a passerby walking on the opposite sidewalk, accompanied by a woman. The second, more unexpected appearance comes at the fifty-fourth minute of the film. In the background, through the room's bay window, a red neon sign reproduces the famous profile that Hitchcock drew of himself and that his TV series would make iconic from the mid-1950s onward. Because the neon sign is difficult to spot, the director decided to include it in the opening shot.

staging techniques employed." Bosley Crowther wrote in the *New York Times* (August 27, 1948) that "the novelty of the picture is not in the drama itself, it being a plainly deliberate and rather thin exercise in suspense, but merely in the method which Mr. Hitchcock has used to stretch the intended tension for the length of the little stunt" for a "story of meager range." *Harrison's Reports*, on the other hand, hailed "an exceptionally fine psychological thriller" (August 28, 1948). Much later, many critics on the other side of the Atlantic would admit that the film, which was not a great popular success at the time, had been underestimated in its day.

"A Dubious Entertainment" for the French

Rope was not distributed in France until February 1950. Here too the reviews were rather harsh. "The whole film gives the impression of being the (dubious) entertainment of its makers. These American 'intellectuals' seen by Americans are a little too simplistic, and we do not quite see the whole point of this painful story," said Jean-Louis Tallenay in *Radio-Cinéma-Télévision* (February 12, 1950). "*Rope* is one of the most unhealthy works imaginable," as one read in *Le Monde* (March 1, 1950). The critic in *Combat* (January 16, 1950), however, praised the technical feat, calling *Rope* "a revolutionary film." Five years after its French release, François Truffaut wrote in *Arts* magazine (May 1955): "*Rope* is not just an experimental film, and in this story of gratuitous crime we find all the themes that Alfred Hitchcock was to spell out more clearly in his later films: the

fascination of one being by another, identification and the exchange of murders."

Hitchcock and His Reversals

The reception of *Rope*, even from Hitchcock's own perspective, changed over the decades. For a long time, the director would claim that it was one of his most exciting films; he even devoted a long text to it, in which he "delighted" in the description of the practical difficulties of shooting and the inventiveness of the crew.[2] That is, until his interviews in the early 1960s, with both Peter Bogdanovich and Truffaut. To Truffaut, he admitted that it was nothing more than a vain technical feat, at odds with his conception of cinema as the art of montage: "I don't know why I let myself get drawn into this *Rope* thing. I can't call it anything but a trick." No doubt he was disappointed by the film's reception and outcome, which, at the time of its release, testified to a genuine lack of critical and popular understanding.

Freeze Frame

One sequence in the film recalls Hitchcock's perverse penchant for placing the audiences on the side of the "bad guy." As the reception slowly draws to a close, the housekeeper begins to clear the lid of the trunk used to hold the food and cutlery. She brings books with her: Will she open the trunk and discover the body it contains? The audience shudders at the thought of the corpse being revealed. The duration of the action, the absence of editing, and the banality of the housekeeper's gestures create a suspense that is both intolerable and ethically equivocal.

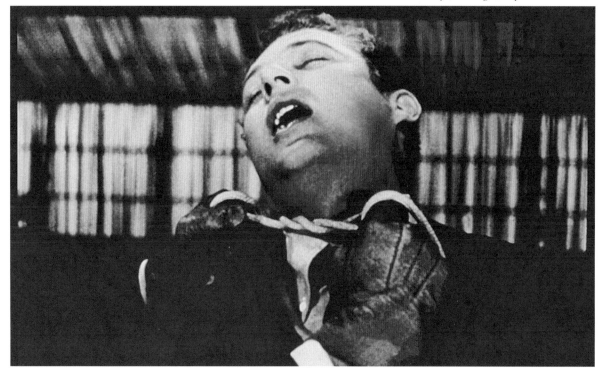

A Variation on the Hitchcock Triangle

With *Rope*, Alfred Hitchcock perversely revisits a familiar pattern in his films of the time: that of the triangle in which one of the vertices (until then a woman, such as Ingrid Bergman in *Spellbound*, 1944, or *Notorious*, 1946) constitutes a power issue for two rival men. In *Rope*, this role is played by Farley Granger (Phillip), also caught between two men: a father figure (Rupert Cadell) and a lover (Brandon).

Shared Guilt

The unease felt by some commentators at the time, as much as the film's commercial failure, undoubtedly stems from the ambiguity of the character played by James Stewart, an actor whose roles until then allowed no moral equivocation. Is he on the side of good or evil?

In *Rope*, although he represents, in extremis, reason in the face of barbarity, he is also and above all considered morally responsible for the murder committed. His long, sanctimonious tirade to the two murderers, ironically reminiscent of the grand declarations of the characters he played in Frank Capra's prewar films (such as *Mr. Smith Goes to Washington*, 1939), only superficially erases the central role played by Rupert Cadell in the perpetration of the crime.

Freeze Frame

The trailer is particularly morbid. At the start, a card over a shot of Central Park announces: "New York, One Spring Afternoon." Then we discover a couple, David Kentley (Dick Hogan) and his amour, Janet (Joan Chandler), sitting on a bench. The man is hoping for an answer to his marriage proposal, and the young woman promises to make up her mind at the reception to which they've been invited later that afternoon. As David walks away, James Stewart's voice comes on: "That's the last time she ever saw him alive." This is followed by a shot of Stewart, facing the camera, addressing the audience: "And that's the last time you'll ever see him alive." Indeed, *Rope* audiences will very briefly see David again at the very beginning of the film, strangled by Brandon and Phillip, then thrown into a trunk.

INGRID BERGMAN SHOWS YOU
THE HEIGHTS *AND THE DEPTHS*
TO WHICH A WOMAN
LIKE THIS
CAN GO!

Strange things happen to
INGRID BERGMAN
JOSEPH COTTEN
MICHAEL WILDING

IN ALFRED HITCHCOCK'S
Under Capricorn
COLOR BY *TECHNICOLOR*

A
TRANSATLANTIC
PICTURE
DIRECTED BY
ALFRED HITCHCOCK

PRESENTED BY
WARNER BROS.

Screen Play by James Bridie   Adaptation by Hume Cronyn   Based on the Play by John Colton and Margaret Linden
From the Novel by Helen Simpson

Under Capricorn

United States / Great Britain · 1 hr 57 · Color (Technicolor) · Mono (Western Electric Recording) · 1.37:1

Production Dates: July 21–October 18, 1948
Release Date in the United States: October 8, 1949

Production: Transatlantic Pictures
Producers: Sidney Bernstein, Alfred Hitchcock
Production Manager: Fred Ahern

Based on a novel of the same name by Helen Simpson (1937) and a play by John Colton and Margaret Linden
Adaptation: Hume Cronyn
Screenplay: James Bridie
Director of Photography: Jack Cardiff
Camera Operators: Dennis Hatt, George Pink
Camera Movement Operators: Paul Beeson, Ian Craig, Jack Haste, David MacNeilly
Sound: Peter Handford
Assistant Director: C. Foster Kemp
Alfred Hitchcock's Assistant: Peggy Robertson
Art Direction: Thomas Morahan
Hair Stylist: Joan Johnstone
Makeup: Charles Parker
Costumes: Roger Furse, Julia Squire
Music: Richard Addinsell
Film Editing: A. S. Bates

Starring: Ingrid Bergman (Lady Henrietta Flusky), Joseph Cotten (Sam Flusky), Michael Wilding (Charles Adare), Margaret Leighton (Milly), Cecil Parker (governor), Denis O'Dea (Mr. Corrigan), Jack Watling (Winter), Harcourt Williams (coachman), John Ruddock (Mr. Potter), Bill Shine (Mr. Banks), Victor Lucas (Reverend Smiley), Ronald Adam (Mr. Riggs), Francis De Wolff (Major Wilkins), G. H. Mulcaster (Dr. Macallister), Olive Sloane (Sal), Maureen Delaney (Flo), Julia Lang (Susan), Betty McDermott (Martha), Alfred Hitchcock (man at the entrance to the palace at the governor's reception)…

SYNOPSIS

The setting is Sydney, 1831. To start a new life, Irishman Charles Adare accompanies his cousin, the new governor of the British colony, to Australia. He meets Sam Flusky, a former convict turned wealthy landowner. Sam invites him to dinner at his home: Charles discovers that all the guests have come without their wives. During the evening, the host's Irish wife, Lady Henrietta Flusky, appears barefoot and drunk. Charles recognizes her as a childhood friend of his sister's. He befriends the couple and tries to restore the young woman's self-esteem. Little by little, he succeeds: Henrietta even causes a sensation at the Governor's Ball, but her husband, on the advice of his housekeeper, Milly, secretly in love with her master, appears and causes a scandal. On the way back home, Henrietta confesses to Charles that she accidentally killed her brother and let her husband take the blame. After the ball scandal, Sam lectures Charles and accidentally shoots him in the arm. Arrested, he faces a return to the penal colony for re-offending. Charles claims to have wounded himself. Henrietta confesses her brother's death to the governor, but Sam refuses to corroborate her version. He realizes Milly's malfeasance in frightening and poisoning his wife, and dismisses her. Eventually, Charles confirms Henrietta's story, clearing Sam's name in the process. On the orders of his cousin, the governor, Charles returns to Ireland, leaving the couple reconciled and free of their demons.

GENESIS

When he founded Transatlantic Pictures with British businessman Sidney Bernstein, Hitchcock wanted to make *Under Capricorn* their independent production company's first Anglo-American film. He imagined giving the lead role to his favorite actress and close friend Ingrid Bergman, who had already appeared in *Spellbound* (1944) and *Notorious* (1946). But the actress was not available at the time the director wanted to film. Unable to imagine the project without her, he patiently waited for her to become available, using the intervening time to shoot *Rope* (1948).

An Unexpected Choice

Published in 1937, *Under Capricorn* is a historical novel by Australian writer Helen Simpson, who died in 1940. Hitchcock had already adapted one of her books for the film *Murder!* (1930), and the author co-wrote *Sabotage* (1936). In 1945, the filmmaker acquired the rights to the book for a derisory sum. The story, about a woman and her husband bound by a terrible secret, is set in 1831 in Sydney, a rapidly developing city populated by pardoned convicts. The *Under Capricorn* adaptation assumes a costume film, a far cry from a breathless Hitchcockian thriller. Although he confessed no particular admiration for this literary work, Hitchcock undoubtedly saw in it an opportunity to stage some of his favorite motifs, as well as a great role for Ingrid Bergman.

Combined Talents

Following his collaboration on the screenplay for *Rope*, actor Hume Cronyn (*Shadow of a Doubt*, 1942; *Lifeboat*, 1943) was again hired by his friend Hitchcock to work on the writing of *Under Capricorn*. In addition to Helen Simpson's text, the two men drew on the play by John Colton and Margaret Linden, returning to their choice of amending certain aspects of the novel, notably its latent racism. Cronyn and Alma Reville, the filmmaker's wife, worked together in Hollywood and completed the writing in England. Hitchcock enlisted the talents of Scottish playwright James Bridie, who wrote the dialogue and fleshed out the characters from Glasgow. Hitchcock and Cronyn, who were responsible for the story structure, struggled to find a satisfying conclusion. Only the housekeeper's unhealthy jealousy, which inevitably evokes the unforgettable Mrs. Danvers from *Rebecca* (1939), seemed to interest Hitchcock. Rather disillusioned, he confided in his collaborator that he thought the film would be a failure.

CASTING

Scheduled to headline the film from the outset, Ingrid Bergman was undoubtedly the main (if not the only) reason why Hitchcock decided to make *Under Capricorn*.

A Battle of Egos

Right from the start of production, Transatlantic put the name of the actress, then at the height of her Hollywood career, in the spotlight. At the time, all the producers were courting her, and Alfred Hitchcock confessed to François Truffaut the possessive impulse behind the film: "I must confess that I made the mistake of thinking that having Ingrid Bergman was the most important thing for me. It was a victory over the business aspect."[1] The star, who knew she was wanted, demanded a salary of $200,000 and 25 percent of the profits. Out of pride, Hitchcock increased his salary to exceed his star's: $250,000 and 30 percent of the profits.

A "Transatlantic" Cast

To play Sam Flusky, the ex-convict, Hitchcock wanted Burt Lancaster, but he was unavailable and in any case too expensive. He finally chose his friend Joseph Cotten (*Shadow of a Doubt*, 1942), but later regretted the actor's lack of credibility as a farmer. As *Under Capricorn* was to be a "transatlantic" film, Hitchcock hired English actor Michael Wilding to play Charles Adare, the Irishman who falls under Henrietta's spell. Having proved more than once his talent for choosing actresses who reveal their evil potential in front of the camera, Hitchcock entrusted the interpretation of the ominous housekeeper to British actress Margaret Leighton, renowned for her roles as a young leading lady at the Old Vic, London's most prestigious theater. To play the governor, Hitchcock also cast the very British Cecil Parker, one of the villains of *The Lady Vanishes* (1938).

FILMING AND PRODUCTION

For his second transatlantic film, Hitchcock chose to film in England, with ambitious sets built in the old MGM British-run studios at Elstree. The prodigal son's return to his homeland earned him a somewhat frosty reception, recorded in newspaper headlines. The British press did not appreciate the "desertion" of England's most talented filmmaker during the war.

For Hitchcock Addicts

Exasperated by the shooting and harboring a strong antipathy for his character, Joseph Cotten renamed the film *Under Cornycrap* before an impassive Hitchcock. According to Cotten, this bad pun explained why the director never called on him again for films. He did, however, entrust him with a role—particularly cruel for Cotten since the character was paralyzed from head to toe—in "Breakdown" (1955), an episode of the *Alfred Hitchcock Presents* series.

A Great Cinematographer

Hitchcock hired the prestigious cinematographer Jack Cardiff, who had been a young "clapper board operator" at the time of *The Skin Game* (1930). Known for his sophisticated lighting and color rendering in Michael Powell's films (*Black Narcissus, The Red Shoes*), Cardiff, to whom Hitchcock showed *Rope*, was eager to reproduce the experience of a film shot in sequence.

Constraints and Obstacles

The budget reached $2.5 million. In addition to Bergman's and Hitchcock's salaries (a fifth of the budget between them), the sum allocated to set construction soared. The Flusky house, the film's central location, had to be built in removable sections to allow the camera to move freely through doors and partitions. This setup, followed by a technicians' strike, delayed the shoot, originally scheduled for mid-June 1948. Hitchcock was still not satisfied with the script, which was struggling to reach a conclusion. If the director agreed to shoot anyway, it was probably because he was more interested in experimenting with his new obsession (the sequence shot) and in his star actress, his other obsession.

False Twins

It is hard to imagine what *Under Capricorn* would have been like if Hitchcock had shot it before *Rope*. Would the filmmaker have conceived it as a succession of long sequence shots? Although the same idea governs the staging of the two films, their tones are quite the opposite. After the inhuman phlegm and misanthropy of the characters in the first, Hitchcock returns to the nobility of great sentiment in the second. In this respect, *Under Capricorn* is the meeting point between the stylistic exercise of *Rope* and the morbid romanticism of *Rebecca*.

A Technical Nightmare

As in *Rope*, the actors' movements were calculated down to the last millimeter, and their positions were marked in chalk on the floor, amid the countless cables that littered it. Set designers pushed furniture and walls during takes so that the big Technicolor camera could move. Electricians moved lights mounted on dollies before quickly exiting the shot. Cardiff would testify to the chaos caused by what at the time seemed a whim of the filmmaker's: "The electric crane ran through the sets like a tank through Sebastopol, whole walls opened up, furniture was retracted by panting prop-men, then put back in its place as the crane made its return trip."[2] He described it as a "technical nightmare," involving endless rehearsals and testing the mettle of the entire team, actors and technicians alike. After each successful take, during which there was a veritable din, the actors had to replay the scene on an empty set so that the sound engineers could record the dialogue properly.

Two Rivals

In Ingrid Bergman's 1980 memoir, *My Life in Film*, the pages devoted to the shooting of *Under Capricorn* reveal a jealousy of a technique that seems to steal the limelight and the filmmaker's attention: the sequence shot. However, the sequence shot was entirely devoted to her acting, and it became a partner that enhanced her persona like no other. For the only time in her career, Bergman broke down and cried on set. But the exhaustion she described was as much that of the actress as of her character. Hitchcock knew this

Hitchcock alongside a very imposing Technicolor camera.

Italian Trip

During the shooting of *Under Capricorn*, Ingrid Bergman's marriage fell apart. She was also tiring of the constraints and limitations of the Holly-wood system. After discovering Rome, in *Open City* (1945) and *Paisà* (*Paisan*) (1946), two films that promised a new way of making cinema, she wrote an impassioned letter to Italian director Roberto Rossellini, expressing her desire to work with him. Shortly before the premiere of *Under Capricorn*, the actress left her husband and child behind to pursue a passionate love affair and pro-fessional career in Italy, pro-voking a worldwide scandal. Hitchcock felt abandoned and betrayed by the woman who had inspired him so much.

and made the most of it, filming the famous sev-en-minute confession scene (the longest in the film) in September 1948, at the very end of the shoot, to take advantage of his actress's state of extreme fatigue. As with the confession by Maxim de Winter (Laurence Olivier) in *Rebecca*, Henrietta Flusky's confession enables the filmmaker to avoid the flash-back cliché in favor of a moment of virtuoso direc-tion. In the end, however, few of the sequences survived the ordeal of the editing room.

RECEPTION

The film was released with some trepidation: Bernstein convinced Hitchcock to shorten some of his sequences. The previews were inconclu-sive. The film was released in the United States a year after shooting was completed. Bergman, who was supposed to be promoting the film, left to join Rossellini in Italy. The adulterous relationship caused a huge scandal, compounded by an out-of-wedlock

Henrietta (Ingrid Bergman), apparently plagued by horrible hallucinations, is in fact being persecuted by Milly, her housekeeper. Alone in her room, she discovers a mummified Indian head under her sheets and faints from fright. Instead of following her fall, the camera caresses the room with its gaze, stopping at the window, where a thunderstorm is rumbling outside. A fade-in opens on a close-up of Henrietta's face, caught in chiaroscuro and showing a glistening tear.

pregnancy. American politicians and Catholic organizations condemned the actress, and some exhibitors were reluctant to show *Under Capricorn.*

Failure and Misunderstanding

In the United States, critics were disappointed in the film, even violently opposed to it. Many found *Under Capricorn* too long and verbose. John McCarten of the *New Yorker* spoke bluntly of a film that "simultaneously succeeds in insulting the Australians, the Irish, and the average intelligence." On the other side of the Atlantic, the *Manchester Guardian* critic criticized the method of long takes, which created "intolerable boredom." The film was a huge commercial failure, the biggest of the director's career, and worsened the already dire situation of Transatlantic Pictures. The banks threatened to seize it. Hitchcock, who did not have kind words for this opus, nevertheless emphasized the wrongheadedness of the Anglo-Saxon critics, who were expecting to see a traditional Hitchcock thriller. On the other hand, in his opinion, the French were able to appreciate the film, "because they looked at it for what it was and not what people expected."[2]

A "Great Sick Film"

Under Capricorn contains many typically Hitchcockian themes: the figure of the false culprit (in this case, deliberately), the transfer of guilt, the secret that binds two souls together, the psychological hold that the poison motif prolongs and symbolizes, morbid jealousy, a couple freeing themselves from the weight of the past. No doubt Hitchcock did not film all the scenes with equal intensity, and the sequences focusing on Ingrid Bergman shine more brightly than the others. This alternation of flashes of brilliance and more disinterested parts makes *Under Capricorn* an uneven, strange film, fascinating in that it bears witness to the work of a filmmaker constantly reinventing his art, at the risk of disappointing his audience's expectations. For *Marnie*, Truffaut coined the expression "great sick film." This phrase, which has remained famous for the fertile paradox it contains, best expresses the idea of a work whose great qualities make us forget its flaws.

Toward the Light

In an issue of *Cahiers du cinéma* in October 1954 devoted entirely to Hitchcock, the French critic Jean Domarchi devoted a long, laudatory article to

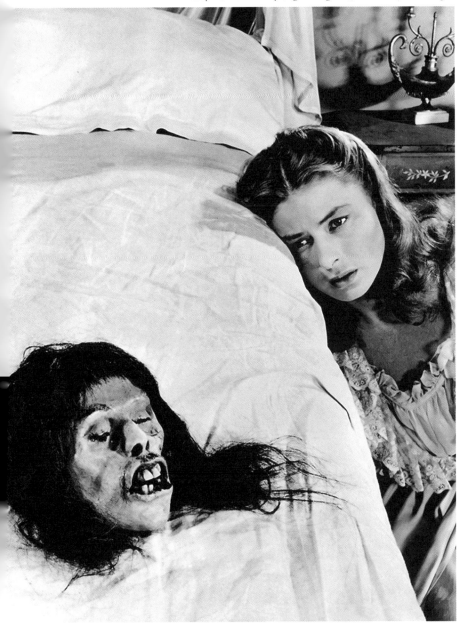

Lady Henrietta Flusky (Ingrid Bergman), or how to survive fright.

Where Is Hitchcock?

The filmmaker, who is difficult to recognize, appears
twice, on both occasions
near the beginning. He appears at the far end of the
screen, wearing a top hat
and in a three-quarter view,
attending a ceremony next
to a soldier in a red uniform.
Then he is at the top of the
steps of the governor's palace as a carriage moves
into the foreground.

the film with the Balzacian title "Le chef-d'œuvre
inconnu" ("The Unknown Masterpiece"). He compared it to the great classics of literature and saw
it as a great work on the theme of freedom. The
Hitchcockian motif of the transfer of guilt is used
here to create a positive conclusion that contrasts
with the filmmaker's usual pessimism. The revelation of Henrietta's crime gives rise to "a succession of beautiful actions, all stamped with the seal
of renunciation." As for the film's darkest character, the housekeeper, Milly, for the critic she is a
revelator in the chemical sense of the word, "who
enables Charles, Sam, and Henrietta to affirm their
greatness in and through sacrifice."[3] Hitchcock has
sublimated his favorite themes in the service of a
surprisingly luminous plot. The characters tear each
other apart, exerting a hold over each other that
is all the stronger because of the passion of their
love. This long, suffocating ordeal, in which words
become action, leads to deliverance, allowing each
of them to bear witness to their nobility and reclaim
their freedom.

Ingrid Bergman, Alfred Hitchcock (London, October 1948).

Ingrid Bergman,
the Cornerstone

Ingrid Bergman (1915–1982) had several lives as an actress, including a Hitchcockian one between 1944 and 1948. Magnified by the director's admiring gaze and the glamour of a film system at its height, she never ceased to remain "natural" and true to herself.

The Birth of a Vocation

Ingrid Bergman was born on August 29, 1915, in Stockholm, Sweden. Her vocation as an actress was born the year she turned eighteen. Although he disapproved of her decision, her uncle (Ingrid had been an orphan since she was a teenager) let her take the entrance exam for Sweden's Royal Dramatic Theatre School. There was one condition: If she failed, she would have to give up her whim. The comic role she played during the audition

earned her a place at the school. She began acting in the theater and then in films. Her Swedish career was interrupted by her departure for Hollywood in 1939.

The First "Natural" Actress

Alfred Hitchcock and Ingrid Bergman had one thing in common: David O. Selznick brought them both to Hollywood. With the idea of directing a remake, the producer was shown *Intermezzo* (1936), by Swedish director Gustaf Molander, on the advice of his representative in New York, Katherine Brown. She drew his attention in particular to the young actress who played the heroine. Selznick's decision was not long in coming: He brought Ingrid Bergman across the Atlantic.

Hitchcock framing Ingrid.

When the actress arrived in Hollywood, the producer wanted her to change her name and face by going to the studio's makeup artists, which she categorically refused to do. Selznick finally changed his strategy: "We're not going to change you one bit. You will remain as you are. You will be the first 'natural' actress."[1] And precisely because no one in Hollywood ever went by their real name, she kept hers. For her first American film, Bergman reprised her role from *Intermezzo* in 1939. Alfred Hitchcock was approached to direct, but in the end Gregory Ratoff was chosen.

Two Stars, One Trio

Before filming together in 1944, Bergman and Hitchcock had already become stars recognized by critics and audiences alike. Selznick had "loaned" his discovery to several studios, resulting in a long list of notable films: *Dr. Jekyll and Mr. Hyde* (Victor Fleming, 1941), *Casablanca* (Michael Curtiz, 1942), *For Whom the Bell Tolls* (Sam Wood, 1943), *Gaslight* (George Cukor, 1944).

The actress and the filmmaker failed to work together on a new version of *The Lodger*, with Jean Gabin, or on the adaptation of John Buchan's *Greenmantle*, with Herbert Marshall and Cary Grant. Their collaboration finally began with *Spellbound*, in which Bergman played a psychiatrist who falls in love with a disturbed doctor played by the new star of the Selznick stable, Gregory Peck. The film proved such a success that the producer wanted to repeat the miracle with the winning trio of Hitchcock, Bergman, and screenwriter Ben Hecht: *Notorious* was shot in 1946. Ingrid Bergman then followed Hitchcock to England for their last film together, *Under Capricorn* (1948).

The Story of a Face

These three films made together, over and above their plots, tell "the story of a face," as filmmaker Claude Chabrol put it in reference to *Notorious* and *Under Capricorn*, a face that hypnotized Hitchcock's camera: "It is the face that the lens scrutinizes, searches, sometimes chisels, sometimes softens. It is to this that the homage of the most beautiful discoveries goes."[2] Ingrid Bergman inspired the filmmaker to create some great formal moments: the interminable kiss filmed in sequence shot in *Notorious*; the extreme close-up on the actress's face, followed by a superimposed shot in which a series of doors are opened under the effect of a first kiss, in *Spellbound*; the scene in *Under Capricorn* where Henrietta is frightened

to discover a mummified head on her bed, as well as the very long sequence shot of the character's confession, the filming of which exhausted its performer. Hitchcock liked to test the actress as much as the heroines she played and, in return, gave her close-ups and sequence shots, tokens of trust and proof of an intimacy that crystallized on the screen. If nothing in the filmmaker's words testifies to his secret passion for Ingrid Bergman, it is enough to observe the way he films her: with devotion, desire, anguish, and fascination.

So Far, So Near

After shooting *Under Capricorn*, Ingrid Bergman flew to Italy to pursue a scandalous love affair with Roberto Rossellini (*Stromboli, Europe 51, Journey to Italy*). Although they never made another film together, the filmmaker and actress continued to see each other throughout their lives. At the evening tribute to Hitchcock organized by the American Film Institute on March 7, 1979, Ingrid Bergman gave a speech expressing her gratitude to him ("an adorable genius") and returned to the director the famous key to the wine cellar of *Notorious*, which she had shared as a good luck charm with Cary Grant for almost thirty-five years. Hitchcock, who had remained impassive throughout the ceremony, took the actress in his arms. The *Los Angeles Times* wrote: "Suddenly it was not a public display of affection, it was the parting of two old friends who thought they would never see each other again."

JANE WYMAN · MARLENE DIETRICH
MICHAEL WILDING · RICHARD TODD

THE
STAGE
IS SET
FOR
WARNER
BROS'.
MOST
EXCITING
HIT
YET!

ALFRED HITCHCOCK'S
Stage Fright

with ALISTAIR SIM · DAME SYBIL THORNDIKE · Screen Play by Whitfield Cook · Adaptation by Alma Reville · Additional Dialogue by James Bridie · Based on a Novel by Selwyn Jepson · A Warner Bros. — First National Picture

Stage Fright

United States • 1 hr 50 • Black and White • Mono (RCA Sound System) • 1.37:1

SYNOPSIS

Production Dates: June 1–end August 1949
Release Date in the United States: April 15, 1950

Production: Warner Bros.
Producer: Alfred Hitchcock
Unit Production Manager: Fred Ahern

Based on a novel by Selwyn Jepson, _Man Running_ (1948)
Adaptation: Alma Reville
Screenplay: Whitfield Cook
Director of Photography: Wilkie Cooper
Camera Operators: Eric Besche, Jack Haste
Sound: Harold V. King
Assistant Director: Jack Martin
Art Direction: Terence Verity
Set Decoration: Bill Beavis, Olga Lehmann
Makeup: Colin Garde
Costumes: Christian Dior, Milo Anderson
Music: Leighton Lucas
Musical Direction: Louis Levy
Film Editing: Edward B. Jarvis

Starring: Jane Wyman (Eve Gill / Doris Tinsdale), Marlene Dietrich (Charlotte Inwood), Michael Wilding (Inspector Wilfred "Ordinary" Smith), Richard Todd (Jonathan Cooper), Alastair Sim (Commodore Gill), Sybil Thorndike (Mrs. Gill), Kay Walsh (Nellie Goode), Miles Malleson (Mr. Fortesque), Hector MacGregor (Freddie Williams), Joyce Grenfell ("Lovely Ducks," owner of the duck-shooting range), Patricia Hitchcock (Chubby Bannister), Alfred Hitchcock (man in the street)…

In London, Jonathan Cooper is suspected of murdering the husband of his mistress, the revue singer Charlotte Inwood, who is in fact the real killer. At least, that is what Jonathan leads his friend, Eve Gill, a trainee actress, to believe. Convinced of the innocence of the man she secretly loves, Eve hides the fugitive at her father's house. Then she arranges to meet Inspector Wilfred Smith, who is in charge of the investigation. Finally, she bribes Nellie, Charlotte Inwood's dresser, and, under the name Doris Tinsdale, takes her place. This puts her in a good position to overhear conversations and to faint when Jonathan returns to the theater where the singer is performing to convince her, in vain, to leave with him, and is almost arrested by the police. Wilfred and Eve, increasingly attracted to each other, exchange a kiss. With her father's help, the young woman, never short of ideas to make Charlotte a suspect, goes so far as to plant a bug in a theater dressing room. Unaware that she was being bugged and provoked by Eve, the singer reveals the truth: She was an accomplice in Jonathan's crime. Jonathan, who is still being hunted, has taken refuge in the basement of the theater, to which he lures Eve. Revealing his insanity to her, he imagines killing her so that he can plead insanity…But she traps him by persuading him to escape through the orchestra pit. Surrounded, he ends up "guillotined" by the iron stage curtain. Eve leaves the theater, supported by Wilfred.

"This is very nice. If you can call mourning, nice. But, isn't there some way we could let it plunge a little in front? I suppose not."

Charlotte Inwood (Marlene Dietrich), in _Stage Fright_

Makeup removal and disguises (Jane Wyman).

GENESIS AND CASTING

In January 1949, Hitchcock signed a contract with Warner Bros. to direct and produce four films. *Stage Fright*, shot in Great Britain, was the first of these. Ten years after his departure for the United States, he made an "English-style" film in memory of his work in the 1930s.

"The Three Hitchcocks"

With his wife, Alma Reville, and their friend the playwright Whitfield Cook, the filmmaker prepared his film in his home on Bellagio Road, Los Angeles. The "three Hitchcocks" adapted a recent thriller novel, *Man Running*, in their own way: They expanded the father's character, changed the murderer (the singer's impresario in the novel), gave the whole thing the tone of a cockney comedy, and invented the thirteen-minute fake flashback that opens the film. Unofficially, their criminal plot was also inspired by an English news item from 1923, the case of the Thompson-Bywaters couple, which had impressed the young Hitchcock.

Marlene…

Although she was second in the credits, Marlene Dietrich was the undisputed star of the film, both in the fiction and on the set. Hitchcock, who modeled his actresses so that their images coincided with his desires (he made a film about them, *Vertigo*, in 1957), knew, in Dietrich's case, that her photogenic qualities were a given and the seal of her fame. A "pupil" of the lighting director Josef von Sternberg, who introduced her to the world (*The Blue Angel, Blonde Venus, The Scarlet Empress*), it was Dietrich who told the cinematographer of *Stage Fright* how to light the film. Hitchcock also allowed her to choose her own jewelry, makeup, and outfits, and reserved Dietrich-style lines for her appearances, to the point of confusing her character with her personality onscreen. The actress, on the other hand, would remember the filmmaker's gentle authority.

…and the Others

The other female star, the young Jane Wyman, feared that the glamour of her "competitor" would overshadow her. Her portrayal of a newcomer who became a real actress meant that she had to wear many disguises, at the risk of looking ugly. Apart from the German Dietrich and the American Wyman, the entire cast was English: Alastair Sim, Sybil Thorndike, Kay Walsh. Joyce Grenfell, the owner of the shooting range, is the most eccentric of them all: "Who wants to shoot lovely ducks!"

FILMING AND PRODUCTION

Most of the filming took place on the largest set at Elstree Studios. But the whole of London is used as a backdrop for this film in praise of the theater: St. Paul's Cathedral, the Royal Academy of Dramatic Art, the Scala Theatre on Charlotte Street…

Fireworks

Richard Todd, who played the villain of the story, recounted Hitchcock's disconcerting method: "Before each take, he gave the first assistant a sketch showing the movements the actors were to make. Then he would leave. When they had finished [rehearsing], Hitchcock would come back and finish the take."[1] It is Hitchcock's direction that gives meaning to the whole thing; it is his direction that indicates that everything here is representation and artifice, that all human behavior (a fortiori that of the characters

The Curtain Rises

As the opening credits of *Stage Fright* roll across the screen, a theater curtain rises over a view of London. In the opening credits of *Rear Window* (1954), three curtains on the same window are successively raised to reveal "reality," in other words, the scenery opposite.

Charlotte Inwood (Marlene Dietrich) onstage at the Scala Theatre.

who are actors) is "cinema," "theater." And only these falsehoods tell a certain truth. The film is a game of masks, disguises, and backstage entrances and exits, and each character has his or her own "big stage." At the Scala Theatre, a feathery Dietrich reclines on the divans to whisper a Cole Porter song, "The Laziest Gal in Town." In "reality," Richard Todd enters a large mansion in a single shot, the door closing invisibly (only in sound) behind him as the camera continues to follow him (twenty takes were needed to complete this sequence shot).

RECEPTION

Although the film's revenue slightly exceeded its cost, American critics, from the *New York Times* to *Harrison's Reports*, found it "moderately exciting."

A Strange Flashback

Hitchcock was often criticized for the opening flashback, which misled the audience. Beyond the audacity of this "deceptive" narrative construction, the filmmaker, by presenting a false "false culprit" for once, pokes fun at his own obsessions and thwarts the viewer's investigative instincts.

Memories

Like a recapitulation before turning to his great Hollywood films of the 1950s, in *Stage Fright* Hitchcock took up two inspirations from his English cinema: on the one hand, the music hall, the theater (*Murder!*, 1930), and the love of actors, whom he is reputed to have always held in low esteem; and on the other, the motif of the young girl who, for the duration of the plot, becomes a woman (*Young and Innocent*, 1937). Here too, she takes stock of her feelings by changing lovers along the way. Above all, she goes from aspiring actress to established one. She learns her craft in action, succeeds in a composition, and overcomes her stage fright.

Where Is Hitchcock?

Eve Gill (Jane Wyman) walks down the street. As an amateur investigator, she rehearses out loud the "role" that will make her look like someone else. Hitchcock passes her and, astonished, turns around.

YOU'LL BE IN THE GRIP OF LOVE'S STRANGEST TRIP!

It begins with the shriek of a train whistle and ends with shrieking excitement! Young America's idol — a good looking stranger in search of sensation — and a girl in love. These are the people around whom Alfred Hitchcock spins his wonderful new web of suspense and surprise. **WARNER BROS.** bring a pounding new tempo to motion picture entertainment.

IT'S OFF THE BEATEN TRACK!

ALFRED HITCHCOCK'S
"Strangers on a Train"

STARRING **FARLEY GRANGER** **RUTH ROMAN** **ROBERT WALKER**

with LEO G. CARROLL   Screen Play by RAYMOND CHANDLER and CZENZI ORMONDE   A WARNER BROS. PICTURE

Strangers on a Train

United States • **1 hr 41** • **Black and White** • **Mono** (RCA Sound System) • **1.37:1**

Production Dates: Mid-October–December 23, 1950
Release Date in the United States: June 30, 1951

Production: Warner Bros.
Producer: Alfred Hitchcock
Associate Producer: Barbara Keon

Based on the novel of the same name by Patricia Highsmith (1950)
Adaptation: Whitfield Cook
Screenplay: Raymond Chandler, Czenzi Ormonde
Director of Photography: Robert Burks
Cameraman: Leonard J. South
Special Effects: H. F. Koenekamp
Sound: Dolph Thomas
Assistant Director: Mel Dellar
Art Direction: Edward S. Haworth
Set Decoration: George James Hopkins
Costumes: Leah Rhodes
Makeup: Gordon Bau
Music: Dimitri Tiomkin
Film Editing: William H. Ziegler

Starring: Farley Granger (Guy Haines), Robert Walker (Bruno Antony), Ruth Roman (Anne Morton), Leo G. Carroll (Senator Morton), Patricia Hitchcock (Barbara Morton), Laura Elliott (Miriam Joyce Haines), Marion Lorne (Mrs. Antony), Jonathan Hale (Mr. Antony), Howard St. John (police captain Turley), John Brown (Professor Collins), Norma Varden (Mrs. Cunningham), Robert Gist (Detective Leslie Hennessey), John Doucette (Detective Hammond), Jack Cushingham (Fred Reynolds, tennis player), Alfred Hitchcock (passenger boarding a train carrying a double bass)…

> "What amuses me about Hitchcock is the way he sets up the film in his head before he knows what the story is."

Raymond Chandler, letter dated September 4, 1950

SYNOPSIS

On a train, Guy Haines, a prominent tennis player, is approached by Bruno Antony, a talkative man with some surprising theories. He believes that a crime without a motive guarantees impunity. So he proposes to his new friend that they swap murderous desires: Bruno will kill Miriam, Guy's horrible wife, for no reason. She refuses to divorce him and prevents him from loving Anne Morton, the daughter of a senator in Washington. And Guy will have to kill Bruno's hated father. Convinced that they have reached an agreement, Bruno goes ahead with the deed: One night at a funfair in the small town of Metcalf, he strangles Miriam and presents Guy, horrified, with a fait accompli. He breaks into Guy's world and, during a party at the senator's house, at the mere sight of Barbara, Anne's younger sister, who wears glasses similar to Miriam's, he nearly kills a guest he was playing at smothering. Despite being pestered to honor his end of the bargain, Guy refuses. Bruno, who has stolen a lighter with Guy's initials on it, threatens to plant the incriminating object at the scene of the crime. A race against time begins: Guy must play his tennis match to avoid arousing the suspicions of the policemen who are tailing him, and win as quickly as possible to get to the funfair in time. He spots Bruno in the crowd, and the two of them start a fight on a merry-go-round that spirals out of control until it crashes. In the midst of the rubble, Bruno again blames his unfortunate sidekick. But he dies and the lighter that incriminates him and exonerates Guy of his wife's murder slips out of his hand.

GENESIS

After three films in which he tried to escape from the "Hitchcock thriller," all of which suffered public and critical setbacks, Alfred Hitchcock was in urgent need of a return to the formula for his success. In February 1950, while traveling by train with his wife, Alma, and their friend Whitfield Cook (*The Paradine Case*, 1947; *Stage Fright*, 1949), Hitchcock read the proofs of Patricia Highsmith's first novel, a story that began on a train. The three passengers immediately exchanged their first ideas.

A Certain Way of Reading a Novel

Hitchcock was interested above all in the situation and the argument: two strangers on a train, the exchange of murders, the untraceable motive, universal guilt (even that of the "innocent"), the theme of the evil and revealing double. He acquired the rights to the novel for the modest sum of $7,500, obtained a production agreement with Warner Bros., and set to work with Cook. In June, they came up with a fairly well-developed treatment: Guy's character was no longer an architect, but a tennis player in search of upward mobility (an evocation of the polished political world of Washington, absent from the novel). Above all, he no longer commits a murder that echoes the one perpetrated by his "partner." As for Bruno, the psychopath, he is no longer an alcoholic, but an educated man who wears clothes that are as extravagant as his theories on mankind.

The Entry and Exit of Raymond Chandler

In July, for the screenplay, Hitchcock began looking for a well-known writer who could grasp the story's cinematic potential. By his own count, he was turned down eight times, including by Dashiell Hammett, the inventor of the novel noir. Finally, Raymond Chandler accepted, and on paper the choice seemed a wise one: the author of *The Big Sleep* and *Farewell, My Lovely*, he was also a screenwriter of film noirs (*Double Indemnity*, *The Blue Dahlia*) and had just republished his essay *The Simple Art of Murder*. Although similar in appearance, the novelist's and the filmmaker's ideas diverged on the essentials. Chandler did not understand that Hitchcock subordinated everything—logic, character motivation, realism—to his visions, camera effects, and suspense, so much so, he wrote to his editor, that "we find ourselves trying to justify the shots he wants to make, rather than building the story. Every time we get into it, he throws

Where Is Hitchcock?

The filmmaker appears ten minutes into the film. As Guy (Farley Granger) gets off at Metcalf station, he boards the train, encumbered by a double bass. The film never ceases to play with all forms of "doubles."

it all away by deciding to do a love scene on top of the Jefferson Memorial or something like that."[1] Hitchcock soon broke off all relations with the writer. Chandler, embittered, finished a script on his own and handed it in to the studio at the end of September. Hitchcock decided not to use it and to start from scratch, even though he did retain an atmosphere, some characters, and the idea of opening his film with a series of shots of feet, Guy's and Bruno's, moving toward each other.

A New Start

Time was running out; filming was due to start in mid-October and the production company was threatening to cancel it. Hitchcock came up with the idea of calling in a virtual stranger, Czenzi Ormonde, assistant to Barbara Keon, the associate producer who had attended the meetings with Chandler. With Keon and under the supervision of the filmmaker, the young woman "forgot" the novel and started from Cook's treatment. She gave life to the character of Bruno's mother and introduced Guy's lighter and Miriam's glasses. Under the guidance of the director and in the manner of *Shadow of a Doubt* (1942), she accentuated the interplay of doubles that punctuate this nightmarish tale: two double whiskeys, two children, two pairs of glasses, two policemen…The fairground setting, present in Highsmith's story at the time of Miriam's murder, returns for the finale, the deranged attraction of the wooden horses, this time inspired by the merry-go-round scene in another crime novel, Edmund Crispin's *The Moving Toyshop*, published in 1946. Hitchcock also devised the sequences and included preparatory drawings in the script. When shooting began on the scheduled date, the script was neither finished (it would be a month later) nor perfect ("flat" scenes served as transitions between the bravura pieces), but it was finally back on track as the director had imagined it from the start.

CASTING

Jack Warner required Hitchcock to take on an actress under contract to his studio, Ruth Roman, a sophisticated brunette deemed to be charmless. In fact, Anne's character was the most boring, her scenes the most static, and her dialogue the most bland. After William Holden declined the role, the filmmaker cast Farley Granger (*Rope*, 1948) in the role of the "good guy."

"The More Successful the Villain, the More Successful the Picture" (Hitchcock)

Having failed to win the case for the casting of the star couple, Hitchcock decided to cast Robert Walker as Bruno. Hitherto cast in sympathetic roles, the actor was in reality a tormented, depressed, and alcoholic man. He threw himself into playing his delirious character, a megalomaniacal failure who had a strange oedipal relationship with his mother. The filmmaker, a former draftsman, created the lobster motif that adorns Bruno's tie when he appears. Like Peter Lorre in *The Man Who Knew Too Much* (1934) or Ray Milland in *Dial M for Murder* (1953), Robert Walker, as Bruno Antony, is the real star of the film: Guy's alter ego, he is his unacknowledged part, Jekyll's Hyde, to the point where this double is one with the "other." And rather than a homoerotic relationship between Guy and Bruno, as many critics have pointed out, it is an autoerotic one.

Friends and an Only Daughter

Hitchcock sought out Marion Lorne, a London theater director, to play Bruno's mother, who was also a crazy and endearing character. In the role of the senator, he brought back Leo G. Carroll, who gave the fifth of his six performances for the director.

Patricia Hitchcock played the cheeky Barbara, eager for intrigue and romance. The filmmaker's daughter would later testify that her father gave her no special treatment on the set. Nevertheless, her character does not exist in the novel, and Hitchcock reserved some of his best lines for her. ("Daddy doesn't mind a little scandal. He's a senator.")

FILMING AND PRODUCTION

For Hitchcock, preproduction and filming provided the opportunity for a decisive meeting and a collaboration that was to last (for twelve films): Robert

For Hitchcock Addicts

Just after *Strangers on a Train*, thirty-two-year-old Robert Walker starred in Leo McCarey's *My Son John*, an anti-communist melodrama. The actor died during the filming. To complete the film, McCarey had to borrow from Hitchcock (with the director's agreement) one of the close-ups in which Walker's character was dying, crushed in the merry-go-round accident.

Burks had been working at Warner Bros. since the age of nineteen and, from the 1930s onward, rose through the ranks to become a renowned postwar cinematographer (King Vidor's *The Fountainhead*).

Robert Burks, the Ideal Partner

An expert in black and white, a specialist in photographic tricks, and an experimenter at heart, Robert Burks had all the qualities needed to make a film as stylized as *Strangers on a Train*. He excelled at visualizing the tormented, dark world of the psychopath, darkening or streaking Robert Walker's close-up face with shadow, while leaving Farley Granger's face in light, even though it was fake. A master of chiaroscuro and lighting (the funfair scenes), Burks turns Bruno into Guy's shadow. Similarly, he and Hitchcock revel in contrasts, as in the shot in which Bruno, decidedly gifted with ubiquity, suddenly appears, a small black dot on the gigantic white marble steps of the Jefferson Memorial in Washington, "like the unseen part of you, somewhere in the world, and he waits in ambush" (Patricia Highsmith).

Mastery

Strangers on a Train leaps from one spectacular moment to the next, rather than progressing steadily, as if Alfred Hitchcock wanted to demonstrate his unparalleled mastery. He imagined the now famous shot in which all the spectators at a tennis match follow a long rally between four players (another double). All the spectators except one: Bruno, with a completely different game in mind, stares intently at Guy. Another well-known shot is Miriam's murder, as seen through a lens of her eyeglasses, which have fallen to the ground. There is also the sequence during the reception at the senator's house, where the young Barbara experiences the unforgettable sensation of being strangled by the sheer force of Bruno's gaze on her. As for the final scene of the wild wooden horses, this is a technical feat and a game of patience, with the camera having to synchronize the action in the foreground at each angle with the edges of the transparent backdrop image to the nearest millimeter. For the merry-go-round accident, Hitchcock filmed the explosion of a model, which he then enlarged, projected, and filmed again, adding panicked extras into the foreground.

Game, Set, and Match

The long, highly segmented sequence of Guy's tennis match, which is edited in alternating cuts with Bruno's decision to return to the funfair, was only

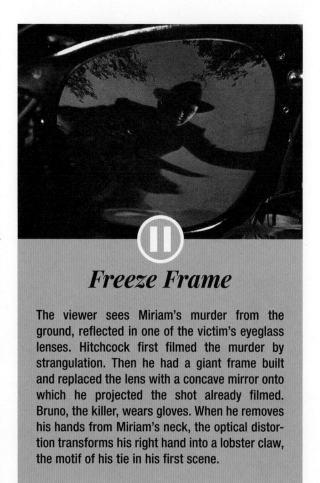

Freeze Frame

The viewer sees Miriam's murder from the ground, reflected in one of the victim's eyeglass lenses. Hitchcock first filmed the murder by strangulation. Then he had a giant frame built and replaced the lens with a concave mirror onto which he projected the shot already filmed. Bruno, the killer, wears gloves. When he removes his hands from Miriam's neck, the optical distortion transforms his right hand into a lobster claw, the motif of his tie in his first scene.

sketched out in Czenzi Ormonde's script. The director developed and refined it during the shooting, and even more so with his film editor William H. Ziegler (who had just edited another tennis drama, Ida Lupino's *Hard, Fast and Beautiful*). Not only did Hitchcock think of this "exchange" between Guy and Bruno as a real match within a match, taking care with every detail (the suspense of the lighter falling through the drain cover), but he also thought of this entire sequence on the scale of the film, making it rhyme with the opening, the shots of Bruno's feet, then Guy's, immediately suggesting a confrontation at a distance.

On the set, Alfred Hitchcock was placid and sometimes gave the impression of being bored. In fact, having previsualized the entire film as usual, he moved quickly and was always one step ahead. In two months, he completed a technically complex shoot, which also required location shots in New York and Washington, but also in Connecticut and at the Warner Bros. studios in Burbank, California. Always calm, he was in fact excited by a film whose power over its viewers he foresaw better than anyone else.

The film begins: a train, two men, and a lighter.
Farley Granger, Robert Walker.

RECEPTION

Strangers on a Train, which cost a million and a half dollars, made twice that amount for Warner Bros. The film marked Hitchcock's return after the setbacks of his previous opuses and reestablished him as the undisputed champion of the thriller.

Yes, but…

Raymond Chandler saw the film and, having considered withdrawing his name from the credits, obviously hated it even more than the original book. Patricia Highsmith was more lenient about this variation on her story, especially appreciating the characterization of Bruno, but regretting that, from the novel to the film, Guy had ceased to be a murderer.

Professional critics were not on the whole appreciative of the film, but in the usual way: They praised its virtuosity and that of its director while still calling for a plausible story, without asking themselves whether that credibility might not detract from the overall look of the film. Bosley Crowther of the *New York Times* (July 4, 1951), who disliked the film and its "tricks," judged the plot implausible in terms close to Chandler's own. In France, André Bazin, who had always considered Hitchcock's technique to be superior to his metaphysics, once again acknowledged his unrivaled skill: "But that's not all!…All the great detective stories go beyond the mere interest of the detective story, whether it's Simenon or Graham Greene, their books have mysteries other than those of the plot" (*Le Parisien libéré*, January 10, 1952).

The Art of the Grotesque

The metaphysics of Hitchcock's work lies in his technical prowess, the very ingenuity that seemed to be a limiting factor for the critics of his time. Indeed, his skill enables him to achieve the grotesque, that aesthetic that accesses the truth of beings through an excess of reality. Hence, for example, in *Strangers on a Train* (and even earlier, in *The Ring*, 1927), the role of the funfair, far more important than its mere value as a popular setting in the novel. The funfair is everyday life itself, but exaggerated as if in a distorting mirror, amplified and deformed to the point of showing the neighing sneer of a wooden horse

in close-up, or putting a spell on Miriam's sentimental illusions, like those of everyone else ("She was a human being," says the senator), which lead her into the "tunnel of love," an attraction that will cost her her life.

The Object of the Century

In Hitchcock's films, familiar or everyday objects also always seem more worrying (the glass of milk in *Suspicion*, 1941), and the filmmaker never hesitates to magnify them optically or actually to the point of making them monstrous (in this case, the telephone to which Anne is moving in the film's penultimate scene). The film is full of unforgettable objects: shoes, a lighter, glasses, a tie, a revolver (a German Luger). So, "maybe ten thousand people remember Cézanne's apple, but a billion viewers will remember the lighter in *Strangers on a Train*...And it is forms that ultimately tell us what lies at the heart of things"[2] (Jean-Luc Godard).

Filming of *Marnie* (1964): Alfred Hitchcock; next to him, Robert Burks, Tippi Hedren.

Robert Burks,
the Man Who Could Do Anything

Between 1950 and 1964, Hitchcock collaborated twelve times with the same director of photography, Robert Burks (1909–1968). A man of boundless skill, so much so that the Master, assisted by this discreet magician, took on his most audacious projects (*Rear Window*, *The Birds*) or could say, on the eve of the shooting of *Vertigo*, that he wanted to rediscover onscreen the gently iridescent quality of a Vermeer painting.

Training

Born in California, Robert Burks found a job at the age of nineteen in the special effects department of Warner Bros., the studio where he stayed for twenty-five years. In 1934 he became a cameraman and from 1938 onward worked on more than thirty films as special effects director of photography, notably including the black-and-white classic *The Fountainhead* (King Vidor, 1949). Until his accidental death, he made forty-four feature films, including twelve with Hitchcock.

Symbiosis

Hitchcock and Burks made three Warner Bros. films in black and white (*Strangers on a Train*, *I Confess*, *The Wrong Man*) and nine others, at Warner Bros., Paramount, MGM, and Universal, in Technicolor (from *Dial M for Murder* to *Marnie*). There was one shoot in 3D (*Dial M for Murder*) and five in VistaVision, Paramount's wide-screen process (from *To Catch a Thief* to *North by Northwest*). In the autumn of 1953, the two men moved from Warner

Bros. to Paramount (*Rear Window*), a sign of their close professional relationship. Burks embodied and symbolized a golden age for Hitchcock, when he was surrounded by a team of professionals such as Herbert Coleman (associate producer), Bernard Herrmann (composer), Edith Head (costume designer), George Tomasini (editor), and Leonard J. South, Burks's cameraman (eleven of the twelve films together).

All-Terrain

Constantly challenged and never found wanting, Robert Burks was as capable of a film noir based on a true story (*The Wrong Man*) as he was of a Hollywood gloss masterpiece (the "brilliant" *To Catch a Thief*). He was equally at home on location (the Quebec setting of *I Confess*) or in the studio (*Rear Window*). Before shooting a film, he and Hitchcock would agree on the visual style of the work to come. For them, a film began to take shape, including in the literal sense (storyboards), before it was actually made. Burks also used models of the set to define camera locations and to plan lighting and shadows for a scene. He went to the huge set of *Rear Window* ten days before the first shot and, with his team, pre-lit each of the thirty-one flats and the large courtyard twenty-four hours a day, switching from night to day in a record time of forty-five minutes. He also knew how to "disguise" the powerful daylighting as natural light.

Finds

On the shooting of *Rear Window*, he placed the camera with a lens of great depth of field in the basket of a crane to cross the courtyard and, without losing definition, maintain James Stewart's point of view as he spied on his neighbor from a distance.

For the traumatic shots of the final flashback in *Marnie*, he combined telephoto and wide-angle lenses. In *Vertigo*, he used a zoom and a tracking shot to create the effect of the void. In the 3D version of *Dial M for Murder*, he worked on the depth of the scene to create a sense of space between characters who were confronting each other from a distance. And although *The Birds* took four months to shoot, Burks devoted a year of his life to the film's optical effects.

Color Chart

In black and white or Technicolor, Burks found the tones he wanted. For *Vertigo*, he designed a special diffusion filter to give Madeleine, who had returned from the dead, a green aura that cast her in an unforgettable light. For *Marnie*, he dulled the colors as if all life had been drained from the heroine by the force of her repression, a desaturation that brought out the only two colors chosen by the filmmaker: yellow (Marnie's bag in the first shot of the film) and the red that invades the screen when memories finally flood in. Suddenly, the color pops up like the memory that returns to the young woman. On the release of *North by Northwest*, *Variety* magazine praised the photography, "whether in the hot yellows of the prairie plain, or the soft green of South Dakota forest."[1]

Tribute

In his own way, Hitchcock paid a tribute to his cinematographer: "If Bob Burks and the rest of us hadn't been technicians ourselves *The Birds* would have cost $5 million [instead of $3 million]."[2] Put another way, for fifteen years the filmmaker found in Robert Burks a man capable of giving shape to all the twists and turns of his imagination.

ALFRED
HITCHCOCK'S
"I Confess"!
IF
YOU
KNEW
WHAT
HE
KNEW-
WHAT
WOULD
YOU
DO?
A shame confessed - a sin concealed! This is
love with the brand of Hitchcock burned in!
All its excitement filmed
in Canada's colorful Quebec
by Warner Bros.
STARRING
MONTGOMERY CLIFT · ANNE BAXTER
KARL MALDEN · BRIAN AHERNE
GEORGE TABORI
WILLIAM ARCHIBALD
A WARNER BROS. PICTURE

I Confess

United States • **1 hr 35** • **Black and White** • **Mono** (RCA Sound System) • **1.37:1**

Production Dates: August 21–October 22, 1952
Release Date in the United States: February 28, 1953

Production: Warner Bros.
Producers: Sidney Bernstein, Alfred Hitchcock
Associate Producer: Barbara Keon
Director of Production: Sherry Shourds

Based on a play by Paul Anthelme, *Nos deux consciences* (1902)
Screenplay: George Tabori, William Archibald
Technical Adviser: Father Paul LaCouline
Director of Photography: Robert Burks
Cameraman: Leonard J. South
Camera Operator: William Schurr
Sound: Oliver S. Garretson
Assistant Director: Don Page
Art Direction: Edward S. Haworth
Set Decoration: George James Hopkins
Hair Stylist: Agnes Flanagan
Makeup: Gordon Bau
Costumes: Orry-Kelly
Music: Dimitri Tiomkin
Musical Direction: Ray Heindorf
Film Editing: Rudi Fehr

Starring: Montgomery Clift (Father Michael Logan), Anne Baxter (Ruth Grandfort), Karl Malden (Inspector Larrue), Brian Aherne (Willy Robertson), O. E. Hasse (Otto Keller), Roger Dann (Pierre Grandfort), Dolly Haas (Alma Keller), Charles Andre (Father Millars), Nan Boardman (maid), Henry Corden (Detective Sergeant Farouche), Ovila Légaré (Monsieur Villette), Gilles Pelletier (Father Benoît), Alfred Hitchcock (man crossing the top of a long staircase) . . .

> "The great misfortune is that the justice of men always intervenes too late; it punishes or denounces acts, without being able to reach higher or further than the person who committed them."

Georges Bernanos, author of *The Diary of a Country Priest*

SYNOPSIS

Disguised as a priest, Otto Keller, the sexton of a church in Quebec City, kills a man, Villette, who caught him in the act of breaking into his house. He confesses his crime to Father Logan. Father Logan has reason to hold a grudge against the murdered man because he was blackmailing Ruth Grandfort, the wife of a politician; before the war, Ruth had been Logan's fiancée. She had married while Logan was on active service, believing that he had forgotten her. When he returned, they met again, Ruth having hidden her married status from him. During one of their walks in the countryside, they were surprised by the blackmailer. Inspector Larrue suspects Logan of the crime. The priest, bound by the seal of the confessional, cannot denounce Keller. Keen to provide him with an alibi, Ruth tells the police about Villette's blackmailing activity, thus providing him with a motive…Logan is arrested. At the end of the trial, the jury finds insufficient evidence to convict him and he is released. Outside the courthouse, surrounded by a hostile crowd, Alma Keller, the murderer's wife, moved by Logan's unjust ordeal, points to her husband as the culprit. He kills her with a pistol and flees. He is trapped in the ballroom of a grand hotel. A policeman shoots him. He dies in the priest's arms.

GENESIS

The gestation of *I Confess* was long and tedious. Hitchcock had been working on the project for a long time, and it was to be produced by his own company, Transatlantic Pictures.

A Contentious Subject

Nos deux consciences (*Our Two Consciences*) is a play by Paul Bourde written in 1902 under the pseudonym Paul Anthelme. Hitchcock discovered it in the London theater in the early 1930s. The filmmaker acquired the rights from the French writer and playwright Louis Verneuil. It is the story of a priest accused and executed for a crime of which he is innocent because, bound by the seal of the confessional, he cannot denounce the real murderer. Warner Bros., in association with Transatlantic, was concerned about the commercial viability of such a subject, as well as the difficulties with the censors. The film was postponed for a long time, delayed by other projects that had come to fruition before it (*Stage Fright, Strangers on a Train*).

In Search of a Screenwriter

Alma Reville wrote a first draft of the adaptation in 1948. Hitchcock then entrusted it to the novelist, playwright, and screenwriter Mabel Margaret Clark, whose pen name was Lesley Storm, whom he had met in London during the filming of *Stage Fright*. But nothing convincing came of it. Then the director presented the script to Graham Greene, an English writer who had converted to Catholicism and whose novels had already been adapted for the screen (Fritz Lang's *The Ministry of Fear*, Carol Reed's *The Third Man*, John Ford's *The Fugitive*). He thought that Greene would be attracted by the issues in a story featuring a theological dilemma. Greene turned down the offer, however, tending generally to avoid film commissions. Hitchcock then tried his luck with Samson Raphaelson, the screenwriter of *Suspicion* (1941), who also refused, feeling too unfamiliar with this type of subject. A version written by Paul Vincent Carroll (David MacDonald's *The Brothers*) also failed to satisfy the director.

William Archibald and George Tabori

After the release of *Strangers on a Train* and a two-month holiday, Hitchcock returned to the story in September 1951. He asked William Archibald and George Tabori to work separately on the script, as well as on another project for Transatlantic, *The Bramble Bush*. Archibald had adapted Henry James's *The Turn of the Screw* for the stage. Tabori, of Hungarian origin but naturalized British, wrote plays and novels about Nazism. He worked with the filmmaker for a long time on the dialogue before realizing that the latter had completely altered his contribution.

Many elements of the script shocked Warner Bros., which was now producing the film entirely after Transatlantic Pictures pulled out due to financial difficulties: the priest, the hero of the film, had an illegitimate child and was unjustly executed at the end. Such situations were unthinkable for the studio, which feared censorship. Hitchcock was therefore forced to make major changes. He also worked with Barbara Keon to flesh out the story with a subplot, and William Archibald reworked the script written by Tabori. A Quebec priest and doctor of theology, Father LaCouline, was hired as a special adviser to authenticate the description of the ecclesiastical world. Father LaCouline made a number of comments and suggestions to Hitchcock about how to avoid Catholic censorship, as he saw it.

CASTING

To reassure Warner Bros., Hitchcock promised to give the lead role to Cary Grant, then to James Stewart. He also suggested Laurence Olivier, but the studio demanded an American actor.

Hitch and Monty

The director then suggested Montgomery Clift, who had become a star after the success of George Stevens's *A Place in the Sun*. The actor had turned down a role in *Rope* (1948) a few years earlier, frightened by his character's obvious homosexuality. After a theatrical debut in New York, he came to prominence with Howard Hawks's *Red River*, in which he co-starred with John Wayne. Relations between the director and the actor became strained very quickly. Clift was anxious and tormented. Trained in the introspective acting methods of the

---

Censored and Banned

Despite all the precautions taken by Hitchcock and the producers, *I Confess* was widely censored during its commercial release in Quebec: Several scenes were cut or removed. The film was completely banned in Ireland.

Montgomery Clift as Father Michael.

Actors Studio, he demanded the permanent presence of his coach, Mira Rostova, on the set and sought her approval after every shot. The actor's alcoholism further complicated the shoot. Yet this was one of his finest film roles, that of Father Logan, a character both complete and intense, a feverish martyr of the faith, inhabited by a subdued and indescribable sadness.

Anne Baxter Rather than Anita Björk

For the female role, Hitchcock considered Swedish actress Anita Björk, who had made a name for herself shortly before in Alf Sjöberg's *Miss Julie* (*Fröken Julie*). The actress arrived in the United States with her lover and a child conceived out of wedlock. Warner Bros. was concerned that the actress might be rejected by puritanical America, which could damage the film's potential. The studio asked her to divorce and marry her lover and the child's father. When she refused, Hitchcock had to give up the idea of this actress. A few days before shooting began, Jack Warner imposed Anne Baxter. The granddaughter of architect Frank Lloyd Wright, she had won an Oscar for Best Supporting Actress for Edmund Goulding's *The Razor's Edge* in 1946 and a nomination for Joseph L. Mankiewicz's *All About Eve* in

1950. Hitchcock had her blond hair dyed even blonder. But he always regretted not having been able to cast Anita Björk, as he confessed to the filmmaker François Truffaut in their conversations.[1]

Two German Actors

The role of the stateless, murderous sexton was played by O. E. Hasse, a very popular German actor who began his career in the early 1930s. He appeared in numerous films in Germany until 1977 (including, in 1954, *Canaris* [*Deadly Decision*], in which he played the title role). He also had a brief career in Hollywood and France: Henri-Georges Clouzot gave him a role in *Les Espions* (*The Spies*), Roger Vadim in *Sait-on jamais…*(*No Sun in Venice*), and Jean Renoir, a brief but unforgettable performance in *Le Caporal épinglé* (*The Elusive Corporal*). Dolly Haas played the moving character of Alma, the murderer's wife. She appeared in many German comedies from the early 1930s. She moved to England in 1936 and married the director John Brahm, whom she divorced to marry the famous cartoonist and caricaturist Al Hirschfeld. Hitchcock spotted her in Brahm's 1936 British remake of Griffith's *Broken Blossoms or The Yellow Man and the Girl*. Having put her career on hold, she accepted Hitchcock's offer.

Dolly Haas, Montgomery Clift.

A Shrewd Policeman

The policeman in charge of the investigation, who soon suspects Father Logan, was played by Karl Malden. After the war, Malden made his film debut in films produced by 20th Century-Fox, but it was Elia Kazan, who knew him from his theater days, who gave him his most notable roles (*Boomerang!*, *A Streetcar Named Desire*, for which he won an Oscar, *On the Waterfront, Baby Doll*). He went on to appear in Marlon Brando's *One-Eyed Jacks*, John Frankenheimer's *Birdman of Alcatraz*, and John Ford's *Cheyenne Autumn* before his role in the television series *The Streets of San Francisco*, between 1972 and 1977, boosted his popularity. In *I Confess*, he succeeded in developing his character as a highly intelligent, instinctive, and rational policeman in just a few scenes.

FILMING AND PRODUCTION

Very early on, Hitchcock had the idea of setting the film in Quebec City, Canada, a city with a strong Catholic influence, both architecturally and spiritually. It was important to him to set the story in a place where it was common, he would say, to see priests in cassocks walking down the street.

A Requirement for Realism

In February 1952, Hitchcock went to Quebec City for location scouting with his wife, Alma Reville. In his quest for realism, he filmed in the streets of Quebec City itself, at the parliament, at the Château Frontenac hotel (where the kitchen staff appeared as themselves during the final chase), at the courthouse, on the Lévis ferryboat, and at Saint-Zéphirin church. The urban setting created an ambiguous atmosphere, giving the viewer the feeling of being in an old metropolis, in the heart of an old world at odds with the topography and architecture of American cities.

Most of the sequences were filmed on real sets, both exteriors and interiors. Shooting away from film sets, in authentic rooms with low ceilings, meant that cinematographer Robert Burks had to reconfigure many of the lights from the floor in order to spread the light more evenly. *I Confess* was the second of twelve Hitchcock films on which Burks worked. His work here was entirely focused on the need for realism, and the film's photography accurately captured the fabric of the houses and streets, the concrete and cobblestones of an old city, as well as the clouds and the distinctive light of the Quebec sky.

padded [and]…suspenseless script," adding that "only the most credulous patron will be worried for very long that the hero will not be delivered from his dilemma by some saving grace." For the *Washington Post* (February 27, 1953), the film "ask[s] for more than the suspension of disbelief" on the part of the audience.

The Interplay of Faith and Doubt

Other papers, however, were more favorable: "In his careful treatment, Hitchcock has gone deeper into human relationships than is usual with him, relying less on the physical chase or on theatrical props like trains or merry-go-rounds [an allusion to the finale of *Strangers on a Train*] than on the interplay of faith and doubt to create his famous brand of suspense" (*Los Angeles Times*, February 28, 1953).

French Incomprehension

I Confess was screened at the Cannes Film Festival in April 1953. The French critical reception was lukewarm. For Jean de Baroncelli, critic at *Le Monde*, it was "a mediocre Hitchcock" (July 3, 1953). *Comœdia* (July 1953) called it "a pseudo-police melodrama that turns into a mundane drama." And according to *Arts* (July 1953), "this perfect watchmaker is no more than a virtuoso. His coldness signifies poetic impotence." Georges Sadoul, in *Les Lettres françaises* (July 1953), barely acknowledged the filmmaker's "veteran expertise" and his ability to "direct his actors well and use Montreal's natural settings brilliantly."

A Great Artist Is Born

It was in *Cahiers du cinéma* (August–September 1953) that we read the praise that gave *I Confess* its rightful place. In a text entitled "L'art de la fugue" ("The Art of Fugue"), Jacques Rivette takes the film as an opportunity to describe the mysterious and unique art of Alfred Hitchcock, who has now entered the pantheon of filmmakers erected by the magazine, alongside Roberto Rossellini, Howard Hawks, and Jean Renoir: "For Hitchcock, directing will never be a 'language,' but a weapon relentlessly aimed at the secret of the body, slipping the sharpest blade into the fault line of gesture and thought." He continues in a lyrical vein: "The black flame that Montgomery Clift has visibly become thus ravages before our incredulous gaze, like the contagion of a tenebrous fire, the flesh of those who approach it, whose husk alone will continue to deceive us." The process of recognizing the filmmaker's work as that of a great artist had begun. And this movement

Where Is Hitchcock?

The filmmaker appears immediately after the credits, a plump human figure passing at the top of a grand staircase filmed from below. The idea of getting the shot of this obligatory appearance out of the way so quickly was undoubtedly determined by the serious nature of the film; this recurring gag would have upset or even contradicted it, had it occurred later in the narrative.

Calvary

Hitchcock did not hesitate to associate Father Logan's fate with the Passion of the Son of God. Before he gives himself up to the police, the priest wanders through the streets of Quebec City, and the director emphasizes the relationship between his frail figure and imposing statues of Christ and stone calvaries.

RECEPTION

Released in the United States at the end of February 1953, the film received some negative reviews, including one by Bosley Crowther in the *New York Times* (March 23, 1953), who called it an "obviously

Anne Baxter and Montgomery Clift aboard the Lévis ferryboat on the St. Lawrence (Quebec). Behind them, the Château Frontenac hotel.

was born in France, within a magazine of dedicated cinephiles.

A Dark Film

In his interviews with François Truffaut in the early 1960s, Hitchcock, who still remembered the difficulties of production and the compromises he had to accept, criticized the film for its lack of humor and finesse. It is true that *I Confess* is one of his darkest and most openly metaphysical works. The filmmaker takes up the motif of the transfer of guilt, but the theme of the wrongly accused innocent is complicated by the idea that this innocent is not quite so innocent, that the murderer performed the act in his place. The film can be seen as a variation on *Strangers on a Train*, or even a continuation of it, which Hitchcock was not really aware of until Truffaut pointed out the similarity between the motifs of the murder swap and the way one man "assumes" the guilt of another.

Montgomery Clift, in an unforgettable performance, invents a haunted and complex character before the viewer's very eyes. A lost look, a subdued

and furtive pain passing over his face, opens up an abyss that the film never openly comments upon or explains. The character he plays, with his almost Christlike quality, seems to have been profoundly changed by his experience as a soldier during the war. It is as if the horror of a merciless century is implicit in him.

A Film Within the Film

In 1995, Canadian playwright and director Robert Lepage directed a drama, *Le Confessionnal*, in which the filming of *I Confess* plays an important role. A young man, returning to Quebec City for his father's funeral, discovers a secret about his own brother's identity that dates back to the filming of Hitchcock's *I Confess*. Past and present merge.

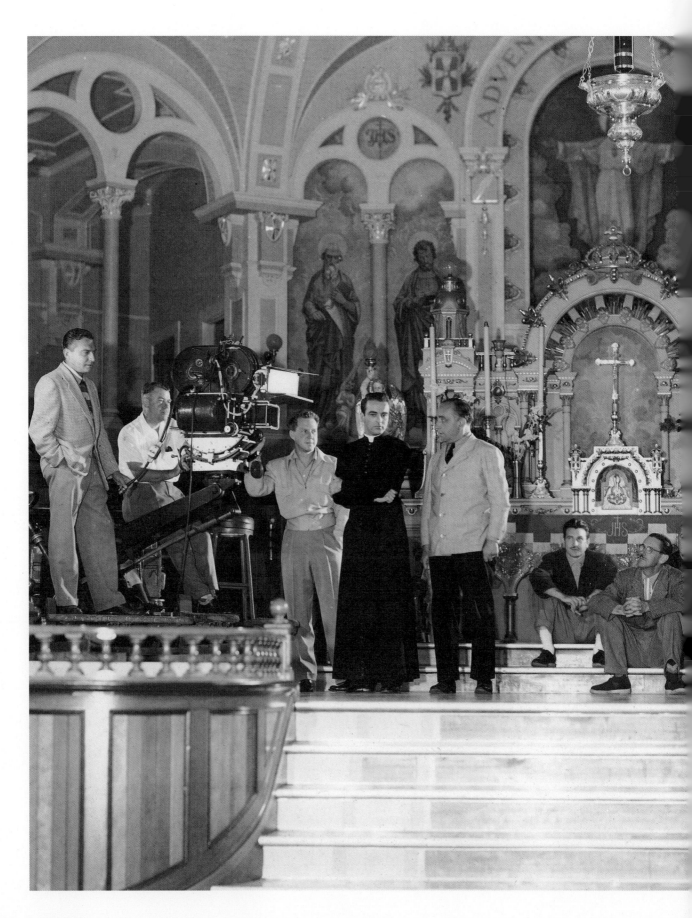

Inside Saint-Zéphirin church (Quebec): Father Logan (Montgomery Clift) and the sacristan (O. E. Hasse); in front of the altar, sitting on a chair, Alfred Hitchcock.

Alfred Hitchcock's

"dial M for Murder"

"...is that you, darling?"

Dial M for Murder

United States · **1 hr 45** · **Color**
(Warnercolor) · **Mono**
(RCA Sound System) · **1.66:1**
(WarnerVision, 3D)

Production Dates: July 30–September 25, 1953
Release Date in the United States: May 29, 1954

Production: Warner Bros.
Producer: Alfred Hitchcock

Based on the play of the same name by Frederick Knott (1952)
Screenplay: Frederick Knott
Director of Photography: Robert Burks
Camera Technician: Leonard J. South
Camera Operator: Wesley Anderson
Sound: Oliver S. Garretson
Assistant Director: Mel Dellar
Art Direction: Edward Carrere
Set Decoration: George James Hopkins
Hair Stylist: Gertrude Wheeler
Makeup: Gordon Bau
Costumes: Moss Mabry
Music: Dimitri Tiomkin
Film Editing: Rudi Fehr

Starring: Ray Milland (Tony Wendice), Grace Kelly (Margot Wendice), Robert
Cummings (Mark Halliday), John Williams (Chief Inspector Hubbard), Anthony
Dawson (Charles Swann), Leo Britt (storyteller), Patrick Allen (Detective Pearson),
George Leigh (Detective Williams), George Alderson (first detective), Robin Hughes
(police sergeant O'Brien), Sanders Clark (detective), Jack Cunningham (bobby),
Robert Dobson (police photographer), Sam Harris (man in phone booth), Alfred
Hitchcock (one of the guests in the group photo)...

"I would gladly shoot an entire film in a telephone box."

Alfred Hitchcock

SYNOPSIS

The setting is a wealthy district of London. Margot Wendice, a moneyed heiress, is the wife of Tony Wendice, a former tennis player, and the mistress of Mark Halliday, an American crime writer. Having discovered his wife's infidelity and the risk of her leaving him, Tony hatches a plan to have her murdered and then inherit her fortune. He blackmails Swann, a former school friend turned shabby con man, promising his silence and a thousand pounds if he kills Margot according to a plan Tony has devised. The next evening, Tony plans to take Mark to dinner at his club, leaving Margot alone in the flat. A phone call to his wife at the end of the evening gets her out of bed and exposes her to the killer, who is hiding in the living room. Swann, who has broken into the house, tries to strangle the young woman, but she defends herself and kills her attacker by stabbing him with a pair of scissors. Tony, who is following the whole scene on the telephone, realizes that he has failed. He returns home to hide a number of incriminating clues. He wants to make a murder committed in self-defense look like Margot's premeditated murder of a blackmailer likely to publicize her affair with Mark. She is arrested and convicted. Just as she is about to be executed, a perceptive police inspector sets a trap for Tony and forces him to unmask himself. Proof is finally found that the husband was behind the murder.

GENESIS

Following the relative success of *I Confess* (1952), the Warner Bros. studio urged Hitchcock, embroiled in writing the script for a film to be called *The Bramble Bush*, to film quickly.

An Adaptation…

Alfred Hitchcock opted for a film adaptation of a successful play recommended to him by cinematographer Jack Cardiff. *Dial M for Murder* premiered in London in June 1952 and was revived in New York at the Plymouth Theatre in September of the same year. It was written by English playwright Frederick Knott. Warner bought the rights from director and producer Alexander Korda for a respectable $30,000. After *Rope* (1948), *Dial M for Murder* was the second play the director had transposed to film.

…in Relief

Hitchcock hoped to shoot in England, at Elstree Studios, which would distance him from the American producers while guaranteeing a certain authenticity of the sets. But Warner Bros. refused, not wanting to send their 3D cameras so far afield. Indeed, studio boss Jack Warner had the idea of having the film made in 3D, a process recently used by some producers in an attempt to counter the competition from television, which had become a mass medium. André De Toth's *House of Wax*, produced in 3D the previous year by the same company, had been a great success. Jack Warner was convinced that a film by Hitchcock shot in 3D could only be a success.

Respecting the Unity of Place

Hitchcock worked on the script with Frederick Knott, whose intelligence he appreciated. He refused to "aerate" the room, retaining the idea, already employed for *Rope*, of a single set built at Warner Bros. Studios. The plot escapes these confines in only a few shots filmed in London, showing the street in front of the Wendice couple's home. The script calls for the action to take place off-screen for a few minutes, at the time of Margot's trial. This effect is evoked by close-ups of Grace Kelly's face, while the background changes color through lighting effects. Later, Hitchcock would explain to François Truffaut in their conversations that attempts to escape the unity of place are often contrivances that scatter the viewer's attention and break the fundamental quality of a play: its concentration. The filmmaker himself chose the furniture and objects placed in the Wendices' apartment.

CASTING

Alfred Hitchcock considered Cary Grant for the role of Tony Wendice, but producer Jack Warner decided against it, fearing public reaction to the casting against type of an actor who had become accustomed to playing sympathetic leads in light comedies.

From One Star to Another

The director chose Ray Milland to play the manipulative husband who ordered his wife's murder. The Welsh-born actor, one of Paramount's biggest stars from 1934 to 1948, won an Oscar for his performance in Billy Wilder's *The Lost Weekend* (1945). In the film, he plays a perfect model of elegant cynicism and suave hypocrisy.

Hitch and Grace: First Meeting

Dial M for Murder marks the first meeting between Alfred Hitchcock and Grace Kelly. It was on seeing a screen test for Gregory Ratoff's *Taxi* (for which she was not ultimately cast) that Hitchcock was

A Frequently Adapted Play

Prior to Hitchcock's film, the play, by British playwright Frederick Knott (1916–2002), was adapted by Julian Amyes for a series of live BBC dramas in the year of its premiere. Transpositions for American television followed, notably by George Schaefer in 1958. Anthony Dawson and John Williams reprised the roles they played in Hitchcock's film and in the theater. There are two other versions, dated 1967 (directed by John Llewellyn Moxey) and 1981 (by Boris Sagal). In the latter version, the central trio is played by Christopher Plummer, Angie Dickinson, and Michael Parks. There are also German, Swedish, and even Soviet adaptations. In 1998, Andrew Davis directed *A Perfect Murder*, starring Michael Douglas, Gwyneth Paltrow, and Viggo Mortensen, a loose remake of Hitchcock's film. The husband suggests murdering his wife to the lover himself.

Frederick Knott, the author of the adapted play, wrote only three plays: *Dial M for Murder* in 1952, *Write Me a Murder* in 1960, and *Wait Until Dark* in 1966. The last, another "claustrophobic" thriller, was successfully transposed to film by Terence Young in 1967, with Audrey Hepburn in the lead role, that of a young blind woman stalked in her apartment.

convinced he had the ideal actress for the role of Margot. The director was truly fascinated by the actress, who embodied the ideal woman in his eyes. He saw in her a blend of sophisticated coolness and hidden sensuality, qualities he particularly appreciated in an actress. He "borrowed" her for $20,000 from MGM, the studio that had her under contract. They got along perfectly during the filming. She became a close friend of Mr. and Mrs. Hitchcock's.

Secondary Roles

To play the lover, Hitchcock cast Robert Cummings, with whom he had a close friendship and whose modesty he appreciated. Cummings had played the lead in one of Hitchcock's films, *Saboteur*, in 1942.

John Williams, a model of British stoicism, had already appeared in *The Paradine Case* (1947). Here, he returned to his stage role as the perceptive police inspector Hubbard, investigating Swann's death. He reappeared in *To Catch a Thief* (1954) and, above all, in ten episodes of the *Alfred Hitchcock Presents* TV series, including three directed by the Master himself: "Banquo's Chair," "Wet Saturday," and "Back for Christmas."

For Hitchcock Addicts

The changing color of Margot's dresses is intended to signify the fatal spiral leading to her imprisonment. We thus move gradually from bright red to dull gray, from a flamboyant evening gown in the first scene to the more ordinary clothes Hitchcock has her buy in the ready-to-wear section of a department store. While he had planned for Grace Kelly to don a velvet robe when she picks up the phone and is mugged, she suggested wearing only a light nightgown. A woman on her own, awakened in the middle of the night by the telephone, would not be dressed in anything more, she said later. So she endures the murderer's onslaught in a splendid pale blue transparent nightdress.

Anthony Dawson, a Scottish-born actor of alarming thinness, also reprised the character he created in the theater, that of the spineless Swann, whom Tony Wendice blackmails into murdering his wife.

Grace Kelly terrified her male partners and is said to have had three affairs on the set, with Frederick Knott, the playwright and screenwriter; Anthony Dawson, the man she stabs onscreen; and above all Ray Milland, who declared himself deeply in love, to the point of jeopardizing his marriage.

FILMING AND PRODUCTION

Filming, which took place over several months, lasted just thirty-six days, but the technical demands

Scandal on the Set

Grace Kelly's affair with Ray Milland (above) sparked a minor scandal during filming, and hostility in puritanical circles. Ray Milland separated from his wife, Muriel, for a time. Hollywood newspapers took up the cause of the neglected wife; Grace Kelly was seen as a "husband-stealer," and she found her reputation tarnished. The studios even worried about her future career. The actress would later say she was affected by the rumors: "I felt like a prostitute." Under pressure from both the media and her family, Grace Kelly left Ray Milland.

of 3D, imposed on the filmmaker by the producer, made things a little more complicated and cumbersome.

Filming in 3D

Hitchcock had to give up some of his directorial ideas and certain types of shots due to material constraints. The process required a bulky camera equipped with two lenses. The camera could only be moved to a limited extent, thereby restricting panning and tracking shots. The filmmaker had a pit built into the set to increase the number of low-angle shots. He avoided the easy spectacular effects often used in 3D films (objects thrown at the audience, etc.). Instead, he used the 3D depth to heighten the sense of confinement (the characters seem to be moving in an aquarium) and to highlight certain objects (telephones, scissors, keys, etc.) that play an important role in the suspense and detective story. Hitchcock wanted a very close-up shot of a telephone dial for the opening credits, which the 3D camera did not permit. He had a giant model built, operated by a gigantic wooden finger. He reused this prop in the scene where Tony Wendice calls his wife from a phone booth.

Staging

The attempted murder scene, a disturbing blend of sexual embrace and absolute brutality, was extremely complicated to shoot. The setup was tricky, as it had to take into account the relief effects required (Grace Kelly's hand stretched out toward the screen, as if asking the viewer for help). Light reflections on the scissors—the murder weapon—also had to be captured. Hitchcock, accustomed to significant fluctuations in weight, lost ten kilos during the rehearsal and filming of these shots.

Another of the film's most remarkable scenes is the one in which Tony convinces Swann to murder his wife. In the space of a few minutes, the viewer witnesses a psychological takeover. The husband subtly but relentlessly manages to sway the would-be murderer through a combination of blackmail and promises. But the audience's support for this unlikely dramatic and psychological progression is due above all to the director's choices. The way in which, through editing, the viewer moves from one character to the next, the way in which Ray Milland's position in space dominates his interlocutor, the use of a vertiginous overhead shot of the two protagonists, all lend a sense of inescapable logic to Tony Wendice's enterprise.

An Invention with No Future

Hitchcock agreed to use 3D but was convinced that the new technique would be out of fashion by the time *Dial M for Murder* came out. In fact, by the time the film was commercially released, it had indeed

On the set, Hitchcock's camera placed in a pit for low-angle shooting.

Anthony Dawson, Grace Kelly.

fallen out of fashion, and *Dial M for Murder* was shown in 3D in only a limited number of theaters in the United States. It was released in a "flat" version in other countries. It was not until the early 1980s that the film was rereleased in theaters, making it possible to see it in 3D and appreciate the filmmaker's original and subtle use of the process.

RECEPTION

When the film was released in the United States, it was a success. It earned over $13 million on a production cost of around $1.4 million.

Mixed Reviews in the United States

The American critics were generally laudatory, with certain reservations. The *New York Times* on July 19, 1954, strangely regretted that "the claustrophobic dimension of the play" could not be maintained in the cinema. The journalist asserts, without much elaboration, that "this kind of exercise in applied mathematics and the emotional tension of suspense are fundamentally incompatible." Other reservations are expressed. For example, the film was considered too verbose: "The chief weakness is that the action is slow, caused by the fact that the story unfolds almost entirely by dialogue" (*Harrison's Reports*, May 1, 1954). For the *Washington Post*, on the other hand, "Hitchcock had a field day with his camera angles, directing our gaze here and then here, inventing tantalizing tricks based on shadows and very, very long shots contrasting with quick close-ups. This is the work of a master having fun with his script" (May 28, 1954).

Recognition in France for the Author?

In France, where the film was released in February 1955, it was fairly well received by critics, sometimes with the reservations one might have when faced with a piece of fine work that lacked real "depth."

Where Is Hitchcock?

Thirteen minutes into the film, Alfred Hitchcock can be recognized in the photograph hanging on the wall of the apartment that Tony (Ray Milland) points out to Swann (Anthony Dawson). It shows the guests at a dinner party at the university where the two characters previously met. Hitchcock is one of the guests.

For example, Jean de Baroncelli wrote in *Le Monde* on February 6, 1955: "Hitchcock is simply displaying the stylistic qualities we have known about him for a long time. *Dial M for Murder* is a good serial work." Conversely, for R. M. Arlaud in *Combat* (February 8, 1955): "This is an extraordinary game of chess in several parts, in which the author loses none of his pawns." For André Bazin, in *France observateur* (February 1955), "Hitchcock's work is, as usual, a marvelous piece of clockwork, and since the pleasure of the mind refers not to the ideal film that could have been made by reworking the script from top to bottom, but to the reality of the play, there is little to criticize." Jacques Doniol-Valcroze's review of the film in *Cahiers du cinéma* (February 1955) provided the opportunity for a crucial interrogation of the value of the filmmaker's body of work as a whole, and the recurrence of themes and motifs deeply embedded in his films. For some French critics, the piece was a milestone in the recognition of Alfred Hitchcock as an auteur.

Minor/Major

Alfred Hitchcock always regarded *Dial M for Murder* as an insignificant title in his filmography, a film of circumstance destined to achieve quick and easy popular success. To François Truffaut, he said, "I could have done it over the phone." While this opinion long convinced critics that it was a rather minor work, albeit a very successful one, the film eventually gained in prominence with the passage of time.

A Web of Guilt

Hitchcock again follows the pattern of the great works of his early American years (*Rebecca, Spellbound, Notorious*). A woman is the object of a struggle between two men who want to possess her. The theme of marital murder is also central to the work, as in *Suspicion* (1941). But *Dial M for Murder* is above all a film that plays with the audience, occasionally making the viewer afraid that the "villains" of the story will *not* succeed in carrying out their terrible deed. Tony Wendice's phone call, intended to wake his wife and trigger the murder, is long delayed by a succession of contingencies: His watch has stopped, and the phone booth he wants to use is already occupied. For his part, the murderer, hiding behind a curtain, is tempted to abandon his evil plan. He waits for the young woman to wake up, until he realizes that the plan is not on schedule. The viewer is thus placed at the center of a complex and contradictory web of guilt. The viewer hopes that Tony Wendice and his accomplice will succeed and that the woman, the target of their plot, will survive.

The Seduction of Evil

Dial M for Murder is without doubt the Hitchcock film that presents the most seductive "villain" in his cinema. Elegant, brilliant, witty, and of superior intelligence (like James Mason's character in *North by Northwest*), Tony Wendice is easily distinguished from his more ordinary love rival, Mark Halliday, the mystery writer played by Robert Cummings. An absolute model of English fair play, Tony, having just been confounded by Inspector Hubbard, offers to serve a glass of whiskey to the other protagonists of the drama in the room, starting with his wife. At this point, it is possible to see, furtively, a flash of admiration in the eyes of the woman he has tried to kill.

Three-Dimensional Cinema

Like the ability to set images in motion, stereoscopy—that is, the possibility of seeing them with the illusion of relief—was born in the early nineteenth century, well before the official birth of cinema. In the early 1950s, competition from television prompted the major Hollywood studios to come up with new cinematographic experiments: enlarging both the image format (CinemaScope) and the screen (Cinerama) and creating the illusion of relief. Between 1953 and 1955, 3D films were distributed, which viewers could watch through special glasses. Hitchcock's film was part of a string of successes that included *Gun Fury* by Raoul Walsh, *Creature from the Black Lagoon* by Jack Arnold, and *Inferno* by Roy Ward Baker. Costly and impractical for exhibitors, the process was abandoned after a few months.

JAMES STEWART
in
ALFRED HITCHCOCK'S
REAR WINDOW
Color by
TECHNICOLOR

co-starring

GRACE
KELLY · COREY · RITTER
WENDELL
THELMA

WITH RAYMOND BURR · DIRECTED BY ALFRED HITCHCOCK · SCREENPLAY BY JOHN MICHAEL HAYES
BASED ON THE SHORT STORY BY CORNELL WOOLRICH · A PARAMOUNT PICTURE

Rear Window

United States · 1 hr 52 · Color · Mono (Western Electric Recording) · 1.37:1 and 1.66:1

Production Dates: November 27, 1953–January 13, 1954
Release Date in the United States: September 1954

Production: Paramount, Alfred J. Hitchcock Productions
Producer: Alfred Hitchcock
Unit Production Manager: C. O. Erickson

**Based on a short story by Cornell Woolrich / William Irish,
"It Had to Be Murder" (1942)**
Screenplay: John Michael Hayes
Director of Photography: Robert Burks
Camera Assistant: Leonard J. South
Camera Operator: William Schurr
Visual Effects: John P. Fulton
Technicolor Adviser: Richard Mueller
Sound: John Cope, Harry Lindgren
Assistant Director: Herbert Coleman
Script: Irene Ives
Artistic Directors: Hal Pereira, Joseph McMillan Johnson
Set Decoration: Sam Comer, Ray Moyer
Makeup: Wally Westmore
Costumes: Edith Head
Music: Franz Waxman
Film Editing: George Tomasini

Starring: James Stewart (L. B. Jefferies, known as Jeff), Grace Kelly (Lisa Carol Fremont), Wendell Corey (Detective Lieutenant Thomas J. Doyle), Thelma Ritter (Stella), Raymond Burr (Lars Thorwald), Judith Evelyn (Miss Lonelyhearts), Ross Bagdasarian (song writer), Georgine Darcy (Miss Torso), Sara Berner (woman on the fire escape), Frank Cady (man on the fire escape), Jesslyn Fax (Miss Hearing Aid—sculptor with hearing aid), Rand Harper (newlywed), Havis Davenport (newlywed), Irene Winston (Emma Thorwald), Iphigenie Castiglioni (woman with bird), Alfred Hitchcock (clock winder)...

SYNOPSIS

——

It is a hot summer in Greenwich Village, New York. L. B. Jefferies, aka Jeff, the great reporter-photographer, is immobilized at home, his leg in a plaster cast. From morning to night, he observes the neighbors who live in the building across the street: a sexy dancer practicing in her kitchen, a young married couple making love all day long, a melancholy single woman in search of her soulmate, a sculptor, a composer-pianist in search of inspiration, an old couple who own a dog and sleep on their balcony because of the heat, another couple, the Thorwalds, who never stop quarreling. One night, Jefferies hears the sound of breaking glass. He notices the Thorwald husband repeatedly leaving the house with suitcases. He suspects him of murdering his wife. He convinces his girlfriend, Lisa Fremont, of this. (She is a famous model who wants nothing more than to marry him.) Despite the skepticism of one of Jefferies's police friends, Lisa decides, after the death of a small dog who had taken too close an interest in a flower bed maintained by Thorwald, to dig in the ground in the vain hope of finding a piece of the deceased's body. She breaks into the presumed murderer's apartment to steal the missing woman's wedding ring, which she believes is proof of her murder. Surprised by Thorwald, Lisa is rescued by policemen who mistake her for a thief. Thorwald, discovering that his neighbor across the street was spying on him, breaks into Jeff's apartment and attempts to push him out the window before being arrested by the police and confessing to everything.

"We are becoming a nation of voyeurs."

——

Stella (Thelma Ritter), in *Rear Window*

GENESIS

In the summer of 1953, through his agent, Lew Wasserman, Alfred Hitchcock signed a contract with Paramount for the direction and co-production of nine films with the studio through his company Alfred J. Hitchcock Productions. Hitchcock would have held exclusive rights to five of them, including *Rear Window*, for eight years.

A Wind of Freedom

For *Rear Window*, the director achieved a freedom he had never enjoyed before, except during the Gaumont British period in the second half of the 1930s. With the exception of *The Wrong Man* (Warner Bros.) and *North by Northwest* (MGM), as well as *Psycho*, a film produced by Hitchcock and only distributed by Paramount, from 1953 to 1958 the director made all his films exclusively for the studio.

Based on a Short Story by William Irish

Rear Window was inspired by "It Had to Be Murder" (1942), a short story by the writer Cornell Woolrich under his pseudonym, William Irish. Joshua Logan, then a theater director, and his producer, Leland Hayward, acquired the rights in 1952. Just as Logan had begun adapting the short story for his first film, Wasserman, the agent he shared with Hitchcock, sold it to the director. At first regarded as the project's co-producer, Logan was eventually dropped.

Filling Out the Short Story

Rear Window marked the beginning of a fruitful collaboration with screenwriter John Michael Hayes, which continued on the next three films. Hayes, author of several screenplays for the cinema, including Anthony Mann's *Thunder Bay* (1953), starring James Stewart, is best known for his adaptations of radio soap operas. According to Hitchcock, he was primarily responsible for the dialogue. In fact, there is every reason to believe that Hitchcock himself had made very precise progress in cutting this film during the shooting of his previous feature, *Dial M for Murder*. Nevertheless, the filmmaker and his screenwriter worked to enrich the original short story by filling in, down to the smallest detail, the lives of the neighbors whom the protagonist spies upon from his window. Logan had already created the character of the voyeur hero's girlfriend, absent from the short story. In the end, Hitchcock was delighted with the scriptwriter's work.

ARRESTATION DU DOCTEUR CRIPPEN ET DE MISS LE NEVE SUR LE PONT DU «MONTROSE»

Macabre Sources

Hitchcock drew on at least two English news stories to envision the murder of a wife by her husband. The first was that of Dr. Crippen, who murdered his wife in 1910, cutting her up into pieces and burying them in the basement of their house, then pretending she had left the marital home. Suspicions were aroused when a piece of jewelry belonging to the missing woman was found worn by the doctor's secretary, his mistress. He tried to escape with her, disguised as a man, on board an ocean liner, but the captain spotted the couple and alerted the Canadian police, who arrested him on arrival. The other case was that of Patrick Mahon, who, in 1924, dismembered his mistress, Emily Kaye, and hid part of the body in a trunk, while trying to dispose of the other organs. Emily Kaye's head was never found.

Newcomers

Hitchcock rehired Robert Burks, with whom he had already made three films, as director of photography. But this first title for Paramount was also the opportunity to meet a number of new collaborators, under contract with the studio, who would from then on follow him loyally: George Tomasini for the editing of his next eight films, Edith Head for costumes (she had already worked on *Notorious*, 1946), and Joseph McMillan Johnson and Hal Pereira for art direction.

CASTING

On the set of *Dial M for Murder*, Hitchcock was already talking to Grace Kelly about his new project, without announcing that she would once again be the female lead.

The Indispensable Grace Kelly

Hitchcock probably never really had any other actress in mind. In October 1953, Grace Kelly learned from her agent that the director was expecting her for the first fittings. She gave up the lead role in *On the Waterfront* offered to her by Elia Kazan. The actress recalls the filmmaker's excitement: "He described to me with great enthusiasm and detail the fabulous setting for this film as we waited for the camera to set up. He would tell me about the people we would see in the apartments across the courtyard, their little stories, how they would appear as real characters and what would be revealed to the viewer. I could see him thinking all the time, and when he had a moment's peace, he would go back to talking about his set. It was a great joy for him."[1]

Hitchcock asked John Michael Hayes to spend some time with her, observing that she "does everything well and pleasantly, but she does not express anything. We must get something out of her, bring her to life."[2] Grace Kelly spent a week with Hayes, who claimed to have modeled the character of Lisa on the 1940s cover girl and model Anita Colby, nicknamed "The Face." He added that he was also inspired by his own wife, Mel Lawrence, also a model. It is also likely that he felt particularly concerned by the tensions between the demands of show business and those of intimate or married life.

Convincing James Stewart

Six years after *Rope*, Hitchcock reunited with James Stewart for the male lead. Stewart was initially reluctant to accept Hitchcock's request. *Rope* had been a technical challenge and a commercial failure, the setup for this next film seemed complicated once again, and, above all, the actor had to deal with the fears of his wife, Gloria, who was worried that the female lead would be Grace Kelly, with her well-established reputation as a seductress. At the insistence of Joshua Logan and Leland Hayward, the actor accepted the role. In return, he required that his fixed salary should be replaced by a share in the film's profits, according to a system developed by the MCA agency to increase the power of actors in Hollywood. Stewart went from comedy actor before the war to neurotic hero of postwar Hollywood cinema. He had just made three Westerns with Anthony Mann in which he played a troubled, masochistic figure. His character in *Rear Window* is both that of a voyeur and that of someone powerless, plagued by an almost insurmountable anguish at the mere prospect of a "normal" love and conjugal life, projecting his own unavowable desires and fantasies into the spectacle of the intimate lives of the inhabitants of the building opposite. The film's trailer identifies this to the viewer. Suddenly addressing the camera, Stewart says, "First I looked at my neighbors to kill time, and then I could not help but go on. As you would have done yourself."

Secondary Roles

Thelma Ritter, the unforgettable informer in Samuel Fuller's *Pickup on South Street*, released a year earlier, was cast in the mocking supporting role of Stella. She plays the nurse and masseuse who, from the very first scene, provides a humorous yet critical commentary on events.

For Hitchcock Addicts

The film's love story is said to have been inspired by Ingrid Bergman's affair with the famous press photographer Robert Capa in the immediate postwar period. At the end of 1945, Capa was working as a set photographer on the set of *Notorious*.

Raymond Burr plays the murderous neighbor. A film noir supporting actor and primarily a television performer, he became famous in the 1950s and 1960s for the TV series *Perry Mason* and, in the 1960s and 1970s, for another series, *Ironside*. Burr was chosen because of his physical resemblance to David O. Selznick, the tyrannical producer with whom Hitchcock made some of his films in the 1940s, under conditions that left him with bad memories.

FILMING AND PRODUCTION

After *Lifeboat*, *Rope*, and *Dial M for Murder*, *Rear Window* takes place behind closed doors. Everything is seen and experienced from the apartment of the main character, L. B. Jefferies, who has an unobstructed view of the courtyard and the windows of the building opposite.

A Gigantic Set

Hitchcock had a gigantic set built at Paramount Studios: fifty-six meters long, eleven meters wide, and twelve meters high. While digging the foundations, the workers even managed to get down to the water table. There were thirty-one apartments, twelve of which were fully furnished, and Hitchcock requested that all those suitable for habitation should have running water and electricity. Production manager "Doc" Erickson was sent to New York by McMillan Johnson, the art director, to take photographs of three Greenwich Village courtyards at different times of the day. Alfred Hitchcock also had the sounds of the places he visited recorded to capture their ambience.

Lighting: A Real Challenge

One thousand giant arc lamps were mobilized to reproduce sunlight, and two thousand spotlights were used for additional lighting.

Lighting a set of this size was a real headache for Robert Burks, who considered the shoot the greatest challenge of his career: "Our main problem was defining the shot. Try to visualize shooting scenes in which the actors are no closer than 70 feet [20 meters] from the camera…On the set, there was a console with switches that looked like the biggest organ ever built." Depending on whether the action took place during the day, at night, or at dusk, three different types of lighting were used: "The problem was to achieve lighting that

The gigantic film set.

gave sufficient light inside the apartments to show the action, but not too much so that you did not get the feeling that the room was lit as if it were night."[3] Burks's assistant confided that it was the first time in his career that he had to adjust the focus when an actor moved from a distance of 50 to 51 feet (15.2 to 15.5 meters).

Despite the cumbersome setup, the shooting was particularly harmonious. James Stewart commented, "The set and every part of the film were so well conceived, and Hitchcock felt so comfortable with everyone involved, that we all believed in his success."[1]

Situational Music

For the music, Hitchcock teamed up once more with Franz Waxman, with whom he had already worked three times. Waxman used almost exclusively situational music (radios on in apartments, a pianist at work, etc.). He borrowed the song "That's Amore" (the newlyweds entering the apartment) and "To See You Is to Love You" (Miss Lonelyhearts) from the repertoire of music to which Paramount owned the rights.

RECEPTION

Rear Window was presented at the Venice Film Festival in August 1954 and released in the US in September of the same year.

An American Success

For a shooting budget estimated at $1 million, the film grossed over $36 million on the American

For Hitchcock Addicts

One day, the heat from the spotlights used to illuminate the film's gigantic set triggered the fire-extinguishing system. Impassively, under the torrents of water drowning a set suddenly plunged into darkness, Hitchcock had an umbrella brought in to wait out the deluge.

market alone. American critics were unanimously favorable. Bosley Crowther, the influential *New York Times* film critic, hailed it as "a tense and exciting exercise," adding: "What it has to say about people and human nature is superficial and glib. But it does expose many facets of the loneliness of city life and it tacitly demonstrates the impulse of morbid curiosity" (August 5, 1954). *Variety* considered it one of Hitchcock's best thrillers, "combining artistic and technical skill to turn a crime mystery into excellent entertainment" (July 14, 1954).

A Nice Piece of Work, According to French Critics

In France, the film was only released on April 1, 1955. The critics in turn recognized the quality of the entertainment. "A nice piece of work, nicely done," said *France-Soir* (April 5, 1955), which crowned Hitchcock "king of virtuosos." R. M. Arlaud in *Combat* hailed "an experimental system in its purest form" and concluded, "What a well-oiled machine!" (April 1, 1955). Journalist Jean de Baroncelli in *Le Monde*, while refraining from "waving the cymbals and tambourines of enthusiasm," alluding to the infatuation with Hitchcock vociferously expressed by a certain French cinephile, was willing to admit that the filmmaker was engaged in a kind of moral investigation with his film, "which consists of taking the mask off humanity" (April 5, 1955). However, the critic from *L'Humanité* deplored the lack of consistency in the characters and the vulgarity of the screenplay, which was only matched by "the vulgarity of the direction and colors" (April 9, 1955).

At the Heart of Cinephile Quarrels

Cahiers du cinéma considered, unlike the critics as a whole, that *Rear Window* was more than just virtuoso entertainment. Future filmmaker Claude Chabrol

reviewed the film in the April 1955 issue. The article, entitled "Les choses sérieuses" ("Serious Matters"), expresses the brilliant intuition of the mental voyage and invites us to consider "the other side of the courtyard...as a multiple projection of James Stewart's preoccupation with love." In November 1955, in the midst of an ideological war with *Cahiers du cinéma*, *Positif* magazine published "Petit bilan pour Alfred Hitchcock" ("Brief Assessment of Alfred Hitchcock"), written by Louis Seguin. Taking aim at the director's last two films, *Dial M for Murder* and *Rear Window*, the author rejects what he sees as a metaphysics at work: "James Stewart spying on his neighbors does not invite contempt, or even compassion, but troubled admiration. The be-all and end-all of Christian morality is indeed this infinite indulgence in the examination of guilty conscience and the voluptuousness of Confession." And the paper concludes with an implacable "Yes, undoubtedly, we must be disdainful of Alfred Hitchcock."

A Very Complete Film

Rear Window is a film that contains all the filmmaker's work and all his obsessions. It is as much a perfect suspense thriller as it is a theoretical film in which the author not only puts into practice a number of techniques for manipulating cinema audiences, but also offers a genuine reflection on his own art. The very notion of spectacle is at the heart of a film whose significance has been the subject of numerous writings (entire books have been devoted to it)[4] and speculations, some of them contradictory.

A Powerless Hero

The film is above all the portrait of an ambiguous character, driven by the irrepressible urge to see what no one wants to show to others: the triviality of everyday life for the average American in the mid-1950s. L. B. Jefferies is a neurotic, impotent hero, both literally (he is confined to a chair by a leg in a plaster cast) and allegorically (sexually, perhaps), refusing the prospect of marriage and finding, in what defines the involuntary spectacle given by his neighbors (sexual exhaustion, indifference, routine, murderous hatred), every reason to see conjugality as an ordinary nightmare. Certain directorial choices (Grace Kelly's shadow passing over Jefferies's sleeping face) succeed in making Lisa Fremont and her desire for marriage truly disturbing. Could it be that the murderer is fulfilling Jefferies's secret desire to annihilate Lisa, embodying the danger of the feminine in all its aspects? This is evidenced by the first shot, a long camera movement describing the setting

412   *Rear Window*

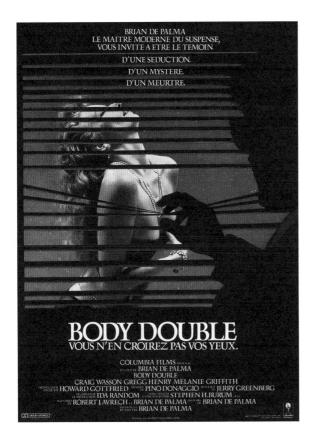

BRIAN DE PALMA
LE MAITRE MODERNE DU SUSPENSE,
VOUS INVITE A ETRE LE TEMOIN

D'UNE SEDUCTION.

D'UN MYSTERE.

D'UN MEURTRE.

BODY DOUBLE
VOUS N'EN CROIREZ PAS VOS YEUX.

COLUMBIA FILMS présente
un film de BRIAN DE PALMA
BODY DOUBLE
CRAIG WASSON GREGG HENRY MELANIE GRIFFITH
producteur exécutif HOWARD GOTTFRIED musique PINO DONAGGIO montage JERRY GREENBERG
producteur délégué IDA RANDOM la photographie STEPHEN H. BURUM a.s.c.
scénario ROBERT J. AVRECH et BRIAN DE PALMA histoire BRIAN DE PALMA
produit et réalisé par BRIAN DE PALMA

An Inspiring Film

Rear Window has served as a matrix for many films that have paid tribute to it, whether deliberately or not. There is *Body Double* (1984), directed by Brian De Palma, a filmmaker accustomed to variations on Hitchcock motifs. Burt Reynolds also claimed the film's influence in *Sharky's Machine* (1981), as did John Badham in *Stakeout* (1987) and Phillip Noyce in *Sliver* (1993). William Irish's estate sued the production of D. J. Caruso's *Disturbia* (2007), a film the estate considered too close to the short story adapted by Hitchcock. There was also an acknowledged remake, filmed in 1998 for television by Jeff Bleckner, starring Daryl Hannah and Christopher Reeve (who had become quadriplegic following a horse-riding accident, making him tragically suited to the role of this "paralyzed" man).

in which the action is to take place, as well as the film's closed-door premise. This movement ends with a close-up of James Stewart's head, a way of moving from the whole to the detail, but also from the content (the hero's fantasies and reveries) to the vessel containing them (his own mind).

The First Zapper?

More generally, *Rear Window* highlights an anthropological shift taking place in modern society at the time. The very notion of intimacy was fundamentally overturned. The film is contemporary with the advent of television as a mass medium and an intruder in every home.

Trapped in his apartment, with one leg in a plaster cast, L. B. Jefferies faces a wall of apartments, as many windows or little boxes, or "skylights." His gaze jumps from one to the next. He has been likened to a cinemagoer satisfying his desire to see (he too is stuck in his armchair). But he can also be seen as the first zapper in the history of cinema, switching from one channel to another as he takes in the different types of scenes offered by the windows of the apartments across the street.

Hitchcock the Visionary

Rear Window was filmed between 1953 and 1954, but the invention of the wired remote control, called "lazybones," dates back to 1950. The wireless remote control, on the other hand, came onto the market five years later. Hitchcock was undeniably an observer of his time and a visionary.

Grace Kelly,
the "Hitchcock Blonde"

Grace Kelly (1929–1982), a filmmaker's feminine ideal, starred in three Hitchcock films, but soon left the cinema for another destiny, leaving her Pygmalion inconsolable, in search of his lost image.

A Model Upbringing

Born into an Irish Catholic family in Philadelphia, Grace Kelly spent her school years in a convent. She continued her studies at the prestigious Bennington College, a private liberal arts university. She then entered the American Academy of Dramatic Arts while pursuing a modeling career. A hard worker, she made her debut on television and Broadway. Her theatrical success opened the door to Hollywood: She appeared in *Fourteen Hours* (1951), where Gary Cooper spotted her and recommended her for the female lead in *High Noon* (1952). In *Mogambo* (1953), the handsome fifty-two-year-old Clark Gable was "split" between brunette Ava Gardner and blonde Grace Kelly—with his performance earning him the Oscar for Best Supporting Actor. Throughout her career, the actress played heroines in relationships with older men.

The Absolute Blonde

Hitchcock discovered the twenty-four-year-old actress at a private screening of *Mogambo*. She was then overlooked by MGM, who agreed to "lease" her to Paramount for a mere $14,000. The Kelly-Hitchcock collaboration lasted three films, making her a star.

Grace Kelly on the set of *Rear Window* (1954).

The filmmaker seems to have found in this blonde with big blue eyes, a perfect figure and bearing, and elegant gestures, the ideal incarnation of the Hitchcock blonde, a dream vision come true. Grace Kelly reconciles opposites: victim and sinner in *Dial M for Murder* (1953), icy and enterprising in *To Catch a Thief* (1954). In *Rear Window* (1954), "Jeff" (James Stewart) hesitates to marry a woman he finds "too talented, too beautiful, too sophisticated, too perfect… too everything!" Hitchcock captures a brief, moving close-up of the actor's face: His gaze expresses deep admiration for the woman who, by dropping in on the neighbor suspected of being a criminal, suddenly gives him proof of her courage and adventurous spirit. Stewart confides: "We were all crazy about Grace Kelly. Everyone was there in the morning waiting for her to arrive so they could watch her."[1]

Fragile, Handle with Care

In *Dial M for Murder*, Hitchcock wants the color of Kelly's outfits to reflect her fate: She goes from brick red to gray, then to black. From *Rear Window* onward, renowned costume designer Edith Head helped him bring his vision of the actress to life. In the film, she must look like "Dresden porcelain, something gracefully untouchable."[1] In the grand masked ball of *To Catch a Thief*, Head has to make her look like a princess: Grace Kelly, a figure half-real, half-fantastical, whom we dream of touching without compromising her perfection.

The Actress and the Princess

Grace Kelly married Prince Rainier III, whom she had met at the 1955 Cannes Film Festival, and put an end to her career, having found, in her opinion, the role of a lifetime. After Ingrid Bergman, this was the second time Hitchcock had seen his favorite actress leave him for another man. But Hitchcock remained hopeful of getting her to play again. He dreamed of reuniting Kelly and Stewart in his remake of *The Man Who Knew Too Much* (1955) and in two ultimately aborted projects, *Flamingo Feather* and *Mary Rose*. He still had her in mind to play the fatal Eve Kendall in *North by Northwest* (1958), but the princess of Monaco was still not ready to leave her principality.

Marnie, or the Dream Lost

In 1962, however, Kelly expressed an interest in playing the heroine of *Marnie*: Hitchcock named the character "HSH" (Her Serene Highness) in the script and postponed shooting until his favorite became available. He made the mistake of announcing her return to Hollywood by praising the actress's sex appeal, "the most wonderful in the world," in the British newspaper the *Daily Express*. The announcement of this sulfurous role caused an uproar among the people of Monaco. Distraught, Kelly had to give up *Marnie* and would never act again. In a letter, she confessed her heartbreak to the filmmaker, who diplomatically tried to appease her: "After all, it was only a film."[1]

The Fleeting Image

Commenting on the filming of *Vertigo* (1957), Kim Novak confided, "Hitchcock hoped to find in me a Grace Kelly blonde, which was not the case, while believing that he would succeed in changing my nature. As a result, we find this resistance on screen."[2] From Novak to Tippi Hedren via Eva Marie Saint, Hitchcock would spend a decade searching the features of his Hitchcock blondes for the face of Grace Kelly, in the manner of an intimate *Vertigo*.

Portrait

PARAMOUNT PRESENTS

CARY GRANT
GRACE KELLY

in

ALFRED HITCHCOCK'S

TO CATCH A THIEF

Color by TECHNICOLOR

VISTAVISION
MOTION PICTURE HIGH-FIDELITY

with
JESSIE ROYCE LANDIS
JOHN WILLIAMS
Directed by
ALFRED HITCHCOCK
Screenplay by
JOHN MICHAEL HAYES
Based on the novel by David Dodge

To Catch a Thief

United States • **1 hr 46** • **Color** • **Mono**
(Western Electric Recording) • **1.85:1** (VistaVision)

Production Dates: May 31–September 4, 1954
Release Date in the United States: August 5, 1955

Production: Paramount
Producer: Alfred Hitchcock

Based on the novel of the same name by David Dodge (1952)
Screenplay: John Michael Hayes
Dialogue Coach: Elsie Foulstone
Director of Photography: Robert Burks
Camera Operator: William Schurr
Visual Effects: John P. Fulton, Farciot Edouart
Technicolor Adviser: Richard Mueller
Sound: Harold Lewis, John Cope
Assistant Director: Daniel J. McCauley
Scripts: Claire Behnke, Sylvette Baudrot
Art Direction: Hal Pereira, Joseph McMillan Johnson
Set Decoration: Sam Comer, Arthur Krams
Makeup: Wally Westmore
Costumes: Edith Head
Music: Lyn Murray
Film Editing: George Tomasini

Starring: Cary Grant (John Robie), Grace Kelly (Frances Stevens), Jessie Royce Landis (Jessie Stevens), John Williams (H. H. Hughson), Charles Vanel (Bertani), Brigitte Auber (Danielle Foussard), Jean Martinelli (Foussard), Georgette Anys (Germaine), George Adrian (detective), John Alderson (detective), Alex Ball (casino manager), Alfred Hitchcock (a man sitting on a bus) . . .

> "For the past month, Hitchcock, based at the Carlton in Cannes, has been shooting his film in all the picturesque locations of the vicinity. Either way, it will be a tourist compendium of Provence."

André Bazin, "Petit journal intime du cinéma," *Cahiers du cinéma*, August 1954

SYNOPSIS

The palaces of the Côte d'Azur are plagued by a series of burglaries. The police suspect John Robie, nicknamed "Le Chat" (The Cat), a former Resistance fighter and retired burglar on the Riviera. Robie visits the restaurant of Bertani, his former network leader, who is also quickly suspected. Danielle Foussard, the daughter of a former burglar, helps Robie lose the police. The Cat obtains a list of the most expensive jewels on the Riviera from H. H. Hughson, an insurance agent. An American widow, Jessie Stevens, and her daughter Frances are among the richest owners. Robie enters the Stevenses' inner circle. Frances seduces the man she thinks is The Cat. One evening, she lures him to her bedroom to watch a fireworks display. The next day, the diamond necklace she was wearing is stolen. The young woman calls the police, but in the meantime, The Cat has disappeared. We learn of the death of Danielle's father, Foussard, who accidentally fell off a cliff and has been identified as the wanted burglar. But knowing that Foussard had a wooden leg, Robie continues his investigations and asks Frances to take him to a masked ball where the false Cat may be found. At the end of the party, Robie stands on the roof of the house. A silhouette appears, and after a perilous struggle, Robie unmasks the burglar, who is none other than Danielle Foussard. The next morning, Frances joins Robie in his apartment and asks him to marry her.

GENESIS

In 1951, Hitchcock read the proofs of *To Catch a Thief*, a novel by British writer David Dodge, and acquired the rights for $15,000. The adaptation was initially to be produced by his company Transatlantic Pictures, but it had lost too much money and his partner, Sidney Bernstein, who decided to give up film production, sold the rights to the novel to Paramount for $105,000. *To Catch a Thief* was the second of nine films Hitchcock signed up for with the studio.

Useful and Enjoyable

Released in 1952, *To Catch a Thief* tells the story of John Robie, a former Resistance fighter and retired burglar nicknamed "The Cat." The man lives a quiet life on the Riviera until a series of jewel thefts is attributed to him, forcing him to investigate to prove his innocence. Hitchcock takes up the distressing theme of the false culprit in a lighthearted, comic vein, but there is another element that catches his eye: the Côte d'Azur, which he had never filmed before. He wanted to mix business with pleasure by filming on the Riviera and was determined to make the French coastline one of the protagonists of his film.

A Screenwriter on the French Riviera

Very happy with John Michael Hayes's work on *Rear Window*, Hitchcock hired him again to write the screenplay. Hitchcock insisted that Hayes should visit the French Riviera before starting work on the adaptation: Hayes and his wife stayed at the Hotel Carlton Nice during postproduction on *Rear Window*. Back in Hollywood, he set to work with the director until late winter 1953. The two men developed the love story between Robie and a young Texan named Frances, heightened the "sexual suspense," and created a comedy. They came up with a 212-page script, translated into French in order to obtain the necessary filming permits. The script was finalized in early May 1954 but went through successive versions, its rewriting dictated in turn by the censors, the actors, and the budget. *To Catch a Thief* ran up against the Production Code Administration (PCA), Hollywood's censorship body, which pointed out the countless sexual allusions and judged the fireworks scene "totally unacceptable." Hitchcock promised that all the problems raised by the commission would be resolved.

Where Is Hitchcock?

Near the beginning of the film, Cary Grant boards a bus and takes a seat in the back row. To his right there sits a birdcage...The actor glances warily at his neighbor on the left, while the camera pans slightly to reveal another passenger: Alfred Hitchcock, impassive (and slimmed down from his recent diet).

CASTING

As was often the case when he thought of a male actor for one of his films, the filmmaker could not imagine *To Catch a Thief* without his favorite star, Cary Grant.

A Premature Retirement

The actor read the novel in 1952 and agreed, with reservations, to star in the film. But filming began just as Grant was retiring. Grant had embarked on a long cruise around the world and turned down every script, no doubt feeling out of step with the times: "It was the period of the blue jeans, the dope addicts, the Method [an allusion to the new Method acting technique], and nobody cared about elegance or comedy at all."[1] However precisely, *To Catch a Thief* is intended to be a sophisticated, nostalgic comedy in which Grant plays a gentleman burglar who has retired. Hitchcock was extremely patient and diplomatic, going so far as to reduce his own salary in order to obtain Grant, who eventually agreed.

High Fidelity

Grace Kelly turned down the female lead in Elia Kazan's black-and-white social drama *On the Waterfront*, preferring instead to play Frances Stevens, the sophisticated blonde in Hitchcock's new color film. *To Catch a Thief* was the actress's third film with the director, and her last before becoming Princess of Monaco. Very keen on actor John Williams, whom he had cast in *The Paradine Case* (1947) and *Dial M for Murder* (1953), Hitchcock entrusted him with the role of Hughson, the insurance agent. On the technical side, Hitchcock was equally faithful: from the

On the Grande-Corniche, Grace Kelly.

cinematographer (Robert Burks) to the editor (George Tomasini), from the assistant director (Herbert Coleman) to the costume designer (Edith Head), Hitchcock used the entire *Rear Window* team.

The Frenchies

The filmmaker assembled the French part of his cast on location. Impressed by Henri-Georges Clouzot's *The Wages of Fear* (*Le Salaire de la peur*) (1953), he chose Charles Vanel to play Bertani, the gang leader turned restaurateur. For Danielle Foussard, Hitchcock, looking for an athletic physique, cast Brigitte Auber, spotted in Julien Duvivier's *Sous le ciel de Paris* (*Under the Paris Sky*) (1951). He later discovered that the actress had acrobatic training, which served her role perfectly as a woman skilled at climbing rooftops.

FILMING AND PRODUCTION

While Hitchcock finalized his French casting in Paris, Herbert Coleman directed his second crew to the Riviera to film transparencies and shots without actors. At the end of May, the entire film crew gathered at the Carlton in Cannes, and filming of *To Catch a Thief* began on the thirty-first, in a vacation atmosphere. The filmmaker took advantage of the opportunity to have Paramount pay for the best restaurants.

A Postcard

According to Herbert Coleman, Hitchcock's philosophy at Paramount could be summed up in a handful of ingredients: "beautiful people, beautiful scenery, a love story and suspense."[1] This was the recipe the filmmaker intended to apply, less concerned with his suspenseful plot than with filming the splendid views of the Riviera and his muse of the moment, Grace Kelly, sublimated by the sumptuous gowns designed by Edith Head. The first shot of the film announces the program: Hitchcock abandons the idea of an opening sequence of hands stealing jewels in favor of a much lighter shot of the front of a travel agency extolling the virtues of the place. An advertising poster proclaims: "If you love life, you'll love France." And the credits are written in pink.

À la Lubitsch

To Catch a Thief is first and foremost a sparkling, sophisticated romantic comedy reminiscent of those by the master of the genre, Ernst Lubitsch (*Bluebeard's Eighth Wife*, a 1938 Paramount film, took place on a studio–re-created French Riviera). So much so, in fact, that this eroticism-tinged lightness ends up taking over from the Hitchcock-style detective story. The film contains a large number of scenes with sexual content, thinly veiled by brilliant double entendres. Among the most memorable is the scene in which Robie and Frances take a break on a ledge after losing the police. The young woman opens her picnic basket and asks the man whether he prefers a leg or a breast. Previously, in *Notorious* (1946), a story about a chicken to be prepared was intertwined with an interminable kissing scene.

Alma Reville at the Wheel

Alma Reville was not on the set to advise Hitchcock, but she was behind the Grande-Corniche chase sequence. Remembering the steep curves of this mountain road, Alma described precisely to her husband how the scene should be shot. She suggested that some shots of the chase should be filmed from a helicopter. *Suspicion* and *Notorious* contained scenes (filmed in transparency) in a speeding car, but this time Alma Reville's ideas turned the chase into a sequence worthy of a modern action film.

The Birth of VistaVision

From 1953 onward, Hollywood studios invented a whole host of devices to counter the growing influence of television and bring audiences back into theaters, including extra-wide-screen formats for films that were intended to be spectacular. In response to 20th Century-Fox's CinemaScope, Paramount in turn patented a "large-format" process, VistaVision, with excellent image definition. As in *Dial M for Murder*, Hitchcock sought to exploit the latest technology, so *To Catch a Thief* was shot in VistaVision. The filmmaker, trained in the days of silent cinema and the almost square image, admitted he was uncomfortable with this imposed format. He confessed to disliking these horizontal screens, which sometimes left both director and viewer perplexed by so much empty space.

Fireworks

VistaVision, still in its infancy, posed a number of problems during filming. As soon as Hitchcock shot a close-up, the background became blurred. Paramount viewed the rushes and sent urgent telegrams to the filmmaker, asking him to shoot transparencies (which would give sharp backgrounds) and to shoot the close-ups later, in Hollywood. Hitchcock accepted the challenge and decided to shoot both close-ups and transparencies on location. Once back at Paramount, he shot different close-ups in front of the transparencies previously shot. Far from seeing the transparency as a mere technical device, the director turned it into a formal experiment, blending artifice with reality.

Painstaking Postproduction

Capricious weather and technical problems delayed filming on the Riviera until the end of June. Hitchcock and his team returned to Hollywood to continue shooting at Paramount Studios. Several scenes had to be reshot, particularly those with VistaVision defects. They also had to rerecord dialogue that could not be heard because of the wind, and dub Charles Vanel, whose English was barely comprehensible. In January 1955, six months after the end of shooting, Hitchcock completed the dubbing in Nice. Over 250 sound loops were corrected.

A Princess Before Her Time

It was in Hollywood, in the second week of August 1954, that Hitchcock began shooting the grand final ball. As he always had very precise requirements for his actresses' costumes, he asked that Grace Kelly look like a fairy-tale princess, and imagined her in a gold lamé gown. Edith Head created an impressive gown braided with gold thread, the highlight of the show. For the costume designer, the sequence was an absolute dream project.

RECEPTION

Released in the US in August 1955, *To Catch a Thief* was a resounding success, benefiting from the favorable reception of *Rear Window*, with which it shared the same female star.

Lightness or Glibness?

American critics perceived a more relaxed Hitchcock, who treated suspenseful plots with nonchalance, preferring instead the "escapist" film. Richard L. Coe of the *Washington Post* paid tribute to this lightness: "one of those de luxe pictures in which everyone lives in glorious workless luxury on the French Riviera, looks wonderful, speaks amusingly and is unconcerned with transit strikes or hurricanes. I loved every minute of it" (August 19, 1955). *The Guardian* was disconcerted by so much casualness and so little tension: "Certainly the 'whodunnit' element in this film is remarkably slack; the unmasking of the master criminal, which is the climax of the story, comes as mildly as bread and milk" (November 1, 1955).

A sun-kissed dress by Edith Head.
Grace Kelly, Alfred Hitchcock.

A "Cat" on the roof: Cary Grant.

A Gastronomic Menu

The film was released in France five months later. In the January 1956 issue of *Cahiers du cinéma*, Claude Chabrol's pseudonym, Jean-Yves Goute, described *To Catch a Thief* as a potpourri of Hitchcock's American work. The critic humorously lists the film's main moments in the manner of a gourmet menu, from the "Provençal hors d'oeuvres" and "salad, niçoise" to the dessert symbolized by the masked ball sequence, described as a "splendid 18th-century set piece, royally adorned and presented...We take coffee on the roof, in a dreamy atmosphere...The whole meal is accompanied by champagne." While the film is intended as a synthesis of Hitchcock's earlier opuses, it is also a field of experimentation for later works: The

chase on the roof and the fireworks scene bathed in green light foreshadow *Vertigo* (1957). A comedy version of *The Wrong Man* and the plane chasing Robie over the Mediterranean returned in *North by Northwest* (1958), again with Cary Grant. After *Suspicion* (1941), *To Catch a Thief* was a new episode in the adventures of the actor, the eternal false culprit who is abused by women.

In Praise of the Hitchcock Blonde

Hitchcock would admit that *To Catch a Thief* is not a serious story. The filmmaker was certainly more interested in sexual suspense, which Grace Kelly, whose performance strikes a perfect balance between fire and ice, reserve and audacity, ideally embodies. *To Catch a Thief* is a monument

to the Hitchcock blonde, a theoretical film on cinematic eroticism. For Hitchcock, sex in the cinema is only interesting if it holds a surprise: "I photographed Grace Kelly impassive, cold, and I show her most often in profile with a classic air, very beautiful and very icy."[2] But when Cary Grant takes her back to her room, she suddenly has an unpredictable impulse: She kisses her partner passionately. And if the censors are surprisingly complacent with such a film, it is because in the meantime the PCA had a new director: Geoffrey Shurlock, known for being more permissive, had replaced the very rigorous Joseph I. Breen. After viewing the film, Shurlock ignored his predecessor's warnings and endorsed *To Catch a Thief.*

Freeze Frame

Invited by Frances (Grace Kelly) to her room to watch a fireworks display, jewel thief Robie, alias "The Cat" (Cary Grant), enters a darkened room. The young woman pesters him to find out how he broke in; meanwhile, the fireworks are in full swing through the wide-open window. The montage alternates between shots of Robie and Frances, closer and closer together on the sofa, and increasingly spectacular colorful explosions, a rapprochement that openly depicts the buildup of excitement. The exchange between Frances and Robie never ceases to be a double entendre. To avoid censorship, Hitchcock asked Lyn Murray to abandon the overly explicit saxophone accompaniment in favor of more classical music.

Cary Grant,
Haute Couture

In a cinematic career spanning more than thirty years and almost eighty feature films, Cary Grant (1904–1986) never ceased to represent and play upon a masculine ideal. Seductive and ironic, elegant and eloquent, graceful in all circumstances, he exuded an irresistible class, an enviable power of seduction: "Everybody wants to be Cary Grant. Even I want to be Cary Grant,"[1] said Cary Grant. Hitchcock too would certainly have wanted to be Grant, to the point of systematically envisioning him, before anyone else, in his American films. Together, they made four major films: *Suspicion* (1941), *Notorious* (1946), *To Catch a Thief* (1954), and *North by Northwest* (1958).

On Tour

Archibald Alec (Alexander) Leach was born on the outskirts of Bristol, in southwest England, to a father who was an ironer and a mother who was a seamstress. The child suffered from a difficult and unstable family environment. An unruly teenager who ran away from home, he was attracted to the theater from an early age, and became a member of a troupe of actors and acrobats, touring the United States at the age of sixteen. He chose to settle in New York. During the 1920s, he crisscrossed the continent, eventually making a name for himself in vaudeville, so much so that one day he decided to try his luck on the West Coast and did a screen test in Hollywood.

Irresistible

In December 1931, twenty-seven-year-old Archibald Leach signed a five-year contract with Paramount, choosing to become Cary Grant to make his name

Portrait

more American and help him reinvent himself. His charm worked right from the start (*Blonde Venus*, 1932, with Marlene Dietrich), but it was with George Cukor's *Sylvia Scarlett* (1935), his first real film, in his own eyes, that his persona asserted itself. The 1930s established him as one of the princes of romantic and zany comedy, with masterpieces by Cukor, Leo McCarey, and Howard Hawks (*The Awful Truth*, *Bringing Up Baby*...) Grant, sparkling and mischievous, acts with his body and his dancer's tempo, the expressiveness of his face and eyes, his "transatlantic" accent, and his art of repartee.

The Science of the Self

Cary Grant was one of those hyper-disciplined, methodical actors who knew the workings of his aura like no one else. He offered a straight profile, knew how best to part his hair, always mastered his lines, and was never mistaken about the lighting or the outfit, which were undeniably to his advantage: his gray suit in *North by Northwest*, his bathing suit in *To Catch a Thief*...Hitchcock did with Grant what he did with other "sacred monsters," Charles Laughton (*Jamaica Inn*, 1938) and Dietrich (*Stage Fright*, 1949): He let them direct themselves. Who better to play Cary Grant?

Seduction and Its Flip Side

Hitchcock embraced Grant's already established image, that unique combination of distinction and casualness, even if it meant subtly undermining it for everyone's sake. Of their four films, the first was the most risky: in *Suspicion*, Cary Grant played an enigmatic character with a venomous charm that went against his audience's expectations. The filmmaker flirted with a limit without being able to go beyond it: It was impossible to turn the actor into a real murderer, the equivalent of Joseph Cotten in *Shadow of a Doubt* (1942). But each time, he managed to counter Grant's image and thereby enrich it. In *Notorious*, he entrusted him with nothing less than a masochistic role, that of an FBI agent witnessing, as a long-powerless spectator, the sexual enslavement of the woman he loves, forced to give in to their common enemy.

Some Abuses

In *To Catch a Thief*, Hitchcock explicitly turned his actor into a sexual object. It is the woman (Grace Kelly) at the wheel and her passenger who suffers the effects of her sporty driving, and it is she who imposes her desire: She kisses the man, smiles at him, and closes her door...leaving the seducer,

somewhat charmed and rather embarrassed, alone in the corridor. "It's as though she'd unzipped Cary's fly," said the director of this scene. And in *North by Northwest*, he is the subject of persecution. Relentlessly pursued, kidnapped, and forced to drink, machine-gunned and thrown into the dust, disguised as a porter, forced to shave with a miniature razor, seduced and deceived, his hand crushed and his body torn apart at the summit of Mount Rushmore, he is denied his very identity: Does he really exist, or is he just an alias, a decoy? Never has Grant's glamour been so abused, only to shine through all the more.

"We Were Very Compatible"

Hitchcock inflicted this "mistreatment" on Cary Grant with the actor's unreserved agreement. Grant would go on to say how much he enjoyed shooting with his fellow Englishman, whose impeccable film preparation he appreciated, among other things. And while Hitchcock confided that Grant was the only actor he had ever loved in his entire life, Cary Grant would describe his artistic collaboration with the filmmaker more laconically, but definitively: "We were very compatible."

THE
UNEXPECTED
FROM
HITCHCOCK!

PARAMOUNT
PRESENTS

ALFRED HITCHCOCK'S
THE
TROUBLE
WITH
HARRY

Color by
TECHNICOLOR

VISTAVISION
MOTION PICTURE HIGH-FIDELITY

starring   and introducing
EDMUND GWENN · JOHN FORSYTHE · SHIRLEY MacLAINE
Directed by ALFRED HITCHCOCK · Screenplay by JOHN MICHAEL HAYES
Based on the Novel by JACK TREVOR STORY · A PARAMOUNT PICTURE

The Trouble with Harry

United States • **1 hr 39** • **Color** • **Mono** (Western Electric Recording) • **1.85:1** (VistaVision)

SYNOPSIS

Production Dates: September 20–October 27, 1954
Release Date in the United States: October 3, 1955

Production: Paramount
Producer: Alfred Hitchcock
Associate Producer: Herbert Coleman

Based on the novel of the same name by
Jack Trevor Story (1949)
Screenplay: John Michael Hayes
Director of Photography: Robert Burks
Camera Operator: Leonard J. South
Visual Effects: John P. Fulton
Paintings: John Ferren
Technicolor Adviser: Richard Mueller
Sound: Harold Lewis, Winston Leverett
Assistant Director: Howard Joslin
Artistic Directors: Hal Pereira, John B. Goodman
Set Decoration: Sam Comer, Emile Kuri
Costumes: Edith Head
Music: Bernard Herrmann
Film Editing: Alma Macrorie

Starring: Edmund Gwenn (Captain Albert Wiles), John Forsythe (Sam Marlowe), Shirley MacLaine (Jennifer Rogers), Mildred Natwick (Miss Ivy Gravely), Mildred Dunnock (Mrs. Wiggs), Jerry Mathers (Arnie Rogers), Royal Dano (Deputy Sheriff Calvin Wiggs), Parker Fennelly (millionaire), Barry Macollum (tramp), Philip Truex (Harry Worp), Leslie Woolf (art critic), Alfred Hitchcock (passerby in a mackintosh)...

It is autumn in a small village in Vermont. A young boy discovers the lifeless body of a man, Harry Worp, in the middle of a clearing. Three villagers stumble upon the dead man in succession, and all imagine themselves responsible for Harry's death. Captain Wiles, a retired sailor, believes he killed Harry accidentally while out hunting. Jennifer Rogers, the boy's mother, remembers hitting him with a milk bottle because he was courting her too insistently. Miss Gravely, a shy spinster, thinks she finished him off with a kick from her heel. As for the misunderstood painter Sam Marlowe, witness to all these versions, he helps Captain Wiles bury the body. Calvin Wiggs, the deputy sheriff, investigates the possible existence of a body. From then on, the four accomplices continue to dig up, move, and rebury the body as the investigation progresses and as their feelings of guilt or innocence change. Finally, a doctor examines the dead man and concludes that Harry Worp died of a heart attack. Relieved, the four "false culprits" place the body back in the middle of the clearing. Sam and Jennifer, who have fallen in love with each other in the course of this imbroglio, are about to marry.

> "With *Harry* I took melodrama out of the pitch-black night and brought it out in the sunshine."
>
> — Alfred Hitchcock

GENESIS AND CASTING

At the beginning of 1954, anticipating the success of *Rear Window* (released in September) and *To Catch a Thief* (shot in the summer), Paramount Studios gave Hitchcock complete freedom for his next film. The filmmaker was struck by the humor of *The Trouble with Harry*, Jack Trevor Story's short first novel, published in 1949. Hitchcock obtained the rights to the book for $11,000; the film's relatively modest budget was set at $1 million, especially since *The Trouble with Harry* was made without using film stars.

A Film in Relaxed Mode

According to screenwriter John Michael Hayes (*Rear Window*, *To Catch a Thief*), Hitchcock wanted to adapt this eccentric pastoral tale "for fun," as a way of relaxing and changing registers.[1] Hayes advised the filmmaker to add suspense and action to the plot, but Hitchcock refused, wishing for once to remain faithful to the novel and the dialogue, which he loved. The two men invented only one character, the deputy sheriff, and replaced the English countryside with New England.

Newcomers and an Old Hand

Hitchcock found most of his cast among stage actors: Mildred Natwick (Miss Gravely), Mildred Dunnock ("Wiggie," the grocer), John Forsythe (Sam, the painter). Spotted in a Broadway musical, the sparkling redhead Shirley MacLaine plays her first film role, the start of a prestigious career. The character of the captain was played by Edmund Gwenn, the last of his four roles for a director he had known twenty-five years earlier (*The Skin Game*). Harry was "played" by Philip Truex, an actor who was somewhat surprised to be given the role of the corpse.

A New Accomplice

The Trouble with Harry inaugurated a brilliant ten-year collaboration between Hitchcock and musician Bernard Herrmann. A renowned composer, Herrmann began working for the cinema in the early 1940s (*Citizen Kane*). Known for his difficult personality, he nevertheless got on perfectly with the filmmaker, who called on him as soon as the script was written.

For Hitchcock Addicts

The year 1955, when the film was released, was also the year of the first season of *Alfred Hitchcock Presents*. *The Trouble with Harry* is a hybrid of film and television. The filmmaker and his composer chose Charles Gounod's "Marche funèbre d'une marionnette" ("Funeral March of a Marionette") (1872) as the film's temporary soundtrack, a little piece of music that was to become the celebrated theme tune for *Alfred Hitchcock Presents*.

John Forsythe, Shirley MacLaine, Mildred Natwick, Edmund Gwenn.

The child (Jerry Mathers) and the dead man (Philip Truex).

FILMING AND PRODUCTION

After filming the summer light of the Riviera (*To Catch a Thief*), Hitchcock turned his attention to the autumnal flamboyance of the northeastern United States, sublimated by the extra-wide format of VistaVision. Twenty-three of the thirty days of shooting were on location.

Autumn Depicted on a Set

Filming began in September near Saint Johnsbury, a village in Vermont. After a storm ravaged the landscape, the crew moved to a nearby town, where the bad weather persisted. By mid-October, the crew was back in Hollywood. John B. Goodman, the set designer, re-created Vermont in the studio using imitation leaves attached to plaster trees.

The Man-Child

The film's famous opening shot features a little boy armed with a plastic pistol, strolling through splendid natural surroundings. The music, initially childlike, turns serious when the boy discovers an inanimate adult body on the ground. One shot, filmed from the corpse's feet, shows the child's torso in line with the dead man's legs: a centaur, half-child, half-adult; half-living, half-dead. The tone is set for this macabre comedy.

RECEPTION

The Trouble with Harry did not have the benefit of a major promotional campaign. On its release, a year after shooting, the film did poorly in the US but was well received in England and France, where "the politics of the author" were in full swing.

The Ease of the Hitchcock Style

In April 1956, *Cahiers du cinéma* devoted no fewer than four articles to the film in a single issue. While the work lacked the usual Hitchcockian sophistication, they all emphasized the filmmaker's rediscovered style. For Éric Rohmer, this freedom of tone is "proof of the supreme ease of a director for whom style is no longer, and indeed never has been, a matter of formulae and processes."[2]

Hitchcock Through the Absurd

Here, Hitchcock attempts an exercise in levity and self-mockery. Death becomes a familiar presence that barely disturbs the course of the love story. The whodunit and the transference of guilt are treated with absurdity: All the characters accuse one another of having killed Harry, as if they had had "their consciences removed."[3] In contrast to this irresponsible behavior, only Bernard Herrmann's music seems to dramatize the events.

Psycho (1960).

Bernard Herrmann,
the Musical Subconscious

Bernard Herrmann (1911–1975) elevated film music to an art form at a time when it was considered merely a musical subgenre. From *Citizen Kane* (1941) to *Taxi Driver* (1976), his work refuted the idea of music paraphrasing action: With him, it dialogued on an equal footing with another art form, namely, film. Herrmann summed up the concept of his art: "Cinema music is the cinema."[1] His scores for Hitchcock are indisputable proof of this. From *The Trouble with Harry* (1954) to *Marnie* (1964) via the synthetic sounds of *The Birds* (1962), eight films mark their ten-year collaboration.

From Radio to the Cinema

A graduate of the prestigious Juilliard School, Bernard Herrmann was destined for a career as a composer and conductor. At the age of twenty-three, he took up both professions at the

innovative CBS radio station, which he left in 1940. The soundtrack to Orson Welles's *Citizen Kane* launched his film career. Memorable scores followed, notably for Joseph L. Mankiewicz's *The Ghost and Mrs. Muir* (1947). In 1944, Hitchcock first approached Herrmann for *Spellbound*, but the composer was busy with another film. Ten years later, Herrmann agreed to work on the comedy *The Trouble with Harry*, composing a score that makes ironic use of music that deliberately underlines each action.

A Moment of Eternity

From the 1950s onward, Hitchcock developed a taste for long, dialogue-free sequences in which Herrmann's genius came to the fore. Referring to the great kissing scene in the hotel room of *Vertigo* (1957), the filmmaker noted mischievously:

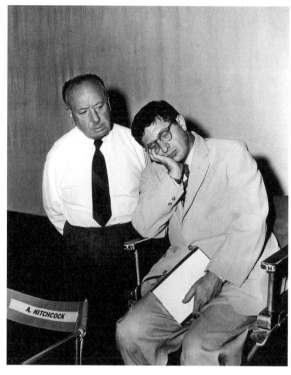
Alfred Hitchcock, Bernard Herrmann, mid-1950s.

"We should let all traffic noises fade, because Mr. Herrmann may have something to say here."[2] The composer conjured up Richard Wagner's opera *Tristan et Isolde* (1865), an evocation of impossible love that can only end in death. He plays the ominous "Tristan chord" and, as Kim Novak emerges transfigured from the bathroom, a passage from Isolde's *Liebestod* ("love death"). The composer slows down this motif as if to stretch it to the dimensions of this fragile moment of eternity. The music follows an upward movement, which, according to Hollywood codes, usually evokes a triumphant happy ending… and which is in this case illusory. For *Vertigo*, which is an immense visual symphony, the merging of the two artists is total.

An Electrifying Fandango

The opening of *North by Northwest* (1958) leaves the audience with no choice: They are immediately hypnotized by Saul Bass's dynamic credits and drawn in by Herrmann's galvanizing score. The composer interweaves two motifs that play cat and mouse with each other. In the second half of the credits, the music contrasts with shots of an ordinary New York office exit: The fandango prepares the viewer for the adventure to come, becoming the theme of an all-powerful, playful filmmaker searching through the crowd for the ideal "wrong man"…who soon emerges from an elevator.

The Violins of Horror

Hitchcock imagined the shower scene in *Psycho* (1960) without music, but Herrmann's strident score, which conveys a sense of great danger to the viewer right from the opening credits, changed his mind. The composer abandoned the symphony orchestra, ill-suited for a low-budget film, and stuck to the ranks of violins to find a sonic equivalent to the stark black-and-white image. In the shower scene, brief bow strokes double the stabbings and blend with the soundtrack, which Hitchcock maintained to further anchor the horror: the victim's screams, the impassive flow of water. The theme recurs with each crime, from the lacerations on the victims to the schizophrenia of Norman Bates (Anthony Perkins).

A Man from Another Time

After supervising the soundtrack and electroacoustic effects for *The Birds*, Herrmann composed a hauntingly romantic score for *Marnie*. Following the film's failure, Herrmann was hired for *Torn Curtain* (1966) only on condition that he wrote a "hit" in tune with the times. Accustomed to total freedom, Herrmann instead created a classic fifty-minute score, even "pumping up" the orchestra. Hitchcock rejected his work and put an end to their collaboration.

Musical Analysis

According to several accounts, after Herrmann, Hitchcock lost interest in the music of his films. Their artistic love affair left a great void. Hitchcock created spaces for Herrmann to express his fiery anger and melancholy. His music took charge of Hitchcock's tragic vision of existence, managing to articulate the filmmaker's unconscious. And, as if by design, the final scene of what would prove to be their last film (Marnie freeing herself from her childhood trauma) culminates in a great cathartic moment.

PARAMOUNT PRESENTS

JAMES STEWART · DORIS DAY

ALFRED HITCHCOCK'S

THE MAN WHO KNEW TOO MUCH

DIRECTED BY
ALFRED HITCHCOCK
SCREENPLAY BY
JOHN MICHAEL HAYES
BASED ON A STORY BY
CHARLES BENNETT AND
D. B. WYNDHAM-LEWIS

COLOR BY TECHNICOLOR

The Man Who Knew Too Much

United States · **2 hrs** · **Color** · **Mono**
(Western Electric Recording) · **1.85:1** (VistaVision)

Production Dates: May 12–August 24, 1955
Release Date in the United States: May 16, 1956 (New York),
June 1, 1956 (United States)

Production: Paramount
Producer: Alfred Hitchcock
Associate Producer: Herbert Coleman

**Based on an original story by Charles Bennett and
D. B. Wyndham Lewis (1934)**
Screenplay: John Michael Hayes, Angus MacPhail
Technical Advisers: Constance Willis, Abdelhaq Chraibi
Director of Photography: Robert Burks
Camera Operator: Leonard J. South
Visual Effects: John P. Fulton, Farciot Edouart
Technicolor Adviser: Richard Mueller
Sound: Paul Franz, Gene Garvin
Assistant Director: Howard Joslin
Art Direction: Hal Pereira, Henry Bumstead
Set Decoration: Sam Comer, Arthur Krams
Makeup: Wally Westmore
Costumes: Edith Head
Music: Bernard Herrmann
Songs: Jay Livingston, Ray Evans ("Whatever Will Be, Will Be";
"We'll Love Again")
Film Editing: George Tomasini

Starring: James Stewart (Dr. Benjamin McKenna, "Ben"), Doris Day (Josephine
Conway McKenna, "Jo"), Brenda de Banzie (Lucy Drayton), Bernard Miles (Edward
Drayton), Ralph Truman (Inspector Buchanan), Daniel Gélin (Louis Bernard),
Mogens Wieth (ambassador), Alan Mowbray (Val Parnell), Hillary Brooke (Jan
Peterson), Christopher Olsen (Hank McKenna), Reggie Nalder (French marksman),
Noel Willman (Woburn), Yves Brainville (French police inspector), Carolyn Jones
(Cindy Fontaine), Bernard Herrmann (conductor), Richard Wordsworth
(Ambrose Jr.), George Howe (Ambrose Sr.), Alfred Hitchcock (man in
Marrakech marketplace)...

SYNOPSIS

———

The McKennas (Jo, Ben, and their son, Hank), an American family, are on vacation in Marrakech. They meet Louis Bernard, a mysterious Frenchman. The next day, at the market, the Frenchman, disguised as an Arab, is stabbed and, in a whisper, warns Ben that a foreign statesman is about to be assassinated in London. He whispers a few last words: "Ambrose Chapel." Ben then receives an anonymous phone call: His son has been kidnapped. He discovers that Hank is being held by the Draytons, an English couple whom the McKennas had befriended at the hotel. Scotland Yard tells Jo and Ben that Bernard was a Deuxième Bureau agent. They travel to London and locate, with some difficulty, the Ambrose Chapel, a church that serves as a hideout for the Draytons. The Draytons knock Ben unconscious and leave with the child, taking refuge in an embassy. Jo joins Inspector Buchanan, in charge of the investigation, at the Royal Albert Hall, where a concert is taking place, attended by a foreign prime minister. As the concert begins, Jo spots the marksman in a dressing room and lets out a scream just before the cymbals are about to sound. The assassin misses and falls to his death. An ambassador, the secret backer of the Draytons and the killer, invites the McKennas to his reception in honor of the statesman. Jo, a retired singer, takes up the piano. She chooses an aria that her son, held upstairs, will recognize. Ben takes advantage of this diversion to explore the premises. He fights Mr. Drayton to the death and saves his son.

At the taxidermist's: James Stewart, George Howe.

GENESIS

As early as 1937, during his first trip to the United States, Alfred Hitchcock spoke of his desire to make a new version of *The Man Who Knew Too Much* (1934). In a portrait of him in the *New Yorker* (September 1938), Hitchcock described an assassination scene in the Moroccan souk that he imagined would feature in the film. In 1940, interested producer David O. Selznick bought the rights to adapt the screenplay from Gaumont British, while Hitchcock set about transposing the plot to American settings. But this remake, judged to be too close to the film he was preparing at the time (*Saboteur*, 1942), was postponed. The filmmaker tried to turn it into a project for Transatlantic Pictures, his production company, but the company went out of business following the commercial failure of *Rope* and *Under Capricorn* (1948).

SOS

In 1953, with a string of successes under his belt and a great deal of freedom at Paramount, Hitchcock was finally able to fulfill a twenty-year-old desire. A letter sent to him in February 1953 seems to have accelerated the process: Angus MacPhail, one of the screenwriters of the first version of *The Man Who Knew Too Much* and a longtime friend, confided that he was suffering from depression and financial difficulties. Hitchcock wanted to help the former head of Gaumont's script department by entrusting him with writing the remake. His name in the credits would make him a member of the Screen Writers Guild, a status that would entitle him to fringe benefits.

From One Script to Another

MacPhail arrived in Hollywood just after Christmas 1954 and took up residence not far from the Hitchcocks' house. The two men reworked a script that had to be modernized and Americanized: the Lawrences, the English couple of the first version, became the McKennas, from the Midwest. The opening on the snowy slopes of Saint Moritz is replaced by a bus scene in Marrakech, where Ben McKenna, who fought in the region during World War II, is on vacation with his family.

The spectacular final shootout disappears in favor of a sequence in an embassy that is far more psychologically violent. The disturbing comic scene at the dentist's is replaced by a zany interlude at the home of a shady-looking taxidermist. By mid-January, the two men had written a seventy-page treatment.

Loyal to His Post

Busy with another project, John Michael Hayes, screenwriter on all three of Hitchcock's Paramount

The grand stage of the Royal Albert Hall. From behind, at the baton: Bernard Herrmann. In a blue dress, soloist Barbara Howitt.

films since *Rear Window* (1954), began work on *The Man Who Knew Too Much* at the end of February 1955. Although he claimed not to have seen the 1934 version, Hitchcock arranged a screening for him before he set to work. In less than a month, Hayes turned in an incomplete first script that stopped at the Ambrose Chapel sequence, but his contribution was decisive in many respects. He brought the McKenna couple and their son Hank to life and toned down direct references to the political context of the Cold War—Paramount demanded that all specific allusions to foreign countries be removed. Under his pen, *The Man Who Knew Too Much* became a more focused spy thriller about the McKennas' family and married life. Hayes also added the scene where Ben, as a wise doctor, forces his wife to take a sedative before telling her that their son has been kidnapped. Suddenly, the dread of an irretrievable loss gives the whole film a different tone.

CASTING

From the very beginning of the project, the role of Benjamin McKenna was planned for James Stewart: The actor had booked his summer of 1955 to shoot the film. Although Hitchcock dreamed of reuniting James Stewart and Grace Kelly onscreen once again, he had to do without his favorite, who became princess of Monaco and retired from acting.

A Blonde Like No Other

In February 1955, Hitchcock considered casting Doris Day in the role of Jo. An extremely popular singer and actress (*Calamity Jane*, *Love Me or Leave Me*), more ordinary or less unattainable in appearance, Doris Day was in stark contrast to the usual hyper-sophisticated Hitchcock blondes. Her contract stipulated that the plot should make no allusion to her character's sex life, so as not to upset her audience. Only a mention of her desire for a second

Longer than the 1934 version (twelve minutes, 124 still shots), the 1955 sequence at the Royal Albert Hall, through the power of editing, interweaves three stories: those of Jo, Ben, and the cymbal player, who becomes a character in his own right and is even mentioned in the film's opening lines. All the emotional power of the sequence converges on Jo, who finds herself, as one version of the script puts it, "on the verge of tears under the combined effect of the singing and the tension to which she is subjected"[1]—even though, contrary to the original version, she is unaware that the gunshot is set to go off at the same time as the cymbal blast (a detonation hidden in a note). Condemned from the start of the film to the status of an observer tossed about by events, Jo emancipates herself from her powerlessness with a cry (which she seems to prepare at the beginning of the sequence, as if she were preparing to sing). This cry throws her into the action, ending twelve dialogue-free minutes.

child was retained in the final version, and the flirtation with Louis Bernard, a role given to French actor Daniel Gélin, disappeared from the script. Hitchcock is said to have appreciated the actress in Stuart Heisler's *Storm Warning* (1951), in which she plays a waitress married to a Ku Klux Klan truck driver. According to composer Jay Livingston, MCA (Music Corporation of America), the artistic agency representing Hitchcock and Day, would have left the filmmaker no choice but to hire the actress in order to get Stewart. With such a star-studded duo, he had two of the most beloved stars of the day, and *The Man Who Knew Too Much* was already destined for a wide family audience.

The Fine Team

Hitchcock's films at Paramount became inconceivable without his loyal team, which also included newcomers who were destined to stay: Robert Burks for pictures, Edith Head for costumes, George Tomasini for editing, and, for music, Bernard Herrmann, who celebrated his second collaboration with the director. The composer even had a cameo appearance as conductor at the Royal Albert Hall, while giant posters bearing his name announced his concert at the entrance. Faced with the scale of the project, Hitchcock wanted to hire Paramount's top designer: for the art direction role, the studio recommended Henry Bumstead, who built the Arab café, the Marrakech hotel, and the interior of the Ambrose Chapel using photos taken in Morocco and London.

Kidnappers and an Assassin

English actors Brenda de Banzie and Bernard Miles played the Draytons, the deceptively sympathetic British couple who kidnap children. Accustomed to villainous roles due to his unsettlingly emaciated and scarred face, Viennese-born actor and dancer Reggie Nalder was given the role of the assassin. Hitchcock, who normally did not direct his actors, advised him to look at his victim "lovingly…, as if you're glancing at a beautiful woman."[2]

FILMING AND PRODUCTION

In mid-May 1955, MacPhail and Hitchcock flew to Marrakech with an unfinished script, on which Hayes had been working day after day from Hollywood. The budget for *The Man Who Knew Too Much* was set at $1.342 million, a sum that did not include the salaries of the filmmaker and his two stars. The shooting schedule spanned forty-eight days (and was thirty-four days late), including seven in Marrakech and twelve in London for exteriors. The rest, close-ups and interiors (with the exception of the Royal Albert Hall), was shot in the studio at Paramount.

An American Woman in Morocco

Right from the opening in the coach, Hitchcock films Morocco as a country with customs that are disconcerting to the American couple: The discovery of local customs seems to be directly inspired by Doris Day's own disorientation. In 1955, the actress had never ventured outside the US, and in her memoirs

she confessed to having been shocked by "the poverty and malnutrition of the inhabitants." The tagine scene, in which the McKennas comically struggle to eat with their hands, was no doubt also inspired by her behavior. She confided, not without naïveté: "Doris Day's habits are quite simple and hygienic, and I certainly wasn't going to dip my hand into the couscous or anything else."[3] Throughout the film, Hitchcock's camera catches the actress's every reaction, and her status as a helpless observer takes on tragic proportions during the assassination attempt at the Royal Albert Hall—a sort of female counterpart to James Stewart in *Rear Window* (1954).

An Opportunity to Make Up for the Economic Conditions

One of the reasons why Hitchcock decided to remake *The Man Who Knew Too Much* was to rework the concert sequence at the Royal Albert Hall, the highlight of the show. The remake represented an opportunity to make up for the economic conditions of the time: This time, the filmmaker

filmed most of the shots on location and benefited from Technicolor and VistaVision, which made this second version more powerful and monumental than the original sequence. Hitchcock acquired the rights to the "Storm Cloud Cantata" by Australian composer Arthur Benjamin, who agreed to extend it by five minutes. Bernard Herrmann took on the task of reorchestrating it, accompanied by the London Symphony Orchestra, the Covent Garden Choir, and mezzo-soprano Barbara Howitt.

An Anthem

Paramount obliged Hitchcock to include a sequence sung by Doris Day in *The Man Who Knew Too Much*. The filmmaker hired composer Ray Evans and lyricist Jay Livingston, both under contract to the studio, to compose a song "simple enough for a child to sing."[4] Livingston was inspired by a scene from Joseph L. Mankiewicz's *The Barefoot Contessa* (1954), where "Che sarà sarà," the motto of the wealthy Italian Torlato-Favrini family, appears engraved in stone. The Spanish translation, easier to pronounce,

Hollywood Tourism

The mid-1950s saw what English critic Raymond Durgnat called "vicarious tourism":[5] Hollywood blockbusters relocated to exotic locations, enabling audiences to travel for the duration of a film without leaving their seats. This was one of the many strategies used by studios to attract audiences and to offset the fierce competition from television. Along with *The Bridge on the River Kwai* (David Lean, 1957), *The Man Who Knew Too Much* is one of the most dazzling examples of this exotic, grand spectacle.

was preferred, and the song was entitled "Que Sera, Sera (Whatever Will Be, Will Be)." Hitchcock was delighted to hear it, but Doris Day hated it and refused to do more than one take of the scene at the embassy. Initially imposed on the filmmaker, this tune nevertheless managed to find its raison d'être within the plot and, by linking a mother to her child like a sonic umbilical cord, constitutes an emotional high point. "Whatever Will Be, Will Be" went on to win the Oscar for Best Original Song and become Doris Day's biggest hit.

The End

At the height of his fame and nominated for an Oscar for Best Screenplay with *Rear Window*, John Michael Hayes refused to share the credits with Angus MacPhail, who, he claimed, had done no work at all and had only benefited from Hitchcock's charity. Hayes turned to the Screen Writers Guild to settle the matter. Its members consulted notes, memos, and drafts and proved him right: MacPhail's name was removed from the credits. Hayes knew that his days with Hitchcock were numbered. The filmmaker tried to lure him into a film project for Warner Bros. (*The Wrong Man*), on condition that he took no salary, a proposal that seemed like a roundabout way of provoking their breakup. The two men, who had penned four films together, would never collaborate again, much to the screenwriter's regret.

RECEPTION

The film was released on June 1, 1956, in the United States, followed by England and many other countries. In less than a week, *The Man Who Knew Too Much* became the biggest financial success of the year, of all Hollywood films.

In the Shadow of the Original

Critics noted Hitchcock's return to the spy thrillers of his English period. But in the eyes of the British press, the film failed to bear comparison with the 1934 version. The *Monthly Film Bulletin* wrote of an entertainment that "is likely to disappoint devotees of the first film. It lacks the earlier pace and excitement; the peculiarly English charm of the original has been exchanged for a vague VistaVision and Technicolor cosmopolitanism" (June 1956). The British press noted that Hitchcock works "in terms of the new gloss and grandeur and slow tempo of the wide screen. But the slower the tempo, the longer the audience's opportunity to see the flaws in the film" (June 23, 1956).

A Contemplative Remake…

In *The Man Who Knew Too Much*, Hitchcock did not choose between action and contemplation, studio film and location shooting, grand spectacle and domestic melodrama, comedy and suspense, artifice and document: Everything blends together. The filmmaker's hybrid, labyrinthine film seems at times to strive for the viewer's undivided attention, at others to leave him pleasantly on his own. While critics identified the "old-style" Hitchcock, the "new-style" Hitchcock still conversed with the former. *The Man Who Knew Too Much* thus combines the effectiveness of the entertainer with the reveries of an auteur who increasingly permitted psychology to haunt the action: *Vertigo* (1957) was not far off.

…and a Metaphysical One

Hitchcock adopted a filming style that leaves much more room for quiet time and observation. At the time of the film's French release, critic Jean-Luc Godard remarked in *Cahiers du cinéma* that the

filmmaker "now looks all around his characters, just as he forces them to look at their surroundings."[6] Capable of fits of heroism, the McKennas are mostly filmed as distant observers, on the margins of the action. Plunging shots of the couple and the grandiose Royal Albert Hall rendered in VistaVision visually testify to Jo and Ben's powerlessness in the face of a dimension beyond them. It is as if the force of destiny suddenly interferes with or enhances ordinary lives. Much more than a remake, *The Man Who Knew Too Much* is, for Éric Rohmer and Claude Chabrol, "a veritable transfiguration"[7] of the original version, with the spy film serving only as a pretext for filming a metaphysical terror.

Where Is Hitchcock?

The filmmaker appears in the sequence in the Marrakech market: From behind, on the left of the picture, he watches the acrobats perform, as do James Stewart and Doris Day.

James Stewart,
or the Shadow of War

He was one of the men Americans identified with most over four decades. An actor in a hundred films, James Stewart (1908–1997) was loyal to some of the great directors: Frank Capra, Anthony Mann, John Ford. He made four films with Hitchcock—four postwar films. And in Stewart's case, there is a before and an after; from one period to the next, he is not the same man, nor the same actor.

Before

Born into a modest and strict family, the young Stewart developed a passion for acting, which he pursued as an amateur. In the early 1930s, he took on small roles on Broadway and, in 1935, landed a contract at MGM Studios. He rose steadily to his first breakthrough: the title role in *Mr. Smith Goes to*

Washington (1939). The actor projected his pleasant face, his clear eyes, and his own values in his character as a man of the people. Both, indiscriminately to the public, represented the sincere, ingenuous, humble yet determined idealist, an unshakable honesty, the common sense of rural America. With *Mr. Smith*, Stewart became the symbol of an "authentic" nation.

During

In March 1941, seven months before the United States entered the war, James Stewart enlisted in the US Army Air Corps. He served his country until his demobilization in September 1945. Meanwhile, aboard B-24 Liberators ("flying fortresses"), he led, then organized and supervised, numerous perilous bombing missions over Germany.[1]

Portrait

After

War changes a man forever: "something I think about almost every day: one of the greatest experiences of my life."[2] It also changed the actor, who was now willing and able to play torment and apprehension. Years after *Vertigo* (1957), Stewart would recall his character's phobia of emptiness: "I'd known people paralyzed by fear."[3] In his most memorable postwar roles, from Anthony Mann's five Westerns to Hitchcock fantasies, he instinctively knew how to impart the necessary emotional experience to his characters. Martin Scorsese summed up this irreversible evolution and broadening of the actor's game: "After the Second World War, a kind of obsession seeped into Stewart's work: a loneliness, a deep anger against the whole universe. If the pre-war Stewart testified to something essentially American, the post-war Stewart touched on a universal dimension."[4]

Rope (1948)

Stewart and Hitchcock, who from 1945 had the same agent, Lew Wasserman, inaugurated their collaboration with a color film, the first for both of them. The shoot was so technically complicated, with very long takes, that Stewart, who came through it thanks to his training as a stage actor, would not remember it fondly. He is reported to have told Hitchcock that viewers would be better off paying for their seats to watch the film being shot…As for his character, Rupert Cadell, he considers himself a superior being. But when he discovers that two of his students have put his extreme theories into practice, the man who thought himself all-powerful suddenly experiences his own powerlessness. *Rope* tells a horrific story that only the post–World War II era could produce.

Rear Window (1954)

Stewart (who helped produce the film) played "Jeff," a character confined to his home, confined to a wheelchair, his leg in a cast. Impotence is evident this time, as is its corollary: compulsive voyeurism. With much of the film focused on his face (his reactions to what he sees through the window), the actor becomes a surface on which sensations are expressed, including distress and emotion when, trapped, he witnesses the attack on his fiancée in the apartment across the street. Trapped in his armchair too, the viewer is literally forced to recognize himself in Stewart.

The Man Who Knew Too Much (1955)

Stewart played Dr. McKenna, on vacation in Morocco with his wife and child. When the child is abducted,

the lost father suddenly looks like a speck in the universe. His world of certainties crumbles before his eyes (and ours). The actor conveys the pain of loss and the dread of insurmountable grief. Stewart, accustomed on this set to Hitchcock's lack of direction, said, "He believed that if you sat down with an actor to analyze a scene, you'd run the danger that the actor would act the scene with his head rather than his heart."[3]

Vertigo (1957)

A masterpiece by Hitchcock and Stewart combined, *Vertigo* elevates impotence and the scopic drive to the level of fine art. The character of Scottie, who closely follows the object of his desire, will never reach it, except to better lose it and enjoy the dream of its return from the dead. *Vertigo* is a film of affliction, and all the time its hero lives in a daze. From prewar to postwar, Stewart moved from the countryside to the city, from near-feminine grace to vacillating masculinity, from euphoria to vertigo.

The Ordinary Man

James Stewart hoped to star in *North by Northwest* (1958), but it was to star Cary Grant and, for good measure, it was a spy comedy. Because the filmmaker described Stewart as "an ordinary man in extraordinary situations," in other words, Stewart was meant to portray the tragic side of the Hitchcock hero.

Alfred Hitchcock
and Television (1955–1965)

By the time Hitchcock became a producer and direc-tor for American television, it had established itself as a truly mass medium. Its irresistible expansion since the late 1940s, due in particular to the expan-sion in the United States of residential suburbs with no cinemas, had overcome the reluctance of the major Hollywood studios. The studios were gradu-ally agreeing to sell their films as audiovisual pro-grams as well as producing directly for the small screen.

A Global Vision

It was Alfred Hitchcock's agent, Lew Wasserman, head of MCA (Music Corporation of America), one of Hollywood's biggest talent agencies, who came up with the idea of introducing the filmmaker to the world of television. This decision was part of a glob-al strategy, which consisted of MCA investing in the new medium in order to transform it into a Trojan horse that would later enable the agency to take over Universal Studios. MCA had already increased the power of actors and weakened the big companies by obliging producers to pay the actors a percentage of the profits from the films in which they appeared, thus emancipating actors from their salaried status.

In 1952, after obtaining authorization from the Screen Actors Guild, then headed by Ronald Reagan and supposedly alert to any risk of mixing genres and conflicts of interest, MCA began producing for television. Its subsidiary, Revue Studios, became one of the largest production companies for the small screen. Very quickly, MCA's turnover as a television

The filmmaker, appearing in publicity images for *Alfred Hitchcock Presents*.

Landmark

producer exceeded that generated by agency commissions alone.

Hitchcock's Brand Image

During a meeting at the end of 1954 or the beginning of 1955, Wasserman suggested "putting Hitchcock on the air." The filmmaker was initially reluctant. His film career was flourishing. He had just had two commercial successes, *Rear Window* and *To Catch a Thief* (1954), and was preparing his remake of *The Man Who Knew Too Much* (1955). Wasserman suggested that Hitchcock use his brand image for television rather than his talents as a filmmaker. Hitchcock was one of the few directors whose name was known to the general public and had even been identified since the early 1940s as the Master of Suspense. For Wasserman, it was a question of using this symbolic status in the service of a popular television series. As for Hitchcock, he had already been tempted, some ten years earlier, to produce radio programs.

Alfred Hitchcock Presents

Persuaded by his agent's arguments as much as by the financial advantages of the project, Hitchcock set up his own production company for the small screen, notably for tax reasons: Shamley Productions, named after the English village where the Hitchcocks, then newlyweds, had bought a country house in 1928.

The series, entitled *Alfred Hitchcock Presents*, was an "anthology," a series of unconnected episodes, short half-hour films shot in black and white and 35 mm, each a self-contained story presented by a master of ceremonies, like other popular series at the time such as *Kraft Television Theatre* (1947–1958). Each episode had to end with a burlesque or macabre twist. An advertiser-sponsor, first the Bristol-Myers pharmaceutical laboratories, then the Lincoln-Mercury car brand, financed the series in exchange for the possibility of broadcasting three advertisements per episode. The sponsor had a say in each script and had the option of refusing certain projects. Bristol-Myers laboratories took a dim view of episodes in which drugs played a harmful role, just as car accidents bothered Lincoln-Mercury.

The Return of an Old Friend

To look after the series, Wasserman and Hitchcock called on Joan Harrison, who became the real linchpin. Hired as a secretary in 1933, at the time of the director's English films, she had become a friend of the Hitchcock couple, to the extent that she followed them to the United States. She worked on the scripts for *Jamaica Inn* (1938), *Rebecca* (1939), *Foreign Correspondent* (1940), *Suspicion* (1941), and *Saboteur* (1942). From 1942, she became an independent producer: Robert Siodmak's *Phantom Lady* and *The Strange Affair of Uncle Harry*; Robert Montgomery's *Ride the Pink Horse*. Above all, in 1954 she produced the successful television series *Janet Dean, Registered Nurse*, which convinced Wasserman and Hitchcock to put her in charge of *Alfred Hitchcock Presents*. In 1957, Norman Lloyd was hired to assist Joan Harrison. An early member of the Mercury Theatre with Orson Welles, and also a close friend of the Hitchcock couple, he played the role of Fry, the Nazi spy, in *Saboteur* and appeared two years later in *Spellbound*.

The role of Joan Harrison and Norman Lloyd was primarily to read and select short stories, detective stories that had already been published rather than original scripts, to summarize them, and then to submit them to Hitchcock, who accepted them, rejected them, or asked, when in doubt, to keep them in reserve. The series thus adapted several writers: Cornell Woolrich (author of the novel that gave rise to *Rear Window*), Ray Bradbury, Stanley Ellin, John Collier, Fredric Brown, Evan Hunter (future screenwriter of *The Birds*), Robert Bloch (author of *Psycho*), Ira Levin, Victor Canning (one of whose novels Hitchcock adapted for his last film, *Family Plot*), A. E. W. Mason, and Ambrose Bierce. The British writer Roald Dahl was adapted six times. Hitchcock was contracted to film a few episodes himself. His involvement as director diminished as the seasons progressed.

Twenty Episodes by Alfred Hitchcock

"Revenge," the first episode of *Alfred Hitchcock Presents*, directed by Hitchcock himself, was broadcast on October 2, 1955. The series ran for seven seasons (1955–1962) and 268 episodes. In 1957, Shamley Productions also produced ten episodes (Hitchcock directed just one, "Four O'Clock") of an NBC series called *Suspicion*, which ran for one season. In 1962, *Alfred Hitchcock Presents* became *The Alfred Hitchcock Hour* (three seasons, 1962–1965, ninety-two episodes). The principle was the same, but each TV film lasted fifty minutes. The filmmaker directed seventeen episodes of *Alfred Hitchcock Presents* and just one of *The Alfred Hitchcock Hour* ("I Saw the Whole Thing," 1962). In 1960 he also directed a color episode of the series *Startime*: "Incident at a Corner."

Birth of a Character

The series gave the filmmaker the opportunity to create a true audiovisual character. He appeared at the beginning and end of each episode, whether he had directed it or not, and each of his appearances gave rise to a burlesque sketch that allowed him to deploy a humor that was sometimes misanthropic and macabre, sometimes in disguise, sometimes in absurd contexts. His introduction to the first episode to be broadcast set the principle and tone of the series: "Good evening. My name is Alfred Hitchcock and tonight I'm going to present the first in a series of suspense and mystery stories, strangely entitled *Alfred Hitchcock Presents*. I will not be acting in these stories but merely appearing. A bit like a witness before and after the fact. To give the title to those who cannot read and explanations to those who do not understand the ending."

Credits and Music

The credits for each film open with a sketch of Hitchcock's profile. This is a drawing he created himself, in eight pencil strokes, in 1927. His shadowy silhouette slips into the lines of this refined caricature and merges with it. The credits were changed when the series became *The Alfred Hitchcock Hour*. After a succession of cross-fades over drawings evoking an atmosphere of Gothic terror (the eyes of an owl, the shadow of a gloomy manor house), Hitchcock's shadow appears on the wooden door of what we guess to be a medieval castle. Such an opening, which reflects Hitchcock's image with the general public, may come as a surprise for a series that makes little use of Gothic horror.

The haunting theme music was chosen by the filmmaker himself: a few notes from the "Marche funèbre d'une marionnette" ("Funeral March of a Marionette"), written in London in 1872 by Charles Gounod. This tune was to become a leitmotif and a gag attached to the filmmaker; it was used in particular during his public appearances at the tribute ceremonies honoring him. Hitchcock said he heard it during a screening of F. W. Murnau's *Sunrise: A Song of Two Humans* (1927), where this piece in a piano version was used to illustrate a sequence in the film.

Written by James B. Allardice

James B. Allardice was responsible for writing the texts Hitchcock presented. Allardice was a playwright and screenwriter who became famous in 1949 for his play *At War with the Army*, which was adapted the following year by Paramount, starring Dean Martin and Jerry Lewis. Before being hired to write Hitchcock's comedy scripts, Allardice worked with the comic George Gobel, for whom he wrote punch lines. In the 1950s and 1960s he worked regularly for

television, on the comedy series *F Troop*, *My Favorite Martian*, *The Munsters*, and *My Three Sons*. To show him what was expected of him, Hitchcock organized a screening of *The Trouble with Harry* (1954), a model of the tone the director wanted to achieve for the small screen. Allardice, who liked to work under pressure, delivered the scripts by the dozen. He received the scripts for the episodes to be illustrated, but very quickly Hitchcock's deadpan presentations bore little relation to the story they were supposed to introduce. Hitchcock was very fond of Allardice, who worked on the entire series. He had him write some of his speeches for various ceremonies. Allardice was also the author of the text that Hitchcock used in the 1960 trailer for *Psycho*, in which he improvised as a tourist guide taking the viewer on a tour of the murder house. Allardice died prematurely in 1966.

Figures of Fun

During his presentations, Hitchcock frequently mocked the advertising cuts imposed by the sponsor. There were numerous jabs at the commercials that concluded the TV episode and that the master of ceremonies described in mocking terms. For example: "Tonight's episode will be preceded by an unselected short film." Or: "Here's something that should put anyone to sleep in under sixty seconds." Or: "Here's a message from someone with their eye on your wallet." Or this: "First, no matter what, you'll get the current equivalent of the torture rack. Please don't scream. After all, I suffer more than you do." At the end of one episode of *The Alfred Hitchcock Hour*, we even see him bury an announcer alive!

The sponsors were annoyed by this irony expressed at their expense. Audiences, however, greatly appreciated Hitchcock's antics and, in the end, he was given free rein in this area.

The filmmaker admitted as much in an interview given to the *Saturday Evening Post* in 1957: "As soon as [the sponsors] realized the commercial effects of my jokes, by looking at their sales figures, they stopped questioning the validity of my quips. But there's no way of forgetting it, it took some time to have me accepted."

Crime Doesn't Pay?

The filmmaker's presentations and, above all, conclusions had another function. Sometimes, at the end of an episode, in the service of a logic that gives everything over to the final twist and the surprise effect, sometimes to the detriment of morality, the crime pays off and, for example, the murderer goes

unpunished. It is then up to the master of ceremonies to make it clear that the guilty parties have been punished after all. Such clarification was of course in line with the demands of the censors, who were particularly vigilant when dealing with a medium that was essentially aimed at a family audience. Hitchcock's explanations were sometimes extravagant. At the end of the "Arthur" episode (1959), he explained that the culprit, having fed the corpse of his murdered fiancée to the hens on his farm, has himself been devoured by a fowl that has become giant as a result of gorging itself. It is a safe bet that audiences were not fooled by these a posteriori justifications, which did nothing to detract from the intrinsic cruelty of certain episodes.

Television helped to profoundly transform the filmmaker's image. His silhouette became known to a very large audience, who associated him with these short, horrific stories broadcast on the small screen installed in everyone's living room. His fame became truly global.

Television as a Laboratory for Cinema

The films Hitchcock made for television were both a continuation of those he had made for the cinema and an outline of some that were to follow. "The Crystal Trench" (1959) is certainly a continuation of

Vertigo (1957). And "One More Mile to Go" (1957) served as a field of experimentation for situations that would find their accomplished form in the film *Psycho* (1960).

A Critique of Everyday Life

Television is also, however, a singular, irreducible aspect of Hitchcock's work. While his films for the cinema feature well-known popular stars (James Stewart, Cary Grant, Grace Kelly), the anonymity of television actors, on the other hand, served the project of stories that are moments in everyday life. The heroes of these TV films are ordinary people plunged into drama or tragedy. A number of motifs in the series, particularly in the episodes directed by Hitchcock, are based on the familiar drama of married life as hell, and describe a banal life haunted by guilt and death. Behind the apparently whimsical and frivolous mask of these short fables, with their sometimes macabre humor and omnipresent cruelty, lies the project of a critique of television itself. This intruder is part of the existence of the average American, who has become the unwilling object of relentless voyeurism: It is the television that is watching him or her. From this point on, everyday life itself becomes the object of a radical critique.

Revenge

Season 1, Episode 1

United States · 26 min · Black and White · Mono (RCA Sound Recording) · 1.33:1

Production Dates: September 15–17, 1955
Broadcast in the United States: October 1955

Production: Shamley Productions
Producer: Alfred Hitchcock
Associate Producer: Joan Harrison

Based on a short story by Samuel Blas (1947)
Screenplay: Francis Cockrell, A. I. Bezzerides
Director of Photography: John L. Russell
Sound: Hugh McDowell
Assistant Director: Jack Corrick
Art Direction: Martin Obzina
Set Decoration: James S. Redd

Makeup: Gale McGarry
Costumes: Vincent Dee
Music: Stanley Wilson
Film Editing: Edward W. Williams, Richard G. Wray

Starring: Vera Miles (Elsa Spann), Ralph Meeker (Carl Spann), Frances Bavier (Mrs. Fergusen), Ray Montgomery (man in a gray suit in room 321), John Gallaudet (doctor), Ray Teal (police lieutenant), Norman Willis (policeman), John Day (policeman), Lillian O'Malley (hotel maid), Herbert Lytton (hotel receptionist), Alfred Hitchcock (himself) . . .

SYNOPSIS

Elsa and Carl Spann live in a mobile home. Elsa's husband goes to work, leaving Elsa alone. That evening, he discovers his wife in a state of shock. She claims that a stranger has attacked her. After the police intervene, they both set off by car, hoping that Elsa will recognize her assailant among the passersby. She suddenly points to a man. Carl follows and kills him in cold blood. He gets back into the car. Later, a dazed Elsa accuses a different man of being her attacker.

A Calculated Beginning

Broadcast on CBS (Columbia Broadcasting System) on October 2, 1955, "Revenge" was the first episode of the television series *Alfred Hitchcock Presents*. Logically, it was a film directed by the Master himself that opened the first season of the series, of which he was both creator and host. "Revenge" was not the first episode Hitchcock filmed (that was "Breakdown"), but for some strategic reason he felt the film was important enough to be shown as the season opener.

A Horror Story

The story was based on a short story by Samuel Blas published in *Collier's* magazine in January 1947 and adapted as a comic strip in the *Witches Tales* magazine in October 1953. This choice was a reminder of the extent to which the series was influenced by horror comics, which were very fashionable in the early 1950s, with their macabre theatrics. Francis Cockrell was commissioned to adapt the short story and went on to write eighteen episodes of the series, five of which were directed by Hitchcock.

A. I. Bezzerides, screenwriter of Nicholas Ray's *They Drive by Night* and *On Dangerous Ground*, as well as Robert Aldrich's *Kiss Me Deadly*, also took part in writing "Revenge," without being credited. He said he was hired to "polish" the script and perfect the dialogue.

Programming a Future Star

If Hitchcock attached so much importance to this episode, to the point of rushing its broadcast, it was because he had big plans for his leading lady. He had spotted Vera Miles in a television advertisement for Pepsi-Cola and wanted to make her his new Grace Kelly. Her character of a fragile, depressed wife foreshadowed the one she would play in *The Wrong Man* the following year. He also planned to give her the lead role in his adaptation of Boileau-Narcejac's novel *D'entre les morts* (*The Living and the Dead*), which would become *Vertigo* two years later. Events did not go according to plan, however, and Kim Novak ended up taking her place. Vera Miles would, on the other hand, reappear in *Psycho* and the TV episode "Incident at a Corner" on the series *Startime* in 1960.

A Virile Male Figure

The male lead was Ralph Meeker, who had played Mike Hammer, the brutal detective in the previous year's *Kiss Me Deadly*. He would appear in three further episodes of the series (not directed by Hitchcock). Specializing in "tough" roles, in the late 1960s he appeared in back-to-back films, including

Alfred Hitchcock Presents...

For the first episode broadcast, Hitchcock sets out the principles of the series, which would consist of "stories of suspense and mystery." At the end of "Revenge," he returns to specify that the husband has been arrested by the police and "has paid his debt to society for taking the law into his own hands." Morality is saved, at the last minute.

Robert Aldrich's *The Dirty Dozen*, Roger Corman's *The St. Valentine's Day Massacre*, and Gordon Douglas's *The Detective*. His main career was in television.

Television as a Theater of Cruelty

"Revenge" is an example of the way in which this new series set out to tell dark, discomforting stories with sometimes atrocious endings. Paradoxically, because censorship was more restrictive than in the cinema, television allowed a freedom of tone and the expression of a pessimism that sometimes liberated itself from the commercial demands of the big screen.

Marital Tragedy

In Hitchcock's cinema, and even more so in his television work, the relationship between husband and wife appears singularly problematic. Elsa's exacerbated imaginary world—an exacerbation that is due to the sexual frustration we sense from the very first images, her husband refusing to make love to her despite her insistence—is contrasted with a masculine pragmatism devoid of horizon or desire. In a caressing shot, Hitchcock's camera then transforms the body of the young woman, dressed only in a swimming costume, into an object of fantasy for the viewer. The viewer is suddenly made guilty of an unspeakable desire that will be fulfilled by the presumed rape of the young woman. The final twist (Elsa Spann, her eyes blank, recognizing her attacker as a man who is not the one killed by her husband) opens up an abyss in the female psyche and dizzyingly challenges the viewer's certainties as he or she realizes that they have been taken for a ride: Is the attack of which Elsa claims to have been the victim even real? This turn of events is perhaps a way of saying that there is no real culprit...or that all men are guilty.

Breakdown

Season 1, Episode 7

United States • **26 min** • **Black and White** • **Mono** (RCA Sound Recording) • **1.33:1**

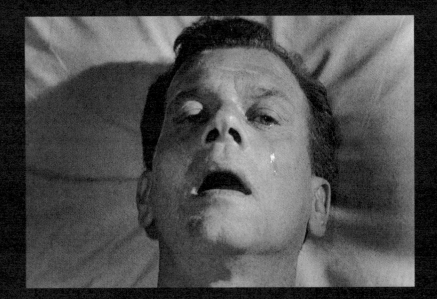

Production Dates: September 7–10, 1955
Broadcast in the United States: November 13, 1955

Production: Shamley Productions
Producer: Alfred Hitchcock
Associate Producer: Joan Harrison

Based on a short story by Louis Pollock (1947)
Screenplay: Francis Cockrell, Louis Pollock
Director of Photography: John L. Russell
Sound: Hugh McDowell
Assistant Director: James Hogan
Art Direction: Martin Obzina
Set Decoration: James S. Redd
Makeup: Garrett Morris
Costumes: Vincent Dee

Music: Stanley Wilson
Film Editing: Edward W. Williams, Richard G. Wray

Starring: Joseph Cotten (William Callew), Raymond Bailey (Ed Johnson), Forrest Stanley (Mr. Hubka), Harry Shannon (Dr. Harner), Lane Chandler (sheriff), James Edwards (convict), Marvin Press (Chessy), Murray Alper (Lloyd), Mike Ragan (White escaped convict), Jim Weldon (guard), Richard Newton (ambulance driver), Aaron Spelling (road worker), Harry Landers (coroner), Elzie Emanuel (Black escaped convict), Ralph Peters (coroner's assistant), Alfred Hitchcock (himself) . . .

SYNOPSIS

Businessman William Callew dismisses an employee over the phone. The man starts to cry. This reaction provokes nothing but contempt in Callew, who has made it a rule not to express any emotion. Shortly afterward, he has an accident that leaves him paralyzed in his car. He looks as if he is dead and is unable to show that he is alive. Escaped prisoners rob him. As far as the rescuers are concerned, Callew is dead. Taken to the morgue, he is saved by a tear running down his cheek.

A Short Story Already Adapted

Although broadcast more than five weeks after "Revenge," "Breakdown" was Hitchcock's first film for his *Alfred Hitchcock Presents* series. The episode was based on a short story by Louis Pollock that appeared in *Collier's* magazine in June 1947. Born in Liverpool, Pollock wrote a number of screenplays, mainly for television, between 1947 and his death in 1964. Until 1945, he was head of publicity and marketing at United Artists, one of the major Hollywood studios. For "Breakdown," he worked on the adaptation of his short story with Francis Cockrell, who also wrote the screenplay for "Revenge." Louis Pollock's story had already been the subject of a radio play in 1945, with Joseph Cotten in the lead role. It also gave rise to a live television drama for the *Suspense* series in 1950. Unusually for his series, Hitchcock mentioned the name of the episode's scriptwriter during the introductory presentation.

Reunion with Joseph Cotten

Joseph Cotten once again played William Callew, a ruthless, misanthropic industrialist. He reunited with Hitchcock thirteen years after *Shadow of a Doubt*, in which he played the lady-killer Uncle Charlie, and seven years after *Under Capricorn*. In the mid-1930s Cotten had befriended Orson Welles, who gave him his film debut in *Too Much Johnson* in 1938, then cast him again in *Citizen Kane* (1941) and *The Magnificent Ambersons* (1942). After an international career, working with the likes of King Vidor, Carol Reed, Robert Aldrich, and even Mario Bava, Joseph Cotten died in 1994 in Los Angeles. He appeared in two other episodes of *Alfred Hitchcock Presents* (not directed by the filmmaker).

Future Extras

Two actors who appeared in this episode went on to become television producers. The first, Richard Newton, who played the ambulance driver, would go on to produce the series *Honey West*, *Hawaii Five-O*, and *Burke's Law*. The second, Aaron Spelling, would go on to become one of the most important developers of television series in the 1970s: *Starsky and Hutch*, *Charlie's Angels*, *Dynasty*, *The Love Boat*, and so on.

The Moral of the Story

"Breakdown" is a perfect example of the morality plays that the films in the series must embody. The unfeeling William Callew must not only learn to feel human emotions, but also understand that they are priceless. The tear that falls from his eye when

everyone thinks he is nothing but a corpse saves him from a real death and, above all, saves him in the eyes of humanity.

Paralysis

The motif of paralysis recurred in other episodes filmed by Hitchcock: "Four O'Clock" (1957), for the *Suspicion* series, and "Poison" (1958), for *Alfred Hitchcock Presents*. This is a recurring theme in Hitchcock's work: *Rear Window* (1954) and *Vertigo* (1957) both feature a man whose circumstances—an injury in one case, a neurosis in the other—prevent him from taking action, weakening him to the point of impotence.

Inconvenient Corpses

In the *New York Herald Tribune* (November 16, 1955), critic John Crosby called it a "marvelous little macabre story" and poked fun at the status of corpses in the filmmaker's mind: "No one seems to mind inert bodies." He pointed out that Hitchcock's last film, *The Trouble with Harry* (1954), featured a dead man's body as the main character.

In 1970, the Italian filmmaker Aldo Lado made *La corta notte delle bambole di vetro* (*Short Night of Glass Dolls*), a film in which the story is told by a paralyzed man whom everyone believes to be dead. The origins of this strange situation for a particularly morbid thriller are perhaps to be found in "Breakdown."

Alfred Hitchcock Presents...

Hitchcock systematically introduced and concluded each of the 19 episodes he directed as well as the 220 or so others he produced for the series. Here, he greets the viewer while reading a detective book, explaining that he finds it very relaxing: "These little books are all very well… but they're only good for reading, they make very poor doorstops." And always with a dry sense of humor, he adds that the little stories he tells are intended "to teach a lesson or point out a moral."

The Case of Mr. Pelham

Season 1, Episode 10

   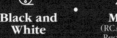

United States · **30 mins** · **Black and White** · **Mono** (RCA Sound Recording) · **1.33:1**

Production Dates: October 7–10, 1955
Broadcast in the United States: December 4, 1955

Production: Shamley Productions
Producer: Alfred Hitchcock
Associate Producer: Joan Harrison

Based on a short story by Anthony Armstrong (1940)
Screenplay: Francis Cockrell
Director of Photography: John L. Russell
Sound: William Brady
Assistant Director: Jack Corrick
Art Direction: James S. Redd
Set Decoration: James S. Redd

Makeup: Leo Lotito Jr.
Costumes: Vincent Dee
Music: Stanley Wilson
Film Editing: Edward W. Williams, Richard G. Wray

Starring: Tom Ewell (Albert Pelham), Raymond Bailey (Dr. Harley), Justice Watson (Henry Peterson), Kirby Smith (Tom Mason), Kay Stewart (Miss Clement), John Compton (Vincent), Jan Arvan (Harry), Norman Willis (barman), Tim Graham (lawyer), Richard Collier (barman), Diane Brewster (secretary), Alfred Hitchcock (himself) . . .

SYNOPSIS

Albert Pelham, a worried man, confides in Dr. Harley: A double is trying to pass himself off as him and replace him both at work and at home. But he cannot differentiate himself from the look-alike or get rid of him. He ends up confronting this stranger who claims to be the real Albert Pelham. In the end, the double, accepted by all as the one and only authentic Pelham, pities the "other," the madman who tried to pass himself off as him and ends up in an asylum.

A Short Story by Anthony Armstrong

"The Case of Mr. Pelham" is based on a short story by Anthony Armstrong written in 1940 and published in June 1955 in *Ellery Queen's Mystery Magazine*. Armstrong, a British-born writer, had worked almost twenty years earlier with Alfred Hitchcock on the screenplay for *Young and Innocent* (1937). His story had already been adapted twice for the BBC, in 1947 and 1955. In 1957, he turned it into a novel, which was adapted for the screen by Basil Dearden in 1970, *The Man Who Haunted Himself*, starring Roger Moore. Once again, Francis Cockrell was commissioned to adapt the story for American television.

Comic Actor

The double lead role is played by Tom Ewell, an actor with a background in theater who became famous for his appearances in lighthearted films. He is best known for his role as the adulterous husband in Billy Wilder's comedy *The Seven Year Itch*, starring Marilyn Monroe, which was released in cinemas five months before the episode was broadcast. It was a reprise of a character he had created in the theater three years earlier. The actor, after his performance as the frustrated, fantasy-ridden Everyman, seemed the ideal choice to play Mr. Pelham, an ordinary American.

A Doctor with Multiple Lives

Dr. Harley, in whom the hapless Pelham confides, is played by Raymond Bailey. This actor lived many lives in his youth: banker, Hollywood extra, sailor, employee on a grapefruit plantation...After 1938, he became a much sought-after supporting actor in films, and then especially on television. He appeared in another episode in the same season, not directed by Hitchcock. In *Vertigo* (1957) he played Scottie's doctor, with James Stewart in the role of Scottie.

The Disconcerting Double

"The Case of Mr. Pelham" returns to the theme of the double, a recurrent motif in Hitchcock's work (*Shadow of a Doubt, Strangers on a Train, The Wrong Man, Vertigo, North by Northwest, Torn Curtain*). This time, the theme is taken literally: It is the existence of a perfect duplicate of himself that distresses the hero. Although the film's literary roots can be found in the works of Edgar Allan Poe ("William Wilson") and Dostoyevsky (*The Double*), Hitchcock and his scriptwriters radically changed the premise. The double does not seem to have the intention

Alfred Hitchcock Presents...

Hitchcock warns the viewer that the story ahead is a frightening one, because "sometimes death is not the worst that can befall a man...little insidious devices that can drive a man out of his mind like putting bubble gum in someone's pocket." At the end of the episode, nurses take away a man claiming to be Hitchcock ("But I'm Alfred Hitchcock, I am, I can prove it") while his double declares that the impostor was almost perfect.

of tormenting Mr. Pelham. He is not the dark, negative face of a worried self. If his existence transforms the man's life into a nightmare, it is because he leads the same life as he does, at his office, at home, in his absence and literally taking his place. "I don't think he's trying to persecute me," says Pelham. Paradoxically, the unease is more intense because this double does not seem to have any malicious intent. He is not hostile; he is just what he is, an impeccable reproduction, and, as such, objectively threatening.

Masochistic Paranoia

The way the film is told casts doubt on the reality of this double's existence. It takes the form of Pelham's increasingly anxious confidences with his doctor, which lead to several flashbacks. A few clues (Pelham's celibacy) suggest a repressed homosexuality leading to masochistic paranoia. The levels of reality remain blurred for the entire episode, at the end of which the viewer wonders whether he or she has lost their bearings. Have we not witnessed the ravings of a madman?

The Unique Original and Their Double

It is paradoxically by trying to distinguish himself from his double in order to confound him that Pelham signs his doom. On Dr. Harley's advice, he wears a fancy tie, in contravention of his characteristic sobriety. When he meets his double, the latter can easily claim that he is the real Pelham, since the "other" is only an imperfect copy thanks to his fancy tie. It is by wanting to assert his unique identity that Pelham is seen as a "double" presence.

Back for Christmas

Season 1, Episode 23

United States • **30 mins** • **Black and White** • **Mono** (RCA Sound Recording) • **1.33:1**

Production Dates: January 13–16, 1956
Broadcast in the United States: March 4, 1956

Production: Shamley Productions
Producer: Alfred Hitchcock
Associate Producer: Joan Harrison

Based on a short story by John Collier (1939)
Screenplay: Francis Cockrell
Director of Photography: John L. Russell
Sound: Earl Crain Sr.
Assistant Director: Richard Birnie
Art Direction: Martin Obzina
Set Decoration: Ralph Sylos
Makeup: Jack Barron
Costumes: Vincent Dee

Music: Stanley Wilson
Film Editing: Edward W. Williams, Richard G. Wray

Starring: John Williams (Herbert Carpenter), Isabel Elsom (Hermione Carpenter), Arthur Gould-Porter (Major Sinclair), Lily Kemble-Cooper (Mrs. Sinclair), Gavin Muir (Mr. Wallingford), Katherine Warren (Mrs. Freda Wallingford), Gerald Hamer (Mr. Hewitt), Irene Tedrow (Mrs. Hewitt), Ross Ford (Mr. Hall), Theresa Harris (Elsie), Mollie Glessing (servant), Alfred Hitchcock (himself) . . .

SYNOPSIS

Herbert Carpenter, a British gentleman, is digging a hole in his cellar for his wife, Hermione. They are due to leave for the United States and will not return until Christmas. Herbert murders and buries his wife. Now settled in California, he writes to friends that they will be staying longer than expected. One day, he receives a letter addressed to Hermione: On her instructions, a company is going to dig a wine cellar in their basement in England. It is a Christmas present for her husband.

Adaptations

"Back for Christmas" is an adaptation of a short story by John Collier published in 1939. Collier was a British writer best known for his acerbic and ironic writing, some of which appeared in the prestigious *New Yorker*. Several of his stories were made into episodes of television series, and seven of them were adapted for *Alfred Hitchcock Presents* (including another by the director in the following season, "Wet Saturday"). Francis Cockrell again adapted the original literary material. Before and after 1956, "Back for Christmas" gave rise to radio adaptations featuring former or future Hitchcock actors such as Peter Lorre (*The Man Who Knew Too Much*, 1934), Herbert Marshall (*Foreign Correspondent*, 1940) and John McIntire (*Psycho*, 1960).

A Favorite Actor

John Williams, a model of British sangfroid, took on the male lead role shortly after playing the perceptive policeman in *Dial M for Murder* (1953) and the insurance inspector in *To Catch a Thief* (1954). Williams, who would appear in a total of ten episodes in the series, including "Wet Saturday," was, according to producer Norman Lloyd, one of Hitchcock's favorite actors. Isobel Elsom (listed in the credits as Isabel), who plays the wife, was a British actress who made her theatrical debut in 1911. She came to the United States in the late 1930s and split her time between the Broadway stage, television, and the cinema (Joseph L. Mankiewicz's masterpiece *The Ghost and Mrs. Muir*; Vincente Minnelli's *Lust for Life*). She appeared in two other episodes of the series, not directed by Hitchcock, including one ("The Three Dreams of Mr. Findlater") in which she and John Williams once again formed a married couple. The actor would once again play a husband tormented by his wife and dreaming of murdering her.

Castration and Erection

"Back for Christmas" is one of those marital dramas that punctuate the filmography, particularly television, of the Master of Suspense. The hero of this macabre comedy, with whom the viewer is asked to identify, is trapped in a marital hell from which he is trying to escape. This hell is reflected in his wife's suffocating perfectionism. The castrating dimension of the wife's control freakery, to the point of directing her husband's every move, is underlined by a scabrous visual gag. After the murder, Herbert Carpenter arrives in New York. He is delighted to contemplate an imposing skyscraper, a veritable phallic motif that causes delight on the face of the freed husband.

Alfred Hitchcock Presents...

Hitchcock appears with a shrunken head beside him: "That's what happens when you fall asleep in the hairdryer." He explains that he would collect them if he had the patience to wait for their owners to die, and announces that the story that follows has nothing to do with shrinking heads—a model of absurd presentation that delights both the filmmaker and the viewers.

A Return to Childhood

From the original story and previous adaptations, the scriptwriter has eliminated a number of details, in particular the presence of Herbert's young mistress, who would have given meaning to the assassin's act. Stripped of this motive, the murder appears stranger and more radical. The murderer yearns for a return to a childhood free of an overly possessive and too gently authoritarian mother. This is how Herbert's instructions to the cleaning lady in the California flat where he has set up house can be interpreted: not to tidy up his things and to preserve a "premarital" disorder, like a little boy who would enjoy not tidying his room.

Bad Impulses

The entire first part of the film is based on suspense, in which the expected murder, the preparation for which the viewer has seen (the hole dug in the cellar to hide the body), is constantly postponed by unexpected events such as the arrival of friends for tea or the request to change the fabric covering the chandelier. In this way, the suspense is not fueled by the fear that a crime will be committed, but rather by the fear that it will not take place! The viewer ends up wishing for the murder of the all-too-perfect Mrs. Carpenter and the impunity of her husband.

The film is also a variation on the particularly Hitchcockian theme of the inconvenient corpse (*Rope*, 1948; *Rear Window*, 1954; *The Trouble with Harry*, 1954; *Psycho*, 1960). The assassin's perfect plan is thwarted by the prospect of the resurgence of a body that never quite manages to disappear for good.

DO <u>YOU</u> HAVE A 'DOUBLE'?

Hitchcock's new hit is a story
taken from life -- and it's <u>doubly</u>
exciting because it's true!

HENRY FONDA and VERA MILES

and the exciting city of New York in ALFRED HITCHCOCK'S

first thriller taken from life

The Wrong Man

Presented by WARNER BROS.

ALFRED HITCHCOCK

The Wrong Man

United States · 1 hr 45 · Black and White · Mono (RCA Sound Recording) · 1.85:1

Production Dates: March 26–June 6, 1956
Release Date in the United States: January 26, 1957

Production: Warner Bros.
Producer: Alfred Hitchcock
Associate Producer: Herbert Coleman

**Based on an article by Herbert Brean, "A Case of Identity," which
appeared in *Life* magazine (June 29, 1953), and a book by Maxwell
Anderson, *The True Story of Christopher Emmanuel Balestrero*,
inspired by a true story**
Screenplay: Maxwell Anderson, Angus MacPhail
Consultants: Frank D. O'Connor (district attorney, Queens County, New York),
George Groves (New York police sergeant)
Director of Photography: Robert Burks
Sound: Earl Crain Sr.
Assistant Director: Daniel J. McCauley
Art Direction: Paul Sylbert
Set Decoration: William L. Kuehl
Makeup: Gordon Bau
Music: Bernard Herrmann
Film Editing: George Tomasini

Starring: Henry Fonda (Manny Balestrero), Vera Miles (Rose Balestrero), Anthony
Quayle (Frank D. O'Connor), Harold J. Stone (Lieutenant Bowers), Charles Cooper
(Detective Matthews), John Heldabrand (prosecutor Tomasini), Esther Minciotti
(Balestrero's mother), Doreen Lang (Ann James), Laurinda Barrett (Constance
Willis), Norma Connolly (Betty Todd), Nehemiah Persoff (Gene Conforti), Lola
D'Annunzio (Olga Conforti), Kippy Campbell (Robert Balestrero), Robert Essen
(Gregory Balestrero), Dayton Lummis (Judge Groat), Peggy Webber (Miss
Dennerly), Sherman Billingsley (himself), Richard Robbins (the guilty man), Alfred
Hitchcock (himself, prologue)...

"*The Wrong Man...* is a roast without the sauce, a raw news item."

François Truffaut

SYNOPSIS

In New York, in the winter of 1953, Manny Balestrero, a quiet, married father, finds himself suspected and then accused of several hold-ups in his neighborhood. To his astonishment, he is identified by several witnesses. Two employees of an insurance company formally recognize him, and a number of clues point to him. What follows is a relentless spiral of charges and court proceedings that condemn him to prison overnight. Despite the best efforts of their lawyer, Manny's wife, devastated by this dramatic situation, gradually sinks into a depression that lands her in a psychiatric hospital. All seems lost. But when the trial is adjourned on a technicality, the real culprit is miraculously arrested and Balestrero is cleared. However, while Balestrero has regained his freedom once and for all, his wife seems to be suffering from incurable sadness, "locked up" forever, unless another miracle occurs. In the very last shot, the viewer learns that she is out of the woods, and the family, which has moved to Miami, is happy and united once again.

GENESIS

A true story: On the evening of January 14, 1953, Christopher Emmanuel "Manny" Balestrero, an Italian American practicing Catholic in his forties, returned to his neighborhood of Jackson Heights (Queens, New York) to be with his wife and two young boys. A bassist earning eighty-five dollars a week, he played every night at the Stork Club, a well-known Manhattan society café. That evening, two policemen stopped him on his doorstep. Recognized by several witnesses as the perpetrator of small-scale holdups in local shops, and confounded by a similarity in his handwriting, he spent a night at the police station, then the morning in Long Island prison. His trial began on April 21 and got off to a bad start but was suspended shortly afterward on a technicality. During this adjournment, on April 29, the real culprit, a man named Charles J. Daniell, was caught red-handed—he confessed to some forty armed robberies in Jackson Heights—and Manny was cleared. The "real man" and the "wrong man" look similar, in the shape of their faces and their slightly bulging eyes.

A Story of Handcuffs

In the June 29, 1953, issue of *Life* magazine, Hitchcock came across the story "A Case of Identity" by journalist Herbert Brean. It was almost the first synopsis of the film, already describing Manny's shifty look once he was handcuffed, the shame that made him look down and see only legs, feet, and the ground around him. This true detail became a sequence during which Manny (Henry Fonda) tries not to stare at anyone. It also foreshadowed the director's ambition: for once, to tell the story from the point of view of the victim rather than the investigator, to reverse the perspective without filming with a subjective camera.

In 1954, in an interview with Chabrol and Truffaut, Hitchcock recounted Manny's sad adventure and told them that the idea of bringing it to the screen "was terribly appealing to him."[1] In truth, this news item served up on a platter what Hitchcock had been devising in fiction after fiction since the 1920s: the story of a man who is unjustly accused, mistaken for someone else, and forced, as if in a nightmare, to expend an insane amount of energy to prove his innocence. The story is also Hitchcockian in its motif, with handcuffs appearing in *The Lodger*, *The 39 Steps*, *Saboteur*…

Time for a New Realism

The story also appealed to Hitchcock because it was timely. For the sake of contrast (he had just shot two Technicolor fantasies, *To Catch a Thief* and *The*

Trouble with Harry) or because he was aware of a change underway in the history of cinematographic forms (neorealism), he was tempted to try his hand at the revolution in the way we look at things initiated by the cinema of Roberto Rossellini. This aesthetic upheaval, which had begun in Italy ten years earlier, brought to the screen the "real life" of an entire people finally liberated from fascist propaganda. Hitchcock had seen and appreciated the "suspense" of Vittorio De Sica's *Bicycle Thieves* (*Ladri di biciclette*), and Paul Sylbert, his art director on *The Wrong Man*, had just arrived from the set of Elia Kazan's *Baby Doll*, which was then seen as an Americanized version of this new realism.

The Presence of Television

At the same time, in the United States, black-and-white television was making its way into homes, and with it the newsreel aesthetic that Hitchcock asked his cinematographer, Robert Burks, to create on the occasion of their eighth collaboration.

Shortly before shooting *The Wrong Man* in the spring of 1956, Hitchcock also became a television director. On October 2, 1955, CBS broadcast the first episode of *Alfred Hitchcock Presents*. The form and content of the TV series permeated *The Wrong Man*, four years before *Psycho*: Both feature stories about ordinary people, everyday lives, a seemingly

Christopher Emmanuel "Manny" Balestrero, the man himself.

familiar context, the supposedly stable world of the American middle class.

A Warner Film

The story of this Italian American musician powerless to assert his innocence, subject to the laws of men and God, appealed to Hitchcock so much that he changed studios for the duration of the film, Warner Bros. having acquired the rights to Herbert Brean's story. A filmmaker at Paramount, Hitchcock opportunely pointed out that he still contractually owed Jack Warner a film. To persuade the studio to definitively commit to the project, he went so far as to waive his salary (bearing in mind that at the time he was earning almost $130,000 per episode of *Alfred Hitchcock Presents*).

Preparations and Investigation

Although Hitchcock made this film for Warner Bros., he was surrounded by his usual collaborators in production (Coleman), cinematography (Burks), music (Herrmann), and editing (Tomasini). The only one missing was screenwriter John Michael Hayes, who was fired at the end of his contract because of a dispute dating back to their previous film. Hitchcock came up with the idea of replacing him with Maxwell Anderson, a screenwriter and above all a playwright, author in particular of *Winterset* (1935), a play inspired by the Sacco and Vanzetti affair opportunely revived in the *Best Plays* programmed on NBC Radio on June 8, 1952. The English screenwriter Angus MacPhail was told to stay in New York, visit the real place, meet the real judge, the real defense lawyer, and the real Balestrero couple. In short, he asked MacPhail to investigate and Anderson to avoid overly literary developments—he would later reproach himself for being afraid to allow himself "the necessary dramatic licence."[2] Obsessed with verisimilitude, he wanted to avoid using his imagination, even if the narrative interest suffered in places; he dreamed of a film in the form of an official report.

CASTING

It was on television, in a program broadcast by ABC, that Hitchcock noticed Vera Miles, his new actress. She first appeared in "Revenge," the first broadcast episode of *Alfred Hitchcock Presents*. Since Grace Kelly had stopped acting, the director had been looking for someone to replace her, and he had high expectations of his new protégée, even if she played an ordinary woman who gradually sank into depression. It was also for Vera Miles that Hitchcock chose

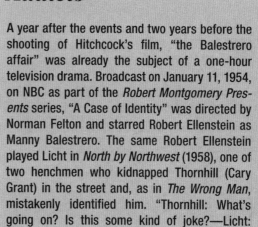

For Hitchcock Addicts

A year after the events and two years before the shooting of Hitchcock's film, "the Balestrero affair" was already the subject of a one-hour television drama. Broadcast on January 11, 1954, on NBC as part of the *Robert Montgomery Presents* series, "A Case of Identity" was directed by Norman Felton and starred Robert Ellenstein as Manny Balestrero. The same Robert Ellenstein played Licht in *North by Northwest* (1958), one of two henchmen who kidnapped Thornhill (Cary Grant) in the street and, as in *The Wrong Man*, mistakenly identified him. "Thornhill: What's going on? Is this some kind of joke?—Licht: That's right, a joke, we're going to have a laugh in the car."

to use black and white in *The Wrong Man*, which he felt was more flattering than the colors that tended to "overwhelm" her, in other words, extinguish her radiance.

The Face of an Honest Man

The Wrong Man was Henry Fonda's first and only film with Hitchcock, who had already considered him for *Foreign Correspondent* (1940) and then *Saboteur* (1942). If the set photos are to be believed, the relationship between the two men was cordial, although it seems that Fonda took some offense at the director's overly exclusive attention to his female lead. Hitchcock asked his two actors to talk to their "doubles," the real Mr. and Mrs. Balestrero, before shooting. In the film, Fonda plays a practically impassive and incredulous Manny, almost mumbling, apart from the childlike astonishment visible in his eyes, passive to the point of masochism or sanctity, the first spectator of his own drama, or "Passion." The actor uses few expressions and essentially offers his bare face to the light as mute proof of his innocence, "an honest man's face that is barely illuminated by a look that is sad and clear to the point of transparency."[3]

FILMING AND PRODUCTION

In February 1956, MacPhail, Coleman, and Hitchcock, occasionally joined by Anderson, went down to the St. Regis hotel to work on the script, study the details of the legal and police procedures, and scout the locations: the route from the Stork Club to Queens, which they timed, the subway station on Fifth Avenue, Manny's usual café (Bickford's), the Victor Moore Arcade, headquarters of the insurance company where he was first "recognized," the drugstores and delicatessen in Jackson Heights, the 110th Street police station and its jail, the George Washington Bridge, the Rose Asylum, the Long Island jail, and the Queensboro Bridge, over which the prisoner van drives…This bridge is the subject of a highly stylized shot in the film that was to catch the eye of the young Jean-Luc Godard (*Cahiers du cinéma*, June 1957): "Let us admire the shot, remarkably photographed by Robert Burks, where the secure vehicle that is taking Balestrero to court passes over a suspension bridge: a small black silhouette, bumping along in the shadow of the immense iron pillars, and strangely reminiscent of *Nosferatu*'s cart arriving in the land of phantoms."

American Neorealism

In all the places Manny Balestrero frequents, Henry Fonda's large body follows in his footsteps. He also crosses paths with shopkeepers, waiters, landlords, and white coats who play their own roles. So the exteriors are real, but so are some of the interiors, even though filming was split between New York (one month) and the Warner Bros. studios in Hollywood (five weeks). This was American-style neorealism, assuming that the original itself was "pure"…Paul Sylbert, the art director, recalled the studio shooting of the scenes in the lawyer's office and Hitchcock's pleasure in creating the illusion, with light and sound, of the subway train passing by. The Balestrero family home was also reconstructed in the studio, with the front door rigged to create an optical effect when Henry Fonda opened it and entered the hallway.[4]

The Appeal of Fiction

How can we resolve this supposed cinematic contradiction between the desire for realism and assumed artifice? The film vacillates between "*more than* fiction," forbidden in the name of Hitchcock's idea of documentary, and "*more than* documentary,"

"This Is a True Story"

Hitchcock forgoes the humorous wink of his traditional appearance in the corner of the screen in favor of a prologue, as he does before each episode of his TV series. But this is unique in the case of one of his feature films. In this serious, stylized opening, filmed on a deserted studio set, he assures the viewer of the veracity of the facts described ("This is a true story—every word of it") and warns them of a new form of suspense in which it is reality, rather than the usual romanticism of his thrillers, that is frightening. Furthermore, in the introduction to "Revenge," Hitchcock had mischievously justified his presence at the beginning and end of each episode: "to give the title to those of you who can't read and to tidy up afterwards for those who don't understand the endings"—endings that are often abrupt and amoral, requiring a reassuring word or, as in the final images of *The Wrong Man*, a text that is supposed to guarantee the viewer a return to order with a happy ending in spite of everything. Referring to the real Mrs. Balestrero in 1962, Hitchcock told Truffaut: "She was locked up in an asylum where she must still be."[2]

limited by the desire for fiction and irrepressible visual ideas. These are all the more desirable because they have been "storyboarded": the close-up on the guard's belly and the large handcuffs dangling from his jacket like butcher's meat hooks; Manny's arrest, when he is wedged in the back of the car between two policemen whose massive profiles suddenly seem like those of two hounds; the interplay of gaze and camera in the insurance company's offices; the wide shot of Manny, still "innocent," coming out of the Stork Club and following in the footsteps, as if in a choreographed dance, of two policemen making their rounds, a sign of the arrest of a man overwhelmed by fate before being saved by providence. In 1957, Truffaut described *The Wrong Man* as a "raw news item." In 1962, the same Truffaut respectfully criticized the Master for a circular camera movement that was as dizzying as it was anti-realist, speeding up and down Henry Fonda's face, his eyes closed, leaning against the wall of his cell to keep from sinking—a foreshadowing of Scottie's (James Stewart's) expressionist nightmare in *Vertigo*.

The Garnelite Effect

Hitchcock and cinematographer Robert Burks shot *The Wrong Man* on sensitive 35 mm film, the Eastman Kodak Tri-X, which came onto the market in 1954. However, Burks needed a lot of light to obtain a documentary photography standard in poorly lit locations (the subway train, Balestrero's house, the police station lobby, etc.), but this should not have prevented the crew from moving quickly from one location to another. To solve this equation, he came up with the idea of using the Garnelite, a recently invented spotlight with an incandescent bulb. Compact, handy, portable, running on ordinary current, and used as a supplementary light for large spotlights on location during the day, the Garnelite also had the merit of being particularly penetrating: "A delicate little lamp, no bigger than a car headlight, but much more powerful," Burks confided to a journalist from the *American Cinematographer* on the shoot.[5] He added that he lit 95 percent of the film in this way and, for one street scene at night, an entire block with forty of these lamps powered by two small portable generators.

The Newsreel Image

For interior scenes, the cinematographer had a diffuser added to soften the luminosity. The Garnelite was used everywhere to obtain an unpolished, slightly rigid image, like that of a news report. In the courtroom where the trial is taking place, Burks admits that he positioned his lights exactly as a newsreel cameraman would have done.

The whole setup serves Hitchcock's desire for an austere, unadorned image, as the title of the *American Cinematographer* report reminds us: "Hitch Didn't Want It Arty." All these efforts also made it possible to ensure the clarity of the opening shots and to achieve a sober, even, and spectacular effect throughout the entire film: capturing and reproducing the light on Henry Fonda's face.

The image of Christ and the shadow of Henry Fonda.

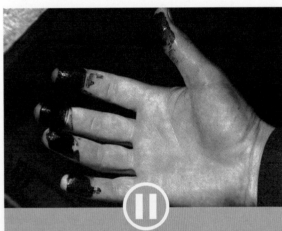

Freeze Frame

Convinced that they have their thief, the police arrest Manny Balestrero. Before the man is put in a cell for the night, Hitchcock emphasizes a detail of the procedure: In silence, a policeman spends a long time fingerprinting Manny, who, incredulous, allows this to happen. A close-up of his right hand shows each ink-stained finger. The black-and-white image helps the character and the viewer to mistake the black ink for red. It is as if Manny has blood on his hands, like a real guilty man. Twenty-five years earlier, in *Blackmail*, the filmmaker had already described the same arrest process and emphasized the fingerprinting aspect.

RECEPTION

In the same tone as the prologue, the director provided the commentary for the trailer. Warner Bros. handled distribution and promotion: "Hitchcock, his first thriller for real!"; "Do you have a 'double'?" Although *The Wrong Man* did not lose money, it was neither a popular nor a critical success. The *Los Angeles Times* (January 24, 1957), for example, criticized the film for "sticking to the story": "Once again, it proves that life can be much more interminable than fiction." Nevertheless, some praised the first part of the film and its demonstration of "the obstinacy of a group of policemen who firmly believe that every man is guilty until proven innocent" (*New Yorker*, January 5, 1957).

A Filmmakers' Film

Convinced that the radical nature of his choices had hindered the film's success, or because of the box-office failure of *The Wrong Man*, Hitchcock was only partially fond of it. It was a different story for other filmmakers, such as Jean-Luc Godard, who made *À bout de souffle* (*Breathless*) four years later and still remembers it in the "Hitchcock moment" in an episode of his *Histoire(s) du cinéma* (1998). *The Wrong Man* returns in Jean-Pierre Melville's *Le Samouraï* (1967), where we find the same police station lineup room and the same appearance of doubles, including in a confrontation where Balestrero finds himself dramatically encumbered by them, and where Jef Costello (Alain Delon) silently recognizes the other soldiers of the same shadow army. The Italian American Martin Scorsese names *The Wrong Man* as one of the influences for *Taxi Driver* (1976), another New York film whose plot seems to be seen

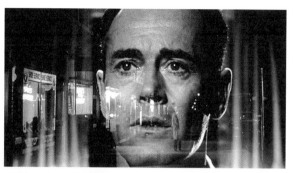

"Certainly the most beautiful shot in Hitchcock's entire oeuvre, and one that sums it up" (Truffaut). The real man cross-fades in to replace the wrong man: Richard Robbins/Henry Fonda.

Who's Who?

On January 15, 1957, three weeks after the New York and Los Angeles premieres of The Wrong Man, Christopher Emmanuel Balestrero took part in a game show on CBS, *To Tell the Truth*. A panel of four judges had to identify the real Balestrero from among three candidates. The presenter recalled in his introduction the police misunderstanding of which man was the victim. When it came to the vote, two jurors picked the right one and the other two got it wrong. This man—whom Hitchcock, to his great disappointment, found emotionally lacking—seemed to have great difficulty not being mistaken for someone else.

through the eyes of its own character, with Bernard Herrmann's heady score that returns to jazz tones from one film to the next... Scorsese explicitly cites as an influence the camera movements in the scene where Manny goes to the insurance company and the interplay of the points of view of the employees behind the counter: "It was the kind of paranoia I wanted to recapture."[6]

Reality and Its Double

Watching *The Wrong Man* again today is still impressive: The mise-en-scène constantly makes us feel, through crossed glances, the invisible but real seesaw between a world in which a man can feel entitled to be there (to see and be seen) and this other world, which is nonetheless the same, where the gaze of others is enough to topple him from it. Even more so in this film, Hitchcock favors the discreet and permanent form of the cross-fade between two scenes. Of course, this technique allows the viewer to move from one space-time to another, but above all, for the space of a few shared images, it causes two realities to overlap in the same shot, making the viewer's eyes uneasy. Which is the real one, which is the double? This continues right up to the film's climax, with a shot that is "certainly the most beautiful of Hitchcock's entire oeuvre, and one that sums it up":[3] the real culprit, coming from the background of the image, advances until the features of his face are superimposed on those of the false culprit, so that the two coexist for a moment.

Wet Saturday

Season 2, Episode 1

United States · **26 mins** · **Black and White** · **Mono** (RCA Sound Recording) · **1.33:1**

SYNOPSIS

Production Dates: August 22–24, 1956
Broadcast in the United States: September 30, 1956

Production: Shamley Productions
Producer: Alfred Hitchcock
Associate Producer: Joan Harrison

Based on a short story by John Collier (1938)
Screenplay: Marian Cockrell
Director of Photography: John L. Russell
Sound: Earl Crain Jr.
Assistant Director: Jack Corrick
Art Direction: Martin Obzina

Set Decoration: James S. Redd
Hair Stylist: Florence Bush
Makeup: Jack Barron
Costumes: Vincent Dee
Music: Stanley Wilson
Film Editing: Edward W. Williams, Richard G. Wray

Starring: Cedric Hardwicke (Mr. Princey), John Williams (Captain Smollet), Tita Purdom (Millicent "Millie" Princey), Kathryn Givney (Mrs. Princey), Jerry Barclay (George Princey), Irene Lang (Jane), Alfred Hitchcock (himself) . . .

In the barn of the family cottage, young Millicent Princey has murdered the man she loved and who told her he was marrying someone else. Millicent's father traps a family friend, Captain Smollet. Holding him at gunpoint, he forces him to put his fingerprints on the murder weapon and throw the body into a pit, making him a prime suspect. He assures Smollet that he will not report him to the police. But Mr. Princey has no intention of keeping his promise.

Season 2, Episode 1

As with the very first episode of the series, it was a film directed by the Master himself that opened the new season of *Alfred Hitchcock Presents*. "Wet Saturday," a short story by John Collier published in the British magazine the *Bystander* in 1938, was the second story by the writer, after "Back for Christmas," to be the subject of an episode directed by Hitchcock. The adaptation for the small screen was written by Marian Cockrell, a Birmingham-born screenwriter and novelist who had written several scripts, mainly for television series (*Suspicion*, *Johnny Staccato*, *Batman*). She wrote eleven scripts for *Alfred Hitchcock Presents*. She also wrote a famous children's book, *Shadow Castle*, published in 1945.

Reunions and Casting Against Character

Alfred Hitchcock reunited with Cedric Hardwicke. This British actor made his film debut in 1913. In the theater, he met the playwright George Bernard Shaw, who considered him his fourth favorite actor. When asked who the first three were, Shaw replied, "The Marx Brothers." Hardwicke, knighted by King George V in 1934, enjoyed a prolific career as a supporting film actor. Hitchcock had already cast him in *Suspicion* (1941) and *Rope* (1948). In "Wet Saturday," he plays Mr. Princey, the cynical family man who sets the trap to incriminate his friend. His character is the polar opposite of the one he played in *Rope*, an honest man who resents the fascist theories of Professor Rupert Cadell, played by James Stewart. The man who seemed to represent moderation, decency, and bonhomie becomes, in this episode, a cold, calculating, and ruthless monster, guided only by the instinct to protect his family.

John Williams was also a regular in Hitchcock films (*Dial M for Murder*, 1953; *To Catch a Thief*, 1954) and between 1955 and 1959 he played in eight episodes of *Alfred Hitchcock Presents*. And he too played a character who was the complete opposite of the one he played in "Back for Christmas." In the previous episode, he was the murderer who buried his wife in the cellar of the marital home, but this time he played Captain Smollet, the unfortunate sacrificial victim of the maneuvers of the father of the family.

Shooting Star

Actress Tita Purdom, alias "Millie" Princey, the hysterical, murderous young woman, had a brief television career, from 1956 to 1959. In films, she played just one role (under the name Tita Phillips), in *Man*

Alfred Hitchcock Presents...

Hitchcock appears reclining on a shelf, taking tea, and is glad that the audience has finally found him: "As you can see, our new quarters are rather modest." As the episode draws to a close, he points out that Captain Smollet did not go quietly when the police arrived and that, in the confusion, young Millicent found a new victim: her own father. All's well that ends well...

in the Attic (1953), a remake of Hitchcock's *The Lodger*. She appeared in another episode of *Alfred Hitchcock Presents*, not directed by the Master, in the following season. In 1951 she married British actor Edmund Purdom, who left her for another actress, Linda Christian. The messy divorce that followed made headlines in 1956.

Cruel Lives, "English Style"

In his famous interviews with Hitchcock in the early 1960s, filmmaker François Truffaut[1] hypothesized an incompatibility between the words "cinema" and "English," considering the British climate, taste for the countryside, and (peaceful, routine) way of life to be anti-cinematographic. "Wet Saturday," which Truffaut may not have seen, seems to stand in stark contradiction to this standpoint. The crime and its visual force emerge specifically at a family reunion in a cottage in the heart of a rainy countryside. These features, which are conducive to a peaceful life, suddenly appear extremely threatening, even provoking the worst. In this respect, "Wet Saturday" is one of Hitchcock's cruelest and most disturbing films. The power of evil lies in the very particularities that François Truffaut enumerates, all the more to repudiate them.

Transference of Guilt

"Wet Saturday" is also a literal illustration of the guilt transference motif that runs throughout the work of the Master of Suspense: One man has to pay for the wrongdoing of another (*Strangers on a Train*, *I Confess*, *The Wrong Man*, etc.). The film thus depicts the fabrication of an ideal culprit. Does the figure of innocence have any chance of existence in Alfred Hitchcock's cinema?

Mr. Blanchard's Secret

Season 2, Episode 13

United States · **26 mins** · **Black and White** · **Mono** (RCA Sound Recording) · **1.33:1**

SYNOPSIS

Production Dates: October 18–22, 1956
Broadcast in the United States: December 23, 1956

Production: Shamley Productions
Producer: Alfred Hitchcock
Associate Producer: Joan Harrison

Based on a short story by Emily Neff
Adaptation: Sarett Rudley (aka Sarett Tobias)
Director of Photography: John L. Russell
Sound: Stephen J. Bass

Assistant Director: Richard Birnie
Art Direction: John J. Lloyd
Set Decoration: James Walters
Hair Stylist: Florence Bush
Makeup: Jack Barron
Costumes: Vincent Dee
Music: Stanley Wilson
Film Editing: Edward W. Williams, Richard G. Wray

Starring: Robert Horton (John Fenton), Meg Mundy (Ellen Blanchard), Mary Scott (Babs Fenton), Dayton Lummis (Charles Blanchard), Alfred Hitchcock (himself) . . .

Babs Fenton, a young woman with a fertile imagination, tells her husband that their neighbor, Mr. Blanchard, killed his wife. Every night, she watches their house. She even breaks in one night, but finds no evidence. She sticks to her idea until Mrs. Blanchard pays her a visit. Babs modifies her imaginary scenario: Mr. Blanchard is watching his wife, sequestering her, planning to murder her, and so on. These fantasies are repeatedly contradicted by reality.

A New Relationship

Broadcast in December 1956, "Mr. Blanchard's Secret" was adapted from a short story by Emily Neff. A journalist with the *New Britain* (CT) *Herald*, then with the *Times-Picayune* in New Orleans, Emily Neff also wrote short stories and short poems, more for recreational purposes than in the hope of launching a literary career. In the 1970s, she opened a communications agency and became involved in New Orleans politics. Three of her stories were adapted for *Alfred Hitchcock Presents*.

Sarett Rudley was responsible for transforming the short story into a screenplay for the series. This screenwriter with a mysterious biography wrote nine episodes for *Alfred Hitchcock Presents*.

TV Actors and a Disappearance

The main female character, Babs Fenton, is played by Mary Scott. This California-born actress played numerous roles on television. She appeared in three other episodes of the series (not directed by Hitchcock). She was the wife of actor Cedric Hardwicke (*Rope*, 1948; "Wet Saturday," 1956), whom she divorced in 1961.

Robert Horton plays the film's irritated and bored husband. This actor with an extensive TV filmography would star, between 1965 and 1966, in the television series *A Man Called Shenandoah*, in which he played an amnesiac cowboy in search of his identity. He made few film appearances. He did, however, make an appearance in Kinji Fukasaku's extravagant American-Japanese science-fiction film *The Green Slime* in 1968. He appeared in six other episodes of the series, not directed by Hitchcock.

The end credits mention the actress Eloise Hardt, credited, depending on the source, with the role of a maid or an old woman. However, she does not appear in the film, which features only four characters. The sequence in which she appeared was probably cut during editing.

A Televisual Variant of *Rear Window*

"Mr. Blanchard's Secret" can obviously be seen as a variant of *Rear Window*. The main character is a Sunday novelist who, like the photographer L. B. Jefferies, played by James Stewart in the 1954 film, projects her own fantasies onto the inhabitants of the house next door. But unlike Jefferies, who interprets a number of signs and events that actually occurred in the apartment across the street as the signature of a crime, the young woman draws her conclusions from the fact that she sees nothing. In her opinion,

Alfred Hitchcock Presents...

Hitchcock stands under an umbrella and asks the viewer to check the fishbowl on the TV set for leaks. Then he announces the film to follow as "a tale of mystery and intrigue laid in middle-class suburbia."

the proof that the neighbor has been murdered is that she is invisible!

Social and Sexual Envy

There are many reasons for Babs Fenton's interest in the couple opposite. One is envy, which arises when, after sneaking into her neighbors' bedroom, she discovers the wardrobe of a woman visibly richer and more sexually fulfilled than herself (as suggested by the silk negligées, signs of obvious sensuality). Her own desire to kill this happier neighbor is reflected in her certainty that the neighbor killed his wife. But reality belies the macabre hypothesis of murder, with Mrs. Blanchard making regular neighborly visits.

Desperate Housewife

Mrs. Fenton's fertile imagination is also rooted in marital dysfunction, a recurring theme in the series. By pretending to be asleep when he is in the same room as her, Babs's husband tries to escape her incessant chatter and morbid fantasies. These are obviously triggered by intense sexual frustration. The young housewife's interest in the couple across the street is a way for her to avoid questioning her own life. The murder fantasy makes up for the emotional or sexual emptiness of her own existence. Moreover, the hypothesis of a murderous neighbor spares her from realizing that this desire for annihilation may be felt by her own husband, whose potential victim she could be. The ordinary, unremarkable life of the average American in the 1950s, the great subject of the series, produces fantasies that are as much desires for catastrophe and death. Lacking mystery in her existence, the wife desperately invents a secret.

One More Mile to Go

Season 2, Episode 28

United States • **26 mins** • **Black and White** • **Mono** (RCA Sound Recording) • **1.33:1**

SYNOPSIS

Production Dates: January 9–11, 1957
Broadcast in the United States: April 7, 1957

Production: Shamley Productions
Producer: Alfred Hitchcock
Associate Producer: Joan Harrison

**Based on a short story by
F. J. Smith (1956)**
Adaptation: James P. Cavanagh
Director of Photography:
John L. Russell
Sound: William Lynch

Assistant Director: Hilton A. Green
Art Direction: John J. Lloyd
Set Decoration: Ralph Sylos
Hair Stylist: Florence Bush
Makeup: Jack Barron
Costumes: Vincent Dee
Music: Stanley Wilson
Film Editing: Edward W. Williams,
Richard G. Wray

Starring: David Wayne (Sam Jacoby),
Steve Brodie (motorcycle cop), Louise
Larabee (Mrs. Jacoby), Norman Leavitt
(gas station attendant), Alfred Hitchcock
(himself) . . .

One night, Sam Jacoby kills his wife in a fit of rage. He puts the corpse in the trunk of his car and looks for a place to dispose of it. A police motorcyclist stops him and points out that his rear light is defective. When the driver is forced to open the trunk to identify the fault, the taillight comes back on. Later, Sam is forced to stop a second time. The policeman reappears and orders him to follow him to the police station to make sure the bulb is changed...

Collaborations

The origin of the film is a short story by F. J. Smith published in *Manhunt* magazine in June 1956. Another short story by this writer gave rise to an episode in season 3 of the series, "Reward to Finder." directed by James Neilson. The adaptation for the small screen is by screenwriter James P. Cavanagh. Born in New York, Cavanagh worked on a number of television serials from 1951 onward, including *Suspense* (fifteen episodes), *Climax!* (nine), *Playhouse 90* (six), and, of course, *Alfred Hitchcock Presents* (no less than fifteen). He also wrote another Hitchcock-directed TV movie, "Arthur" (the first of season 5), in 1959.

The Prey and the Hunter

The film's lead role was played by David Wayne, who would go on to enjoy a prolific career, especially in television. He played the hero of the *Ellery Queen* (1975–1976) and *House Calls* (1979–1982) television series. On the silver screen, he appeared in William Dieterle's *Portrait of Jennie*, George Cukor's *Adam's Rib*, and Samuel Fuller's *Hell and High Water*. His most memorable role was undoubtedly that of the child killer in Joseph Losey's *M* (1951), the American remake of Fritz Lang's German film *M*. "One More Mile to Go" was his only appearance on *Alfred Hitchcock Presents*.

The motorcycle policeman is played by Steve Brodie. Accustomed to playing tough guys in a number of A- and B-level films, he appeared in Jacques Tourneur's *Out of the Past*, Anthony Mann's *Winchester '73*, and Samuel Fuller's *The Steel Helmet*. The second half of his career was spent almost exclusively on television. Coincidentally, he also played a police lieutenant in Joseph Losey's *M*, in which he tracked down the assassin played by David Wayne.

The Eternal Struggle Between Men and Women

The first image of "One More Mile to Go," the one that immediately follows the episode's introduction, shows a house in the dark, with a lighted window that seems to symbolize the small window of the TV screen. The camera slowly approaches and catches, on the other side of the glass, a couple in the middle of a domestic dispute. The woman seems to be harassing the man, who, after a few minutes, clearly fed up with the torture, reflexively strikes his wife's skull with a poker. Throughout the scene, the dialogue is inaudible. No matter what is said, it is the immanent, immemorial struggle of men and women that the spectator witnesses, reduced to a position of

Alfred Hitchcock Presents...

The filmmaker appears with his own severed head in hand and declares, in verse: "Most of you are wondering how Anne Boleyn lost her head. King Henry VIII, fed up with her, said, 'Let her be beheaded.'" Again in verse, he describes the episode to follow: "Our tale tonight is about modern life and how to get rid of a problem… the wife."

voyeur of the intimacy of others, like the photographer in *Rear Window* (1954).

How to Make a Corpse Disappear

The second part of the film, in which we have to wait some ten minutes before hearing the first dialogue, is a new variation on the motif of dealing with a corpse. How do you make a troublesome corpse disappear? This question, already humorously at the heart of *The Trouble with Harry* (1954), will also be posed for the killer in *Psycho*, filmed three years later. But this is not the only similarity between "One More Mile to Go" and the 1960 film.

A Sketch for *Psycho*

In fact, this episode is the testing ground for the kind of suspense that Hitchcock would bring to a high degree of intensity and perfection later in his career. The viewer identifies with the "hero," who is regularly stopped by a policeman who wants to help him repair his rear light, putting him at risk of having to open his trunk and reveal a corpse, and hopes to see him escape his fate. Hitchcock thus places the viewer on the side of the "bad guy," speculating on the ontological fear of the law that is one of the driving forces behind his work. With unrestrained sadism, the audience is manipulated, regularly distressed, then relieved when Sam Jacoby escapes the trunk search through a series of lucky breaks. It is impossible not to identify "One More Mile to Go" and the suspense it develops as an outline of the sequence from *Psycho* in which Marion Crane (Janet Leigh), who has just stolen a large sum of money, is stopped on the road by a suspicious motorcyclist. The episode demonstrates just how ideal a medium television was for experimenting with Hitchcock's cinematographic work.

The Perfect Crime

Season 3, Episode 3

United States • **25 mins** • **Black and White** • **Mono** (RCA Sound Recording) • **1.33:1**

SYNOPSIS

Production Dates: July 17–19, 1957
Broadcast in the United States: October 20, 1957

Production: Shamley Productions
Producer: Alfred Hitchcock
Associate Producer: Joan Harrison

Based on a short story by Ben Ray Redman (1928)
Adaptation: Stirling Silliphant
Director of Photography: John L. Russell
Sound: William Lynch
Assistant Director: Hilton A. Green
Art Direction: John J. Lloyd
Set Decoration: James S. Redd
Hair Stylist: Florence Bush

Makeup: Robert Dawn
Costumes: Vincent Dee
Music: Stanley Wilson
Film Editing: Edward W. Williams, Richard G. Wray

Starring: Vincent Price (Charles Courtney), James Gregory (John Gregory), Gavin Gordon (Ernest West), Marianne Stewart (Alice West), Mark Dana (Harrington), Charles Webster (reporter), John Zaremba (photographer), Nick Nicholson (reporter), Therese Lyon (the Wests' housekeeper), Alfred Hitchcock (himself) . . .

Charles Courtney is a prominent detective who has solved numerous criminal cases. One evening, he receives a visit from lawyer John Gregory. Gregory demonstrates to him that Harrington, a man recently executed on the strength of Courtney's deductions, was innocent. Courtney murders Gregory and after throwing the body into his ceramic kiln transforms it into a vase that he displays on a shelf, alongside other objects linked to bloody events, as an exemplary illustration of the perfect crime.

Season 3, Episode 3

It was not an episode directed by Hitchcock that opened the third season of *Alfred Hitchcock Presents*. "The Perfect Crime" was broadcast on October 20, 1957, after two episodes, including the bizarre Robert Stevens–directed "Glass Eye," whose weirdness was a spectacular start to the new season. The screenplay for "The Perfect Crime" is based on a short story by Ben Ray Redman, first published in *Harper's Bazaar* in August 1928. Redman was a New York–born writer, editor, and literary critic. He contributed to the *New York Times*, *Harper's Bazaar*, the *American Mercury* and, above all, the *Saturday Review of Literature*. None of his other short stories were adapted for the screen, and he committed suicide in 1961. The story was adapted by Stirling Silliphant. Originally from Canada, Silliphant started out as an advertising executive for Walt Disney and began writing screenplays in 1955. After working extensively in television, he went on to contribute to the screenplays of numerous Hollywood films. He wrote eleven episodes of the *Alfred Hitchcock Presents* series.

A Perfect Role for Vincent Price

The Perfect Crime benefits from the presence of Vincent Price. Born in Missouri, this actor with an impressive filmography, a suave voice, and a sharp sense of humor, capable of moving from the sophisticated to the grotesque, played in several masterpieces of postwar Hollywood cinema, including Otto Preminger's *Laura*, Samuel Fuller's *The Baron of Arizona*, and Fritz Lang's *While the City Sleeps*. In the late 1950s, under the impetus of filmmakers such as William Castle and Roger Corman, he became a mythical figure in horror cinema. He appeared only once in the *Alfred Hitchcock Presents* series, in this episode, where his role as a pompous, incompetent, and murderous criminologist suited him perfectly. He recalled with humor his work with the director, who, he said, would sometimes ask James Gregory and him (Price) to "go faster," before falling asleep in his chair.

An Ideal Stooge

James Gregory provides the perfect foil for Vincent Price. Born in New York, he was a perennial supporting actor. He appeared in numerous TV series, including *Danger*, *The Lawless Years* (in which he played the main character, a policeman at war with organized crime in the 1920s), *Thriller*, *The Twilight Zone*, and, of course, *Alfred Hitchcock Presents* (in three episodes). He also played the notable role of a

fiercely anti-communist US senator in John Frankenheimer's 1962 film *The Manchurian Candidate*.

The Fabrication of a Culprit

Much more than the story of a miscarriage of justice caused by incompetence, which takes the form of a dialogue between Gregory and Courtney and a few silent flashbacks, "The Perfect Crime" is about the fabrication of a culprit. Here, it is the arrogance of an overconfident detective, unable to decipher the signs (footprints in the mud, the peculiarity of the murder weapon), that determines the fate of an innocent man. As for the motif of transference of guilt, frequently present in Hitchcock's work (*Strangers on a Train*, 1950; *I Confess*, 1952), it is embodied here in the way Harrington, the "wrong man," allows himself to be convicted in place of the woman he loves.

Treatment of the Body

In the film's final sequence, the audience understands that, after murdering Gregory, Courtney has thrown his corpse into a ceramic kiln and reduced it to a kind of clay, from which he has made a vase. This vase is displayed for journalists to see when they come to interview him. The transformation of the corpse into an everyday or even consumable object will be the subject of a later episode, "Arthur" (season 5). This operation of transmutation is perhaps the exemplary success of a project of many assassins in Hitchcock's cinema. "The absence of the *corpus delicti* is curiously troublesome to the police," declares the detective, who then puts this truth into practice by transforming his victim's body into an object, the display of which will cynically remind us of the possibility of the perfect crime.

Four O'Clock

Season 1, Episode 1

United States • 50 mins • Black and White • Mono (RCA Sound Recording) • 1.33:1

SYNOPSIS

Production Dates: July 29–August 2, 1957
Broadcast in the United States: September 30, 1957

Production: Shamley Productions
Executive Producer: Alfred Hitchcock
Associate Producer: Joan Harrison

Based on a short story by Cornell Woolrich (1938)
Adaptation: Francis Cockrell
Director of Photography: John L. Russell
Sound: William Lynch
Assistant Director: Hilton A. Green
Art Direction: John J. Lloyd

Set Decoration: James S. Redd
Hair Stylist: Florence Bush
Makeup: Jack Barron
Costumes: Vincent Dee
Music: Stanley Wilson
Film Editing: Edward W. Williams, Richard G. Wray

Starring: Nancy Kelly (Fran Steppe), E. G. Marshall (Paul Steppe), Richard Long (Dave), Tom Pittman (Joe), Harry Dean Stanton (Bill), Charles Seel (client), Jesslyn Fax (woman), Vernon Rich (doctor), David Armstrong (policeman), Juney Ellis (mother), Brian Corcoran (boy), Chuck Webster (boy), Dennis O'Keefe (himself) . . .

Paul Steppe, a watchmaker, suspects his wife of cheating on him. He installs a time bomb of his own making in their cellar, whose explosion is intended to kill both his wife and her alleged lover. But two burglars bind and gag him in the basement in front of the deadly device. He tries in vain to raise the alarm. A blown fuse prevents the bomb from exploding. But the jealous husband, terrorized and subjected all this time to an infernal countdown, has lapsed into a state of madness.

Suspicion

In 1957, Shamley Productions, the company created by Hitchcock for television, signed a contract with NBC to produce ten episodes out of forty for a new series called *Suspicion*. Another ten episodes would come from Revue Productions, and twenty would be dramas shot live on the East Coast. These were almost hour-long stories, foreshadowing *The Alfred Hitchcock Hour*, the television series upon which the filmmaker would embark in 1962. He directed only one episode of the series, which lasted one season. The film is presented by actor Dennis O'Keefe.

A Short Story by Cornell Woolrich

"Four O'Clock" is the first episode in the *Suspicion* series. It is an adaptation of a short story by Cornell Woolrich published in *Detective Fiction Weekly* in October 1938. Woolrich was the author of the story that gave rise to *Rear Window* (1954). Many of his short stories were adapted for television (six episodes of the *Suspense* series between 1949 and 1950, three episodes of *Alfred Hitchcock Presents* between 1956 and 1958, three episodes of *Thriller* in 1961, and one episode of *The Alfred Hitchcock Hour* in 1962). Several of his novels, often published under the pseudonym William Irish, were adapted for the cinema: Jacques Tourneur's *The Leopard Man*, Robert Siodmak's *Phantom Lady*, François Truffaut's *The Bride Wore Black*, and *Mississippi Mermaid*. Francis Cockrell, an American television Stakhanovite (eighteen collaborations on *Alfred Hitchcock Presents*), was in charge of bringing the short story to the small screen. He also worked on another episode of the *Suspicion* series, "Lord Arthur Savile's Crime," based on a work by Oscar Wilde.

Husband and Wife

The lead role, that of the paranoid husband and murderer consumed by jealousy, went to E. G. Marshall. An actor with a rich career in both film and television, he made his mark in Delbert Mann's *The Bachelor Party* and Sidney Lumet's *12 Angry Men* in 1957. He also played memorable roles in Edward Dmytryk's *Broken Lance* and Richard Fleischer's *Compulsion*. He twice played President Eisenhower on television: in *Ike* in 1986 and *War and Remembrance* in 1988.

Nancy Kelly played the wife suspected of adultery by her husband. She appeared in a number of unremarkable films, with the exception of Henry King's *Jesse James* in 1939, before switching to television.

She appeared in an episode of *The Alfred Hitchcock Hour* series, the frightening "The Lonely Hours," directed by Jack Smight in 1963.

Youth of a Future Star

Harry Dean Stanton (named Dean Stanton in the credits) started filming in 1954 as one of the thugs who bullies Nancy's husband. His late stardom came with roles in Sam Peckinpah's *Pat Garrett and Billy the Kid* and John Milius's *Dillinger* in 1973, Ridley Scott's *Alien* in 1979, and, above all, Wim Wenders's *Paris, Texas* in 1984. He also starred in four David Lynch films: *Wild at Heart*, *Twin Peaks: Fire Walk with Me*, *The Straight Story*, and *Inland Empire*, as well as appearing in the *Twin Peaks* series.

An Overlong Film?

The episode was the subject of a harsh critical review in *Daily Variety* (October 2, 1957), which lamented an unnecessarily drawn-out story: "The talented directing techniques we associate with Hitchcock are adapted to the necessity of spreading over an hour what could last only half an hour. The middle of the film is particularly sluggish, despite efforts to heighten tension through various means of raising false hopes for the victim played by E. G. Marshall. The problem is that it is all too obvious from the outset that these are false hopes." But it could also be argued that the length of the episode, devoted first to the meticulous construction of a device of death, then to the spectacle of a relentless countdown, precisely increases the intolerable nature of the torment inflicted on the man caught in his own trap.

The Rules of Suspense

"Four O'Clock" is a kind of variation on the rules of suspense established by Hitchcock himself. What Hitchcock criticized about his 1936 film *Sabotage*—a bomb explosion that kills a child left alone in ignorance of imminent danger—is this time averted by the protagonist's awareness of his terrible fate. Audience and character share the same knowledge, the same anguish, and the same physical position. Paul Steppe, reduced to impotence, thus joins the club of paralyzed male figures, the first spectators of the possibility of their own destruction: L. B. Jefferies in *Rear Window*, Scottie in *Vertigo* (1957), William Callew in "Breakdown" (1955), Harry Pope in "Poison" (1958).

PARAMOUNT PRESENTS

JAMES STEWART
KIM NOVAK
IN ALFRED HITCHCOCK'S

'VERTIGO'

CO-STARRING BARBARA BEL GEDDES WITH TOM HELMORE · HENRY JONES DIRECTED BY ALFRED HITCHCOCK SCREENPLAY BY ALEC COPPEL & SAMUEL TAYLOR TECHNICOLOR® VISTAVISION®
BASED UPON THE NOVEL D'ENTRE LES MORTS BY PIERRE BOILEAU AND THOMAS NARCEJAC MUSIC BY BERNARD HERRMANN

Vertigo

 United States • **2 hrs 8** • **Color** • **Mono**
(Westrex Recording System) • **1.85:1**
(VistaVision)

Production Dates: September 30–December 19, 1957
Release Date in the United States: May 9, 1958 (premiere, San Francisco),
May 28, 1958 (United States)

Production: Paramount, Alfred J. Hitchcock Productions
Producer: Alfred Hitchcock
Associate Producer: Herbert Coleman

Based on a novel by Pierre Boileau and Thomas Narcejac,
***D'entre les morts* (*The Living and the Dead*) (1954)**
Screenplay: Alec Coppel, Samuel Taylor
Director of Photography: Robert Burks
Camera Operator: Leonard J. South
Titles Designer: Saul Bass
Special Sequence (nightmare scene): John Ferren
Visual Effects: John P. Fulton, Farciot Edouart, Wallace Kelley
Technicolor Adviser: Richard Mueller
Sound: Harold Lewis, Winston Leverett
Assistant Director: Daniel J. McCauley
Continuity: Peggy Robertson
Art Direction: Hal Pereira, Henry Bumstead
Set Decoration: Sam Comer, Frank McKelvy
Hair Stylist: Nellie Manley
Makeup: Wally Westmore
Costumes: Edith Head
Music: Bernard Herrmann
Film Editing: George Tomasini

Starring: James Stewart (John "Scottie" Ferguson), Kim Novak (Madeleine Elster/
Judy Barton), Barbara Bel Geddes (Midge Wood), Tom Helmore (Gavin Elster),
Henry Jones (coroner), Raymond Bailey (doctor), Ellen Corby (manager of the
McKittrick hotel), Konstantin Shayne (Pop Leibel), Lee Patrick (car owner mistaken
for Madeleine), Nina Shipman (woman mistaken for Madeleine in the museum),
Dori Simmons (woman mistaken for Madeleine at Ernie's), David Ahdar (priest),
Margaret Bacon (nun), Margaret Brayton (Ransohoff saleslady), Jean Corbett
(Madeleine Elster), Fred Graham (policeman on the roof),
Alfred Hitchcock (passerby)...

SYNOPSIS

——

The setting is San Francisco. Because of his fear of heights, which accidentally led to the death of a policeman during a rooftop chase, Detective Scottie Ferguson resigns. Midge, an ex-fiancée, looks after him. Knowing that he is unemployed, his old friend Gavin Elster asks him to shadow Madeleine, his young, blond wife. Madeleine is said to be haunted by the spirit of Carlotta Valdes, a great-grandmother who committed suicide when she was Madeleine's age. Skeptical, Scottie follows Madeleine by car: She visits a florist, her ancestor's grave, her portrait in a museum, a hotel room, then she goes under the Golden Gate Bridge, where she throws herself into the water. Scottie saves her and falls in love with her and her story. He accompanies her to the seaside, where they kiss, then into a forest, and finally to the Spanish mission where Carlotta once lived. But his fear of heights prevents him from reaching her before she falls from the top of the church tower. Scottie falls into a depression. He drifts along until one day he meets Judy, a young dark-haired woman who reminds him of Madeleine. A flashback tells the viewer that Judy must have been playing a role: She is Madeleine, and Madeleine is an invention of Elster's to get rid of his real wife by throwing her off the church tower in front of Scottie, who has been deceived about the identity of the suicide victim. Scottie obliges Judy to look exactly like Madeleine, which she agrees to out of love. But a necklace she has kept betrays her. Scottie forces her back to the scene of the crime and, together this time, they reach the summit. Judy, frightened, falls to her death, leaving Scottie cured of his vertigo and on the verge of madness.

"Suspense is like a woman. The greater the part played by the imagination, the greater the emotion."

——

Alfred Hitchcock

GENESIS

Hitchcock closely followed the publications of the two writers Boileau-Narcejac. In 1954, one of their thrillers was adapted as *Les Diaboliques* by Henri-Georges Clouzot, hastily dubbed "the French Hitchcock" by the press. The same year saw the publication of another of their stories, *D'entre les morts* (*The Living and the Dead*). Even before it had been translated, Paramount Studios provided the Master with a summary, and he expressed an interest in this story of a man who is madly in love with the "ideal woman," who has been elevated to iconic status after her death, to the point where he dreams of resurrecting her image by any means possible.

First Attempts

The novel takes place between Paris and Marseille, first in 1940, then in 1944. Hitchcock retained this two-stage structure but set the plot in the mid-1950s in San Francisco, "an American Paris,"[1] as he put it. He insisted on entrusting the adaptation to playwright Maxwell Anderson (*The Wrong Man*), who, in September 1956, delivered a first draft that already included the Mission Dolores Cemetery (where the grave of Carlotta Valdes, Madeleine's "ancestor," is located), but which Hitchcock and Herbert Coleman, his associate producer, found disappointing. A longtime friend of the director, Angus MacPhail, intimidated by the scope of the subject ("a fascinating story," he told Coleman), gave up on trying to improve on it. He did, however, write a two-page plan that began, like the film to come, with a manhunt on the rooftops of San Francisco.

Vertigo Tour

From the summer of 1956, Herbert Coleman crisscrossed the city and the surrounding area, spotting places with Hitchcock that would become unforgettable stations on the sad hero's way of the cross: Ernie's (Scottie and Madeleine's first meeting in the restaurant); Podesta Baldocchi, the florist on Grant Avenue; the museum in Lincoln Park where Carlotta's portrait is on display; the Gothic-style hotel in Gough Street (Madeleine's appearance at the window); the Golden Gate Bridge (Madeleine's "suicide"); the steep streets of San Francisco (car shadowing); the seaside road in Monterey (first kiss); the Spanish mission of San Juan Bautista with its doubly fatal bell tower…

Scriptwriter Number Three

From September to the end of November 1956, the production hired a third scriptwriter, Alec Coppel, who at the time had several stories lined up for episodes of *Alfred Hitchcock Presents*. His version, among other advances, contained the "swirling kiss" scene in Judy/Madeleine's bedroom, including the indication of a 360-degree pan. Hitchcock, Coleman, and James Stewart, selected for the lead role and involved in the production of *Vertigo*, felt that the "Coppel version" was still unsatisfactory, too mechanical.

A Story Coming to Life

A fourth and final writer, whom Hitchcock asked not to read the novel, was to prove decisive. Samuel Taylor had an intimate knowledge of San Francisco and, in turn, was able to identify locations. Above all, he brought the love story to life. He also invented the characters of the bookseller and Midge, Scottie's confidante, the everyday, down-to-earth side of the ethereal and inaccessible Madeleine. Taylor worked from February to July 1957, sometimes with the director and sometimes alone (Hitchcock underwent two operations in quick succession). In any case, in May the two men made a decisive change.

Where Is Hitchcock?

Hitchcock appears shortly after the film begins. A bugle case in hand, he walks past the entrance to a shipyard (Paramount Studios' paint shop), where Gavin Elster (Tom Helmore), the husband of the "possessed" woman, has his office. Unbeknownst to anyone else, Hitchcock's mere presence there indicates the location of the "director" of the diabolical fiction to come. This was the final scene shot on December 19, 1957, the last day of filming for *Vertigo*.

Barbara Bel Geddes, James Stewart, and a view of San Francisco.

A Coup de Force, a Stroke of Genius

Hitchcock convinced Taylor (or vice versa, depending on what they each had to say on the subject) to "twist" the structure of the novel. In *D'entre les morts* (*The Living and the Dead*), the revelation of the plot that ruins Scottie's fateful fantasy traditionally comes at the end. In *Vertigo*, two-thirds of the way through the story, there is a sudden reversal of point of view (the film switches from "male" to "female"): Judy's camera gaze and a flashback that reveals the truth to the audience alone. In this way, the filmmaker replaces the final surprise with suspense: How will Scottie learn what only he now does not know, and how will he react? As for the character of Judy/Madeleine, it immediately assumes a whole new dimension. And in a brilliant stroke of genius, Judy's confession forces the audience to replay the first part of the film in their heads while they eagerly follow the events of the second part: They "see" the film again as they watch it.

Three years later, this narrative audacity would be matched only by the brutal death of Janet Leigh at the forty-sixth minute of *Psycho*. And Hitchcock was so doubtful about his idea for *Vertigo* that, shortly before the film's release in 1958, he cut

the entire scene before reinstating it at the last minute.[2]

CASTING

Although at the start of the project Hitchcock dreamed (as always) of casting Cary Grant, it was not long before James Stewart landed the role of the hapless Scottie. Accustomed to the Master's methods (this was their fourth and last collaboration), the actor was to remain a stable and reassuring element of a constantly thwarted project throughout preproduction and shooting.

Exit Vera Miles

From the outset, Hitchcock dedicated the role of Madeleine to Vera Miles, whom he had introduced to the world ("Revenge" 1955; *The Wrong Man*, 1956). *Vertigo*, of course, was to make her a star. The actress tried on costumes and even served as a model for the first version of Carlotta's painted portrait. But the twists and turns in the script meant that filming had to be postponed several times, and soon she could no longer hide the fact that she was pregnant (March 1957). Depending on whose version of

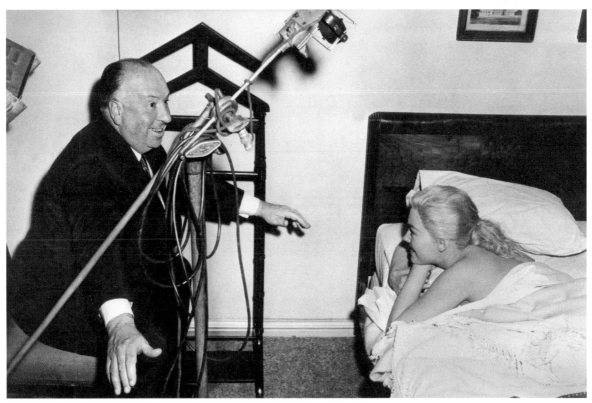

the story is told, Hitchcock was either furious or distraught—probably both.

From One Madeleine to the Other

Harry Cohn, head of Columbia, and Lew Wasserman, Hitchcock's and Stewart's agent, made a deal: Kim Novak, a young Columbia star, would star in *Vertigo* if, in return, Stewart starred in a Columbia film with Novak (*Bell, Book and Candle*, Richard Quine, 1958). Hitchcock had no choice. He certainly found her too overtly sexual, as he preferred a sense of fire under the ice. Above all, Novak arrived with preconceived ideas about her character: her hairstyle, her hair color, her outfits. The filmmaker remained adamant: She was to be blond with a spiral bun, then brunette, then blond again. She wore the entire wardrobe designed for her by Edith Head, a "fashion show" that would have a devastating effect on Scottie's (and the audience's) gaze and his mind: gray suit, green and purple evening gown, red dressing gown with white polka dots, white coat and black scarf, beige and brown pumps…

Pygmalion at the Helm

Just as Scottie modeled Judy in *Vertigo* so that she became Madeleine (again), Hitchcock shaped Kim Novak's look and acting so that she became a Hitchcockian actress: He controlled the rhythm of her diction, deliberately giving her very few cues. To break her resistance, he asked for a face like a blank page, an empty surface capable of holding a "legible" emotion instead of a jumble of expressions. Barbara Bel Geddes, hired for the role of Midge, also remembered the only instruction the director ever gave her: "Don't act! Don't act!" The character of Gavin Elster, the Machiavellian husband, was played by Tom Helmore, who, twenty years earlier, appeared in one of the director's English films, *Secret Agent*.

FILMING AND PRODUCTION

The film script dates from September 12, 1957, a fortnight before the first exterior shots, followed by two months in the studio (October 16–December 19). Delayed for a year, *Vertigo* took advantage of everything that had delayed it; rarely had Hitchcock made a film that was so premeditated.

Dreams and Nightmares

A variation on the myths of Pygmalion and Orpheus (Hitchcock asked set designer Henry Bumstead to use lots of mirrors), *Vertigo* is a dreamlike film. Everything, down to the smallest detail, contributes to creating an unreal atmosphere—for example, the unusual, hypnotic duration of Scottie's shadowing as he "marries" Madeleine with his eyes, a reverie

reinforced by the combination of shots taken in the city and transparencies. Cinematographer Robert Burks played with different filters to diffuse light (in the cemetery, in the forest) and emphasize certain colors (Madeleine's blond hair, the neon green of the Empire Hotel). For Scottie's nightmare, a sequence the like of which he had not dared to try since Salvador Dalí and *Spellbound* (1944), Hitchcock called on John Ferren, an abstract expressionist painter.

The Vertigo of Love

The film's two climaxes, each time in the Spanish mission tower, involve the creation of a spectacular special effect. To make the sensations of vertigo and disorientation very sensitive to the eye, the technical team made a model of the circular staircase and filmed its empty core by combining a zoom-in with a tracking shot (a "trombone shot"). This double countermovement also represents the male character's attraction/repulsion to/from his own desire: "He hates her and hates himself for loving her," wrote Hitchcock on the last page of his shooting script.

The Living and the Dead

With the scene at the Empire Hotel, Scottie's and Hitchcock's obsessions reach their climax. Swathed in an otherworldly light, enveloped in elegiac music, the "dead" Madeleine returns, intact, as if the force of man's desire and the powers of cinema were converging to reverse death. For the vertiginous kiss that ensues between Scottie and Judy, now Madeleine once again, the filmmaker placed the two actors on a turntable and in front of an overhead projection of an earlier scene from the film. The violins go wild, (Hitchcock told his composer, for this scene: "We'll only have the camera and you.")[4] At the sight of this "déjà vu," Scottie thinks he is reaching his highest point of fulfillment. In fact, he plunges into the depths of the tragic illusion in which he indulges.

Freeze Frame

One scene in *Vertigo* takes place in a bookshop in San Francisco's Union Square (also the setting for *The Birds*, 1962). Inspired by a real bookshop in the city, the location was built on a Paramount set where, using the available projectors, Hitchcock discreetly demonstrated his poetic art. As the bookseller tells Carlotta's sad story, daylight gradually fades in a long, fixed shot looking down on the street through the shop window. The filmmaker achieves a perfect studio effect of reality. In a single shot, he repeats what he has achieved on the scale of a film. In *Rope* (1948), a film made in "real time," the action begins in daylight and ends at night: "The change in lighting was so well done that nobody noticed it" (Hitchcock).[3]

For Hitchcock Addicts

In 1962, Chris Marker's *La Jetée*, an apocalyptic photo-novel, also summoned the poetic power of *Vertigo*. In *Sans soleil* (1982), the same filmmaker travels extensively, including in time: During an entire sequence, he lovingly walks in the footsteps of *Vertigo* in San Francisco, referring in the commentary to "a film seen nineteen times." In June 1994, Marker published a lengthy letter about Hitchcock's film in *Positif*, ending with the words: "This text is only for those who know *Vertigo* by heart. But are the others worthy of being addressed?" An incentive to watch the film over and over again, or in a spiral (loop)…

Spirals…

From Christmas 1957 to January 1958, Hitchcock and George Tomasini worked on editing *Vertigo* while Bernard Herrmann created one of his most sumptuous and haunting scores in the period leading up to February. In all, the film contains more than seventy minutes of these musical spirals, inspired by Wagner's *Tristan und Isolde*, and perhaps also by a Norman O'Neill composition for a J. M. Barrie play, *Mary Rose*, heard by Hitchcock in 1920…and of which he asked the studio to unearth a recording.

RECEPTION

At the end of its first run, the film covered its costs (a budget of $2.5 million); in other words, it was a failure for both the studio and the filmmaker. Looking for someone to blame (the film itself, too modern…?), Paramount attacked the conceptual poster designed by Saul Bass, and the East Coast marketing office tried to replace it with more conventional publicity material.

An Infinite Film

Apart from some isolated praise (Hitchcock was an "absolute genius" for the *Hollywood Reporter*), the critical reception was far from warm: The film was too long, too slow and reveals its ending before the end, and there is no happy ending. For the *New Yorker*, "Hitchcock, who produced and directed this thing, had never before indulged in such absurdities." In France, the film was better perceived, particularly in *Cahiers du cinéma* (March 1959), where, among other insights, critic Éric Rohmer scrutinized the spiral motif (Madeleine's bun, the staircase in the tower, Saul Bass's credits, the cutaway trunk of the thousand-year-old sequoia): "Everything comes full circle, but the loop never loops completely; the revolution always leads us a little deeper into reminiscence."

The Grand Illusion

Slowly at first, then with each rerelease and restoration (1983, 1996, 2014), *Vertigo* has continued to be rediscovered, reevaluated, and acclaimed until today, when it is now the object of a cinephile cult. A 2012 poll in *Sight and Sound* named it the greatest film of all time. Indeed, for its admirers, *Vertigo* expressed, like no film before it, their fascination with cinema itself. Scottie is a spectator in the first part; in the second, he becomes a "director." By its very plot and its impossible repetition, Vertigo reveals cinematic time: that of theatrical projection (a deceptively looping duration), during which the audience also experiences the passage of their own existence, the slow, true nightmare of "the spiral of time [that] never stops swallowing the present and widening the contours of the past."[5] And if love and cinema dream of eternalizing the present, Hitchcock's cinema alone denounces the illusion of time regained. In other words, *Vertigo* indulges in unbridled romanticism, relentlessly deconstructing its high hopes. The filmmaker does not exclude himself from this fascination, where woman and cinema are one and the same. On the contrary, he creates a necrophiliac fairy tale in which he performs an autopsy on the forms of his mind and perception.

ne at the museum (Kim Novak).

Edith Head,
Supreme Elegance

She was the woman who made more than a thousand films and won eight Oscars. The queen of costume designers, Edith Head (1897–1981) was intimately involved in Hitchcock's direction, all the better to sublimate it.

A Newcomer

Born in California, Edith Claire Posener kept the name of her first husband, Charles Head, throughout her life, having divorced him in 1936. After studying literature, Edith Head taught art and French at an all-girls school and perfected her drawing skills in evening classes. Specializing in landscapes, the young woman knew nothing about costume design when she interviewed for a job at Paramount in 1924. She was hired on the strength of a portfolio of sketches borrowed from her classmates.

Paramount Girl

Howard Greer and Travis Banton, who headed Paramount's costume department, took the young woman under their wing. At a time when no experience was required to break into the industry, Edith Head rose through the ranks thanks to her flair and inventiveness. Following Howard Greer's alcoholism problems, the young assistant became Travis Banton's right-hand woman. When Banton left Paramount in 1938, she naturally took over as head of the department.

The Birth of a Profession

Hollywood studios set up costume departments in 1918: Before then, actors drew directly from their own wardrobes. Banton and Greer at Paramount, Erté and Adrian at MGM, gave the profession its

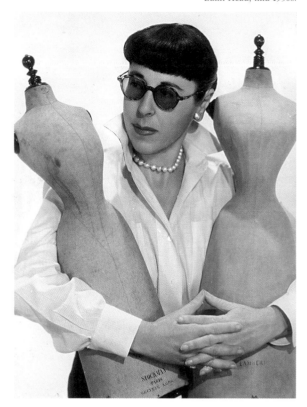

Edith Head, mid-1950s.

letters of nobility; the general public knew their names and, like the filmmakers, they were the artisans of Hollywood glamour. From Greta Garbo to Marlene Dietrich, they helped forge its most beautiful myths. In turn, Edith Head became a star costume designer, creating memorable outfits for Clara Bow, Jean Harlow, and Barbara Stanwyck. At this time, the moguls wanted to make Hollywood the fashion capital of the world.

Creator of Visions

In 1945, Edith Head was "loaned" by RKO to dress Ingrid Bergman in *Notorious*, creating the provocative zebra blouse that revealed her belly. Head and Hitchcock met again for *To Catch a Thief* (1954) and were to remain close until the director's last film (*Family Plot*, 1975). Their highly respectful collaboration spanned almost thirty years and eleven films. Edith Head knew how to give shape to the filmmaker's visions. In her words, Hitchcock "spoke the language of the stylist, even though he knew nothing about clothes. He would specify colors in the script if they were important. If he wanted a skirt that grazed a desk when a woman walked by, he'd specify that too."[1]

Show Dresses

In the enclosed world of *Rear Window* (1954), Grace Kelly's every outfit is a jewel of refinement, reflecting her character's social origins. But the costume designer had a favorite film: *To Catch a Thief*, a veritable haute couture fashion show that imbues the actress and the shots with unreality. Head makes Hitchcock's wishes come true, and vice versa: *To Catch a Thief* was "a costume designer's dream," crowned by the masked ball and the gold-thread-stitched dress worn by Grace Kelly.

The Art of Disappearing

Costumes can be the highlight of the show, but Edith Head also knew how to keep things simple. In *To Catch a Thief*, Hitchcock wanted dresses with simple lines so as not to detract from the brilliance of Kelly's finery. In *The Birds* (1962), he asked Head to ensure that the audience paid no attention to Tippi Hedren's clothes, so as not to be distracted from the spectacle of her terror. Any brightly colored clothing must be justified in advance.

The Little Gray Suit

In *Vertigo* (1957), Scottie (James Stewart) takes Judy (Kim Novak) shopping and forces her to wear a gray suit. On set, Kim Novak agreed to wear any color except gray—even though gray was stipulated in the script. Head explained that "[When] Hitch paints a picture in his films, that color is as important to him as it is to any artist."[2] The filmmaker's response could have been a line from Scottie: "I don't care what she wears as long as it's a gray suit."[2]

The Undresser

If Hitchcock, according to Head, was the most precise of filmmakers, it was because every female silhouette (and every shot) must take the shape of a mental image. Like Scottie, he does not compromise on his visions—even when it comes to choosing his actresses' underwear. His fascinating conception of costume could be summed up in this confession to François Truffaut about *Vertigo*: "All James Stewart's efforts to re-create woman, cinematographically, are shown as if he were trying to undress her instead of dressing her." When Judy slips away to add the final touch (the bun) to her outfit, "Stewart expects her to return naked this time, ready for love."[3]

Lamb to the Slaughter

Season 3, Episode 28

 • • • • □

United States • **30 mins** • **Black and White** • **Mono** (RCA Sound Recording) • **1.33:1**

SYNOPSIS

Production Dates: February 18–19, 1958
Broadcast in the United States: April 13, 1958

Production: Shamley Productions
Producer: Joan Harrison
Associate Producer: Norman Lloyd

Based on a short story by Roald Dahl (1953)
Adaptation: Roald Dahl
Director of Photography: John L. Russell
Sound: William Lynch
Assistant Director: Hilton A. Green

Art Direction: John J. Lloyd
Set Decoration: James S. Redd
Hair Stylist: Florence Bush
Makeup: Jack Barron
Costumes: Vincent Dee
Film Editing: Edward W. Williams, Richard G. Wray

Starring: Barbara Bel Geddes (Mary Maloney), Harold J. Stone (Lieutenant Jack Noonan), Allan Lane (Patrick Maloney), Ken Clark (Mike, lieutenant's assistant), Robert C. Ross (forensic doctor), William Keene (policeman), Thomas Wild (policeman), Otto Waldis (Sam), Alfred Hitchcock (himself) . . .

One night, policeman Patrick Maloney tells his pregnant wife, Mary, that he is leaving her for someone else, and she kills him by knocking him unconscious with a frozen leg of lamb, then puts the meat in the oven. She tells the police that she found her husband's body when she came home from shopping. The puzzled investigators wonder how the murder was committed. She offers them dinner, and they eat the (finally) cooked leg of lamb, still wondering about the weapon that killed Maloney.

First Collaboration with Roald Dahl

"Lamb to the Slaughter" marked Alfred Hitchcock's first collaboration with writer Roald Dahl, who adapted his own short story for the small screen. Six of Dahl's stories were later adapted for *Alfred Hitchcock Presents*, including four in episodes directed by Hitchcock himself. Roald Dahl was born in Wales, became a fighter pilot and then a member of the British secret service at the start of World War II, and began writing in 1942. Although he is best known for his children's stories (*Charlie and the Chocolate Factory*), he also wrote numerous short stories for adults, sarcastic and gritty, sometimes with a hint of the fantastic and often with surprising endings. It is hardly surprising that Hitchcock appreciated his style and his cruel stories with their incredible coups de theatre. His writings were adapted for television, even before the Hitchcock-produced drama. Later, between 1979 and 1988, the English series *Tales of the Unexpected*, after the title of one of his collections of short stories, featured episodes inspired by his work. The writer introduced each film in the first two seasons. Roald Dahl also contributed to the writing of a James Bond adventure, *You Only Live Twice* (1967).

The Model Wife

The lead role, that of Mary Maloney, was played by Barbara Bel Geddes, who returned to Alfred Hitchcock just after *Vertigo*, where she played Midge, the friend in love with Scottie (James Stewart) but unwanted in return. Her role as the "exemplary" wife in "Lamb to the Slaughter" can be seen as the darker side of her *Vertigo* character, in which she represented the prosaic real world from which a man trapped by his imagination wanted to escape. The episode continues to make her a symbol—this time to the point of madness—of the horizonless reality of everyday married life. She appeared in three further episodes of *Alfred Hitchcock Presents*. Then, between 1978 and 1990, she played the character of Ellie Ewing in *Dallas*, the famous TV drama series.

Male Figures

The hapless husband was played by Allan Lane, who played intrepid Wild West heroes in countless B movies from the mid-1940s onward. He was also the voice of Mr. Ed, "the talking horse," in the hit TV series of the same name, produced between 1961 and 1966. This was his only appearance in the *Alfred Hitchcock Presents* series. The police lieutenant was played by Harold J. Stone, a familiar face on American TV and a supporting actor in a number of

notable films (Stanley Kubrick's *Spartacus*, George Cukor's *The Chapman Report*). His assistant was played by Ken Clark, who started out in B movies and continued his career in Italy, appearing in James Bond genre imitations and spaghetti Westerns.

Conjugal Murder

"Lamb to the Slaughter" opens with a scene of conjugal murder, a recurring theme in the series. Mary greets her husband, showering him with attention, to the extent of suffocating him with a torrent of words. He remains silent for a long time, then tells her that he is going to leave her for another woman. The strangeness of the scene lies in the sensation of witnessing a model of suave domestic hell, making the man's murder all the more shocking. After a moment's daze, as if unaware of her husband's announcement, the wife continues to act like an automaton, like an exemplary housewife. Then, still in a daze, she knocks him unconscious with a frozen leg of lamb.

The Monstrous Leg of Lamb

Food plays a central role in this episode. It is a recurrent motif in the director's filmography, where greed and repulsion often merge. By becoming the weapon of a crime, the leg of lamb suddenly acquires a special status. At the start of the episode, Mary reminds her husband that she is pregnant. This information undoubtedly serves two purposes: to heighten the viewer's compassion in the face of the young woman's abandonment, and to give a new dimension to this mother-to-be, the most menacing entity in Hitchcock's work. In one shot, when the leg of lamb is removed from the oven to feed the policemen, it becomes a kind of monstrous embryo. The idea of death mingles furtively with that of maternity.

Alfred Hitchcock Presents...

In a supermarket, Hitchcock, holding a shopping cart, is ticketed by a policeman. He says he was punished "for parking in a store aisle at rush hour." At the end of the episode, he announces that Mary has been arrested after trying to kill her second husband in the same way as her first. This time, however, the freezer had not been plugged in, so "the meat was too soft."

Dip in the Pool

Season 3, Episode 35

United States · 26 mins · Black and White · Mono (RCA Sound Recording) · 1.33:1

SYNOPSIS

Production Dates: February 18–19, 1958
Broadcast in the United States: June 1, 1958

Production: Shamley Productions
Producer: Joan Harrison
Associate Producer: Norman Lloyd

Based on a short story by Roald Dahl (1952)
Adaptation: Robert C. Dennis
Director of Photography: John F. Warren
Sound: Stephen J. Bass
Assistant Director: Hilton A. Green

Art Direction: John J. Lloyd
Set Decoration: James S. Redd
Hair Stylist: Florence Bush
Makeup: Leo Lotito Jr.
Costumes: Vincent Dee
Film Editing: Edward W. Williams, Richard G. Wray

Starring: Keenan Wynn (William Botibol), Fay Wray (Mrs. Renshaw), Philip Bourneuf (Mr. Renshaw), Louise Platt (Ethel Botibol), Doreen Lang (Emily), Ralph Clanton (ship's purser), Doris Lloyd (Emily's mother), Ashley Cowan (captain), Owen Cunningham (auctioneer), Alfred Hitchcock (himself) . . .

Mr. and Mrs. Botibol are on an Atlantic cruise. To get away from his wife, the cash-strapped husband takes part in a bet to guess how far the transatlantic liner will travel in twenty-four hours. Realizing that the favorable weather conditions would make him lose his bet, he decides to slow the boat down by throwing himself into the water in front of a witness, who will sound the alarm. Alas, the woman who witnesses his dive is a simple-minded woman whom no one takes seriously.

A "Children's" Author and Prolific Screenwriter

After "Lamb to the Slaughter," Hitchcock directed the adaptation of another Roald Dahl short story, "Dip in the Pool," published in 1952 in the *New Yorker*. Dahl was the author of numerous short stories, some for children, others for adults in the know. Robert C. Dennis, who wrote the adaptation, was a Canadian-born screenwriter working mainly for television. In all, he wrote some thirty episodes for the *Alfred Hitchcock Presents* series.

Husband and Wife

The leading male role, that of William Botibol, was played by Keenan Wynn, who would have a long career in Hollywood, usually in supporting roles. Born in New York, he made his film debut in the early 1940s, appearing in numerous Hollywood films of all genres. Two of his most famous performances were as Colonel Guano in Stanley Kubrick's *Dr. Strangelove* and as the auctioneer in Sergio Leone's *Once Upon a Time in the West*. He also appeared in numerous TV series, including two episodes of *Alfred Hitchcock Presents*.

Ethel Botibol was played by Louise Platt. She is remembered for her role as the officer's pregnant young wife in John Ford's *Stagecoach*. She also appeared in an episode of the second season of *Alfred Hitchcock Presents*.

A Grande Dame of Cinema

Fay Wray (Mrs. Renshaw, one of the ship's passengers) also starred in this episode. Born in Canada, she began her career in silent films in 1923. Her most memorable role was that of Mitzi in Erich von Stroheim's *The Wedding March* in 1928. She made the transition to talking pictures without difficulty, and her career lasted until the 1960s, with an eclipse between 1942 and 1953. Her real claims to fame were the roles of Eve in Schoedsack and Pichel's *The Most Dangerous Game* in 1932 and, above all, Ann Darrow, the "screaming girl," in Schoedsack and Cooper's *King Kong* in 1933.

A Hitchcockian Supporting Role

Emily, the woman who witnesses the unfortunate gambler plunge into the ocean, was played by Doreen Lang. She appeared in three Hitchcock features: *The Wrong Man*, 1956 (one of the insurance company employees); *North by Northwest*, 1958 (Roger Thornhill / Cary Grant's secretary); and *The Birds* 1962 (the anxious mother in the restaurant).

Alfred Hitchcock Presents...

Lying on the deck of a transatlantic liner, the filmmaker reads an issue of *Alfred Hitchcock's Mystery Magazine*, and his photo appears prominently on the cover. Concluding the episode, he adds that the story had a happy ending: The ship having been delayed by an engine problem, Mr. Botibol won his bet. "Unfortunately, he was no longer around to enjoy his money, but his wife and her second husband enjoyed it."

Conjugal Incompatibility

"Dip in the Pool" is another tale of marital disharmony. Spending a small family inheritance during a cruise, the Botibol couple express very different conceptions of existence, most likely determined by a difference in social background. Ethel Botibol lists the monuments of Florence she wishes to visit, while her husband scoffs at this costly cultural trip, expressing a common sense far too prosaic for her: "If you can't drink it, wear it, or drive it, it's of no value to you," she reproaches him. In his wife's eyes, Mr. Botibol is nothing more than a peasant to be ashamed of. In another scene, the wife sets out the couple's schedule for their imminent trip to Paris, demonstrating a particularly suffocating desire for control.

Castrating Wife-Mother Figure and a Man-Child

Following on from "Back for Christmas," "Dip in the Pool" is a variation on the couple composed of a castrating wife-mother figure and a man-child, who here indulges in a compulsive passion for gambling. For him, the expected gain is a way of acquiring autonomy, of becoming like the passenger on the boat who gave him the idea for the bet, Mr. Renshaw, an expert in stock market operations, and thus no longer being dependent on his wife and her inheritance, which enabled them to go on this cruise. Such a desire leads him to an action that gives Hitchcock the opportunity for a terrifying wide shot: Suddenly, out at sea, a man disappears.

Poison

Season 4, Episode 1

 • • • •

United States • **26 mins** • **Black and White** • **Mono** (RCA Sound Recording) • **1.33:1**

SYNOPSIS

I n south Malaaysia, Harry Pope, lying in bed, calls in a whisper to his partner, Timber Woods. An asp, he says, has curled up between the sheet and his stomach. Woods torments the man who was once his lucky rival in love but eventually sends for a doctor. The doctor diffuses chloroform under the sheet to put the reptile to sleep. But there is no snake. The whole thing is blamed on Pope's hallucinations. Woods lies laughing on the bed and is bitten. He asks Pope for help, and Pope replies that the doctor has left.

Production Dates: August 21–22, 1958
Broadcast in the United States: October 5, 1958

Production: Shamley Productions
Producer: Joan Harrison
Associate Producer: Norman Lloyd

Based on a short story by Roald Dahl (1950)
Adaptation: Casey Robinson
Director of Photography: John L. Russell
Sound: William Lynch

Assistant Director: Hilton A. Green
Art Direction: John J. Lloyd
Set Decoration: James S. Redd
Hair Stylist: Florence Bush
Makeup: Jack Barron
Costumes: Vincent Dee
Film Editing: Edward W. Williams, Richard G. Wray

Starring: Wendell Corey (Timber Woods), James Donald (Harry Pope), Arnold Moss (Dr. Ganderbay), Weaver Levy (assistant to Dr. Ganderbay), Alfred Hitchcock (himself)...

A Storyteller and a Specialist in the Feminine Melodrama Genre

"Poison" opens the fourth season of *Alfred Hitchcock Presents*. This was the third time that Hitchcock had filmed an adaptation of a short story by the Englishman Roald Dahl, author of children's stories and cruel denouement "twists in the tail." The adaptation was entrusted to Casey Robinson. Described by one critic as a "master of adaptation," Robinson started out in Hollywood in 1927, writing intertitles for silent films. He became a director in the early 1930s, penning short films with comedians Joe Smith and Charles Dale. He then turned to screenwriting. Among the many Hollywood films he scripted were several "women's melodramas," some starring Bette Davis (Edmund Goulding's *Dark Victory* and *The Old Maid*, Anatole Litvak's *All This, and Heaven Too*, Irving Rapper's *Now, Voyager* and *The Corn Is Green*). He also wrote the screenplay for Fritz Lang's *While the City Sleeps*. He was involved in the writing of two episodes of season 4 of *Alfred Hitchcock Presents*.

A Male Cast

James Donald played Harry Pope, trapped in bed by the fear of a snake coiled on his stomach. The Scottish-born actor made his film debut in the late 1930s, appearing in numerous British war films (*One of Our Aircraft Is Missing, In Which We Serve, The Way Ahead*). In an essentially British career, he also played Dr. Roney in Roy Ward Baker's impressive 1967 film *Quatermass and the Pit*. He also starred under Hitchcock's direction in another episode of the series, the shocking "The Crystal Trench," in 1959.

Wendell Corey, in the role of Timber Woods, played opposite him. He made his theatrical debut in the late 1930s at the Federal Theatre Project, created by the Roosevelt administration. Discovered by producer Hal Wallis, he played his first film role in 1948, that of a gangster in Lewis Allen's *Desert Fury*. He appeared, mainly as a supporting actor, in several notable films, including Anatole Litvak's *Sorry, Wrong Number* and Anthony Mann's *The Furies*. He also played the frightening psychopathic murderer in Budd Boetticher's *The Killer Is Loose*. For Hitchcock, he had already played police lieutenant Doyle, friend of L. B. Jefferies (James Stewart), in *Rear Window* (1954), but "Poison" would be his only *Alfred Hitchcock Presents* appearance. A year earlier, he had starred in a TV series about the coast guard, *Harbor Command*, which lasted one season (1957–1958). He

Alfred Hitchcock Presents...

Hitchcock extols the virtues of a new alarm system against pickpockets: a rattlesnake, with its distinctive sound, to be placed in his jacket pocket! Just as he is about to reintroduce his anti-theft system, he reaches into his pocket and discovers that the reptile has been stolen...

died of cirrhosis at the age of fifty-three, after appearing in a number of low-budget productions.

At the end of the episode, the filmmaker announces that Harry has, of course, served some time for not calling the doctor when his friend was bitten by a snake...

Paralysis and Impotence

"Poison" takes up the motif of paralysis, already present in Hitchcock's film (*Rear Window*) and television work ("Breakdown," 1955; "Four O'Clock," 1957). The episode sets up a singular device in which one man, unable to move, finds himself entirely at the mercy of another. The paralysis is an unexpected litmus test that reveals the true nature of the relationship between the two main protagonists.

Sadism

The unequal situation in which the two characters of "Poison" find themselves allows one of them to express a long-buried resentment. Both men love the same woman, who has chosen Harry Pope. From that moment on, Pope is tortured by Timber Woods, who decides to postpone the doctor's arrival by feigning clumsiness. Woods is a kind of evil demiurge. He takes the place of a director abusing his power, deciding how events should unfold, how they should look, and how they should be enacted. The suspense at work in this episode is created subjectively by a sadistic character.

METRO-GOLDWYN-MAYER presents
CARY GRANT
EVA MARIE SAINT
JAMES MASON
IN ALFRED HITCHCOCK'S
NORTH BY NORTHWEST
VISTAVISION · TECHNICOLOR
ONLY CARY GRANT AND ALFRED HITCHCOCK EVER GAVE YOU SO MUCH SUSPENSE IN SO MANY DIRECTIONS
so we brought it back!
CO-STARRING
JESSIE ROYCE LANDIS
WRITTEN BY
ERNEST LEHMAN
DIRECTED BY
ALFRED HITCHCOCK

North by Northwest

United States · **2 hrs 16** · **Color** · **Mono**
(Westrex Recording
System)
· **1.85:1**
(VistaVision)

Production Dates: August 27–December 24, 1958
Release Date in the United States: July 1, 1959 (Chicago, preview),
July 17, 1959 (United States)

Production: Metro-Goldwyn-Mayer
Producer: Alfred Hitchcock
Associate Producer: Herbert Coleman

Screenplay: Ernest Lehman
Director of Photography: Robert Burks
Camera Operator: Leonard J. South
Titles: Saul Bass
Special Effects: A. Arnold Gillespie, Lee LeBlanc
Technicolor Adviser: Charles K. Hagedon
Sound: Franklin Milton
Assistant Director: Robert Saunders
Continuity: Peggy Robertson
Production Designer: Robert Boyle
Art Direction: William A. Horning, Merrill Pye
Set Decoration: Henry Grace, Frank McKelvy
Hair Stylist: Sydney Guilaroff
Makeup: William Tuttle
Costumes: Harry Kress
Music: Bernard Herrmann
Film Editing: George Tomasini

Starring: Cary Grant (Roger O. Thornhill), Eva Marie Saint (Eve Kendall), James
Mason (Phillip Vandamm), Jessie Royce Landis (Clara Thornhill), Leo G. Carroll (the
"Professor"), Josephine Hutchinson (Mrs. Townsend), Philip Ober (Lester
Townsend), Martin Landau (Leonard), Adam Williams (Valerian), Edward Platt
(Victor Larrabee), Robert Ellenstein (Licht), Les Tremayne (auctioneer), Philip
Coolidge (Dr. Cross), Patrick McVey (Sergeant Flamm), Edward Binns (Captain
Junket), Ken Lynch (Charley), Malcolm Atterbury (man waiting for the bus), Jesslyn
Fax (woman in the train), Alfred Hitchcock (man who misses the bus)...

SYNOPSIS

R oger O. Thornhill, a New York advertising executive, is kidnapped by two killers. Mistaking him for the spy George Kaplan, they hand him over to the criminal Phillip Vandamm, who is waiting for him in a mansion. Drugged by his captors, Thornhill manages to outrun them, risking his life in the process. On the trail of Kaplan, his double, he meets the real owner of the mansion at the UN, who collapses in his arms, a dagger in his back. Thornhill flees and jumps on a train. He meets the seductive Eve Kendall. Knowing him to be on the run, she hides him in her sleeping car. Arriving in Chicago, Eve tells Thornhill that Kaplan has arranged to meet her at a bus stop in Indiana. Alone on an almost deserted road in open country, Thornhill narrowly escapes attack by a machine-gunner. He then realizes that Kendall is working for Vandamm. He finds them both at an auction and, once again, narrowly escapes arrest by the police, who take him to the "Professor." The "Professor" reveals that Kaplan is a spy invented by the American counterespionage services to deceive Vandamm, and Kendall is a CIA double agent. Thornhill agrees to be Kaplan long enough to prevent Vandamm from leaving the US with microfilms containing state secrets. In Rapid City, South Dakota, he manages to wrest Eve from the hands of their enemy. As they flee, the couple slide down Mount Rushmore. A perilous chase ensues, during which Thornhill saves Eve at the last minute…and helps her onto the bunk of the sleeping car that carries them away.

"…the crazy dance about to take place between Cary Grant and the world."

—

Bernard Herrmann, on the music for *North by Northwest*

GENESIS

Under a nonexclusive contract with Paramount, Alfred Hitchcock was hired by Metro-Goldwyn-Mayer for one film. After enjoying its golden age in the 1930s–1940s, the studio, which had "more stars than in heaven," had made a poor start to the 1950s and, in 1957, recorded losses for the first time in its history. MGM bought the "Hitchcock signature" to restore its reputation and made screenwriter Ernest Lehman available to the Master. The two men worked on a short adaptation of Hammond Innes's novel *The Wreck of the Mary Deare*, at the same time as the director was preparing to shoot *Vertigo* (1957). But more so than by Innes's bestseller, Hitchcock was enthused by the development of an original idea that obsessed him. Its working title: *The Man on Lincoln's Nose.*

A Set-Based Film

The story would be that of an imaginary spy created from scratch by the CIA to lure the enemy. An ordinary man, mistaken for this spy, would become embroiled in an assassination at the UN and end up on Mount Rushmore, the granite memorial depicting the monumental faces of four of the most important presidents in US history. Somehow, the hunted man would end up hidden in one of Lincoln's nostrils. Hitchcock envisioned the film as a tour of a series of continental settings traversed by his false culprit on the run.

A Filmmaker Worth His Weight in Gold

Expecting to read the script for *The Wreck of the Mary Deare*, MGM received a two-page summary of the next Hitchcock film: *In a Northwesterly Direction.* The filmmaker signed a "golden" contract that gave him the final cut and a say in all aspects of the production. He would receive $300,000 and 10 percent of the receipts when the film had earned twice its cost, set at $3.1 million.

Of the $25,000 allocated to the screenplay, Alfred Hitchcock set aside $1,000 for Otis Guernsey. He wanted to pay the eminent theater critic of the *New York Herald Tribune*, who had suggested the idea for the film at a luncheon in New York. In a letter to the filmmaker, Guernsey recounts the origin of the idea, a true story from the Middle East during World War II. Two secretaries at an English embassy had invented a spy and spread information about him in order to attract the attention of the Nazis: "The enemy gobbled the bait and spent some valuable time and energy trying to hunt down the non-existent operative."[1] In his letter, Guernsey had freely offered this script idea to Hitchcock.

On the Road...

After shooting *Vertigo*, Hitchcock took a family vacation, while Lehman set about writing *In a Northwesterly Direction.* For two weeks, the screenwriter visited New York, Chicago, and Rapid City, South Dakota, and immersed himself in the plot locations. He wrote seventy-five pages and met up

Cary Grant at the UN, or the nightmare of the wrongfully accused.

A Modern Hamlet

Several title ideas were considered: *Breathless*, *The CIA Story*, *The Man on Lincoln's Nose*, but also *The Bed in Which No One Slept*, *It's Good to Be Alive…North by Northwest* was among the first suggestions. This phrase is taken from a line in Shakespeare's *Hamlet*, which Hitchcock must have known: "I am but mad north-north-west. When the wind is southerly, I know a hawk from a handsaw."

again with the director on February 3, 1958. After six months of thought, discussion, and hard work, the final version of the script was completed on August 8, 1958.

CASTING

Ernest Lehman worked on what became *North by Northwest* with a view to James Stewart, who was himself enthusiastic about it, playing the role of Roger O. Thornhill. But filming was delayed and the actor began work on *Bell, Book and Candle* (Richard Quine, 1958), where he was reunited with Kim Novak (*Vertigo*). For Hitchcock, only the equally popular and charismatic Cary Grant could replace James Stewart. *North by Northwest* would be their fourth and final collaboration. Hitchcock first considered Russian-born actor Yul Brynner for the role of Vandamm, the crook involved in the import-export of government secrets, but he was reluctant before opting for the British sophistication of James Mason. He cast Martin Landau as the devoted accomplice secretly in love with his boss, whom the censors deemed too effeminate…Barely older than

Cary Grant, the ironic Jessie Royce Landis played Thornhill's mother, having previously played Grace Kelly's in *To Catch a Thief* (1954).

Vertigo, Second Season

Still haunted by Grace Kelly, Hitchcock dreamed of his favorite actress to play the sultry Eve Kendall. Then brunettes Cyd Charisse, Taina Elg, and Elizabeth Taylor were suggested, but Hitchcock chose Eva Marie Saint, known for her role opposite Marlon Brando in *On the Waterfront* (Elia Kazan, 1954). Hitchcock transformed her into a Hitchcock blonde. This time dispensing with the services of his favorite costume designer, Edith Head (who was, however, consulted), he took the actress shopping at Bergdorf Goodman, a luxury New York department store, and chose her outfits, behaving, in his own words, like James Stewart with Kim Novak in *Vertigo*. The idea was to dress her "in bright colors when the mood of the scene [was] dark, and in neutral colors when the mood [was] exciting."[2] The filmmaker gave Eva Marie Saint three acting instructions: to speak in a low voice, not to use her hands, and to look Cary Grant straight in the eye.

Loyal to Their Posts

While *North by Northwest* was the first and only film in MGM's history to be shot in VistaVision (a widescreen process owned by Paramount), cinematographer Robert Burks marked his tenth collaboration with Hitchcock, and George Tomasini his sixth edit. After *Vertigo*, Hitchcock again called upon graphic artist Saul Bass to design the opening credits. For their fifth film together, Bernard Herrmann composed a memorable score, a heady fandango that conveys a sense of adventure, danger, and desperate flight.

FILMING AND PRODUCTION

The filmmaker had already announced to the press that *North by Northwest* "would meet viewer expectations about what constituted the quintessential Hitchcock film."[3] This was his way of reassuring his audience, after having made two highly personal films, *The Wrong Man* (1956) and *Vertigo* (1957).

Freeze Frame

Screenwriter Ernest Lehman precisely describes the introductory scene, which is intended to capture the tempo of Madison Avenue in the 1950s: "Revolving doors of sleek new glass-and-steel office buildings spewing out streams of supercharged New-Yorkers, hurrying for cabs and buses and subways and cocktail bars."[3] This urban chaos is contrasted with the geometric harmony of Saul Bass's credits: Against a green background, arrows intersect to form a grid that gradually contours to the surface of a skyscraper, itself a reflection of New York traffic.

Obstacle Course

Filming began on August 27, 1958, in front of the United Nations building, but Hitchcock had to circumvent the ban on filming an assassination scene inside the building. Ever the ingenious filmmaker, he pretended to visit the site in the company of a photographer. Guided by the hand of the Master, the photographer took photos in preparation for an exact studio reconstruction. A stolen shot from the back of a truck of Cary Grant entering the building completed the illusion. In *North by Northwest*, Hitchcock pushed the mix of real sets and studio reconstructions to a greater extent than ever before, the combination of the real and the fake that always gives his films the appearance of a daydream.

Peril in Full Sunlight

In one afternoon, Hitchcock wrote the famous open-country scene in which Cary Grant is chased through a cornfield by a crop duster. It was born of a desire to break a cinematic cliché: that of a peril that would only appear in the dark of night, to the sound of ominous music. On the contrary, what was needed was "a deserted plain, in full sunlight, no music, no black cat,

"A succession of shots bordering on abstraction": Eva Marie Saint. Right: Cary Grant and Malcolm Atterbury.

Under the Eye of the Censors

Hitchcock was forced to change a line spoken by Eva Marie Saint during her first meeting with Cary Grant: "I never make love on an empty stomach" (which can still be read on the actress's lips) becomes, post-synched: "I never discuss love on an empty stomach." He also had to find a way to make the last scene, in which Thornhill and Eve Kendall are about to spend the night together—unmarried—appear less sultry. The solution came from the director of censorship, Geoffrey Shurlock, who suggested that Cary Grant should say: "Come along, Mrs. Thornhill," before hoisting her onto his bunk.

no mysterious face behind the windows!"[4] The shoot took place at Lost Hills, in the San Joaquin Valley in Northern California, in hundred-degree weather. The sequence creates the perfect illusion of continuity, between transparencies and real shots, between Cary Grant and his double. Having already played with time in the sequence at the Royal Albert Hall in *The Man Who Knew Too Much* (1955), Hitchcock now plays with space, showing the distance between Thornhill and each element of the set in a succession of shots that verge on abstraction (and refer to the geometric lines in the credits). In the end, the filmmaker eliminated the shots filmed from a helicopter, that is, from the pilot's point of view, so that the viewer could experience the scene solely from the perspective of the threatened hero.

Splendid Desecration

Having been banned by the UN, Hitchcock had to face up to a further ban on filming violent scenes on Mount Rushmore, "the shrine of democracy." The filmmaker and his screenwriter each tried to calm the officials' apprehension, Lehman by writing a

highly patriotic letter and Hitchcock by reporting to the press on his heroes' journey to the monument. But the Department of the Interior, in charge of national parks, saw this as a "flagrant desecration" and banned the filming. Robert Boyle, MGM's chief set designer, took it upon himself to re-create life-size sections of Mount Rushmore in rubber. After the Statue of Liberty in *Saboteur* (1942), Hitchcock mobilized another great national symbol for a choreography of bodies and figures climbing, clawing, and falling. Reminiscent of *Young and Innocent* (1937), Cary Grant reaches out a helping hand to Eva Marie Saint to keep her from falling into the void and hoist her up to him. The sequence culminates in a brilliantly elliptical shot of Mr. Thornhill helping the new Mrs. Thornhill to climb into their cabin berth, a return to the ordinary.

RECEPTION

Sol Siegel, head of MGM, was worried about budget overruns and sent countless memorandums urging Hitchcock to shorten the shoot. The filmmaker dreamed of an overture featuring Cary Grant as an advertising executive: The camera would pan across the tables of the designers in an advertising agency, and from their sketches the credits would emerge. Grant agreed to shoot the scene for no extra fee, but Hitchcock had to give up the $20,000 opening. Siegel felt it would weigh down a film already full of bravura moments. At the beginning of April 1959, production put the finishing touches to *North by Northwest*, with a budget in excess of $4 million.

The Power of Illogic

Preceded by a major advertising campaign and eagerly awaited, *North by Northwest* was a success. In the US, it became the sixth-highest-grossing film of the year, unanimously hailed as great entertainment. A. H. Weiler of the *New York Times* celebrated the "year's most scenic, intriguing and merriest chase" (August 7, 1959). *Time* called the plot "smoothly troweled and thoroughly entertaining" (August 17, 1959). The illogicality they all point out did not prevent *North by Northwest* from ticking all the boxes of a great Hitchcock: suspense, adventure, romance, and comedy.

Cary Grant and Alfred Hitchcock on the set of *North by Northwest*.

The Religion of Gratuitousness

North by Northwest's script is merely a pretext for a succession of visions that only the cinematic medium can embody. This is what François Truffaut admires when he emphasizes the absolute gratuitousness of the plane scene, a sequence that, since it does nothing to advance the action, can only be a filmmaker's notion. For the French critic, himself a young director at the time, cinema practiced in this way becomes an abstract art, "like music."

A Celebration of the Chase

At the time of the film's release in France, Hitchcock returned to his eternal motif of the chase for *Cahiers du cinéma*: The theme of the false culprit on the run serves his staging by enabling a great deal of movement and inducing numerous changes of scenery. Far from being mere backdrops, the scenery in *North by Northwest* has a dynamic function, as the action has to emerge from the particularities of the environment: "When there is movement, you have to ask yourself: what, in this particular scenery, is going in the direction of this movement?"[6]

Hitchcock on Hitchcock

Hitchcock again: "Painters always paint the same flower. They begin by painting it when they have no experience, and then they paint it with all the experience they have gained."[6] In this sense, *North by Northwest* represents the culmination of an artistic quest for maximum expressivity. The filmmaker copies himself in order to surpass himself, and dialogues with the great motifs of his filmography: the chase, the distant, sensual blonde, the war of the sexes, the double, the monumental, existence as dream and nightmare. In short, *North by Northwest* remains "the ultimate specimen of a genre whose rules Hitchcock himself created and set as if for eternity."[7]

An American *39 Steps*

For the director, the film was his American *39 Steps*. All its whimsy is summed up by its original title, *The Man on Lincoln's Nose*: "There is no such thing as north-by-northwest on the compass."[5] Illogicality, abstraction, and gratuitousness, far from working against the film, become the preconditions for sequences of pure cinema. With *North by Northwest*, Hitchcock reached a point of incandescence in his art, where form is totally liberated from verisimilitude and content. Hitchcock himself would confess to having conceived his most effective MacGuffin for this film, because it was the emptiest and most nonexistent—and also the most meaningful: microfilms, in other words, scraps of film…Emptied of his identity, Roger "O." ("O" as a sign of emptiness) Thornhill is himself reduced to a moving silhouette, purely a figure.

Where Is Hitchcock?

The filmmaker appears at the very end of the credits, at the same time as his name: He rushes to catch a bus that pulls away, closing the door in his face.

On the train, from New York to Chicago, Cary Grant in pursuit of Eva Marie Saint, or maybe the other way around (*North by Northwest*).

Set (Mount Rushmore, Eva Marie Saint, Cary Grant). Right: Transparency (the plane, Cary Grant on the ground).

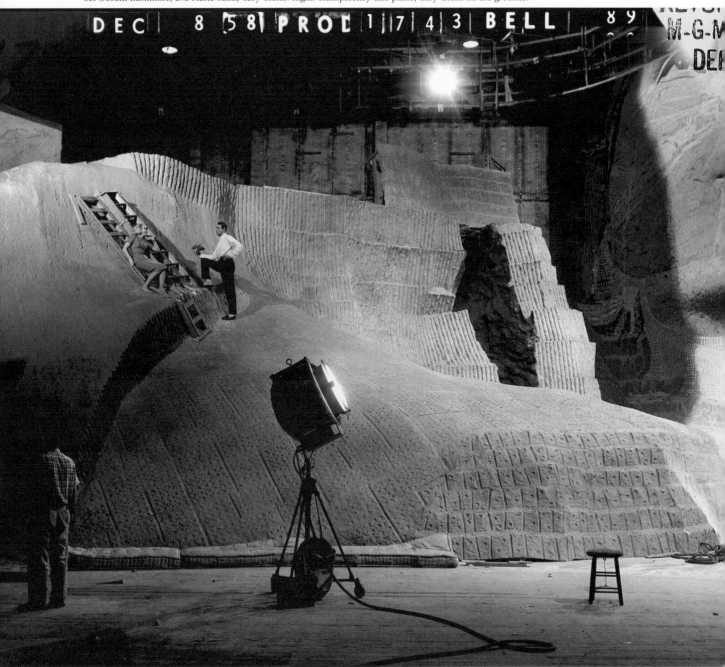

Two men hanging from a stone hand (*Saboteur*, 1942).

Monuments,
at the Summit of the Drama

Alfred Hitchcock always proceeded by means of "visions": He visualized a place and a situation, to which the plot was then subordinated, forced to pass through it. The starting point for *North by Northwest* (1958) was the image of a character being chased up Mount Rushmore, a monumental sculpture of the faces of four US presidents, and taking refuge in Abraham Lincoln's giant nostril. Such excesses, by capturing the imagination, have contributed to the reputation of Hitchcock's films. In the course of the action or at its climax, a famous building or cultural landmark appears, suddenly forcing the characters to go there to be saved or condemned. The appearance of this monument, its size, its volume, its motionless power, impresses the audience. Follow the guide...

The List

Hitchcock was neither the first nor the only film-maker to make use of the spectacular value of a monument; one need look no further, for example, than the Empire State Building at the end of *King Kong* (1933). But he is unique in the frequency of his use of the monumental, in both his English and American periods. His work includes the British Museum (*Blackmail*, 1929), the Royal Albert Hall (*The Ring*, 1927, and the two versions of *The Man Who Knew Too Much*, 1934 and 1955), Westminster Abbey (*Foreign Correspondent*, 1940), Radio City Music Hall and the Statue of Liberty (*Saboteur*, 1942), the Jefferson Memorial (*Strangers on a Train*, 1950), the Golden Gate Bridge, Coit Tower, and the Palace of the Legion of Honor (*Vertigo*, 1957), the

A man and a woman on the head of President Jefferson (*North by Northwest*, 1958).

UN building, a Frank Lloyd Wright–style house, and Mount Rushmore (*North by Northwest*), Tower Bridge (*Frenzy*, 1971) …This non-exhaustive list extends to other countries: In *Rich and Strange* (1931), the English couple on a stopover in Paris gaze in amazement at the Eiffel Tower, the Arc de Triomphe, Notre-Dame, and the Folies Bergère show. In *Torn Curtain* (1966), Paul Newman "visits" the East Berlin Museum with a killer on his tail.

A Point on the Map

Mr. and Mrs. Hitchcock had always traveled the world, and the Master's films deliberately reflected this taste for tourism. For the filmmaker, a monument is first and foremost a postcard, a cliché that he quotes literally and at the same time hijacks from its everyday use. For characters and viewers alike, a famous building is also a landmark, a place that Hitchcock is careful to show in its entirety and to pinpoint. In the center of the first shot of *Stage Fright* (1949) stands St. Paul's Cathedral: Welcome to the heart of London. Hitchcock's films are like maps drawn by a strange topographer, using locations that are both recognizable and faked: models, miniatures, transparencies, concealments, and matte paintings (the *Blackmail* and *Torn Curtain* museums), life-size replicas of parts (the arm and head of the Statue of Liberty), studio sets (Mount Rushmore)…

Justice Is Done

The monumental space is also a dramatic space (murderous pursuits, deadly chases, threats of attack), in which the characters, like tightrope walkers, are always in danger of falling, thereby precipitating the story's conclusion. By stepping onto the summit of a monument, the Hitchcockian hero finds refuge and salvation, while the traitor falls into a fatal trap and faces a speedy trial: "These scenes are trial scenes…But here, Hitchcock has turned the staging of the trial on its head, thanks to the violence of the action and the sequence of pursuit, capture, sentence and condemnation."[1] But the "innocent" can also be punished, as in the case of Scottie, who never stops falling from the beginning to the end of *Vertigo*, as if the entire film were the monument from which he constantly throws himself.

The Eye of God

There is the judgment of men and the judgment of heaven. The term "fall" must also be understood in its biblical sense (Adam and Eve driven from the Garden of Eden). Hitchcock's world is always a post-lapsarian world—a world after the fall. From then on, the gigantism of a monument brings the human being down to scale: an ant under the yoke of an abstract force that surpasses it and decides its life or death. It is as if a stern, silent God were manifesting Himself from the heights of His grandeur to remind the individual of his earthly condition, or to punish him irremediably. In *Blackmail*, the blackmailer, under the gaze of an Egyptian face several times his size, has no chance of escape. In *North by Northwest*, the heads of American presidents certainly contribute to the villain's vertiginous death. And in *Saboteur*, the saboteur finds himself hanging from the hand of the Statue of Liberty. Hitchcock uses several low-angle shots on the colossal head of the stone woman, so that she seems to be throwing the traitor into the void despite the hero's efforts to prevent the worst. In Hitchcock's world, the monument reigns supreme.

Banquo's Chair

Season 4, Episode 29

United States · **30 mins** · **Black and White** · **Mono** (RCA Sound Recording) · **1.33:1**

SYNOPSIS

William Brent, a retired policeman, is convinced that John Bedford killed his aunt two years ago. To find the man out, he organizes a dinner party at the murder house and invites the young man. He hires an actress who, dressed as the dead aunt, appears at the dinner. The other guests are accomplices who pretend not to see her. Bedford, believing her to be a ghost, denounces himself. Brent's hired actress then enters, apologizing for her tardiness. She had only just arrived.

Production Dates: March 25–26, 1959
Broadcast in the United States: May 3, 1959

Production: Shamley Productions
Producer: Joan Harrison
Associate Producer: Norman Lloyd

Based on a short story by Rupert Croft-Cooke (1937)
Adaptation: Francis Cockrell
Director of Photography: John L. Russell
Sound: William Russell
Assistant Director: Hilton A. Green

Art Direction: John J. Lloyd
Set Decoration: George Milo
Hair Stylist: Florence Bush
Makeup: Jack Barron
Costumes: Vincent Dee
Music: Frederick Herbert
Film Editing: Edward W. Williams, Richard G. Wray

Starring: John Williams (Inspector Brent), Kenneth Haigh (John Bedford), Reginald Gardiner (Major Cook-Finch), Max Adrian (Robert Stone), Thomas P. Dillon (Sergeant Balton), Hilda Plowright (Mae Thorpe), George Pelling (Lane), Alfred Hitchcock (himself)...

An Eclectic Novelist

"Banquo's Chair" is based on a short story by Rupert Croft-Cooke. This British writer had published poetry, plays, novels, short stories, biographies, and essays since the 1920s at an extraordinary pace. Under the name Leo Bruce, he wrote numerous crime novels evocative of the underworld. Croft-Cooke served in the secret service during World War II but left England in 1952 after being imprisoned for six months for homosexual practices. He would not return until 1968, when homosexuality was decriminalized. Several of his books were translated into French for the "Série noire" collection published by Gallimard, and three of his novels were made into films. "Banquo's Chair" is the only television adaptation of one of his works. Francis Cockrell, who had already worked on four films directed by Hitchcock, was responsible for the adaptation.

An "All British and Irish" Male Cast

The audience once again found the faithful John Williams in the lead role. He had already worked several times with Hitchcock, who appreciated him greatly: *The Paradine Case* (uncredited, 1947), *Dial M for Murder* (1953), and *To Catch a Thief* (1954) for the cinema; "Back for Christmas" and "Wet Saturday" for television in 1956. The murderous nephew was played by Kenneth Haigh. The son of a miner, he made his name in John Osborne's play *Look Back in Anger* in 1956. He appeared in another episode of the 1958–1959 season of *Alfred Hitchcock Presents*, not directed by the Master. In the early 1960s, he starred as Brutus in Joseph L. Mankiewicz's *Cleopatra*. Haigh became popular with British television audiences for his portrayal of explorer Sir Richard Burton in the 1971 miniseries *The Search for the Nile*. Reginald Gardiner (Major Cook-Finch) made an uncredited appearance in Alfred Hitchcock's *The Lodger* in 1926. He also appeared in Charlie Chaplin's *The Great Dictator* and Ernst Lubitsch's *Cluny Brown*. Irishman Max Adrian is another guest at this singular dinner party. A major star of the stage, he appeared in three films directed by Ken Russell in 1971: *The Music Lovers*, *The Devils*, and *The Boy Friend*.

The Supernatural Exception

"Banquo's Chair" is an episode that makes exceptional use of the supernatural in a series essentially devoted to telling very realistic murder stories, mostly set in familiar surroundings. Here, the punch line makes the protagonists—and the audience—realize that the appearance of a ghost has

Alfred Hitchcock Presents...

Hitchcock appears in African hunter's garb, on a sedan chair, welcoming viewers to the Hollywood jungle. He announces that the story to follow will take the safari "from the Hollywood smog to the London fog." At the episode's conclusion, he claims to have hired a local guide to track the game. The guide turns up with a sign reading "Address of the Stars," an allusion to the maps of Los Angeles sold to tourists, showing the homes of movie stars.

served to confound the culprit. This recourse to the fantastical, which he always refused to use, is also quite a curiosity in the filmmaker's work (*The Birds*, in 1962, being the exception that proves the rule). A film like *Vertigo* represents a kind of manifesto in this sense: The hypothesis of supernatural manifestations (Carlotta, Madeleine's ancestor, back from the dead) is swept aside by the discovery that everything the film's hero (and the audience) thought he was seeing was merely a very prosaic spectacle designed to entrap him.

The Burden of Guilt

The fright provoked by the presence of a ghost reveals the awareness of guilt and remorse that drives the sinner to confession. These are all reminders of the filmmaker's Catholicism, lending a metaphysical dimension to the criminal's guilt. It is upon this assumption, of course, that police officer William Brent's stratagem is based: to frighten the culprit.

The Flabbergasted Demiurge

In "Banquo's Chair," the audience is placed in the opposite position to the one in Hitchcock's *Vertigo*. They are no longer on the side of the duped victim, but on that of the manipulator, putting on a show designed to surprise an individual. The discussion that takes place at dinner conveniently revolves around theater. Brent's character thus appears as a demiurge. He is the image of the director building a trompe l'oeil universe that the ultimate revelation of the story will reduce to nothing.

Four Films
with Alfred Hitchcock (1959–1969)

Between 1959 and 1969, Alfred Hitchcock made five feature films and eight suspense episodes for television, not to mention media interviews, public appearances, and major talks. At the height of his activity, he also responded favorably to special requests, such as during World War II, to place his fame at the service of an event or a cause. His involvement, for reasons that he kept secret or disclosed on camera, often revealed an autobiographical and sentimental dimension.[1]

Tactic (1959)
Co-produced by the American Cancer Society, filmed in New York, and broadcast on NBC on May 2, 1959, this thirty-eight-minute film tackles the taboo of cancer in the society of its time,

encouraging everyone to have themselves screened and treated. Hitchcock takes part in the first part of the program (about twelve minutes). He first talks about the "fear of fear" of cancer, which leads to a denial of reality in the face of the disease. Then, on a bare set ("one door, one desk, two chairs, a paper-knife," in his words), he reappears to direct a two-character scene with three cameras: a doctor (William Shatner) announcing to a young woman (Diana Van der Vlis) the urgency of operating on her for breast cancer. The director intervenes twice "live," the first time addressing the actress and one of the cameramen to request and obtain a close-up of her onscreen as the terrible news is announced. The second time, he asks Shatner to take hold of the letter opener on the desk at the same time

The Westcliff Cine Club Visits Mr. Hitchcock in Hollywood (1963).

as he evokes the surgical act to come, as "a little subconscious act." A cutaway shot from another angle brings the knife into focus. To *Tactic* director and co-producer George Lefferts, who scripted the film right down to the filmmaker's "improvisations," Hitchcock confided that he agreed to this shoot because his own mother died of breast cancer in 1942.

The Westcliff Cine Club Visits Mr. Hitchcock in Hollywood (1963)

In anticipation of a "Hitchcock session," members of the Westcliff film club in Essex wrote to the director at the end of 1962, asking for a few introductory lines. Instead, he sent an eleven-minute filmed message, shot at Universal in 16 mm color. As he admits at the start of his speech, the idea was "inspired by a touch of nostalgia." Westcliff-on-Sea is not far from Leytonstone, where he was born and raised. And while this little film also offers a tour of Universal Studios (where he had just completed *The Birds*), Hitchcock turns first and foremost to the camera to indulge in a free-form evocation of his youth, almost a reverie: the Thames Estuary, the railway lines of his childhood (London, Tilbury, and Southend Railway; Great Eastern Railway), his London years at the time of *The 39 Steps* (1935), and his attraction to bleak winter landscapes…Hitchcock's intimate knowledge of Essex remains intact, with the names of railway stations and seaside resorts cited as memorable stops. All his life, Hitchcock, who became a naturalized American citizen in 1955, remained an Englishman. The film was shown at the Westcliff Cine Club on June 19, 1963.

The Will Rogers Appeal (1966)

Will Rogers (1879–1935) was a popular American comedian and actor. After his death, a hospital in his name specialized in the treatment of tuberculosis, and Hitchcock was one of the stars called upon to raise funds for it. In the appeal the filmmaker appears on a movie set, with the name "Warren"—John F. Warren, cinematographer on *Torn Curtain*—written on the opening clapperboard, still in the picture. We deduce that this little shoot must have taken place in early 1966. Hitchcock rises from his director's chair and speaks into the camera. His speech, which is extremely amusing, finds a way of making fun of the Method, the acting technique popularized by Lee Strasberg, which makes every actor want to know his character's innermost motivations.

This is a technique that Hitchcock did not believe in (according to him, only editing gives meaning and depth to actions), but which he had just experienced with Paul Newman on the set of *Torn Curtain*. *The Will Rogers Appeal* was released in cinemas in summer 1966.

Hitchcock on Grierson (1969)

Alfred Hitchcock, the Master of Suspense, paid tribute in this appeal to John Grierson (1898–1972), the "Father of Documentary." He had been approached by Scottish television and immediately agreed to take part. In the film, recorded during the shooting of *Topaz*, he narrates a heartfelt tribute to the Scottish-born English director and producer. Hitchcock's remarks are accompanied by large excerpts from films shot or conceived by Grierson (*Drifters*, 1929; *Night Mail*, 1936; *The Big Mill*, 1963), evoking his attachment to the documentary method, the period—common to both directors—of their intellectual training and their shared belief in the power of film editing.

Above all, the filmmaker's presence and involvement are a reminder of his indelible link with English cinema.

Arthur

Season 5, Episode 1

United States • **30 mins** • **Black and White** • **Mono** (RCA Sound Recording) • **1.33:1**

SYNOPSIS

Production Dates: July 7–9, 1959
Broadcast in the United States: September 27, 1959

Production: Shamley Productions
Producer: Joan Harrison
Associated producer: Norman Lloyd

Based on a short story by Arthur Williams (1948)
Adaptation: James P. Cavanagh
Director of Photography: John L. Russell
Sound: William Lynch
Assistant Director: Hilton A. Green

Art Direction: John J. Lloyd
Set Decoration: James S. Redd
Hair Stylist: Florence Bush
Makeup: Jack Barron
Costumes: Vincent Dee
Music: Frederick Herbert
Film Editing: Edward W. Williams, Richard G. Wray

Starring: Laurence Harvey (Arthur Williams), Hazel Court (Helen Brathwaite), Robert Douglas (Inspector Ben Liebenberg), Patrick Macnee (Sergeant John Theron), Barry G. Harvey (Constable Barry), Alfred Hitchcock (himself)…

The fiancée of Arthur, a chicken farmer in New Zealand, leaves him for a richer man. A year later, abandoned by her lover, she returns to Arthur's home, where he strangles her. Later, returning from a trip, he comes across police investigating her disappearance at his home. They find no trace of the body. Arthur offers them some chickens, which he assures them have been well fed. They suspect that he has made his fiancée disappear in a poultry feed crushing machine.

Author of a Single Short Story

The fifth season of *Alfred Hitchcock Presents* opens with another Alfred Hitchcock film. The story from which it is taken, "Being a Murderer Myself," published in 1948 in *Ellery Queen's Mystery Magazine*, was written by Arthur Williams, whose real name was Peter Barry Way, an Englishman who worked for a travel agency. In the letter he sent with his story to the monthly for publication, he stated that he did not want the story to appear under his real name, adding that "the effect of the story might be lost should my real name be given." "Being a Murderer Myself" is his only known literary work. It was also published in French in an anthology, by Marabout, under the title *Chère de poules*. The prolific James P. Cavanagh (some fifteen episodes in the series, including "One More Mile to Go," directed by Hitchcock) adapted it for the small screen.

A Role for Laurence Harvey

The lead role was played by Laurence Harvey. Of Lithuanian-Jewish origin, he began his acting career after the war in South Africa, where he had lived with his family since 1934, before moving to London, where he performed in the theater and found his first film roles. This was his only appearance in *Alfred Hitchcock Presents*. At the time, the actor was also being considered for a role in *No Bail for the Judge*, a Hitchcock film that was never made. In 1960, he played Colonel Travis in John Wayne's *The Alamo*. His performance in *The Manchurian Candidate* (John Frankenheimer, 1962) as Sergeant Raymond Shaw, brainwashed in Korea and programmed to carry out a political assassination in the United States, was one of his most remarkable. He went on to direct three films and died prematurely in 1973.

Scream Queen and Future TV Stars

The episode's acerbic heroine was played by British actress Hazel Court. A regular on TV, she was also a scream queen starlet. Between 1954 and 1964, she appeared in David MacDonald's *Devil Girl from Mars*, Terence Fisher's *The Curse of Frankenstein* and *The Man Who Could Cheat Death*, and Roger Corman's *Premature Burial* and *The Mask of the Red Death*. Robert Douglas, who played the police inspector, was a prolific television director from 1960 onward. London-born Patrick Macnee played Sergeant Theron. Macnee's television career was intense in the 1950s; however, he achieved great popularity a little later, due to the series *The Avengers*, in which he

played the role of John Steed from 1961 to 1969. He appeared in another episode of the *Alfred Hitchcock Presents* series directed by the Master himself, "The Crystal Trench," (1959).

The (Deadly) War of the Sexes

The main character, Arthur Williams, appears immediately after the credits, addressing the viewer. He is thus in the same position as the filmmaker when he introduces each film in the series. He assumes the role of narrator as much as that of assassin, with whom the viewer will identify. *Arthur* is yet another example of the battle to the death between the sexes in Hitchcock's work. The criminal, a surrogate for the director, enunciates a certain philosophy of marriage: "They marry and spend the rest of their lives wondering why they are so miserable." Murder reduces women to poultry whose necks have been twisted. (Is that a tragic clucking sound we hear at the fatal moment…?)

The Abject Nature of Food

Another recurring Hitchcock motif lies in the way the murderer makes his victim's corpse disappear. He crushes it in a machine designed to produce chicken feed. Once again, food is associated with death and the corpse (*Sabotage*, 1936; "Lamb to the Slaughter," 1958; "Banquo's Chair" 1959; *Frenzy*, 1971).

Alfred Hitchcock Presents…

Hitchcock shows viewers a new design for eggs, polyhedral in shape: "Its advantages are obvious. No more eggs rolling off the table." Nevertheless, "the hens seem rather slow at grasping new ideas." After the episode, he announces that the murderer, by dint of feeding his hens flesh and bone, has caused them to grow to spectacular size. And, horrified, he cannot bring himself to describe what happened the day Arthur passed among his starving chickens…

The Crystal Trench

Season 5, Episode 2

United States • **30 mins** • **Black and White** • **Mono** (RCA Sound Recording) • **1.33:1**

Production Dates: August 25–27, 1959
Broadcast in the United States: October 4, 1959

Production: Shamley Productions
Producer: Joan Harrison
Associate Producer: Norman Lloyd

Based on a short story by A. E. W. Mason (1917)
Adaptation: Stirling Silliphant
Director of Photography: John F. Warren
Sound: William Russell
Assistant Director: Hilton A. Green
Art Direction: John J. Lloyd

Set Decoration: Julia Heron
Hair Stylist: Florence Bush
Makeup: Robert Dawn
Costumes: Vincent Dee
Music: Frederick Herbert
Film Editing: Edward W. Williams, Richard G. Wray

Starring: James Donald (Mark Cavendish), Patricia Owens (Stella Ballister), Werner Klemperer (Mr. Ranks), Ben Astar (Swiss innkeeper), Patrick Macnee (Professor Kersley), Harald O. Dyrenforth (Frederic Blauer), Oscar Beregi Jr. (man with the telescope), Alfred Hitchcock (himself)…

SYNOPSIS

Mark Cavendish meets recently married Stella Ballister, whose husband has just died in a mountain accident. The body is trapped in a glacier. The young woman refuses Cavendish's proposal of marriage and lives only in anticipation of recovering her husband's remains. Forty years later, when he is removed from the ice, she discovers on his body a locket containing the portrait of an unknown young woman.

An Adventurous Novelist

Broadcast on October 4, 1959, "The Crystal Trench" is the second episode of the fifth season of *Alfred Hitchcock Presents*, following "Arthur," also directed by the filmmaker. The film is based on a short story by Alfred Edward Woodley Mason, a London author known for his historical novels, the most famous of which is undoubtedly *The Four Feathers* (1902), a tale of colonial adventure dealing with the themes of courage and cowardice, adapted several times for the cinema (by Schoedsack and Cooper in 1929, Zoltan Korda in 1939 and 1955, Don Sharp in 1978). Actor and cricket champion before becoming a writer, Mason was a Liberal MP between 1906 and 1910, joined the navy during World War I, and took part in espionage missions in Spain and Mexico. The short story is part of a collection, *The Four Corners of the World*, published in 1917. Stirling Silliphant, who worked on Hitchcock's 1957 episode "The Perfect Crime" and was later a screenwriter for the cinema (*In the Heat of the Night, The Liberation of L.B. Jones, The New Centurions*), was commissioned to adapt the story.

Men...

In the leading male role, viewers will find British actor James Donald ("Poison," 1958). The mountain guide was played by Werner Klemperer. Son of the famous conductor Otto Klemperer, he fled Nazi Germany with his family in the 1930s and served in the US Army during World War II. Three years before "The Crystal Trench," he appeared in Alfred Hitchcock's *The Wrong Man* (1956) as Dr. Bannay. Stanley Kramer's *Judgment at Nuremberg* (1961) drew attention for his performance as an arrogant Nazi, and he is best known for his portrayal of the clumsy and stupid Colonel Klink, commander of the prisoner-of-war camp in the hit series *Hogan's Heroes*.

Actor Patrick Macnee, already seen in "Arthur," played Professor Kersley. He achieved lasting fame as John Steed in the British TV series *The Avengers*, broadcast between 1961 and 1969, and again in 1976

and 1977. The hotel manager was played by actor Ben Astar. Born in Palestine, a specialist in sometimes picturesque supporting roles in films (*On the Double, Five Weeks in a Balloon, Bye Bye Birdie*) and television (*The Untouchables, The Young Marrieds, Mission: Impossible, It Takes a Thief*), this is his only appearance in *Alfred Hitchcock Presents*.

...and a Starlet

The film's only female character is Patricia Owens, present only in this episode of the series. Born in Canada, she moved to London with her parents in 1933. In a filmography rich in TV drama series, she had a short film career, for example, in Robert Rossen's *Island in the Sun* in 1957, Joshua Logan's *Sayonara* with Marlon Brando, and John Sturges's *The Law and Jake Wade* the following year. Her most memorable role was that of Hélène Delambre in Kurt Neumann's 1958 horror film *The Fly*, starring Vincent Price.

A Little-Known Masterpiece

For the few commentators on the series, "The Crystal Trench" is one of the best films ever made by the Master. Indeed, this episode can legitimately be considered one of the masterpieces of the *Alfred Hitchcock Presents* series, and perhaps of the filmmaker's entire filmography.

It forms an essential link between two major works, *Vertigo* (1957) and *Psycho* (1960). With this film, the role of television in Hitchcock's career becomes more obvious. For him, the small screen was a place of experimentation, offering the possibility of imposing a singular aesthetic (economy, brevity, theatricality), an unexpected and obligatory passage that would determine, as *Psycho* exemplifies, the entire end of his work.

The Living and the Dead

As in *Vertigo*, the story is constructed around the mad desire to bring a loved one back from the dead. While waiting for the glacier to melt, Stella Ballister is consumed by the idea of finding her husband, dead but preserved, frozen in the beauty of his youth, an impulse similar to that of Scottie (James Stewart) re-creating Judy in the image of Madeleine in the 1957 film. This obsession with preservation foreshadows the psychotic project of Norman Bates in *Psycho*, who mummifies his mother to keep her close to him.

Stage Entrance

In the first shot of Stella Ballister, seated in the hotel dining room, the filmmaker frames the actress in a perfect, almost frozen profile. This shot is reminiscent of the one that first showed Madeleine (Kim Novak) in *Vertigo*, like a medal profile, idealizing her in the eyes of the male character and the viewer. Shortly afterward, when Stella hears the news of her husband's death, she offers her neck to the camera, filmed as Kim Novak's was in *Vertigo*, as an object of desire beyond reach. Her gaze is elsewhere, beyond this world.

Challenging Time

"The Crystal Trench" tells the story of a young woman who challenges time. Caught up in the memory of the idealized six months of her marriage, Stella withdraws from life and waits forty years for the glacier to return her husband to her, while another man nurtures vain hopes at her side. While the *Alfred Hitchcock Presents* series usually tells stories over a few days, or even hours, this episode spans several decades. Here, time has different values. There is the time of the events described and the time of waiting, a protracted ellipsis during which the female character lives only in the memory of one man. From the outset, past and present are intertwined through montage and repetition. The train taking Mark Cavendish to the mountain station is also the one that will transport him forty years later to discover the frozen man's body. For a few moments, the montage blurs temporal markers, merging the two moments. The viewer understands that he is going back in time. And it is the vain hope of a return to the past that is at stake, at the end of forty years of

suspense: a return to the past that will prove to be only an illusion for Stella Ballister.

"Man Is a Flaw in the Diamond of the World" (Merleau-Ponty)

The diamond is the film's true metaphor. Stella prefers the diamond in the ice coffin containing her husband's body to the brilliant one offered by Mark Cavendish, the narrator, who is in love with her and wants to propose to her. But this diamond has a flaw, a "toad," the photo in the young man's locket revealing that he was in love with another woman. This detail shatters the ideal scenario of absolute, shared love that the young woman had constructed. The flaw in the gemstone is proof of the world's ontological imperfection. "The Crystal Trench" is undoubtedly one of the author's cruelest films, insofar as it denounces all romantic illusion through the chimeras of a female character trapped in her own blindness. Stella Ballister is in love with an image, and a false one at that. This is how the face of her dead husband appears to her. His frozen body, intact and still young, is but a mirage constructed by Stella. Her gaze has frozen the beloved object in a deceptive process of crystallization.

Paradoxical Guilt

The question of guilt also comes up in this episode when Stella meets Ranks, the mountain guide played by Werner Klemperer, who led her husband on the fatal expedition. This admission of his responsibility, far from calming the young woman, plunges her into a terrible rage. This anger is probably less the consequence of a lie told by the man than of the paradoxical pride he seems to take in his confession. For him, the confession is a way of asserting both his superior physical strength and endurance (he survived the climatic conditions that claimed the life of his fellow climber) and a humility in which he takes an obscene pride. This reflection on the meaning of confession, very explicit in Mason's short story, is reminiscent of the filmmaker's Catholicism.

In memory of Vertigo*…Stella's neck (Patricia Owens).*

Alfred Hitchcock Presents…

On a snow-covered mountainside, Hitchcock cuts a rope. We hear the sound of a body falling into the void: "My, my, I seem to have made a faux pas. My friend was at the other end of that rope. Rotten luck. He was also my business partner." At the end of the episode, Hitchcock has a rope around his waist: "I think I shall begin my descent…before I become the source of a legend about an abdominable snowman." He begins his descent and disappears from the frame. A man in tattered clothes, his partner, comes crawling back and cuts the rope that is holding his "friend."

A new— and altogether different— screen excitement!!!

starring
ANTHONY
PERKINS
VERA
MILES
JOHN
GAVIN
co-starring
MARTIN
BALSAM
JOHN
McINTIRE

and
JANET
LEIGH
as
MARION
CRANE

Directed by
ALFRED
HITCHCOCK
Screenplay by
JOSEPH
STEFANO
A PARAMOUNT
Release

ALFRED
HITCHCOCK'S
PSYCHO
PSYCHO

Copyright ©1960 by Shamley Productions, Inc. Country of Origin U.S.A.   60-1048   LITHO. IN U.S.A.   Property of National Screen Service Corp. Licensed for display only in connection with the exhibition of this picture at your theatre. Must be returned immediately thereafter.   60/319

Psycho

🏳 **United States** • 🕐 **1 hr 49** • ⊚ **Black and White** • 🔇 **Mono** (Westrex Recording System) • ▭ **1.85:1**

Production Dates: November 11, 1959–January 1960
Release Date in the United States: June 16, 1960 (New York, preview),
September 8, 1960 (United States)

Production: Shamley Productions
Producer: Alfred Hitchcock
Unit Manager: Lew Leary

Based on the novel of the same name by Robert Bloch (1959)
Screenplay: Joseph Stefano
Director of Photography: John L. Russell
Camera Operator: Leonard J. South
Titles and pictorial consultant: Saul Bass
Special Effects: Clarence Champagne
Sound: Waldon O. Watson, William Russell
Assistant Director: Hilton A. Green
Art Direction: Joseph Hurley, Robert Clatworthy
Set Decoration: George Milo
Hair Stylist: Florence Bush
Makeup: Jack Barron, Robert Dawn
Costumes: Helen Colvig, Rita Riggs
Music: Bernard Herrmann
Film Editing: George Tomasini

Starring: Anthony Perkins (Norman Bates), Vera Miles (Lila Crane), John Gavin (Sam Loomis), Janet Leigh (Marion Crane), Martin Balsam (Detective Milton Arbogast), John McIntire (Sheriff Al Chambers), Simon Oakland (Dr. Fred Richman), Frank Albertson (Tom Cassidy), Patricia Hitchcock (Caroline), Vaughn Taylor (George Lowery), Lurene Tuttle (Mrs. Chambers), John Anderson (California Charlie), Mort Mills (highway patrol officer), Alfred Hitchcock (man in the street outside the real estate office)...

SYNOPSIS

———

Marion Crane, a young employee at a Phoenix, Arizona, real estate agency, longs to marry her lover, Sam Loomis. But he is too deeply in debt to contemplate such a prospect. Marion steals a large sum of money from her boss. She flees by car, hoping to find Sam in California. On the way, at night, in the torrential rain, she stops at a motel off the main road. The place is run by Norman Bates, a shy, psychologically fragile young man, a taxidermist in his spare time, who says he lives in the large mansion overlooking the motel with a mother to whom he is excessively attached. After dining with him, Marion seems determined to leave at dawn to return the stolen money. That evening, she is stabbed to death in the shower. Norman, discovering the scene, makes the body and the car (and the money) disappear into a pond. He erases all traces of the crime to protect his mother, who appears to be the murderer. Lila Crane, with Sam's help, hires a detective to track down her sister. When the detective arrives at the motel, he is brutally murdered. With no news of him, Lila and Sam go to the scene, having learned from the sheriff that Mrs. Bates has in fact been dead for ten years. Lila discovers the mummified corpse of the old woman in the cellar of the house. She escapes a murder attempt, helped by Sam, who subdues the assailant at the last moment. At the police station, the psychoanalyst reveals the truth: The murderer is in fact Norman, who used his mother's clothes to commit his terrible crimes.

"Psycho won't be a blockbuster, but it will be a very strange film. It will be a film full of charm and blood. There will be lots and lots of blood."

———

Alfred Hitchcock, October 1959

Anthony Perkins.

GENESIS

The film that was to become Alfred Hitchcock's greatest commercial success was conceived in doubt, an understandable doubt, since it was, in many respects, a quasi-experimental work in the context of the Hollywood production system of the late 1950s.

A Horror B Movie?

In the summer of 1959, Hitchcock bought the rights to a short terror novel, *Psycho*, written by Robert Bloch and inspired by the murders of a serial killer, Ed Gein, arrested in 1957 after murdering several women, digging up corpses, and creating macabre artifacts with the remains of his victims (lampshades, gloves, and masks made of human skin). The man worshipped his abusive mother, who died in 1949.

The choice of such a novel came as a surprise to Hitchcock's entourage, with him seeming to want to move away from the sophistication of his earlier work. In fact, Hitchcock was intrigued by the commercial success of low-budget terror films such as those by William Castle, American International

Pictures, and Roger Corman, which often appealed to teenage audiences, a new consumer mass demographic in the late 1950s.

Introducing Joseph Stefano

Robert Bloch, the author of the novel, had several of his short stories adapted for *Alfred Hitchcock Presents*. Although Bloch was approached by the director to adapt *Psycho*, the task fell to screenwriter James P. Cavanagh. Cavanagh had already worked on a script for the series, "One More Mile to Go" (1957), an episode that foreshadowed a particular sequence in *Psycho* (the police stop). At this stage of the conception, the filmmaker hesitated: Should he make a work for the cinema or produce a drama for television? Unhappy with Cavanagh's work, Hitchcock turned, at the suggestion of MCA's agents, to Joseph Stefano. Originally an operetta dancer and singer, the man had little experience of writing for the cinema with the exception of *The Black Orchid* (Martin Ritt, 1958). He worked mainly for television. Hitchcock was delighted with his ideas, particularly that of giving Marion Crane's character more depth. He got on wonderfully well with him.

For Hitchcock Addicts

The voice of Mrs. Bates, heard on several occasions, comes from three different sources: two actresses, Jeanette Nolan, already seen in three episodes of *Alfred Hitchcock Presents*, and Virginia Gregg, who appeared four times in the series, but also a young actor, Paul Jasmin, a close friend of Anthony Perkins.

Produced by Hitchcock, Distributed by Paramount

When Hitchcock submitted his adaptation project to Paramount, the company's executives were reluctant. All the indications were that the idea of bringing to the screen a novel with violent twists and turns frightened them. Hitchcock decided to produce the film himself, with his own television company, Shamley Productions. *Psycho* was shot on MCA's newly acquired sets, the former Universal Studios. Paramount would simply distribute the film. It seems, moreover, that this configuration was the result of pressure exerted by Lew Wasserman, head of MCA, who made Paramount an offer it could not refuse… This setup was in fact the result of a strategy enabling MCA to rent out its recently acquired film sets while guaranteeing its client high profits in the event of commercial success.

CASTING

Although the actors chosen to play the main roles were well-known to the public, they were not big stars. *Psycho* was to be a film without stars.

Anthony Perkins, the Role of a Lifetime

The main male character, Norman Bates, is in his forties in Bloch's novel. He is bald and paunchy. Hitchcock and Stefano wanted him to be a fragile, shy young man. Anthony Perkins was their first choice. He already had a few films to his credit: William Wyler's *Friendly Persuasion*, Robert Mulligan's *Fear Strikes Out*, Anthony Mann's *The Tin Star*. He had become a popular actor with teenage audiences who could identify with his characters. By agreeing to play a cross-dressing killer, he made a courageous choice that changed his career forever. Norman Bates was to be the role of a lifetime.

The Entry of Janet Leigh and Return of Vera Miles

For the role of Marion Crane, names like Eva Marie Saint (*North by Northwest*), Piper Laurie, Hope Lange, Martha Hyer, and Shirley Jones were discussed. Even Lana Turner was briefly considered. Hitchcock's choice fell on Janet Leigh: Although not a star at the time, she was sufficiently well-known to the public, who had seen her in a few historical fantasies (*Prince Valiant*, *The Vikings*) or an Anthony Mann Western (*The Naked Spur*), that they did not expect the sudden disappearance of her character a third of the way through the film and were left bewildered. Marion Crane's sister was played by Vera Miles, with whom Hitchcock reunited after *The Wrong Man* (1956).

Male Characters

Marion's fiancé was played by the young John Gavin (*Imitation of Life*, Douglas Sirk). Hitchcock was unhappy with his performance, deeming it too "stiff," and after the film's release referred to him unkindly as "The Stiff." At Stefano's suggestion, Martin Balsam was hired to play the detective and Simon Oakland the psychiatrist. Until then, both actors had had mainly television careers. The character of the psychiatrist appears at the end of the film: In a long monologue, he gives the viewer a psychiatric explanation of Norman Bates's demented behavior and actions. After the scene was shot, Hitchcock congratulated the actor: "Mr. Oakland, you just saved my movie." Such a reaction—and there would be others during the shoot—betrayed the filmmaker's uncertainty about the commercial potential of the film in progress.

Who Will Play the Mother?

In order to mislead the media, Hitchcock made it appear that he was looking for an actress to play Norman Bates's (dead) mother. The names of Judith Anderson (the housekeeper in *Rebecca*, 1939) and Helen Hayes, among others, were floated. In fact, Hitchcock used stand-ins Margo Epper and Ann Dore to portray the figure of Mrs. Bates passing behind her bedroom window and appearing menacingly through the shower curtain. And it was a little person stuntwoman, Mitzi Koestner, whom Anthony

Money, the real interest for the character (Janet Leigh) and a red herring for the viewer.

Perkins holds in his arms as he takes his "mother" into the cellar of the house.

FILMING AND PRODUCTION

The filmmaker used a technical team drawn mainly from *Alfred Hitchcock Presents*. Scenes were sometimes shot with two cameras, using small-screen methods.

Like a TV Series Episode

John L. Russell, the cinematographer, used to black and white, had already worked on more than ten episodes directed by Hitchcock. Set designer George Milo, makeup artists Jack Barron and Robert Dawn, hairstylist Florence Bush, sound engineer William Russell, and assistant director Hilton A. Green, all employees of Revue Studios, worked regularly on the series.

Hitchcock also brought back his editor of six films, George Tomasini, and hired Joseph Hurley on the recommendation of set designer Robert Boyle (*North by Northwest*, 1958), who was unavailable. Hurley teamed up with Robert Clatworthy to create, among other things, a large American Gothic–style house, inspired as much by Edward Hopper's painting *House by the Railroad* (1925) as by the house in *The Addams Family*, the famous *New Yorker* comic strip.

Controlled Shooting and Sensitive Scenes

During the six-week shoot, the set was closed to visitors, with security guards at the entrance. The director resisted a request from Paramount's publicity department to take photos. He instructed the crew not to reveal anything about the script. The actors, for the most part, had only part of the script, and often did not know how the film would end. Some sequences proved complicated to shoot, particularly the murder scenes. The shower scene, involving both violence and nudity, had to avoid censorship restrictions while expressing a brutality never before seen in cinema. Hitchcock commissioned Saul Bass, who was also in charge of designing the credits, to storyboard the two murder scenes (the knife scene in the shower and the violent death of the detective played by Martin Balsam). Saul Bass would later take credit for the Marion Crane murder scene. Most eyewitness accounts from collaborators present on the set affirm that Hitchcock did indeed direct these shots himself, based on Bass's cut. The shower sequence was filmed with a body double, Las Vegas stripper Marli Renfro, who replaced Janet Leigh for certain close-ups requiring total nudity. Leigh's breasts are sometimes covered by a moleskin jumpsuit. Chocolate syrup gives the illusion of flowing blood.

Where Is Hitchcock?

Hitchcock appears in the sixth minute. He is seen through the glass of Marion Crane's (Janet Leigh's) office door. With his back in three-quarter profile, he is smoking a cigar on the sidewalk, wearing a cowboy hat.

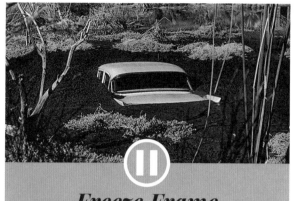

Freeze Frame

To hide his "mother's" crime, Norman Bates puts Marion Crane's corpse in the trunk of her car and pushes it into a pond. She is gradually engulfed, until the immersion movement is suspended for a few seconds. At this moment, the audience, who up to that point had identified with the young woman and trembled for her fate, fears that Norman will not succeed in his aim (to conceal the crime). The audience becomes his accomplice in thought, moving from dread to compassion for a psychopath, in a tried-and-tested paradox from Hitchcock's cinema.

Saved by the Music?

Once again, Hitchcock commissioned Bernard Herrmann to compose the music. While a jazz orchestration was originally planned, the composer invented a jerky melody, punctuated by strident violin riffs likely to play on the audience's nerves. The director was so pleased and reassured by Herrmann's work that he doubled his salary.

RECEPTION

At the first screenings for some of the director's collaborators, *Psycho* provoked frightened reactions. Robert Bloch, the novel's author, was torn between frustration at no longer being able to recognize his work and admiration for the graphic violence onscreen: "It's either going to be your biggest success or your biggest flop,"[1] he told Hitchcock.

Original Marketing

Hitchcock orchestrated an original publicity campaign, urging audiences not to reveal the story's ending and requiring exhibitors not to let anyone in after the screening had begun. He conceived a long trailer, written by his accomplice James B. Allardice, in which, transformed into a tour guide, he takes viewers on a tour of the film's settings: the gloomy Bates house, Norman's motel, the bathroom...suggesting that bloody events have taken place there. Here too he urges the audience not to recount the ending.

A Phenomenal Success, Criticisms Superseded

The film was an immediate and phenomenal success. Theaters were packed. *Psycho*, which cost $800,000, made tens of millions. Hitchcock forced journalists to see the film in a commercial screening with the public. American critics were initially disappointed, if not shocked. Bosley Crowther of the *New York Times* called it a blot on an honorable career. The *Esquire* critic wrote that the film was "merely one of those television shows padded out to two hours by adding pointless subplots and realistic details." He saw in it only "a reflection of a most unpleasant mind, a mean, sly, sadistic little mind." The *Village Voice*'s Andrew Sarris, however, called it "the first American movie since *Touch of Evil* to stand in the same creative rank as the great European films." Bosley Crowther, like others, changed his mind shortly afterward, ranking the film among the most important of the year. *Psycho* was accused of encouraging violence, and on several occasions Hitchcock had to respond to this accusation.

A Failure or a Masterpiece?

French critics were equally disconcerted by the film. Michel Capdenac in *Les Lettres françaises* urged his readers not to "follow the bluff." For *La Saison cinématographique 1961*, "the Master gives in to the bargain basement and has just produced some film reels that will go down in the annals of failure and mediocrity." Louis Seguin, of *Positif* magazine (December 1960), as anti-Hitchcock as ever, revealed the ending and described *Psycho* as a neat little horror film that could be enjoyed furtively "if the secrets didn't leak out in the first half-hour." Unsurprisingly, the film made the cover of the November 1960 issue of *Cahiers du cinéma*. An article by American critic and researcher Robin Wood, "Psychanalyse de *Psycho*" ("Psychoanalysis of *Psycho*"), opened the issue. Jean Douchet, meanwhile, analyzed the way the filmmaker played with the audience's nerves and mind, and saw in the skill of the mise-en-scène, from the very first shots, a way of speaking "of the eternal and the finite, of

existence and nothingness, of life and death, but seen in their naked truth."

An Audacious Film

Psycho was one of Alfred Hitchcock's most audacious undertakings, an incredible challenge that provoked doubt and perplexity in those around him. In undertaking this project, the filmmaker took the risk of disappointing audiences by moving away from the humor, sophistication, and elegance associated with his most recent successes (*To Catch a Thief*, *The Man Who Knew Too Much*, *North by Northwest*). The film marks a crucial stage in the history of cinema, paving the way for a new way of showing violence and bringing terror to the heart of a world that is familiar to the point of triviality (people being killed in a bathroom) and deceptively reassuring. A lesson inherited from the success of his TV series? No doubt. But the terror aroused by the film is also based on the sensation, for those who watch it, of being faced with the work of a filmmaker who is both ahead of his time ("right on time," in fact, as his success in the cinemas testifies) and so in control of his art that no detail in *Psycho* seems devoid of meaning.

The Absurdity of Existence

Hitchcock would say that in a film of this kind, it is the camera that does all the work. *Psycho* is indeed a work in which the audience's emotions are aroused simply by the specific resources of cinema, by a unique way of combining image and sound, framing and editing. The film contains, as if reduced to their essence, the most profound motifs of the filmmaker's universe: voyeurism, here indisputably sexual, and guilt, constantly questioned by events. *Psycho* is a machine for terrorizing the audience, not only for its shock effects and violence, but also for its astonishing mastery and profound sadness. In fact, it expresses a tragic sense of existence, brought on by Marion Crane's death in the middle of the story, a death that is both contingent and absurd (is she not, by chance, in the wrong place at the wrong time?). Beyond its function of controlling the audience's mind and nerves, suspense appears as a veritable metaphysical construct.

78 Shots and 45 Seconds
That Changed the History of Cinema

It is one of the most famous scenes in the history of cinema. It has become part of popular culture, even beyond the film that contains it. It has been imitated, deconstructed, and parodied countless times. It marks a milestone in the representation of violence onscreen.

The Shock of the Unexpected

When they first saw *Psycho* in 1960, audiences were particularly shocked and disoriented by the murder of Marion Crane (Janet Leigh) in her shower. It was a scene that at the time was unimaginable in an American film. The main character, the one with whom viewers have identified and whose emotions they have shared, disappears, brutally murdered, after forty-six minutes. It was this very departure from the rules of Hollywood storytelling that

persuaded Hitchcock to adapt Robert Bloch's book: "I think that the thing that appealed to me and made me decide to do the picture was the suddenness of the murder in the shower,"[1] he told François Truffaut in an interview.

Suggesting Without Showing

But such a scene was particularly difficult to film. The brutality of the scene had to be conveyed without transgressing Hollywood's prohibitions on the depiction of violence and nudity (no blades penetrating flesh, blood spurting, breasts, buttocks, or genitalia visible). "I'm going to shoot and cut it staccato, so the audience won't know what the hell is going on,"[2] said Hitchcock.

Hitchcock commissioned Saul Bass, not only as creator of the credits but also as pictorial consultant, to design the scene. Bass recalled: "I had a kind of constraint in my head, the requirement to produce a horrific murder devoid of blood."[2] He drew up a series of shots whose editing alone would create the sensation of violence, and shot some of them himself using an old camera.

A Puzzle

Hitchcock commissioned Robert Clatworthy and Joseph Hurley to build a set consisting of a bathtub topped by a showerhead and surrounded by four walls, each of them removable to allow for different camera positions.

The nudity of Marion Crane's character was a puzzle. Hitchcock and Bass showed Janet Leigh the storyboard of the scene to reassure her. The character's nudity had to be suggested while remaining within the limits allowed by the censors and preserving the actress's modesty. In some shots, Janet Leigh's breasts are covered with moleskin. In others that required the actress to be nude, Hitchcock used a double, Marli Renfro, a Las Vegas stripper for whom being nude on set posed no problem.

In this black-and-white film, chocolate syrup could be used to represent the blood dripping into the bathtub. To find the right sound effect to simulate the sound of a knife penetrating flesh, Hitchcock had his sound engineer plant blades in different kinds of melons, until he settled on a particular variety. The sound of a knife plunging into a huge steak alternates with that of the melon being mangled.

An Abstract Brutality

Based on the storyboard drawn by Bass, Hitchcock created an interplay of medium and extreme close-ups, with oblique and unusual frames. Geometric abstraction (the water gushing diagonally from the shower and colliding with the movement of the assassin's arm) is combined with off-camera shots designed to arouse the audience's anxiety. Some shots last less than a second, and many viewers will swear they have seen what is not shown. The stridency of Bernard Herrmann's violins accentuates the savagery of the images.

A Sequence of Disputed Provenance

There are several urban legends about the filming of this scene: Anthony Perkins is said to have been present on the set (Margo Epper, an actress-stuntwoman whose face has been blackened, holds the knife); Janet Leigh is said to have been completely naked, which is not true. Even more bizarrely, it is said to have been shot by a foreign crew from Japan or Germany.

In the mid-1970s, Saul Bass claimed to have filmed the sequence himself. Hitchcock, having seen the test shots filmed by his pictorial consultant, suggested he shoot it. Such an assertion would always be denied by the filmmaker himself and by witnesses present on the set during the shooting of the scene, such as assistant director Hilton A. Green and Rita Riggs, the dresser. Janet Leigh remembered the presence of Saul Bass but asserted that he never directed her in place of Hitchcock.

If the shower scene in *Psycho* is one of the most famous sequences in the history of cinema, it is due to the virtuosity of its editing and the morbid beauty of its shots, to its unprecedented violence that pushes back the limits of representation. Above all, it is a moment of pure cinema.

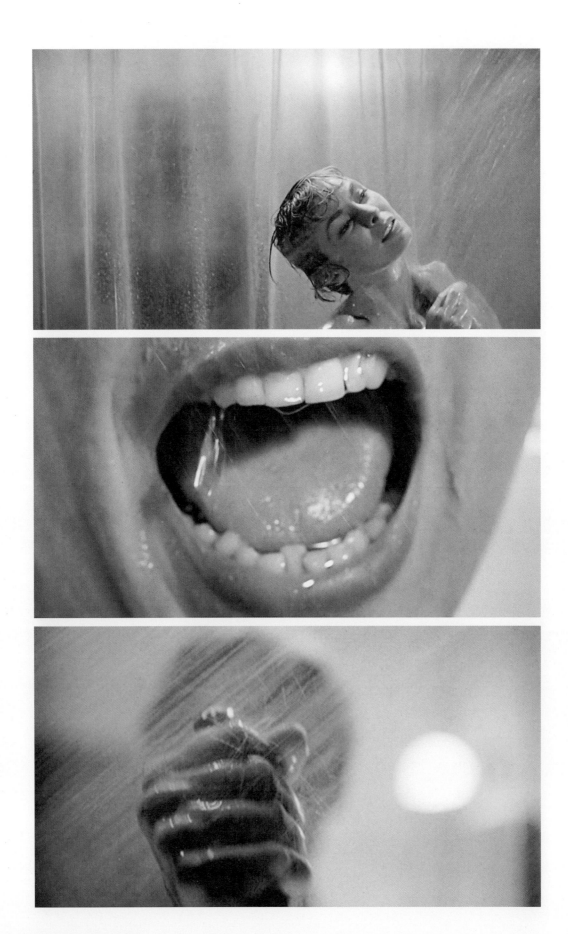

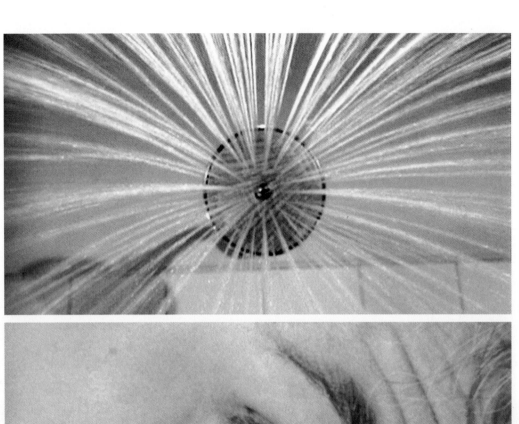

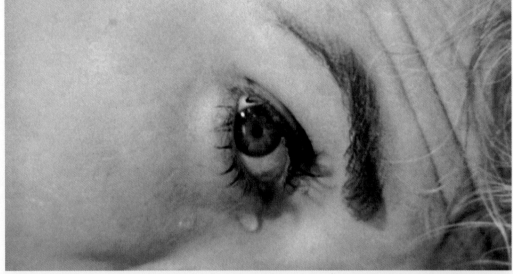

Saul Bass, *Psycho* storyboard.

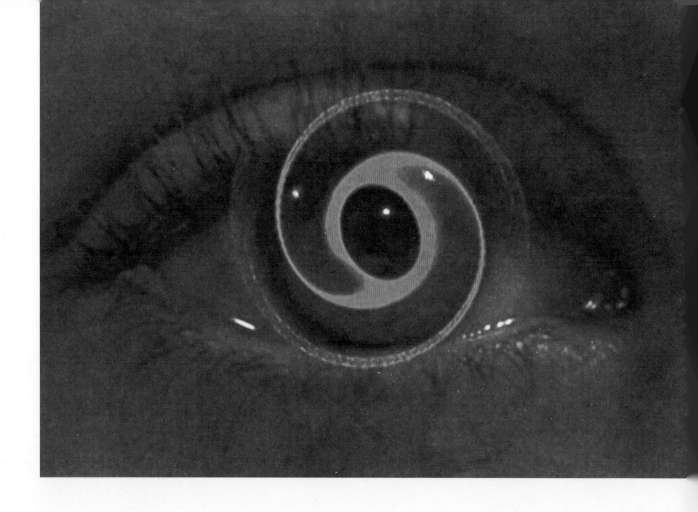

Saul Bass,
the Art of the Opening Sequence

Graphic artist, designer, poster artist, logo creator, storyboard artist, visual consultant, and filmmaker, Saul Bass (1920–1996) was an inventor of forms, many of which permeated and shaped postwar American visual culture. His innovative film credits include three for Hitchcock in the late 1950s: *Vertigo*, *North by Northwest*, and *Psycho*.

Design at the Service of Cinema

Born in the Bronx, New York, to Jewish parents of Russian origin, Saul Bass developed a passion for drawing and the graphic arts. He attended the Art Students League and, in 1942 at Brooklyn College, met the painter and art theorist György Kepes (*Language of Vision*, 1944), who introduced him to the German Bauhaus movement, the modern art of

his time. An assiduous reader of Freud, an admirer of Eisenstein's films, and a young man with ideological leanings toward the left, Bass wanted to place his talent at the service of the good and the beautiful. In 1952, he set up his own advertising and design company in Los Angeles. Four years later, he began a forty-year collaboration of protean activity with his future wife, Elaine Bass. In 1954 and 1955, filmmaker Otto Preminger (thirteen films between them) commissioned him to design the credits for *Carmen Jones* and *The Man with the Golden Arm*, whose bold graphics earned him prominence. Over the course of four decades, Saul Bass would go on to produce more than fifty opening titles for directors such as Billy Wilder (*The Seven Year Itch*), Robert Aldrich (*The Big Knife*), Robert Wise (*West Side Story*),

John Frankenheimer (*Grand Prix*), Martin Scorsese (*Casino*), and many more.

The Spirit of the Film

Before Saul Bass, almost all film credits consisted of a succession of names to be read off the screen; no one paid any attention to them, neither the projectionist nor the audience. Bass invented moving credits, whether drawn, animated, shot on film, or a combination of several approaches. He conceived the sequence as the entry point to the feature film, immediately capturing the audience's attention and concentration, involving them in an experience in which the extraordinary nature of the projection upends the ordinariness of everyday life. Bass also saw this beginning as a prologue, a "film within a film," and each time sought a spectacular form that indicated the spirit, tone, and idea of what was to come. In two or three minutes, using signs, shapes, figures, colors, symbols, metaphors, optical tricks, and the resources of typography, he delivered a dynamic foreword and a slightly cryptic interpretation of the work to come. Ahead of the film's "big secret," he mischievously introduced its enigma.

Three Unforgettable Opening Credits

Vertigo: a female face seen in pieces, like a jigsaw puzzle—a mouth, two eyes, an eye in extreme close-up from which the title emerges. From the eye too come colored spirals, hypnotic and dizzying shapes, redoubled by the tragic swirls of Bernard Herrmann's music. Against an all-black background, these swirling rings seem to unfold in cosmic space, or in the inner world of a man obsessed by the impossible reconstruction of an imaginary woman. At the end of the credits, we return to the eye, from which the filmmaker's name emerges.

North by Northwest: Blue lines on a green background crisscross the screen, like a grid or structure on which the names in the credits rise and fall, as in an elevator, to the rhythm of Herrmann's fandango. The lines merge with the outline of a glass skyscraper that reflects the traffic on Madison Avenue: the world and its double, or mirror image, a perfect introduction to a spy movie.

Psycho: In symbiosis with the strident music by the same composer, the opening credits go into a frenzy: Lines coming successively from each edge of the screen speed across the title and credits that appear, cutting them in two, disconnecting and expelling them, with Janet Leigh's first and last names ending up separated, and "Anthony Perkins"

torn between the top and bottom of the image—a figuration of dismemberment and schizophrenia?

Later Tributes

Between 1990 and 1995, Martin Scorsese called on Saul and Elaine Bass five times, in particular for the credits of *Cape Fear*, *The Age of Innocence*, and *Casino*. In 1998, Gus Van Sant remade *Psycho* "identically," using the same iconic opening, but with one difference: The lines were no longer gray, but green, a green reminiscent of *North by Northwest*... In 2002, Steven Spielberg's *Catch Me If You Can* began with a Saul Bass–style prologue. From 2007 to 2015, the *Mad Men* television series had seven seasons, ninety-two episodes, and a theme song: In less than a minute, we have a combination of *North by Northwest* (a Madison Avenue skyscraper) and *Vertigo* (a man falls into the void of his madness), a tribute to Alfred Hitchcock and Saul Bass combined. To be continued...

Portrait

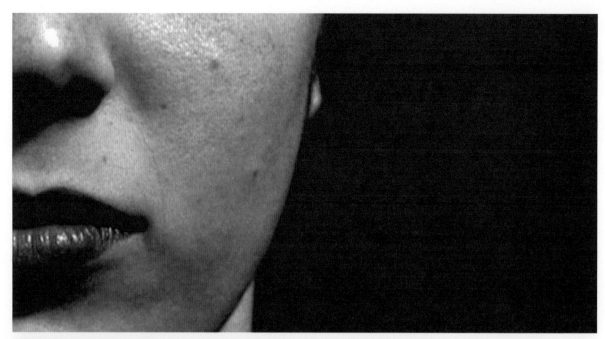

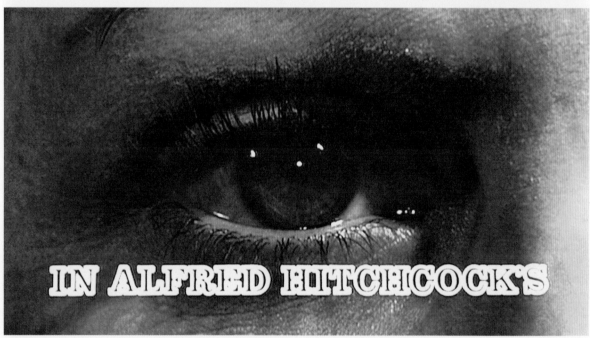

Vertigo, 1957.

ART DIRECTION **HAL PEREIRA**
& HENRY BUMSTEAD
SPECIAL PHOTOGRAPHIC EFFECTS
JOHN P. FULTON, A.S.C.
PROCESS PHOTOGRAPHY
FARCIOT EDOUART, A.S.C.
& WALLACE KELLEY, A.S.C.
SET DECORATION **SAM COMER**
& FRANK McKELVY
TITLES DESIGNED BY **SAUL BASS**

MUSIC BY **BERNARD HERRMANN**

In 1958, during postproduction, Saul Bass asked John Whitney, an experimental filmmaker and pioneer of computer art, to compose the sinusoidal part of the *Vertigo* credits, based on the Lissajous curve (the figuration of a mathematical equation elaborated by a nineteenth-century French physicist). Using a mechanical computer derived from World War II military technology and producing the infinite rotation of a platform, itself synchronized to the swing of a suspended pendulum and equipped with a paint pen, Whitney created the spiral patterns of the opening sequence.

Incident at a Corner

Season 1, Episode 27

 United States • 1 hr • Color •   Mono • 1.33:1

SYNOPSIS

Production Dates: February 8–17, 1960
Broadcast in the United States: April 5, 1960

Production: Shamley Productions
Producer: Joan Harrison
Associate Producer: Norman Lloyd

Based on a short story by Charlotte Armstrong (1959)
Screenplay: Charlotte Armstrong
Director of Photography: John L. Russell
Sound: William Russell
Assistant Director: Hilton A. Green
Art Direction: John J. Lloyd

Set Decoration: George Milo
Hair Stylist: Florence Bush
Makeup: Jack Barron
Costumes: Vincent Dee
Music: Frederick Herbert
Film Editing: Edward W. Williams, Richard G. Wray

Starring: Vera Miles (Jean Medwick), George Peppard (Pat Lawrence), Paul Hartman (James Medwick), Bob Sweeney (Uncle Jeffrey), Leora Dana (Mrs. Tawley), Warren Berlinger (Ron Tawley), Philip Ober (Malcolm Tawley), Jerry Paris (W. E. Grimes, prosecutor), Jack Albertson (Harry Crane), Eve McVeagh (Georgia Crane) . . .

An incident, seen from three different angles, occurs at a small-town crossroads. As a result of this banal altercation, a traffic cop is slandered, accused, and laid off. His granddaughter, accompanied by her fiancé, leads the investigation. She solicits testimony and understanding from friends, neighbors, and notables but encounters attitudes ranging from resignation to hostility. The couple will have their work cut out to exonerate the policeman.

Startime

"Incident at a Corner" is the twenty-seventh episode of the thirty-three-part _Startime_ TV series. Sponsored by the Ford Motor Company, it ran for just one season (1959–1960), broadcast on NBC. The all-powerful Lew Wasserman, head of the MCA agency and Revue Studios, enabled the series to feature movie stars such as Ingrid Bergman and James Stewart, justifying its title: _Startime_. Wasserman convinced Alfred Hitchcock, whose agent he was, to direct this medium-length film. "Incident at a Corner," Hitchcock's only color television production, was shot in under ten days.

From One Set to Another

From the mid-1950s to 1962, Hitchcock alternated between film and television. Many of his colleagues switched from one medium to the other. The cinematographer, set designer, assistant director, sound engineer, makeup artist, and hairdresser of "Incident at a Corner" all came from _Psycho_, which had concluded shooting a week earlier in Universal's nearby studio, under the technical and economic conditions of a TV movie.

A Movie Cast

The logic of the communicating channels between cinema and television also applied to the casting of "Incident at a Corner" While George Peppard played for the first and only time under Hitchcock's direction, Vera Miles came from _Psycho_ and previously from "Revenge" as well as _The Wrong Man_. The same went for Bob Sweeney (soon to appear in _Marnie_), Philip Ober (the man stabbed at UN headquarters in _North by Northwest_), and Alexander Lockwood (_Saboteur_, _North by Northwest_).

Who Saw What?

The film opens in an original way: The same scene is presented three times from three different angles. This interplay of repetition and difference launches the plot: What really happened? What was really said? Who saw what? But this decentering of the single point of view also sums up the philosophical issue at stake: The truth eludes those who think they know it and is often only revealed, as in "Incident at a Corner," following a series of misinterpretations.

A Message for the Audience

In another eye-catching moment, suddenly Hitchcock films the whole family gathered in the living room. This is a bird's-eye shot, with five splices that enable the camera to get closer and closer to

Pat Lawrence (George Peppard), drawing attention to his leap of faith: If the injustice done in this small town to an ordinary man goes unremedied, then no one will ever be safe from slander. No one—in other words, not the Medwick family in their living room, or the audience, also in their living room, watching "Incident at a Corner."

For the _Hollywood Reporter_ magazine, this investigation by a handful of citizens, which reveals the dysfunctions and narrow-mindedness of an apparently blameless community, is "Hitchcock at his non-violent best" (April 7, 1960). On the same day, _Daily Variety_ lamented the thin plot, lack of dramatic tension, and artificial ending.

In the Land of Denunciation

At the time, nobody saw, or wanted to see, a thinly disguised commentary on McCarthyism, the "witch hunt" that, in the first half of the 1950s and in the name of the fight against communist ideology, spread an atmosphere of denunciation and fear in the United States. The whole country was rife with rumors, suspicions, lies, and accusations, and every American could denounce his neighbor as well as be denounced by him. Four successive shots in the credits of "Incident at a Corner" show an anonymous mouth whispering in the hollow of an attentive ear, the explicit expression of widespread rumormongering. And then there is this exchange in the prosecutor's office:

Pat Lawrence: "I'm not prepared to have a man's life ruined by a lie."

Prosecutor: "It would not be the first time."

Seen!

In _Rear Window_ (1954), a man spies on his neighbors from his window. In "Incident at a Corner," a man finds himself at the crossroads of his neighbors' gazes and their prejudices. In Hitchcock's world, peaceful only in appearance, every human being is "caught" in a gaze: Either they are voyeurs or they are seen. And to be seen is often to be frowned upon.

Mrs. Bixby and the Colonel's Coat

Season 6, Episode 1

United States • **30 mins** • **Black and White** • **Mono** (RCA Sound Recording) • **1.33:1**

SYNOPSIS

Production Dates: August 17–19, 1960
Broadcast in the United States: September 27, 1960

Production: Shamley Productions
Producer: Joan Harrison
Associate Producer: Norman Lloyd

Based on a short story by Roald Dahl (1959)
Adaptation: Halsted Welles
Director of Photography: John L. Russell
Sound: Lyle Cain
Assistant Director: James H. Brown

Art Direction: Martin Obzina
Set Decoration: James S. Redd
Hair Stylist: Florence Bush
Makeup: Robert Dawn
Costumes: Vincent Dee
Music: Frederick Herbert
Film Editing: Edward W. Williams, David J. O'Connell

Starring: Audrey Meadows (Mrs. Bixby), Les Tremayne (Dr. Fred Bixby), Stephen Chase (colonel), Sally Hughes (Miss Putney), Howard Caine (pawnbroker), Maidie Norman (Éloise), Bernie Hamilton (Dawson), Alfred Hitchcock (himself) . . .

Mrs. Bixby tells her husband, a dentist, that she will be spending the weekend at her aunt's place, as she does every month, whereas she actually sets off to a rendezvous. In the morning, her lover, the colonel, departs but leaves her a mink coat. She pawns it, then asks her husband to retrieve the pawned item. Mr. Bixby returns with a thin $50 fur stole. Mrs. Bixby then discovers that her husband's employee is wearing the expensive coat.

Another Story by Roald Dahl

"Mrs. Bixby and the Colonel's Coat" opens the sixth season of *Alfred Hitchcock Presents*. It was the fourth short story by British writer Roald Dahl to be adapted for the series, following "Lamb to the Slaughter," "Dip in the Pool," and "Poison." Halsted Welles was in charge of the adaptation. This prolific screenwriter made his film debut with the script for *The Lady Gambles*, starring Barbara Stanwyck, in 1949. He also wrote the screenplays for two fine Delmer Daves Westerns, *3:10 to Yuma*, after Elmore Leonard (1957), and *The Hanging Tree* (1960). But he devoted himself above all to television, participating in numerous series such as *Suspense* (1949–1953), *Danger* (1954–1955), *Kraft Suspense Theatre* (1964), and *Night Gallery* (1971–1973). He wrote six adaptations for *Alfred Hitchcock Presents*.

Roald Dahl's short story was published in 1959 in *Nugget* magazine. Jacques Rivette's short film *Fool's Mate*, made in 1956, told the same story. No doubt the French filmmaker was inspired, as Dahl was after him, by an urban legend that had been around since the 1930s.

Hitchcock and the Starving Actress

The role of the unfaithful wife was played by Audrey Meadows. This actress, who began her career in 1950, appeared mainly on television, in series such as *The Honeymooners* (1955–1956), *The Red Skelton Show* (1960–1971), *Too Close for Comfort* (1982–1986), and *Uncle Buck* (1990–1991). This would be her only participation in the series. She recalled shooting the breakfast scene with her lover: "I had to get up at five in the morning, and I was very hungry. Mr. Hitchcock noticed that I was nervously devouring the toast and jam between takes. So he said to me: "Mrs. Meadows, we can add bacon and eggs if you're still hungry."[1]

The Husband and the Lover

For the role of Dr. Bixby, Hitchcock hired Les Tremayne. The filmmaker wanted an actor who could give the impression, at the beginning of the story, that his character was rather conservative, but who we discover at the end is also given to trifles. Tremayne began his career in 1949, appearing in numerous films of varying ambition, including John Cromwell's *The Racket* and *The Unguarded Moment*. He played the auctioneer in the auction sequence of *North by Northwest* (1958). He often lent his voice as narrator or commentator, notably for Fred Wilcox's *Forbidden Planet* and George Cukor's *Bhowani Junction*. He

Alfred Hitchcock Presents...

In the episode's introduction, Hitchcock sums up the series's philosophy: "As usual, we're going to present little domestic stories of an unusual nature…Where crime is involved, it is crime committed by ordinary people, like your neighbor." He then claims to have settled all his differences with the show's sponsor, whom he endorses entirely. A halo appears over his head when he announces that a wonderful little film (the commercial) will be shown before the episode. In conclusion, he claims still to have no problems with the show's sponsor, even though a noose is hanging over his neck.

also appeared in the sixth season of *Alfred Hitchcock Presents*.

The role of the colonel was given to Stephen Chase, for his only appearance in the series. Since 1933, he had appeared in films (Rudolph Maté's *When Worlds Collide*, Douglas Sirk's *No Room for the Groom*, Raoul Walsh's *The Lawless Breed*) and numerous TV serials.

Lies and Hypocrisy

"Mrs. Bixby and the Colonel's Coat" presents a world where relationships between men and women are governed by lies. It is a world determined first and foremost by adultery, but also by cowardice—the cowardice of the lover who does not tell his mistress that he is going to leave her. Thus, the colonel prefers to give Mrs. Bixby a mink coat as a parting gift, which quickly consoles the neglected wife. The apparent marital harmony described at the beginning of the episode (Mrs. Bixby brings her husband his lunch, and he worries about being bored in her absence) is built on a hypocrisy whose mutual nature the story's punch line will prove. Marital boredom and domestic subservience are denounced by the wife in a lament with almost feminist overtones, Mrs. Bixby justifying the adultery of which she is guilty as follows: "No man really pays any attention to you, unless you wash his shirts, bring him his lunch or fight the creditors."

The Horse Player

Season 6, Episode 22

 United States • 30 mins • ⊛ Black and White • 🔇 Mono • 1.33:1

Production Dates: January 4–6, 1961
Broadcast in the United States: March 14, 1961

Production: Shamley Productions
Producer: Joan Harrison
Associate Producer: Norman Lloyd

Based on a short story by Henry Slesar (1960)
Adaptation: Henry Slesar
Director of Photography: John L. Russell
Sound: William Russell
Assistant Director: James H. Brown
Art Direction: Martin Obzina

Set Decoration: John McCarthy, Julia Heron
Hair Stylist: Florence Bush
Makeup: Jack Barron
Costumes: Vincent Dee
Music: Joseph E. Romero
Film Editing: Edward W. Williams, David J. O'Connell

Starring: Claude Rains (Father Amion), Ed Gardner (Sheridan), Percy Helton (Morton), Mike Ragan (Mr. Cheever), William Newell (bank teller), David Carlile (bank teller), Ada Murphy (old lady), Kenneth MacKenna (Bishop Cannon), Alfred Hitchcock (himself)...

SYNOPSIS

Father Amion tries to dissuade one of his parishioners, Sheridan, from using prayer to win at games of chance. Father Amion is tempted, however, and asks Sheridan to bet for him in a horse race, hoping to win enough money to repair the roof of his church. Sheridan bets on the horse to place rather than to win, and is able to give Father Amion the money he had hoped for.

Henry Slesar, Mainstay of the Series

Hitchcock's second film for season 6 of *Alfred Hitchcock Presents*, "The Horse Player" is an adaptation of a short story by Henry Slesar. Slesar wrote short, fast-paced detective and science-fiction stories with a twist at the end, published in a variety of magazines including *Playboy*, *Ellery Queen's Mystery Magazine*, and, of course, *Alfred Hitchcock's Mystery Magazine*. Spotted by the series' production team, he became one of its most active and loyal writers, often adapting his own stories for the small screen. Between 1957 and 1962, he collaborated on thirty-seven episodes of *Alfred Hitchcock Presents*. Between 1962 and 1964, he wrote ten more for *The Alfred Hitchcock Hour*. Two of Slesar's stories were also adapted for *The Twilight Zone*. Above all, Slesar was the creator and main scriptwriter of the series *The Edge of Night* from 1968 to 1983.

A Mostly Male Cast

In the role of Father Amion, Hitchcock reunited with Claude Rains, fifteen years after *Notorious*. Famous for playing the Invisible Man in James Whale's film of the same name (1933) and Captain Renault in Michael Curtiz's *Casablanca* (1942), the actor had already made three appearances in *Alfred Hitchcock Presents* and would make one more the following year. Ed Gardner, who played the professional turf player, was a radio producer, writer, and actor in the early 1940s. He created the character of Archie, a picturesque Brooklyn barkeeper in the radio series *Duffy's Tavern*, which won him great popularity. In 1945, the radio series became a film directed by Hal Walker, with many of the stars as themselves. *Duffy's Tavern* was also made into a TV series, again starring Ed Gardner, in 1954. Gardner would return in an episode of *Alfred Hitchcock Presents* the following season. Kenneth MacKenna, who played Bishop Cannon, began his career in 1925 and appeared until 1933 in several now somewhat forgotten films. He also directed a few during this period. The Metro-Goldwyn-Mayer studio hired him in 1936 as story editor. Returning to acting in Blake Edwards's *High Time* in 1960, he went on to appear in TV series (*Bonanza*, *Hong Kong*, *The Barbara Stanwyck Show*). In 1961, he played Judge Norris in Stanley Kramer's *Judgment at Nuremberg*. The same year, he again played a bishop in an episode of *Dr. Kildare*. "The Horse Player" would be his only participation in Hitchcock's series.

Alfred Hitchcock Presents...

Hitchcock stands next to a man dressed as a horse. He holds the back of the animal costume in his hand. He claims that someone had the bright idea of making him wear it to illustrate the film to follow. The man with the horse's head pretends to leave. Hitchcock calls him back and gives him his part of the costume. At the end of the episode, he announces that the sponsor really insisted that he play this game. After the commercial break, the "horse" appears, galloping in front of the camera before splitting in two, each part going in the direction opposite the other.

A Comical Remake of *I Confess*?

"The Horse Player" can be interpreted as a frivolous, humorous remake of *I Confess* (1952). The main character is also a Catholic priest, the victim of an insoluble theological contradiction. The story focuses on a man who commits a sin to fulfill his vows, then repents. But his contrition allows him to have it both ways, ultimately ensuring both moral and financial gain. The script unfolds a series of events that take him down a particularly winding, and one might say Jesuitical, path. To what extent is man guilty? What is fault? Did Father Amion win because he prayed not to? Or does the final twist of fate, with a result that excludes any metaphysical determination, place him face-to-face with his own freedom?

Innocent or Guilty?

In *I Confess*, was the priest, the film's hero, truly innocent of the murder of which he was accused? Or was he already guilty of the desire to see the man who was blackmailing him disappear? In the same way, "The Horse Player" gives no answers to a series of spiritual questions that may not have any, and illustrates the impossibility of distinguishing innocence from guilt.

At the end of the film, the priest raises his eyes to heaven. Is he questioning God on the inscrutability of his ways? The subjective shot that follows shows the hole in the church roof that lets in the rainwater. In the absence of an answer, the divine inscrutability is replaced by the prosaic but real image of a leaky roof.

Bang! You're Dead

Season 7, Episode 2

United States · **30 mins** · **Black and White** · **Mono** · **1.33:1**

Production Dates: July 25–27, 1961
Broadcast in the United States:
October 17, 1961

Production: Shamley Productions
Producer: Joan Harrison
Associate Producer: Norman Lloyd

Based on a short story by Margery Vosper (1961)
Adaptation: Harold Swanton
Director of Photography:
John L. Russell
Sound: William Russell
Assistant Director: Wallace Worsley
Art Direction: Martin Obzina
Set Decoration: John McCarthy, Julia Heron

Hair Stylist: Florence Bush
Makeup: Jack Barron
Costumes: Vincent Dee
Music: Joseph E. Romero
Film Editing: Edward W. Williams, David J. O'Connell

Starring: Billy Mumy (Jackie Chester), Steve Dunne (Rick Sheffield), Biff Elliott (Fred Chester), Lucy Prentiss (Amy Chester), Juanita Moore (Cleo), Marta Kristen (seller in the supermarket), John Zaremba (supermarket manager), Karl Lukas (postman), Olan Soulé (little girl's father), Craig Duncan (supermarket employee), Thayer Burton (cashier), Alfred Hitchcock (himself)…

SYNOPSIS

A solitary young boy borrows a revolver belonging to his uncle, believing it to be a toy. He goes out into the street, has fun pointing it at passersby, then goes to a supermarket. He periodically adds a bullet to the gun's barrel. His parents try to find him before there is a fatal accident. Back home, he aims at the cleaning lady, when his father intervenes at the last moment, with the bullet narrowly missing the maid.

An Unassuming Author Adapted by a Television Stakhanovite

"Bang! You're Dead," the filmmaker's only episode for the series' seventh season, is based on a short story by Margery Vosper. The London-born Vosper was the sister and literary agent of actor, screenwriter, and playwright Frank Vosper, who died in 1937. Harold Swanton wrote the adaptation. The screenwriter, who made his film debut in 1948 (*Appointment with Murder*), would devote most of his time to writing television scripts until the early 1980s. He took part in series such as *The Whistler* (1955), *Panic!* (1957–1958), *Buckskin*, of which he was the creator (1958), and *Wagon Train* (1960–1961). He collaborated on ten episodes of *Alfred Hitchcock Presents* and one episode of *The Alfred Hitchcock Hour*.

The Restless Child

The film's lead role, that of little Jackie Chester, was given to Billy Mumy, who went on to become an American TV star with the series *Lost in Space* (1965–1968). He did not have fond memories of the shoot, and particularly of Alfred Hitchcock. One day, annoyed by this kid who could not stand still while the crew was adjusting the lighting for a scene, the director is said to have terrorized him by whispering in his ear that he was going to drive a nail through his foot and that the blood would start to flow.

The Icon of a Great Melodrama

Juanita Moore played Cleo, the Chester family maid. She made a particularly lasting impression as Annie Johnson in Douglas Sirk's masterpiece *Imitation of Life* (1959). Her career began in the late 1930s, and the actress accumulated a series of small roles, for which she was often not mentioned in the credits, until Sirk's melodrama, which deals openly with the Black question in the United States. As is the case in "Bang! You're Dead," despite appearances.

A Short Treatise on Suspense

"Bang! You're Dead" seems to be an instruction manual for cinematic suspense, as Hitchcock understood it. The film sets up a particular situation: The audience is in possession of information that the characters do not have. Like the little boy in *Sabotage* (1936) who unknowingly carried a bomb that could explode at any moment, the kid in the film is the unconscious bearer of a possible catastrophe. In a sadistic and unstoppable way, suspense is heightened by increasing the probability of a fatal accident

Alfred Hitchcock Presents...

Hitchcock is manning the cash register at a movie theater. He steps out of the booth and brandishes a pistol. When he pulls the trigger, a small flag bearing the word "Bang!" emerges from the barrel. The filmmaker warns the audience that, despite its humorous presentation, the film deals with a serious subject. At the end of the episode, he reiterates that this story is not to be taken lightly, hoping that parents are now aware of the need to keep firearms out of the reach of children. The introduction to some episodes of the series is a serious warning to the viewer; Hitchcock abandons his flippancy for a few moments to warn the audience of the evils of alcohol or the need to obey traffic regulations.

every time Jackie adds another bullet to the gun's barrel. Another way of heightening the tension: The discovery of the boy in time by his distraught parents is constantly postponed by random everyday events (the mother delayed by a flippant customer, the manager answering the phone before calling the child over the public address system…)

Violence in History

This little object lesson on how to create effective suspense in cinema can also be seen as a metaphor for the place of violence in American culture and history, as well as a relocation of the question of guilt. By playing a cowboy, the little boy in the film returns to a primitive history that has never really been digested. The film's monotonous backdrop, the residential suburbs of the 1950s, reflects a postwar desire to "escape from history," to repress a fundamental violence (the massacre of Native Americans, Black slavery) that banal, childish games and social reality tend to mimic or unwittingly recall. The uncle in possession of the lethal weapon has just returned from a trip to Africa. This detail would seem insignificant were it not for the fact that Africa is also the cradle of an original history and a primitive brutality that is purely American. Subliminally, the Black question recurs in the twists and turns of a story that ends with the armed child endangering the Chesters' maid.

Lew Wasserman,
the Great Strategist

Sometimes called "the King of Hollywood" or "the Last Baron," Lew Wasserman (1913–2002) was Alfred Hitchcock's agent. He was also his last producer, one of the most decisive, after Michael Balcon in England and David O. Selznick. Wasserman gave the Master unrivaled power and recognition. He is the man who shaped the second half of Hitchcock's American career, the man who helped build his image as much as enrich it.

The Wasserman Method

The Music Corporation of America (MCA), headed by Jules Stein, was founded in Chicago in 1924 to negotiate contracts for jazz orchestras. In 1939, it set up offices in Beverly Hills. Lew Wasserman, who had come over from the advertising department, was put in charge of prospecting for new clients to gain a foothold in the film industry. Bette Davis, Errol Flynn, James Stewart, and Joan Crawford, among others, would now be represented by MCA.

Wasserman's men, the producers' bêtes noires, fiercely negotiated the contracts of actors and actresses on the studios' payroll. They sometimes encouraged them to forgo their salaries in order to claim a percentage of their films' profits. By increasing the power of the stars, MCA's methods gradually transformed a system in which the producer had previously been all-powerful.

Lew Wasserman became Alfred Hitchcock's agent in 1945, following MCA's purchase of Leland Hayward's company, which looked after the director's interests. It was through him that the director

Portrait

hired James Stewart for *Rope* in 1948: Wasserman convinced the actor to opt for a percentage of the film's profits rather than a fee that Transatlantic Pictures, Hitchcock's production company, would not have been able to pay.

By Way of Television

In 1953, Lew Wasserman signed Hitchcock to a ten-film contract with Paramount; the director would have exclusive rights to five of them. The agent succeeded in increasing his client's salary and expense limits. He also convinced him to take American citizenship in order to obtain tax benefits (the filmmaker became a US citizen on April 20, 1955).

Hitchcock maintained a friendly relationship with his agent, even commissioning Bernard Buffet to paint his portrait. To one of the MCA executives' astonishment at the painting of a seated Lew Wasserman in a black suit, a tall, lean, and disquieting man with gaunt hands reminiscent of spider's legs, Hitchcock responded with an enigmatic smile.

Wasserman was a shrewd strategist who used the Master of Suspense's reputation to make strategic choices for MCA. The company wanted to move into production. It was doing so by betting on the future of the new mass medium of television. Revue Studios, a subsidiary of MCA, became one of the most important television producers of the 1950s. Several of the agency's clients became stars of the small screen. Wasserman also encouraged Hitchcock to direct a television series. The result was the 1955 series *Alfred Hitchcock Presents* (which became *The Alfred Hitchcock Hour* in 1962), produced by Revue Productions and Shamley Productions. The latter company was created by the director on the advice of his agent. The small screen enabled him to increase both his income and his popularity.

Hitchcock Under Control

Television became MCA's Trojan horse, giving it increasing power at the heart of a struggling Hollywood system. Audiences were declining, exacerbated by the antitrust decree forcing major companies to sell off their movie theaters.

In 1958, MCA bought Universal International's 180 hectares of studios. This is where *Psycho* was filmed the following year. Wasserman pressured

Paramount not to produce the film but to distribute it. This enabled Hitchcock, who produced the film with Shamley Productions, to cash in on its considerable success.

In 1962, MCA bought the Decca company, which owned Universal. Wasserman found himself at the head of a major company, MCA/Universal. He took on Hitchcock under contract and acquired the rights to Paramount's TV series and films, which he himself had negotiated for the director. It also made him the studio's third-largest shareholder. But what appeared to be economic security and an increase in power turned into a golden prison. After the commercial failure of *Marnie* (1964), Wasserman obliged the director to direct several films and to hire certain actors. Above all, he refused to give the green light to projects Hitchcock felt strongly about (*Kaleidoscope*, 1967). The relationship between the two men deteriorated. Wasserman had gone from being Hitchcock's agent to being his employer, a boss who could prevent certain projects, such as *Mary Rose*, from going ahead, a fact that particularly affected the director. Lew Wasserman, the man who revolutionized the Hollywood system, became a cautious, conservative producer.

"It could be the most terrifying motion picture
I have ever made!"— *Alfred Hitchcock*

"...and
remember,
the next
scream
you hear
may be
your own!"

ALFRED HITCHCOCK'S
"The Birds"
TECHNICOLOR®

A Fascinating
New Personality

STARRING

ROD TAYLOR · JESSICA TANDY
SUZANNE PLESHETTE *and Introducing* 'TIPPI' HEDREN

Based on Daphne Du Maurier's Classic Suspense Story!

Screenplay by EVAN HUNTER · Directed by ALFRED HITCHCOCK

The Birds

United States · **1 hr 59** · **Color**
(Technicolor) · **Mono**
(Westrex Recording
System) · **1.85:1**

Production Dates: March 5–July 10, 1962
Release Date in the United States: March 28, 1963 (New York premiere),
March 29, 1963 (United States)

Production: Universal Pictures
Producer: Alfred Hitchcock
Production Manager: Norman Deming

Based on the short story of the same name by Daphne Du Maurier (1952)
Screenplay: Evan Hunter
Titles: James S. Pollak
Director of Photography: Robert Burks
Camera Operator: Leonard J. South
Visual Effects: Ub Iwerks, Albert Whitlock
Special Effects: Lawrence A. Hampton, Clarence Champagne, Dave Fleischer,
Chuck Gaspar, Don Wolz, Petro Vlahos
Sound: Waldon O. Watson, William Russell
Electronic Sound Production and Composition: Remi Gassmann, Oskar Sala,
Bernard Herrmann (consultant)
Assistant Director: James H. Brown
Alfred Hitchcock's Assistant: Peggy Robertson
Art Direction: Robert Boyle
Set Decoration: George Milo
Hair Stylist: Virginia Darcy
Makeup: Howard Smit
Costumes: Edith Head, Rita Riggs
Bird Trainer: Ray Berwick
Film Editing: George Tomasini

Starring: Tippi Hedren (Melanie Daniels), Rod Taylor (Mitch Brenner), Jessica
Tandy (Lydia Brenner), Suzanne Pleshette (Annie Hayworth), Veronica Cartwright
(Cathy Brenner), Ethel Griffies (Mrs. Bundy), Charles McGraw (Sebastian Sholes),
Ruth McDevitt (Mrs. MacGruder), Lonny Chapman (Deke Carter), Elizabeth Wilson
(Helen Carter), Malcolm Atterbury (Deputy Al Malone), William Quinn (Sam),
Doreen Lang (hysterical mother in the diner), Alfred Hitchcock (man walking dogs
out of a pet shop)...

"*The Birds*...A lyrical, tragic poem whose episodes are like stanzas that reinforce a single theme on an emotional level."

—

Federico Fellini

SYNOPSIS

——

In a pet shop in San Francisco, Melanie Daniels clashes with lawyer Mitch Brenner, who has come to order a pair of inseparable parakeets for his younger sister's birthday. Mitch recognizes her as a wealthy heiress whose extravagance has been the talk of the town. Both annoyed and seduced by the young man, Melanie buys a pair of parakeets and discreetly drops them off at the Brenner family home, not far from the coastal village of Bodega Bay. Slightly injured in the head by a seagull, she is rescued by Mitch, who then introduces her to his mother, whose attitude is icy. Melanie finds refuge with Bodega Bay's schoolteacher, Annie. Annie, a former girlfriend of Mitch's who is still in love with him, explains to the newcomer that Mrs. Brenner has always prevented her son from having a serious relationship with a woman. Melanie's departure is constantly jeopardized by swarms of birds attacking the inhabitants of Bodega Bay. These increasingly violent attacks lead to Annie's death. Melanie joins the Brenners, who are barricading their home against the next onslaught. But during the night, she is seriously injured by seagulls that have invaded the attic. The Brenners take advantage of a lull to take her to their car and take her to the hospital. The car sets off in a landscape covered with birds, massed in silence.

GENESIS

In 1961, Hitchcock decided to adapt Winston Graham's novel *Marnie* into a film that would mark Grace Kelly's return to the silver screen. However, Grace Kelly, now princess of Monaco, announced that she would not be available for another year or two. In the meantime, the filmmaker planned to bring other stories to the screen, including Fredric Brown's *The Mind Thing*, a science fiction story centered on an alien with the power to mentally dominate living creatures. In the book's final scene, the hero is assaulted by various animals commanded by the invader. In the end, the project never saw the light of day, but Hitchcock took up the idea of nature's revolt against man in what was to become *Alfred Hitchcock's "The Birds."*

A True Story and a Long Short Story

Reading a newspaper article about the destruction of a small California town by a sudden attack of birds reminded the filmmaker of Daphne Du Maurier's short story "The Birds," which Hitchcock had published in the United States in a collection of his favorite suspense stories.[1] He decided to move the action from English Cornwall to a coastal hamlet in Northern California, Bodega Bay, which he had discovered during the filming of *Shadow of a Doubt* (1942). But while he did pick up on key elements of the short story (the behavior of birds silently massing between two raids, the final section where a family huddles in their house for protection), the filmmaker found little depth to the characters, simple farmers trying to survive. To develop the story, he called on writer Evan Hunter (one of Ed McBain's many pseudonyms), whose first novel, *The Blackboard Jungle*, was adapted into a film in 1955. On the strength of this success, Hunter became a screenwriter, working on a TV series based on his *87th Precinct* crime novels, which he published under the name Ed McBain.

Why?

Evan Hunter had known his new boss for about two years, having seen his short story "Vicious Circle" adapted for the TV series *Alfred Hitchcock Presents* and having himself scripted the episode "Appointment at Eleven." Together, the two men invented original characters for the film of *The Birds*. The story begins with a love affair between a whimsical heiress and a dashing lawyer. She sets off to find him in his hometown, Bodega Bay, where she discovers him in the company of a possessive mother and a young schoolteacher who has long been in love with him… The idea was to build a situation captivating enough to sustain interest before the first attacks, the audience having come to the movie theater to see the killer birds promised by the publicity. However, Hitchcock stumbled over the reason for the birds' hostile behavior, knowing that believers in verisimilitude would demand to know. Various explanations were considered, such as a Soviet plot or nature's revenge against human pollution, but in the end, the film failed to shed any light on the matter, returning to the roots of Daphne Du Maurier's short story.

CASTING

Long before the script was completed, Hitchcock decided that the lead role would be played by model Tippi Hedren. Having arrived in Los Angeles to become an actress and recently divorced, she was the mother of a four-year-old child, Melanie, a name Hunter and the filmmaker gave to the character she played in *The Birds*. The little girl would later become a famous actress (Melanie Griffith) and the mother of star actress Dakota Johnson. In fact, Tippi Hedren is none other than the grandmother of the heroine of the *Fifty Shades of Grey* saga.

Training a Newcomer

After spotting Tippi Hedren in a commercial, Hitchcock signed her to a seven-year contract. The aspiring actress then followed the same path as the other actresses associated with the director. She was placed in the hands of hairdressers, stylists, jewelers, and makeup artists who precisely designed her physical appearance. Above all, she rehearsed iconic scenes from previous Hitchcock films, both in private and in front of the camera. But Hedren's screen test was the object of particular care: Shot in color and in conditions worthy of a feature film (Martin Balsam, the detective in *Psycho*, acted opposite her, while Robert Burks took care of the photography), it cost the princely sum of $30,000. Yet the young woman still thought she was just going to appear in episodes of *Alfred Hitchcock Presents*. So it came as a great surprise when her Pygmalion informed her that she was to star in *The Birds*. Indeed, Tippi Hedren had hardly ever acted in her life. But the filmmaker made up for her lack of experience by arranging for her to attend all the film's preparatory meetings, an unusual privilege for an actress.

Freeze Frame

One of the film's shocking moments is directly inspired by Daphne Du Maurier's short story. Mrs. Brenner (Jessica Tandy) visits a neighboring farmer and discovers that he has been killed when she catches a glimpse of his legs stretched out on the ground through a doorway. Hitchcock heightens the horror of the situation with a rapid series of increasingly close-up shots, culminating in a corpse's head with hollowed-out eye sockets.

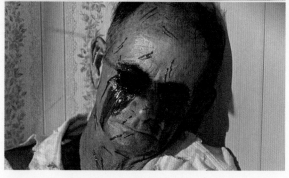

The Real Stars: "The Birds and Me"

Confident in his ability to turn a perfect stranger into the lead, Hitchcock did not hesitate to declare that the real stars of the film would be the birds, his own name as director, and the script written with Hunter. From then on, he ruled out the idea of using famous performers. The role of Mitch, intended for a time for Cary Grant, fell to Rod Taylor, an Australian actor spotted two years earlier in George Pal's *The Time Machine*. The only exception to this discreet casting is perhaps Jessica Tandy. Hitchcock knew her well, as she was the wife of his actor and author friend Hume Cronyn, seen in *Shadow of a Doubt* (1942) and *Lifeboat* (1943) before becoming screenwriter for *Rope* and *Under Capricorn* (1948). In *The Birds*, Tandy convincingly played Mitch's tormented mother. It is one of her few screen appearances, her long career having been devoted primarily to the theater. For *Driving Miss Daisy*, however, she went on to win the 1990 Oscar for Best Actress, of which she remains the oldest winner—she was eighty at the time of the ceremony.

FILMING AND PRODUCTION

At $3.3 million, the budget for *The Birds* was Hitchcock's biggest to date. This inflation was largely due to the number of shots featuring photographic effects: four hundred out of a total of fifteen hundred, a proportion unmatched at the time. Such a deployment of forces required many months of preparation, involving cinematographer Robert Burks, Robert Boyle's team of set designers (who created highly detailed storyboards), and artist Albert Whitlock, a specialist in background paintings. This was followed by six months of shooting and another year of postproduction, during which Walt Disney's loyal technician Ub Iwerks superimposed images of birds on shots of the actors.

Real Birds by the Hundreds

At first, Hitchcock had mechanical birds made, but the result was so unconvincing that they only appear on rare occasions in the final version of the film. Hundreds of real birds were used for foregrounds and interior scenes. They were directed by the famous animal trainer Ray Berwick, but this did not prevent numerous injuries: On some days, a dozen crew members suffered scratches. The climax was reached during the shooting of the scene in which Melanie, attracted by suspicious noises, enters the Brenner attic, which is overrun by seagulls. For this sequence, which lasts two minutes onscreen, Tippi Hedren spent five days being hit in the face by the

Hitchcock directs Rod Taylor in the death scene of the schoolteacher, played by Suzanne Pleshette.

Filmmaker and finches.

birds thrown by propmen positioned off camera. At the end of what she considers to be the worst week of her life, she suffered a fit of hysteria after her eyelid was slashed by a seagull. Visiting the set, Cary Grant declared himself impressed by the actress's fearlessness. Hedren surmised that Hitchcock had hired lesser-known actors so they would not have sufficient influence to refuse to be subjected to such treatment.

Uncustomary Improvisations

Despite his penchant for precise scripts and rigorous shooting plans, Hitchcock, driven by a sudden nervousness, indulged in some unusual improvisations on the set. In particular, he revised the staging of a number of sequences to make them more sympathetic to Melanie's subjective point of view. At the last minute, he also wrote the dialogue in which the heroine tells Mitch that she hasn't seen her mother since she was eleven, under the jealous gaze of Mrs. Brenner and in the presence of Annie, the schoolteacher. Set just before the birds' attack at the children's party, this passage contributes to the overall rhythm of the film, in which the birds' assaults are systematically preceded by the evocation of the anxieties of the three women surrounding Mitch: His mother and Annie fear that he will be taken away from them by Melanie, who is gradually becoming aware of the emptiness of her past existence. In this way, the bird raids seem to materialize the fears expressed by the characters. However, Evan Hunter would be furious at the addition of this dialogue, as well as at the deletion of the ending he wrote.[2]

The Most Difficult Shot

Hunter's script ended with the main protagonists suffering a final attack as they fled by car. At the very end of shooting, Hitchcock abandoned this part of the film and replaced it with a brief scene: At dawn, Melanie and the Brenners venture out of the family home, surrounded by silent birds. The film then closes with a long shot of the car driving off into a landscape covered in hundreds of feathered predators. Considered by the filmmaker to be his most difficult shot to date, this final shot mixes real birds, dummy birds, and superimposed birds. With the help of Robert Burks and his team, he achieved a composition that brought together no less than thirty-two elements filmed separately, including a splendid sky painting by Albert Whitlock.

RECEPTION

Screened out of competition at the opening of the 1963 Cannes Film Festival, *The Birds* was very well received in Europe. But Hitchcock's international recognition as a major artist (it was while this film was being finished that François Truffaut contacted him for a book of interviews) was perhaps counterproductive in the United States. Two months before the Cannes screening, the results in American cinemas were mixed: While not a commercial failure, the film made only a small profit, given its high production and promotional costs.

Another Cohesive Construct

In interviews at the time, Hitchcock attributed the birds' aggressiveness to a rabies infection, returning to the news item that inspired the story. In the trailer, which includes very little footage from the film, the director addresses the audience with an ironic reference to human mistreatment of harmless birds. But these attempts at diversion did not prevent the reaction feared: Most American critics and viewers criticized the film for never explaining or justifying the attacks. Of course, the film's cohesion lies on another level, where the characters' individual anxieties are linked to their fear of the birds' onslaught

For Hitchcock Addicts

The film has no music in the traditional sense. However, Hitchcock commissioned his loyal composer Bernard Herrmann to oversee a highly sophisticated soundtrack, combining natural bird calls with electronically altered ones. The mix is achieved using an instrument the filmmaker discovered in Berlin in the 1920s, the trautonium. Two specialists in the use of this electroacoustic device, Remi Gassmann and Oskar Sala, created the sound effects that accompany the fury of the birds (crows, sparrows, seagulls…).

Suspense in Images and Sound

When Melanie picks up little Cathy Brenner from school, she waits for her on a bench. The editing alternates between close-ups of the heroine and shots of a "chicken cage," a children's playground, behind her. With each occurrence of the second frame, the metal structure serves as a perch for more and more silent crows, their numbers steadily increasing and indicating an imminent attack. The suspense thus created is supported by a sound element: Inside, the children finish their school day by singing a nursery rhyme that they repeat over and over, adding a new stanza each time. Each return to the beginning of the melody, delaying the end of the lesson, increases the anxiety of Melanie, now aware of the danger, and that of the audience.

by a system of narrative riddles. For example, when Melanie meets Mitch, she accidentally lets a canary escape from its cage. Referring to her existence as a spoiled heiress, the young man tells her that she herself lives in a gilded cage. Later, the metaphor becomes concrete, but in reverse, when Melanie must take refuge in a cramped telephone booth to escape the beaks of angry birds.

A Metaphysical Danger

By the end of the film, a transformed Melanie has acquired a sense of responsibility. Wounded, she is comforted by Mitch's mother, who has become less possessive of her son—the beginning of the late-stage redemption of Hitchcock's terrible mothers, which continues in *Marnie* (1964). However, this resolution of conflicts remains uncertain, due to the somber note of the finale imposed by Hitchcock. Throughout his career, Hitchcock never had his hero die, but *The Birds* could be the exception. Of course, Melanie and the Brenners are still alive in the final shot. But the conclusion suggests that the killer birds may soon overwhelm the planet. Ultimately, then, the film is about humankind's impotence in the face of the uncontrollable power of the universe, represented here by an unexplained, quasi-metaphysical threat. Significantly, Hitchcock requested that the last frame should not include the words "THE END."

Where Is Hitchcock?

At the very beginning of the film, just before Melanie (Tippi Hedren) enters the pet shop in San Francisco, Hitchcock emerges. He is holding the leads of two white Sealyham terriers, which are in fact his own dogs, named Geoffrey and Stanley.

Tippi Hedren, order and disorder.

Alfred Hitchcock,
a French Invention?

In the aftermath of World War II, the artistic value of Alfred Hitchcock's cinema was the subject of lively debate in French cinephile circles. Considered at best a skillful director, a king of entertainment likely to produce commercial success with films in the detective or spy genres, Hitchcock was not a major director in the eyes of those who felt that only the use of "great subjects" could give him that legitimacy.

In Praise of Style

Hitchcock's French supporters, from the ranks of the young critics of the time, emphasized the cinematographic writing and mise-en-scène, rather than the social or psychological dimension of the themes tackled. Controversy raged within the weekly *L'Écran français*, the scene of both generational and

ideological clashes. In January 1949, shortly after the release of *Rope*, Jean-Charles Tacchella and Roger Thérond published an article entitled "Hitchcock se confie" ("Hitchcock Confides"), in which they praised—in opposition to the diktat of the "great subject"—what they saw as the main quality of the films of the author of *Notorious*, namely: style. *L'Écran français* encompassed a wide range of sensibilities. Journalists who were members of or close to the Communist Party, and those who were very much opposed to it, responded to those who were apologists for the Hollywood cinema. It was Louis Daquin who responded to Tacchella and Thérond by reminding them that, "without a subject, there can be no films," and criticizing any vision that was too formalist. André Bazin, who also wrote for the weekly, responded in turn, stressing the urgent need for a formal analysis of cinema. Reined in by the communist fringe of its editorial staff, *L'Écran français* abandoned these arguments, adopting only an anti-American stance determined by the geo-political situation of the time, particularly the start of the Korean War, which exacerbated ideological positions.

The Politics of the "Auteur"

The defense of Alfred Hitchcock's cinema found another arena, that of a new magazine, *Cahiers du cinéma*, created in 1951, with André Bazin as one of its editors in chief. Although he was not the most ardent defender of the Master, young critics gathered there who saw the filmmaker not only as a great formalist, but also as the author ("auteur") of a work of particularly intense thematic richness. The publication in October 1954 of an issue devoted entirely to Hitchcock, featuring a two-part interview with François Truffaut and Claude Chabrol, made the point even more strongly. In February 1955, Bazin tried to temper the enthusiasm of his protégés while considering their opinion "respectable and fertile." As the Master's films were released, articles in the magazine by Jacques Rivette, Jean-Luc Godard, and Éric Rohmer emphasized the metaphysical dimension of a body of work built around the themes of the fall, guilt, and redemption. *Positif* magazine, influenced by surrealism, attacked such a vision and, with a lack of nuance typical of this period rich in ideological battles, criticized the "Sulpician"—almost "religious" iconic—conception of the *Cahiers* editors, as well as a way, as Ado Kyrou wrote, of dragging Hitchcock to heights that could be "those of fascism." The publication in 1957 by Éric Rohmer and Claude Chabrol of a book devoted to the filmmaker, essentially focused on the metaphysical dimension of his work, marked an essential step in his recognition.[1]

Hitchcock/Truffaut

Now a film director, François Truffaut was astonished by the indifference, even hostility, of American critics toward a director who was even more underrated in the United States than in France, to such an extent that the idea of a retrospective of Hitchcock's films at New York's Museum of Modern Art in 1963 provoked controversy. He came up with

Psycho on the cover of *Cahiers du cinéma*.

the idea of a book of interviews with the filmmaker, in which his working methods would be discussed in a very pragmatic way. For Truffaut, the book was intended to change Americans' opinion of Hitchcock's films. Hitchcock, moved and delighted by this proposal, agreed to receive the young director, accompanied by Helen Scott, the fluently bilingual American press attaché at the French Film Office in New York, who provided translations as the conversation progressed. From August 14 to 20, 1962, the two men met at Universal's offices. Truffaut obtained from his publisher Robert Laffont the right to illustrate the book with photos and photograms. The design of the book took months, then years. In the meantime, Laffont, frightened by the thickness of the manuscript and Truffaut's demands, considered abandoning the project, but Truffaut succeeded in convincing him of the singularity of the book, which was finally published in November 1966 (1967 in the US). The recognition of Alfred Hitchcock's work has been, for the most part, a French affair.

Focus

I Saw the Whole Thing

Season 1, Episode 4

United States

1 hr

Black and White

Mono

1.33:1

Production Dates: July 23–27, 1962
Broadcast in the United States:
October 11, 1962

Production: Shamley Productions
Producer: Joan Harrison
Associate Producer: Gordon Hessler

Based on a radio play by Henry Cecil (1958)
Adaptation: Henry Slesar
Director of Photography:
Benjamin H. Kline
Sound: Edwin Somers
Assistant Director: Ronnie Rondell
Art Direction: Martin Obzina
Set Decoration: John McCarthy, Glen L. Daniels
Hair Stylist: Florence Bush
Makeup: Jack Barron
Costumes: Vincent Dee

Music: Lyn Murray
Film Editing: Edward W. Williams, David J. O'Connell

Starring: John Forsythe (Michael Barnes), Kent Smith (Jerry O'Hara), Evans Evans (Penny Sanford), John Fiedler (Malcolm Stuart), Philip Ober (Colonel Hoey), John Zaremba (Richard Anderson), Barney Phillips (Lieutenant Sweet), William Newell (Sam Peterson), Willis Bouchey (Judge Neilson), Rusty Lane (Judge Martin), Billy Wells (George Peabody), Robert Karnes (police sergeant), Alfred Hitchcock (himself) . . .

SYNOPSIS

Michael Barnes gives himself up to the police for a hit-and-run after hitting a motorcyclist. However, he claims to have complied with a stop sign, an assertion contested by five eyewitnesses. The rider succumbs to his injuries. During the trial, Barnes manages to undermine the opposing versions but refuses to answer the judge's questions. A new witness definitively exonerates him. At the maternity hospital, Barnes confesses to a friend that he was not behind the wheel of his car, which was in fact being driven by his pregnant wife.

A Singular Case

"I Saw the Whole Thing" is the only episode of *The Alfred Hitchcock Hour* directed by the filmmaker. The series, which lasted three seasons, adopted the format of *Alfred Hitchcock Presents* in 1962, extending the length of the episodes from thirty to fifty minutes.

A Loyal Screenwriter

Henry Slesar adapted a short story by Henry Cecil, a British magistrate and novelist specializing in trial stories. Beginning in 1957, Slesar collaborated on thirty-seven episodes of *Alfred Hitchcock Presents*. He worked again on scripts, mostly adapted from his own stories, for ten episodes of *The Alfred Hitchcock Hour*.

Reunions

John Forsythe played Michael Barnes, the accused motorist. Hitchcock worked with him again eight years after *The Trouble with Harry*. Forsythe was by then a regular TV star (*Climax!*, *Bachelor Father*, *To Rome with Love*). He even had his own series, *The John Forsythe Show*, between 1965 and 1966, in which he played a retired serviceman running a girls' school. Forsythe was also the voice of Charlie, a demiurgic, invisible character in the series *Charlie's Angels*.

A Man's World

Kent Smith, who played Barnes's friend, was a young leading man in the 1940s: He appeared in Jacques Tourneur's *Cat People*, Jean Renoir's *This Land Is Mine*, Robert Siodmak's *The Spiral Staircase*, and King Vidor's *The Fountainhead*. He then pursued a career of supporting roles in films and television (*The Invaders*) until 1978. Judge Neilson was played by Willis Bouchey. This long-serving actor was no stranger to John Ford films. He was part of the director's regular cast from the mid-1950s onward: *The Long Gray Line*, *The Wings of Eagles*, *The Horse Soldiers*, *Sergeant Rutledge*, *Two Rode Together*, *The Man Who Shot Liberty Valance*, *Cheyenne Autumn*.

A Picturesque Female Character

Actress Evans Evans, who played Penny, the scatterbrained young woman, worked mainly in television. She appeared in Arthur Penn's *Bonnie and Clyde* (1967) and in five John Frankenheimer films (*Grand Prix*, *Impossible Object*, *The Iceman Cometh*, *Prophecy*, *Dead Bang*).

Alfred Hitchcock Presents...

Hitchcock holds a gigantic key in his hand and announces the creation of a club open only to women. Everyone will find what they desire... including him. At the end of the episode, he announces that the sheriff is now the sole member of this club...which has just closed.

Human Error

Borrowing the dramatic structure of the courtroom film, "I Saw the Whole Thing" impressively combines the filmmaker's motifs and obsessions. The film can be seen as a fable about the precariousness of human testimony, about the uncertainty that taints any conviction built on the feeling of having seen something. "To look is not the same as seeing" is one of the lessons of Hitchcock's cinema, which often showed characters as victims of illusions built on a false belief. Hitchcock's obsession with the miscarriage of justice caused by a hasty and untruthful denunciation is reminiscent of his 1956 film *The Wrong Man*.

Guilt Transference

The episode also offers a new variation on the theme of guilt transfer. By denouncing himself in his wife's place, Barnes assumes responsibility for an act he did not commit. This is what Father Logan, played by Montgomery Clift, voluntarily does in *I Confess* (1952). But surely Barnes is also the modern version of Sam Flusky, played by Joseph Cotten, in *Under Capricorn* (1948)? Did he not already accuse himself, out of love for his wife, of a crime (murder) committed by her? "I Saw the Whole Thing" appears as a familiar, contemporary version of the historical-romantic drama, with the road accident becoming the ordinary tragedy of modern times, replacing the crime of passion. Barnes blames himself instead of his wife, because she is pregnant and their child's imminent birth has caused her to worry and hit the road. The end of the episode shows Barnes's smiling infant daughter, but whose existence is immediately linked to a lie, itself the result of a man's death. Innocence is already tainted by guilt.

Hitchcock and the MGM lion, circa 1958.

A Genius for Publicity:
Hitchcock at the Helm

Hitchcock was not the first director to become a household name: D. W. Griffith, Cecil B. DeMille, S. M. Eisenstein, Frank Capra… But he was undoubtedly one of the most conscious of his fame and reputation, which he viewed first as a lever and then as a guarantee of wide distribution for his films. He never hesitated to appeal to viewers, using every available means of communication, and, like no other filmmaker, never hesitated to "fight his own cause."

In Profile

In December 1927, as a young English filmmaker with a few films to his credit, Hitchcock had the idea of creating a self-promotional Christmas card: He sent friends and acquaintances a wooden puzzle in a small linen bag. Assembled, the pieces formed his profile, which he designed himself and which, in the 1950s and 1960s, became famous the world over, to the point of becoming his logo. He never ceased to

play on his silhouette, his shadow, his stoutness, his allure, his generous speech, and his distinctive diction, never ceasing to multiply the effects of recognition. He championed his own appearance.

Appearances

Uniquely in the history of cinema, Hitchcock appears in person in thirty-eight of his fifty-three feature films. He finds ways of insinuating himself into his films in every conceivable way. What may have started out as the appearance of a cheap extra, a quip or a wink to journalist friends, became an unparalleled publicity stunt, a sign of recognition and complicity between a man and his millions of viewers, a signature effect as well as a theoretical minute ("This is a film"). This play on audience expectations reached unprecedented proportions with the presentation of each of the 361 episodes of *Alfred Hitchcock Presents* and *The Alfred Hitchcock Hour.* For ten years (1955–1965), the Master of

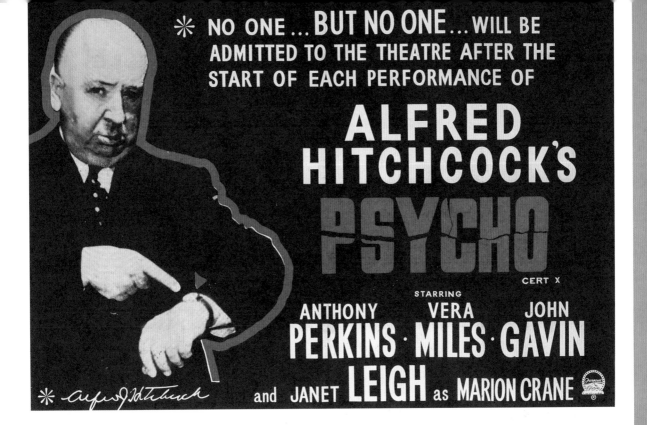

Suspense (a publicist's expression) proved to be a master of entertainment, a star of television. His surname became a brand that he coined (*Alfred Hitchcock's Mystery Magazine*).

Deus ex Machina

The filmmaker's television appearances on camera set the tone for the program; the man and the series merge. Viewer mail received by Shamley Productions bears witness to this: For most viewers, there was no doubt that Hitchcock was the creator, writer, and director of *every* episode.[1] Even more than in his feature films, his customary appearances in the prologue and epilogue gave him a magical power: that of the deus ex machina for all these macabre, tragic stories. For everyone, he embodied the force of destiny.

Addressing the Public

Hitchcock gave hundreds of interviews throughout his life, in every country and on every medium (press, radio, television), and in return generated thousands of articles. He was photographed in every situation, position, and outfit (disguised as a woman for a photo thriller published in *This Week Magazine* on August 4, 1957). He gave lectures and published numerous papers on his actresses, his films, and his conception of music, censorship, suspense, and action.[2] He continued to practice what he called "audience management," the high art of manipulating mass emotions and buying impulses.

Similarly, he addressed some of his trailers to them, such as those for *The Wrong Man* ("This is Alfred Hitchcock speaking…"), *Psycho* ("Good afternoon…"), *Marnie* ("How do you do?"), and *Frenzy*, where he is floating in the Thames: "I daresay you are wondering why I am floating around London like this…"

The Art of the Launch

In March 1962, a year before the release of *The Birds*, William Blowitz, head of the New York agency responsible for the film's publicity strategy, wrote in a memo: "The star of this film is Alfred Hitchcock." *The Birds* opened the Cannes Film Festival (May 1963), in the presence of the director, his actress, dozens of photographers, and hundreds of birds released into the Côte d'Azur sky. And it was Hitchcock who came up with the launch slogan, which memorably combines a title in the plural and a verb in the singular: "*The Birds* is coming!" Quite an art.

Warhol/Hitchcock

On Friday April 26, 1974, Andy Warhol met Alfred Hitchcock for an interview. Impressed, the artist, who also knew a thing or two about films and communication, asked the filmmaker some questions:
AW: Will you ever play the absolute star in one of your films? The big lead role?
AH: It was suggested once, years ago.
AW: Really? You should do it now. That is what you should be doing.[3]

ALFRED HITCHCOCK'S
SUSPENSEFUL SEX MYSTERY

"MARNIE"

Starring 'TIPPI' HEDREN · SEAN CONNERY

Co-starring DIANE BAKER · MARTIN GABEL · Screenplay by JAY PRESSON ALLEN From the Novel by WINSTON GRAHAM

Directed by ALFRED HITCHCOCK · A Universal Release TECHNICOLOR®

UNIVERSAL
CITY STUDIOS

Marnie

United States · 2 hrs 10 · **Color** (Technicolor) · **Mono** (Westrex Recording System) · 1.85:1

Production Dates: November 26, 1963–March 14, 1964
Release Date in the United States: July 22, 1964 (New York)

Production: Universal Pictures
Producer: Alfred Hitchcock
Unit Manager: Hilton A. Green

Based on the novel by Winston Graham, *Marnie* **(1961)**
Screenplay: Jay Presson Allen
Director of Photography: Robert Burks
Camera Operator: Leonard J. South
Visual Effects: Albert Whitlock
Sound: Waldon O. Watson, William Russell
Assistant Director: James H. Brown
Alfred Hitchcock's Assistant: Peggy Robertson
Art Direction: Robert Boyle
Set Decoration: George Milo
Hair Stylist: Alexandre de Paris, Virginia Darcy
Makeup: Jack Barron, Howard Smit, Robert Dawn
Costumes: Edith Head, Vincent Dee, Rita Riggs, James Linn
Music: Bernard Herrmann
Film Editing: George Tomasini

Starring: Tippi Hedren (Marnie Edgar), Sean Connery (Mark Rutland), Diane Baker (Lil Mainwaring), Martin Gabel (Sidney Strutt), Louise Latham (Bernice Edgar), Bob Sweeney (cousin Bob), Milton Selzer (man at the racetrack), Alan Napier (Mr. Rutland), Henry Beckman (detective), Edith Evanson (Rita), Mariette Hartley (Susan Clabon), Bruce Dern (sailor), S. John Launer (Sam Ward), Meg Wyllie (Miss Turpin), Alfred Hitchcock (man leaving a hotel room) …

SYNOPSIS

In an American town, under an assumed name, brunette Margaret ("Marnie") Edgar steals a large sum of money from the safe of her employer, Sidney Strutt, and disappears. In Philadelphia, now a brunette under a new identity, Marnie applies for a job with the wealthy Mark Rutland: Strutt's client has recognized the thief. Fascinated, he hires her and behaves like a psychoanalyst. Raised by her mother to hate men, terrified of thunderstorms, with a phobia for the color red, and a kleptomaniac, Marnie runs off again with the cashbox. Mark finds her again, this time as a blonde, and gives her a choice: She marries him or he turns her in. The couple spend their honeymoon at sea, but Marnie resists her husband, who takes her by force. She attempts suicide. Back in Philadelphia, Rutland hires a detective to look into Marnie's past and has the young woman's horse, which she loves passionately, brought to her. During a hunting trip, she panics at the sight of a red jacket. She has a fall, forcing her to shoot the wounded animal. Dazed, she tries to rob Mark. Mark takes the young woman back to her native Baltimore. Marnie, in a daze, remembers: One stormy evening, her mother, too busy with a sailor, left her little girl alone with her fright. Trying to calm Marnie down, the man cuddled her too closely and the mother killed him in front of the child. Freed from this traumatic memory, Marnie leaves with her husband, liberated.

"You Freud, me Jane!"

Tippi Hedren's line from *Marnie*

GENESIS

In 1961, Alfred Hitchcock was interested in several projects for his first film produced entirely by Universal. He was particularly enthusiastic about *Marnie*, a novel by English writer Winston Graham, author of Poldark, a series of historical novels set in eighteenth-century Cornwall.

Back to Analysis

Published in early 1961, *Marnie* was named after its heroine, a frigid kleptomaniac woman who, unmasked by a man, is forced to marry him. The novel was acclaimed by critics for its accurate female point of view and psychoanalytically informed psychological suspense. In Graham's book, the filmmaker found material for an unofficial remake of *Spellbound* (1944), in which the roles are reversed: This time, it is the man who helps the woman free herself from an unconscious trauma. From March onward, Hitchcock worked every day for three months on the *Marnie* script with Joseph Stefano, who had written *Psycho* (1960). The two men transposed the plot from England to the United States, in particular to Grace Kelly's hometown of Philadelphia…On June 9, Stefano and Hitchcock completed a 161-page treatment.

"Our Dear Marnie"

In 1962, Hitchcock called upon Evan Hunter, the screenwriter of *The Birds* (1962), to continue the work begun with Stefano, who was tied up with another project. Enthralled by the novel and its heroine, Hunter set to work just as Hitchcock began shooting *The Birds*, and even consulted a psychologist, who helped him understand the woman he already referred to as "our dear Marnie."[1] However, when Hitchcock took over the reins of the project, Hunter found him more inclined to impose his ideas than to accept those of his collaborator.

A Sultry Scene

Although an admirer of Winston Graham's novel, Hunter was reluctant to include the scene in which Mark Rutland rapes Marnie after their wedding. In his opinion, this scene causes the audience to lose all sympathy for the male hero. He considered it obscene and ridiculous. But the filmmaker already had a very precise idea in mind, which he dictated in minute detail to his scriptwriter. Attempting to respect Hitchcock's demands while expressing his misgivings, Hunter finally learned that he had been ousted from the project on May 1, 1963, by

a phone call from Peggy Robertson, the director's assistant.

Miss Allen

Looking for a new writer, Hitchcock met Jay Presson Allen, a forty-year-old screenwriter. After starting out as an actress, Allen devoted herself entirely to writing. The filmmaker took a liking to this witty and funny partner, who offered him a female perspective on his screenplay. Allen learned the Master's unorthodox writing methods: off-the-cuff conversations and a nonlinear treatment of the plot. Among Allen's most significant contributions was the removal of Marnie's two loving cousins in favor of two women in love with the same man. Allen also eliminated the character of the psychoanalyst, turning Mark Rutland into an amateur zoologist who performs a "crude analysis" on his wife. Unlike Evan Hunter, she was not embarrassed by the rape scene, which she wrote herself. Allen and Hitchcock worked together from June to September 1963. Allen would remember it as her most formative collaboration.

CASTING

For Hitchcock, the adaptation of *Marnie* was to coincide with Grace Kelly's return to the screen. The Princess of Monaco said she was interested, but also unavailable for the whole of 1962. In the meantime, Hitchcock put the film on hold and worked on his television episodes, as well as on his new project, the adaptation of *The Birds*, based on Daphne Du Maurier's short story.

Inspired by Real Women

Winston Graham claimed that Marnie was inspired by three real-life women: a babysitter wary of men who had a passion for horses; a criminal who changed her physical appearance after every offense; and a mother, acquitted of killing her newborn by reason of insanity, who had a child who became a kleptomaniac.

No Springtime for Kelly

In an article in the *Daily Express* dated March 21, 1962, entitled "Grace Kelly: Ice That Burns Your Hands," Hitchcock announced the production of *Marnie* and prematurely mentioned the star's participation; he said she would play a "passionate and most unusual love scene." On learning of her return to the screen, MGM recalled that Kelly, still under contract, had unfulfilled commitments to the studio. The director tried to schedule the shoot to coincide with the princely couple's annual visit to the US, but the actress had difficulty freeing herself. Faced with the scale of the problems and the unpopularity of the project among the people of Monaco, she reluctantly gave it up.

In Search of Marnie

Concealing his disappointment, Hitchcock went in search of a replacement. Eva Marie Saint and even Marilyn Monroe expressed interest. The director considered actress Claire Griswold, with whom he had rehearsed scenes from films made with Grace Kelly. He continued to hesitate before settling on the latest Hitchcock blonde, Tippi Hedren (*The Birds*). For his most psychological film, Hitchcock broke with his usual practice and worked closely with his actress. Together, they analyzed each scene, "feeling by feeling, reaction by reaction," as Hedren put it, with the filmmaker going so far as to specify the tone and rhythm of her lines.

Far from James Bond

Eager to cast an actor as charismatic as Cary Grant or James Stewart, Hitchcock auditioned Rock Hudson before awarding the role of Mark Rutland to Scottish actor Sean Connery, made famous by the first two James Bond films. Connery asked to read the script, however, to make sure that *Marnie* was not a *North by Northwest*–style spy movie: The actor wanted to escape the playboy image that now clung to him. Jay Presson Allen recommended Louise Latham to the filmmaker as Marnie's mother, while brunette Diane Baker—whose resemblance to Grace Kelly was emphasized by Alma Reville—was chosen to play Rutland's infatuated sister-in-law.

Final Laps

Marnie was the last film in a fruitful collaboration with cinematographer Robert Burks and editor George Tomasini, both of whom died shortly afterward. It was also the last time Bernard Herrmann composed the music for a Hitchcock film, a score of aggressive romanticism. Edith Head was once again

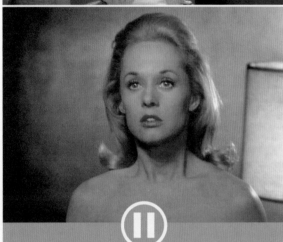

Freeze Frame

Exasperated by his wife's refusal to accept him on their honeymoon, Rutland finally enters the room where Marnie ensconces herself every night. He expresses his desire before ripping off her nightgown: We see a shot of the young woman's bare legs. Oscillating between bestiality and tenderness, Rutland apologizes, dresses her again in her robe, and embraces her passionately. Dazed, she seems to fall in slow motion and, as if prompted by an unspoken order, lies down on the bed. The camera takes in a close-up of her face, then returns to Rutland, who menacingly approaches her as Bernard Herrmann's passionate, tragic score plays. At the moment of embrace and rape, without any apparent struggle, the camera pulls away and glides along the wall to fix itself on the cabin window overlooking a very calm sea.

hired to sublimate Tippi Hedren, whose every detail of appearance (nails, bag, hairstyle, shoes) was the occasion for a fetishistic fixation.

FILMING AND PRODUCTION

Shooting began at the end of November 1963, by which time a second crew had already filmed exteriors and transparencies in Philadelphia, Baltimore, and Hartford, Connecticut. After a series of works featuring exteriors, *Marnie* rarely left the studio. In the midst of preparation, Hitchcock summed up the plot to Peter Bogdanovich: "It is the story of a girl who doesn't know who she is. She is a psychotic, a compulsive thief, and afraid of sex, and in the end she finds out why. In terms of style, it will be a bit like *Notorious*."[2]

Empowerment

Until Christmas, filming went smoothly, but Hitchcock's mood darkened when the crew went back to work after the New Year. In love with his actress since *The Birds*, Hitchcock first alienated Hedren, as much for the sake of the character as out of cruelty, preferring to devote his attention to Diane Baker. When, at the end of January 1964, Hedren asked him for four days' leave to travel to New York to receive a press award and appear on Johnny Carson's famous *Tonight Show*, he flatly refused. Infuriated, Hedren committed the ultimate sin, calling him a "fat pig." ("She did what no one is permitted to do. She referred to my weight.")[3] Hedren demanded to be released from her exclusive contract with Hitchcock: He replied that before letting her go, he would destroy her career.

Bestiality

With *Marnie*, romanticism (*Rebecca*) and badinage (*North by Northwest*) are out of the picture, and Hitchcock's vision of the relationship between men and women is marked by a harsh bestiality. Since *Psycho* and *The Birds*, Hitchcock had been filming characters with irrepressible impulses, like wild beasts at the mercy of their instincts. Mark Rutland's knowledge of zoology should help him understand Marnie...Evoking sexual life in the wild, the man confides to the thief that "lady animals figure very largely as predators." In *The Birds*, Rod Taylor had already invited Tippi Hedren to get back into her gilded cage...

Where Is Hitchcock?

In the fifth minute of the film, the filmmaker emerges from a hotel room, notices the elegant Marnie crossing the hallway, then gives a quick glance at the camera as if to say to the viewer: "Follow that girl."

A Female Norman Bates?

A kleptomaniac, mythomaniac, and frigid (except for her orgasm on horseback), Marnie's character is a collection of behavioral aberrations. In the end, she is a far less horrific female counterpart to *Psycho*'s Norman Bates. After *Spellbound*, Hitchcock returned to the psychoanalytic drama in his own way: The plot is resolved through a crudely Freudian analysis that brings the childhood trauma to the surface of the picture. Far from seeking to make plausible use of this discipline, the filmmaker uses psychoanalysis for its expressive qualities: His heroine's phobia of red allows him to reconnect with his passion for signifying objects and narratively justify the color that invades the image with each new crisis. As for Forio, the horse, the only living being for whom Marnie seems to feel desire and empathy, he represents, according to Hitchcock, the image of the father. By putting an end to the animal, injured in a fall, Marnie takes the first step toward healing, intimately consenting to gradually transfer her affection to Mark, her husband.

RECEPTION

Shocked by the filming, undoubtedly the most disturbing of his career, Hitchcock lost interest in *Marnie*, which he seemed to want to fail. Tippi Hedren was to be Hitchcock's last blonde, and despite the director's insistence that she remain captive to her exclusive contract for two years, she refused every role he offered her.

A Guilty Enjoyment

Marnie was released in July 1964. The majority of American critics rejected a film that did not live up to their expectations of Hitchcock entertainment, even though the result might prove captivating. For

The house of misfortune: Marnie (Tippi Hedren) and her mother (Louise Latham).

Eugene Archer of the *New York Times*, it was "at once a fascinating study of a sexual relationship and the master's most disappointing film in years" (July 23, 1964). Edith Oliver of the *New Yorker* called it "an idiotic and trashy movie with two terrible performances in the leading roles," but concedes that she "had quite a good time watching it. There is something bracing about Hitchcock at work, even when he is at his worst." The film earned just over $3 million in North America, more than *Vertigo*. It fared better in Europe, particularly England, due to Sean Connery's great popularity.

The Impossible Woman

A few months after the film's release in France, Michel Delahaye considered *Marnie* to be yet another variation on the two Hitchcockian themes of "the terrible mother and the impossible woman" (*Cahiers du cinéma*, February 1965). But the impossible woman seems in fact to be more coveted by Hitchcock than by the character of the husband: His staging reflects a fascination tinged with a desire for total control. On the set, he sought to control both Tippi Hedren's clothes and her

company. On the one hand, he had a bottle of champagne delivered to her dressing room every evening; on the other, he hired a graphologist to analyze the actress's handwriting and obtain proof of her duplicity.

That Obscure Object of Desire

Impossible, duplicitous, and desirable—this is Marnie from the very first image: dyed brunette, filmed from behind, walking away from the camera in her high heels, with a close-up of a bright yellow bag under her arm, split down the middle like a female sexual organ. Faced with this mystery, the eye of the filmmaker and audience has never been so close to touching the actress. Robert Burks obeys some astonishing guidelines when filming Hedren's face: The camera must approach her as if making love to her. Similarly, never before has Hitchcock's mise-en-scène so isolated parts of his star's body: her feet, her hands, her hair. The filmmaker is entirely caught up in an erotic vision: "We go to close-up to show her hair blowing in the wind while she's riding the horse—that's a leitmotiv that goes through the film."[4]

A Love Poem

Hitchcock devoted his second film with Tippi Hedren to celebrating and persecuting her, both in reality and in fiction. The filmmaker's moods toward her were reminiscent of those of his male hero, an ambiguous character, odious and noble, who rescues *Marnie* from the clutches of her past (like Cary Grant in *Notorious*) but does not hesitate to rape her. A sadistic love poem, Marnie evokes the surrealism-tinged cinema of Luis Buñuel. The film needs to be seen in the context of Hitchcock's oeuvre and compared with its twin, *Vertigo* (1957), whose painful, hallucinatory lyricism it shares. The filmmaker suddenly abandons all modesty and the art of suggestion to deliver a disarming cinematic confession in public. *Marnie*, a distinguished and brutal film, is the testimony of a filmmaker madly in love, who hesitates in deciding whether to embrace or destroy his beloved. He records and fixes Tippi Hedren's beauty and allure for eternity, while his staging fragments the actress's body, satisfying his fetishist impulse. This fragmentation recalls another: the shower scene in *Psycho*. *Marnie* has all the makings of a symbolic murder.

Passion and violence: Tippi Hedren.

Eva Marie Saint (*North by Northwest*, 1958).
Right: Grace Kelly (*Dial M for Murder*, 1953).

Blondes,
Mirage—Image

Blond hair is a projection surface, like a bright screen that plays host to all kinds of fantasies. In the Western imagination, blond hair, a rare hue reserved for fairy-tale princesses, is synonymous with fertility, wealth, and purity. But platinum blond (artificial, bordering on white) is a sign of dissolute morals. This is precisely what Hitchcock is interested in: manipulating the contradictions of blondness (virtue and vice, innocence and manipulation) to forge the "complete woman," a cinematic chimera born of an intimate obsession.

The Ideal Victim

A frightened woman cries out: Filmed in close-up, her face is encircled by an abundance of blond hair. The opening shot of *The Lodger* (1926) reveals one of the victims of the Avenger, the London killer who preyed exclusively on young women with "golden hair." Word of his serial crimes spreads through the newspapers and backstage at a cabaret, where dancers in a line reveal short, dark hair beneath their blond wigs— the theme of their show, *Golden Curls*. That is, all but one: a real blonde, and therefore a potential victim. In the same film, Hitchcock designates the blonde as his object of choice, adoration, and persecution. She is the ideal victim who inspires murderous (*Dial M for Murder*, 1953), fetishistic (*Vertigo*, 1957), and sadistic (*Marnie*, 1964) impulses. For him, "Blondes make the best victims. They're like virgin snow that shows up the bloody footprints."[1]

In Black and Blond

Like a sculptor repeating the same motif, Hitchcock devoted his filmography to shaping, theorizing, and perfecting his image of blondness. With their crimped hair and adventurous spirit, Madeleine Carroll (*The 39 Steps*, *Secret Agent*, 1935) and Nova Pilbeam (*Young and Innocent*, 1937) represent a "first draft" of the Hitchcock blonde. But the latter lacks an essential quality: the dangerous duplicity of an explosive, subterranean sex appeal. And both lack an indispensable ingredient: the image in color.

The Theory of the Hitchcock Blonde

Apparently indifferent to Cary Grant's charms, Grace Kelly kisses him as he escorts her back to her hotel room. This scene from *To Catch a Thief* (1954) is Hitchcock's exact illustration of the blonde: the empress of "indirect sex" who, unlike Marilyn Monroe, conceals her mad sensuality beneath a sophisticated, icy exterior. A true apparition, she had to be single and childless: Nothing could make her too real. With Grace Kelly or Eva Marie Saint in *North by Northwest* (1958), whom he dressed, styled, lit, and applied makeup to, Hitchcock gave substance to his theory of the luminous blonde, a theory that would darken in subsequent films.

The Color Blond

With Technicolor, and with the help of cinematographer Robert Burks and his hairdressers, Hitchcock succeeded, from 1953 onward, in making his actresses' blond hair (ideally the color of wheat) glow with an unearthly radiance. Slightly undulating hairstyles and intricate chignons created a play of shapes and reflections that transformed hair into a poetic, labyrinthine, hypnotic, and autonomous surface.

The "Hair Shot"

In Hitchcock's filmography, many shots linger dreamily on an actress's hair: Over time, the filmmaker increasingly stretched the duration of the "hair shot." The shot of Tippi Hedren recurs like a refrain in *Marnie*; when she sheds her brown dye, Hitchcock films a simple wash with a sink tap as a liberation bordering on pleasure: Marnie becomes blond again. And the filmmaker captures the actress from behind when her character, in the throes of one of her crises, tries to escape the camera's gaze.

Counterfeits

For Hitchcock, one is born a blonde; one does not become one. A woman may dye her hair, but she is determined by her natural color. So there is every reason to be wary of a brunette pretending to be a blonde (*Vertigo*; *Family Plot*, 1975) and vice versa (*Marnie*). This change of hue, this feminine taste for metamorphosis, is proof of the duplicity of women who, through the fascination they exert, set visual traps for gullible men.

The Mirage Woman

From *Vertigo* onward, the filmmaker more clearly dissociated the female face from her hair, as if one did not necessarily logically refer to the other. The growing doubt that surrounds an image and its reverse gives rise to deep anguish: Madeleine's vertiginous chignon is that of a lost woman, the image of an abyss. Norman Bates's mother's hair in *Psycho* (1960) ultimately reveals a skull. A symbol of life, hair becomes a trompe l'oeil that adorns vanished figures.

IT
TEARS
YOU APART
WITH
SUSPENSE!

PAUL NEWMAN JULIE ANDREWS

ALFRED HITCHCOCK'S

'TORN CURTAIN'

TECHNICOLOR®

co-starring

LILA KEDROVA · HANSJOERG FELMY · TAMARA TOUMANOVA
LUDWIG DONATH · DAVID OPATOSHU

Music by
JOHN ADDISON

Written by
BRIAN MOORE

Directed by ALFRED HITCHCOCK · A Universal Picture

Torn Curtain

United States • **2 hrs 8** • **Color**
(Technicolor) • **Mono**
(Westrex Recording
System) • **1.85:1**

Production Dates: October 18, 1965–February 16, 1966
Release Date in the United States: July 27, 1966

Production: Universal Pictures
Producer: Alfred Hitchcock
Unit Production Manager: Jack Corrick
Screenplay: Brian Moore, Willis Hall, Keith Waterhouse
Director of Photography: John F. Warren
Camera Operator: Leonard J. South
Visual Effects: Albert Whitlock
Credit Titles: Mel Statler
Sound: Waldon O. Watson, William Russell
Assistant Director: Donald Baer
Alfred Hitchcock's Assistant: Peggy Robertson
Script: Lois Thurman
Art Direction: Hein Heckroth
Set Decoration: Frank Arrigo, George Milo
Hair Stylist: Lorraine Roberson, Hal Saunders (Julie Andrews)
Makeup: Jack Barron
Costumes: Grady Hunt, Edith Head (Julie Andrews)
Music: John Addison
Film Editing: Bud Hoffman

Starring: Paul Newman (Professor Michael Armstrong), Julie Andrews (Sarah
Sherman), Lila Kedrova (Countess Kuchinska), Hansjörg Felmy (Heinrich Gerhard),
Tamara Toumanova (ballerina), Ludwig Donath (Professor Gustav Lindt), Wolfgang
Kieling (Hermann Gromek), Günter Strack (Professor Karl Manfred), David
Opatoshu (Mr. Jacobi), Gisela Fischer (Dr. Koska), Mort Mills (farmer), Carolyn
Conwell (farmer's wife), Arthur Gould-Porter (Freddy), Gloria Govrin (Fräulein
Mann), Peter Bourne (Professor Olaf Hengström), Alfred Hitchcock (man with a
baby on his knees)...

> "During the Cold War, we observed each other in a mirror while looking at the guy in front of us. We fantasised about everything."

John Le Carré

SYNOPSIS

—

American nuclear physicist Professor Armstrong, accompanied by his assistant and fiancée, Sarah Sherman, attends an international conference in Norway. Sarah discovers that Armstrong is preparing to go to East Berlin. She follows him against his will. Armstrong has decided to share his knowledge with the Soviet bloc, guided, he says, by a desire to contribute to world peace. While Sarah regards him as a traitor, Armstrong makes contact with dissidents: His real aim is to steal the scientific formula for a defense system that an East German scientist, Professor Lindt, is said to have developed. Armstrong thinks he has escaped the policeman assigned to keep an eye on him. He is caught by the policeman just as he is making contact with a network in a farmhouse intended to facilitate his escape. He kills him, with the complicity of the peasant woman who has taken him in. Back at the University of Leipzig, he manages to obtain the formula from the scientist. Pursued, Armstrong and Sarah, now aware of her fiancé's true activities, flee. They are taken away in a fake bus on the regular Leipzig–Berlin line, whose passengers are all members of the resistance. In Berlin, they create panic in a theater to escape the police, then hide in a ship bound for Sweden. They are almost unmasked before jumping into the water in Stockholm harbor and finding safety.

GENESIS

Hitchcock's fiftieth feature film was born of his desire to revive the theme of marital suspicion, one of the key motifs in his work. The Master was fascinated by the story of Guy Burgess and Donald Maclean, British diplomats recruited as spies by the USSR, to whom they passed state secrets. It is the wife's point of view, her pain and anguish when she learns of her husband's betrayal, that mainly interested the filmmaker. The moral conflicts at play—made more complex by the homosexuality of the protagonists—provided ample inspiration for the author of *Suspicion*.

A Political Thriller

After an unsuccessful attempt to convince playwright James Goldman to write the screenplay, Hitchcock asked Vladimir Nabokov to imagine a political thriller based on "the problem of the woman who is associated, either by marriage or commitment, with a defector," as he wrote in a letter to the author of *Lolita*. The writer declined, claiming a lack of knowledge of the workings of

The "Cambridge Five"

Torn Curtain was inspired by the real-life story of Kim Philby (center of photo, 1955), Guy Burgess, Donald Maclean, Anthony Blunt, and John Cairncross, which fascinated Hitchcock. These five well-to-do Cambridge University students, sympathetic to Marxist ideals, were recruited by the Soviet state police and provided secret intelligence to the USSR as early as the 1930s, and later during World War II and the Cold War. Their careers in journalism, diplomacy, and the British state apparatus gave them access to a wealth of classified information. In 1951, on the verge of being discovered, Burgess and Maclean fled to Moscow, where they ended their lives in alcohol and disillusionment.

the British secret service. Hitchcock then turned to Brian Moore, a Catholic author of Irish origin living in New York and esteemed by Graham Greene. He enjoyed Moore's novels, which resonated with his own childhood experiences, notably *The Feast of Lupercal*, set in a religious school. In an interview with *Cahiers du cinéma* (February 1966), Moore explained: "Hitchcock had once worked successfully with a writer like Thornton Wilder—at the time of *Shadow of a Doubt*—so he asked me if I'd be interested in repeating the experience." Moore initially refused but was persuaded by a substantial increase in the remuneration offered. From then on, the two men met every day in Hitchcock's office to finalize the script, a first draft of which was completed in June 1965.

CASTING

Universal, still reeling from the commercial failure of *Marnie*, cast Julie Andrews (*Mary Poppins*, which won her an Oscar, *The Sound of Music*) and Paul Newman (*The Outrage*, *The Prize*) as the two main characters. These big stars of the time were intended to guarantee the film's success with the public.

A Poor Choice?

Hitchcock had previously tried to convince Cary Grant to accept the male lead role, but Grant was too old for the character anyway and had decided to call

time on his career. Hitchcock was particularly disappointed by the choice of the female lead, as Julie Andrews seemed to him to have little credibility as a scientist. At first, Newman seemed more suitable. But during the shoot, the filmmaker became prodigiously annoyed by the actor's innumerable questions, which, like a true disciple of the Actors Studio, required him to know his character's every motivation. For Hitchcock, Newman proved incapable of "giving neutral looks, those looks that allow me to edit a scene."[1]

A Question of a Point of View

It seems that the choice of lead actors and other studio requirements substantially transformed the original project. Any hint of homosexuality disappears, but more importantly, the character of the defector's wife was gradually eclipsed by her husband's exploits. Only the staging of the first third of the film is built around her point of view. After obtaining a first version of the script, Hitchcock demanded more from Moore, who became impatient and criticized the lack of depth in the characters. Hitchcock contacted English screenwriters Keith Waterhouse and Willis Hall and asked them to make a few changes to the script. The latter reworked some of the dialogue even though filming had already begun. They were not included in the credits, however, the Writers Guild having judged their contribution to be less than essential.

Paul Newman in search of explanations and Hitchcock, pondering.

The New Cohort of Familiar Colleagues

The team behind his television series *Alfred Hitchcock Presents* provided the director with a number of colleagues. For example, editor Bud Hoffman made his first move into feature films, replacing George Tomasini, who had recently died. John F. Warren, cinematographer, also arrived from the TV series, succeeding Robert Burks (who died in 1968). And the faithful Edith Head was put in charge of Julie Andrews's costumes and hairstyles.

FILMING AND PRODUCTION

Filming took place mainly in California, at Universal Studios. Hitchcock hired a German crew to bring back authentic views of East Germany, on the pretext of making a tourist documentary, but this material was never used. The film was criticized for its outrageously artificial studio and California exteriors.

A Particular Photographic Bias

Hitchcock asked John F. Warren to filter the lighting with gauze curtains to give the impression of a gray, anodyne world. Semi-matte white canvases of various sizes were deployed to reflect the light. In an interview for the May 1967 issue of *American Cinematographer* magazine, Hitchcock explained, "I looked for a photographic style that would help us tell this story in a more realistic and less seductive way." This rejection of the flamboyant Technicolor of the previous decade in favor of greater visual austerity would be criticized by some critics.

A Film Without Bernard Herrmann

Once filming was complete, Hitchcock called on the inescapable Bernard Herrmann for the music. He gave him specific and surprising instructions: He wanted the music to suit the times. Indeed, the studio heads asked for a popular melody. They mentioned the name of Henry Mancini (*The Pink Panther*) and even imagined a theme song sung by Julie Andrews. Whether out of conviction or to achieve public success, Hitchcock agreed to go with the times, even though he wanted to keep his usual musician. But Herrmann proved not to be the best choice, his symphonic music having fallen out of fashion in contemporary thrillers. Perhaps also fed up with Herrmann's style, Hitchcock declared himself dissatisfied with his proposals and turned them down. This marked the end of a ten-year collaboration. A score was then urgently commissioned from British composer John Addison, who won an Oscar for his score to *Tom Jones* in 1963. Addison's music is fairly conventional. However, there is the memorable ominous melody in the opening credits, which is happily repeated at several points in the film, including the escape on the bus.

Avant-Garde Credits

Hitchcock entrusted Mel Statler with the design of the credits, asking him to draw inspiration from the kinetic and sensory works of Argentine artist Julio Le Parc, whose first exhibition was held in New York in 1966. While the left-hand side of the screen was occupied by a continuous stream of smoke reminiscent of a rocket taking off, the right-hand side showed, behind a colored filter, certain close-ups of the faces of the characters who would appear in the film. A whole range of emotions and attitudes are expressed, from anguish to pain, from surprise to meditation.

Chronicle of a Failure Anticipated

Filming began under gloomy auspices. Testimonials from contributors unanimously evoke a certain skepticism and anticipated disappointment. Even before the first crank of the handle, many saw the project as nothing more than a vain attempt by a filmmaker whose time had passed to adapt, awkwardly, to current tastes. But *Torn Curtain* does not resemble the cynical, disillusioned spy tales spawned in the wake of Martin Ritt's *The Spy Who Came in from the Cold*, nor the glib exploits of a James Bond. Brian Moore, who found the plot implausible, did not wish to appear in the credits,

For Hitchcock Addicts

Hitchcock was irritated by Paul Newman's casual manner on their first meeting. The actor went in shirtsleeves to the dinner to which Hitchcock had invited him, preferring to drink beer rather than the fine wines selected by the Master.

Julie Andrews carried away by a panicking crowd.

apprehensive about the film's reception. As for Waterhouse and Hall, they saw the script as a collection of errors and naïvetés. Julie Andrews hated the script, which reduced her role from rewrite to rewrite. Filming was gloomy, and some claimed that the director worked without conviction. Paul Newman declared: "We all knew we had a loser on our hands and that the film would be a turnip." Hitchcock, for his part, explained the film's failure by the choice of actors: "We would have done a much better job without Julie Andrews and Paul Newman. Bad cooking, that's what it was. If you count the overheads, they cost a million eight hundred thousand dollars, which I think is a disgrace. To spend so much money on a casting error!"[2]

RECEPTION

The first preview screening in the United States took place on July 14, 1966. The film, which had cost $6 million, brought in $13 million, a result considered disappointing by the studio.

A Unanimous Rejection in the United States

American critics were unanimously harsh: "Hitchcock is so tired that what once seemed to be a highly personal style is now no more than a repetition of past triumphs," wrote Richard Schickel in *Life*. In the *New York Times* (July 28, 1966), Bosley Crowther judged that it "is a pathetically undistinguished spy picture, and the obvious reason is that the script is a collection of what Mr. Hitchcock most eschews, clichés...He is so badly burdened with a blah script...and a hero and a heroine...who seem to miss the point that he has come up with a film that plows through grimly, without any real surprises, suspense or fun."

French Ideology

Released in France in November, the film received a more nuanced reception. This may be explained by the fact that Hitchcock was then almost unanimously recognized as a major artist in the history of cinema, which represented a vital intellectual issue for French critics. Reticence was essentially ideological. As Alain Vannier wrote in *Les Lettres françaises* (December 1, 1966), "Hitchcock, in his own way, in an icy, slow film with an infantile scenario, is trying to revive the Cold War all by himself." Samuel Lachize, in *L'Humanité* (November 26, 1966), repeats the expected commonplace: "What is bad about this film is the way

Hitchcock mocks an audience that has come to be entertained at his heels and finds, by way of film, nothing more than a mediocre rehash of his previous works." For *La Saison cinématographique* (1967), Alfred Hitchcock had bungled his fiftieth film. *Positif* magazine (May 1967) remained hostile to Hitchcock: Louis Seguin called the filmmaker a minor director, "quite unworthy of the bookish respect lavished upon him." As for the film, he considered it a failure, revealing "his contempt for the audience, his grocer's snobbery, his conformism, and his misogyny."

A Small Defense Committee

However, other critics were more favorable. Yvonne Baby, in *Le Monde* (November 23, 1966), said, "While knowing full well that he has made better films than this one, we can say, to paraphrase the words of one of his characters, that he has once again managed to reconcile 'the mathematical logic' of 'suspense' with 'the romantic illogic of adventure.'" True to their "auteur" stance, *Cahiers du cinéma* devoted several pages to the film in their January 1967 issue, under the title "Défense de *Torn Curtain*" ("Defense of *Torn Curtain*"). No fewer than four editors offered learned and poetic praise for a film that cites Cocteau (Jean Narboni and André Téchiné), but also Bresson (Sylvain Godet), while seeing in it a reflection on language (Jean-Louis Comolli).

And Today?

Today, *Torn Curtain* still seems an unloved, negligible work among the director's other filmography. The film is often seen as the production of a

For Hitchcock Addicts

Hitchcock imagined that Paul Newman's character would throw away the stolen scientific formula to express detachment from the Cold War.

tired artist reduced to repeating old formulae that no longer work. The memory of earlier masterpieces (*Notorious*, *The Man Who Knew Too Much*, *North by Northwest*) is summoned to the detriment of this latest delivery. Nevertheless, the beauty of *Torn Curtain*, which despite its shortcomings can be counted among the filmmaker's great titles, is as inseparable from its era as it is from its place in Hitchcock's career. What happens to Hitchcock's motifs and obsessions when the production system that gave them form has changed? Certainly, the film opens with a marital suspicion (what is behind Professor Armstrong's / Newman's lies to his fiancée?), but above all, by exhibiting a morally dubious hero (Armstrong, by unscrupulously stealing the secrets of a scientist who knows more than he does, becomes the man "who did not know enough"), the narrative bears witness to a change in the irreproachable ethics of supposedly heroic characters. And Paul Newman's acting adds a note of strangeness by confusing, even rendering opaque, the psychology of an individual who seems perpetually haggard, less actively involved than merely carried along by events.

Toward Abstraction

The criticism that the film reconstructed an "exotic" universe in a California studio is probably unfounded. To appreciate its importance, one must consider its flaws as qualities. Transparencies, matte paintings, and painted backgrounds are artificial processes that had become all too visible to viewers in the mid-1960s. Paradoxically, this use disrupted the classical aesthetic on which Hitchcock's art was based. What was once perceived as natural was no longer so. This all-too-obvious falseness pushes the film toward an abstraction already touched upon in *North by Northwest*, and taken to a higher level in this film.

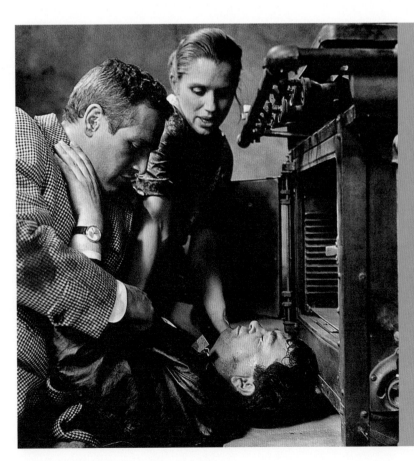

Freeze Frame

In his pursuit of a paradoxical effect of truth, Hitchcock "denaturalizes" established ways of depicting violence in cinema. The filmmaker dilates time in the Gromek murder sequence. He also eliminates the dramatic music (originally intended) that this brutal scene would typically call for. Originally conceived to show how difficult and laborious it is to kill a man, this murder scene (at the end of which the villain ends up asphyxiated by gas from a kitchen oven) is considered by Hitchcock to be symbolic.

Paul Newman.

With *Torn Curtain*, Hitchcock produced a mannerist version of his own cinema. By hollowing out and desertifying shots, by crushing and miniaturizing his characters in sets that are too big for them and obviously artificial, by stretching time in certain sequences, the filmmaker marks a melancholy end of an era for his cinema.

Through the Looking Glass

The Iron Curtain is a mirror through which characters pass on an orphic journey in search of their own reflection. The motif of duplication is thus logically present, expressed notably by the two buses chasing each other (the fake one hiding the fleeing spies, and the one on the regular line, which resembles the first and follows it until it catches up). Hitchcock declared that he wanted to treat these two vehicles as characters (the good guy and the bad guy). The humans become frozen, metaphysical figures out of a De Chirico canvas. This refined abstraction, which completes a so-called classical style already abused in *Psycho* and *The Birds*, would continue, less happily, in the next film, *Topaz*. Conversely, what had long been concealed or treated allegorically in Hitchcock's cinema finally asserts itself directly in the triviality of his last two films, *Frenzy* and *Family Plot*.

Where Is Hitchcock?

The filmmaker appears in the seventh minute of the film. He is sitting in the lobby of the Hotel d'Angleterre in Copenhagen. He holds a baby in his lap, then moves it onto his other leg while wiping his trousers...

Unrealized Projects

The list of all the unfinished Hitchcock projects in his fifty-year career would be a long one: script or production problems, rights issues, vetoes from financiers, unavailable stars, the filmmaker's loss of interest…Some are barely developed, others more advanced: These are just a few of the best-known or most evocative examples, sometimes dear to the filmmaker's heart—a list that resembles the remnants of half-remembered dreams upon awakening.

Life of a City or London (End of the 1920s)

Inspired by the documentary *Berlin: Symphony of a Metropolis* (*Berlin: Die Sinfonie der Großstadt*, Walter Ruttmann, 1927), Hitchcock dreamed of filming twenty-four hours in the life of a metropolis, somewhere between documentary and fiction. He gave up, unable to find the plot to serve such a subject.

Greenmantle (1935–1939)

Hitchcock was looking for a sequel to the screen adventures of Richard Hannay, the hero of *The 39 Steps*, which he would adapt from another spy novel by John Buchan. But the rights were too expensive. According to other sources, it was *Greenmantle*'s adaptation project that preceded *The 39 Steps*, but the filmmaker abandoned it, preferring a shorter story.

Titanic (1938)

The famous sinking of the transatlantic liner was to be the subject of Hitchcock's first American film. A twenty-page treatment exists. But, among other difficulties, producer David O. Selznick's plans to buy a real ocean liner came to nothing.

The Bramble Bush (1951–1953)

Based on a novel by David Duncan (1948), this is the story of an activist on the run who steals a passport, only to realize that his new identity is that of a man wanted for murder. But the script left the filmmaker unsatisfied.

Flamingo Feather (1955–1956)

Based on a novel by Laurens van der Post, this adaptation project led Hitchcock and his wife on an expedition to the plot's location in South Africa. The study trip turned into a pleasure trip once the director was convinced of the impossibility of shooting in situ.

The Wreck of the Mary Deare (1957)

In the summer of 1957, Hitchcock met screenwriter Ernest Lehman, and together they planned to adapt a bestseller by Hammond Innes (1956), with Gary Cooper in the lead role. Apart from the idea of a spectacular opening (a deserted ship adrift), they felt unable to avoid "boring courtroom drama." The film was made without them (but with Cooper), in 1959, while they devoted themselves to an original screenplay: *North by Northwest*.

No Bail for the Judge (1959)

Based on a novel by Henry Cecil (1952), this is the story of a lawyer charged with exonerating her father, himself a judge, accused of murdering a prostitute. Samuel Taylor (*Vertigo*) wrote the screenplay, and actors Audrey Hepburn, Laurence Harvey, and John Williams were approached. When Hepburn withdrew, Hitchcock lost interest.

Blind Man (1960)

In this original screenplay, written with Ernest Lehman (*North by Northwest*), a blind pianist regains his sight after having the eyes of a man killed in an accident transplanted into him. The donor was in fact murdered, and the image of his killer remained imprinted in the pianist's new retinas...Part of the plot was to take place at Disneyland, but after seeing and hating *Psycho*, Walt Disney strongly objected. In the end, Lehman was unable to create a plot around an idea for a sequence that Hitchcock had had: Onstage at Covent Garden, Maria Callas is singing an aria when she sees a man stabbed in a dressing room. She lets out a scream, the highest note she's ever reached, and the whole audience applauds. The film was to end with a chase on the *Queen Mary* ocean liner.

Village of Stars (1960)

Based on a suspense novel by Paul Stanton, this is the story of a pilot who is carrying a bomb that will go off below a certain altitude. But the release mechanism jams and the plane runs out of fuel...

Trap for a Lonely Man (1960)

In this project, based on a French play by Robert Thomas, a young married couple are on vacation in the Alps. The wife disappears, the police find her, and she is happy to be reunited with her husband, who fails to recognize this unknown woman.

Mary Rose (1964)

This is undoubtedly the project that meant the most to Hitchcock. As a young Londoner, he saw J. M. Barrie's play (1920) and never forgot it: A "lady vanishes" on an island, for a few days in the first instance, then for several decades, and returns unchanged while her family has aged. In 1964, Jay Presson Allen (*Marnie*) was commissioned to write the screenplay, Albert Whitlock made several preparatory drawings, and the filmmaker dreamed of shooting this "horror story" on the Scottish coast. "If I were making the film," he said, "I would dress the girl in a gray dress, and inside the hem I would place a neon light so that the glow would reflect only on the heroine. When she moved, her silhouette would cast no shadows on the walls, only a blue light."[1]

Universal doubted the commercial value of this dark ghost story and refused to authorize the film.

The Three Hostages (1964)

Following on the adventures of Richard Hannay, the hero of *The 39 Steps*, in this story, three children are hypnotized, kidnapped, and hidden in three different countries. Once again, the rights to the novel proved prohibitive. But the filmmaker also believed that it was impossible to make people believe in hypnosis in cinema, which always comes across as acting.

R.R.R.R. (1964)

In this comedy project with the famous Italian screenwriters Age and Scarpelli, an Italian immigrant goes from elevator attendant to manager of a large American hotel. He brings in and houses his family of thieves, who prey on the hotel's wealthy guests. Unable to structure the story, Hitchcock gave up.

Kaleidoscope or Frenzy (1964–1967)

In the mid-1960s, Hitchcock watched films by Polanski (*Repulsion*), Godard (*Masculin féminin*), and Antonioni (*Red Desert / Deserto rosso*) and saw the advent of a new modernity. With several successive screenwriters, he set out to create a cinematic experiment (low budget, high-sensitivity color film, visual effects) about a serial killer who commits murders in different New York locations: Central Park, Shea Stadium, a warship cemetery on the Hudson River, a giant installation of storage tanks. In early 1967, the filmmaker spent three months on the East Coast, commissioning Arthur Schatz to shoot location photos and film tests with unknown actors (the photos and tests still exist). Lew Wasserman, the head of Universal, put an end to the project, which was well advanced but too "bizarre." Hitchcock is said to have wept with disappointment.

The Short Night (1968–1979)

At the end of the 1960s, Hitchcock was thinking of adapting a novel inspired by the 1966 escape of George Blake, an English spy in the pay of the Soviets. But it was in 1977 that preproduction really got underway, right up to the storyboard stage. Four scriptwriters took turns, location scouting took place in Finland, and those close to the filmmaker prepared themselves: producers Hilton A. Green and Norman Lloyd, art directors Robert Boyle and Albert Whitlock, costume designer Edith Head. But in May 1979, exhausted and ill, Hitchcock summoned Green: "I want you to do me a favour. I want you to call Mr Wasserman and tell him I'm never going to make another movie."[2]

When in Southern California visit Universal Studios

HITCHCOCK TAKES YOU BEHIND THE ACTUAL HEADLINES TO EXPOSE THE MOST EXPLOSIVE SPY SCANDAL OF THIS CENTURY!

ALFRED HITCHCOCK'S

From LEON URIS' inflammatory best seller

Suggested for MATURE audiences (parental discretion advised).

STARRING

FREDERICK STAFFORD · DANY ROBIN · JOHN VERNON · KARIN DOR · MICHEL PICCOLI · PHILIPPE NOIRET · CLAUDE JADE

MICHEL SUBOR AND JOHN FORSYTHE · MUSIC ~ MAURICE JARRE · SCREENPLAY BY SAMUEL TAYLOR · DIRECTED BY ALFRED HITCHCOCK

A UNIVERSAL PICTURE · TECHNICOLOR®

69/378

Topaz

United States • 2 hrs 23 • Color (Technicolor) • Mono (Westrex Recording System) • 1.85:1

SYNOPSIS

Production Dates: September 25, 1968–April 1969
Release Date in the United States: December 19, 1969

Production: Universal Pictures
Producer: Alfred Hitchcock
Associate Producer: Herbert Coleman

**Based on the novel of the same name by
Leon Uris (1967)**
Screenplay: Samuel Taylor
Director of Photography: Jack Hildyard
Visual Effects: Albert Whitlock
Sound: Waldon O. Watson, Robert R. Bertrand
Assistant Directors: Douglas Green, James Westman
Alfred Hitchcock's Assistant: Peggy Robertson
Art Direction: Henry Bumstead
Set Decoration: John Austin
Costumes: Edith Head
Music: Maurice Jarre
Film Editing: William H. Ziegler

Starring: Frederick Stafford (André Devereaux), Dany Robin (Nicole Devereaux), John Vernon (Rico Parra), Karin Dor (Juanita de Cordoba), Michel Piccoli (Jacques Granville), Philippe Noiret (Henri Jarré), Claude Jade (Michèle Picard), Michel Subor (François Picard), Per-Axel Arosenius (Boris Kusenov), Roscoe Lee Browne (Philippe Dubois), Sonja Kolthoff (Mrs. Kusenova), Tina Hedström (Tamara Kusenova), Donald Randolph (Luis Iribe), John Forsythe (Michael Nordstrom), Alfred Hitchcock (man in a wheelchair)…

In 1962, a high-ranking KGB official, having left his country with his wife and daughter, is picked up in Copenhagen by CIA agents. On the basis of his revelations, André Devereaux, a French secret service agent who had supplied the CIA with a copy of a treaty on the conditions of collaboration between the USSR and Fidel Castro, leaves for Cuba to gather evidence of the presence of Soviet missiles on the island. There he meets up with his informer and mistress, Juanita de Cordoba, head of a resistance network against the Castro regime. After gathering evidence of Soviet activity, she is denounced by a woman in her employ who has talked under torture. Juanita is executed by Rico Parra, a leader of the Cuban revolution who is in love with her, in a gesture where vengeance mingles with compassion, thereby sparing her torture. Back in Washington, Devereaux, in possession of the microfilms attesting to the presence of the missiles, learns from the Soviet defector that an espionage network exists at the top of the French secret service. He knows the name of one of its members, Henri Jarré. Following a meeting at which Devereaux expresses his suspicions, Jarré goes to the home of Jacques Granville, another French secret service agent who turns out to be the leader of the spy ring. Granville has Jarré killed. Devereaux discovers Granville's identity through his wife, the spy's mistress. The unmasked spy commits suicide.

> "For me, espionage is much more the preserve of the gentleman; but, naturally, I am of the old school."

Graham Greene

The death of Juanita (Karin Dor).
Right: Alfred Hitchcock, Claude Jade.

GENESIS AND CASTING

While the preparation of *Kaleidoscope*, an audacious cinematographic project, bogged down (the film never saw the light of day), Hitchcock was going through a gloomy, depressive period marked by the loss of several friends in the space of a few years: his cardiologist, Dr. Ralph Tandowsky, editor George Tomasini, director of photography Robert Burks, and author of comic TV monologues James B. Allardice. Under pressure from Universal, the filmmaker turned to adapting a spy bestseller.

Uris-Hitchcock, a Lost Encounter

Leon Uris's book was fueled as much by the Cuban Missile Crisis as by the anti-Gaullism of an American diplomatic corps irritated by France's desire for independence. Hitchcock asked the author of the novel, already responsible for several successful adaptations, to write the screenplay. The writer had painful memories of a collaboration in which the filmmaker was nostalgic for his former glory. Their relationship became conflictual, with Hitchcock, according to Uris, unable to understand the modern issues of espionage, and Uris, according to Hitchcock, conceiving characters without human depth, poor caricatures. After their separation, the director turned to his friend Samuel Taylor (*Vertigo*, 1957).

An International Cast

The lead role, that of André Devereaux, was played by Frederick Stafford, an actor who began his career in semi-parodies of James Bond films. The most complex and moving character, Rico Parra, was played by actor John Vernon, primarily a television actor. German actress Karin Dor, who played Juanita de Cordoba, mistress of Devereaux and Parra, was a star of German popular cinema. The cast included

For Hitchcock Addicts

The film's story is based on real events: the Cuban Missile Crisis (1962), but also the Georges Pâques affair. Pâques was director of studies at the Institut des Hautes Études de Défense Nationale before working for NATO. Recruited by the Soviet secret services in 1943, he passed military information to them. He was arrested in 1963 following an investigation by an agent of the SDECE (Service de documentation extérieure et de contre-espionnage), the model for Devereaux's character.

several French actors: Dany Robin and Claude Jade (the latter recommended to Hitchcock by François Truffaut, who had just filmed *Baisers volés* [*Stolen kisses*] with her), Michel Piccoli, Philippe Noiret, and Michel Subor.

FILMING AND PRODUCTION

Shooting began even though the script had not yet been completed. Filming was chaotic, marked by much hesitation. According to several witnesses, Hitchcock showed signs of fatigue. Many passages of the novel were changed. Vexed by the anti-Gaullist tone of the story, the French authorities refused to grant permission to film in the streets of Paris, allowing it only after the intervention of the American ambassador.

Three Different Endings

Hitchcock's intended ending (an old-fashioned duel between the hero and the traitor) was perceived as anachronistic, and disliked during screening tests. The filmmaker envisaged another, more amoral ending (the spy returns to the Soviet Union). Forced by Universal, Taylor and Hitchcock settled on a third conclusion: the suicide of Granville, the traitor, evoked by a shot heard behind a door.

RECEPTION

Released for Christmas 1969, the film was a huge commercial and critical failure.

A Sullen Critique

The film "lacks humor and animation" (the *Washington Post*). Hitchcock produces "the same damn spy movie that he has been making since the 1930s, only longer, slower, and duller" (Pauline Kael,

the *New Yorker*). Vincent Canby, writing in the *New York Times*, nonetheless acknowledged the filmmaker's mark in every detail.

Three months after its American release, *Topaz* was distributed in France. Its shooting in Paris prompted reports and interviews with the Master and his actors. But the film was attacked for its ideology. For *L'Express*, "if the style is Hitchcock, the level of thought is John Wayne." Henry Chapier, in *Combat*, found the film "brilliant, and lame."

Aesthetic Experiments

Hitchcock regarded *Topaz* as a total disaster. Yet, despite its patchiness, it contains intense poetic moments as much as it serves as a field of experimentation, with the filmmaker indulging in subtle color work. A floral motif runs throughout the film: from the opening sequence, with the petal-by-petal fabrication of porcelain roses, to the execution of Juanita, whose dress opens into a corolla as she falls to the ground, the climax of a moving Liebestod ("love death").

Where Is Hitchcock?

At the thirtieth minute of the film, in the New York airport lobby, Hitchcock is being pushed in a wheelchair. He gets up to greet a man and leaves. Should the wheelchair be seen as a metaphor for a film struggling to stand on its own two legs?

From the Master of Shock! A Shocking Masterpiece!

HITCHCOCK'S FRENZY

A deadly new twist from the original Hitchcock

ALFRED HITCHCOCK'S "FRENZY"

starring JON FINCH · ALEC McCOWEN · BARRY FOSTER

co-starring BILLIE WHITELAW · ANNA MASSEY · BARBARA LEIGH-HUNT · BERNARD CRIBBINS · VIVIEN MERCHANT

Screenplay by **ANTHONY SHAFFER** · Directed by **ALFRED HITCHCOCK**

Frenzy

United States • 1 hr 56 • Color
(Technicolor) • Mono
(Westrex Recording System) • 1.85:1

Production Dates: July 26–October 26, 1971
Release Date in Great Britain: May 25, 1972
Release Date in the United States: June 21, 1972

Production: Universal Pictures
Producer: Alfred Hitchcock
Associate Producer: William Hill

Based on a novel by Arthur La Bern, *Goodbye Piccadilly, Farewell Leicester Square* (1966)
Screenplay: Anthony Shaffer
Director of Photography: Gilbert Taylor
Visual Effects: Albert Whitlock
Sound: Gordon K. McCallum, Peter Handford
Casting: Sally Nicholl
Assistant Director: Colin M. Brewer
Alfred Hitchcock's Assistant: Peggy Robertson
Art Direction: Syd Cain
Set Decoration: Robert W. Laing
Hair Stylist: Pat McDermott
Makeup: Harry Frampton
Costumes: Julie Harris, Dulcie Midwinter
Music: Ron Goodwin
Film Editing: John Jympson

Starring: Jon Finch (Richard Blaney), Barry Foster (Robert Rusk), Barbara Leigh-Hunt (Brenda Blaney), Anna Massey (Barbara "Babs" Milligan), Alec McCowen (Chief Inspector Tim Oxford), Vivien Merchant (Mrs. Oxford), Billie Whitelaw (Hetty Porter), Clive Swift (Johnny Porter), Bernard Cribbins (Felix Forsythe), Michael Bates (Sergeant Spearman), Jean Marsh (Monica Barling), Madge Ryan (Mrs. Davison), Elsie Randolph (Gladys), John Boxer (Sir George), George Tovey (Neville Salt), Alfred Hitchcock (a skeptical onlooker at the minister of health's speech)...

"It's the picture of a young man!"

Norman Lloyd

As in the days of Jack the Ripper, a killer is on the loose in London. A special feature: He strangles his victims with a necktie. Richard Blaney, ex–Royal Air Force pilot, ex-bartender, finds himself penniless. He confides in his friend Robert Rusk, a greengrocer in Covent Garden, but refuses his financial help. He then turns to his ex-wife, Brenda, whom he bullies in full view of several witnesses. Shortly afterward, Rusk in turn visits Brenda alone, rapes her, and strangles her with his tie. Blaney is suspected of the murder. Only Barbara, his partner, still believes in him and their love. While Blaney hides out at a friend's house, Rusk lures Barbara into his home and kills her. That same evening, he dumps her body in the back of a truck loaded with sacks of potatoes that is about to set off. One detail might give him away (his tiepin, with its initial, in the young woman's stiffened fist), but, after an improbable journey, he recovers the object and manages to have Blaney arrested in his place. Blaney, who understands too late the true nature of his "friend," proclaims his innocence. Only Inspector Oxford has any doubts. He opens up at home to his wife, a calamitous cook convinced that she is a Le Cordon Bleu chef, who convinces him of the miscarriage of justice. Oxford takes over the investigation, confounds Rusk, and exonerates Blaney just as the latter, having escaped from prison, is about to take justice into his own hands.

GENESIS

On August 27, 1970, Hitchcock wrote to François Truffaut that he was looking in vain for a new subject for a film, and humorously complained about Universal's script department, which kept sending him supposedly Hitchcockian stories. Yet it was through this same channel, or that of a literary agent, that *Goodbye Piccadilly, Farewell Leicester Square* arrived on the filmmaker's desk, a detective story published four years earlier by Englishman Arthur La Bern, a former crime reporter turned writer and screenwriter. On December 10, Lew Wasserman, head of Universal, gave the go-ahead for the acquisition of the book rights. The adaptation work was to avoid the mistakes responsible for the costly and traumatic failure of *Topaz* (1969) and enable the return to the usual Hitchcockian precision of the preparatory phase.

The Ingredients for Success

Many of the ingredients for a successful film by the Master were present or in the making within this short novel: a false culprit, a villain more "seductive" than the sad hero, an acerbic critique of married life, (very) dark humor, and, above all, several shocking scenes, in particular the hectic journey of a corpse in the back of a truck loaded with sacks of potatoes. Hitchcock described *Frenzy*, renamed after one of his unrealized 1960s projects, as "the story of a powerless man who expresses himself through murder."[1] The plot also takes place in the vicinity of Covent Garden, a large open-air market in old London soon to disappear, where the filmmaker's father, William Hitchcock, himself a greengrocer, used to take his son, forever marked by all the bustle and profusion. By returning home and shooting far from Universal, without the American stars weighing on the budget, Hitchcock (the film's producer) saw not only the potential for promoting the return of the prodigal son, but also the possibility of making a decent, profitable film.

Scouting

On December 31, 1970, in New York, Anthony Shaffer, English playwright and author of the hit play *Sleuth*, received a call from Alfred Hitchcock—at first he thought it was a hoax—offering to collaborate. The two men traveled together to London to discuss the forthcoming script and to scout locations in Leicester Square, on the banks of the Thames, at the Old Bailey courthouse, in the alleyways overlooking Oxford Street, and in the New Scotland Yard

For Hitchcock Addicts

During the shooting of *Frenzy*, Hitchcock entrusted Barry Foster, the actor who played the murderer, with books from his personal library devoted to John Christie and Neville Heath, two English psychopaths who made headlines in their day.

building on Victoria Embankment. And, of course, in Covent Garden, where the murderer lives and works, which places the market at the heart of the suspense and makes it the natural source of memorable motifs: the grapes crushed by Richard Blaney's poor hero, the potatoes, all kinds of food suggesting abundance and withering, life and its decay. Far from the abstract aesthetic of a fiction like *Torn Curtain* (1966), Hitchcock imagined *Frenzy* as a trivial film.

Intersecting Texts

From January 22 to February 24, 1971, the screenwriter and filmmaker locked themselves away in Universal's bungalow, where they began a dialogue, with Shaffer drafting a first version of the screenplay. Hitchcock read books on sexual pathology, which inspired a scene in the film (in the pub, a discussion on perverts between a lawyer and a doctor, with Blaney nearby). They also had a screening of Richard Fleischer's *10 Rillington Place*, a Columbia film released in England in January 1971 and inspired by the story of John Christie, a necrophiliac strangler in postwar London.

At another work session, in April, the two men understood each other quickly and well; by May 1971, a script was ready. The plot had been condensed (no more escapades of the false culprit in Paris; the trial was only a short scene instead of forty pages), Blaney's character had been rejuvenated, the role of Inspector Oxford had been expanded, and he had a wife who concocted inedible meals every evening. The policeman's dinners serve as a humorous counterpoint to the violent scenes. And by virtue of being shown, the food seems to have a troubled link with the sexual or criminal acts that Oxford and his wife discuss at the dinner table. The investigation progresses at home rather than in the offices of Scotland Yard, an idea Hitchcock came up with to avoid a crime-movie cliché. Likewise, the filmmaker imagines a denouement that brings together his three protagonists—the real man and the "wrong man," plus the inspector—in a bedroom where the truth falls like a cleaver.

CASTING

Hitchcock attended a screening of *Twisted Nerve*, a "Hitchcockian" English thriller from 1968, with music by Bernard Herrmann, one of whose posters proclaimed: "Enough to make even Hitchcock jump!" He retained two actors: Billie Whitelaw to play a "fury" convinced of the innocent man's guilt, and Barry Foster, who was given the role of the tie-wearing killer after Michael Caine turned it down as too unsavory. However, in 1972, Caine starred in *Sleuth*, Shaffer's film adaptation of his own play, alongside Laurence Olivier, another prestigious actor who had been approached by Hitchcock to play Inspector Oxford. Glenda Jackson was considered for the part of Brenda, while Helen Mirren declined to play Barbara.

A 100 Percent British Team

The final cast, drawn in part from the theater, was exclusively British. The names were unknown to the American public, the film's main audience, but the faces caught the eye. The filmmaker was surprised by these actors, who knew all their lines even before the first rehearsal, and some of whom, like Barry Foster and Vivien Merchant (wife of playwright Harold Pinter), often made pertinent acting suggestions.

For this first film shot in the director's native country since *Stage Fright* (1949), all Hitchcock's crew were English, and some were old acquaintances: Peter Handford (*Under Capricorn*, 1948) on sound, Albert Whitlock (eleven films to date, since *The Man Who Knew Too Much* in 1934) on special effects, Elsie Randolph (*Rich and Strange*, 1931) in a small role. Gilbert Taylor, the cinematographer, had been a clapper loader on the set of *Number Seventeen* in 1932 before working as cinematographer on *Repulsion* (1965), an English film by Polanski that Hitchcock had seen and appreciated. From Taylor, in fact, he asked for a realistic picture of the kind, as he put it, that would portray "a day in Covent Garden," in other words, a picture without glamour. In the same spirit, *Frenzy* is devoid of all traces of any sophisticated Hitchcock blondes…

FILMING AND PRODUCTION

The indoor scenes were shot at Pinewood Studios, where the Master, age seventy-two in 1971, had filmed *Young and Innocent* thirty-four years earlier.

Back Home

By all accounts, the filming of *Frenzy* began in a state of excitement: for Hitchcock, his return to London. The opening credits scene is a humorous and spectacular account of this enthusiastic homecoming: A single shot, taken from a helicopter, flies over the Thames like a great bird, approaching Tower Bridge, the gateway to the city. When the filmmaker's name appears in capital letters, the deck of the bascule bridge opens its two parts to allow the prestigious patronymic to pass through. A glorious score by Ron Goodwin—after Hitchcock had rejected Henry Mancini's score as too macabre—then blows the trumpet of fame, leaving no doubt as to the nature of this comeback. If he had misled Mancini with his lack of precision, the filmmaker made his expectations clear to Goodwin in a "music note" dated January 1, 1972: "Grandiose in style." The composer would confirm the intention of this fanfare opening: "Hitchcock wanted no suggestion of the horror to come."[2] So, this "grandiose style" opening also serves as a counterpoint to the scene that follows, when the horror comes.

A Shadow over the Filming

After the failures of *Marnie, Torn Curtain*, and *Topaz*, Hitchcock was—by all accounts—back in top form. Shooting, between summer and autumn 1971, went off without a hitch, despite an event that took place shortly beforehand and left the filmmaker distraught: At the beginning of June, his wife, Alma, suffered a stroke that left her temporarily incapacitated. Less than a year later, however, she was able to attend the London premiere. Caught up in his fear of sudden catastrophe, an anxiety that hangs over so many of his works, Hitchcock seemed to lose interest for a while in the preparation of the film. He ate and drank more than usual, his arthritis caused him pain, he had bouts of melancholy and perhaps a few instances of drowsiness on the set. *Frenzy*, in its final form, betrays none of these difficulties. On the contrary, it contains a number of remarkably lively and daring scenes, bravura pieces that demonstrate an undiminished taste and flair for visual and aural experimentation.[3]

Brenda's Death

The scene of the first rape with murder by strangulation, which alone took at least three and a half days to shoot, is one of Hitchcock's great editing moments. Never before had Hitchcock proposed or imposed such an explicit vision of violence (with the possible exception of Gromek's death in *Torn Curtain*), never before had he been so frontal; certainly, in this case, the film crosses a line that the evolution of Western mores and representations allowed. But the filmmaker had always played with this limit, constantly challenging it. In fact, this scene shows what the shower sequence in *Psycho* would have looked like if it had been shot not in 1960, but in 1972, or reveals what the viewer was already "seeing" at the time of the attempted rape and murder behind the curtain in *Blackmail* in 1929.

In a Truck Full of Potatoes

The other murder, Barbara's, or rather its unexpected twists and turns, is another tour de force. The equivalent of twelve days' shooting and one hundred and eighteen shots, according to Hitchcock, were required to achieve the long scene in which the assassin attempts to take from the dead woman, hidden in the back of a potato truck, an incriminating object that she is holding tightly in her clenched hand (a key in the novel, a tiepin in the film). By delighting in sordid and funny details (the protruding foot), by associating a naked corpse with potatoes as a reminder that all things are doomed to expire and putrefy, Hitchcock emphasizes the film's profoundly pessimistic meaning and at the same time achieves a small masterpiece of black humor.

Goodbye to Babs

In contrast to the two major sequences (Brenda's murder and the truck), which were meticulously storyboarded and heavily edited, Hitchcock had the idea of a one-shot scene to evoke the murder of Richard's fiancée. The murderer has convinced Barbara, known as Babs, to come to his apartment. Unsuspecting, she agrees. When he opens the door and says, just as he did to his first victim: "You know,

you're my kind of woman," the viewer knows that the worst is about to follow. Bolstered by this complicity with the audience, and not wanting to repeat the form of the first murder, the director does not let the camera in. It remains at the door, where it silently begins a long tracking shot down the empty staircase, which Hitchcock dubbed "Goodbye to Babs." This entire section was shot in the studio. The camera continues to move backward until it reaches the front door of the house, where the passage of a pedestrian with a sack of potatoes on his back provides an invisible link, and the sequence continues to move backward, this time in a real exterior shot, all the way to Henrietta Street. The camera crosses the street, finally stopping and showing the façade, while the noise of the traffic returns and grows louder, covering Babs's screams, which the viewer hears only in his head. Previously, by the time the necktie strangler had approached Babs, the street noise had suddenly disappeared. Filmmaker's comment: "Dead silence."

Reverse Tracking Shots

Martin Scorsese would remember this extensive reverse tracking shot through a staircase and corridor for the finale of *Taxi Driver* (1976). Perhaps the idea for this single movement lasting almost a minute and a half came to Hitchcock from his experiments with *Rope* (1948) or his 1967 New York project, *Kaleidoscope*, renamed *Frenzy* at the time, whose psychedelic aesthetic was the antithesis of the English film, but which also depicted the fatal journey of a serial killer. Studying one of the scripts for this early *Frenzy*, film historian Bill Krohn noted this intention: "As for the question of gore, Hitchcock began to address it by moving the camera back during the park murder to a very high height, bringing it back close to the ground only after Caroline [the first victim] had died."[4]

RECEPTION

In January 1972, Hitchcock returned to London to supervise the post-synchronization and music. He fine-tuned the trailer, in which he amused himself by appearing three times: in close-up and at the water's edge after his mannequin is seen floating on the Thames, then in front of a Covent Garden transparency where he shoves a recalcitrant leg into a sack of potatoes. Finally, he has the audacity to retrieve his

Hitchcock, Beknighted

On January 14, 1971, Alfred Hitchcock went to Paris to be awarded the Legion of Honor. The filmmaker insisted that it should be presented to him by Henri Langlois, founder of *La Cinémathèque française*, three years after Langlois had been dismissed by the Gaullist government, then reinstated to quell a revolt in film circles to which Hitchcock had lent his support. In front of the cameras, the filmmaker thanked Langlois for having done so much to safeguard and promote films. Ten years earlier, Langlois had written of Hitchcock: "Behind the mask that hides him better than any other, there is the Devil, quite simply, the admirable face of Lucifer, who sees all, knows all, is fooled by nothing and no one, and whose humor is intact. This marvellous sense of humour explains everything about Hitchcock."[5]

tie from what is supposed to be Babs's corpse, then, by virtue of the editing, asks Brenda if she likes his tie: A connection is then made to the film's close-up shot of the first victim screaming blue murder.

R Classification

The film had its world premiere at the Cannes Film Festival on May 19, 1972, and was enthusiastically received. Universal, a firm believer in the film, promoted it in every possible way: "From the Master of Shock...A shocking masterpiece!" In fact, *Frenzy*, which cost the studio $2.5 million, grossed $16 million three years later, including TV sales. And all this despite the fact that it was the first Hitchcock film to be given an 18 certificate in Great Britain, and rated R (restricted) by the Motion Picture Association of America. It was also the first Hitchcock film to contain female nudity (the reason for the censorship, but also the film's success in the movie theaters...?), with doubles for Brenda's breasts (Barbara Leigh-Hunt) and Babs's body (Anna Massey).

Unanimous...or Almost

With the exception of a few negative papers, the American reviews were excellent. From the *New York Times* to the *Los Angeles Times*, everyone was openly astonished by this return to form. In the English newspaper *The Times*, John Russell Taylor, later author of an authorized biography of Hitchcock,[6] published an enthusiastic article entitled "The Hitchcock Magic Is Intact" (May 23, 1972). Six days later, and four days after the film's London release, Arthur La Bern, clearly unable to hold out any longer, responded to this article in the same newspaper: "I endured one hundred and sixteen minutes of it during a press screening and it was, as far as I was concerned, a most painful experience." This attack undoubtedly conceals his frustration at having been left out of the adaptation of his novel. On January 11, 1971, Arthur La Bern had written to the filmmaker to express his delight at his new film project and propose a meeting, an invitation that Hitchcock apparently did not take up.

With the Compliments of Alfred

In anticipation of *Frenzy*'s American release, Universal held some press screenings. Its publicity department sent journalists a large envelope containing a gift and a note. The gift was a necktie, an allusion to the murder weapon. It was accompanied by a note from the Master: "This tie is presented to you compliments of Alfred Hitchcock as a souvenir of his latest thriller, *Frenzy*."

A Malaise for Civilization

Since the film's release, many critics have wondered about Hitchcock's obsession with food. Certainly, Hitchcock regards eating as a sexual and criminal act, to the extent that rape and murder whet the killer's appetite, and he bites into an apple or any other food he can get his hands on. Far from idealizing the human being, *Frenzy* reduces him to a predator, an organism entirely governed by his instincts, and even by his intestines. The only moral difference between human beings lies in the extent to which they are repressed. At the end of his great dialogue with Truffaut, recorded in the early 1960s, when *Frenzy* was not even a novel, Hitchcock recounted a dream film, impossible and total: "twenty-four hours in the life of a city. [...] I want to try to film an anthology of food. The arrival of food in the city. [...] The action of eating. [...] Gradually, toward the end of the film, there will be sewers and garbage pouring into the ocean. [...] At that point, [...] the general theme becomes the rottenness of humanity. [...] The task is enormous, but I still feel the need to make this film."[7]

Where Is Hitchcock?

Just after the credits roll, on the banks of the Thames, Sir George makes a rousing speech about the reducing river pollution. Hitchcock, in black suit and bowler hat, appears in two shots among the small crowd listening. His presence becomes ironic when the floating corpse of a naked young woman with a tie around her neck appears—a "pollution" that immediately, contradicts the politician's optimism.

Family Plot

United States • 2 hrs • Color
(Technicolor) • Mono
(Westrex Recording
System) • 1.85:1

Production Dates: May 12–August 18, 1975
Release Date in the United States: April 9, 1976

Production: Universal Pictures
Producer: Alfred Hitchcock

Bsed on a novel by Victor Canning, *The Rainbird Pattern* (1972)
Screenplay: Ernest Lehman
Director of Photography: Leonard J. South
Visual Effects: Albert Whitlock
Sound: James Alexander, Robert L. Hoyt
Assistant Director: Howard G. Kazanjian
Alfred Hitchcock's Assistant: Peggy Robertson
Art Direction: Henry Bumstead
Set Decoration: James W. Payne
Makeup: Jack Barron
Costumes: Edith Head
Music: John Williams
Film Editing: J. Terry Williams

Starring: Karen Black (Fran), Bruce Dern (George Lumley), Barbara Harris
(Blanche Tyler), William Devane (Arthur Adamson), Ed Lauter (Joseph Maloney),
Cathleen Nesbitt (Julia Rainbird), Katherine Helmond (Mrs. Maloney), Warren J.
Kemmerling (Grandison), Edith Atwater (Mrs. Clay), William Prince (Bishop Wood),
Nicholas Colasanto (Constantine), Marge Redmond (Vera Hannagan), John Lehne
(Andy Bush), Charles Tyner (Wheeler), Alexander Lockwood (Parson), Martin West
(Sanger), Alfred Hitchcock (a Chinese shadow) . . .

SYNOPSIS

Julia Rainbird, a wealthy old lady, enlists Blanche Tyler's clairvoyant talents to track down her late sister's illegitimate son. She wishes to make him her heir and asks Blanche to bring him back in exchange for a reward. With the help of her taxi-driver companion George Lumley, Blanche, more con artist than fortune-teller, sets out to find the nephew and discovers that he has been posing as dead. The man, who murdered his adoptive parents, thrives as a jeweler under the name of Arthur Adamson and runs a criminal business on the side with his partner, Fran: kidnapping celebrities, releasing them in exchange for a diamond ransom. The couple have just found a priceless stone that Adamson has hidden in the center of a chandelier. Learning that he is wanted, the jeweler hires a criminal friend to eliminate the couple: Blanche and George narrowly escape death. The "fortune-teller" visits every Arthur Adamson in town before finding the right one: She tells him that he is his wealthy aunt's heir apparent but discovers the body of Adamson and Fran's latest victim, a bishop. Adamson drugs her and locks her away in a basement. George searches for Blanche and sees her car outside Adamson's house. He frees her and together they push the criminal couple into the basement "cell." In a daze, Blanche heads for the entrance staircase and locates the famous diamond: The fake clairvoyant discovers her talent as a medium.

"I would like to die with a clear conscience."

Julia Rainbird (Cathleen Nesbitt)
in *Family Plot*

GENESIS

To efface the memory of the recent failures of *Torn Curtain* (1966) and *Topaz* (1969), Hitchcock began looking for a new spy story. Not satisfied with any of his previous readings, he met William Link and Richard Levinson, two screenwriters who had worked on the *Alfred Hitchcock Presents* series. They recommended that he read *The Rainbird Pattern* by Victor Canning, a bestselling British author. Published in 1972, the novel crosses the paths of two pairs of crooks and criminals. *The Rainbird Pattern* is not an espionage thriller, but, in the view of the two screenwriters, a perfect Hitchcock plot.

A Farce

Hitchcock reunited with Ernest Lehman, who had collaborated on *North by Northwest* (1958) and had become a much-sought-after screenwriter. As usual, the Master wanted to take every possible liberty with the novel, confiding in Lehman: "I have no respect for the book. It is our story, not the book's."[1] They transposed the British plot to California and called the film *Alfred Hitchcock's Deceit.* The filmmaker suffered a series of health problems, absenting himself for various tribute events and often finding himself at odds with Lehman. The script was not finalized until April 1975.

CASTING

Hitchcock's casting was drawn from a generation of actors associated with the new Hollywood and adept at the psychologizing Method of the Actors Studio.

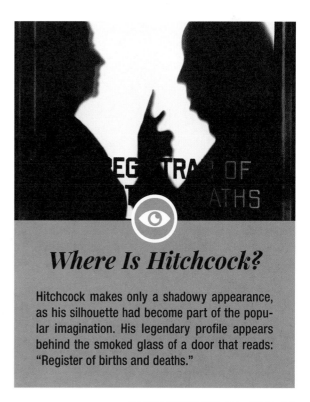

Where Is Hitchcock?

Hitchcock makes only a shadowy appearance, as his silhouette had become part of the popular imagination. His legendary profile appears behind the smoked glass of a door that reads: "Register of births and deaths."

DIRECTED BY ALFRED HITCHCOCK

Freeze Frame

In a somnambulistic moment, Blanche (Barbara Harris) climbs a staircase and points to the diamond hidden in the chandelier. The fake clairvoyant discovers a paranormal power. This final scene is the most Hitchcockian: a staircase, close-ups of the gloved finger and the diamond. Hitchcock follows this scene with the actress winking at the camera, a subject of disagreement between himself and Lehman. Until now, the camera gaze had been reserved only for the filmmaker's appearances. But he decided to give his audience one last knowing look. The credits roll during a freeze frame on the diamond, the filmmaker's final shot, the perfect symbol of a sparkling filmography.

A New Generation

Bruce Dern (*The King of Marvin Gardens*, Bob Rafelson, 1972) and Barbara Harris (*Nashville*, Robert Altman, 1975) play the sympathetic crook couple. Rising star Karen Black (*Easy Rider*, Dennis Hopper, 1969; *Nashville*) takes on the role of Fran, wife of Arthur Adamson, the jeweler and crook originally played by Roy Thinnes, star of the TV series *The Invaders*. Dissatisfied with his performance, Hitchcock replaced Thinnes during filming with William Devane (*McCabe & Mrs. Miller*, Robert Altman, 1971).

FILMING AND PRODUCTION

Filming began in mid-May. Universal Studios invited the press to a grand reception, where each guest was surprised to discover a tombstone engraved with his or her name. When he was not filming, Hitchcock put on a show for the journalists invited to the set and had no hesitation in showing off his pacemaker.

More Air

According to Lehman, the filmmaker purged the novel of all its Hitchcockian elements: the police investigation, the punishment inflicted on the villains, against whom no figure of good emerges by contrast. His mise-en-scène confined itself to wide, general shots and almost entirely dispensed with his famous close-ups, which are loaded with meaning. This time, Hitchcock invited his young actors, accustomed to following his storyboard, to improvise and propose their ideas. This unprecedented method is a sign that the artist was trying to embrace the zeitgeist and bring the present into his latest fiction.

RECEPTION

For what is now called *Family Plot*, Universal organized a grand preview in Los Angeles, where the film's reels were transported in a hearse. This was followed by a press conference at which the director assured everyone that this was not his last film.

A More Tranquil Film?

Family Plot was a failure with the public. American critics were torn between a respectful attitude and disappointment with a film at odds with the rest of Hitchcock's oeuvre, closer to its era than to its filmmaker. The most sensitive review came from William S. Pechter for *Commentary* magazine: "Perhaps it is true that *Family Plot* reflects the tranquility of an older artist, a serene wisdom in which all his childhood terrors have finally been exorcised and set aside. If so, then so much the better for Hitchcock. And too bad for us."

Making Way for the Younger Generations

Hitchcock entrusted the soundtrack to John Williams, the new star composer who had just scored Universal's latest hit, *Jaws* (Steven Spielberg, 1975). Williams sought the approval of Bernard Herrmann, who was angry with Hitchcock, before accepting the job. Herrmann also rubbed shoulders with the new generation, writing the music for Brian De Palma's *Obsession*—a "remake" of *Vertigo*—and Martin Scorsese's *Taxi Driver* (1976).

The Final Years

Hitchcock went in search of a final commercial success. He began work on a screenplay, *The Short Night*, the true story of an English spy who escapes from prison to reach the Soviet Union. The director considered casting Sean Connery and Ingmar Bergman's actress Liv Ullmann. He alternated between phases of enthusiasm and discouragement, writing sessions and stays in the hospital, when he was not with Alma, whose state of health was worsening. On March 7, 1979, the American Film Institute presented him with a Life Achievement Award. Hitchcock was apprehensive about this celebration, which seemed like a farewell from the film industry. At the end of 1979, he was made a Commander of the Order of the British Empire, an award from his native country that moved him even more. Despite the honors, and notwithstanding his state of health, Hitchcock made regular visits to his Universal office and worked on his fifty-fourth feature film with screenwriter David Freeman, who took the opportunity to keep a diary, published after the filmmaker's death (*The Last Days of Alfred Hitchcock*, 1984). Their collaboration lasted five months and, at the end of winter, Hitchcock emptied his office to settle permanently in Bellagio Road, where he died on April 29, 1980, at the age of eighty.

Sylvie Vartan, *L'Ange noir*
(Jean-Claude Brisseau, 1992
Right: Angie Dickinson,
Dressed to Kill (Brian
De Palma, 1980).).

Hitchcock After Hitchcock
(Legacy)

What film could not claim a debt to the author of *Psycho*? Hitchcock's work never ceases to inspire remakes, rereadings, playful imitations, and conceptual variations.

Is There Such a Thing as Hitchcock Cinema?

In the history of what is known as classic American cinema (1930–1960), there was a moment when, at the height of its aesthetic plenitude, it produced films that became matrix works, bearing witness to a kind of formal culmination that profoundly determined the cinema of the years that followed. Do we say that a film is "Fordian," "Langian," "Hawksian," or, of course, "Hitchcockian"? But while many masterpieces have inevitably inspired a generation of great filmmakers to follow in the footsteps of the great masters, what can be said of the films Hitchcock made in his professional maturity? What thriller today does not continue to draw on the sources of *Vertigo* or *North by Northwest*? What modern horror film is not a direct descendant of *Psycho* or *The Birds*? It is not so much the themes addressed by the filmmaker as the means employed to condition the viewer that serve as a lesson, if not a method, for the entertainment industry, even though it sometimes entails losing sight along the way of the metaphysical dimension that also characterizes the cinema of the author of *Frenzy*.

Remakes

First and foremost, of course, there are the remakes. Whether a remake of a film or a new transposition of a novel already adapted by Hitchcock, the challenge is often a daunting one for those who attempt to remake his masterpieces. But one should rather see these films as a playful journey, and be amused by the comparisons between titles, and sometimes astonished by the way in which some, adopting stances totally opposed to those of the Master, manage to avoid the danger of inevitably disappointing repetition. Among other examples, there are two adaptations of Marie Belloc Lowndes's novel *The Lodger*, by John Brahm (1944) and Hugo Fregonese (*Man in the Attic*, 1953), as well as two new versions of *The 39 Steps,* after John Buchan, one by Ralph Thomas (1959) and the other by Don Sharp (1978). But were these filmmakers thinking of adapting Belloc Lowndes and Buchan, or were they also thinking of Hitchcock?

A Conceptual Approach

By choosing to remake *Psycho* in color, almost shot by shot, in 1998, Gus Van Sant succeeded in producing a conceptual object, further sharpening critical apprehension of the original film through the discovery of what is at stake, in the relationship with this new version, between repetition and difference, and above all between two eras (1960 and 1998). But with *Homicide*, among others, did not filmmaker William Castle, as early as 1961, produce an opportunistic variation on *Psycho* that could also appear conceptual?

Plagiarisms and Rereadings

A number of stories filmed by Hitchcock have been taken up, reworked, and sometimes "trivialized" by exploitation cinema, inventive in its plagiarism and lacking in inhibitions. The structure of *Vertigo* can be found in two screenplays by Italian filmmaker Lucio Fulci: Riccardo Freda's *A doppia faccia* (*Double Face*),

in 1969, and his own film *Una sull'altra* (*Perversion Story*) made the same year. In both cases, a man is reunited with a beloved woman he thought dead.

Brian De Palma

Brian De Palma is the man who has most spectacularly, and endlessly, appropriated the cinema of Hitchcock to create a fascinating rereading, both erudite and romantic. *Obsession*, in 1976, takes the structure of *Vertigo* and turns it into a meditation on cinema, on the impossibility of finding an object of fixation lost forever, and the necessity of seeking it anyway. *Rear Window*, *Vertigo*, and *Psycho* are given an original treatment in *Dressed to Kill* (1980) and *Body Double* (1984). De Palma's entire oeuvre could be summoned up in this way. The cinephile enters into Hitchcock's images, not only to dissect them, but also to amplify their meaning.

Paranoia and Fetishism

Mario Bava's *Rosso segno della follia* (*Hatchet for the Honeymoon*, 1969), a sort of Mannerist throwback to *Psycho*, evokes cross-dressing and a maladjusted Oedipus. As for Roman Polanski's paranoid thriller *Frantic* (1988), it is easy to see the extent to which the subtlety of the mise-en-scène serves the description of a reality that has become alien to the film's hero, as in *North by Northwest*.

French Filmmakers

Great French filmmakers have had an intimate, precise, and accurate knowledge of Hitchcock. The connection seems inexhaustible, from François Truffaut, in *La mariée était en noir (The Bride Wore Black)* in 1967, who uses a number of Hitchcock formulae, to Claude Chabrol, in *Masques* in 1987, who takes up and varies the structure of *Notorious*, via Jean-Claude Brisseau and his magnificent *L'Ange noir, (The Black Angel)* which, in 1994, paid its debt to the inexhaustible *Vertigo*…

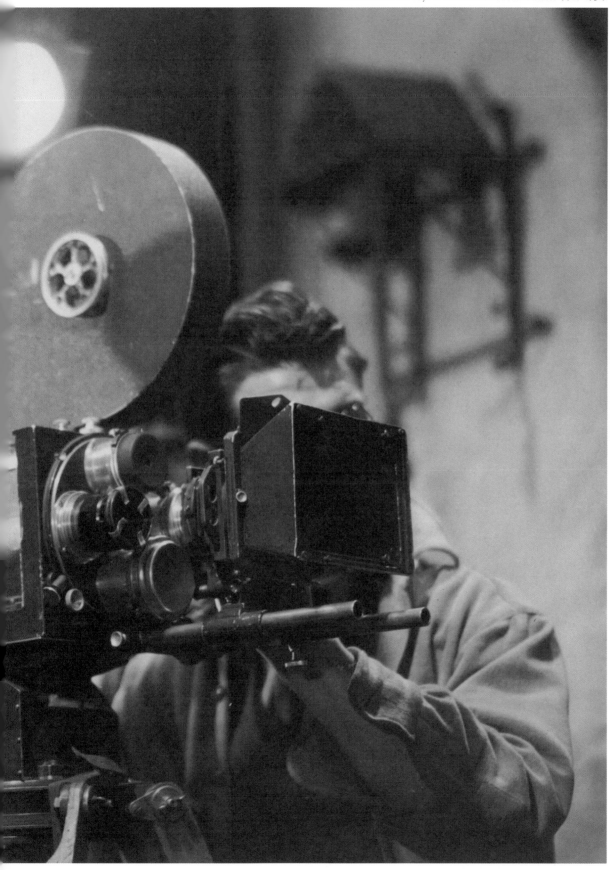

Hitchcock in the days of British International Pictures (1927–1932).

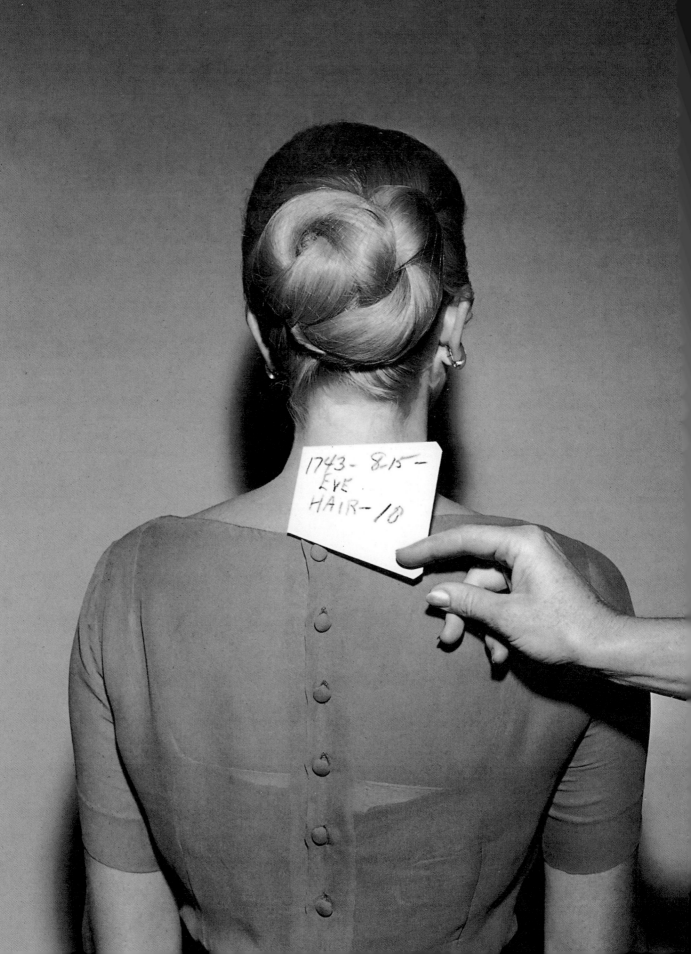

Glossary

Cameo: a brief appearance in a film by an actor, director, or well-known public figure. The cameo may be part of the plot, but it is also a wink to the audience and a signature effect. Alfred Hitchcock featured in cameos of himself in thirty-eight of his fifty-three feature films.

Camera shot sizes: general or overall shot (landscape), full shot (a character from head to toe), medium full shot (head to knee), "cowboy" shot (framing at the mid-thigh, "below the holster"), medium shot (head to waist), chest shot / medium close-up (head to chest), close-up (neck and face), extreme close-up (eyes and top of the head), etc., and how a film can play with the succession of these different scales.

CinemaScope: America's first wide-screen film process (*The Robe*, Henry Koster, 20th Century-Fox, 1953) to produce a gigantic effect. The technique is based on an early optical process known as anamorphosis, which compresses the image before restoring it to its full width on projection. Following CinemaScope, many studios and countries (France, Italy, USSR…) developed their own wide-screen techniques (SuperScope, DyaliScope, FranScope, VistaVision, TechniScope, Kinopanorama, etc.). Hitchcock never filmed in CinemaScope but did film five times in VistaVision, the Paramount process (*To Catch a Thief, The Trouble with Harry, The Man Who Knew Too Much, Vertigo, North by Northwest*).

Cinematographer: also referred to as director of photography. Responsible for the technical and creative aspects of the shoot: choice of film, cameras, and lenses (in consultation with the director), lighting and shadows (in consultation with the art director and set designers), color rendering, optical tricks performed during the shoot, as well as framing, which they may perform themselves or entrust to an associate.

Cinerama: a projection process experimented with in the American documentary *This Is Cinerama* (1952). During filming, the camera was equipped with a triple lens, while projection was carried out on an "extra-wide" curved screen using three projection devices. The word "Cinerama" is a contraction of "cinema" and "panorama" (it also happens to be an anagram of "American").

Clapper loader: the person who holds the clapperboard, a "slate" used during filming to identify each shot and number each take, then used in editing to synchronize image and sound, recorded separately. The clapper board is filmed by the camera before the start of a take and marks the beginning of the take.

Continuity: the job of the script supervisor, which consists in ensuring the visual and sound coherence of a film, its continuity. This means making sure that two shots that follow each other are connected in every way (sets, costumes, props, movements) and can be "edited" together. This is a task that Alma Reville, Hitchcock's wife, often took care of, officially or unofficially, on her husband's shoots in the 1920s and 1930s.

Continuity (shot/editing): an editing term referring to the joining and linking of two successive shots, giving the impression of a seamless filmed space, continuity of movement, and speed of action.

Dive shot: an angle of view. The camera is positioned (high) above what it is filming, giving the impression of "dwarfing" the subject, object, or space filmed.

Field: a portion of space framed by the camera and rendered onscreen.

Insert: small object or part of an object or body (a hand, an ear, etc.) framed in extreme close-up and inserted during editing between wider shots. Onscreen, the insert creates a change of scale and deliberately draws attention to this object or partial object.

Intercutting (or alternating editing): shots edited to show alternating actions taking place simultaneously. These actions may share the same space or take place in different spaces but are linked through editing.

Intertitle (or title card): text filmed during the silent era. It appears between two shots and provides the viewer with additional written information: commentary, location of the action in space and time, information about a character (at the same time as the actor's or actress's name); the intertitle makes up for the absence of sound by also transcribing dialogue. Hitchcock made his film debut in 1920 as an intertitle illustrator.

Koulechov effect: named after the Soviet filmmaker who, in the early 1920s, postulated the suggestive power of editing. In this film experiment (which has never been found, if it ever existed in this form), a close-up of an actor's impassive face is preceded or followed by shots of a plate of soup, a child in a coffin, a woman lying on a sofa. It is the editing that "plays" by suggesting to the viewer that the actor is experiencing hunger, sadness, and desire, respectively (meaning is deduced from the interaction of the shots). Hitchcock often cited this experiment as an example of the effectiveness of editing and an explanation for his rejection of psychology in acting.

Low angle: an angle of view. The camera is positioned below what it is filming, giving the impression of enlarging the subject, object, or space filmed.

MacGuffin: see p. 154.

Magazine (camera): fixed or removable camera accessory that contains the blank film to be recorded at the time of shooting and protects it from accidental exposure to light, which would fog it.

Matte painting: see p. 202.

Panning shot: horizontal or vertical movement of a camera around its axis. What is captured by the rotation of the camera, held at a fixed point (panoramic view).

Postproduction: after shooting, this stage in the creation of a film includes image and sound editing, post-synchronization, dubbing, sound effects, mixing, the addition of special effects, and color grading.

Preproduction: phase of preparation for the shoot (financing, casting, assembling the technical crew, technical structuring, location scouting, storyboarding, drawing up the work plan, etc.).

Reverse angle: portion of space located opposite that which appears in the field and which faces it in a play of alternation.

Rushes: images and sounds produced by the camera during filming, in other words, all the shots taken to produce a film. By extension, rushes refer to regular screenings or viewings of these elements by the director and part of the crew. Each of these sessions is used to check the technical and artistic quality of the shots and to decide which ones will be used by the laboratory in preparation for editing.

Schüfftan process (or Schüfftan effect): named after the German cinematographer who invented it in the 1920s. A tilted mirror is used to combine a life-size set and a model in the same shot, giving the illusion of a continuous, larger-than-life sequence. For crowd scenes or monumental scenes, this trick or trompe l'oeil technique saves on extras (silhouettes drawn to represent an audience) and sets (addition of painted buildings). Hitchcock used this technique in several of his English films: *The Ring, Blackmail, The Man Who Knew Too Much, The 39 Steps.*

Sequence shot: a shot characterized by its duration, taking up a large footage of film and showing the entire action without any splices. Hitchcock was so fond of this aesthetic that he made a film entirely out of sequence shots: *Rope.*

Stereoscopy: from the Greek *stereos* (στερεός), "firm," "solid," and *scopeo* (σκοπέω), "to look, or see." This is the totality of techniques and methods used to reproduce the impression of a relief perception from two flat images. In common parlance, rather than "stereoscopic film," reference is made to a "3D" (three-dimensional) film effect. Hitchcock shot one film in 3D: *Dial M for Murder.*

Storyboard: see p. 316.

Story editor: responsible for writing a script, ensuring its progress and compatibility with production conditions. A privileged interlocutor with the scriptwriter(s).

Tinting: silent film technique used to give a shot a specific color. The printed film is dipped in a dye that tints the gelatin without damaging the image. Several shades are codified and used: blue or violet (night), yellow (sun and interiors), fiery red (fires, battles), green (vegetation), etc. This practice ceased with the advent of talking pictures, as dyes impaired the audio tape.

Transparency: in the studio, using a projector placed behind a translucent screen, previously filmed images are used as a background for one or more actors acting out a scene in front of the same screen. The camera films both the foreground and the background, so that the actor actually appears to be in the scene. This illusion has been used extensively to show characters in cars (the vehicle is motionless on the set, while the scenery scrolls by). Transparency is an economical process, but it can also be an artistic decision.

Traveling shot: movement in space of a camera placed on a crane, trolley, or rails. It can be forward, backward, lateral, or vertical.

Treatment: the stage preceding the screenplay. This is the first outline version of the plot structure, often divided into short, numbered paragraphs, without the dialogue (written later, based on the treatment).

Notes

**Alfred Hitchcock,
a Life in the Making**   **9**

1. Alfred Hitchcock, "Enjoying Fear," *Good Housekeeping*, February 1949. Quoted in Sidney Gottlieb, *Hitchcock on Hitchcock: Selected Writings and Interviews*, University of California Press, 1995.

2. Claude Chabrol and Éric Rohmer, *Hitchcock* [1957], Ramsay, 2006.

**Hitchcock Before Hitchcock
(1899–1925)**   **14**

1. All quotations in this text are Alfred Hitchcock's own words, taken mainly from his own articles (edited by Sidney Gottlieb), his biographies (John Russell Taylor, Donald Spoto, Patrick McGilligan, Charlotte Chandler, etc.), interviews (Peter Bogdanovich, François Truffaut), dictionaries (Howard Maxford), and studies of the filmmaker (Bill Krohn, Alain Kerzoncuf, and Charles Barr). See "Selected Bibliography."

The Mountain Eagle   **41**

1. Summary based on existing film stills and written sources: *The Bioscope*, October 7, 1926; *Kinematograph Weekly*, October 7, 1926; Maurice Yacowar, *Hitchcock's British Films* [1977], Wayne State University Press, 2010.

2. Alfred Hitchcock, "Life Among the Stars: Nita Naldi, Vamp," *London News Chronicle*, March 2, 1937.

The Lodger   **47**

1. Alfred Hitchcock, lecture at Columbia University, March 30, 1939, *Trafic*, spring 2002, previously published in Sidney Gottlieb, *Hitchcock on Hitchcock: Selected Writings and Interviews*, University of California Press, 1995.

2. Ivor Montagu, "Working with Hitchcock," *Sight & Sound*, vol. 49, summer 1980.

The Farmer's Wife   **75**

1. Claude Chabrol and Éric Rohmer, *Hitchcock* [1957], Ramsay, 2006.

Champagne   **79**

1. Peter Bogdanovich, *The Cinema of Alfred Hitchcock*, MoMA, 1963; *Les Maîtres d'Hollywood*, vol. 2, Capricci, 2018.

2. Interview with Alfred Roome, in Patrick McGilligan, *Alfred Hitchcock, une vie d'ombres et de lumière*, Institut Lumière / Actes Sud, 2011.

The Manxman   **83**

1. Claude Chabrol and Éric Rohmer, *Hitchcock* [1957], Ramsay, 2006.

Blackmail   **89**

1. Patrick McGilligan, *Backstory: Interviews with Screenwriters of Hollywood's Golden Age*, University of California Press, 1986.

Juno and the Paycock   **99**

1. Peter Bogdanovich, *The Cinema of Alfred Hitchcock*, MoMA, 1963; *Les Maîtres d'Hollywood*, vol. 2, Capricci, 2018.

2. Sean O'Casey, *Autobiographies*, vol. 4, *Rose et Couronne* [1926–1935], Belfond, 1996.

3. Cited in Donald Spoto, *La Face cachée d'un génie, la vraie vie d'Alfred Hitchcock* [1983], Albin Michel, 2004.

An Elastic Affair   **104**

1. Alain Kerzoncuf and Charles Barr, *Hitchcock Lost & Found: The Forgotten Films*, University Press of Kentucky, 2015.

Elstree Calling   **106**

1. Alain Kerzoncuf and Charles Barr, *Hitchcock Lost & Found: The Forgotten Films*, University Press of Kentucky, 2015.

2. Adrian Brunel, *Nice Work*, Forbes Robertson, 1949.

3. John Russell Taylor, *Hitch: The Life and Work of Alfred Hitchcock*, Faber & Faber, 1978.

Murder! / Mary   **109**

1. Charles Landstone, *I Gate-Crashed*, Stainer & Bell, 1976.

2. Maurice Yacowar, *Hitchcock's British Films* [1977], Wayne State University Press, 2010.

3. Jacques Lourcelles, *Dictionnaire du cinéma*, vol. 3, *Les Films*, Robert Laffont, 1992.

The Skin Game   **121**

1. Claude Chabrol and Éric Rohmer, *Hitchcock* [1957], Ramsay, 2006.

Waltzes from Vienna   **139**

1. Jessie Matthews and Muriel Burgess, *Over My Shoulder: An Autobiography*, W. H. Allen, 1974.

2. Esmond Knight, *Seeking the Bubble*, Hutchinson & Co., 1943.

3. Stephen Watts, "Alfred Hitchcock on Music in Films," *Cinema Quarterly*, winter 1933–1934.

**Michael Balcon, the Man Who
Knew a Thing or Two**   **142**

1. Michael Balcon, "Thirty Years of British Film Production," *British Kinematography*, October 1949.

2. Michael Balcon, "Putting the Real Britain on the Screen," *Evening News*, October 1, 1936.

The Man Who Knew Too Much   **145**

1. Peter Bogdanovich, *The Cinema of Alfred Hitchcock*, MoMA, 1963; *Les Maîtres d'Hollywood*, vol. 2, Capricci, 2018.

2. Cited in James Chapman, *Hitchcock and the Spy Film*, I. B. Tauris, 2018.

3. Claude Chabrol and Éric Rohmer, *Hitchcock* [1957], Ramsay, 2006.

**The MacGuffin, a Very
Ridiculous Secret**   **154**

1. François Truffaut, *Hitchcock/Truffaut* [1966], Gallimard, 2003.

The 39 Steps   **157**

1. François Truffaut, *Hitchcock/Truffaut* [1966], Gallimard, 2003.

Secret Agent   **169**

1. Alfred Hitchcock, "My Screen Memories," *Film Weekly*, May 1936.

2. Ivor Montagu, "Working with Hitchcock," *Sight & Sound*, vol. 49, summer 1980.

3. James Chapman, *Hitchcock and the Spy Film*, I. B. Tauris, 2018.

4. Alfred Hitchcock, "Director's Problems," *The Listener*, February 2, 1938.

5. Elisabeth Weis, *The Silent Scream: Alfred Hitchcock's Sound Track*, Associated University Presses, 1982.

6. Graham Greene, *The Pleasure Dome: The Collected Film Criticism, 1935–1940*, edited by John Russell Taylor, Secker & Warburg, 1972.

Sabotage   **181**

1. Patrick McGilligan, *Backstory: Interviews with Screenwriters of Hollywood's Golden Age*, University of California Press, 1986.

2. Charles Barr, *English Hitchcock*, Cameron & Hollis, 1999.

3. Ivor Montagu, "Working with Hitchcock," *Sight & Sound*, vol. 49, summer 1980.

Young and Innocent   **193**

1. Cited in Patrick McGilligan, *Alfred Hitchcock, une vie d'ombres et de lumière*, Institut Lumière / Actes Sud, 2011.

2. Alfred Hitchcock, "Nouvel éclat de Nova," *Film Weekly*, December 5, 1938.

3. Alain Bergala, *Young and Innocent*, Les Enfants de cinéma / Yellow Now, coll. "Les cahiers de notes," 1997.

Albert Whitlock, the Illusionist   **202**

1. Bill Krohn, "Ils ont fabriqué *The Birds*," table ronde avec les décorateurs d'Hitchcock (Albert Whitlock, Robert Boyle, Harold Michelson), *Cahiers du cinéma*, June 1982.

2. Mark Cotta Vaz and Craig Barron, *The Invisible Art: The Legends of Movie Matte Painting*, Chronicle Books, 2002. See also the documentary by Mark Horowitz, *Albert Whitlock: A Master of Illusion*, 1981.

The Lady Vanishes　　　**205**

1. James Chapman, *Hitchcock and the Spy Film*, I. B. Tauris, 2018.

2. Margaret Lockwood, *Lucky Star*, Odhams Press, 1955.

3. Michael Redgrave, *In My Mind's I: An Actor's Autobiography*, Viking, 1983.

David O. Selznick, or the Perfect Disharmony　　　**222**

1. David O. Selznick, *Cinéma*, textes choisis et réunis par Rudy Behlmer, Ramsay, 1984.

2. Cited in Leonard J. Leff, *Hitchcock & Selznick*, Ramsay Cinéma, 1990.

Rebecca　　　**225**

1. Cited in Patrick McGilligan, *Alfred Hitchcock, une vie d'ombres et de lumière*, Institut Lumière / Actes Sud, 2011.

2. Cited in Leonard J. Leff, *Hitchcock & Selznick*, Ramsay Cinéma, 1990.

3. François Truffaut, *Hitchcock/Truffaut* [1966], Gallimard, 2003.

Foreign Correspondent　　　**235**

1. Patrick McGilligan, *Backstory: Interviews with Screenwriters of Hollywood's Golden Age*, University of California Press, 1986.

2. Cited in James Chapman, *Hitchcock and the Spy Film*, I. B. Tauris, 2018.

Mr. & Mrs. Smith　　　**245**

1. Stanley Cavell, *À la recherche du bonheur, Hollywood et la comédie du remariage*, Cahiers du cinéma, 1993.

2. Bill Krohn, *Hitchcock au travail*, Cahiers du cinéma, 1999.

Suspicion　　　**249**

1. Bill Krohn, "Ambivalence (*Suspicion*)," *Trafic*, no. 41, spring 2002, P.O.L.

2. Peter Bogdanovich, *The Cinema of Alfred Hitchcock*, MoMA, 1963; *Les Maîtres d'Hollywood*, vol. 2, Capricci, 2018.

3. François Truffaut, *Hitchcock/Truffaut* [1966], Gallimard, 2003.

4. Pascal Kané, *Cahiers du cinéma*, March–April 1971.

Hitchcock at War　　　**258**

1. Alain Kerzoncuf and Charles Barr, *Hitchcock Lost & Found: The Forgotten Films*, University Press of Kentucky, 2015.

Saboteur　　　**261**

1. François Truffaut, *Hitchcock/Truffaut* [1966], Gallimard, 2003.

2. George Turner, "*Saboteur*: Hitchcock Set Free," *American Cinematographer*, November 1993.

Shadow of a Doubt　　　**277**

1. George Turner, "Hitchcock's Mastery Is Beyond Doubt in *Shadow*," *American Cinematographer*, May 1993.

2. Cited in Donald Spoto, *La Face cachée d'un génie, la vraie vie d'Alfred Hitchcock* [1983], Albin Michel, 2004.

3. Cited in Patrick McGilligan, *Alfred Hitchcock, une vie d'ombres et de lumière*, Institut Lumière / Actes Sud, 2011.

Lifeboat　　　**289**

1. Cited in Patrick McGilligan, *Alfred Hitchcock, une vie d'ombres et de lumière*, Institut Lumière / Actes Sud, 2011.

2. Cited in Donald Spoto, *La Face cachée d'un génie, la vraie vie d'Alfred Hitchcock* [1983], Albin Michel, 2004.

3. flavorwire.com/256717/john-steinbeck-wanted-his-name-taken-off-hitchcocks-lifeboat.

Bon voyage　　　**300**

1. Alain Kerzoncuf and Charles Barr, *Hitchcock Lost & Found: The Forgotten Films*, University Press of Kentucky, 2015.

Psychoanalysis According to Hitchcock　　　**302**

1. Sigmund Freud, letter dated June 9, 1925, to Karl Abraham, *Freud/Abraham, correspondance*, Gallimard, 1969.

2. Two of the better known examples: Raymond Bellour, "Le blocage symbolique," *Communications*, Seuil, 1975; Slavoj Žižek (dir.), *Tout ce que vous avez toujours voulu savoir sur Lacan sans jamais oser le demander à Hitchcock* [1988], Capricci, 2010.

Spellbound　　　**307**

1. François Truffaut, *Hitchcock/Truffaut* [1966], Gallimard, 2003.

2. Guy Cogeval and Dominique Païni (dir.), *Hitchcock et l'art, coïncidences fatales*, Mazzotta, 2000.

Storyboards, Films on Paper　　　**316**

1. Bill Krohn, *Hitchcock au travail*, Cahiers du cinéma, 1999.

Memory of the Camps / German Concentration Camps Factual Survey　　　**321**

1. Meyer Levin, *In Search* [1950], Constellation Books, 1951. Cited in Annette Wieviorka, *1945, la découverte*, Seuil, 2015.

2. Sidney Bernstein, interviewed in *A Painful Reminder*, Brian Blake (production), 1985.

3. Cited in Toby Haggith, *The Making of German Concentration Camps Factual Survey*, booklet for the box set containing the restored version of the film, Imperial War Museums / British Film Institute, 2017.

4. Caroline Moorehead, "What Hitch Saw, Filmed—and Hid," *The Times*, December 12, 1983; Caroline Moorehead, *Sidney Bernstein: A Biography*, Jonathan Cape Ltd, 1984.

5. Dai Vaughan, *Portrait of an Invisible Man: The Working Life of Stewart McAllister, Film Editor*, BFI Publishing, 1983.

6. The film can be viewed at the Frontline website: www.pbs.org/wgbh/frontline/film/memory-of-the-camps.

7. www.bfi.org.uk/news-opinion/news-bfi/features/night-will-fall-story-file-number-f3080.

8. Robin Wood, *Hitchcock's Films* [1965], Columbia University Press, 1989.

Notorious　　　**329**

1. Bill Krohn, *Hitchcock au travail*, Cahiers du cinéma, 1999.

2. Claude Chabrol and Éric Rohmer, *Hitchcock* [1957], Ramsay, 2006.

3. "Hitchcock/Bogdanovich," *La Conquête de l'indépendance*, DVD box set *Les Années Selznick*, Carlotta, 2017.

4. Cited in Donald Spoto, *La Face cachée d'un génie, la vraie vie d'Alfred Hitchcock* [1983], Albin Michel, 2004.

Rope　　　**347**

1. Michael Munn, *Jimmy Stewart: The Truth Behind the Legend*, Skyhorse Publishing, 2006.

2. Alfred Hitchcock, "My Most Exciting Picture," *Popular Photography*, November 1948.

Under Capricorn　　　**357**

1. François Truffaut, *Hitchcock/Truffaut* [1966], Gallimard, 2003.

2. Cited in Patrick McGilligan, *Alfred Hitchcock, une vie d'ombres et de lumière*, Institut Lumière / Actes Sud, 2011.

3. Jean Domarchi, "Le chef-d'œuvre inconnu," *Cahiers du cinéma*, October 1954.

Ingrid Bergman, the Cornerstone　　　**366**

1. Ingrid Bergman and Alan Burgess, *Ma vie*, Fayard, 1980.

2. Claude Chabrol and Éric Rohmer, *Hitchcock* [1957], Ramsay, 2006.

Stage Fright　　　**369**

1. Bruno Villien, *Hitchcock*, Colona, 1982.

Strangers on a Train　　　**373**

1. Raymond Chandler, *Lettres*, Christian Bourgois, 1984.

2. Jean-Luc Godard, "Le contrôle de l'univers," *Histoire(s) du cinéma*, 1998.

Robert Burks, the Man Who Could Do Anything　　　**382**

1. Howard Maxford, *The A–Z of Hitchcock: The Ultimate Reference Guide*, B. T. Batsford, 2002.

2. Letter to Peter Bogdanovich (1963), cited in Tony Lee Moral, *The Making of Hitchcock's "The Birds,"* Kamera Books, 2013.

I Confess　　　**385**

1. François Truffaut, *Hitchcock/Truffaut* [1966], Gallimard, 2003.

Rear Window　　　**405**

1. Cited in Donald Spoto, *La Face cachée d'un génie, la vraie vie d'Alfred Hitchcock* [1983], Albin Michel, 2004.

2. Cited in Patrick McGilligan, *Alfred Hitchcock, une vie d'ombres et de lumière*, Institut Lumière / Actes Sud, 2011.

3. Arthur E. Gavin, "Rear Window," *American Cinematographer*, February 1954.

4. Francis Montcoffe, *Rear Window*, Nathan, 1990; Stefan Sharff, *The Art of Looking*, Limelight Editions, 1997; John Fawell, *Hitchcock's "Rear Window": The Well-Made Film*, Southern Illinois University Press, 2001.

Grace Kelly, the "Hitchcock Blonde"   **414**

1. Cited in Patrick McGilligan, *Alfred Hitchcock, une vie d'ombres et de lumière*, Institut Lumière / Actes Sud, 2011.

2. Cited in Patrick Brion, *Hitchcock*, Éditions de La Martinière, 2000.

To Catch a Thief   **417**

1. Cited in Patrick McGilligan, *Alfred Hitchcock, une vie d'ombres et de lumière*, Institut Lumière / Actes Sud, 2011.

2. François Truffaut, *Hitchcock/Truffaut* [1966], Gallimard, 2003.

Cary Grant, Haute Couture   **426**

1. All quotations in this text come from Graham McCann, *Cary Grant: A Class Apart*, Columbia University Press, 1996, and from Nancy Nelson, *Evenings with Cary Grant*, Warner Books, 1993.

The Trouble with Harry   **429**

1. Steven DeRosa, *Writing with Hitchcock: The Collaboration of Alfred Hitchcock and John Michael Hayes* [2001], CineScribe Media, 2011.

2. Éric Rohmer, "Castigat Ridendo…," *Cahiers du cinéma*, April 1956.

3. Jean Domarchi, "Humain, trop humain…," *Cahiers du cinéma*, April 1956.

Bernard Herrmann, the Musical Subconscious   **432**

1. www.bernardherrmann.org/articles/an-interview-with-bernard-herrmann.

2. Steven C. Smith, *A Heart at Fire's Center: The Life and Music of Bernard Herrmann* [1991], University of California Press, 2002.

The Man Who Knew Too Much   **435**

1. Bill Krohn, *Hitchcock au travail*, Cahiers du cinéma, 1999.

2. Cited in Donald Spoto, *La Face cachée d'un génie, la vraie vie d'Alfred Hitchcock* [1983], Albin Michel, 2004.

3. A. E. Hotchner, *Doris Day: Her Own Story*, William Morrow and Company, 1975.

4. Cited in Patrick McGilligan, *Alfred Hitchcock, une vie d'ombres et de lumière*, Institut Lumière / Actes Sud, 2011.

5. Raymond Durgnat, *The Strange Case of Alfred Hitchcock*, MIT Press, 1974.

6. Jean-Luc Godard, "Le chemin des écoliers," *Cahiers du cinéma*, November 1956.

7. Claude Chabrol et Éric Rohmer, *Hitchcock* [1957], Ramsay, 2006.

James Stewart, or the Shadow of War   **444**

1. Starr Smith, *Jimmy Stewart: Bomber Pilot*, Zenith Press, 2005.

2. Jonathan Coe, *James Stewart, une biographie de l'Amérique* [1994], Cahiers du cinéma, 2004.

3. Howard Maxford, *The A–Z of Hitchcock: The Ultimate Reference Guide*, B. T. Batsford, 2002.

4. Martin Scorsese, "James Stewart, Robert Mitchum," *Cahiers du cinéma*, September 1997.

The Wrong Man   **461**

1. Interview recorded in August 1954 and published in February 1955 in *Cahiers du cinéma*.

2. François Truffaut, *Hitchcock/Truffaut* [1966], Gallimard, 2003.

3. François Truffaut, *Les Films de ma vie*, Flammarion, 1975.

4. Laurent Bouzereau (production), *Guilt Trip: Hitchcock and "The Wrong Man,"* 2004.

5. Frederick Foster, "'Hitch' Didn't Want It Arty," *American Cinematographer*, February 1957.

6. Ian Christie and David Thompson, *Scorsese on Scorsese* [1989], Faber & Faber, 2004.

"Wet Saturday"   **470**

1. François Truffaut, *Hitchcock/Truffaut* [1966], Gallimard, 2003.

Vertigo   **481**

1. *Obsessed with "Vertigo"*: Harrison Engle (production), 1997.

2. Dan Auiler, *"Vertigo": The Making of a Hitchcock Classic*, St. Martin's Press, 1998; Charles Barr, *Vertigo* [2002], BFI / Palgrave Macmillan, 2012.

3. Éric Rohmer, "L'hélice et l'Idée," *Cahiers du cinéma*, March 1959.

4. Cited in Patrick McGilligan, *Alfred Hitchcock, une vie d'ombres et de lumière*, Institut Lumière / Actes Sud, 2011.

5. Chris Marker, "A Free Replay (Notes sur *Vertigo*)," *Positif*, June 1994.

Edith Head, Supreme Elegance   **492**

1. Cited in Patrick McGilligan, *Alfred Hitchcock, une vie d'ombres et de lumière*, Institut Lumière / Actes Sud, 2011.

2. Paddy Calistro and Edith Head, *Edith Head's Hollywood*, Angel City Press, 1983.

3. François Truffaut, *Hitchcock/Truffaut* [1966], Gallimard, 2003.

North by Northwest   **501**

1. Letter from Otis Guernsey to Alfred Hitchcock, October 14, 1957.

2. "Alfred Hitchcock Talking," *Films and Filming*, July 1959.

3. Cited in James Chapman, *Hitchcock and the Spy Film*, I. B. Tauris, 2018.

4. François Truffaut, *Hitchcock/Truffaut* [1966], Gallimard, 2003.

5. Peter Bogdanovich, *The Cinema of Alfred Hitchcock*, MoMA, 1963; *Les Maîtres d'Hollywood*, vol. 2, Capricci, 2018.

6. Jean Domarchi and Jean Douchet, "Entretien avec Alfred Hitchcock," *Cahiers du cinéma*, December 1959.

7. Jacques Lourcelles, *Dictionnaire du cinéma*, vol. 3, *Les Films*, Robert Laffont, 1992.

Monuments, at the Summit of the Drama   **512**

1. Marc Vernet, "Hitchcock et le monumental," *Conférences du collège d'histoire de l'art cinématographique*, La Cinémathèque française, no. 6, winter 1994. *See also*: Cosmo Vitelli [Nicole Brenez], "Hitchcock, le monument," *Admiranda*, no. 2, 1988.

Four Films with Alfred Hitchcock   **516**

1. Most of the information about these four films comes from Alain Kerzoncuf and Charles Barr, *Hitchcock Lost & Found: The Forgotten Films*, University Press of Kentucky, 2015.

Psycho   **525**

1. Cited in Stephen Rebello, *Alfred Hitchcock and the Making of "Psycho"* [1990], Marion Boyars Publishers, 2013.

78 Shots and 45 Seconds That Changed the History of Cinema   **534**

1. François Truffaut, *Hitchcock/Truffaut* [1966], Gallimard, 2003.

2. Stephen Rebello, *Alfred Hitchcock and the Making of "Psycho"* [1990], Marion Boyars Publishers, 2013.

"Mrs. Bixby and the Colonel's Coat"   **546**

1. Martin Grams Jr. and Patrik Wikstrom, *The "Alfred Hitchcock Presents" Companion*, OTR Publishing, 2001.

The Birds   **555**

1. Alfred Hitchcock, *Alfred Hitchcock Presents: My Favorites in Suspense*, Random House, 1959.

2. Evan Hunter, *Me and Hitch*, Faber, 1997.

Alfred Hitchcock, a French Invention?   **566**

1. Claude Chabrol and Éric Rohmer, *Hitchcock* [1957], Ramsay, 2006.

A Genius for Publicity: Hitchcock at the Helm   **570**

1. Robert E. Kapsis, *Hitchcock: The Making of a Reputation*, University of Chicago Press, 1992.

2. Sidney Gottlieb, *Hitchcock on Hitchcock: Selected Writings and Interviews*, University of California Press, 1995.

3. *Warhol/Hitchcock*, Marest, publisher, 2016.

Marnie   **573**

1. Cited in Tony Lee Moral, *Hitchcock and the Making of "Marnie"* [2002], Scarecrow Press, 2013.

2. Peter Bogdanovich, *The Cinema of Alfred Hitchcock*, MoMA, 1963; *Les Maîtres d'Hollywood*, vol. 2, Capricci, 2018.

3. Cited in John Russell Taylor, *Hitch: The Life and Work of Alfred Hitchcock*, Faber & Faber, 1978.

4. Cited in Donald Spoto, *La Face cachée d'un génie, la vraie vie d'Alfred Hitchcock* [1983], Albin Michel, 2004.

Blondes, Mirage—Image   **584**

1. Interview given to CBS TV (February 20, 1977).

Torn Curtain   **587**

1. François Truffaut, *Hitchcock/Truffaut* [1966], Gallimard, 2003.

2. Cited in Donald Spoto, *La Face cachée d'un génie, la vraie vie d'Alfred Hitchcock* [1983], Albin Michel, 2004.

Unrealized Projects   **596**

1. François Truffaut, *Hitchcock/Truffaut* [1966], Gallimard, 2003.

2. Tim Kirby (production), *Hitch: Alfred the Great*, BBC, 1999.

Frenzy   **603**

1. Cited in Donald Spoto, *La Face cachée d'un génie, la vraie vie d'Alfred Hitchcock* [1983], Albin Michel, 2004.

2. Cited in Patrick McGilligan, *Alfred Hitchcock, une vie d'ombres et de lumière*, Institut Lumière / Actes Sud, 2011.

3. Raymond Foery, *Alfred Hitchcock's "Frenzy": The Last Masterpiece*, Scarecrow Press, 2012.

4. Bill Krohn, "*Kaleidoscope*: L'histoire secrète du premier *Frenzy*," *Cahiers du cinéma*, February 2011.

5. Henri Langlois, *Écrits de cinéma (1931–1977)*, Flammarion / La Cinémathèque française, 2014.

6. John Russell Taylor, *Hitch: The Life and Work of Alfred Hitchcock*, Faber & Faber, 1978.

7. François Truffaut, *Hitchcock/Truffaut* [1966], Gallimard, 2003.

Family Plot   **615**

1. Cited in Patrick McGilligan, *Alfred Hitchcock, une vie d'ombres et de lumière*, Institut Lumière / Actes Sud, 2011.

Hitchcock at work… (1960).

Cary Grant and Alfred Hitchcock on the set of *North by Northwest* (1958).

Selected Bibliography

Site

The Alfred Hitchcock Wiki:
the.hitchcock.zone/wiki/Main_Page

Published Works

Dan Auiler, *Hitchcock's Notebooks*, Avon Books, 1999.

Michael Balcon, *Michael Balcon Presents...A Lifetime of Films*, Hutchinson & Co., 1969.

Charles Barr, *English Hitchcock*, Cameron & Hollis, 1999.

Alain Bergala and Anne Marquez (dir.), *Brune/Blonde*, Skira Flammarion / La Cinémathèque française, 2010.

Peter Bogdanovich, *The Cinema of Alfred Hitchcock*, MoMA, 1963; *Les Maîtres d'Hollywood*, vol. 2, Capricci, 2018.

Claude Chabrol and Éric Rohmer, *Hitchcock* [1957], Ramsay, 2006.

Charlotte Chandler, *It's Only a Movie: Alfred Hitchcock: A Personal Biography*, Simon & Schuster, 2005.

James Chapman, *Hitchcock and the Spy Film*, I. B. Tauris, 2018.

Guy Cogeval and Dominique Païni (dir.), *Hitchcock et l'art, coïncidences fatales*, Mazzotta, 2000.

Steven DeRosa, *Writing with Hitchcock: The Collaboration of Alfred Hitchcock and John Michael Hayes* [2001], CineScribe Media, 2011.

Jean Douchet, *Hitchcock* [1967], Cahiers du cinéma, 1999.

Sidney Gottlieb, *Hitchcock on Hitchcock: Selected Writings and Interviews*, University of California Press, 1995. Translated into French: *Ferme les yeux et vois!* and *Quoi est qui?*, Mares, publisher, 2017.

Martin Grams Jr. and Patrik Wikstrom, *The "Alfred Hitchcock Presents" Companion*, OTR Publishing, 2001.

Vincent Haegele, *Bernard Herrmann, un génie de la musique de film*, Minerve, 2016.

Pat Hitchcock O'Connell and Laurent Bouzereau, *Alma Hitchcock: The Woman Behind the Man*, Berkley Publishing Group, 2003.

Alain Kerzoncuf and Charles Barr, *Hitchcock Lost & Found: The Forgotten Films*, University Press of Kentucky, 2015.

Bill Krohn, *Hitchcock au travail*, Cahiers du cinéma, 1999.

Alfred Hitchcock, Janet Leigh: rehearsal for the shooting of one of the seventy-eight shots that make up the shower scene (*Psycho*, 1960).

Leonard J. Leff, *Hitchcock & Selznick*, Ramsay Cinéma, 1990.

Howard Maxford, *The A–Z of Hitchcock: The Ultimate Reference Guide*, B. T. Batsford, 2002.

Dennis McDougal, *The Last Mogul: Lew Wasserman, MCA, and the Hidden History of Hollywood*, Crown Publishers, 1998.

Patrick McGilligan, *Alfred Hitchcock: A Life in Darkness and Light*, HarperCollins Publishers, 2003; *Alfred Hitchcock, une vie d'ombres et de lumière*, Institut Lumière / Actes Sud, 2011.

Murray Pomerance, *Alfred Hitchcock's America*, Polity Press, 2013.

Jean-François Rauger, *L'oeil domestique, Alfred Hitchcock et la télévision*, Rouge Profond, 2014.

Donald Spoto, *The Dark Side of Genius: The Life of Alfred Hitchcock*, Little, Brown and Company, 1983; *La Face cachée d'un genie, la vraie vie d'Alfred Hitchcock* [1983], Albin Michel, 2004.

John Russell Taylor, *Hitch: The Life and Work of Alfred Hitchcock*, Faber & Faber, 1978.

François Truffaut, *Hitchcock/Truffaut* [1966], Gallimard, 2003.

Bruno Villien, *Hitchcock*, Colona, 1982.

Michael Walker, *Hitchcock's Motifs*, Amsterdam University Press, 2005.

Robin Wood, *Hitchcock's Films* [1965], Columbia University Press, 1989.

Maurice Yacowar, *Hitchcock's British Films* [1977], Wayne State University Press, 2010.

Slavoj Žižek, *Tout ce que vous avez toujours voulu savoir sur Lacan sans jamais oser le demander à Hitchcock* [1988], Capricci, 2010.

Index

Pages referring to the film and television works as well as portraits that are the subject of a detailed analysis are in **bold**.

Stannard, Eliot 24, 31, 33, 41, 43, 47, 49, 57, 61, 65, 70, 75, 76, 79, 80, 81, 83, 84
Stanton, Harry Dean 478, 479
Stanton, Paul 597
Stanwyck, Barbara 240, 264, 493, 547, 549
Starkey, Dewey 245, 249
Statler, Mel 587, 592
Stefano, Joseph 525, 527, 528, 575
Stein, Jules 552
Stein, Lotte 109
Steinbeck, John 289, 291, 293, 295, 297
Stendhal 146
Sterler, Hermine 109
Sternberg, Josef von 185, 240, 311, 370
Stevens, George 327, 387
Stevens, Robert 477
Stevenson, Edward 249
Stewart, Gloria 408
Stewart, Hugh St. C. 145, 150
Stewart, James 11, 347, 349, 350, 351, 353, 355, 383, 387, 405, 407, 408, 409, 411, 412, 413, 415, 435, 437, 438, 439, 440, 443, **444-445**, 450, 457, 467, 471, 473, 481, 483, 484, 487, 493, 495, 499, 504, 505, 522, 545, 552, 553, 576
Stewart, James G. 343
Stewart, Kay 456
Stewart, Marianne 476
Stewart, Sally 205, 208
Stone, Harold J. 461, 494, 495
Storm, Lesley 387
Story, Jack Trevor 429, 430
Strachey, Jack 106
Strack, Günter 587
Stradling, Harry 215, 219, 245, 247, 249, 252
Strasberg, Lee 517
Strassner, Joe 157, 169, 181
Strauss, Johann, fils 139, 140, 141
Strauss, Johann, père 139
Stroheim, Erich von 37, 497
Stuart, John 31, 33, 134, 135, 136

Sturges, John 521
Sturges, Preston 223
Subor, Michel 599, 601
Sullavan, Margaret 264
Swanton, Harold 550, 551
Sweeney, Bob 544, 545, 573
Swerling, Jo 289, 293
Swift, Clive 603
Sylbert, Paul 461, 463, 466
Sylos, Ralph 458, 474
Tabori, George 385, 387
Tacchella, Jean-Charles 566
Tallenay, Jean-Louis 345, 354
Tandowsky, Ralph 600
Tandy, Jessica 340, 341, 555, 558
Tanner, Peter 321, 323, 324, 325, 327
Tarantino, Quentin 191
Taylor, Elizabeth 505
Taylor, Gilbert 603, 606
Taylor, Gordon 321, 323
Taylor, John Russell 107, 612
Taylor, Rod 340, 341, 555, 558, 559, 579
Taylor, Samuel 481, 483, 484, 597, 599, 600, 601
Taylor, Vaughn 525
Teal, Ray 452
Tearle, Godfrey 157
Téchiné, André 594
Tedrow, Irene 458
Tennyson, Penrose 143, 145, 150, 157, 169, 181, 193, 200
Terry-Lewis, Mabel 215
Terry, Harry 65, 83
Tester, Desmond 181, 185
Tetzel, Joan 343
Tetzlaff, Ted 329, 332, 334
Tey, Josephine 193, 195
Thatcher, Torin 181
Thérond, Roger 566
Thesiger, Ernest 23
Thinnes, Roy 618
Thomas, Dolph 373
Thomas, Jameson 75, 76, 77, 106, 107
Thomas, Ralph 163, 621
Thomas, Robert 597
Thompson, Dorothy 290, 297

Thompson, Edith 24, 370
Thorndike, Sybil 369, 370
Thornton, Cecil V. 99, 109
Thurman, Lois 587
Tiomkin, Dimitri 277, 282, 373, 385, 395
Todd, Ann 343, 345
Todd, Richard 369, 370, 371
Toland, Gregg 259, 329
Tom Jones 592
Tomasini, George 383, 405, 408, 417, 420, 435, 439, 461, 465, 481, 490, 501, 505, 525, 530, 555, 573, 576, 592, 600
Toomey, Regis 307
Toumanova, Tamara 587
Tourneur, Jacques 310, 332, 475, 479, 569
Tourneur, Maurice 33
Tovey, George 603
Tracy, William 245
Travers, Henry 277, 281
Travers, Linden 205
Tremaine, Kathleen 205
Tremayne, Les 501, 546, 547
Trevelyan, Hilda 157, 163
Trevor, Austin 181
Trevor, Jack 79
Tribby, John E. 245, 249, 329
Trier, Lars von 140
Triesault, Ivan 329, 332
Tripp, June 47, 49
Truex, Philip 429, 430, 431
Truffaut, François 37, 50, 58, 63, 71, 95, 119, 123, 130, 154, 155, 159, 188, 190, 255, 282, 310, 312, 313, 330, 338, 353, 354, 359, 364, 388, 391, 396, 397, 403, 462, 463, 466, 467, 469, 471, 479, 493, 508, 534, 560, 567, 601, 605, 613, 621
Truman, Ralph 435
Tschechowa, Olga 109, 113
Tucker, George Loane 84
Tummel, William 277
Turner, Lana 528
Tuttle, Lurene 525
Tuttle, William 501
Twist, Derek N. 157

Tyner, Charles 615
Ullmann, Liv 619
Uris, Leon 599, 600
Vadim, Roger 388
Valentine, A. D. 135
Valentine, Joseph 261, 264, 277, 282, 347
Valentine, Val 106, 125, 127
Valentino, Rudolph 43, 50
Valli, Alida 343, 344
Valli, Virginia 31, 33, 35, 37
Van der Post, Laurens 596
Van der Vlis, Diana 516
Van Hessen, Richard 343
Van Sant, Gus 541, 621
Vanel, Charles 417, 420, 422
Vannier, Alain 593
Vanzetti, Bartolomeo 465
Varden, Norma 373, 378
Vaz Dias, Selma 205
Verity, Terence 369
Vermeer, Johannes 382
Verneuil, Louis 387
Verno, Jerry 157, 193
Vernon, John 599, 600
Vetchinsky, Alex 205, 207
Vibert, Marcel 79
Victoria, reine 14
Vidor, King 33, 185, 241, 378, 382, 455, 569
Viertel, Peter 261, 262, 263
Vlahos, Petro 555
Voight, Ed 347
Vosper, Frank 139, 145, 148, 551
Vosper, Margery 550, 551
Wagenheim, Charles 235, 241, 242
Wagner, Richard 114, 433, 490
Wakefield, Hugh 145
Waldis, Otto 494
Walker, Brandy 65
Walker, Hal 549
Walker, Robert 305, 373, 376, 378, 380, 381
Walker, Vernon L. 245, 249, 329
Wallis, Hal 332, 499
Walsh, David 321
Walsh, Kay 369, 370
Walsh, Raoul 293, 403, 547

Walters, James 472
Wanger, Walter 235, 237, 238, 242
Ward, Charles B. 140
Ward, Edward 245
Warhol, Andy 571
Warmington, S. J. 109, 181
Warner, Jack 172, 376, 388, 397, 465
Warren, John F. 307, 496, 517, 520, 587, 592
Warren, Katherine 458
Warrington, Bill 135
Warth, Theron 329, 332
Wasserman, Lew 350, 407, 445, 446, 447, 487, 528, 545, **552-553**, 597, 605
Waterhouse, Keith 587, 590, 593
Watling, Jack 357
Watson, Justice 456
Watson, Lucile 245
Watson, Waldon O. 525, 555, 573, 587, 599
Watson, Wylie 157, 215, 219
Watt, Harry 215
Watts, Haward 75
Waxman, Franz 225, 232, 249, 252, 343, 405, 411
Way, Peter Barry 519
Wayne, David 474, 475
Wayne, John 387, 519, 601
Wayne, Naunton 205, 208, 210
Webb, Roy 329
Webber, Peggy 461
Weber, Carl Maria von 218
Webster, Ben 57
Webster, Charles 476
Webster, Chuck 478
Weiler, A. H. 507
Weldon, Jim 454
Welles, Halsted 546, 547
Welles, Orson 158, 223, 227, 241, 252, 253, 263, 264, 281, 293, 312, 432, 447, 455, 531
Wells, Billy 65, 568
Wenders, Wim 479
Werndorff, Oscar Friedrich 139, 143, 157, 160, 169, 173, 181
West, Martin 615
West, Vera 277
Westman, James 599
Westmore, Ern 215
Westmore, Monte 225

Westmore, Perc 347
Westmore, Wally 405, 417, 435, 481
Weston, Garnett 91
Whale, James 549
Wheeler, Gertrude 395
Wheeler, Lyle 225, 228
Whelan, Emma Jane 14
White, Ethel Lina 205, 207
Whitehead, Jack 157
Whitelaw, Billie 603, 606
Whitlock, Albert 145, 150, 157, 160, 181, 193, **202-203**, 205, 207, 215, 555, 558, 560, 573, 587, 597, 599, 603, 606, 615
Whitty, Dame May 205, 208, 213, 249, 252
Wiene, Robert 26
Wieth, Mogens 435
Wilcox, Fred 547
Wild, Thomas 494
Wilde, Oscar 479
Wilder, Billy 323, 327, 397, 457, 540
Wilder, Thornton 277, 279, 280, 281, 283, 291, 590
Wilding, Michael 357, 359, 361, 369
Wiles, Sydney 205
Williams, Adam 501
Williams, Arthur 518, 519
Williams, Charles 205
Williams, Derick 89, 99
Williams, Edward W. 452, 454, 456, 458, 470, 472, 474, 476, 478, 494, 496, 498, 514, 518, 520, 544, 546, 548, 550, 568
Williams, Emlyn 145, 147, 215, 219
Williams, Eric Bransby 61
Williams, Harcourt 357
Williams, J. Terry 615
Williams, John (acteur) 343, 395, 397, 398, 417, 419, 458, 459, 470, 471, 514, 515, 597
Williams, John (compositeur) 615, 618
Williams, Lawrence P. 245
Willis, Constance 435
Willis, Norman 452, 456
Willman, Noel 435

Acknowledgments

Maud Ameline, Valentine Benoliel, Emma Duperier, Bernard Eisenschitz, Peggy Hannon,

Bénédicte Bortoli (editor), Laurence Lehoux (E/P/A), assisted by Amédine Sèdes,

Laurence Basset (iconographer), Daniel Bouteiller (T.C.D.)

Joëlle Cammas, Franck Lubet, Magali Paul, Claudia Pellegrini, Vincent Spillmann (La Cinémathèque de Toulouse),

Véronique Chauvet, Amandine Dongois, Jean-Philippe Jonchères, Bertrand Keraël, Sandra Laupa, Laurent Mannoni, Cécile Verguin (La Cinémathèque française, Paris),

Jean-Pierre Verscheure (Cinévolution),

Espen Bale, John Curran, Briony Dixon (British Film Institute, London),

Elizabeth Cathcart, Kristine Krueger, Edda Manriquez, Taylor Morales (Academy of Motion Picture Arts and Sciences, Beverly Hills),

and Le Square Gardette (Paris, 11e arrondissement).

Photo Credits

ACADEMY OF MOTION PICTURE ARTS AND SCIENCES

© Academy War Film Collection, restored by the Academy Film Archive 258
© Alfred Hitchcock papers, Margaret Herrick Library / Metro-Goldwyn-Mayer production / Warner Bros. Entertainment Inc. 21, 43
© Alfred Hitchcock papers, Margaret Herrick Library / Photo James Manatt / Metro-Goldwyn-Mayer production / Warner Bros. Entertainment Inc. 624
© Alfred Hitchcock papers, Margaret Herrick Library / Photo Kenny Bell / Metro-Goldwyn-Mayer production / Warner Bros. Entertainment Inc. 511
© Alfred Hitchcock papers, Margaret Herrick Library 582, 596
© Core production photographs, Margaret Herrick Library / Metro-Goldwyn-Mayer production / Warner Bros. Entertainment Inc. 13
© Metro-Goldwyn-Mayer set reference photographs, Margaret Herrick Library / Metro-Goldwyn-Mayer production / Warner Bros. Entertainment Inc. 510
© Robert Boyle papers, Margaret Herrick Library / Metro-Goldwyn-Mayer production / Warner Bros. Entertainment Inc. / DR 318
© Robert Boyle papers, Margaret Herrick Library 203
© Saul Bass papers, Margaret Herrick Library 539

AURIMAGES

© 1930 Studiocanal Films Ltd. All Rights Reserved / The Kobal Collection 108
© Gaumont British / The Kobal Collection 177
© Mary Evans 28–29, 67, 104
© Paramount / The Kobal Collection 428, 445
© Warner Bros. / The Kobal Collection 394

With kind permission of BFI NATIONAL ARCHIVE

© British International Pictures (BIP) / DR 77, 78, 103
© Gainsborough Pictures (Gaumont British) / DR 51, 197, 213
© Gaumont British Picture Corporation / DR 161, 165
© Paramount Pictures / DR 440
© Selznick International Pictures, Vanguard Films / United Artists / DR 345 bottom, 516

Coll. CINÉMATHÈQUE FRANÇAISE

© Alfred Junge 148

© Barry Richardson / Warner Bros. / DR 467
© British International Pictures (BIP) / DR 64, 68–69, 85, 91, 95, 96, 97, 102, 106, 115, 118, 122, 123, 128, 132–133, 134, 623
© British International Pictures (BIP) / Südfilm / DR 111, 113
© Gainsborough Pictures / DR 34, 40, 44, 52, 53, 212
© Gainsborough Pictures (Gaumont British) / DR 198 right, 199, 200, 209
© Gaumont British Picture Corporation—Tom Arnold Films Ltd. / DR 140
© Gaumont British Picture Corporation / DR 149 top, 150, 162, 166, 173, 175, 176, 186, 188, 189
© Les Films du Carrosse (Paris) / Universal Pictures / DR 282
© Mayflower Pictures / DR 217
© Paramount Pictures / Filwite Productions / DR 443
© Paramount Pictures / DR 411, 437
© RKO / DR 251, 253, 254, 256, 336
© Selznick International Pictures / DR 313
© The Rank Organisation / Gainsborough Pictures (Gaumont British) / DR 210, 211
© Transatlantic Pictures / Warner Bros. / DR 352, 356
© Universal Pictures / DR 155, 341, 263, 265, 269, 285, 559 top, 561, 562, 580, 617 top
© Walter Wanger Productions / DR 238–239
© Warner Bros. / DR 370, 371, 379, 384, 392–393, 400, 468 right, 383

GETTY IMAGES

© AmerAnglo 49
© Archives / Walt Disney Television 202
© Bettmann 7, 86, 201, 552, 559 bottom, 570, 589
© CBS Photo Archive 449, 451
© Eliot Elisofon / The LIFE Picture Collection 270 right, 271–274
© Evening Standard 27
© Frank Barratt / Keystone 607
© George Rinhart / Corbis 466
© Gjon Mili / The LIFE Picture Collection 281
© Harry Benson / Express 601
© Herbert Dorfman / Corbis 554
© Hulton Archive 101, 160, 493
© Hulton Deutsch Collection / Corbis 142, 366
© J. R. Eyerman / LIFE Magazine / The LIFE Picture Collection 280, 402
© John Florea / The LIFE Picture Collection 294
© John Kobal Foundation 223, 427, 489, 508
© John Springer Collection / Corbis 208, 246, 388, 529, 591, 627
© Lisa Larsen / The LIFE Picture Collection 464

© LMPC 244, 342, 480, 614
© March Of Time / The LIFE Picture Collection 171
© Michel Ginfray / Sygma 611
© Mondadori 391
© Movie Poster Image Art 30, 168, 180, 192, 204, 248, 276, 288, 328, 346, 372, 404, 416, 460, 500, 524, 571, 572
© Paramount Pictures / Archive Photos 414
© Paramount Pictures / Sunset Boulevard / Corbis 415, 423
© Peter Stackpole / The LIFE Picture Collection 222, 230
© Popperfoto 407
© Stuart Macgladrie / The Sydney Morning Herald /Fairfax Media 631
© Sunset Boulevard / Corbis 191, 283, 333, 375, 377, 504, 609
© Transatlantic Pictures / Warner Bros. / Sunset Boulevard / Corbis 360
© Twentieth Century-Fox Film Corporation / Corbis 298
© Ullstein Bild 93, 117, 487, 527
© Universal History Archive / UIG 224, 602
© Universal Pictures / Sunset Boulevard / Corbis 578, 581, 583
© Warner Bros. / Archive Photos 380

HEMIS.FR

© Markives / Alamy 553
© Pictorial Press Ltd / Alamy 399
© PictureLux / The Hollywood Archive / Alamy 398
© RGR Collection / Alamy 567
© Warner Bros. / AF archive / Alamy 390
© Warner Bros. / United Archives GmbH / Alamy 381

PROD DB

© 20th Century-Fox / DR 292, 296, 316
© British International Pictures (BIP) / DR 71, 72, 74, 76 left, 82, 84, 88, 92, 94 top, 98, 116, 120, 124, 129, 130, 131, 136, 137
© British International Pictures / Südfilm / DR 114
© Columbia Pict. / DR 413
© Gainsborough Pictures / DR 35, 36, 46, 55, 56, 58, 59, 60, 62, 63
© Gaumont British Picture Corporation—Tom Arnold Films Ltd. / DR 138, 141
© Gaumont British Picture Corporation / DR 143, 144, 149 bottom, 151, 156, 163, 184, 198 left
© Les Films Alain Sarde / DR 620
© Mayflower Pictures / DR 214, 218
© MGM—Filmways Pict. / DR 621
© MGM / DR 426, 503, 505, 506, 507, 509, 513, 584
© Panoramic Productions / DR 50

© Paramount Pictures / DR 18, 409, 420, 421, 424, 425, 430, 431, 434, 438, 441, 444, 484, 486, 488, 491, 492, 540, 542, 543
© Rank Organisation—Gaumont British / DR 178, 179
© RKO / DR 220, 247, 255, 334, 335, 339
© Selznick International Pictures / DR 228, 229, 231, 233, 304, 306, 310, 311, 312, 314, 315, 367
© Selznick International Pictures, Vanguard Films / United Artists / DR 344, 345 top
© Shamley Productions / DR 305, 432, 446, 452, 454, 456, 458, 470, 472, 474, 476, 478, 494, 496, 498, 514, 518, 520, 523, 530, 531, 532, 534, 536, 537, 538, 544, 546, 548, 550, 568, 635
© Universal Pictures / DR 10, 154, 260, 266–267, 268, 286, 340, 382, 512, 558, 564, 565, 576, 577, 586, 590, 593, 594, 595, 598, 600, 610, 613, 617 bottom, 618, 619
© Universum Film (UFA)—Gainsborough Pictures / DR 23
© Walter Wanger Production / DR 237, 241, 243
© Warner Bros. / DR 15, 16, 349, 350, 351, 353, 354, 355, 364, 365, 368, 378, 389, 401, 468 left, 469, 585
DR 8, 25, 183, 433, 485, 541

OTHER SOURCES

© Bertram Park / Camerapress / Gamma-Rapho 19
© Bridgeman Images 363, 632
© British International Pictures (BIP) / DR 70, 76 right, 80, 94 bottom
© Gainsborough Pictures / DR 38–39, 45
© H M Bateman Designs www. hmbateman.com 153
© Imperial War Museum [GOV 41 (a), GOV 41 (b), GOV 41 (c), GOV 41 (d), GOV 41 (e)] 320–326
© Matt Greene / DR 275
© MEPL / Bridgeman Images 73
© Ministry of Information (MoI) / Phoenix Films / DR 300, 302
© Paramount Pictures / DR 319
© Philippe Halsman / Magnum Photos 87, 563, 566
© Pierre Pigeot—Collections La Cinémathèque de Toulouse 234
© Universal Pictures / DR 317
© Walter Sanders / Black Star / DR 270 left, DR 362
From the pages of LIFE. © 1942 The Picture Collection Inc. All rights reserved. Reprinted from LIFE and published with permission of The Picture Collection Inc. Reproduction in any manner in any language in whole or in part without written permission is prohibited. 270–275

About the Authors

Bernard Benoliel is the director of art and culture at the Cinématheque Française. He is the co-author of books devoted to the work of Anthony Mann, Clint Eastwood, and Bruce Lee.

Gilles Esposito is a journalist who writes for magazines including *Mad Movies* and *So Film*. He has also contributed to collections devoted to the work of Samuel Fuller, Leo McCarey, John Ford, and Universal Pictures.

Murielle Joudet is a film critic for *Le Monde* as well as for TV and radio. She has written essays on Isabelle Huppert and Gena Rowlands.

Jean-François Rauger is the director of programming at the Cinématheque Française. He is a journalist at *Le Monde* and the author of *The Domestic Eye: Hitchcock and Television*.

Copyright © 2024, Éditions E/P/A—Hachette Livre
Translation copyright © 2024 by Black Dog and Leventhal Publishers
Cover copyright © 2024 by Hachette Book Group, Inc.
Front cover credits PictureLux/The Hollywood Archive/Alamy Stock Photo
Back cover credits Entertainment Pictures/Alamy Stock Photo

Translation by Paul Ratcliffe by arrangement with Jackie Dobbyne of Jacaranda Publishing Services

Original title: *Hitchcock, La Totale*
Texts: Bernard Benoliel, Gilles Esposito, Murielle Joudet, Jean-François Rauger
Published by Éditions E/P/A—Hachette Livre, 2019

Black Dog & Leventhal Publishers
Hachette Book Group
1290 Avenue of the Americas, New York, NY 10104
www.blackdogandleventhal.com
 BlackDogandLeventhal   @BDLev

First English-language Edition: October 2024

Published by Black Dog & Leventhal Publishers, an imprint of Hachette Book Group, Inc.
The Black Dog & Leventhal Publishers name and logo are trademarks of Hachette Book Group, Inc.

The Hachette Speakers Bureau provides a wide range of authors for speaking events. To find out more, go to hachettespeakersbureau.com or email HachetteSpeakers@hbgusa.com.

Black Dog & Leventhal books may be purchased in bulk for business, educational, or promotional use. For more information, please contact your local bookseller or the Hachette Book Group Special Markets Department at Special.Markets@hbgusa.com.

The publisher is not responsible for websites (or their content) that are not owned by the publisher.

Additional copyright/credits information is on page 647.

Print book cover and interior design by Katie Benezra. Production design by Clea Chmela.

LCCN: 2024930239

ISBNs: 978-0-7624-8868-1 (hardcover), 978-0-7624-8869-8 (ebook)

Printed in China

10 9 8 7 6 5 4 3 2 1